OXFORD READERS

Fascism

Roger Griffin is Principal Lecturer in History at Oxford Brookes University. His publications include *The Nature of Fascism* (1991, 1993) and contributions to *Contemporary Political Ideologies* (ed. R. Eatwell and A. Wright, 1993); *Fascism and Theatre: Comparative Studies on the Aesthetics and Politics of Performance in Inter-War Europe* (ed. G. Berghaus, forthcoming); *Was there Fascism outside Europe?* (ed. S. U. Larsen, forthcoming); and *The Failure of British Fascism* (ed. M. Cronin, forthcoming).

OXFORD **READERS**

Fascism

Edited by Roger Griffin

Oxford · New York
OXFORD UNIVERSITY PRESS
1995

Oxford University Press, Walton Street, Oxford OX2 6DP

Oxford New York
Athens Auckland Bangkok Bombay
Calcutta Cape Town Dar es Salaam Delhi
Florence Hong Kong Istanbul Karachi
Kuala Lumpur Madras Madrid Melbourne
Mexico City Nairobi Paris Singapore
Taipei Tokyo Toronto

and associated companies in
Berlin Ibadan

Oxford is a trade mark of Oxford University Press

Introduction, selection, and editorial matter © Roger Griffin 1995
For further copyright details see pages 397–9
First published as an Oxford University Press paperback 1995

British Library Cataloguing in Publication Data
Data available

Library of Congress Cataloging-in-Publication Data
Fascism / edited by Roger Griffin.
    p. cm. — (Oxford readers)
    Includes bibliographical references and index.
    1. Fascism. 2. Fascism—History—20th century.
I. Griffin, Roger. II. Series.
JC481.F3334 1995 320.5´33—dc20 94–44039
ISBN 0–19–289249–5

10 9 8 7 6 5 4 3 2 1

Typeset by Pure Tech Corporation, Pondicherry, India
Printed in Great Britain
on acid-free paper by
Bookcraft (Bath) Ltd
Midsomer Norton, Avon

Preface

When this century was still young, a brand-new ideological force which came to be known as 'fascism' burst upon a Europe just recovering from the body-blows of the First World War and the Russian Revolution. Before long it had brutally put paid to any dreams which liberals, democratic socialists, and communists might have had that a new era of international progress and harmony had dawned in the wake of so much pointless suffering and death. It might have seemed that after the horrors of Nazism and the Second World War the time of fascism had passed, yet it has survived to become a permanent, if generally highly marginalized, part of the political subcultures of most Westernized countries. Indeed, as we approach the end of the twentieth century it appears to be actually increasing in virulence wherever local socio-economic conditions fail to sustain the ideal of the multi-ethnic civil society. It even shows signs of contaminating the discourse of a number of party politicians of the extreme and not-so-extreme right on matters of immigration and cultural identity.

The central focus of this volume is the ideological kinship between the major forms of inter-war fascism, and the continuity of these with its post-war manifestations. This kinship is revealed by concentrating on texts which suggest the characteristic way fascist ideologues diagnose what they see as the current political and cultural crisis, a diagnosis which involves the utopian vision of an entirely new order. The premiss underlying this anthology is that, no matter how nebulous, irrational, or repugnant such a vision may be, it plays a crucial role in motivating fascism's activists and shaping its policies. The sample texts which have been culled from a wide range of movements and assembled in this Reader will, I hope, promote a better understanding of the ideological dynamics of generic fascism. Together they illuminate a frequently neglected causal dimension of what the Fascist and Nazi regimes attempted to achieve, and point to a rationale behind their apparently wanton destruction of liberty and life. The Reader also highlights how far these regimes were linked at the level of core ideas, both with each other, and with scores of other fascist movements which fortunately for humanity have withered on the vine before achieving power.

The selection would have been less comprehensive without the assistance of a number of academics and librarians who responded patiently when pestered for help in tracking down original samples of fascism in places or in languages to which I had no access. The routine efficiency of the staff of Oxford Brookes University library, the Bodleian, and St Antony's College library was impressive. The help of individuals in obtaining or translating particular extracts is acknowledged below, but I would especially like to thank Professor Ian Kershaw, Professor Adrian Lyttelton, Professor Jeremy Noakes, Professor Martin Blinkhorn, Dr Detlef Mühlberger, and Dr Roger Eatwell for providing useful feedback to draft sections of the manuscript which related to their specialism. I must assume sole responsibility for the selection of the texts and the theory of fascism underlying it, as well as for any inaccuracies in the translations (all of which are by me except where otherwise stated) or factual errors contained in the notes. I would much appreciate being alerted in writing to such blemishes. My thanks also go to Catherine Clarke and George Miller of OUP for accommodating the modifications to the format demanded by this volume in the Oxford Readers series. Moreover, George Miller contributed much to making the introductions and notes more comprehensible. Pauline Tobin's skill and patience in word processing scores of English texts were also invaluable.

Lastly, I would also like to acknowledge the support of my colleagues in the School of Humanities at Oxford Brookes University while I was working on this book, as well as the indirect contribution of the hundreds of students who over the years have taken my course on generic fascism, thereby enabling me to refine my theories on the subject. But it is to Mariella that this book is dedicated.

The cover photograph shows a bronze Goggle Head by the British sculptress Elizabeth Frink, made in 1969. It is one of a series of studies inspired by newspaper photographs of General Oufkir, implicated in a presumed plot between the French and Moroccan States to have the revolutionary democrat Ben Barka 'disappeared' in 1965. Frink commented that 'Oufkir had an extraordinarily sinister face: always in dark sunglasses.' The Goggle Heads became for Frink 'a symbol of evil and destruction in North Africa, and, in the end, everywhere.' In the context of this Reader the image is intended to suggest how attempts by a 'total' State to create a 'new order' or to induce the rebirth of the nation inevitably give rise, not to a heroic élite of 'new men', but to a breed of fanatical or cynical henchmen.

Acknowledgements

I am grateful to the following individuals for their help with obtaining or translating the texts specified below by their number in this volume. Numbers in italic signify translations; numbers in bold indicate that information was supplied in addition to obtaining or translating the text concerned.

Dr David Baker, Nottingham Trent University, 175; Sarah Berg, Centre de Recherches, d'Informations et de Documentations Antiracistes, Paris, **203**; Dr Rheinhold Brender, Frankfurter Allgemeine, **106**; Dr Luciano Cheles, Lancaster University, 211; Dr Mike Cronin, Sheffield Hallam University, **97**; Professor Hans Dahl, University of Oslo, 110; A. Dantoing, Centre de Recherches et d'Études Historiques, Brussels, 108, 109; Professor Mikhail Dumitzashco, Institute of Advanced Management in Agriculture, Moldova, *207*; Dr Roger Eatwell, University of Bath, 179, 184, 186, 200, 208; Emanuel Godin, Oxford Brookes University, 198; William Goodall, Oxford, *122, 123*; Paul Hockenos, RFE/RL Research Institute, Munich, **207**; Professor Lauri Karvonen, Åbo Academy, Finland, *113, 114*; Andres Kasekamp, University of London, *115*; Alex Kershaw, London, **199**; Andrea Laczik, Oxford, *118*; Elizabeth Lowry, University of Oxford, *119, 206*; Dr Donal Lowry, Oxford Brookes University, 119, 206; Dr Detlef Mühlberger, Oxford Brookes University, **60**; Dr Rob Pope, Oxford Brookes University, 212; Dr Mario Sznajder, Hebrew University of Jerusalem, 120, 121; George Taylor, Centre for Democratic Renewal, Atlanta Georgia, 204; Dr Richard Thurlow, University of Sheffield, 94; Professor Antonio Costa Pinto, Instituto Superior de Ciencias do Trabalho e da Empresa, Lisbon, 102, 103; Satomi Tomishima, Tokyo, *124, 125*; Andreas Umland, University of Oxford, **212**.

Contents

B. Fascism in Power January 1925–April 1945

PART II: FASCISM IN GERMANY

PART III: ABORTIVE FASCISMS 1922–1945

A. European Fascisms

i Britain

ii Ireland

iii Spain

iv Portugal

v France

vi Belgium

vii Norway

viii Finland

ix Estonia

x Latvia

xi Romania

xii Hungary

B. Non-European Fascisms

i South Africa

PART IV: THEORIES OF FASCISM

EPILOGUE

General Introduction

....

This volume in the Oxford Reader series is designed to make available in English a wide selection of texts written by fascist thinkers, ideologues, and propagandists both inside and outside Europe before and after the Second World War. To my knowledge it is the first ever attempt to produce a comprehensive anthology of fascist texts. Why should this be?

One reason is the dubious nature of the exercise itself. To have a Reader in Ethics or Ecology raises no eyebrows, because both subjects are generally associated with potentially positive, life-asserting areas of human endeavour which encompass a rich variety of different arguments and insights from authors ancient and modern. On the other hand, fascism is very much a product of the modern age. (Throughout the notes to the texts I capitalize Mussolini's Fascism, though both upper and lower case were used by contemporaries, and use lower-case 'fascism' to refer to the generic phenomenon. The corresponding adjectives are 'Fascist' and 'fascist' respectively.) Moreover, it is identified with a whole range of forces which crush any genuine human creativity of word or deed: totalitarianism, brainwashing, state terror, social engineering, fanaticism, orchestrated violence, blind obedience. A Reader devoted to fascism might thus be construed as endowing with a bogus aura of serious theoretical content, and even dignity, something which is best regarded as a perversion of the human mind and spirit. Yet there is no reason in principle why primary sources relating to negative aspects of the human condition should be any less worthy of scholarly or general interest than positive ones, a point underlined by the fact that one of the companion volumes in the Oxford Readers series is devoted to war. Moreover, with fascism back in the headlines as a phenomenon in the ascendant, it is arguably high time to renew rather than suspend attempts to come to grips with the ideas and mind-set which lie behind it.

A second argument against such a Reader is the chronic lack of consensus among specialists about what constitutes the 'fascist minimum', that is, the lowest common denominator of defining features to be found in all manifestations of fascism. This is bound up with another unresolved issue, namely whether fascism possesses anything resembling a coherent ideology. Many would be tempted to agree with the historian Hugh Trevor-Roper's verdict that fascist 'ideology' is at bottom no more than 'an ill-sorted hodge-podge of ideas' (Woolf 1981: 20). More recently the social scientist Stephen Turner conceded that:

The puzzle of fascism remains, half a century after the conclusion of the war against the fascist regimes. [. . .] No sociology of the interwar era grasped fascism fully or produced an unambiguously 'correct' political recipe for dealing with it. The continuing dispute over the character of fascism and the interwar 'fascist' regimes suggests that these are inappropriately high standards for social science. But the failure to meet them indicates that the pretensions to political wisdom of social science are inappropriate as well (Turner and Käsler 1992: 11–12).

Fortunately for me, and, I hope, for the reader, I was able to accept Oxford University Press's invitation to prepare this volume without compromising deep-seated convictions about the nature of fascism, convictions which make an anthology of excerpts from primary sources not just feasible but highly desirable. Indeed, in the book which staked my own claim to provide a more cogent and useful definition of fascism than previous ones, I declared that a 'regrettable lacuna in this text is an appendix providing extensive and wide-ranging samples of fascist ideology, both inter-and post-war, to illustrate the highly nuanced and varied permutations that the same core of ideas can generate' (Griffin 1993: 20).

The background to such a remark is the central importance which my theory attributes to the role of ideology in the definition and dynamics of fascism. I am one of a minority of academics concerned with generic fascism who take its ideas seriously as a key to understanding the characteristic policies, institutions, and style of its politics (though it should be stressed that other members of this fairly exclusive 'club', such as Ernst Nolte, Zeev Sternhell, Stanley Payne, George Mosse, Emilio Gentile, James Gregor, and Roger Eatwell, are far from seeing eye to eye on what these ideas actually are). Moreover, my approach happens to be restrictive enough to exclude many ultra-right movements and regimes, but inclusive enough to encompass phenomena from outside Europe, as well as treating post-war fascism as a prolific source of important variations on the inter-war models. This makes the range of phenomena sampled in this book strictly delimited while being richly variegated.

What are the essentials of this approach? To summarize the elaborate method-ological argument put forward in *The Nature of Fascism*, it starts by assuming that there can be no objective definition of fascism, since, like all generic concepts in the human sciences, 'fascism' is at bottom an ideal type. In other words, it ultimately results from an act of idealizing abstraction which produces an artificially tidy model of the kinship that exists within a group of phenomena which, despite their differences, are sensed to have certain features in common. The assumption that some such ideal-typical common denominator exists arguably lies at the basis of all Readers in political thought, be it liberalism, anarchism, socialism, communism, ecologism, feminism, conservatism, or any other 'ism'. To turn fascism into a taxonomic term which can be used in scientific enquiry is to select certain attributes of phenomena associated with fascism as definitional or essential (thereby relegat-ing others to being secondary or peripheral), and assemble these in sterile labora-tory conditions into an artificially tidy conceptual model. As Max Weber, who pioneered 'ideal type' theory, recognized, such a model is at bottom a utopia, since it cannot correspond exactly to anything in empirical reality, which is always irreducibly complex, 'messy', and unique. Definitions of generic terms can thus never be 'true' to reality, but they can be more or less useful in investigating it ('heuristically useful') when applied as conceptual tools of analysis. The continuing debate over what constitutes fascism merely indicates that no academic consensus has so far grown up about which of the many available ideal types of it is the most useful (see Griffin 1993: 8–22).

The second premiss of my approach is that it is possible to define fascism, or identify the 'fascist minimum', in terms not of a common ideological component, but of a common mythic core. This suggests that it is just as misguided to seek to establish that there is a common denominator between all forms of fascism at the level of articulated ideas as to deny fascism any coherent ideological content. The coherence exists not at the surface level of specific, verbalized 'ideas', but at the structural level of the core myth which underlies them, serving as a matrix which determines which types of thought are selected in certain national cultures and how they are arranged into a political ideology, whether at the level of theory, policies, propaganda, culture, or of semiotic 'behaviour', such as the use of symbols or the enactment of ritual. The term 'myth' here draws attention, not to the utopianism, irrationalism, or sheer madness of the claim it makes to interpret contemporary reality, but to its power to unleash strong affective energies through the evocative force of the image or vision of reality it contains for those susceptible to it. This generic mythic image, laden with potential mobilizing, and even mass-mobilizing, force, may, like any psychological matrix or archetype (such as the Hero, or Paradise), take on a wide variety of surface formulations according to the particular cultural and historical context in which it is expressed.

The mythic core that forms the basis of my ideal type of generic fascism is the vision of the (perceived) crisis of the nation as betokening the birth-pangs of a new order. It crystallizes in the image of the national community, once purged and rejuvenated, rising phoenix-like from the ashes of a morally bankrupt state system and the decadent culture associated with it. I was drawn to exploring the heuristic value of this ideal type as a result of noticing recurrent references in Fascist texts to the alleged decay of the 'old Italy' (its senility, decadence, sickness, decline, disinte-gration, collapse, debilitation, etc.) and the urgent need for its rebirth (reawaken-ing, regeneration, health, revival, rejuvenation, invigoration, etc.) in a 'new' Italy. Such *topoi* bore an uncanny resemblance to the slogans of other 'putative' fascist movements, such as the Nazis' cry of 'Germany awake', the British Union of Fascists' campaign for a 'Greater Britain', or the Romanian Iron Guard's call for the appearance of *omul nou*, the New Man.

The idea that a 'nation' is an entity which can 'decay' and be 'regenerated' implies something diametrically opposed to what liberals understand by it. It connotes an organism with its own life-cycle, collective psyche, and communal destiny, embracing in principle the whole people (not just its ruling élites), and in practice all those who ethnically or culturally are 'natural' members of it, and are not contaminated by forces hostile to nationhood. In this way of conceiving the nation—sometimes referred to by academics as 'integral nationalism', 'hyper-nationalism' or 'illiberal nationalism'—it becomes a higher reality transcending the individual's life, which only acquires meaning and value in so far as it contributes directly to its vitality and well-being. Extensive study of the primary sources of Fascism and of other fascisms convinced me that at the core of its mentality was the *idée fixe* of devoting, and, if necessary sacrificing, individual existence to the struggle against the forces of degeneration which had seemingly brought the nation low, and of helping relaunch it towards greatness and glory. The fascist felt he (and it generally was a 'he') had been fatefully born at a watershed between national decline and national regeneration, a feeling that alchemically converted all pessim-ism and cultural despair into a manic sense of purpose and optimism. He knew himself to be one of the 'chosen' of an otherwise lost generation. His task it was to prepare the ground for the new breed of man, the *homo fascistus*, who would instinctively form part of the revitalized national community without having first to purge himself of the selfish reflexes inculcated by a civilization sapped by egotism and materialism.

Within fascist studies the recurrent obsession with national rebirth and the need for a 'new man' seemed to have been frequently noted without being recognized as a candidate for the 'fascist minimum'. A deliberate exercise in 'idealizing abstraction' turned this theme into fascism's sole necessary definitional trait. To sum up the mythic core in a single concept involved resuscitating what is an obscure and obsolescent word in English, 'palingenesis' (meaning rebirth), and coining the expression 'palingenetic ultra-nationalism'. The premiss of this Reader is thus that generic fascism can be defined in terms of this expression, or to repeat the formula expounded at length elsewhere (Griffin 1993: 2): *Fascism is a genus of political ideology whose mythic core in its various permutations is a palingenetic form of populist ultra-nationalism*. From this premiss about the matrix of fascist ideology, a number of features of generic fascism follow which have a profound bearing on how it operates in practice both as an opposition movement and as a regime.

1. *Fascism is anti-liberal*. Fascism's call for the regeneration of the national community through a heroic struggle against its alleged enemies and the forces undermining it involves the radical rejection of liberalism in all its aspects: pluralism, tolerance, individualism, gradualism, pacifism, parliamentary democracy, the separation of powers, the doctrine of 'natural rights', egalitarianism, the rectilinear theory of progress, the open society, cosmopolitanism, one-worldism, etc. The important proviso to this aspect of fascist movements is that, though they oppose parliamentary democracy and their policies would in practice inevitably lead to its destruction, they may well choose to operate tactically as democratic, electoral parties. Indeed, they may go to considerable lengths to camouflage the extent of their hostility to liberalism through euphemism and dishonesty, reserving their rhetoric of destruction of the 'system' and of revolution for the initiated.

2. *Fascism is anti-conservative*. The centrality to fascism of a myth of the nation's regeneration within a new order implies a rejection of illiberal conservative politics (for example, an absolutist system in which sovereignty is invested in a hereditary monarchy or oligarchy), as well as of liberal and authoritarian conservative solutions to the current crisis which imply a restoration of law and order that does not involve social renewal. In other words, in the context of fascism 'rebirth' means 'new birth', a 'new order', one which might draw inspiration from the past but does not seek to turn the clock back. However, two factors have obscured fascism's revolutionary, forward-looking thrust. First, in order to achieve power in the inter-war period fascism was forced to ally itself or collude with conservative forces (the army, Civil Service, Church, industrialists, reactionary bourgeois, etc.) on the basis of common enemies (such as communism, cosmopolitanism) and common priorities (such as law and order, the family).

Second, fascist ideologues frequently attach great importance to allegedly glorious epochs in the nation's past and the heroes which embody them. They do so not out of nostalgia, but to remind the people of the nation's 'true' nature and its destiny to rise once more to historical greatness. In *The Eighteenth Brumaire of Louis Bonaparte* Marx expressed an insight into the readiness of Napoleon III's regime to use myths based on the past to enlist popular support for the Second Empire which is equally pertinent to fascism. He saw that the 'awakening of the dead [. . .] served the purpose of glorifying the new struggles, not parodying the old; of magnifying the given task in imagination, not fleeing from its solution in reality; of finding once more the spirit of revolution, not making a ghost walk around again'.

3. *Fascism tends to operate as a charismatic form of politics*. Since, to use Weberian terminology, fascism rejects both the traditional politics of the *ancien régime* and the legal-rational politics of liberalism and socialism, it follows that it is predisposed to function as a *charismatic* form of politics. This does not necessarily involve the epitome of such politics, the leader cult. Historically, some forms of fascism (for example Valois's *Le Faisceau*) have opted for a technocratic, managerial model of the planned society, while others (for example, the French New Right) focus exclusively on the battle for cultural hegemony of ideas which would form the basis of a new order. In practice, though, there has been a marked tendency for fascist movements not to be containable within the framework of conventional party politics and to take the form of cadre or mass 'movements' with strong liturgical or cultic elements overtly appealing to highly charged collective emotions rather than to the individual's capacity for reasoned judgement.

All political ideologies are prone to assume a charismatic aspect when they operate as revolutionary forces—liberalism did, for example, in the French Revolution. It is significant, though, that fascism *remained* a charismatic form of politics in the two cases where it managed to install itself in power. Symptoms of this trait are the 'oceanic assemblies' and all-pervasive *littorio* (the *fasces*, or axe and rods carried as a symbol of power by lictors in ancient Rome) in the New Italy, and the Nuremberg rallies and the omnipresent *Hakenkreuz* (swastika) in the Third Reich. Both Fascism and Nazism as regimes were characterized by the centrality of the leader cult, the celebration of public over private space and time, and the constant attempt to use social engineering to regiment people into organizations with an ethos of activism and enthusiasm.

Such phenomena have often led specialists to use religious terminology in the analysis of fascism, claiming that it is a 'secular', 'civic', 'lay', or 'political' religion, replete with 'millenarian' or 'eschatological' energies. Such phrases are in order only so long as it is borne in mind that fascism sets out to operate on human society through human agency and within human history. It thus lacks a genuine metaphysical dimension and is the utter antithesis and destroyer of all genuine religious faith. Its compulsive use of the religious language of sacrifice, belief, resurrection, redemption, spirit, and its attacks on scepticism, doubt, materialism, consumerism, hedonism as the signs of moral decay are to be understood as the hallmarks of a modern political ideology seeking to offer a panacea to the malaise and anomie of contemporary society. They do not signify a literal regression to an earlier age of religious certainties (in which the nation as the focus of populist energies and the concept of the State as the creator of the ideal society did not exist).

4. *Fascism is anti-rational*. Consistent with its tendentially charismatic nature is fascism's frequent repudiation of rationalism and its overt celebration of myth. It is not so much irrational as anti-rational, seeing the most distinctive human faculty not in the reason celebrated in the Enlightenment, humanist, and positivist tradition, but in the capacity to be inspired to heroic action and self-sacrifice through the power of belief, myth, symbols, and *idées-forces* such as the nation, the leader, identity, or the regeneration of history. It should be stressed that fascism's anti-rationalism has not prevented it from producing a vast amount of highly articulate ideological writings, some of them displaying great erudition and theoretical verve, nor from turning selected components of the Western philosophical and scientific traditions into grist for its own mill.

5. *Fascist 'socialism'*. If it is the core mobilizing myth of the imminent (or, under a regime, ongoing) rebirth of the nation that forms the definitional core of fascism, it follows that the various fascist negations (anti-communism, anti-liberalism, etc.) are corollaries of this 'positive' belief, not definitional components. The same myth explains the recurrent claim by fascist ideologues that their vision of the new order is far from anti-socialist. Clearly it axiomatically rejects the internationalism and materialism of Marxism, but may well present the rejuvenation of the national community as transcending class conflict, destroying traditional hierarchy, expunging parasitism, rewarding all productive members of the new nation, and harnessing the energies of capitalism and technology in a new order in which they cease to be exploitative and enslaving. Indeed, in the inter-war period, when Bolsheviks were confident that their cause represented the next stage of human progress, many fascists made the counter-claim that their solution to the crisis of civilization embodied the only 'true' socialism, an assertion often associated with a commitment to corporatist economics, national syndicalism, and a high degree of state planning.

6. *Fascism's link to totalitarianism*. Also implicit in fascism's mythic core is the drive towards totalitarianism. Far from being driven by nihilism or barbarism, the convinced fascist is a utopian, conceiving the homogeneous, perfectly co-ordinated national community as a total solution to the problems of modern society. Yet any attempt to expunge all decadence necessarily leads to the creation of a highly centralized 'total' State with draconian powers to carry out a comprehensive scheme of social engineering. This will involve massive exercises in regimenting people's lives, and the creation of an elaborate machinery for manufacturing consensus through propaganda and indoctrination combined with repression and terror directed against alleged enemies, both internal and external, of the new order.

In this way any regime's attempt to realize the fascist utopia would lead in practice to an Orwellian dystopia, though the actual scale of destruction and atrocities it caused would vary considerably according to how the ideal 'national community' was conceived and the degree of co-operation in the general public and crucial areas of State power that it could count on. As a result the 'totalitarian State' in Italy became a grim travesty of what Mussolini intended, namely a new order in which the individual's life was to be infused with moral purpose and heroism by becoming symbiotically linked to that of the State. The term thus acquired instead its chilling post-war connotations. It is worth remembering, however, that modern society is intrinsically and irreducibly heterogeneous, and that no 'totalitarian' regime, fascist or not, has ever managed to stamp out elements of pluralism and polycentrism, no matter what lengths it has gone to.

Fortunately for humanity only two fascist movements have been in a position to attempt to implement their total solutions to society's alleged woes, namely Fascism and Nazism. All others have so far in one way or another been marginalized, emasculated, or crushed, though in the inter-war period some conservative authoritarian regimes (such as Franco's Spain or Antonescu's Romania) temporarily incorporated fascist movements, a ploy used by the Third Reich in several of its puppet states (for example, Norway and Hungary).

7. *The heterogeneity of fascism's social support*. The sociological implication of this ideal type of fascism is that it has no specific class basis in its support. If the middle classes were over-represented in the membership of Fascism and Nazism, this is because specific socio-political conditions made a significant percentage of them more susceptible to a palingenetic form of ultra-nationalism than to a palingenetic form of Marxism or liberalism. There is nothing in principle which precludes an employed or unemployed member of the working classes or an aristocrat, a city-dweller or a peasant, a graduate, or someone 'educationally challenged' from being susceptible to fascist myth. Nor is the fascist mentality exclusively the domain of men or the young, though its stress on heroism and the need for a new élite easily lends itself to militarism and hence to male chauvinism, especially when heroism is associated with physical courage, violence, war, and imperialism.

8. *Fascist racism*. By its nature fascism is racist, since all ultra-nationalisms are racist in their celebration of the alleged virtues and greatness of an organically conceived nation or culture. However, fascist ultra-nationalism does not necessarily involve biological or Social Darwinian concepts of race leading to eugenics, euthanasia, and attempted genocide. Nor does it necessarily involve anti-Semitism, or hatred directed against any particular group perceived as culturally or genetically different, or simply 'internal enemies' of the nation (such as Roma/Gypsies, Muslims, Hungarians, homosexuals, blacks). Obviously, if such elements of 'heterophobia' (fear and hatred of those felt to be 'different') are already present in the particular political culture of the nation where fascism arises, it is more than likely that they will be incorporated into its myth of national decadence and hence into the policies for creating the new order.

Fascism is also intrinsically anti-cosmopolitan, axiomatically rejecting as decadent the liberal vision of the multi-cultural, multi-religious, multi-racial society. However, this does not necessarily lead to a call for other races to be persecuted *per se*, but may express itself 'merely' in a campaign of propaganda and violence against their presence as 'immigrants' who have abandoned their 'natural' homeland. This type of fascism thus tends to produce an *apartheid* mentality calling for ethnically pure nation-states, for 'foreigners' to go back, or be returned, to 'where they belong', and a vitriolic hatred of 'mixed marriages' and cultural 'bastardization'.

9. *Fascist internationalism.* Fascism, though anti-internationalist in the sense of regarding national distinctiveness and identity as primordial values, is quite capable of generating its own form of universalism or internationalism by fostering a kindred spirit and bond with fascists in other countries engaged in an equivalent struggle for their own nation's palingenesis, often against common enemies (for example, liberals, communists, and, if they are white supremacists, non-white races). In Europe this may well lead to a sense of fighting for a common European homeland on the basis of Europe's alleged cultural, historical, or even genetic unity in contrast to non-Christian, non-Indo-European / Aryan peoples (for instance, Muslims, 'Asian' Soviet or Chinese communists) or degenerate ones (citizens of the USA or the 'Third World'). Within such a Europe, national or ethnic identities would, according to the fascist blueprint, be strengthened, not diluted. (The practical impossibility of realizing such a scheme does not worry fascists, since the nebulousness and impracticality of all their long-term goals is crucial to the mythic power they exert.)

10. *Fascist eclecticism.* Perhaps the most important corollary of our ideal type for the purposes of this Reader, however, is its suggestion that fascism pre-exists any particular externalization in the form of articulated or concretized thought. Inevitably each fascism will be made in the image or 'imagining' of a particular national culture, but even within the same movement or party its most influential ideologues will inevitably represent a wide range of ideas and theories, sometimes quite incompatible with each other *except at the level of a shared mythic core of palingenetic ultra-nationalism.* Fascism is thus inherently syncretic, bringing heterogeneous currents of ideas into a loose alliance united only by the common struggle for a new order. As a result there is in fascist thought a recurrent element of (and sometimes declared intention of) synthesis. This befits a latecomer to the European political scene which not only had to fight for its own political space against rival modern ideologies (liberalism, conservatism, socialism, communism), but legitimate itself ideologically in a culture teeming with well-established ideas and thinkers. What conditions the content and thrust of fascist eclecticism is the myth of national rebirth.

It is worth adding that, in its self-creation through synthesis, fascist ideology can draw just as easily on right-wing forms of thought (such as mutations of Christianity, racism, élitist and decadent aesthetics, Nietzscheanism, occultism, forms of illiberalism, integral nationalism, etc.) as on forms of left-wing thought (for example, derivatives of anti-materialist or utopian socialism, such as syndicalism). It is also implicit in what has been said that fascism is not necessarily confined to inter-war Europe, but can flourish wherever the stability of Western-style liberal democracy is threatened by a particular conjuncture of destabilizing forces (see Griffin 1993: ch. 8).

If read in the light of the above considerations, many of the excerpts of fascist writings assembled in this volume will not appear simply as isolated samples of an aberrant genus of political thought. They should cumulatively acquire a deeper resonance as different products of the same ideological matrix, as permutations of the same rationale for a war of 'creative destruction' to be waged against a particular status quo. Within the shell of their utopianism lies the seed of a totalitarian nightmare for all those who in one way or other are not deemed to belong within the regenerated national community or fit into the new order. Whether their author is a lone dreamer, the mouthpiece of a purely 'cultural' think-tank, the spokesman of an activist paramilitary movement, the propagandist of a compaigning electoral party, the policy-maker of an organization within a fascist regime, or the charismatic leader himself, he is giving specific form to the latent mythic core which defines fascism and determines its various attributes in historical reality.

It is this mythic core which accounts for the sharp distinction which this volume implicitly draws between the fascist regimes in Italy and Germany bent on creating a revolutionary new social and ethical order on the basis of mass mobilization, and the many authoritarian right-wing regimes which have been spawned by the twentieth century whose fundamental aim is the reactionary one of using mechanisms of intensive social engineering and repression to maintain the social status quo. Many military dictatorships fit into this latter category, and are characterized by an absence of genuine ideology or myth of renewal: when they have recourse to a leader cult, appeal to populist nationalist sentiment, or stress traditional family or religious values, it is simply to manufacture consensus and conceal an ideological vacuum. In the inter-war period, however, a number of authoritarian regimes consciously adopted some of the trappings and style of Fascism or Nazism to generate an illusion of national rejuvenation while resolutely resisting any populist pressures to change the system from below. Examples are Salazar's Portugal, Franco's Spain, Pétain's 'Vichy' France, Dollfuss's Austria, Horthy's Hungary, Antonescu's Romania, Vargas's Brazil, and Tōjō's Japan. The creation of a single-party state, the founding of a youth movement or a 'shirted' militia, and the rhetoric of national reawakening do not in themselves constitute fascism unless they are associated with a core ideology of rebirth which is as anti-conservative as it is anti-liberal or anti-Bolshevik, whatever compromises it has had to make with existing élites and institutions to achieve and retain power in practice. Such regimes I have termed elsewhere 'para-fascist' (Griffin 1993: 120–4). They have been ignored in this volume as a source of original texts.

From what has been said, the organization of the Reader should hold few surprises. Part I is an attempt to bring together texts which afford glimpses into the mythic core and the historical evolution of the only phenomenon to which any definition of fascism must apply, namely the Fascist movement led by Benito Mussolini. In it the lens provided by the ideal type has been used to focus attention on currents of thought which flowed into infant Fascism, or contributed to its adolescence, its maturity, and the rapid onset of its senility. The same approach is used for National Socialism (Part II). Several major experts deny fascist status altogether to the Third Reich. However, as the extracts suggest, Nazism not only amply fulfils the definitional criteria established by the ideal type, but turns out to have been only the most successful of a plethora of German fascisms of the period. Samples of these have also been included to underline the fact that in its formative period Nazism was able to draw on a political culture already saturated with forms of palingenetic ultra-nationalist myth.

This is followed in Part III by a survey of abortive fascisms of the inter-war period. As explained, the ideal type used in this volume denies fascist status to all authoritarian regimes other than Fascist Italy (including the Italian Social Republic) and Nazi Germany. It also excludes many movements which have sometimes been associated with fascism, either because they lacked a genuine, radical, palingenetic thrust (for example, the French Croix de Feu), or because they pursued the separatist goal of creating a new nation, and not of rejuvenating an existing nation-state (such as the Croatian Ustasha). However, enough European movements do fit the prescribed criteria to illustrate the adaptability of fascism to individual national cultures, and while very few movements outside Europe qualify, there are sufficient to refute the notion that fascism is an exclusively European phenomenon.

The Reader then considers an assortment of inter-war and post-war theories of fascism (Part IV), underlining the wide diversity of reactions and approaches it has provoked over the decades. Such an excursus into definitions is particularly necessary since the theory of generic fascism is inextricably bound up with the phenomenon itself, and should serve to emphasize the strictly tentative, heuristic nature of my own approach. Part V then focuses on post-war manifestations of fascism, and should convince all those naïve enough to assume fascism died in 1945 that it is in fact like a super-virus which constantly evolves to accommodate changes in its habitat, producing a wide variety of new strains resistant to traditional prophylactics.

A few further points might usefully be made here before readers embark on, or dip into, the texts which follow. It is in the nature of the exercise of assembling such an anthology that it can only scratch the surface of fascism as a textual phenomenon, and that it has both a degree of Anglophone and Anglocentric bias (particularly evident in Parts IV and V) in the materials selected. What is less self-evident is that a fundamental editorial decision has been made to sample as many forms of fascism as possible rather than offer a few lengthy specimens of it. This has meant a series of heavily cropped snapshots to illustrate fascism's extraordinarily protean quality rather than some more detailed portraits. Even so, countless smaller movements have been left out of the album, ranging from insignificant ones, like the Fascist Brown Shirts in Canada, to much more important ones like the Dutch National Socialists led by Mussert, eventually nominal head of state under the Nazis. I would urge readers who want to go into more depth than this volume permits to study any full-length primary source(s) available to them, hopefully with renewed curiosity and a sharpened eye for the typical features of its 'discourse'. (Incidentally, I would be grateful to receive samples of primary sources relating to fascisms I have omitted.)

On a quite different tack, I would like to emphasize that this is an academic work, not a journalistic one. It necessarily involves operating a particular ideal type of the term 'fascist' as a taxonomic category of political analysis. As such it is not being used as a term of personal abuse, nor does the selection of a particular passage imply its author's guilt by association for the suffering inflicted on millions of people as a result of the policies pursued by the two fascist regimes half a century ago, nor for the acts of criminality and violence carried out by contemporary fascist movements committed to racist or terrorist violence. The subject under investigation here is 'fascism' as a political myth and an ideology, not the 'fascist' as a personality type or historical actor. Clearly there is a casual connection between the two, but the connection is not immediate or simple. In particular, there are numerous cases of modern ideologues who produce texts which my ideal type identifies as fascist, but who stay aloof from paramilitary or mass movements and repudiate violence, seeing culture, not the streets or parliament, as the prime arena in which the battle for national, European, or Aryan regeneration is to be fought. They would be likely to resent their ideas being categorized as fascist, whatever the structural links between their ideas and the mythic matrix I have identified. Moreover, it is quite possible to contribute to some of the newer discourses of fascism, such as revisionism or the New Right, without harbouring any sympathy with organized fascism at all, but simply by having written works which can be cited as mitigating circumstances for the atrocities committed by Nazism, or as theoretical justification for the rejection of egalitarian ideals.

By now the reader should be assured that this anthology has no 'revisionist' intent of euphemizing fascism, let alone vindicating it. To grant fascism full ideological status, to claim that the well-springs of fascism are idealism and the longing for a new and better age, or to defend its compatibility with modernity, is not to rehabilitate it. In a sense, assembling this volume has been like preparing scores of laboratory slides to exhibit different species of the same genus of disease for the benefit of those concerned by the damage it can wreak or engaged in the search for a cure. If fascists were to peruse this volume I trust they would have no difficulty alighting on passages which chime in with their diagnosis of the ills of contemporary society, but that they would find that the accompanying notes smack unpleasantly of the decadent liberal values which they reject. The 'true' readers are all those who want to understand better the fascist syndrome in order to inoculate themselves, and even others, against it.

As I write in the summer of 1994, 'post-fascist' politicians have recently been elected to the new Italian Government and to the European Parliament, while radically fascist sentiments are being openly expressed by the publicity machine of Vladimir Zhirinovky, who according to some Pundits might just conceivably become the next Russian president. Meanwhile, all over the world groups of population are retrenching into their ethnic or cultural identity, many in a spirit of radical intolerance of the equivalent identity of others. I would like to think that by the time these lines are read this volume will have lost rather than increased its relevance, so that it can be seen as a companion to historical studies rather than to current affairs. But this is probably to indulge in wishful thinking. A close causal relationship exists in modern societies between political and economic crises and the growth of ultra-nationalism. Given the structural forces now generating such crises in various parts of the globe, I fear that not many years will pass before this selection requires an appendix of new passages to bring it up to date, or someone is commissioned to compile an anthology entirely devoted to contemporary forms of rebirth ultra-nationalism. This may be the first Reader in fascism. It is a sign of the times that it seems destined not to be the last.

PART I

Fascism in Italy

There is one respect in which selecting samples of writing symptomatic of fascism in Italy is less problematic than for any other country. At least it is undeniable that a movement, a loose body of political myth (I have deliberately avoided the term 'doctrine'), and in due course a party and a regime, arose in inter-war Italy referred to by supporters and opponents alike as 'Fascismo'. (Italians write both 'Fascismo' and 'fascismo', though the adjective 'fascista' is never capitalized. I nevertheless capitalize both noun and adjective in the context of Mussolini's movement, as explained above, p. 1.) As a result Part I is unencumbered by the problem of defining (generic) fascism which is implicit in Parts II, III, and V.

Yet this simplifying factor is more than compensated for by a number of others peculiar to the Italian situation which complicate both exposition and analysis. Firstly, the Fascist regime was fully in power for some eighteen years (1925–43), six years longer than Nazism and thus with even more time to undergo radical shifts in structure, policy, and ethos, as well as to continue pouring out expositions of its principles and goals. Secondly, Fascism has an even more complex and drawn-out career than Nazism. In contrast to Hitler, Mussolini was well established as a political leader and national figure before the First World War, and took a conspicuous part in the interventionist campaign which finally helped push Italy into the war in the 'radiant' days of May 1915. This campaign for the first time brought together various currents of ultra-nationalism which were eventually to converge and lend impetus to the Fascist movement and regime. Indeed, interventionism can be said to prefigure Fascism in a way which has no equivalent in the case of Nazism (whose many pre-war *völkisch* thinkers and so-called cultural pessimists, rightly seen as laying the ideological foundation of Nazism, never coalesced into a uniform political force).

After the First World War Fascism started out as a revolutionary movement pledged to carry the generation of the trenches and of the 'new Italy' into power via extra-parliamentary 'Fasci di combattimento', a name deliberately chosen to evoke the interventionist campaign (whose main organizational body had been the '*Fasci* [leagues] of revolutionary action'), the Parliamentary Fascio of National Defence formed in December 1917, and the key role of veterans (*combattenti*) as the nucleus of the new ruling élite. However, it remained negligible as a political factor, despite its energetic use of paramilitary violence, propaganda, and electioneering to create a power base in Milan. In fact, Mussolini's exploits were vastly overshadowed by D'Annunzio's occupation in September 1919 of Fiume, an Adriatic city claimed by Italy in reward for its support of the Entente powers, but decreed a free port by the Paris Peace Conference. It was only when 'maximalist' socialists resorted to radical action to bring about *their* transformation of Italy during the 'red two years' (*biennio rosso*) of 1919–20, thereby provoking a violent right-wing backlash, that Fascism took off as a mass movement and a national political force. This was because a major component in both the original Fasci and the new 'action squads' (*squadre d'azione*) were veteran soldiers, especially former members of the élite combat troops, the Arditi, formed in the First World War. In November 1921 Fascism officially became a party-political force with the formation of the Partito Nazionale Fascista, and the dual aspect this gave Fascism as both a paramilitary, extra-systemic and an electoral, systemic organization helped Mussolini to pull off in October 1922 the remarkable gamble for the 'conquest of power' that became known as the March on Rome. As a result of the 'deal' struck with the king, Victor Emmanuel III, for him to call off what amounted to a threatened *putsch*, Mussolini became at the same time the leader of a revolutionary paramilitary force and Prime Minister of a coalition government operating within a parliamentary system.

The next two years saw a conflict develop between the violent 'manganello' (rubber truncheon), 'intransigent' aspect of Fascists and the 'doppio petto' (double-breasted waistcoat), constitutional one. The *squadristi* had in theory been neutralized by their absorption into a Voluntary Militia of National Security (MVSN), but the most radical elements were not content to see their revolution emasculated and in June 1924 'took out', possibly at Mussolini's instigation, his most courageous and outspoken parliamentary critic, the socialist deputy Matteotti. This provoked a prolonged political malaise at the heart of state power which was only resolved when Mussolini, realizing the opportunity afforded him by the inertia of his opponents, suppressed parliamentary opposition parties and created an authoritarian government made up entirely of Fascists. It is only at this point that it is possible to talk of Italy being under a 'Fascist regime', and even here a number of overlapping 'phases' can be discerned: the establishment of a 'totalitarian' system (1925–9); the period of consolidation and of growing confidence that Italy was the only European nation which had solved the economic, social, and state crises which seemed to be afflicting the whole developed world in the wake of the First World War and the Depression (1930–4); the move towards African imperialism and rapprochement with Nazism (1935–9), and war (1940–3).

The regime's comprehensive failure to 'Fascistize' (inculcate with Fascist values) all but a minority of Italians, or to establish the social cohesion, economic and industrial dynamism, or military strength claimed by the exorbitant rhetoric of 'totalitarian' Italy was to seal its fate. In July 1943 some of the Fascist 'hierarchs', appalled at the progress of the war and the disastrous consequences of the Anglo-American onslaught being allowed to continue, colluded with the king to oust Mussolini as head of government and to negotiate an armistice. Fascism as a monarchical and national regime was therefore finished. Yet, just as it had a shadowy pre-existence in two years of coalition government, regime-Fascism was also granted a shadowy, and in terms of state terror much more brutal, two years of after-life in the form of the Italian Social Republic. This regime, also referred to sarcastically as the 'Republic of Salò' after the small town on Lake Garda from which official propaganda emanated, was set up by the Third Reich and garrisoned by the German army (though nominally governed by intransigent Fascists), only to be gradually squeezed out of existence as the Allies fought their way up the peninsula. It is worth adding that since the war Fascism has enjoyed a continuous existence in Italy both as a party-political and extra-systemic (and sometimes terrorist) force, during which time it has continued to undergo considerable ideological evolution (see Texts 171, 188, 211).

To offer representative samples of Fascist thought is far from straightforward. Fascism is notorious for the wide range of conflicting positions which it adopted over time: propounding anti-clericalism and forging a pact with the Vatican; upholding both republicanism and monarchism; asserting the rights of the proletariat in theory and of the bourgeoisie and big business in practice; claiming to be destroying class barriers in a democratic and populist spirit, while also boasting its hierarchical, authoritarian, and 'totalitarian' nature; venting its scorn on all political parties yet forming one; claiming Fascism was uniquely Italian and hence 'not for export' and yet asserting its validity as a role model for all modern nations; celebrating the modern in an iconoclastic, Futurist spirit and yet imposing the cult of 'Romanness' based on the glories of the Classical world; boasting of the uniqueness of Italy as the sole regenerating force of civilization and acknowledging Nazism to be its twin manifestation of revolutionary nationalism. Mussolini even signed a Pacification Pact with the Italian Socialist Party in August 1921 before the decisive shift towards compromise with the force of monarchism, the Church, and big business thereafter, only to revive the rhetoric of 'socialism' in the Italian Social Republic (though by now this meant a national socialism forged in the spirit of Nazism).

Some of these contradictions can be explained by Mussolini's belief that, in his own words, 'the equivalence of all ideologies, all equally fictions' gave him 'the right to create his own and to impose it with all the energy of which he was capable' (quoted Lyttelton 1987: 365). In practice this meant he felt at liberty to chop and change his programme to adapt to shifts in the objective conditions in which he sought to gain or consolidate power. He thus had no scruples about arriving at an accommodation with the monarchy, the army, the Church, and big business despite his socialist origins. This accommodation was essential for Fascism, always a minority movement in terms of hard-core followers, to form a government (Hitler's back-pedalling on the anti-capitalist elements of the official Nazi programme was prompted by similar considerations). Many biographers of Mussolini would also stress the fickleness and cynicism of Mussolini as a political leader, which would seem to be borne out by his promotion of Nazi-style race laws in 1938 after several earlier speeches had mocked Germanic fantasies of Aryan purity. However, the documentary evidence adduced by major experts on Fascism such as Emilio Gentile, Renzo de Felice, and Walter Adamson about Mussolini's intellectual development before 1914 suggest that he stayed remarkably faithful to a single core myth, that of the creation of a new Italy based on a regenerated national community. It was a vision nebulous enough to allow him to appropriate a number of conflicting components of thought and policy as long as they had this vital ingredient.

This would explain why he encouraged the confluence within Fascism of several discrete currents of pre-1914 ultra-nationalism, without ever trying to resolve their contradictions: proponents of 'Vocean' nationalism (e.g. Papini), the nationalist permutation of revolutionary syndicalism (e.g. Panunzio), and political Futurism (e.g. Marinetti) were all welcomed into the open arms of early Fascism, where in time they were to commingle with the nationalism of the Italian National Association (e.g. Rocco), Dannunzianism, Gentilean idealism, 'universal Fascism' (e.g. Gravelli), and racism, not to mention a whole range of aesthetics ranging from abstract art and modernism (e.g. Bontempelli) to vernacular primitivism (e.g. Maccari). Given this pluralism, so strikingly at odds with the monolithic uniformity of what is generally imagined to constitute totalitarianism, it is not surprising if the legion attempts by enthusiastic Fascist intellectuals to formulate Fascist doctrines on a vast range of political, social, cultural, economic, and philosophical issues produced a welter of conflicting ideas. No wonder, then, if one commentator, Augusto Lanzillo in his 1922 book *La rivoluzione del dopoguerra* [The Post-War Revolution] was observing on the eve of the March on Rome that there was not one Fascism but various Fascisms, a point echoed in the title of Adrian Lyttelton's anthology of Fascist writings (1973), *Italian Fascisms from Pareto to Gentile*. Indeed, after 1925 Fascism is best approached ideologically as a loose alliance of schemes for national renewal, linked in turn to various brands of conservatism, in particular monarchism and Catholicism. Other important ingredients were the strong current of imperialism and urge to become a Great Power which had emerged in the late nineteenth century under liberalism, and a genuine populist nationalism aroused by the later stages of the First World War and the frustrations of the 'mutilated victory'.

If the refusal of Mussolini to impose a rigid doctrinal orthodoxy on his movement contributed to his regime's durability, it also helps explains its failure to Fascistize society to any meaningful degree. If Fascism could mean all things to all (patriotic, anti-communist and chauvinistic) men (and some women), then it was relatively easy for it to enlist sufficient support to function on a day-to-day basis once it had seized power, but equally easy for it to mean little more than an inflated sense of national pride and unthinking support of a regime which seemed at last to be making Italy a modern, powerful, internationally respected nation. No deep-seated conversion or transformation was called for: as a mass phenomenon the *homo fascistus*, the Fascist New Man, was still-born. The fatal tendency of Fascist leaders, first and foremost Mussolini himself, to confuse rhetoric with reality, encouraged by Fascism's stress on the primacy of moral and spiritual transformation, meant that the New Italy ultimately remained little more than a myth, one which evaporated almost without trace for all but a minority of 'intransigents' like Farinacci once the Allies invaded the peninsula.

It would be tempting to infer from this situation, as many have done, that Fascism lacked an ideology. If this term is taken to mean an internally cohesive and rigorous body of political theory then this is doubtless correct. But if ideology is interpreted as a normative and mobilizing myth then its core emerges clearly from every type of writing associated with Fascism, whatever their surface differences. It is the vision of a heroic, youthful 'new Italy' arising from the collapse of the played-out liberal order incarnated in the Giolittian era. In other words Fascist ideology consisted of numerous permutations of the 'palingenetic ultra-nationalism' which we have proposed as the defining trait of generic fascism (see the General Introduction above). It was a myth sufficiently cogent to inform a broad front of policy-making, inspire an elaborate civic liturgy (or 'political religion'), and secure a wide degree of (admittedly somewhat perfunctory and superficial) popular consensus as long as the harsh realities of war and defeat were kept at a safe distance from public conscience.

The documentary legacy of Fascist ideology is constituted by millions of words deposited in thousands of academic texts, works of propaganda, journals, newspapers, pamphlets, manifestos, novels, poems, diaries, and letters, not to mention the important semiotic testimonies of the visual arts, architecture, films, newsreels, photographs, and posters, and another abundant and interesting source material, namely post-war memoirs. The selection which follows: (i) presents forty-five short passages rather than reproduce a few lengthy excerpts from a handful of sources; (ii) omits texts already available in English in Adrian Lyttelton's *Italian Fascisms* (1973), which includes the (perhaps over-)famous, but still essential, *Enciclopedia Italiana* article 'Fascism' by Giovanni Gentile and Mussolini; (iii) includes passages written at various stages of Fascism's history from pre-Fascism to the Italian Social Republic, several of them marking pivotal events (such as the foundation of Fascism or the rapprochement with Hitler); (iv) illustrates different currents of thought within Fascism, sometimes at a stage prior to their formal amalgamation with it; (vi) represents several types of source, namely programmatic statements, books, journal and newspaper articles, speeches, and interviews; (vii) concentrates on writings by figures who were or were to become leading Fascists. Pride of place has been given to articles and speeches by Mussolini himself, for not only have they yet to be comprehensively translated into English (there are two editions of his voluminous collected writings in Italian), but they played a particularly important part both in creating the illusion of the dynamism of his movement and regime, and in charting the contorted evolution of official Fascist thinking on a wide range of issues.

What I hope will emerge cumulatively in reading these texts is the extraordinary diversity of Fascist thought; the considerable degree of convergence among Fascist ideologues on the central palingenetic myth of the new Italy, the new state, the new Italian man, the new (European) civilization; the emphatically renovating and modernizing thrust of most strands of Fascism; the fact that Fascism is not to be reduced to 'Mussolinism'; the fecundity of Fascism as a source of theories and doctrines despite its markedly rhetorical and mythic thrust.

If I have succeeded in my intention, readers may be persuaded that Fascism did have an ideological dimension, albeit of an overtly anti-rational kind typical of charismatic politics. They may also sense some of the *revolutionary* excitement that it inspired in genuine converts. With some historical awareness of the human tragedies and atrocities for which Fascism was responsible or co-responsible from the invasion of Ethiopia onwards, they may also have a chilling sense of the shadow which inevitably fell between the Fascist dream that a new era was dawning and the grim historical realities it actually generated.

Section A

Fascism as an Opposition Movement

INTRODUCTION

The first part of this section (Ai) opens with a flavour of the various brands of ultra-nationalism with their own project for the renewal of Italy which came together in the interventionist campaign that helped generate support for the government's decision to enter the war on the side of the Entente powers in May 1915. It samples the nationalism formulated by G. Papini and his entourage (notably Prezzolini and Corradini) ever since the founding of the periodicals *Il Leonardo* and *La Voce*, here expressed in the Futurist magazine *Lacerba* on the eve of the war (Text 1); revolutionary syndicalist thought in the manifesto of the main organization of interventionism, the Fascio rivoluzionario d'azione internazionalista: the 'international' was soon dropped, but the term 'Fascio' became closely associated with the interventionist spirit (Text 2); Marinetti's characteristic brand of political Futurism (Text 3), and Mussolini's call for intervention published in the first issue of his newly founded *Il Popolo d'Italia*, which went on to be the main daily newspaper of official Fascism (Text 4). The way these components of political myth converged on the idea of the war as the catalyst to national renewal and thereby prefigured Fascism is discussed in an important article by Adamson (1992).

The war consolidated the interventionist myth of the imminent transition from the old Italy to the new while adding a new component to it: so-called *combattentismo*, or the spirit of the trenches kept alive by war veterans. This vital ingredient of what would become Fascism's foundation myth is illustrated by Mussolini's piece on the 'trenchocracy' (Text 5), the manifesto of the Political Futurist Party (Text 6), the article on the New Italy by Rocco (Text 7), another major protagonist of interventionism, and a passage from the history of the Fascist conquest of the state by Farinacci (Text 8), one of the most 'intransigent' recruits to the early Fasci and a stalwart of the Salò Republic.

Section Aii opens with the three short declarations of the principles of Fascism on its foundation which show its debt to *combattentismo* (Text 9). It then moves to the Carnaro Charter, the constitution of the Fiume 'regency', imbued with the 'leftist' spirit of syndicalism imparted by the theoretician De Ambris and with the 'rightist' visionary register characteristic of the poet D'Annunzio (Text 10), one of the most important interventionists and now a national war hero. The organic, hierarchic conception of the new nation promoted as a solution to the country's ills by the Nationalists (i.e. members of the Italian Nationalist Association) can then be gleaned from Text 11, while a diary entry (Text 12) underlines how important this myth was to the outbreak of paramilitary violence against socialism known as *squadrismo*, which catapulted Fascism into becoming a major force in national politics. Three texts testify to the rapid way Fascism was changing in the run up to the 'conquest of the state' of October 1922, one by ANI leader and now Fascist deputy Federzoni to parliament (Text 13), and two by Mussolini himself. The first gives his own account of the significance of the sudden way Fascist support had taken off in the countryside (Text 14), while the second is a major statement of Fascism's core myth made in Naples three days before the March on Rome (Text 15).

The two-year lull before the Fascist storm during which Mussolini was Prime Minister of a coalition government (Section Aiii) was characterized by intense ideological and publicistic activity by Fascists concerned to give some theoretical focus to the revolution they were now more convinced than ever they were carrying out. We find Marinetti claiming Mussolini as a Futurist leader (Text 16), former socialist and now Fascist syndicalist Panunzio giving an account of the new synthesis which Fascism embodied (Text 17), and Malaparte's own vision of the revolutionary task of 'national syndicalism' (Text 18). The section concludes with excerpts from Mussolini's crucial speech in which he announces to an inert parliament his own draconian measure for resolving the crisis created by the assassination of Matteotti: the establishment of a Fascist dictatorship (Text 19).

i. Pre-1918 Tributaries of Fascism

GIOVANNI PAPINI

1 The War as a Source of National Renewal

Giovanni Papini (1881–1956) was one of the most prolific and influential publicists in the pre-1915 campaign for a new Italy based on the spread of a new aesthetic sensibility and the emergence of a new political class of homines novi *(new men). Under the Fascists he became professor of Literature, editor of the arts magazine* Il Frontespizio, *member of the Royal Academy, and spokesman of racial policies (though he distanced himself from Nazism). He embodied much of the 'rightist' aspect of Fascism which rejected both social-ism and liberalism for their 'materialism', and was naturally drawn to the interventionist campaign for which he wrote this article (see Adamson 1993).*

Italy, even if it was no longer a geographical expression, was quickly becoming a metaphysical expression.

A great power, but the weakest of all; armed, but incapable of waging war; full of social unrest, but with no serious will to change regime; conservative, but spineless whenever there was a hint of threat to stability. Cavour had understood the situation well: nothing great can be made with shit. Italy of 1860 had been shit dragged kicking and screaming towards unification by a daring minority, and shit it remained throughout fifty years of unification, urged on by the occasional outbursts of zeal from small minorities either in favour of an imperial mission in Africa or of a liberating transformation in its domestic politics.

We are a country of botched attempts: everything is tried and nothing comes off. A nation which constantly fails through the lack of a mobilizing force.

Those who hold power are of three types: the old, the incapable, the charlatans. Old and hence impotent; incapable and hence disasters; charlatans and hence traitors.[. . .]

Now we propose to make new pacts with you, our Italy. We have not loved you enough. We abandoned you because, in our puerile fantasies, you were not pure and perfect like in the apocalypses painted by old masters. We surrendered you to the clutches of those without backbone, to tricksters, racketeers, shady solicitors, mercenary shopkeepers, foreigners, cretins, thieves, and garrulous lawyers. We abandoned you, and because you were soiled we allowed you to be soiled even more. You were in the hands of imbecility and of vested interest, and we, with our intelligence and disinterest, we wandered off in a huff.

We acknowledge our guilt, and do not deny our pangs of conscience. Even if you are what you are, we should not have taken refuge in more ethereal worlds to descend, as yesterday, as today, only when rifles started flashing. Italy, as an invalid, you need the best to stand by you in the living flesh. We know which side we are on.

A new generation exists which is more gifted, stronger, more spirited, more cultured, more honest than the one which precedes us and now governs us. This generation has the right henceforth to take up its proper place in society. Others have brought our country into a terrible state: the least they can do is let us make the effort to raise her up again. The war will not suffice. But it is enough to start with. Afterwards there will be a total change in the ruling classes, of the caste which holds power. We are laying the foundations for this change. We will not only be its poets, but its theorists. We will not only read books, but also its balance sheets. We want to know how things stand. We have the right finally to know precisely what you have done to this people from whom you have always demanded blood and money without ever granting it an ounce more happiness or an ounce more glory.

Now we are here. We know what is our duty and our place. There is work for all to do. When the moment is right we will take off our jacket, roll up our sleeves and see whether this old Italian shit can finally be turned into a fine stone statue.

['Il nostro impegno' [Our task], *Lacerba*, 15 Nov. 1914; repr. in *Lacerba* (Gabriele Mazzotta: Milan, 1970), 305–7.]

REVOLUTIONARY SYNDICALISM

2 The War as a Proletarian Cause

The Revolutionary League (Fascio) for International Action (later transformed into the Leagues (Fasci) of Revolutionary Action) was formed by revolutionary syndicalists in October 1914 to campaign for Italy's intervention in the First World War, an issue which split the working-class movement into neutralists and interventionists. It was joined by a number of Mazzinian republicans and influential Socialists, and in November by Mussolini himself. A number of the activists of the Fasci (e.g. A. Olivetti) went on to become prominent advocates of the 'leftist' strand of corporativism under Fascism (see Texts 10, 17, 18, 28, 31, 37; Roberts 1979; Sternhell et al. 1994: chs. 3 and 4).

The war is today a tragic reality, one which we cannot watch as indifferent onlookers without betraying the very cause of the revolution, without denying our socialist principles which speak to the peoples in the name of civilization and freedom. Thus it is useful to ask if the most vital interests of the working class of various countries, if the cause of social revolution, are better served by the position of strict neutrality desired for Italy by the official Socialist Party, in full accord with clerical opinion, and working completely to the advantage of the German military, or whether they are not furthered instead by intervention to support those States[1] which represent in Europe the cause of liberty and peace: to support France which is the cradle of a hundred revolutions; England, safeguard of every political freedom; and Belgium, so generous and heroic. The reply cannot be in doubt for us revolutionaries, because, true to the teaching of our masters, we believe that the

---

[1] In all these texts the use of capitals in the original will be respected, notably the capitalization of 'State', except for *fascismo* and *fascista* which will always be capitalized in translation to indicate Italian fascism.

limits of national revolutions cannot be transcended without first reaching them, and for this reason the class struggle remains an empty formula, not a vital and fertile force, unless every people is first integrated within its own natural borders of language and race, and unless, once the question of nationality has been definitively resolved, the historical climate has formed necessary for the normal development of the class movement, and for the progress and triumph of the ideas which inspire working-class internationalism. The triumph of the Austro-German bloc in Europe would mean the renewed triumph of the Holy Alliance, the reinforcement of the cause of reaction and militarism over that of revolution, in a word the perpetuation and consolidation of the forces of militaristic and feudal conservatism which have brought about the present enormous catastrophe, which will produce other wars tomorrow, and with them more sorrow and misery for the working classes, who have been stopped in the midst of their march onwards and upwards towards the conquest of their own economic emancipation.[. . .]

Not to co-operate with the best means to give help to the worst. Revolutionaries can be in no doubt as to their choice.[. . .] All the vital forces of the world, all those who wish a better future for working humanity, and are struggling for the triumph of the proletarian cause and the social revolution, for the fraternity of all peoples and the end of all wars, must resolutely join the fray. We must force our government either to stop dishonouring us or to leave office. We meanwhile must allocate tasks and prepare ourselves for action.

['Ai lavoratori d'Italia' [To the workers of Italy], *Pagine Libere*, 6/1 (10 Oct. 1914); repr. as an appendix to Renzo de Felice, *Mussolini il rivoluzionario 1883–1920* (Einaudi: Turin, 1965), 679–81.]

FILIPPO T. MARINETTI

3 The War as the Catharsis of Italian Society

Filippo Marinetti (1876–1944) was the leading theoretician, poet, and propagandist of the Italian Futurist movement, which he launched with the famous manifesto published on 20 February 1909. His extreme cult of Italy, the machine age, and war led him to become an eloquent advocate of interventionism, as well as an ardent collaborator with, then supporter of, early Fascism (see Text 16). Despite his contempt for academies he was made member of the Royal Academy of Italy in 1929 and accepted honours from the Salò Republic. As well as illustrating the metapolitical, aestheticizing nature of much fascist ideology, Marinetti is the extreme embodiment of the modernist, anti-conservative thrust of Fascism.[2]

Italian students!
Since an illustrious past was crushing Italy and an infinitely more glorious future seethed in her breast, six years ago, under our all too voluptuous skies, Futurist

[2] See J. Joll, 'F. T. Marinetti: Futurism and Fascism', in *Three Intellectuals in Politics* (Pantheon Books: New York, 1965).

energy was to be born, to organize itself, to be channelled, to find in us her motors, her vehicles of illumination and propagation. Italy, more than any other country, was in dire need of Futurism, because she was dying of pastism.[3] The patient invented its own remedy. *We happen to be its doctors.* The remedy is valid for any country.

Our immediate programme was a relentless war against Italian pastism: archaeology, academicism, senilism, quietism, the obsession with sex, the tourist industry, etc. Our ultra-violent, anti-clerical, and anti-traditionalist nationalism is based on the inexhaustible vitality of Italian blood and the struggle against the ancestor-cult, which, far from cementing the race, makes it anaemic and putrid. But we were to move beyond this immediate programme, already (partly) realized in six years of ceaseless battles.[. . .]

Italian students!
Dynamic and aggressive, Futurism is now being fully realized in the great world war which it—alone—foresaw and glorified before it broke out. *The present war is the most beautiful Futurist poem which has so far been seen*; what Futurism signified was precisely the irruption of war into art, as embodied in the creation of the phenomenon of the Futurist Soirée (an extremely efficient means for propagating courage). Futurism was the militarization of innovating artists. Today we are witnessing an immense Futurist explosion of dynamic and aggressive contexts within which we soon wish to make our entrance and show what we are.[. . .]

Fatherland = expansion + multiplication of the *ego*. Italian patriotism = to contain and feel in oneself the whole of Italy and all the Italians of tomorrow.

The War will sweep from power all her foes: diplomats, professors, philosophers, archaeologists, critics, cultural obsession, Greek, Latin, history, senilism, museums, libraries, the tourist industry. The War will promote gymnastics, sport, practical schools of agriculture, business, and industrialists. The War will rejuvenate Italy, will enrich her with men of action, will force her to live no longer off the past, off ruins and the mild climate, but off her own national forces.

[Manifesto agli studenti of 29 Nov. 1914; published in *Futurismo e fascismo* (Franco Campitelli: Foligno, 1914); repr. in F. T. Marinetti, *Teorie e invenzione futurista* (Mondadori: Milan, 1968), 91–7.]

BENITO MUSSOLINI

....

4   The War as a Revolutionary Event

The two years spent in Switzerland (1902–4) had initiated Mussolini into a form of revolutionary socialism, based not on materialism or orthodox Marxism, but on a cocktail of voluntarist and anti-rational principles derived from Pareto, Le Bon, Nietzsche, and Sorel.

---

[3] A stifling preoccupation with the past diametrically opposed to Futurism.

This predisposed him to succumb after 1908 to the calls of the Papinian periodical La Voce for national renewal through a new élite of homines novi *(new men), as well as to the arguments of heterodox syndicalists for a 'revolutionary war'. Such an extensive 'revision' of his socialism along nationalist and voluntarist lines helps explain the famous volte-face of November 1914 when Mussolini broke with the neutral stance of the Socialists, resigned as editor of their paper* Avanti! *and founded his own,* Il Popolo d'Italia, *which soon became the most influential voice of interventionism. The most significant article in the first issue, from which this extract is taken, is his strident call for Italian intervention couched in the discourse of palingenetic myth (see Gregor 1979; Adamson 1993; Sternhell et al., 1994, ch. 5).*

Today—I will shout it out loud—anti-war propaganda is the propaganda of cowardice. It works because it titillates and excites the instinct for self-preservation. But this in itself makes it anti-revolutionary propaganda. It is fine coming from lay priests and Jesuits who have a material and spiritual stake in the conservation of the Austrian Empire; it is fine coming from bourgeois, black-marketeers, or worse who—especially in Italy—show their pitiful political and moral inadequacy; it is fine coming from royalists who, especially if they are decorated with the laticlave,[4] cannot bring themselves to tear up the treaty of the Triple Alliance which guaranteed—apart from peace (and we have seen what sort of peace!)—the continued existence of the throne. This coalition of pacifists knows exactly what it wants and we can form a clear picture of the motives which inspire its attitude. But we socialists, we have always represented—except in the dark periods of mercantile and Giolittian reformism—one of the 'living' forces of the new Italy: do we now want to attach our destiny to these 'dead' forces in the name of a 'peace' which does not save us from the disasters of war today and will not save us from the infinitely greater ones tomorrow, and which in any case will not save us from shame and from the universal derision of peoples who have lived through this great tragedy of history? Do we want to drag out our miserable day-by-day existence—content with the royalist and bourgeois status quo—or do we want instead to break up this murky conspiracy of dull-witted schemers and cowards?[. . .] These disturbing questions (which I, for my part, have replied to) explain the origin and purpose of this newspaper. What I have undertaken is an act of audacity, and I have no illusions about the difficulties of the undertaking. They are many and complex, but I have a firm faith in my ability to overcome them. I am not alone. Not all my friends of yesterday will follow me; but many other rebellious spirits will gather around me. I will create a newspaper which is independent, totally free, personal, *mine*. I harbour no aggression towards the Socialist Party, or against the organs of the Party, in which I intend to stay, but I am prepared to fight anyone who tries to stop me freely criticizing a cast of mind which for various reasons I consider disastrous to the national and international interests of the Proletariat.[. . .]

I am on my way! And taking up my march once more—after what was a brief respite—it is you, the young of Italy, the young of the workplace and the universities, the young in years and in spirit, the young who belong to the generation

---

[4] A badge consisting of two purple stripes worn as a sign of high office.

which destiny has charged with 'making' history, it is you that I hail with a cry of greeting, in the certainty that it will not fall on deaf ears in your ranks, but summon forth a powerful response.

The cry is a word which I would never have uttered in normal times, but which today I shout out loud, at the top of my voice, with absolute sincerity and steadfast conviction, a word which is both dreadful and awesome: *war!*

['Audacia!' [Courage!], *Il Popolo d'Italia*, 15 Nov. 1914; repr. in *Omnia Opera di Benito Mussolini*, ed. E. and D. Susmel (La Fenice: Florence, 1951–81), vii. 5–7.]

BENITO MUSSOLINI

5 'Trenchocracy'

One of the crucial contributions of the First World War to the rise of Fascism was the myth that the trenches had forged a heroic, youthful, and classless élite which after the war would sweep away the sclerotic 'old order', so out of touch with the minds and aspirations of the war generation. This myth, which was to have an even more significant impact on the rise of Nazism, played a major role in winning over veterans to D'Annunzio's cause when he occupied Fiume (see Text 10) and in mobilizing the paramilitary action squads (squadre d'azione) which took on the 'Bolsheviks' in the 'red two years' (1919–20) and turned Fascism into a mass movement. It was also perpetuated within the military ethos which became such a prominent feature of the Fascist regime's myth of renewal. Note the prescient suggestion that the new force (not yet termed 'Fascism') could be a form of national socialism.

The word is ugly. No matter. There are uglier ones which have long enjoyed citizenship rights in the Italian language. We don't give a fig about 'purists' who snarl at 'neologisms'. It's all part of the eternal conflict between the old sensibility and the new! The trenchocracy is the aristocracy of the trenches. It is the aristocracy of tomorrow! It is the aristocracy in action. It comes from the depths. Its 'quarterings of nobility' are a splendid blood red. On its coat of arms there may be depicted a 'Frisian horse',[5] a dugout, a hand-grenade.[. . .]

A new aristocracy is emerging. The blinkered and the idiot do not see it. Yet, this aristocracy has already taken its first steps. It is already claiming its birthright. It is already planning in detail its attempts to 'take possession' of social positions. It is clandestine, intense labour of preparation, reminiscent of that carried out by the French bourgeoisie before 1789.[. . .]

In Milan the whole movement of propaganda and resistance is in the hands of the Committee of Action run by disabled and wounded servicemen. In Turin a fully fledged party has been formed for 'survivors of the front' with the rigorous exclusion of draft-dodgers. In Bologna the forthcoming publication has been announced of a newspaper called *The Voice of the Veterans*.[. . .] What an immense moral force is contained in the patriotic spirit of those who come back from the front.[. . .]

[5] A mobile obstacle used in the battlefields and fortification systems of the First World War.

The disabled servicemen of today are the vanguard of the great army who will return tomorrow. They are the thousands who await millions of demobilized soldiers. This enormous mass—conscious of what it has achieved—is bound to cause shifts in the equilibrium of society.

The brutal and bloody apprenticeship of the trenches will mean something. It will mean more courage, more faith, more tenacity.

The old parties, the old men who carry on with the *exploitation*[6] of the political Italy of tomorrow will be swept aside. The music of tomorrow will have another tempo. It will be an *andantino sostenuto*, and a hot-blooded *fortissimo* is not ruled out. There will also be many a *diesis in chiave*.[7] It is this prediction which makes us observe with a certain contempt everything which is said and done by the old windbags who govern us, so full of presumption, sacred formulas, and senile imbecility.[. . .]

The words 'republic', 'democracy', 'radicalism', 'liberalism', the word 'socialism' itself, have no sense any longer: they will have one tomorrow, but it will be the one given them by the millions of 'those who returned'. And it could be something quite different.

It could, for example, be an anti-Marxist and national socialism. The millions of workers who return to the furrow in their fields, after being in the furrows of the trenches, will realize the synthesis of the antithesis: class and nation.[. . .]

Those who in eleven battles chased Austria back beyond the Isonzo; those who stopped Austria and Germany, Bulgaria and Turkey on the Piave,[8] watch, listen, understand.

The Italy of today is here. The Italy of tomorrow is too.

We are pooling the passions of the soldiers and we will be with them tomorrow to see that the highest justice is done.

['Trincerocrazia', *Il Popolo d'Italia*, 15 Dec. 1917; repr. in *Omnia Opera di Benito Mussolini* (see Text 4), x. 140–3.]

6   The Futurist Vision of the New Italy

The Political Futurist Party was founded in Rome in September 1918 two months before the end of the First World War. Though it was to have minimal impact on the Italian electorate, its programme is worth citing as one of the earliest attempts to capitalize on what since the defeat at Caporetto had become a wave of popular enthusiasm for the war and translate it into a formal political organization dedicated to the 'renewal' of Italy. Significant too are several aspects of the programme which, quite independently of Mussolini,

---

[6] French word in the original.

[7] (In music) a sustained slow tempo.

[8] In the wake of the disastrous defeat at Caporetto in Oct. 1917, the Italian forces retreated to the River Piave where they successfully created a line of defence.

adumbrate aspects both of Fascism and of generic fascism: the concern with the nation's strength, special destiny, and need for autonomy, the emphasis on the need for the Italians to become a rejuvenated and physically healthy race, the fusion of élitism with a concern for the people (populism), the call for nationalism to become a 'political religion', the embracing of technology and the radical thrust towards a (nebulously defined) future (see also Text 3).

1. The Futurist Political Party which we are founding wants an Italy which is free, strong, which no longer lives in the shadow of its great past, or has to submit to foreigners whom it loves too much or to priests whom it tolerates too much: an Italy that can fend for herself, absolute mistress of her resources and intent on realizing her great future.

2. No other sovereign but Italy herself. Revolutionary nationalism for the freedom, well-being, physical and intellectual development, strength, progress, greatness, and pride of the whole Italian people.

3. The patriotic education of the proletariat. Struggle to abolish illiteracy, construction of communications, new roads, and railways. Compulsory lay primary education enforced by law. Abolition of many useless universities and institutes of classical education. Compulsory gymnastics enforced by law. Sports and military education in the open air. Schools of courage and Italianness.[. . .]

5. [. . .] The only religion: the Italy of tomorrow.[. . .]

6. [. . .] Our war must be waged till the point of total victory, i.e. till the Austro-Hungarian Empire has been dismembered and our natural borders by land and sea have been assured, without which we could not have a free hand in sorting out, cleaning up, and renewing Italy and increasing her territory.[. . .]

   We must abolish commemorative patriotism, monument-mania, and every pastist interference of the State in art.[. . .]

10. Industrialization and modernization of the dead cities which still live off their past. Less reliance on the dangerous and precarious tourist industry. Development of the merchant navy and river navigation. Improved water supplies and drainage system including the reclamation of malaria-infested areas.[. . .]

The Futurist Political Party, which we are founding now to be organized after the war has ended, will be clearly distinct from the Futurist artistic movement. This will continue in its work of rejuvenating[9] and fostering the Italian creative genius. The Futurist artistic movement is always necessarily in advance of the sluggish sensibility of the people. Therefore it remains an avant-garde which is often misunderstood and resisted by the majority who cannot understand its stupefying discoveries, the violence of its polemics, and the bold leaps of its intuitions.

In contrast, the Political Futurist Party intuits present needs and articulates precisely the consciousness of the whole race in its purging revolutionary momentum. The party can be joined by all Italians, men or women, of any class or age, even if artistic and literary concepts are beyond them.

[9] Literally 'de-ageing'.

This political programme marks the birth of the Political Futurist Party called for by all Italians who are fighting today for a more youthful Italy, freed from the weight of the past and of the foreigner.

[Manifesto of the Political Futurist Party (Sept. 1918), appendix to Renzo de Felice, *Mussolini il rivoluzionario 1883–1920* (Einaudi: Turin, 1965), 738–41.]

ALFREDO ROCCO

7 From the Old Italy to the New

Alfredo Rocco (1875–1935), an academic lawyer by profession, established himself on the eve of the First World War as one of the leading ideologues of the Italian National Association (ANI—see Text 11), which seemed to provide the ideal vehicle for the realization of his programme of national renewal. It was based on the replacement of the 'bankrupt' liberal system by a strong, supra-individual, hierarchically structured state compatible with the spiritual authority of the Vatican and embracing Italy's Roman past (in marked contrast to the one conceived by the Futurists). As Fascist minister of justice between January 1925 and July 1932 he was given the chance to put his theories into practice by drafting or shaping many of the laws which established the juridic foundation of the Fascist regime (see De Grand 1978). Here he captures the palingenetic expectancy of the war generation.

The outbreak of the Great War in the last days of July 1914 caught the Italian people in a phase of its spiritual life and its development as a nation which is still critical. Fifty years of unification have not eradicated the traces, inevitably profound, of hundreds of years in which it had fought no wars and remained disunited and servile. It was impossible that the struggle for the *Risorgimento*, which had lasted but a few decades and achieved success too easily, at the cost of too few true and great sacrifices, could change overnight the spirit of a people that had not fought for fifteen hundred years, namely since the third century AD, when the Roman State was already recruiting its soldiers among barbarians because its degenerate citizens would not deign to take up arms in its defence; a people which for thirteen centuries, namely since the fall of the Western Empire, lived in a state of general decay, because the Middle Ages, the age of individualism and of social and political dissolution, had not yet come to an end; a people which for four hundred years groaned under the weight of the most ignoble political serfdom and had become the laughing-stock of Europe; which for two hundred years had not even had an intellectual life of its own, but thought with the brain and felt with the soul of foreigners.[. . .]

All these negative forces of dissolution were still having a profound effect on Italian life when the European conflagration burst out.[. . .] Nevertheless, almost a century had passed since the Italian national conscience began its reawakening.[. . .] In protest against the intrigues of the pettifogging politicians, against the rationalized baseness of pacifism, against individual, cynical, and materialistic egoism, which found in socialist ideology its fullest concrete expression, there rose up those élites which had been forming in cultural and intellectual circles outside the by now played-out organs of official politics, élites which easily carried with them the masses, always ready to follow men of resolution and faith. Thus Italy, abandoning a neutrality which would have condemned it to decadence and ruination, intervened in the war. And the Italian war came about.[10][. . .]

The revitalization of national energies, of national consciousness, of the national spirit has been proceeding at an unexpected pace since the war and since the victory. The old Italy, heir of the old materialistic, cynical, and divisive individualism, is beginning to give way to the new Italy, which has nationally come of age and is full of historical and political purpose.[. . .]

One of the most significant manifestations of this new, higher life which Italy, now purified and renewed by the war and by victory, is preparing to enjoy is the official and open entry of Italian Catholics into political life. The 'Partito popolare italiano', whose formation was recently announced and whose programme was published a few days ago, marks a new era in Italian life.[. . .] The divorce between State and Church, in both theory and practice, has been transcended.[11] The national State, for the first time, gathers within itself the participation and support of the whole of Italian society.

> ['Dalla vecchia alla nuova Italia' [From the old Italy to the new], *La Politica*, 19 Jan. 1919; repr. in *Scritti e discorsi politici di Alfredo Rocco* (Dott. A. Giuffrè Editori: Milan, 1938), 545–7, 564–5.]

ROBERTO FARINACCI

8 The War as the Midwife of a New Italian People

Roberto Farinacci (1892–1945) had been the leader of Cremona's interventionist lobby and a front-line soldier in the war. One of the founding members of Fascism in March 1919, he then became the undisputed ras *(leader) of the Cremona Fascio, whose squadristi he led in numerous punitive expeditions against 'Bolsheviks' during the near civil war conditions of the* biennio rosso *(the 'red two years' of 1919–20). An admirer of Nazism in the 1930s, he became the most vociferous advocate of anti-Semitic laws in 1938 and of rapprochement with Germany. Under the Salò Republic he ran Cremona for the Nazis, and was eventually shot by partisans while escaping to Switzerland. This passage is taken from his autobiography, published in 1937, and records the intoxicating sense of national renewal experienced nearly two decades earlier.*

Even if the pre-revolutionary action of interventionism was not the exclusive work of Mussolini and Corridoni[12] and his friends, [. . .] it is worth remembering that the

---

[10] A phrase modelled on the phrase from the Book of Genesis, 'And there was light'.

[11] This rift would in fact only be healed under Mussolini by the Lateran Pacts of 1929.

[12] A major syndicalist interventionist who died in the trenches reputedly shouting 'Long Live Italy!'

most clear-sighted of all the political leaders was Mussolini. He saw in the war the real beginning of the revolution, the intervention of the whole Italian people in the history of Italy, the premiss of a new political and moral life.[. . .]

It was not only the war, but the immediate post-war events which caused the reasons and the passions which had been pent up and suffocated during the conflict to explode, separating the true interventionists who had wanted the war for Italy and the Italians from all the others who had asked for it or rejected it for other reasons.[. . .]

The war also revealed the magnanimous spirit, the *élan* and the fraternal heart of our reserve officers who had learned to fight by fighting, and taught our peasants to do likewise, mindful only of their own honour.[. . .]

The war revealed the value of our technicians, who improvised extensively, provided everything necessary, often meeting needs before they were expressed.[. . .]

The war brought into contact Italians separated by differences of culture, social background, and region, making them live in the same trench, the same mud, sharing the breath of the same agony, in the presence of the same dead who were the dead of all; and, by making them love and suffer, hope and work together, it fused them in the same pride and the same love of their Fatherland,[13] their shared experience making them communicate very different customs, character traits, and dialects. But it also enabled them to recognize each other's virtues, to search for and find the common elements of the same nation and civilization, enriching all of them with each other's qualities. It made defects intelligible and forgivable, purging many men of any arrogance and of regional or provincial narrow-mindedness and vanity.

[. . .] The war had thrown into relief the horrific and grotesque results of a centralized administration and bureaucracy which, like a malignant tumour, replaced the organic discipline of the whole people under a simple, strong, clear, and properly supervised discipline, leading to waste, corruption, and the poor co-ordination of materials, men, and actions. Officials went out of their way to provoke us with their display of growing negligence, procrastination, superficiality, ineptitude, officiousness, arbitrariness, and dishonesty.[. . .]

Now that the war had taken place, Mussolini did not change his mind. Blood had cemented the idea of Italy with the force of work.[. . .] He celebrated a new Italy, a new people, more worthy and glorious. He celebrated the imminent end of the old Italy.

[*Storia della Rivoluzione Fascista* [History of the Fascist Revolution] (Cremona Nuova: Cremona, 1937), iii. 230–40.]

---

[13] The Italian 'patria' will be translated throughout as Fatherland, even if, as a feminine noun, it also has connotations of 'mother country'.

ii. Currents of Italian Ultra-Nationalism in Fascism's Opposition Period (23 March 1918–27 October 1922)

9 San Sepulcro Fascism

Mussolini formed the first Fascio di combattimento at a meeting held in Piazza San Sepulcro in Milan on 23 March 1919 attended by a small gathering of war-veterans, syndicalists, Futurists, and Mussolinian socialists. There was a conspicuous presence too of former Arditi, the blackshirted assault troops who played an important role in supporting D'Annunzio, leading the Fascist squadre d'azione, *and providing the role model for the Fascist Militia. The Fascio was specifically conceived not as a party-political force but as the beginning of a nation-wide cellular network of extra-parliamentary opposition inspired by the spirit of the trenches. More important than the deliberately vague programme was the tenor of revolutionary nationalism set by the speeches by Mussolini and others that accompanied these declarations. These were fully reported in* Il Popolo d'Italia, *which now focused its energies on rallying all the 'productive forces' of Italy to the cause of the new Italy.*

First Declaration

The meeting of 23 March extends its first greeting, its love, and its reverent thoughts to the sons of Italy who fell for the greatness of the Fatherland and the freedom of the World, to the disabled and invalids, to all the veterans, to the ex-prisoners who have done their duty, and it declares itself prepared energetically to uphold the material and moral claims which will be made by the associations of ex-servicemen.

Because we do not want to found a veterans' party, since something of the sort is already being created in various Italian cities, we cannot specify the programme based on these claims. We leave this to those concerned.[. . .]

We can declare with total certainty that the Fatherland today is greater [. . .] because we feel greater, because we have experienced this war, in as much as we have wanted it, it was not imposed on us, and we could have avoided it. [. . .] The war [. . .] has produced positive results because no victorious nation has witnessed the triumph of reaction. In every case there is progress to greater political and economic democracy.[. . .]

Second Declaration

The meeting of 23 March declares its opposition to the imperialism of other peoples which is pursued at the expense of Italy and any Italian imperialism which is at the expense of other peoples; it accepts the supreme postulate of the League of Nations which presupposes the integration of each nation, an integration which in the case of Italy must be carried out in the Alps and in the Adriatic with the reclaiming and annexation of Fiume and Dalmatia.

We have 40 million inhabitants on an area of 287,000 square kilometres. This area is divided by the Apennines, which reduce even more the amount of our territory which can be put to use: in ten or twenty years our population will be 60 million and we only have one and a half million square kilometres of colonies, mostly desert, which could never absorb our population. But if we look around we see England which, with 47 million inhabitants, has a colonial empire of 55 million square kilometres.[. . .] We want our place in the world because we have a right to have it.[. . .]

Third Declaration

The meeting of 23 March commits Fascists to sabotaging with every means open to them the candidature of the neutralists[14] of all parties.[. . .] We do not know the date or the system which will be used, but within a year the paper battle of the elections will be fought. Whether we want it or not, the war will be the central issue. In other words, since the war has been the dominant fact of our national life, it is clear that it will be impossible to avoid talking about it.

Well, we will campaign precisely on the issue of the war, because we have not repented for what we have done.[. . .]

[*Il Popolo d'Italia,* 83 (24 Mar. 1919); repr. in *Omnia Opera di Benito Mussolini* (see Text 4), xii. 321–4.]

10   **The Regency of Fiume as the Harbinger of the New Italy**

It was not Mussolini but D'Annunzio (1863–1938) who first demonstrated the revolutionary potential of the populist ultra-nationalism whipped up by the war and the post-war crisis. A major literary figure, he had made the transition from the cult of decadence to a pseudo-Nietzschean nationalism in the 1890s, which in turn led to him becoming a flamboyant nationalist politician, interventionist, and war hero. In September 1919 he capitalized on his fame and charisma by leading a group of veterans to occupy the Adriatic port of Fiume, which had been declared a free city by the Paris Peace Conference. D'Annunzio's self-declared Regency was effectively ended by the Treaty of Rapallo (November 1920). When he eventually endorsed Fascism he was showered with honours by the regime. The constitution of Fiume, the Carnaro Charter, is a blend of D'Annunzio's own visionary and aesthetic nationalism with the corporativism promoted by the revolutionary syndicalist De Ambris. For those unfamiliar with the concept of the corporativist state, D'Annunzio's idiosyncratic

---

[14] Neutralists are those who opposed Italy's intervention in the First World War and are thus identified with the 'old Italy'.

breakdown of the whole of economic life into discrete sectors is given as an example (see Ledeen 1977; Sznajder 1989).

The people of the free city of Fiume, ever mindful of its Latin fate and ever intent on realizing its legitimate wishes, has decided to renew its governing principles in the spirit of its new life, [. . .] offering them for fraternal election by those Adriatic communities which desire to put an end to all procrastination, to shake off oppressive subjugation, and rise up and be resurrected in the name of the new Italy.

Hence, in the name of the new Italy, the people of Fiume, constituted in justice and in liberty, solemnly swears to fight to the last with all its force to maintain against any opponent the integrity of its land with its mother country, the upholder and perpetual defender of the Alpine territory which bears the sign of God and Rome.

The Corporations

xviii. The State is the collective will and the common effort of the people towards an ever increasing level of material and spiritual vitality.

Only producers concerned with communal wealth and creators concerned with communal power are full citizens of the Regency and with it constitute a single working body of increasing fulfilment.

Whatever the type of labour produced by hand or creative imagination, by industry or art, by planning or execution, all are obliged to be registered members of one of the ten newly created Corporations which derive their form from the Commune,[15] but unfold their energies freely and freely determine their mutual duties and the provisions which govern them.

xix. In the first Corporation are registered the salaried workers of industry, agriculture, commerce, transport; and the independent artisans and small landowners who also carry out work on the land or have few helpers and casual labourers.

The second Corporation groups together all the employees of technical and administrative bodies working for all private industrial and rural companies, excluding the joint-owners of such companies.

The third covers all the commercial employees who are not real workers; and co-owners are also excluded from this one.

The fourth Corporation brings together employers in industrial, agricultural, commercial and transport companies, as long as they are not only owners but—in the spirit of the new statutes—wise leaders who work hard to promote the company.

In the fifth are included all municipal and State employees working in the public sector in whatever capacity.

The sixth includes the intellectual flower of the people: the studious youth and its masters: teachers in State schools and the students in colleges of further educa-

[15] The autonomous city-states of the late Middle Ages and the Renaissance such as Siena and Florence.

tion; sculptors, painters, decorators, architects, musicians, all those who work in fine art, pictorial arts, decorative arts.

The seventh is made up of all those who are freelance professionals not covered in the previous categories.

The eighth is constituted by industrial and agrarian co-operative societies of production, work, and consumption; and only the administrators of such societies can be members.

The ninth incorporates all the people who work at sea.

The tenth has no category, no title, no name. Its fulfilment is awaited like that of the tenth Muse. It is reserved for the mysterious forces of a people which labours and rises up. It is like a votive statue consecrated to the unknown genius, to the appearance of a man who is utterly new [*novissimo*], to the ideal transfigurations of works and days, to the total liberation of the spirit from soul-destroying exertion and the sweat of blood.

It is represented in the civic sanctuary by a burning lamp which bears an ancient Tuscan motto from the epoch of the Communes, a stupendous allusion to a spiritualized form of human labour:

> *Toil without toil.*

[The Constitution of Fiume, promulgated 8 Sept. 1920, in *La Carta del Carnaro nei testi di Alceste de Ambris e di Gabriele D'Annunzio*, ed. R. De Felice (Il Mulino: Bologna, 1973), 35–47.]

....

11   The Nationalist Blueprint for a New Italy

Set up in December 1910 by Enrico Corradini (an associate of Papini) and Luigi Federzoni, the Italian National Association (ANI) was the major forum for rightist, statist ultra-nationalism in pre-Fascist Italy. The Nationalists promoted a fiercely anti-socialist and anti-liberal vision of an organic, industrially advanced, and imperial Italy able to pursue its destiny as a great power and put an end to the hegemony of the 'older' plutocratic nations Britain and France. Inevitably, it became a major force in the interventionist campaign. Its imperialist and productivist ideas influenced Mussolini, but it was only in March 1923 (after the March on Rome) that the ANI merged with Fascism, now moving to the right, which enabled several Nationalists, notably Federzoni and Rocco, to gain high office within the regime in its formative phase (see De Grand 1978). Noteworthy in this passage are the organic conception of the nation (cf. Text 117) and the advocacy of a rightist form of syndicalism, which under Rocco would effectively eclipse the leftist version.

The fundamental thesis of Nationalism,[16] which places the Nationalist doctrine in a special relationship with respect to all other political doctrines, is that the various

---

[16] 'Nationalism' refers specifically to the statist, neo-conservative brand of palingenetic ultra-nationalism espoused by the ANI.

societies existing on earth are true organisms endowed with a life which far transcends that of individuals and which is sustained for centuries and millennia.

Thus the Italian nation does not only contain the 36 million Italians alive now, but all the hundreds of thousands of millions of Italians who will live in future centuries, and who are conceived as components of a single whole. In this conception each generation and every individual within a generation is but a transient and infinitesimal part of the nation, and is the cell of the national organism. Just as cells are born, live, and die, while the organism remains the same, so individuals are born, live, and die, while the nation continues to live out its millennial existence.[. . .]

For many years Italians lived with the illusion that the problem of renewal and social and economic recovery was an exclusively *domestic* issue, that could and had to be resolved as if Italy was cut off from the world, indeed, as if Italy was the only country in the whole world. No one ever cast an eye across the borders to see what was going on there. As a result a mistake was made and became ever more widespread, namely of seeing the country's economic and social problem as one of *internal* distribution of wealth.[. . .] Nationalism was perhaps the only movement of ideas in Italy which, to Italians absorbed in the problem of *internal distribution of wealth*, raised the issue of the *international distribution of wealth*. It proclaimed out loud that, alongside *internal justice*, there also exists *international justice*, and asked for justice for the Italian nation too. In this sense Nationalism deserved the name *socialism of the nations*. Indeed, if there is a nation which has the right and the duty to behave nationalistically it is precisely the Italian nation, the *proletarian* nation *par excellence*, suffocated in a world dominated by the high-handedness and greed of capitalist and plutocratic nations.[. . .]

But Nationalism, which is an integral doctrine of social life, takes full account of the inevitable and irrepressible conflicts between classes and does not ignore the problem of the internal distribution of wealth. It recognizes that hand in hand with the increase in production must go the equitable distribution of its profit among those who contributed to achieve it.

Hence it recognizes the need for the working class to be organized, just as it recognizes the need for employers to be organized. Indeed, Nationalism, going beyond the economic conceptions of a now superseded liberalism, has pinned its colours firmly to the mast of syndicalism. Taking a bold but logical step, Nationalism believes that the syndicate must become the basis of economic life and wants to bring this about.[. . .]

Nationalism considers the expansion of Italy's power in the world not only as a process of promoting national productivity and bringing the highest economic and political benefits to all its citizens, but above all as a duty. It is a moral law which calls upon a people destined, for geographic, historical, and demographic reasons, either to perish or to expand and dominate, to embrace its destiny and be unflinching in the struggle with competing nations, a struggle which will be hard but, with victory assured, also glorious.

['Associazione Nazionalista Italiana', in *Il nazionalismo* (ANI: Rome, 1920), 6–9, 14–15.]

12 The *Squadristi* as the Revolutionaries of the New Italy

The diary kept by the Florentine squadrista Mario Piazzesi was published in 1980 at the wish of the author, by then living in Mexico. It is one of the few diaries to offer an authentic and articulate testimony (though one written with an eye to posterity) of the experiences and motivation of those who joined the Fascist squads for reasons other than pure anti-Bolshevism and a longing for 'action'. Piazzesi went on to take part in the March on Rome, fought in Ethiopia, and after the regime's collapse in 1943 rose to be Prefect of the Italian Social Republic. Passages such as this, in which the author remembers a conversation with his father, throw into relief the prevalent feeling among squadristi that they were fighting not just against Bolshevism, but for a new Italy, a palingenetic vision of Fascism's mission to which Piazzesi remained faithful till the end.

'For some time', he said to me, 'a new Italy has been forming, an Italy born of professionals, petty bourgeois artisans, peasants, the common people, of all those who fought in the war, and have patiently put up with things. But after a period of uncertainty it is realizing what it has achieved and experiencing a vague feeling of pride at having destroyed a huge empire, for having overcome the age-old awe of the foreigner who for centuries was able to roam at will pillaging our country, at having shaken off a certain sense of inferiority with regard to other Europeans. It feels that the spirit of Victory is an idea which can nourish even simple souls.

'New classes are forming who are leap-frogging the political and economic generations of before the war, most of them belonging to the small and middling bourgeoisie and artisan class. These have held military rank and have no intention of being absorbed back into the anonymous masses, but want to create new types of business, new companies, new trades in which to project the sense of leadership and organization they learnt and applied in the war.

'There are also people who, though with no interests to defend, are capable of being converted to this new idea [of Fascism], which is developing and focusing feelings and states of mind that have been latent for some time, but are now taking shape and gathering ever greater momentum.[. . .]

'In short, the vast majority of the nation, which before was holding its breath awaiting the imminent catastrophe, now feels that the Red tempest is about to be blown away thanks to the action of our anti-hail rockets, and those who live in the Augean Stables of the political parties have noticed the raging flood which the new Hercules is liable to unleash on them. The old liberal democracy, which in its day worked so efficiently for the good of the nation, had given ground on all fronts so as to ingratiate itself with the popular classes after the end of the war, and in so doing reduced its prestige to a minimum. But one of our great thinkers, Machiavelli, warns that "the people has contempt for the weak and respects the strong".

'In a word, neither the old ruling class nor the Reds have understood the revolution which is taking place above all in the generation of the war, a revolution which in practical terms started in 1915, which witnessed the interventionist campaign and forced the country to enter the conflict, despite the visiting-cards which 300 parliamentary deputies left in the house of the neutralist Giovanni Giolitti[17] as a sign of solidarity. The new generations realized that only if the country were put through a severe ordeal could the new forces of the nation develop.[. . .]

'But the most interesting phenomenon of all is taking place, as it were, higher up. The whole peripheral structure of the State, namely all the provincial authorities, from the Prefect to the Quaestor, from the magistrates to the police and the *carabinieri* (who for years and years have been held in contempt by the Reds), realize the ever widening gulf which separates them from the centre, feel that the barrier between them and Rome is growing more and more impenetrable, and thus they are being instinctively drawn towards the Fascist movement.

'Let's be clear on this: they are not Fascists, perhaps their mentality even precludes this, but they realize that Fascism offers them the last hope that the powers and responsibilities entrusted to them will not be swept away by the chaos and demagogy, and the motives for their shift in allegiance are honest ones.

'Perhaps, Mario,' my father concluded, 'in this brief synthesis resides the essence of the situation and the reason why this movement made up of what are, let's face it, hotheads when examined dispassionately, is winning the support of the majority of the nation.'

[Diary entry for 24 Nov. 1921, *Diario di uno squadrista*, ed. M. Toscano (Bonnacci: Rome, 1981), 208–11.]

LUIGI FEDERZONI
....

13 Fascism as the Victory of the New Italy

Convinced nationalist of a statist and monarchist disposition, Luigi Federzoni (1878–1967) was co-founder of the Italian Nationalist Association (ANI) in 1910, and after serving in the First World War became the Nationalists' most radical spokesman. As Fascist minister of the interior he played a key role in suppressing freedom of the press and in reorganizing local government under the Podestà, who replaced the elected mayor, communal council, and executive committee instituted under liberalism. His ministry also oversaw the introduction of the Fascist police state as well as its apparatus of social welfare. In this speech, written four months before the March on Rome and nine months before the PNF's absorption of the ANI, Federzoni already portrays Fascism as the vehicle for the Nationalist cause now that it has won a genuine popular following (De Grand 1978).

In the face of the profound crisis of conscience and loss of direction which is afflicting our Country at this time, Nationalism must take its responsibilities seriously.[. . .]

Up to now all Nationalism has had a history of being isolated, rejected, derided, and disregarded. It was treated like a prophet simply ignored as a nuisance when it urged the Italians to prepare their weapons and spirits for the inevitable ordeal of a

[17] The liberal Prime Minister who incarnated for Fascists the 'old Italy' to be superseded.

war, a war which most believed was the morbid dream of perverse imaginations. Ignored when it reminded the nation of its historical tasks to complete the integration of its territory and pursue political expansion within a more just hierarchy of power; when it provided sound critical foundations for the struggle against democratic reformism, humanitarian anti-militarism, universalism, and Masonic anti-clericalism. Ignored when it became the first to launch the anti-socialist counter-offensive to rid Italian life of the double tyranny of utopianism and demagogy.[. . .] And yet time and again we witnessed the strange phenomenon of a vast wave of support for our cause drowning out in a triumphant but fleeting moment of consensus the voices of those who first raised the alarm: the first flag was lost from view in the throng. After which, on every occasion, Nationalism had to start the struggle on its own all over again.

Now the situation seems to have changed, but that bitter experience has chastened us.[. . .]

The national uprising has won. It has routed and humiliated those who only yesterday were the rulers of the spirit and life of the nation. It takes its name and character from the overwhelming reality of the hour, which is called Fascism, a remarkable movement, instinctive and dynamic, which will be counted among the most profound and original revolutions of contemporary history. At bottom it is nothing other than the regenerating properties of the war which have taken effect miraculously and mysteriously in the soul of the Italian people.[. . .]

The Italian crisis [. . .] has had three successive phases.[. . .] The first was the struggle which the nation had to engage in against those who sought to stop it from obeying its own law by entering the war. The new Italy, self-aware and self-reliant, forced the old Italy, faint-hearted and sceptical, to perform an act of will. The second phase came after the glorious outcome of the war, when the nation had once more to engage in a struggle, this time to defend its own life and its own victory from those who begrudged it both. And once more the Italy of young men bearing arms won the day against sedition. The third phase we are living through now: resisting the manifest and insistent will of the country and the natural logic of events, there are those who are doing everything they can do to lure Italy back into supine obedience to the very parties which held it in such a shameful state of servility before.

['Nuove ipocrisie legalitarie' [New constitutional hypocrisies], speech made in the Chamber of Deputies 29 June 1922, in *Presagi alla Nazione* [Portents to the Nation] (Casa ed. Imperia della PNF: Milan, 1924), 327–9.]

BENITO MUSSOLINI
....

14   **The Incorporation of the Peasantry into the Italian Nation**

It was the biennio rosso, *the two years of near civil war in rural areas between socialists and the ultra-right, which in the course of 1920 transformed Fascism from a highly marginalized movement concentrated in Northern cities into the beginnings of a nation-*

wide mass movement. Here Mussolini, writing in the lead-up to the March on Rome,
ignores the violence of the blackshirted action squads which were the driving force of
Fascism's dramatic expansion, to focus on the peasant-farmers, claiming that his movement
had enabled them to be fully incorporated into the nation for the first time. Note the
emphasis on the war as the origin of Fascism and national revival, and the claim that
Fascism was completing the Risorgimento by finally making Italians feel an integral part
of the nation. This was a recurrent theme of Fascist rhetoric, emphasized, for example, by the
Fascist leader Dino Grandi at the Rome Congress in November 1921 (cf. also Texts 15, 22, 34).

The history of Italian Fascism, which is short, but already full of incident, can be
divided into three distinct periods: the first goes from March 1919 to November–
December 1920; the second from November–December 1920 to the Rome Congress
of 1921; the third from then till now. It has been asserted, and the assertion is true,
that in the first period of its existence Fascism was a prevalently urban phenomenon.[. . .] In the autumn–winter of 1920, Italian Fascism does not lose its 'urban'
character, because its most active centres remain the urban ones, but it becomes
rural as well; that is, it spreads into small villages, it gathers followers among the
inhabitants of the countryside and tends to change from a minority into a mass
movement. There is no doubt that the flow of so many new elements into the
movement alters more or less profoundly aspects of the original profile of Fascism:
the integration of these new forces, of this sort of great spiritual and material
mobilization takes place a bit chaotically, but it is not permissible to reject these
rebels, or possible to select them carefully. This will only happen in the third part
of the story, when Fascism transforms itself from a movement into a party.[. . .]

Profound economic motives [. . .] have drawn masses of rural populations to
Fascism in impressive numbers. But this alone is not enough to explain the 'liking'
of the new rural petty bourgeoisie for Fascism. Psychological factors also played a
role.[. . .] There is no doubt that during the last year of the war, between Caporetto
and Vittorio Veneto, a profound psychological transformation took place in the
masses of 'rurals'[18] who held the front. Among the assault troops there were
thousand upon thousand peasant-farmers. Many of those who fought in the first
and second battle of the Piave were potential Fascists.[. . .] It is certain that almost
all the political secretaries of the small rural *Fasci* are veterans, and often officers or
non-commissioned officers used to exercising command. It is thus undeniable that
rural Fascism derives much of its moral strength from the war and from victory, but
that at the same time it keeps alive this moral force, of incalculable historic value,
throughout the country. The new petty bourgeoisie of rural producers, concentrated in the *Fasci*, is destined to become, as in France, a force of stability and solid
patriotism. A guarantee of the continuity of national life.[. . .]

In a sense this is the miracle which has been awaited for centuries. During the
Risorgimento the rural populations were either left out of account or hostile. The
unification of Italy is the work of the intellectual bourgeoisie and certain artisan
sectors of the cities.[. . .] But the Great War of 1915–18 incorporates the peasants in

---

[18] Soldiers recruited from rural areas.

their millions. Still their participation in it is generally passive. Once again they had been dragged along by the cities. Now Fascism is transforming this rural passivity [. . .] into active participation in the reality and sanctity of the nation. Patriotism is no longer a feeling monopolized (or exploited) by the city, but becomes the heritage of the countryside as well. The tricolour flag, ignored for a century, is now waving in the most remote villages. Not everything that is flourishing, and almost exploding into life, in this springtime of the race is destined to last. We know this: but we also know that some spiritual upheavals leave deep traces. We will leave to the faint-hearted or the whiter-than-white the boring task of cavilling about the sincerity of rural patriotism. We are just at the beginning of a new period of Italian history.

And before long the immense operation attempted and carried out by Fascism in these years will be understood and properly assessed.

['Il fascismo e i rurali' [Fascism and the countryside], *Gerarchia*, 5 (25 May 1922); *Il Popolo d'Italia*, 130 (1 June 1922); repr. in *Omnia Opera di Benito Mussolini* (see Text 4), xviii. 201–7.]

BENITO MUSSOLINI
....

15 Fascism's Myth: The Nation

This speech was made by Mussolini at the Fascist Congress held in Naples three days before the March on Rome and on the very day on which he drew up plans for the March in his hotel. In retrospect the speech is a clear pointer to the imminent show of strength. It also adumbrates the creation of a 'total (itarian)' state, and the cult of Italy's Roman legacy (Romanità) under the eventual regime, both in the tenor of official cultural and political life and in the drive to create an Adriatic and African empire. Its main interest, however, lies in Mussolini's lucid formulation of the focus of fascist 'myth' of the nation as a supra-individual spiritual entity capable of infusing with heroism and purpose the lives of those who fight for it. A recurrent trait of generic fascism is its overt anti-rationalism and celebration of 'myth', a term which ever since Georges Sorel's highly influential theories on the subject had acquired for the ultra-right positive connotations.

We Fascists have no intention of coming to power by the tradesman's entrance; we Fascists do not intend to turn our backs on the first recruits of our movement, such fearsome and ideal followers, for a miserable dish of ministerial pottage! [*Prolonged and enthusiastic applause*] Because we have a vision of the problem which could be called historical, in contrast to that other vision which could be called political and parliamentary.

It is not a matter of assembling any old government, more dead than alive: it is a question of injecting into the liberal State—which has fulfilled tasks which were magnificent and which we will not forget—all the force of the new Italian generations which resulted from the war and our victory.

This is essential not just in the interests of the State, but in the interests of the nation's history.

Well, gentlemen, once the problem is not understood in historical terms, it is transformed into a problem of force. Besides, every time in history deep clashes of interest and ideas surface, it is force which finally decides the issue. This is why we have gathered and tightly organized the ranks of our legions and established an iron discipline in them: to make sure that if the conflict should ever be decided by force, victory will be ours. We deserve it [*applause*]: it is for the Italian people which has the right, which has the duty, to rid its political and spiritual life of all the parasitic encrustations of the past which cannot carry on existing indefinitely in the present because this would kill the future.[. . .]

We have created our myth. The myth is a faith, a passion. It is not necessary for it to be a reality. It is a reality in the sense that it is a stimulus, is hope, is faith, is courage. Our myth is the nation, our myth is the greatness of the nation! And to this myth, this greatness, which we want to translate into a total reality, we subordinate everything else.

For us the nation is not just territory, but something spiritual. There are States which have had immense territories and which have left no trace in human history. It is not just a question of size, because there have been minute, microscopic States in history which have bequeathed memorable, immortal specimens of art and philosophy.

The greatness of the nation is the totality of all these qualities, of all these conditions. A nation is great when it translates into reality the force of its spirit. Rome becomes great when, starting out as a small rural democracy, it gradually spreads out across the whole of Italy in accordance with its spirit, till it encounters the warriors of Carthage and must fight them. It is the first war in history, one of the first. Then, gradually, it bears its standards to the ends of the earth, but at every turn the Roman Empire is the creation of the spirit, since the weapons were aimed, not just by the arms of the Roman legionaries, but by their spirit. Now, therefore, we desire the greatness of the nation, both material and spiritual.[. . .]

['Il discorso di Napoli' [The Naples speech], 24 Oct. 1922, *Il Popolo d'Italia*, 255, 25 Oct. 1922; repr. in *Omnia Opera di Benito Mussolini* (see Text 4), xviii. 453–8.]

iii. The Coalition Government 30 October 1922–3 January 1925

FILIPPO T. MARINETTI

16 **A Futurist Portrait of the New Prime Minister of Italy**

Beltramelli's book The New Man *is an account of the Fascist conquest of the state. It prefigures the later leader cult (ducismo) by presenting Mussolini as the embodiment of the mythic figure alluded to in the title, the theme of so much revolutionary discourse. The appendix was written by Marinetti (see Text 3), who strains his rhetorical powers to the utmost in his celebration of Mussolini's superman status, but at the same time seizes the opportunity to portray Fascism and its leader as archetypally Futurist phenomena. Much of Fascism's success in enlisting support can be attributed to the way that the nebulousness of its palingenetic vision allowed proponents of quite conflicting brands of revolutionary nationalism to project onto it their own specific scheme for a rejuvenated Italy.*

Vittorio Veneto[19] and the coming to power of Fascism represent the realization of the minimum Futurist programme (which has a maximum programme yet to be achieved) launched fourteen years ago by a group of daring young men who put forward convincing arguments to indict the whole nation, brought low by a senility and mediocrity which made it afraid of the foreigner.

This minimum programme asserted Italian pride, unlimited confidence in the future of the Italians, the destruction of the Austro-Hungarian Empire, everyday heroism, love of danger, violence rehabilitated as a decisive argument, the glorification of war, sole hygiene of the world,[20] the religion of speed, of novelty, optimism, originality, the access of the young to power to combat the parliamentary, bureaucratic, academic, and pessimist spirit.

Our influence in Italy and the world has been and remains enormous. Italian Futurism, typically patriotic, which has generated countless Futurisms abroad, has nothing to do with their political positions, such as the Bolshevism of Russian Futurism which has become the official art of the State.

Futurism is a genuinely artistic and ideological movement. It intervenes in political struggles only in hours of grave danger for the nation.

We were the first of the first interventionists.[. . .] we created the first associations of the *Arditi* and many of us were members of the first Fasci di combattimento.

Prophets and harbingers of the great Italy of today, we Futurists are delighted to salute in the Prime Minister, not yet 40, a marvellous Futurist temperament.[. . .]

---

[19] Vittorio Veneto, a small town in Venetia, was the decisive battle in which the Italians finally inflicted a significant defeat on the Austrians in the last month of the war.

[20] This phrase is taken directly from the original Futurist Manifesto of 1909, and sums up the claim that war plays a purging and invigorating role in history.

Mussolini has a formidable Futurist temperament, but is not an ideologue. If he was an ideologue he would be a prisoner of ideas. Instead he is free, untrammelled. He was a socialist and internationalist, but only in theory. A revolutionary, to be sure, but never a pacifist. He had to end up obeying his special brand of patriotism, which I call physiological.

Physiological patriotism, because it is physically constructed in the best Italian tradition, fashioned out of the craggy rocks of our peninsula into dressed blocks of stone.

Lips made prominent, contemptuous by an audacity, a pugnaciousness, which spits on everything which is vain, slow, cumbersome, useless. Massive head, but ultra-dynamic eyes which vie with the speed of the cars racing across the plains of Lombardy. The bowler hat squashed down over his eyes like the black clouds which hang heavily over the inky blackness of ravines in the Apennines. The lapel of his overcoat always raised in an instinct for disguise which smacks of a conspiracy being hatched in the Romagna.

A baton in his pocket like an ever-ready sword. Bent over his writing-desk with elbows wide, his arms poised like levers to strike out at someone who is bothering him—or his enemy.

The square head, a new type of shell or box full of powerful explosive, or simply the cubic will of the State, the head ready to charge into someone's chest like a bull.

A Futurist orator, who prunes, cuts down, drills through, ties back the opponent's argument, methodically shearing away all the tangled weeds of objections, cutting through the crowd like a torpedo-boat, like a torpedo.

['Benito Mussolini', appendix to Antonio Beltramelli, *L'uomo nuovo* (Mondadori: Milan, 1923), pp. iii–vi.]

SERGIO PANUNZIO

17 The New State Born of Syndicalism and Statism

Sergio Panunzio (1886–1944) was a major representative of the current of revolutionary syndicalism which took up the interventionist cause and eventually became a tributary of Fascism. He became a major spokesman of the leftist, populist (as opposed to the Nationalists' rightist, statist) strand of corporativist thinking, which he refined as head of the Fascist Faculty of Political Sciences at Perugia University, but here it is the impact of Hegelian state theory and dialectics which is most in evidence. He was a prolific apologist of Fascism's corporative state and the genius of its leader right up till the regime's collapse in 1943 (see Roberts 1979; Sternhell et al. 1994: ch. 3).

The State, which seemed, especially after the strenuous exertions of Hegelian dialectic and German academic journals, a *monumentum aere perennius*,[21] is in a

---

[21] A monument more lasting than bronze.

condition of complete dissolution.[. . .] Pathology or social physiology? And in reply we ask insistently, is puberty and the adolescent crisis of the individual organism a matter of pathology or physiology? Without a divine grain of madness in an individual there can be no intelligence, no genius. Without a divine grain of madness [. . .] the creative genius of history is extinguished.

A tide [*ricorso*[22]] of pristine, healthy primitive energies [*barbarie*]—so different from an influx of barbarity [*imbarbimento*] and decadence!—is the greatest guarantee (just as the immortal teachings of the great G. B. Vico tell us) of the perpetuation and vital process of human Society.

There is no need, then, for consternation at the apparent dissolution of contemporary Society. The so-called and appropriately termed 'Syndicalist madness' is life and lust for life, and is a symptom of vitality and not of death.[. . .] Like all original historical movements destined to make history, Syndicalism, in its first phase, is a movement of reaction, yet not a destructive and degenerative reaction, but one which stimulates and generates fresh forces and new social institutions.[. . .] What matters now is to see if Syndicalism, once it has transcended its adolescent phase and become mature, is capable of reconstructing the State, which means producing a new stable juridical and political system for Society.[. . .]

Amidst so much destruction and chaos, among so many broken and diverging lines, to the trained eye of a sociologist and jurist there is one line visible which is clear and unbroken: the syndical organization—a true 'madreporic rock'[23] jutting out in the middle of the immense sea—and the 'syndical' reorganization of the State. Syndicalism is not only something quite different from destructive lust and madness, but we believe it to be the sole, true reconstituent crisis of the modern State, one which is not extrinsic and artificial, but intrinsic and natural. Nowadays all men are organizing themselves and retrenching within their Syndicates—as in earlier epochs they did within Cloisters, Castles, Communes[24]—as a refuge from isolation and to avoid some truly terrible, sinister, fatal, irreparable disaster; furthermore, nowadays everyone feels that the Syndicates on their own are not enough, that *something more* is necessary, something stronger, higher, more authoritative and venerable, in a word that what is needed is a return *to* the State and *of* the State, which for some time now has disappeared from view.[. . .]

The new synthesis is the unity of the State and the Syndicate, of Statism and Syndicalism. It is the State which is the ultimate destination and expression of Syndicalism once it has overcome its initial negative phase. This is how the social process reintegrates itself in the unity of its two moments: there is a transition from society to the State; the State then breaks down into society as the source of its constituent elements and vital plasma; society then reconstitutes itself, restores itself, reconnects itself, rebuilds itself in the State. This is not a contingent or ephemeral State, not *this* or *that* State, but *the* State, as an idea, as the eternal State

[22] A reference to the theory of cultural decay and renewal (*corso* and *ricorso*: roughly ebb and flow) developed by the Italian philosopher Giambattista Vico (1688–1744).

[23] The coral-like material built up by skeletons of aquatic animals called madrepores, which over time can form oceanic barrier reefs and atolls.

[24] 'Communes' refers to the free city-states of early Renaissance Italy.

which lives eternally and never dies, the symbol and expression of the juridic need for social unity, living incarnation of the social idea, the only thing that, while Kingdoms, Republics, and Empires dissolve, never dies or fades away.

['Stato e sindacato', *Rivista internazionale di filosofia del diritto* [International Review of the Philosophy of Law], 3/1 (Jan.–Mar. 1923), 4–9; written Nov. 1922.]

CURZIO MALAPARTE

18   Fascism's European Mission

Curzio Malaparte (né Suckert) joined the PNF in 1921 and took part in the March on Rome as a squadrista. Through his journal La Conquista dello Stato *founded in 1924 he became a major publicist of the* squadrismo *myth, claiming that its spartan provincial radicalism represented the essence of Fascism, and attacking the urban, statist, bourgeois, and hyper-modern (Futurist) strands. He went on to be an advocate of the rural and populist aesthetic associated with the aesthetic current called* Strapaese *(see Text 25) and with the arts review* Il Selvaggio *(see Lyttelton 1987: ch. 14). A notable feature of this passage is the way the characteristic Fascist myth of the reborn (Italian) national community is already linked to the need to resolve the crisis of European civilization. In this context liberal democracy is argued to be an alien import in terms reminiscent of the anti-democratic arguments of* völkisch *and Conservative Revolutionary thinkers of German fascism (cf. Texts 47, 48).*

We have no fear of flying in the face of common assumptions when we affirm that Fascism, in its first phase, was profoundly Sorelian:[25] the justification of its violence is completely historical, not political; it is the Sorelian ethic which assigns to the proletariat the function of creating a modern myth and a favourable climate which aids and accelerates the maturation of the new society in accord with the natural order embodied in the first Ionic and Asiatic cities. The new Fascist ethic is born of the Sorelian one, but at the same time marks a break with it by transforming the concept of social class into that of national class, and the economic premiss into a historical one. When Sorel assigns syndicalism the task of preparing and stabilizing the new proletarian civilization on the ruins of bourgeois civilization, he is equating the modern function of producers, industrial workers, and agricultural workers with the primitive function of the shepherds who gave rise to heroic civilizations. Carried away by the broad scope of his class myth, he considers the shepherd people who founded the first cities as a class, as a social group, thereby ignoring the wonderful equality which prevailed between citizens in heroic times: instead it is to be considered a *gens*, a nation, a racial group, almost, rather than a social one.

The modern function of producers cannot be that of creating a new order of social values, but a new order of civic values. Fascist syndicalism, in contrast to Sorelian syndicalism, distinguishes between society and civilization: and it there-

---

[25] See introduction to Text 15.

fore does not set itself the task of preparing and establishing the new proletarian civilization on the ruins of the bourgeois one [. . .] but of preparing for and ushering in the return of a national civilization, both genuinely Italian and deeply historical, on the ruins of the modern, anti-national, class-based one of Anglo-Saxon origin which ever since the Reformation has suffocated our indigenous natural force, enjoying its latest triumphs in the form of liberal democracy and socialism.[. . .]

We firmly believe that syndicalism will destroy social classes and bring about the emergence of a single class, of a new nation, of a new *gens*, which subsumes in itself, just as in a new race born of mysterious fusion of different and conflicting races (classes), all the forms and all the ethnic, political, economic values of our race. We believe in the coming not of a new society, but of a new civilization: and we are certain that it will be neither bourgeois nor proletarian. We have equal contempt for both.[. . .]

Fascism has appropriated the revolutionary spirit of syndicalist violence to carry out the profound transformation of the modern social order (founded on the economic and political struggle between the bourgeoisie and proletariat), from which will emerge, welded into a powerful organism, a single national class. Fascism already represents this new class.

Its profound and implacable anti-socialist, anti-liberal, anti-democratic, anti-humanitarian spirit, is a decidedly anti-modern spirit, we might almost say anti-European, if we did not fear giving the term 'European' the connotations which Slavophile Russians give it.[. . .] The force of Fascism is in the people, is in the irrepressible tradition of our culture, of our religious life, is in the very nature of our race, and not, it is to be stressed, in balancing acts or games of political compromise. Its mission in the world is not to take on board and transform the political, social, and economic factors of modern civilization, it is not to assimilate the cultural and mechanical forms of modern civil existence, but is still as ever our deeply historical Catholic mission of implacable and sustained resistance to the modern spirit, born of the Reformation.[. . .]

> [*Europa Vivente. Teoria storica del sindacalismo nazionale* [Living Europe: The History and Theory of National Syndicalism] (Vallecchi: Florence, 1961; first pub. 1923), 463–7.]

BENITO MUSSOLINI

19 The End of the Liberal Regime

The disappearance in May 1924 of Giacomo Matteotti, reformist socialist and the Chamber of Deputies' most outspoken critic of the Fascists' recent electoral success, was widely and correctly assumed to be the work of Fascist hard-liners, and plunged Mussolini's premiership into crisis. The king's inertia and the opposition's insistence on using the legalistic tactic of boycotting parliament (the 'Aventine Secession') meant that the revolutionary faction within Fascism embodied in ex-squadristi such as Farinacci gained the confidence to demand that Mussolini take the initiative. This he finally did in the speech to the

Chamber from which this extract is taken. Despite the sarcasm of the language, the sinister implications of the promise to restore stable government 'with force if necessary' would soon become apparent. Immediately after this speech the sitting of Parliament was suspended and the process of establishing a Fascist dictatorship had begun.

I declare before this Assembly and before the whole Italian people that I and I alone assume political, moral, historical responsibility for everything that has happened. [*Loud and sustained applause. Many shouts of 'We are all with you! We are all with you!'*]

If more or less garbled phrases are enough to hang a man, then out with the gallows and out with the rope! If Fascism has been nothing other than castor oil,[26] and if it is not instead the superb passion of the best of Italian youth, it is my fault! [*Applause*] If Fascism has been an association of delinquents, then I am the head of this association of delinquents! [*Loud applause. Many shouts of 'We are all with you!'*]

If all the acts of violence have been the result of a particular historical, political, and moral climate, well it is my responsibility, because it is I who have created this historical, political, moral climate with a propaganda campaign which has lasted ever since the intervention.

In the last few days not only Fascists, but many citizens have been wondering 'is there a Government?' [*Sounds of approval*] Are they men or are they puppets? Have these men the dignity of men? And have they the dignity of a government? [*Sounds of approval*]

I deliberately wanted things to come to a head, and, with my wealth of experience of life, I have assayed the Party like a goldsmith over the last six months. And, just as to establish the quality of certain metals it is necessary to strike them with a hammer, in the same way I have tested the mettle of certain men, I have seen what they are worth and the reasons why at a certain moment, when the wind starts changing they run for cover? [*Loud applause*]

I have put myself to the test, and understand that I would not have taken these measures if the interests of the nation were not at stake. But a people does not respect a government which allows itself to be held in contempt! [*Sounds of approval*] The people want its dignity to be reflected in the dignity of the government, and the people, even before I said it, has said: Enough is enough![. . .]

Italy, gentlemen, wants peace, wants calm, wants a stability which allows work to continue. This calm, this stability we will give her with love, and, if necessary, with force. [*Loud sounds of approval*]

You can be certain that within forty-eight hours of this speech the situation will have been clarified in every respect. [*Loud and sustained applause. Comments*]

We all know that what motivates me is not a personal whim, it is not lust for power, it is not an ignoble passion, but only an unlimited and burning love for the Fatherland. [*Loud, sustained and repeated applause. Repeated cries of 'Long live Mussolini'. The right honourable ministers congratulate the Prime Minister. The sitting is suspended*]

[Speech to Parliament of 3 Jan. 1925, in *Omnia Opera di Benito Mussolini* (see Text 4), xxi. 439–44.]

---

[26] A favourite technique used by *squadristi* for punishing their enemies was to force them to drink castor oil, with dramatically unpleasant physical effects.

Section B

Fascism in Power January 1925–April 1945

INTRODUCTION

It is convenient to divide the two decades of Fascism in power into several phases. The formative years of the totalitarian regime (Section Bi) encompassed a stream of innovative constitutional and institutional measures. Aspects of the mythic rationale for these structural changes are glimpsed in excerpts from the lecture on the nature of Fascism by Giovanni Gentile (Text 20), an article on the religious spirit of Fascism incarnated in the Militia (Text 21), Mussolini's speech to commemorate victory in the First World War (Text 22), the celebration of the leader figure in a book by ex-*ras* and then secretary of the PNF, Augusto Turati (Text 23), an article by Mussolini in which he expresses his fears for the physical survival of the Italian and white race (Text 24), a statement by one of the regime's aesthetic ruralizers (Text 25), a pronouncement by an aesthetic modernizer (Text 26), a lecture on the role of the university under Fascism by Giuseppe Bottai, one of the regime's most zealous technocratic 'modernizers' (Text 27), and Mussolini's own summary of the achievements of the regime in its first five years (Text 28).

The period of consolidation up to 1934 (Section Bii) is represented by the vision of Fascism's pan-European role promoted by the periodical *Antieuropea* (Text 29), a speech on the role of youth, published in the weekly of the newly founded Fasci Giovanili (Text 30), the interpretation of the revolutionary mission of Fascist corporativism by one of its major theorists, Ugo Spirito (Text 31), Bottai's ecstatic reception of Mussolini's (and Gentile's) 'Doctrine of Fascism' (Text 32), the guiding principles of the Dopolavoro movement set out by another party secretary, Achille Starace (Text 33), and one of Mussolini's many declarations to the effect that Fascism marked the birth of a new civilization (Text 34).

After 1934 (Section Biii) Fascist Italy embarked in earnest on fulfilling its 'imperial mission' and moved ever closer to alliance with Nazism. This is reflected in Mussolini's rationale for the Italo-Ethiopian conflict (Text 35), two marching songs which emerged from the Ethiopian War and Spanish Civil War respectively (Text 36), the characterization by the minister of agriculture Edmundo Rossoni of the 'autarkic mentality' necessary for Italy to wage war (Text 37), Mussolini's declaration of the bond between Nazism and Fascism (Text 38), and an account of the introduction of Fascist racial policy (Text 39).

A flavour of Fascist thought once the regime was at war (Section Biv) is given by Mussolini's speech the day it was declared (Text 40), a legal expert's justification of the war as a battle to defend the racial integrity of European peoples (Text 41), and a vision of the new European order which intransigent Fascists still believed was being forged by the Axis powers (Text 42).

In Section Bv there follows part of what is effectively the constitution of the Italian Social Republic (Text 43), Mussolini's rousing speech to Republican Blackshirts when he still could entertain illusions that the Allies would be defeated (Text 44), and his defiant and wistful musings on the benefits to Italy and Europe which an Axis victory would have brought, as expressed in an interview given only days before his murder by Partisans (Text 45).

i. The Formative Years of the 'Totalitarian' Regime January 1925–February 1929

20 **Fascism as a Total Conception of Life**

Giovanni Gentile (1875–1944) was a neo-idealist philosopher who became increasingly concerned with the rooting of individual moral will in the ethical state to overcome the contemporary decadence of existence under liberalism. This converted him progressively to Nationalism, interventionism, and, after the March on Rome, to Fascism. Between 1923 and 1929 a stream of prestigious appointments and honours encouraged his prolific activities as the self-appointed philosopher of Fascism, his two most notable being to write the Manifesto of Fascist Intellectuals and the first part of the article on Fascism in the Enciclopedia Italiana *(1932), which he edited. After the controversy caused by his attacks on the Lateran Pacts in 1929 (he wanted Fascist spirituality to replace Christianity), he withdrew from active politics, only to resume them again at the end of the regime and under the Salò Republic. In this passage he gives his gloss on the myth of the 'two Italies' which was first propagated by the Florentine avant-garde (see Adamson 1993). It articulates two important themes of regime Fascism: its function as an (ersatz) religion, and as a 'totalitarian' state.*

We see two Italies before us: an old one and a new one: Italy of the past centuries which is our glory but it also a sad legacy which weighs on our shoulders and our spirits: let's be frank, it is also our shame, a shame we want to expunge and make up for. It is precisely that great Italy which occupies such an important place in the history of the world. The only Italy, one might say, which is known, studied, and researched by all civilized peoples, and whose history is not a particular history, but an epoch in universal history: the Renaissance.[. . .] The Italy of foreigners, and not of Italians. Italians without faith, and hence absent. Is not this the old Italy of decadence?[. . .]

   Let us add new monuments to the old ones if we feel like it. Let us erect them on our squares to steel our characters, to honour the living more than the dead in the consecration of recent memories, which at bottom are more glorious than any which Italian history has to offer, and, paying tribute to generous memories, to raise our consciousness of being the free citizens of a great nation. For where 'nation' is understood in this way, even liberty is less a right than a duty: a prize which is only achieved through the self-denial of the citizen prepared to give everything to his Fatherland without asking for anything in return.

   Even this concept of the nation, which we see as central, is not a Fascist invention. It is the soul of the new Italy which slowly but surely will prevail over the old. Fascism, with its keen sense of the wave of nationalism which drew Italians to the fire of the Great War and enabled them to endure victoriously the tragic ordeal, with its radical reaction against the materialists of yesterday who tried to pooh pooh the value of that ordeal [. . .] Fascism does everything to remind the people of the greatness and beauty of the sacrifice that has been made as its greatest legacy for the future.[. . .]

How many times has Fascism been accused with obtuse malevolence of barbarity? Well yes: once you understand the true significance of this barbarity we will boast of it, as the expression of the healthy energies which shatter false and baleful idols, and restore the health of the nation within the power of a State conscious of its sovereign rights which are its duties.[. . .]

Do not forget, the ethical State of the Fascist is no longer the agnostic State of the old liberalism. Its ethics derive from spirituality: a personality which is awareness; a system which is will.[. . .] The State is the will of the nation writ large, and hence its intelligence. It ignores nothing, and it involves itself in everything which has a bearing on the interests of the citizen—which are its own interests—either economically or morally. *Nihil humani a se alienum putat.*[27] The State is neither a huge façade, nor an empty building. It is man himself: the house is built, inhabited and animated by the joys and sorrows which derive from the labour and from the whole life of the human spirit.[. . .]

Gentlemen, Fascism is a party, a political doctrine. But Fascism [. . .] while being a party, a political doctrine, is above all a total conception of life. Like the Catholic, if he is Catholic, invests with his religious feelings the whole of his life [. . .] so the Fascist, whether he is writing in newspapers or reading them, going about his private life or talking to others, looking to the future or remembering the past and the past of his people, must always remember he is a Fascist!

Thus he fulfils what can really be said to be the main characteristic of Fascism, to take life seriously. Life is toil, is effort, is sacrifice, is hard work; it is a life which we know full well is not for fun: there is no time for fun.

Before us there always lies an ideal to realize: an ideal which gives us no rest. We cannot waste time.

['Che cosa è il fascismo?' [What is fascism?], lecture delivered in Florence on 8 Mar. 1925, repr. in *Che cosa è il fascismo* (Vallecchi: Florence, 1925), 14, 28, 32–3, 36, 38, 63.]

21   **Fascist Mysticism**

This anonymous article, published in a magazine written for consumption by Fasci set up by expatriates outside Italy, illustrates a major aspect of Fascist and fascist thought and exhibits an unmistakable symptom of its charismatic style of politics, namely the appropriation of religious language and mystical imagery to shroud the regime's institutions and actions in a pseudo-spirituality. The resulting travesty is particularly grotesque in this case

---

[27] It considers nothing human to be alien to it.

since religiosity is being used to sanctify the MVSN (the Voluntary Militia for National Security) created in February 1923 to subordinate the squadre d'azione to PNF control. It hence became the main repository under the Fascist regime of the Blackshirt cult of violence and contempt for humanist (and hence Christian) values, the centrality of which to the foundation myth of the regime was displayed in the Exhibition of the Fascist Revolution of 1932 (see Stone 1993). The Militia was disbanded by King Victor Emmanuel III in December 1943, but was revived under the Italian Social Republic first as the Republican National Guard and then the Black Brigades (see Text 44), in which role this 'holy' force was implicated in numerous atrocities.

The mysticism of Fascism is the proof of its triumph. Reasoning does not communicate, emotion does. Reasoning convinces, it does not attract. Blood is stronger than syllogisms. Science claims to explain away miracles, but in the eyes of the crowd the miracle remains: it seduces and creates converts. Perhaps, a hundred years on, people will say that in Italy a Messiah arose who started by talking to fifty and ended up evangelizing a million: that those thus illuminated spread in Italy and through faith, through devotion, through sacrifice won the hearts of the masses: that their words were unfamiliar, coming from so far away that they were forgotten, talking of duties when everyone talked of rights, of discipline when everyone dedicated themselves to licence, of the family when individualism was in the ascendant, of property when wealth was becoming anonymous, of the Fatherland, when hatred was rife among citizens and self-interest triumphed over all restraint, of religion when everyone denied it out of fear of the ultimate judge. But they eventually succeeded. Because they gave good in return for evil, because they defended their own enemies, because every day they worked miracles of love, because every hour they told the story of their humble acts of heroism, because on contact with them men became better and through their actions Italy became more orderly, quieter, more prosperous, greater, because they expressed in their song the joy of their goodness and in their eyes the light of their sacrifice, because when they fell it was with a cry of faith and for every one who fell a hundred rose up, because when truth shines out on all sides, not even recluses can deny it.

It is in this way that Fascism has triumphed, through the efforts of its Militia.[. . .] The cup of sacrifice is held out to the 'best' and we must drink from it. Then we can say with Christ when he drank from the sponge soaked in vinegar and gall: 'Consummatum est'. His sacrifice is the salvation of others. What does the individual matter? It is the Race which counts, it is its renewal which is necessary for the good of the Country and the world. The Duce has spoken.[. . .] His command is our law, which is already in us. The struggle continues and is bitter. All over the world Italy is looked to as a beacon of light, which guides humanity to salvation.[. . .] We are princes and triarii[28] of the new legions of civilization.

['Santa Milizia' [Holy Militia], *I fasci italiani all'estero*, 2 May 1925.]

---

[28] A special section of Roman legionaries.

22 Fascism as the Creator of the Third Italian Civilization

In this speech Mussolini underscores a number of key Fascist myths central to its relatively successful campaign to nationalize the masses (their attempted Fascistization was far less successful): the way the liberal state had ignored ordinary Italians (and thus was undemocratic); the achievement of Fascism in building on the revolutionary change in national sentiments brought about by the war and creating a fully united nation; the vitalistic (and anti-bourgeois) stress on the need to realize ever greater goals; the claim that Fascism was completing the Mazzinian Risorgimento by creating for the first time an Italian people fully conscious of its identity and destiny, integrated within the state; and the notion that Fascism was ushering in a third flowering of Italian civilization (after the Roman Empire and the Renaissance).

Why do I say that it is only today that the people have a sense of victory?

[. . .] The political regime preceding ours, the liberal democratic [*demoliberale*] regime, ignored the masses. Later it no longer ignored them, but abandoned them to the mercies of others who whipped them up against the State.[29]

Now, when you see veterans marching two or three abreast, when you see the magnificent discipline within the Italian people, no longer moving through the streets like herds of sheep as they used to, but in tight formation, you realize that a profound transformation has come about in their hearts, you realize that the Italian people is about to enter the State, or has already become part of it. Gentlemen, this is something to be proud of! After the war, who, by working with the raw materials of the war, on the passions, the triumphs, but also the disappointments of the war, succeeded in bringing this neglected people, grown hostile or indifferent, back into the fold of the State? Who? The Fascists, not liberalism, not socialism.

The masses, now reconciled with the nation, enter the State through the main gate which the Fascist revolution opened wide. And the State, with the monarchy at the top, has enormously widened its base. There are no longer just subjects, but citizens; there is not only just a nation, but a people conscious of its destinies.

It is this achievement, this fruit of victory, which nourishes the self-confidence of the Italian people.

But, fellow soldiers, victory is not a final destination: it is a starting-point; it is not a goal: it is a stage. Victory is not a comfortable armchair to flop down in during commemorative ceremonies. No. It is a stimulus, a goad, which urges onwards towards strenuous heights and more arduous duties.[. . .]

Let us look, with one eye, at the dove of peace, even though it only takes to the air from far-off horizons; but with the other eye, let us observe the concrete necessities of life, and history, which shows us the rise, growth, and decline of individuals and peoples, creating major imbalances with fatal consequences. I do not exclude the possibility that tomorrow history will follow a different course

[29] The Bolsheviks in the *biennio rosso* (1919–20).

from yesterday, but, while we are waiting for this miracle, we must have a powerful and respected Army, a proper Navy, an Air Force with air superiority, an intense spirit of discipline and sacrifice in every class of people. In 1836, after the abortive Savoy expedition, Giuseppe Mazzini asked, 'Supposing this Fatherland was nothing but an illusion? Supposing Italy, exhausted after two epochs of civilization, was now condemned to lie supine with no name or mission, yoked to a younger, more vital nation?'

When Mazzini dictated these words, his soul was overwhelmed by what could be called a storm of doubt. Now, a century later, it is an ineffable experience for us, the Italians of this generation, to be able to dispel such distressing doubt and, mindful of Vittorio Veneto,[30] give a triumphant reply to the terrible question.

The Fatherland is no illusion! It is the sweetest, greatest, most human, most divine of realities! No! Italy did not exhaust itself in creating its first and second civilization, but is already creating a third.

Fellow soldiers!

We will create it in the name of the king, in the name of Italy, with physical effort, with the spirit, with blood and with life.[31]

['Celebrazione della vittoria' [Commemoration of victory], speech given to the Associazione nazionale mutilati di guerra in Rome, 4 Nov. 1925]; repr. in *Omnia Opera di Benito Mussolini* (see Text 4), xxix. 439–41.]

AUGUSTO TURATI

23   The Leader as the Voice of the Reborn Race

Augusto Turati (1888–1955) had been an interventionist and fought in the First World War before becoming the ras (leader) of the Brescia Fascio. He agitated for a form of national syndicalism which would genuinely represent workers' interests and sought to realize this when appointed as vice-secretary of the PNF. When he was general secretary of the PNF (1926–9), his efforts to turn the party into the basis of state power which would outlast Mussolini ended in his expulsion from it in 1932, permanently ending his career as a prominent Fascist. This passage from a work of propaganda written while at the peak of his influence points to the presence of a Fascist equivalent of the Nazi 'leader principle' some years before the fanatical ducismo of the 1930s.

It is always fascinating, even for non-academics, to observe the life of races, the tumultuous dramas which unfold in the life of peoples who appear as victorious conquerors on the stage of history and then suddenly plunge back into a state of

---

[30]   The Vittorio Veneto offensive of Oct.–Nov. 1918 finally defeated the Austrian army and partially avenged the costly defeat inflicted at Caporetto a year before.

[31]   Mussolini's speech concluded with the playing of the Arditi song 'Giovinezza' (Youth), which by now had become a Fascist anthem.

obscurity and oblivion as if they were condemned to a wretched and inexorable fate. Occasionally one of these peoples suddenly rises up again: it desperately takes its stand once more on the shining shore; it ascends once more to join battle and achieve domination. The reasons for the resurrection?[. . .] It seems as if each of these peoples has heard a superhuman voice which shouted out its orders.[. . .] What miracle has been achieved? An idea. Which idea? The idea which in that moment represented the possibility of rebirth. The idea which expressed the direct sensation of [. . .] the voice of the race. [. . .]

But in the battles between peoples for victory, will alone is not always enough, the Idea does not suffice to unite them. What is still missing? A man.[. . .] Which is the race which has generally won? The one which combined three forces: a people, an idea, a man. In other words when the figure of the Leader expressed in its most complete form the essence of the two other elements: that of the Race and that of the Idea.[. . .]

Only when pain turned us into brothers were we able to hear in the will of the Man now acknowledged as Leader the sacred, eternal voice of the Race.

[*Una rivoluzione e un capo* [One Revolution and One Leader] (Libreria del Littorio: Rome/Milan, 1927), 181–94.]

BENITO MUSSOLINI

24 The Strength in Numbers

It was a natural expression of Mussolini's palingenetic temperament that he became increasingly preoccupied with reversing the depopulation and cosmopolitanism which reading the Italian demographer Corrado Gini and Oswald Spengler's Decline of the West *convinced him were crucial factors in Italy's contemporary national weakness, just as they had been in the decline of the Roman Empire. Accordingly, on 26 May 1927 he made a major speech outlining an ambitious scheme of 'ruralization' (measures to discourage the rural exodus) and 'demographic power' (a campaign for big families so as to achieve a population of 60 million by 1950). Typical of Mussolini's capacity for double-think, he regularly legitimated the need for an Italian Empire in terms of Italy's over-population (see Texts 9, 35). The following text originally appeared in the preface to the Italian edition of a book by Richard Korherr. Korherr went on to be Himmler's chief statistician during the Second World War, charged with keeping a rough tally of victims of the Final Solution in the East. It is thus in keeping if the Duce strikes a markedly white supremacist note, belying the common opinion that Fascism was not racist before its rapproachement with Nazism.*

The way the book demonstrates that a drop in birth-rates initially affects the power which peoples exercise and eventually leads to their death is irrefutable. It even gives a precise overview of the various phases of this process of disease and death, and the author gives them names which sum up everything: urbanization or metropolitanism. At a certain point the city starts growing in a diseased, pathological way, not through its own resources but through external support. The more the city increases and expands into a metropolis the more sterile it becomes.

The increasing infertility of citizens stands in a direct relationship to the rapid and monstrous growth of the cities.[. . .] The metropolis spreads, attracting the population from the countryside which, immediately it has become urbanized, becomes sterile just like the population which is already there. The fields are deserted, but once the desert of abandoned, burnt regions reaches a certain extent the metropolis is suddenly up against the wall: its businesses, its industries, its oceans of stone and reinforced concrete are unable to restore a balance which is now shattered for good: catastrophe has struck.

The city dies, the nation—deprived of the young life-blood of new generations— is now made up of people who are old and degenerate and cannot defend itself against a younger people which launches an attack on the now unguarded frontiers. This has happened. It can happen again. This will happen, and not just to cities and nations, but on an infinitely greater scale: the whole White race, the Western race can be submerged by other coloured races which are multiplying at a rate unknown in our race.

Are the black and yellow races at the gates, then? Yes, they are at the gates, and not just because of their fertility, but because of the keen awareness they have of their race and its future place in the world. For example, while the Whites in the USA have a miserable birth-rate—which would be even more so if it were not for the injection of more fertile races such as the Irish, the Jews and the Italians—the Negroes are extremely fertile, and already number an impressive 14 million, which is a sixth of the population of the country. There is a large quarter of New York populated exclusively by Negroes. A serious revolt of Negroes which broke out last July was only quelled after a night of bloody street battles with police who found themselves confronted by serried ranks of Negroes.[. . .]

I believe that demographic laws—both negative and positive—can cancel out or at least slow down [the decline in the birth-rate] if the social organism to which they are applied is still capable of reacting. In this case what counts even more than formal laws is the moral tradition, and above all the religious conscience, of the individual. If a man does not feel the joy and pride of being 'perpetuated' as an individual, as a family, and as a people; or on the other hand, if a man does not feel sadness and shame at the prospect of dying as an individual, a family, and a people, laws in themselves can do nothing, even, I would say especially, if they are draconian.[. . .]

A nation does not only exist as a history and a territory, but also as a mass of human beings who reproduce from generation to generation. Otherwise the result is slavery or destruction. Italian Fascists: the philosopher of the state, Hegel, once said that he who is not a father is not a man!

In a Fascist Italy where marshes have been drained, the land has been irrigated and cultivated; where life has become disciplined, there is space and food for another 10 million men. Sixty million Italians will have the numbers and strength to make an impact on the history of the world.

[*Gerarchia*, 8/9 (9 Sept. 1928); repr. in *Omnia Opera di Benito Mussolini* (see Text 4), xxii. 209–11, 215–16.]

25 The Anti-Modernist Aesthetic of *Strapaese*

The ruralizing policies of Fascism corresponded ideologically to the populist ideas of two prominent Florentine intellectuals, Ardengo Soffici and Curzio Malaparte (see Text 18), who for a time published articles in Il Selvaggio [The Primitive] celebrating the purity of regional and rural life in contrast to urban rootlessness and corruption. Artistic explorations of this theme came to be known as Strapaese (literally 'hyper-village'), one of whose most radical articulators was the editor of Il Selvaggio, Mino Maccari (1898–1989). His sublimation of the revolutionary spirit of the provincial squadristi in their defence of 'true' Italian values could at times produce unmistakably xenophobic, racist, anti-modernist, and anti-Semitic outbursts reminiscent of the völkisch-nationalist aesthetic which was officially promoted by the Nazis under the Third Reich (see Text 48). Note that Maccari claims that he is not opposed to modernity as such, but is keen to foster an alternative, more healthy modernity purged of its decadent components.

We have no desire to 'abolish' modernity; we are not nostalgic for any past century; it is just that we would like to see a modernity which is more Italian than American or German, and our century more in harmony with the traditional Italian spirit, with customs, with a mentality, with habits which are peculiar to our people and rooted in generations of Italians.

It seems to us that modernity, in the form it is taking, namely as something bastard, international, external, mechanical—a racket manipulated by Jewish bankers, pederasts, war-profiteers, brothel keepers—if it were to be taken on board by us in its entirety just as it is, could poison, corrupt, and extensively cancel out the heritage of our race, which has been conserved, passed down from century to century by that great friend and protector of peoples which is tradition, and against which failed artists stupidly direct their wrath as well as those who, unable to sell the joint roasted in the fire of tradition, sell instead the grey smoke of *Novecentismo*.[32]

[*Il Selvaggio*, 2 (1927), quoted in S. Guglielmini, *Guida al Novecento* (Principato: Milan, 1971), 334–5.]

26 The Modernist Aesthetic of *Novecento*

In stark contrast to the Third Reich, Fascist Italy accommodated various shades of modernism (including the international movement, Futurism, and abstraction), alongside neo-classical or openly anti-modernist ones. Though there were deep conflicts between

[32] See Text 26.

the representatives of different aesthetic creeds, Mussolini was happy to harness the energies of all creative individuals who convinced themselves that his regime was the vehicle for the social transformation which they saw it as the mission of their art to promote. Novecento (Twentieth Century) celebrated the dynamism of modern city life, an aesthetic which came to be referred to as Stracittà (hyper-city) to contrast it with Strapaese. In architecture Novecento developed a modernized neo-classical (Roman) aesthetic to symbolize the renewal of Italy. In this passage taken from the movement's influential journal, one of its foremost theoreticians illustrates how successfully Fascism had created a mythic climate which abolished any clear distinction between art and life.

At bottom, *Novecentismo* is above all a cultural history. To put it better, the creation and inspirer of cultural history. Of a culture which is intensely Italian and modern.

It is the eternal and fatal Mediterranean tendency to the streamlined, the airy, to the wealth which comes from perpetual motion, always to want to see a bit of sky mixed in with things of the earth and a bit of mystery blended in with the most precise realities, to turn each hour of everyday life into the strophe of a poetic myth. There is a strange and spontaneous correspondence [. . .] between the theoretical ideals which *Novecentismo* espoused from the outset in a purely literary sphere, and the whole spirit in which Italian life has been renewed. We called for the deliberate creation of the myths for the new era: and is it not true to say that today the whole of Italy at every level, in every walk of life, in the most prosaic of activities, in politics and industry, in agriculture and fashion, is working as if intent on writing a mythic poem, with a precise sense of its role as the protagonist on the stage of a theatre, which is the theatre of history?

[900, July 1928, quoted in S. Guglielmini, *Guida al Novecento* (Principato: Milan, 1971), 336.]

GIUSEPPE BOTTAI

27 The University as the Incubator of a Fascist Élite

Giuseppe Bottai (1895–1959) served in the Arditi and after the war was attracted by Futurism and combattentismo before joining the Fascist Party. As minister of corporations (1929–32) and minister of education (1936–43) he worked to create a technocratic and managerial élite while fostering the technical and craft skills necessary to feed the productive revolution he saw promised by corporativism. After 1938 he also endorsed the regime's adoption of biological racism by applying anti-Semitic legislation to education. In the cultural sphere he encouraged the adherence of avant-garde artists and intellectuals to the regime especially through his literary review Primato (1940–3). In this speech Bottai expresses his belief in Fascism's power to create a cultural revolution which will transform higher education from within. Bottai's overtly modernizing conception of Fascism is akin to the celebration of twentieth-century dynamism by the Stracittà movement (see Text 26).

It is in these terms that, as I see it, the problem of culture in the present phase of Fascism is to be framed. Fascism-as-culture, in which, as we saw, Fascism-as-action is not denied but integrated, is the foundation of Fascism-as-State. In our type of State, which is not an arid bureaucratic construction (whether we are talking about the old bureaucracy or the one now emerging within the framework of syndical-ism), professional skills based on the mentality of the accountant is not enough. Our State engages the spirit and conscience of our citizens; it is with their spirit and conscience that they must operate in order to serve it. In the syndical laws,[33] in the Charter of Labour,[34] the framing of problems relating to material interests and to contractual guarantees is bound up with a higher order of principles, such as the training and education of individuals and the overriding interest of production, principles on which a manager must be in a position to form a judgement. For this to be possible it is important that he knows not only how those laws are put into immediate effect, but how to calculate, with at least some degree of foresight, the possible consequences of their application. In short, the manager must be in possession of that higher form of skill which involves being able to look ahead so as not to go down the wrong avenue or lose it altogether.

It is in this precise point that, in my view, the role of the university under Fascism lies: in laying the basis for a living culture, one which creates a class of men able to provide leadership in politics, science, and art. The university must adapt so as to be able to fulfil a task of this sort. All the great aspects of a civilization, from religion to philosophy, from science to literature, from political institutions to economic organizations, are reducible to a single, unique principle which informs all of them. The animating principle of Fascism must be raised to the common denominator of every branch of study. Of every branch, for, if the need for a cultural revolution is above all palpable in legal, political, economic, and social studies, it is no less urgent in other types of study, which often pursue lines of enquiry which still conflict with the Fascist training of the character and mind of Italians.

['Cultura e azione' [Culture and action], Inaugural lecture on opening of the course on Corporative Legislation at the University of Pisa, 13 Nov. 1928; repr. in *Giovanni Bottai. Scritti*, ed. R. Bartolozzi and R. del Giudice (Capelli: Bologna 1965), 64–8.]

BENITO MUSSOLINI

28   The Achievements of the Fascist Revolution

When Mussolini gave this speech on the 'state of the nation' in 1929, the eradication of liberalism and socialism as political threats was complete and institutional foundations of the Fascist state were in place, including the recently signed Lateran Pacts. These for the first time since the Risorgimento *reconciled the Vatican to the Italian state. It would be simplistic to dismiss such a passage simply as propaganda, for it captures a feeling which*

---

[33] Passed by Rocco in Apr. 1926.   [34] Drafted by Rocco and Bottai and issued Apr. 1927.

spread far beyond the circles of 'intransigent' Fascists that the new regime was successfully creating a dynamic, progressive, fully integrated national community, a creative synthesis of nationalism with socialism which was a role model for all modern nations. Notable is the stress on the State, which in Fascist theory played the pivotal role in the new order which the Volk played in Nazi thought (see Text 20). The allusion to the creation of an empire is also significant, in the light of the subsequent invasion of Ethiopia.

This, the first quinquennial assembly of the regime, is a new and unprecedented event in the history of Italy and the world.[. . .] It is an assembly because it brings together all the vital and productive forces of national society, all the men who carry out specific responsibilities and functions at the top of the hierarchies and converge on a sole objective.[. . .]

The new electoral law,[35] which is the logical and legitimate consequence of the profound constitutional transformation of the State and the creation of new corporative institutions, has worked excellently. The new Chamber is formed via a two-stage process of selection and its ratification[36] by the people.[. . .] Gone for good is the depressing succession of deceptions, frauds, and acts of violence which inevitably accompanied the so-called electoral campaigns of the past: the election itself has been abolished. People now vote for an idea, for a regime, not for men.[. . .]

A nation exists only in so far as it is a people. A people rises only in so far as it has a healthy birth-rate, is industrious, and is disciplined. Power is the product of these three basic factors. We need to start applying them at the beginning of each life. This is the function of a newly created organization which typifies the regime: the National Institute for Maternity and Childhood [Opera nazionale per la maternità e l'infanzia].[. . .]

The whole educational system in Italy is pervaded by the spirit of the victorious war and of the Fascist revolution. Alongside the schools, and complementing them, youth is organized into the Balilla and Avanguardisti,[37] the hope and pride of the Fatherland.

The employed are integrated within the institutions of the regime: syndicalism and corporatism enable the whole nation to be organized. The system is based on the legal recognition of professional unions, on collective contracts, on the prohibition of strikes and lock-outs, on the Charter of Labour (a fundamental document the importance of whose provisions will come to be appreciated more and more), on the Magistrature of Labour. It is one which has already borne fruit. Labour and capital have ceased to consider their antagonism an inexorable fact of history: the conflicts which inevitably arise are solved peacefully thanks to an increasing degree

[35] The law of 17 May 1928, creating a new system of election to the Chamber of Deputies under which candidates were selected by the Fascist Grand Council and approved by plebiscite.

[36] Lit. 'consecration'.

[37] The Balilla was for boys aged 8 to 14, the Avanguardisti for adolescents from 15 to 17. See Text 30.

of conscious class collaboration. The social legislation of Italy is the most advanced in the world: it ranges from the law on the eight-hour day to compulsory insurance against tuberculosis.[. . .]

Communications in Italy have in the last few years made impressive progress.[. . .]

The malaise of the past is no more. For the regime north and south do not exist: only Italy exists and the Italian people.[. . .]

Squadrismo became the Militia and every trace of *squadrismo* disappeared.[. . .]

Efficient armed forces and sound finances are the precondition for the foreign policy of a State.[. . .]

Let us remember that Italy's energies are totally absorbed in the effort to create new institutions, a new type of civilization which reconciles traditions with modernity, progress with faith, the machine with the spirit, and which synthesizes the thought and advances of two centuries. This Italy does not want to disturb the peace, but is ready to defend its interests in any part of the world.[. . .]

This portrait of everything the regime has achieved for the State and the people is far from complete. There are other spheres of activity to be remembered: the promotion of sport and physical education, with stadiums and gymnasiums built on a scale not unworthy of ancient Rome; the 'Dopolavoro',[38] the full range of artistic spectacles, no longer left to individuals or groups, but instituted by law; the renewed dignity of our greatest theatres; the restoration and rediscovery of ancient remains which bear witness to the marvellous history which, both before and after Christ, is the history of Rome.[. . .]

Rome had to be the capital of a resurrected Italy,[. . .] but the fatal conclusion of the first phase of the *Risorgimento* brought about a deep division which ever since 1870 has tormented the conscience of the Italians. This division, a true thorn in the side of the nation, has been healed with the pacts of the 11 February,[39] [. . .] even-handed and precise pacts which create between Italy and the Holy See a situation, not of confusion or hypocrisy, but of differentiation and loyalty. I think that it is far from absurd to maintain that only in a regime based on this Concordat can the logical, normal, healthy separation between Church and State become a reality, thus delimiting clearly the tasks and functions of each. Each has its own rights, its own duties, its own authority, its own sphere of competence. Only on this premiss can the two collaborate on certain issues on the basis of their own sovereignty.[. . .]

The peace between the Quirinal and the Vatican is an event of supreme importance, not only for Italy, but for the world. For Italians it is enough to remember that on 11 February 1929 the Kingdom of Italy, ruled over by the House of Savoy and with Rome as the capital of the Italian State, was finally and solemnly recognized by the Supreme Pontiff. (*The assembly rises to its feet and applauds at length*).[. . .]

It is the incontestable merit of Fascism to have given Italians a sense of State. All our achievements which we have summarized to you today fade in comparison with what we have achieved by creating the State. For Fascism the State is not a

---

[38] See Text 33.   [39] The Lateran Pacts.

'night-watchman' which merely concerns itself with the personal security of its citizens. Nor is it an organization with a purely material end, such as that of guaranteeing a certain level of well-being and of relative social harmony, which could be achieved simply through an executive council; nor has it been created as a purely political entity, completely unconnected with the complex, ever-changing reality of individuals and peoples. The State as Fascism conceives and actualizes it, is a spiritual and moral entity, because it is the concrete political, juridic, and economic organization of the nation. This organization has emerged and continues to develop as a manifestation of the spirit. The State is the guarantor of internal and external security, but it also safeguards and perpetuates the spirit of the people as it has evolved over the centuries in language, customs, and faith.

The State is not only present, but past, and, above all, future. It is the State which, transcending the brief limits of individual lives, embodies the conscience of the nation. It is the State which, in Italy, is subsumed and elevated in the House of Savoy, and in the sacred, august person of the king.

The forms in which States express themselves change, but the necessity for the State remains. It is the State which teaches its citizens civil virtues; makes them aware of their mission; calls upon them to be united; harmonizes their interests through justice; enables men to progress from the elemental life of the tribe to the highest expression of human power which is empire; immortalizes the names of those who died to defend its integrity or obey its laws; holds up as an example for future generations the military leaders who increased its territory, or the geniuses who enhance its glory. (*Enthusiastic applause*)

When the sense of State declines and disintegrating, centrifugal pressures exerted by individuals or groups prevail, national societies are destined to decline. Can you doubt the future having heard this account of what has been accomplished, (*No! No!*), having heard the doctrinal principles to which we will adhere? You can have no such doubts, and nor can the Italian people to whom you convey your impression of this great assembly.[. . .]

When we meet in Rome five years hence, the report on the regime's achievements will be even fuller than today's. It is with this certainty that you and the people will vote 'yes'.[40] The short monosyllable will show the world that Italy is Fascist and Fascism is Italy.

[Speech to the Quinquennial Assembly of the regime, 10 Mar. 1929, *Il Popolo d'Italia*, 69 (12 Mar. 1929), Rpr. in *Omnia Opera di Benito Mussolini* (see Text 4), xxiv. 5–16.]

[40] In the forthcoming plebiscite.

29 | ASVERO GRAVELLI
Towards a Fascist Europe

Asvero Gravelli, director of Antieuropa, *founded in 1928, was one of a number of enthusiastic advocates of Fascism's 'universal' mission (see Texts 30, 31, 32, 34). In other words, he saw 'totalitarian' Italy as the pioneer of a new type of nation-state whose emulation by other countries would enable the crisis of Western civilization to be solved and a new Europe to emerge. However, the utopian nature of such publicism and of the moves towards organizing a fascist International (for example at the time an unbridgeable gulf separated Fascism from Nazism on issues of race) doomed such 'universal Fascism' to failure. By the mid-1930s even its rhetoric of international harmony was officially abandoned as Italy entered its phase of imperialism and was drawn ever more ineluctably into the orbit of Nazi belligerence. Here Gravelli reiterates the founding principles of his peculiar brand of Eurovision (see Ledeen 1972).*

We have declared and reconfirm!

1. That Fascism is anti-European, because contemporary Europe, afflicted by a spiritual crisis, by a material crisis, is still partly under the influence of the immortal principles,[41] while vast segments of the population look to Moscow for guidance. Given *this* Europe, Fascism is anti-European.

2. The anti-Europeanism of Fascism is not an end in itself, but a provisional historical position which will last until Fascism has helped Europe regain an equilibrium of ideas and spirit, the precondition for a new European role in the world.

3. In expounding its anti-Europeanism the Fascist Revolution cannot be considered merely a movement of reaction, of counter-reformation, of anti-democracy, or anti-liberalism, ideas which are unacceptable because they are being swept away by the incessant development of human civilization.

4. Precisely because the development of the process of civilization is incessant, the ideas of democracy and liberalism cannot be considered final destinations, as if human civilization had exhausted its capacity and potential for progress. The ideas of democracy and liberalism can be seen as temporary stages, but History keeps moving, and entrusts the task of realizing progress to those ideas which are capable of interpreting the new life, the new situations determined by its irresistible course.

5. Fascism transcends democracy and liberalism. Its regenerating action is based on granite foundations: the concept of hierarchy, the participation of the whole people in the life of the State, social justice through the equitable distribution of

---

[41] The liberal principles of the French Revolution.

rights and duties, the injection of morality into public life, the prestige of the family, the moral interpretation of the ideas of order, authority, and freedom.

Guided by this act of transcendence Europe will find its way within the new era of History.

[*Antieuropa*, 2/5 (May 1930), 1018.]

GIOVANNI GIURATI

30   The Role of Youth under Fascism

The setting up of organizations to cater for every age group of Italian youth of both sexes was an important aspect of the regime's programme for the Fascistization of society and its perpetuation by those who had not participated in the original 'Fascist Revolution'. In an attempt to ensure a steady supply of working-class recruits to the PNF and Militia, the Fasci Giovanili were set up by the Fascist Grand Council in October 1930. This extract from its fortnightly bulletin Gioventù Fascista *[Fascist Youth] reproduces a speech by Giovanni Giurati (1876–1970), former squadrista, president of the Chamber of Deputies, and now secretary of the PNF, a post he held from October 1930 until December 1931. It contains several typical features of Fascist thought and propaganda: the importance of squadrista violence as the foundation myth of the regime, the concern for Fascism's perpetuation as a permanent revolution, the blend of élitism and populism, the sacralization and militarization of politics, the stress on youth, and the belief in Fascism's universal and imperial mission modelled on the Roman Empire (see Koon 1985).*

The Fascist Party must be aristocratic, in the sense that it must embrace the flower of the race in terms of moral purity, intellectual training, discipline, devotion to the Duce, dedication to the Fatherland. But it must also be a mass party if it wants to provide tens of thousands of Blackshirts able to hold the supreme offices of the State, run the local councils and provinces, regiment the working masses, instruct the youth, in a word bear the enormous burden of constructing a modern State. All the more burdensome because the Party does not want to be the cretinous copy of the type familiar from the past. It wants to be a model to all those who must one day embrace the principles of the Fascist Revolution.[. . .]

The Party [. . .] had to concern itself with the new generation which the Regime in the course of its sustained rule was raising to meet the responsibilities of adult life. The system followed till the end of Year VIII[42] had not proved effective.[. . .] Thus it was necessary to found the Fasci Giovanili, as direct heirs of the Action Squads, as a great training ground for the spirits and muscles to rear the future soldiers of the Fatherland. On 4 November 328,000 young men in every corner of Italy, wearing their Blackshirts and carrying the colours of Rome, affirmed in their oath the imperial will of Fascism.

[42] i.e. 1930: in imitation of the French Revolution, the Fascist calendar was restarted to commemorate 1922, year of the March on Rome, as the beginning of a new era.

This unexpected influx of recruits pleasantly surprised the older generation. *Squadrista* songs rang out with the gusto of the past. Each of us felt he was reliving the days of fever and struggle. It was just as when once a temporary dam is broken down and the stagnant water pours into a thousand tumultuous channels to make the surrounding valleys fertile. While we watched this moving spectacle of spontaneity and enthusiasm, we thought how the Young Fascists gave another damning reply to those who foretold disaster for the movement. It is among the young that all the great movements in history have found their prophets, their soldiers, their martyrs. It is well known that the more life is held in contempt, the more value it acquires, and the young, since they are more prepared to embrace a faith are precisely for this reason more prepared to pay the final sacrifice for it. Hence it is the unquestioning support of the young which vouches for the value and universality of a movement. Seeing the Young Fascists in the squares of Italy and hearing their songs, we who are concerned for the fate of the Regime have our conviction reaffirmed—if it was ever necessary—that Fascism is universal, and that no force will ever stop its progress.

['I giovani e il partito' [The young and the party], *Gioventù Fascista*, 1/6 (26 Apr. 1931), 3.]

UGO SPIRITO

31 Fascist Corporativism as the Key to a New International Order

A major component of Fascist's revolutionary programme consisted in replacing liberal (laissez-faire) economics by a corporative system which avoided the centralizing bureaucracy of the Soviet planned economy. That this was no mere propaganda ploy is testified to by the heated debate which grew up, against the background of the Depression and the failure of actually existing capitalism which it betokened, over which of the many theories of corporativism, leftist and rightist, provided the best model. The academic philosopher Ugo Spirito became a prolific exponent of what he termed 'integral corporatism', in which ownership would pass from stockholders to producers, a controversial interpretation which exposed him to the charge of 'Bolshevism' by some fellow Fascists. In this passage he shows the unbounded faith he had in the capacity of corporativism to create the basis of a harmonious new international order in which nations would not lose their identity. This was a permutation of Fascist internationalism, and one at loggerheads with the drive for autarky which the regime was increasingly pursuing (see Text 37).

The distinctiveness of the new corporative concept when compared to liberalism and socialism can perhaps be seen best in the international sphere. If the term *international* is taken to mean in concrete terms *the relationship between nations*, it can definitely be asserted that only under corporativism can there be any serious talk of an 'International'. The liberal and socialist international were really only *anti-national*.

The truth of this assertion is demonstrated especially in economics, where the major problem has emerged and various solutions have been attempted. The *laissez-faire* school of traditional economics denied the existence of frontiers and therefore of nations: at least as far as everything to do with economic life is concerned (that is, the immediately concrete and visible interests of each citizen), the nation has no significance.[. . .]

But the opposite, abstractly statist demands of socialism lead to the same conclusion. In practice the State in which each must trust to obtain justice and liberty is a State which abolishes differences between individuals and, along with them, nations. 'Proletarians of the whole world unite' is the cry of the socialists, which means 'deny your Fatherland for humanity, deny the States for the State which will be your redemption.'

In contrast, Fascism recognizes the value of the universalist demand which lies at the heart of the so-called ideology of the liberal and socialist International, and proclaims the need for a genuine International based on corporative principles.

By moving from the individual to the State, from corporation to corporation, we finally arrive at the national corporation. But confronted by the myopic naturalistic nationalism which asserts the dogma of economic independence [. . .] and only knows the weapon of protectionism, Fascism has understood that the true triumph of corporativism lies in bringing about the triumph of the corporative idea throughout the whole world. And, while the use of protective import duties is forced on us by present conditions, it campaigns against customs barriers and against the egotistic limitations of international commerce. This is not, of course, to encourage the anarchy of individualistic *laissez-faire*, but to establish a system of collaboration between nations under which every country, by organizing its own economy in a planned way, takes account of the organization prevailing in other countries and comes to an arrangement with them on how best to co-ordinate different programmes.[. . .] Just as it does not abolish distinctions between individuals, corporativism is not a levelling force between nations, and just as it recognizes the value of every individual's work and his[43] need to affirm his personality freely, so it recognizes, within an international system, every country's peculiar contribution to the creation of a new civilization.

> ['Il corporativismo come liberalismo assoluto e socialismo assoluto' [Corporativism as absolute liberalism and absolute socialism], *Nuovi studi di diritto, economia e politica* [New Studies in Law, Economics, and Politics], 6 (1932), 285–98; repr. in *Capitalismo e corporativismo* (Sansoni: Florence, 1934), 66–7.]

GIUSEPPE BOTTAI
....

32 Mussolini's Century

Closely associated with the Ministry of Corporations in its formative phase, Bottai was another enthusiastic believer in Fascist economics and frequently used his periodical Critica

---

[43] Italian does not have gender-specific possessive adjectives, but to translate them with the masculine 'his' is certainly in keeping with the pervasive chauvinism of Fascist thought (which is why extracts by women writers under the regime would be unrepresentative). On the role of women under Fascism see Grazia (1994).

Fascista to extol its virtues as the solution to key problems of the modern world. Here, however, he devotes his leader to a eulogy of the second part of the article 'Fascism', 'Political and Social Doctrine', which appeared in vol. xiv of the Enciclopedia Italiana. *It was published in the Fascist press on 5 August 1932 and went through numerous editions. It has been subsequently established that the first part ('Fundamentals') had been written by the Encyclopedia's editor, Giovanni Gentile, but that the second was indeed written by Mussolini himself. Note the supreme confidence that Fascism is inaugurating a new phase of world history ('universalism' was still officially endorsed), and the uncritical* ducismo *(adulation of the Duce's superhuman powers), both symptomatic of the sense of boundless and (until Nazism appeared on the scene) unrivalled potential as a revolutionary form of modern politics which Fascism generated among its most ardent supporters (for the full text of the article see Lyttelton 1973).*

The head of a political movement, of a vast ethico-political revolution such as Fascism, is not in the best position to trace its doctrinal features, to provide a theoretical profile of the movement itself. He interprets intuitively the needs in the realm of ideals which animate social life and which move and compel him to lead the movement itself. With his intuitive vision, he has no need to know the inter-connections which bind it into a conceptual whole which interprets social life and which gives it its true place in the history of the spirit.[. . .]

However, Mussolini, the originator and leader of Fascism—His spirit had this new surprise in store for us—reveals in his pronouncement[44] a lucid theoretical awareness, because it defines in precise, clear, and organic terms the essential foundations of the revolution. It is yet another proof of the exceptional conceptual power of this exceptional Man. The doctrinal vision outlined by Mussolini not only satisfies the cultural sensibility and demands of more serious academics, but also those of cultural critics concerned with the history of modern thought.[. . .] It is very significant that the Duce has Himself felt the need to give an account of the *doctrine* of Fascism. This confirms what He has been at pains to point out on other occasions, namely that he is not indifferent to whether or not the Fascist Revolution has a theory, a doctrine, and that, indeed, these are the demonstrations of the spiritual value and historical substance of Fascism, the true guarantees of its univer-sality and of the possibility that it can be accepted by all men, all over the world. Indeed, now Mussolini feels the need to affirm that Fascism has a universal value which 'represents a stage in the history of the human spirit'. What is hereby being affirmed, in the words of the Duce and in a doctrinal context, is that Fascism is an integral part of the history of the modern world: it is not a sudden explosion with no historical roots or context, but is a stage in an organic process, which is what gives it its spiritual nobility and historical legitimacy.[. . .]

The doctrine of Fascism, which takes account of both the democratic and the socialist experience, conceives the State as the system of rights and duties of individuals organized in such a way that they can achieve the highest ethical goals of the human personality (in its concrete national manifestation), a State which cannot help promoting social justice which under a liberal regime was inevitably

---

[44] His *Dottrina del fascismo.*

trodden underfoot. In this sense if, as Mussolini says, this century will be a century *of the right* [. . .] it will also be a century *of the left*.[. . .]

The 'doctrine of Fascism', dictated by Mussolini, is the 'Manifesto' of a revolution of ideas which will invade the world. The Duce says that our century will be the Fascist century: we think with pride and emotion that it will be the century of Mussolini.

['Il secolo di Mussolini' [The century of Mussolini], *Critica Fascista*, 10/16 (15 Aug. 1932).]

ACHILLE STARACE

33   Going to the People

Achille Starace (1889–1945) fought in the First World War and was a leading squadrista in the recently 'redeemed' Trento and Alto Adige before becoming vice-secretary of the PNF on its creation. He also played a conspicuous role in the events leading to the 'conquest of the state' in October 1922. From 1931 to 1939 he was national secretary of the party, a position he used energetically to permeate public life with choreographic, ritual, and symbolic expressions of the 'new Italy', thus creating what has been called after Rousseau a 'civic religion'. Starace's drive to Fascistize the masses in the spirit of Mussolini's phrase 'Andare al popolo' (going to the people) led him to take his responsibility for the Opera nazionale dopolavoro (roughly 'the National Leisure System') especially seriously. Set up in 1925, this was the main agency for the regulation of the 'free time' (literally 'after work') of millions of 'ordinary' Italians who through the legion activities it organized came to have a somewhat diluted experience of Fascism as a part of everyday normality and a modern lifestyle.

Go to the people, to educate them, to raise them, to improve them physically and morally; to encourage them to love their land, their village, their family, their home; to impart the desire to know the true face of the Fatherland by travelling along its roads and pausing with fresh eyes to admire its infinite beauties, allowing them to know the mountains and seas, the impressive geographical features, varied and unchanging, which mark the limits of their country; to make them expert at swimming and climbing, and in the skills which may be necessary in a future war! To loosen their muscles in joyful and simple sporting contests, to familiarize them once more with the glorious and charming traditions of their people [*gente*], whether expressed in a colourful costume, the harmony of a song, or a religious procession which wends its way chanting psalms, or a churchyard watched over by a bell tower constantly ringing out its message to the faithful, or a simple country dance held on a threshing-floor freshly swept clean and decked with flags.

To teach them and enthuse them with the love of music, song, dance, painting, sculpture, poetry, all the arts in which Italy has always led the way and whose banners were unfurled by its people and raised high in all the skies of the world.

To perfect their trade and teach them that the paths to success are opened by effort and not absurd pretensions and useless words.

Finally to help them affectionately in every step of their lives, guaranteeing individuals and their families that moral and economic well-being to which the Italian people, renewed by Fascism, have for the first time been granted the right thanks to a new and full understanding of their duties.

These are the aims which inspire the daily activities of the OND.

[*L'Opera nazionale dopolavoro* (A. Mondadori: Milan, 1934), 12–13.]

BENITO MUSSOLINI

34   The Birth of a New Civilization

In this article, initially written for American consumption, Mussolini gives yet another testimony to a belief which he had already enshrined in the Enciclopedia Italiana *article (see Text 32), and which was a constantly asserted theme in the publicism of Fascist ideologues in the early 1930s: each country could be seen to be developing its own permutation of the new Italian state (that is, of generic fascism). Thus the Fascist revolution marked the dawn of a new civilization on a par with the Roman Empire, Christianity, and the Renaissance, significantly all Italian contributions to the glory of human history. Mussolini is also at pains to stress Fascism's peaceful intentions on the international stage, a claim which Goering would make for Germany (Text 68) and Mosley would make for his British form of fascism (Text 92).*

We have entered fully into a period which can be called the transition from one type of civilization to another. The ideologies of the nineteenth century are collapsing and find no one to defend them. Is it not symptomatic of this that there are socialists tired of the socialism which had been mummified by Marxist dogma? In the same way there are democrats who no longer want to have anything to do with democracy, and liberals who believe the demo-liberal phase of Western States is over. There are both negative and positive reasons for the decay and demise of demo-liberal civilization. The negative ones can be summed up as Capital's evolution into an impersonal form, which was thus in a certain sense already socialized and ready to fall into the arms of the State; in the impotence of executive power, in the arrogance of parliaments, in the class mysticism and mythology of the proletariat. The last four years of crisis[45] have accentuated the characteristics of the situation. But the new Fascist ideas, which are active in every nation in the world, would not have reached their present state of maturity without the impact of what I would call positive reasons. In order of time and importance the most significant of these has been the decennial celebrations of the Fascist Revolution.[46] Millions of people in every country have finally seen and understood.[. . .]

---

[45] The world Depression.

[46] The Mostra della Rivoluzione Fascista, a vast exhibition held in Rome in 1932 to commemorate the *squadrista* 'conquest of power'. The architectural style was a blend of Futurism and *Novecento* modernism and the whole enterprise a major event in the establishment of Fascism as a 'civic religion' (see Stone 1993).

Many who considered Fascism an ephemeral movement within Italian politics have now started studying it seriously. All have been able to recognize—by seeing with their own eyes—the profound transformation which Fascism has brought about, not only in the material lives of the Italian people, but in their spirit. As ever the *fait accompli* has spoken volumes, and the Italian example inspired in many countries near and far the urge to emulate it.[. . .] The event which has placed in mortal danger all the principles of the last century has been the triumph of the Hitlerian forces in Germany. Here is another great country in the process of creating a unitary, authoritarian, totalitarian State, i.e. a fascist one, but one which has accentuated certain features differently which Fascism was spared by virtue of having operated in a different historical context. This is not the place to establish analogies or differences between the two regimes. The undeniable fact is that the actions and innovations undertaken by both are taking place outside any sort of demo-liberal conception of things, and that both have annihilated demo-social-liberal forces. The very word socialism would be unknown to the Germans by now if it did not figure in the very name of Hitler's party. What can be called fascist seeds of political and spiritual renewal of the world can be now seen at work in every country, even in England. There is no doubt that even France, the last citadel in the defence of the 'immortal principles', will one day soon have to raise the flag of surrender. America itself is abandoning them. Roosevelt is moving, acting, giving orders independently of the decisions or wishes of the Senate or Congress. There are no longer intermediaries between him and the nation. There is no longer a parliament but an 'état majeur'. There are no longer parties, but a single party. A sole will silences dissenting voices. This has nothing to do with any demo-liberal conception of things.

The appeal to the forces of youth sounds out on all sides: the nation which is way out in front, anticipating by a decade the action of other countries, is Italy. Nothing leads us to believe or make others believe that the young who have become the ruling class of fascist States—and therefore authoritarian, unitarian, totalitarian—will disturb the peace: it is to be predicted that they will guarantee peace to the world. There is nothing, therefore, more interesting and dramatic than a civilization whose sun is setting, and which—amidst many mistakes, much squandering of energy, and many massacres—has left a deep imprint on history. And there is nothing more auspicious and fascinating than the glow on the horizon of a new civilization.

['Fra due civiltà' [Between two civilizations], article published in the journal of *Universal Service* in the United States, in *Il Popolo d'Italia*, 198, 22 Aug. 1933, and in *Omnia Opera di Benito Mussolini* (see Text 4), xxvi. 44–5.]

iii. Imperialist Expansion and Alignment with Nazism 1935–1939

BENITO MUSSOLINI

35 **The Vital Need for Empire**

The colonization of Ethiopia marked the end of the purely domestic phase of Italy's transformation in which it was possible to believe, however naïvely, that Fascism had been able to pioneer a radically innovative type of State without upsetting the international community, and (even more naïvely) that its emulation was the basis of a harmonious new world order. Mussolini had already alluded to Italy's imperial mission in his 'Quinquennial' speech (Text 28), though planning for the Abyssinian campaign had started only in 1932. In this article, written two months before the invasion began, Mussolini plays down (but does not deny) arguments asserting the cultural and racial superiority of Italy over Ethiopia. He chooses instead to legitimate the coming war in terms of the need for 'vital space' for Italian settlement and the necessity to secure the existing colonies of Eritrea and Libya once Italy behaved proactively as a Great Power in international affairs. This last point is an allusion to the regime's growing territorial ambitions in the Mediterranean. It is typical of fascism in its aggressive, expansionist mode to present such imaginary needs and mythic ambitions as a 'problem' and then offer totalitarian and military action as the 'solution'. Trapped within this destructive and ultimately self-destructive logic, the parabola of Fascism was now destined to fall, even if in the short term the creation of an 'African Empire' (an old dream of liberal Italy) generated for the regime and its leader the mass popularity it was intended to secure (see Sbacchi 1989).

Some reasons which have been put forward for the Italo-Ethiopian conflict by the Italian press to repudiate those alleged in the foreign press are of secondary importance on which it is unnecessary to dwell.

That in Ethiopia slavery exists, that is the buying and selling of human beings, is admitted by the negus[47] himself. That this trade takes atrocious forms is documented in a thousand reports, mostly carried out by the English, the latest being published in 1932.[. . .]

Another non-essential reason: race. Firstly Ethiopians still do not consider themselves Negroes but Semites.[48] Secondly there are thousands of Negroes who fight as soldiers under the Italian flag and who have always fought magnificently for us and themselves. This can be said too of the Arabs, some of whom are organizing an 'Arab youth of the *Littorio*'. We Fascists acknowledge the existence of races, their differences and their hierarchy, but we do not propose to present ourselves to the world as the embodiment of the White race set against other races, we do not intend to make

---

[47] Haile Selassie, emperor of Ethiopia.
[48] Ethiopia's imperial dynasty claimed descent from the Queen of Sheba and King Solomon.

ourselves the preachers of segregation and of racial hatreds when we see that our fiercest critics are not the Negroes of Harlem—who could profitably use their time to take care of their colleagues who are daily and Christianly lynched in the United States—but are mostly genuine Whites in Europe and America.

Similarly the theme of 'civilization' should not be overemphasized.[. . .]

The essential arguments, absolutely irrefutable and enough to put an end to any attempt to censure us, are twofold: the vital needs of the Italian people and its military security in Eastern Africa.[. . .] The second of these is the decisive one.[. . .]

It is blindingly obvious that the strategic situation of our colonies, precarious enough in normal times, would become untenable in exceptional times, if ever Italy was to become a player on the chessboard of Europe. The solution of the problem must be a totalitarian one.[. . .]

Posed in military terms, the Italo-Abyssinian problem is one of striking simplicity, of an absolute logic; posed in military terms, the problem only admits—with Geneva,[49] without Geneva, against Geneva—one solution.

All the other arguments are important, but not decisive: it is in this last fact that the policy of Fascist Italy finds its supreme historical and human justification.

> ['Il "dato" irrefutabile' [The irrefutable 'fact'], *Il Popolo d'Italia*, 182 (31 July 1935); repr. in *Omnia Opera di Benito Mussolini* (see Text 4), xxvii. 110–11.]

TWO MARCHING SONGS OF FASCIST SOLDIERS ABROAD

36

These two songs give a glimpse of the popular myths which rationalized the colonization of Abyssinia (bringing civilization to a barbarous people while simultaneously renewing the Roman legacy), and intervention on the side of Franco's forces in the Spanish Civil War (fighting Communism to defend Christian civilization and bring about a Fascist Europe). Four hundred thousand Italian troops were sent to Ethiopia, which became 'Italian' on 9 May 1936, the war and subsequent colonization causing some 200,000 Ethiopian deaths (see Sbacchi 1989). Over 50,000 soldiers (of whom 4,000 died) were sent to Spain between January 1937 and mid-1938. By then European democracies and the League of Nations had fatally demonstrated their impotence to stop nationalist acts of military aggression directed against legal governments and other countries, and Fascist Italy and the Third Reich (which also actively supported Franco) were brothers-in-arms.

(a) From the Abyssinian Campaign

La Patria ci ha chiamati,	The Fatherland has called us,
e intorno al tricolor,	And we all have formed ranks
noi tutti siam schierati	Around the tricolor
con fede e amor.	With faith and love.

[49] Seat of the League of Nations.

Noi siamo balde schiere,	We are valiant formations
indomiti guerrier,	Of indomitable warriors
portiamo le bandiere	Carrying the flags
nell'Africa Orientale.	Into Eastern Africa.
Il simbolo di gloria,	The symbol of glory,
di pace e civiltà,	Of peace and civilization
l'Italica Vittoria	Will be made to shine once more
rifulgere farà!	By the Italic Victory.
Oh Roma, eterna Roma,	Oh Rome, eternal Rome,
tu sai che i figli tuoi	You know that your sons
rispondono all'appello	Will answer the call,
al solo grido 'A noi!'	The single cry 'Come to us'.
Di Roma il grande impero	We want to renew
vogliamo rinnovar,	The great Empire of Rome,
marciando sul sentiero	Marching on the path
che il Duce sa indicar.	Which the Duce has shown us.
Gli schiavi e la barbarie	Slavery and barbarity
dovranno scomparir,	Are doomed to vanish
dell'aquile romane	The very moment
al subito apparir.	The Roman eagles appear.
Il popolo italiano	The Italian people
nel cuor custodirà,	In its heart will keep
splendente quella fede	The faith shining
che indomito lo fa!	Which makes it invincible.
È bello il sacrificio,	Sacrifice is beautiful
per te saremo eroi:	For you we will be heroes:
Oh Roma eterna Roma.	Oh eternal Rome.
noi siamo i figli tuoi.	We are your sons!

(b) From the Spanish Campaign: 'Arriba España!' [Long live Spain]

Al grido dei fratelli di Spagna	Hearing the cry of our Spanish brothers
Noi siam corsi compatti e serrati	We lined up in the serried ranks
A Legioni di Camicie Nere	Of the Blackshirt Legions
Per difender l'Iberico suol.	To defend the Iberian soil.
Or squilli l'adunata dell'assalto,	Now let the bugle muster us for the attack,
Echeggi il grido di battaglia,	Let the cry of battle ring out,
Con forza leonina e furente	With leonine and furious force
Ci scagliamo sul bieco oppressor!	We will hurl ourselves against our sullen foe.

Chorus	*Chorus*
Salve, Duce, per Te noi pugniamo,	Hail, Duce, it is for You we fight,
Legionari del fascismo siam.	We are Legionaries of Fascism.
In alto il pugnale, da forti	We raise our daggers, and through our strength
Noi vogliamo la Spagna liberar.	We want to liberate Spain!
Mai ci tremi né braccio né core,	May our arm and our heart never tremble,
Messager di nuova Storia noi siam	We are the messengers of the new History.

In alto le Insegne, da prodi,	We hold our Colours aloft, and through our valour
Noi vogliamo la Civiltà salvar!	We want to save Civilization.

Ognor ci sorrega la Fede	Faith sustains us always
Che ci sprona a tutti i cimenti	It spurs us on to face any danger,
Dell'eterna Luce di Roma	We are the daring bearers
Noi ne siamo i baldi apportator.	Of the eternal Light of Rome.

L'Europa Fascista noi vogliamo	We want a Fascist Europe
Che desti i popoli oppressi	Which rouses oppressed people from their sleep,
E torni il sorriso alle genti	And returns a smile to the face of nations
Martoriate dal rosso insidiator.	Tormented by the treacherous Reds.

[Quoted in A. V. Savona and M. L. Straniero, *Canti dell'Italia fascista* (1919–1945)
(Garzanti: Milan, 1979), 272–3, 306–7.]

EDMONDO ROSSONI

37 The Autarkic Mentality and the New Fascist Order

*The drive for autarky, or economic self-sufficiency and independence from foreign im-
ports, was first introduced in 1929 in the context of the world Depression, but in the
course of the 1930s it was increasingly bound up with safeguarding the regime's colonial
and territorial ambitions in the event of war (a need underlined by the League of Nation's economic sanctions against Italy during the Ethiopian War). Edmondo Rossoni
(1884–1965) was the head of the Fascist syndicates between 1922 and 1925, after which
the regime created a form of corporativism which betrayed the proletarian radicalism of
his 'integral syndicalism' by exclusively serving the interests of the employers and the
state. This 'directive', written when he was minister of agriculture, gives a sample of the
way the nebulous Fascist discourse of militarism, ducismo, and utopian nationalism could
be used to paper over the enormous cracks which had opened up in Italian economic life,
particularly under the burden of the Ethiopian and Spanish campaigns (see Tannenbaum
1972).*

Free competition can be no more than a sham in a State like ours, which needs to
know not only what is being produced, but also the conditions in which it is
produced. The basic mechanisms of economic problems have to be seen clearly,
and clear solutions must be imposed, because the economic struggle for bread or
wealth, for a single cent or a million, inevitably gives rise to political struggles,
something ruled out absolutely by the needs of the Fatherland and the inexorable
will of Fascism.

These considerations have given birth to the Fascist economic doctrine, and the
same considerations have determined the organization of the Fascist economy.
They find concrete expression on the one hand in the practical collaboration of all
the elements of society and on the other in the productive efficiency and autarky of
the nation.[. . .]

Once the political and social conscience has been perfected, the Duce commands us to develop an *autarkic mentality*.

The initiative must start with individuals, especially Leaders, and with provincial centres, to arrive at a national plan.

Every Provincial Council of the Corporations must create an inventory of what is produced and what the needs are in every province.[. . .]

A new instrument of the Fascist economy for the perfect knowledge of the productive process, for establishing plans, and for the just assessment of the value of work, are the consortiums [*consorzi*].[50] While general economic policy is made by the Corporations, in every specific branch of activity employers and workers assembled in these economic bodies establish the quantity of production and oversee the products, though they are still under the control of the Corporative State, which represents all the economic interests and social groups.[. . .]

The Italian economic world henceforth marches in step with the Blackshirts and the Legionaries who have conquered the Empire. Even the economy, illuminated by the Fascist idea, is no longer arid, opaque, materialistic: it is being transformed and reorganized to become a system of human relations between men [*uomini*] belonging to the same country.

It is in this atmosphere that it is necessary to renew and be renewed, and with this will that we must prepare Italians for the life of tomorrow. In this way Mussolini will not only have created the new power and the new glory of Italy, but also the new social order for the centuries to come.

[*Direttive fasciste all'agricoltura* (La Stirpe: Rome, 1939), 138–41.]

BENITO MUSSOLINI

38   Blood-Brothers: Fascism and Nazism

Mussolini had first referred to a Rome–Berlin Axis in November 1936 and, by the time he visited Berlin in a display of solidarity, the co-operation agreed in foreign policy had already taken concrete form in the Fascist and Nazi intervention on the side of Franco. The Axis was to have enormous consequences for Italy in the introduction of racial legislation in 1938, the ultimately unsustainable human and military cost of committing troops after 1940 to the Russian and North African fronts in the wake of the Nazis' imperialist aggression, and the declaration of war on the United States in December 1941. These events were to lead eventually to Italy's crushing defeat on all fronts and the transformation of much of its territory into a battleground for the Allies' momentous onslaught against the Third Reich from July 1943 till April 1945. Though the degree of underlying kinship between the Third Rome and the Third Reich is a matter of academic debate, it would be naïve to dismiss the parallels of world-view which Mussolini identifies here as pure propaganda, since there is

---

[50] By 1937 there were some 280 of these price-fixing cartels, made compulsory by the State in 1932 but operating largely beyond its control. See Tannenbaum 1972: 105–6.

evidence that both he and Hitler spontaneously recognized a deep affinity with each other as the (only) leaders of genuinely populist and revolutionary movements of national regeneration. Mussolini gave this speech in German.

It is not only in my capacity as the head of the Italian government that I have come among you, but above all in my capacity as head of a national revolution who has wanted to give proof of open and unequivocal solidarity with your revolution. And even if the course of the two revolutions has not been the same, the objective which both wanted to achieve, and have achieved, is the same: the unity and greatness of the people.

Fascism and Nazism are two manifestations of the parallel historical situations which link the life of our nations, resurrected to unity in the same century and through the same action.

As has been said, my journey to Germany has no hidden agenda. Nothing is being plotted to divide a Europe already sufficiently divided. The solemn reaffirmation of the existence and solidity of the Rome–Berlin Axis is not directed at other States, because we, Nazis and Fascists alike, want peace and are always ready to work for peace, for a real and fruitful peace which does not ignore but resolves the problems of the coexistence of peoples.

Just as fifteen years of Fascism have given a new material and spiritual countenance to Italy, so your revolution has given a new face to Germany: new, even if, as in Italy, it is based on the most noble and eternal traditions which can be reconciled with the necessities of modern life.[. . .]

We have many elements of *Weltanschauung* in common.

Not only have Nazism and Fascism everywhere the same enemies who serve the same masters, the Third International, but they share many conceptions of life and history. Both believe in violence as a force determining the life of peoples, as the dynamo of their history, and hence reject the doctrines of so-called historical materialism and their political and philosophical by-products. Both of us exalt work in its countless manifestations as the sign of the nobility of man; both of us count on youth, from which we demand the virtues of discipline, courage, tenacity, patriotism, and scorn for the comfortable life.[. . .]

Twenty years ago your great Führer launched the rallying-cry which was to become the battle-cry of the German people: 'Deutschland erwache!' Germany has awakened. The Third Reich has arisen.

I do not know when Europe will awaken, as was said at the Party Congress in Nuremberg, because dark but readily identifiable forces[51] are at work to provoke war from within and without. The important thing is that our two great peoples, which form an impressive, ever growing mass of 150 million souls, are united in a single unshakable resolve.

This momentous display of solidarity bears witness of this unity to the world.

['Il discorso di Berlino' [The Berlin speech], 29 Sept. 1937, in *Omnia Opera di Benito Mussolini* (see Text 4), xxviii. 248–53.]

---

[51] An allusion (among other alleged internal 'enemies') to the Jews.

39 **The Introduction of Fascist Racial Policy**

Gioacchino Volpe (1876–1971) held chairs in history from 1905 till 1946 and wrote what can be seen as the official history of the Fascist movement, which first appeared in 1939. This passage deals with the publication in July 1938 of the Manifesto of Fascist Racism claiming that Italians were Aryans and biologically distinct from Jews, a document completely out of keeping with official Fascist policies hitherto (which had often ridiculed the eugenic fantasies of the Nazis), even if (as Volpe admits) undercurrents of anti-Semitism had always been present. Measures designed to remove Jews from civil society followed but in the main anti-Semitism struck no chord with Italians. Note how the passage is a blend of critical detachment from Fascist racial policies (Volpe was progressively to abandon Fascism as the war wore on), yet at the same time an apologia for it—for example, the last sentence supports the notion that Jews are a separate race (see Michaelis 1978).

This word [*razza* or 'race'] had recurred for some time in the writings and speeches of many Fascists, including Mussolini, from which collections of quotations were assembled to demonstrate the complete consistency both of his thought and of Fascism. Actually race had been talked about more often than not in the sense of 'people' [*popolo*], 'nation' [*nazione*] or 'nationality' [*stirpe*], with essentially moral characteristics. Now,[52] however, efforts were made to identify the materialistic content of this concept and a group of academics, mostly physiologists, zoologists, and biologists, formulated the Italian doctrine of race, which had all the hallmarks of an official doctrine and was published in all the newspapers. In contrast to the racism of German Nazism and, although they have never theorized about it extensively, of the Anglo-Saxons, Italian racism, at least in its first formulation, did not talk about superior and inferior races, and did not establish a relationship between biological and moral values. But, like German Nazism, Italian racism immediately trained all its heavy artillery on the Jewish target. In doing so it did not forget the importance of explaining its appearance in terms of the new situation created by the Empire and the new needs of the Italian nation, now a great colonial power, and hence in close contact with coloured races, and bent on creating in citizens a keen awareness of their individuality, while keen to keep at bay the danger posed by the half-caste with all the political and moral disasters associated with him.[. . .]

Even the voice of anti-Semitism was not entirely new in Italy. It had been heard for some time, for example, in the periodical *Vita Italiana* edited by Dr Preziosi. But it cannot be said that there was a widespread sense of a Semitic or Jewish problem in Italy.[. . .] Yet as Fascism developed and clarified its own principles to itself, there was an increasing emphasis on arguments which were nationalistic, anti-cosmopolitan, anti-humanitarian and anti-pacifist, anti-plutocratic, anti-democratic, anti-liberal, anti-Masonic, anti-Bolshevik: all of them, more or less implicitly or explicitly

[52] When the Manifesto of Fascist Racism was published.

anti-Jewish, or which could express themselves in an anti-Semitic movement.[. . .] It thus appeared—and other facts and circumstances may have contributed which were not thought advisable to make public—that a Jewish problem existed in Italy too. (Is it out of place to think that there was among other things the desire to counteract German racism, which had a grudge against all Mediterranean races, the Italian included, and against Rome, both Classical and Christian: to counteract it with a doctrine which singled the Italians out among the Mediterranean races and claimed for them a place within the noble Aryan family?)[. . .]

Some voiced the concern whether in a moment of grave international tension such as this it was really appropriate to add to Italy's enemies and make them even more embittered. Another secret fear was this: that Fascism might simply follow in the footsteps of Nazism on racial matters, and thus lose some elements of its original, pure Italianness [italianitá]. These and similar misgivings, fears, objections could be heard on the grapevine at the time, while open criticisms and objections on matters of principle were published in the Vatican newspaper *L'Osservatore Romano*, expressed both by the Pope himself, as well as by some high-ranking prelates who had up till then been generally well-disposed to Fascism. The press reacted by intensifying the campaign against Jews and reasserting the primacy of Fascism in this development too. Responding in particular to foreign critics, Mussolini repeated the phrase which he uttered at the time of the sanctions imposed by the League of Nations, and which had remained both famous and inspiring: 'we will carry right on regardless' [noi tireremo diritto].

And soon words turned into facts: withdrawal of the right of boys and youths both of whose parents were Jews from attending state schools even if they were baptized, and the setting up of special primary and secondary schools; the ban on Jews holding academic or teaching posts, on belonging to academies of science or art, on publishing academic books; restrictions imposed on their activities as writers; the removal of Jews from public office and managerial positions within large business enterprises; the forbidding of mixed marriages; the expulsion of Jews who had immigrated to Italy since the war. Having declared that there was absolutely no intention of going so far as a policy of persecution against the Jews, the measures concerning them were presented as part of a larger battle which imperial Italy was waging: within its peninsular and African frontiers, for the integrity of the race; against the danger of miscegenation or 'contamination' by heterogeneous elements; as an aspect of the demographic campaign not only to increase the quantity but also the quality of the Italian people; as the latest effort to nationalize Italian culture, removing it from the influence of trends or currents in literature or art with a negative, innovative impact, these being represented to a considerable degree by Jews, namely by foreigners who were also of a different stock, resistant to any assimilation and proud of its superiority to any other race.[. . .]

[*Storia del movimento fascista* (Istituto per gli Studi di Politica Internazionale: Milan, Mar. 1943), 238–41.]

iv. Fascism at War 1940–1943

BENITO MUSSOLINI

40   **People of Italy! Run to your Arms!**

Mussolini's decision to abandon his status as 'non-belligerent' ally of Germany by declaring war on France was cynically calculated to wrest territorial and material advantages from an already conquered nation with minimal cost to Italy. It backfired because of the lamentable unpreparedness of the Italian forces to attack France when ordered to a few days later, a failure which prefigured the two years of military débâcles which were to ensue right up to the armistice of September 1943, thereby cruelly exposing the hollowness of the cult of Romanità (Romanness). The gap between Fascist rhetoric and reality by now was yawning dangerously wide in other respects too. Despite the ecstatic responses of the crowd reported in Il Popolo d'Italia, appeals to the vision of Fascist aggression as the struggle between old plutocratic and youthful dispossessed states fell on deaf ears. This myth, used by Nationalists before the First World War (see Text 11), was to become central to official Fascist interpretations of the war right till the end.

An hour marked by destiny is striking in the skies of our Fatherland. [*Loud cheers*] The hour of irrevocable decisions. The declaration of war has been sent [*cheers, loud shouts of 'War! War!'*] to the ambassadors of Great Britain and France. We are entering the field of battle against the plutocratic and reactionary democracies of the West, who at every turn have impeded the march, and often threatened the very existence of the Italian people.[. . .]

This gigantic struggle is but a phase in the logical development of our revolution. It is the struggle of poor, densely populated countries against those who cause starvation and ferociously preserve the monopoly of all the wealth and all the gold of the earth. It is the struggle of fertile and young peoples against those who have become sterile and are destined to decline. It is the struggle between two centuries and two ideas.[. . .]

In a memorable meeting in Berlin, I said that Fascist morality dictates that, when you have a friend, you march with him to the end. [*'Duce! Duce! Duce!'*] This we have done and will do with Germany, with her people, with her marvellous armed forces.

On the eve of an event of monumental consequences, let us turn our thoughts to the Majesty of the king and emperor [*the crowd breaks out into great cheers for the House of Savoy*], who, as ever, has read the souls of the Fatherland. And let us salute with our voices the Führer, the leader of our great German ally. [*The people break out in sustained cheers for Hitler*]

Italy, proletarian and Fascist, has risen to its feet for a third time, strong, proud, and united as never before. [*The crowd shouts with a single voice 'Yes'!*] The order of the day is a single, categorical word which is imperative for all. It is one which is already soaring from the Alps to the Indian Ocean setting hearts aflame along the way: win! [*The people break into ecstatic cheers.*] And we will win, so as finally to assure a long period of peace with justice to Italy, Europe, the world.

People of Italy!

Run to your arms and display your tenacity, your courage, and your worth!

> ['Corri alle armi', speech of 10 June 1940, published in *Il Popolo d'Italia*, 160 (11 June 1940); repr. in *Omnia Opera di Benito Mussolini* (see Text 4), xxix. 403–5.]

ALFREDO CIOFFI

41   **Safeguarding Europe's Birthright against the Jewish Conspiracy**

This article is symptomatic of how the official doctrine of Fascism had been modified to conform with Nazism's very different myth of national rebirth. The periodical from which it is taken was published in German and Italian, and is part of a drive to co-ordinate the Italian with the Nazi regime on the basis of shared racial and juridic principles which goes far beyond mere propaganda. Alfredo Cioffi, president of the Court of Appeal and lecturer in Administrative Law at Rome University, portrays Britain and the USA (still a neutral country when this article was written) as having been infiltrated by Jews working as part of an international conspiracy, a typically Nazi claim. Nevertheless, the author still implies the primacy of Italy, Fascism, and Mussolini over Germany, Nazism, and Hitler.

Judaism, now that it has succeeded in infiltrating the richest countries in the world, the United States and England, is able to communicate its political directives to its communities in other nations to influence their regimes so as to achieve ever greater penetration into finance, into commerce, into the war industry, into agriculture, into mining, and into high State offices.

The English plutocracy had two armies to maintain its ascendancy, one armed and open, the other covertly and insidiously co-operating with its plans for domination.

Since the unity of Jewish racial feeling prevailed over the *citizenship* acquired in the various States as a label, to be able to operate there freely according the universal directives mentioned earlier, this imposed on European peoples the continuing duty to defend their own civilization, their own race, their own right to life within their own 'vital space', which is inseparable from it.

This war to defend such an inviolable right is also inevitably and intrinsically a war of defence against plutocratic and political exploitation.

This accounts for the racial legislation in Germany and Italy which is now being adopted in Romania, Bulgaria, Slovakia, Croatia, and now in France and other nations of continental Europe.

It is Europe, cradle of civilization, which is reasserting its nobility and heroic spirit, reclaiming the beauty of its ideals of humanity and art, and rejecting subjugation to the Judaeo-Anglo-Saxon utilitarianism.

Italy has the glory and privilege of constituting a race, with its own biophysical structure, its own purity passed down by tradition. It has the glory of having its own race chosen by God, who is worshipped within the Catholic faith of which it is the seat. It takes pride in being an inextinguishable civilization, in having been the beacon of the Mediterranean, and now, under the aegis of Fascism, in resuming its path, and its mission to establish a higher justice among peoples.

These are the contents and the significance of the racial legislation, whose necessity Mussolini was yet again the first to recognize.

> ['Osservazioni politiche sullo Stato razziale in Italia' [Political observations on the racial State in Italy], *Il diritto razzista* [Racist Law], 2/5–6 (Sept.–Dec. 1941), 174–5.]

CARLO COSTAMAGNA
....

42   The New Europe which will Arise from the Axis Victory

Carlo Costamagna (1881–1965) was a major academic theorist of corporativist law of a statist and anti-populist disposition. He also edited Lo Stato *[The State] from which this article is taken. Its interest lies in the tenacity of neo-Hegelian theorizing about the ethical nature of the national community and the inevitability of an Axis victory on the very eve of the defeat of Fascism. In insisting on the rights to self-determination of 'young' national cultures Costamagna renews the traditional Fascist and Nazi attack on 'plutocratic' Great Powers (see Texts 11, 41, 76). He also anticipates (albeit in fascist, not liberal, key) the widespread fears of the 1990s that national sovereignty and identity are threatened by the emergence of a united Europe. It is symptomatic of the vitality of neo-fascism that it was reprinted with other articles by Costamagna in the 1980s.*

British power principally manifested itself as an attack on Roman civilization [romanità] and Catholicism, and hence it established itself as the intransigent defender of the state of political fragmentation into which the European continent had fallen since the dissolution of the Holy Roman Empire [impero-chiesa], expending its energies negatively in the maintenance of territorial balance while the spirit of the British people wasted itself in equally negative rhetorical claims to constituting a 'universal' civilization.[. . .]

It needed the entry of the masses into the constitutional life of States and the transfer of the existential problems of peoples onto the world stage, on which new threatening configurations of power located physically outside Europe now played a role in the shape of Russia and North America. It was only then that some nations grown fully aware of and hostile to the 'old world' dared denounce the disastrous consequences which the balance of power system on the continent and the imperial politics of Britain had had on the fates of the far too many peoples, condemned to compete with each other in the narrow confines of central and western Europe. Only then was the necessity met for a political system capable of assuring through mutual agreement [consorzialmente] the conditions needed to safeguard the autarchy of the individual nations which represented these peoples within the framework of a larger communal space, and to impose respect for the new system on those, both within and without, who inevitably opposed it.[. . .]

The reasons for the present war are exclusively 'national', and cannot be traced back to the goal of realizing a cosmopolitan idea thinly veiled through the use of the adjective 'European'. Even worse, there are attempts in some quarters to discount the significance of the military factor and the necessity of military victory to reach the final objective, which must be conceived as the creation of a clearly defined and co-ordinated political system in which all the peoples allied within it, and only those, satisfy their aspirations, and are able to resolve the social and imperial issues raised by the assertion of their unique spirit.[. . .]

According to the propositions which derive from our doctrine, only the national community can operate not just as a political and economic entity, but as a moral one. As an ethical personality it is the compendium of all the values of the spirit and the only yardstick for the validity of a world-view. Even from a cultural point of view, only the individual nation constitutes a *universum*, that is, a 'concrete universal'; because in it, and only in it, the fluctuating and contradictory motives of the supposed universal spirit are resolved into unity. Only the individual in its practical reality possesses a specific style, soul, and genius which make it a concrete manifestation of humanity; hence the great works which express national genius are simultaneously universal monuments of the spirit, whether we are thinking of Dante, Cervantes, or Goethe.[. . .]

The new order, which the 'Axis' powers and their allies propose, has grown out of the processes which unified Italy and Germany in the nineteenth century in the face of the treaty rights which some wanted to foist on us as the rights of the European 'order'. It revealed itself morally in the twentieth century with the national and popular revolutions of two countries, in the teeth of the dictates of the League of Nations: cosmopolitan dictates in the service of English imperialism. Today it is bursting forth, without waiting for the permission of the 'learned', from the blood of the fallen and the sufferings of the population, and is being tempered through lengthy trials and tribulations. It merely needs victory to define its external form, one appropriate to its essentially national essence.

If the new order, a bond [*fascio*] of the force of several peoples, countering the opposition of external hostile forces, merits the name European, it will do so only by virtue of the fact that its material confines coincide with a vague region which is geographically European, and its moral limits cover the nebulous cultural sphere associated with Europe.

['L'idea de Europa e la guerra' [The idea of Europe and the War], *Lo Stato*, 1943; repr. in Gennaro Malgieri, *Carlo Costamagna* (Settecolori: Vibo Valentia, 1981), 128–34.]

v. The Italian Socialist Republic 1943–1945

43 | **Fascism Reborn**

The Fascist Republican Party was set up by Mussolini in September 1943 as the core organization of the Italian Social Republic (RSI). The party programme was elaborated by pro-Nazi Alessandro Pavolini and former communist Nicola Bombacci, and promulgated at its first congress in November 1943. Its ideology is not just a revival of early Fascism, but a curious mixture of revolutionary socialism, republican ultra-nationalism, anti-Semitism, and Catholicism. It also envisages a European Community underpinned by the colonization of sub-Saharan Africa. The brute fact was that Northern Italy became a shrinking puppet-state of the Nazis in economic and agricultural production, in foreign affairs, and in the military campaign against the Allies. The RSI's only effective sphere of action was in the reign of terror carried out against partisans, Jews, and army deserters by the blackshirted Militia, now renamed the Republican National Guard.

1. The Constituent Assembly is convoked, a sovereign power of popular origin, to declare the decadence of the Monarchy, and solemnly condemn the treachery of the last king,[53] to proclaim the Social Republic and nominate its Leader.[. . .]

3. The Republican Constituent assembly has the duty to guarantee to citizens, soldiers, workers, and taxpayers the right to exercise control and responsible criticism of the acts of the public administrations; every five years the citizen will be called upon to pronounce on the nomination of the Leader of the Republic.[. . .]

5. The organization which is responsible for the education of the People in political matters is a single body. The Party, an order of fighters and believers, must form an organism of absolute political purity, worthy of being the custodian of the revolutionary idea.[. . .]

6. The religion of the Republic is the Roman Catholic Apostolic faith. Every other religion which does not conflict with the laws is respected.

7. Those belonging to the Jewish faith are foreigners. For the duration of this war they belong to an enemy nationality.[. . .]

8. The essential goal of the foreign policy of the Republic must be the unity, independence, and territorial integrity of the Fatherland within its maritime and Alpine frontiers constituted by nature, blood sacrifice, and history, frontiers threatened by the enemy both with the invasion and with the promises made by the government which has taken refuge in London.

---

[53] Victor Emmanuel III, who, having allowed Mussolini to become head of state in October 1922, helped remove him from power in July 1943.

Another essential goal consists in achieving recognition of the vital space indispensable for a people of 45 million inhabitants living in an area inadequate to feed it. This policy will be furthered through the creation of a 'European community' through the Federation of all nations which accept the following principles:

(a) the elimination of the centuries-old British intrigues from our continent;

(b) the abolition of the whole internal capitalist system and the struggle against plutocratic nations;

(c) the exploitation for the benefit both of the European peoples and native inhabitants of Africa's natural resources, while maintaining absolute respect for peoples, especially Muslim ones which, like Egypt, are already civilized and have centralized organizations.[. . .]

18. With this preamble to the Constituent Assembly, the Party shows not only that it is going to the people, but that it stands by the people. For its part, the Italian people must realize that there is only one way for it to defend its conquests of yesterday, today, tomorrow, namely to repel the enslaving invasion of Anglo-American plutocracies, which have given a thousand signs of their desire to increase the distress and misery of Italian life. There is only one way to achieve all its social goals: fight, work, win.

[Il manifesto di Verona del Partito fascista repubblicano [The Verona manifesto of the Republican Fascist Party], appendix to Felice Bellotti, *La Repubblica di Mussolini 26 July 1943–25 April 1945* (Zagara: Milan, 1947), 223–8.]

44 The Greatest Massacre of All Time: Democracy

Though nominally the leader of the Italian Social Republic, Mussolini, demoralized and ill since the twin humiliations of his removal by his own regime and rescue by the SS, lived effectively in a state of house arrest in the Villa Feltrinelli in Gargnano on Lake Garda, 'protected' by Nazi soldiers and stripped of any real executive power or influence. His sole remaining function was to be a symbolic figure supplying rousing speeches on behalf of the RSI leaders and their Nazi masters. In July 1944 Pavolini created the Black Brigades as an élite anti-partisan force, their name deliberately evoking the original black-shirted squadristi. It is one of these brigades which Mussolini here regales with hollow promises of victory in the Fascist war they are fighting to destroy Jewish capitalism, alongside Germans displaying Roman valour. (What is not said is that only a month before his despair at the situation had made him contemplate suing for a separate peace with the Allies.)

At the meeting of Verona the Fascist Republican Party set out its founding principles. If the events of the war have delayed the application of some of them, this does not mean they are changed. They remain.[. . .]

To those who still ask 'what do you want?' we answer with three words which sum up our programme. They are these: Italy, Republic, socialization.[. . .]

Now is precisely the moment when Germany is committed to a supreme struggle, and 80 million Germans are becoming 80 million soldiers, engaged in an effort of resistance which has something superhuman about it. It is precisely now that the enemies anticipate, in hopes and illusions—a victory which they can never achieve, because Germany will never capitulate, because to capitulate for Germany would mean politically, morally, and even physically to 'die'—it is in this moment that we reaffirm our complete, total solidarity with National Socialist Germany, which is a Germany fighting with a courage and valour which could be called 'Roman', one which wrests recognition and admiration even from its enemies if they have not been made completely blind and stupid by hate.[. . .]

The greatest massacre of all times has a name: democracy. This word hides the voracity of Jewish capitalism which, through the butchery of men and the ruin of Christian civilization, wants to carry out the scientific exploitation of the world.[. . .]

It is in vain that, under the protection of foreign bayonets and mercenaries, men who had the discretion, that is to say the infamy and the cowardice, to choose surrender, throw themselves into the persecution of Fascists and Fascism. They do no more than document its irrepressible continuity.[. . .]

They do so because they feel that what was presumed dead is alive.[. . .] No human force can cancel from history something which entered history as a reality and a faith. In a mere twenty years, tens of thousands of Fascists, the flower of the Italian race, have fallen in peace and in war, in Italy, in Europe, in Africa in the shadow of black pennants.[54] They are the heroic expression of Fascism. They bear witness to it. They are its eternal bastion.

Take back to my comrades in Milan, along with my greetings, testimony to my certainty about the victorious outcome for Italy, and for Europe, of this colossal clash of civilizations which takes its name from Fascism.

['Alle Camicie Nere della Brigata Nera "Aldo Resega" ' [Speech to the Blackshirts of the Black Brigade 'Aldo Resega'], 14 Oct. 1944, *Corriere della Sera*, 247 (15 Oct. 1944); repr. in *Omnia Opera di Benito Mussolini* (see Text 4), xxxii. 112–16.]

BENITO MUSSOLINI

45   What Might have Been: Axis Europe

In this interview, given eight days before he was shot by partisans, Mussolini evokes his grandiose vision of what an Axis victory would have achieved. As the hegemonic nation in the south of a Europe divided into two vast geopolitical spheres, Italy would finally have gained the wealth and power so far denied it by the old plutocracies. Noteworthy are his admission that even in these conditions it would have then taken Italy a hundred years of

[54]   Part of the uniform of the Militia.

Fascist rule to become Nazism's equal, his vision of a Fortress Europe able to counteract the enemy forces of Asia and the USA (a key fascist myth in the post-war period), and his faith in the eventual triumph of the Fascist idea.

I spoke constantly with the Führer about the new order to be established in Europe and Africa. We never had any divergence of views.[. . .] Europe would have been divided in two great zones of influence: north and north-east a Germanic sphere of influence; south, south-east, and south-west an Italian sphere of influence. A hundred or more years of work to bring to fruition this gigantic plan. However, a hundred years of peace and well-being. Was I not to look forward with hope and love to a solution of this type realized on this grandiose scale?

In a hundred years of Fascist education and material well-being, the Italian people would have had the possibility, the numerical strength, and the spirit to enable them to act as an effective counter-weight to the power of Germany, a power which is now overwhelming. A force of 300 million Europeans, real Europeans, because I refuse to count as European the populations of the Balkans and of certain zones of Russia, even those near the Vistula: a material and spiritual force to mobilize against the eventual enemies of Asia and America.

Only an Axis victory could have entitled us to lay claim to our share of the world's resources, of resources which are in the hands of a small number of greedy nations who are the cause of all the evils, all sufferings, and all the wars. The victory of the so-called Allied Powers will give to the world only an ephemeral and illusory peace.

For this, you, those who have remained faithful to me, must survive and maintain faith in your hearts. The world, once I have disappeared, will still need the idea which has been and will be the most daring, the most original, and the most Mediterranean and European of ideas.

I was not bluffing when I declared that the Fascist idea will be the idea of the twentieth century. An eclipse of five years, or even ten, has absolutely no importance. It is partly events, partly men with their weaknesses which today are bringing about this eclipse. History will vindicate me.

[Interview with the journalist Gian Gaetano Cabella, director of *Popolo di Alessandria*, 20 Apr. 1945, printed in *Testamento politico di Mussolini* (Tosi: Rome, 1948) and in *Omnia Opera di Benito Mussolini* (see Text 4), xxxii. 191–9.]

PART II

Fascism in Germany

Once we cross the Alps we leave behind us the sole area of generic fascism which poses no taxonomic problems, and enter the far more contentious sphere of the German ultra-right. In the past there has been considerable debate about whether Nazism can be fruitfully approached as a manifestation of fascism, and some major scholars exercised by the problems of defining this concept have expressed doubts on the issue, notably Renzo De Felice and Ledeen (1976), Zeev Sternhell (1979), and Gilbert Allardyce (see Text 166), doubts shared by a number of major German historians whose starting-point is the study of Nazism itself, including Klaus Hilde-brand and Andreas Hillgruber. It is not surprising then if the seminal text on the scholarly debate over the nature of the Third Reich, Ian Kershaw's *The Nazi Dictatorship* (1993), includes in the chapter on the 'Essence of Nazism' a sustained discussion as to whether it is to be considered a 'unique phenomenon' or a 'form of fascism'. His own verdict on the question is that when Nazism is seen 'in a European-wide context of radical anti-socialist, national-integrationist movements [its] similarities with other brands of fascism are profound' (see Kershaw 1993: 34–9).

In the course of arriving at this judgement, Kershaw makes a basic point which has seemingly eluded many of those at pains to stress Nazism's extreme degree of racial fanaticism, expansionism, and destructiveness, namely that 'there need be no contradiction [. . .] between acceptance of Nazism as (the most extreme manifestation of) fascism and recognition of its own unique characteristics within this category, which can only properly be comprehended within the framework of German national development' (1993: 37). It might be added that, as argued above in the General Introduction, all historical singularities are unique phenomena, and that whenever any generic concepts are used as tools for their analysis it is only common patterns, tendencies, and affinities that are being observed, not exact replications. To treat Nazism as a form of fascism is not to deny its uniqueness, but to claim that some of its causal factors and empirical aspects are thrown into relief if it is seen as a permutation of a generic phenomenon called 'fascism'. In the light of the ideal type being used in this Reader, what emerges about Nazism is the structural affinity at the level of world-view which linked it with Fascism, as well as with the other movements of national rebirth surveyed in Part III.

The ideal type of 'palingenetic ultra-nationalism' does more, however, than provide a basis for direct comparison between Nazism and generic fascism. It also casts a particular light on Nazism itself. Applied to German culture since the mid-nineteenth century it highlights a prolific literary and political subculture expressing despair at the state of contemporary German society and the course which history seemed to be taking. However, this was no 'cultural pessimism', for the radical disenchantment with the present was accompanied by equally radical schemes for society's regeneration. Once translated into overtly political calls for a new order, these currents of palingenetic myth represent permutations of German fascism, and thus have a direct kinship with Nazism itself. These new forms of the ultra-right, equivalents of which can be found in ideas if not in strength in many Westernized nations by the end of the nineteenth century, and would have remained just as marginalized and impotent as they did in every other country but Italy, had not an exceptional conjuncture of factors emerged which enabled its Nazi variant not only to become a mass movement, but to go on to establish a regime of unprecedented destructiveness and modernized barbarity.

A comparatively small role was played in this conjuncture by Germany's *Sonderweg* or 'special path' to nationhood, for every such path is unique, all nations have bred ultra-nationalists, and few can claim to have achieved the status of a nation-state on the basis of a healthy liberalism. As for the assumption of a pathological cultural tradition dating back to Luther or earlier, or of a particular German national character which predisposed Germany to fascism, this points to a racist rather than scientific approach to historical realities which has no room in academic analysis unless it points cautiously to recurrent features of Germany's political culture. Even then such elements played a small role in the seizure of power by Hitler's Nationalsozialistische Deutsche Arbeiterpartei (NSDAP). By far the most important factors were direct results of Germany's defeat in the war, which weakened the resistance of its liberal institutions to an onslaught from the extreme left and right. They include the sudden collapse of the Second Reich and the Hohenzollern dynasty, the 'imposition' of a new republican constitution associated with the acceptance of a humiliating and draconian peace settlement by a government led by the SDP (Sozialdemokratische Partei Deutschlands) Government, and the temporary establishment of a Soviet-style administration in Munich, events occurring in the midst of unprecedented social and economic chaos in the aftermath of the First World War. The new state was also unwittingly provided with certain constitutional features which could be turned into fatal flaws by administrations or presidents not committed to the upholding of democratic principles.

In a recently unified country whose official liberalism had been even shallower on the eve of the 'Great' War than that of the British and French nation-states it was to fight, the confluence of a well-established ultra-nationalist subculture with this set of circumstances inevitably gave rise to political movements advocating a government based on authoritarian and racist principles. Even so the fledgling Republic, born in the most unpropitious circumstances, weathered the acute storm of the first four years and the *Los-von-Weimar* (Out of Weimar) movement abated as stability grew. It took a second phase of virulent political crisis, this time sparked off by the extrinsic factor of the world Depression, for one of these movements, the NSDAP, which had established itself as the lingua franca of the many dialects of the palingenetic ultra-right, to move out of its condition of extreme marginalization and seize power in 1933. A crucial role was played in this end-game by decisions taken by the presidential government and by sheer luck. That it was the NSDAP that took advantage of the situation and not another party was, however, no coincidence. Its leadership had worked long and hard to prepare for precisely such a contingency. Nor is it a coincidence if its core myth was the inevitable collapse of the Weimar Republic and the creation of a totally new type of order rooted in primordial Germanness (see Kershaw 1990).

This approach not only rejects the idea that Nazism was a uniquely and peculiarly German phenomenon, but also repudiates (though it cannot refute) as fallacies numerous other strategies which have been found to account for the eventual transformation into killing-fields of large tracts of Europe by the government and armed forces of one of the most culturally, scientifically, and technologically 'advanced' nations on earth: (i) contrary to the Hitler-centric fallacy, Nazism was not even primarily the product of the psychopathic fantasies of a single individual called Adolf Hitler; (ii) contrary to some psycho-historical fallacies, Nazism was not the wanton eruption of demonic, psychic, or simply 'decadent' forces in the heart of an excessively secularized, rational, materialistic, or 'civilized' Europe; (iii) contrary to Marxist fallacies (Text 135), Nazism was not a desperate attempt by monopoly capital or the bourgeoisie to preserve power in the face of an imminent socialist revolution; (iv) contrary to the 'nihilist' fallacy, Nazism was not the expression of metaphysical evil, or of an unbridled will to destroy, but of a (meta-)political ideology whose 'positive' goals involved a preliminary stage of cathartic destruction; (v) contrary to one 'revisionist' fallacy (Text 185), the imperialist aggression and mass murder of the Nazis were not a symbiotic response to the barbaric onslaught of Stalinist Russia in a 'European Civil War'; (vi) contrary to some neo-fascist claims (Text 193), Nazism was not the degenerate 'Stalinist' form of what would otherwise have been a healthy 'Trotskyite' German Revolution, for the attempt to translate any form of 'German nihilism' into practice would have led to systematic state terrorism, even if not on the scale of the Third Reich.

Given these premisses, it is appropriate that Part II should open with samples of non-Nazi fascism before turning to National Socialism itself. To do so is fully consistent with the aim of this Reader, which is to provide primary source material relating to generic fascism, and not to contribute directly to a scholarly understanding of Nazism. However, the decision not to concentrate exclusively on Nazism in this section is considerably eased by the existence of an abundance of primary source material relating to the Third Reich already made available in English (see the Select Bibliography), of which the Noakes and Pridham anthologies (1974, 1984, 1988) must be seen as essential reading for any serious study of the Third Reich undertaken by those with no linguistic access to German sources. The vast amount of Hitler's own writings, speeches, and conversations already available in English has also enabled this selection to concentrate on other Nazi ideologues, while attempting, as in Part I, to cull samples from a wide variety of sources which simultaneously trace the historical evolution of political events.

It is sobering to reflect that the world-view they represent still has the power to inspire in some a sense of reality and purpose, despite the atrocities which the attempt to implement it brought about (see Texts 177, 182, 204).

German Fascism before the Nazi Seizure of Power

INTRODUCTION

The texts of Section Ai are a small sample of the many currents of ultra-nationalism which abounded under the Second Reich and the Weimar Republic, and whose prevalence provided a necessary (but not sufficient) condition for the rise of fully-fledged fascist movements, not least Nazism itself. In each case the diatribes against the rationalism, liberalism, and materialism of the modern world (though not against modernity as such), and the longing for a new order or Reich, is too élitist and remote from the arena of party-political activism to constitute fascism, though the dividing-line between this 'proto-fascism' and fascism is ultimately arbitrary.

The next eight passages (Section Aii) are all written in the aftermath of the First World War, and are inspired by a sense of the bankruptcy of the new Republic, as well as the conviction that the 'revolution' which created it on the collapse of the German war effort and of the Hohenzollern Empire was a travesty of any 'true' revolution. The more significant common denominator is the sense that this true German revolution is finally taking place, one which offers the only source of hope for the regeneration of Europe, the West, or humankind itself. However, even such brief extracts hopefully bring out just how variegated non-Nazi German fascism could (and can) be: ranging from the Conservative Revolutionary position of Moeller van den Bruck (Text 52), or the vision of an organic national order influenced by Catholic precepts (Text 53), to the youthful, almost anarchic, nationalism of former front-line soldiers (Texts 54, 55), and the technocratic vision of the new German born of the trenches (Text 56). These passages should underline how far the world-view expressed in such passages is from 'cultural despair', even when the author is Oswald Spengler himself (Text 57), who had become widely synonymous with pessimism, and was portrayed as such by the Nazis themselves to discredit his alternative vision of a new Germany and a new age. Meanwhile, the evocation of the knight as the inspiration of a European federation (Text 58) shows how misleading concepts such as 'nationalist' and 'anti-modern' can be when used uncritically to characterize fascist thought.

The eight Nazi sources cited in Section Aiii, all written before the seizure of power in 1933, can be clearly sensed to belong to the same mind-set and ideological structure as the foregoing in their unshakeable belief both in the utter decadence of contemporary 'liberal democratic' Germany and in the imminent emergence of a new order. However, the central stress on biological racism and anti-Semitism in some of the texts sets them apart as a distinctive brand of fascism. More crucially, they are associated with a political movement and organization bent on achieving power in the most ruthless and pragmatic of spirits.

46 **The Redemptive Mission of German Culture**

Richard Wagner (1813–83) dedicated his life to overcoming the tendency of the modern age towards compartmentalization, cosmopolitanism, and 'soulless' materialism. The concern with drawing on native sources of mythology and creativity led him, not only to write major celebrations of German and Germanic culture in such musical dramas as Lohengrin *(1850),* The Ring of the Nibelung *(1854–74), and* Parsifal *(1882), but to write art criticism which was steeped in racist ultra-nationalism and anti-Semitism, such as the 1850 essay 'The Jews in Music'. Apart from becoming Hitler's favourite composer, Wagner thus supplied to the Nazis both a major source of the regime's 'civic religion' and a model of 'healthy' German aesthetics in theory and practice. In this essay, first of a series published in the Süddeutsche Presse in 1867, three years before the Franco-Prussian War and Germany's unification, the longing for national rebirth is expressed in terms which can already be seen as prefiguring themes of German fascism. It is no coincidence if he enjoyed a close relationship with his son-in-law, H. S. Chamberlain, a major prophet of Nazi racism.*

In that period [the seventeenth century] Louis XIV and his courtiers even established the laws for what was beautiful, and in their basic way of seeing things even the French living under Napoleon III[1] have not progressed beyond these laws: this explains their forgetting of national history, the eradication of their own seeds of a national art, the corruption of the art and poetry introduced from Italy and Spain, the transformation of beauty into elegance, grace into *bienséance*.[. . .]

Once the true damage to freedom caused by the influence [of French civilization] is assessed, an influence which so completely dominated even the most characteristically German political genius of modern times, Frederick the Great, that he actually looked down on all things German [*deutsches Wesen*] with passionate contempt, then we must admit that redemption from the demonstrable depravity of European humanity could be compared in importance to the destruction of the Roman Empire with its levelling, and ultimately lethal, civilization. Just as complete regeneration of the blood of European peoples [*Völkerblut*] was necessary in that case, so here too a rebirth of national spirits [*Völkergeist*] is arguably necessary, and it really does seem to fall to the same nation which provided the source of that regeneration that time to carry out this rebirth as well. For hardly any event in history is as palpably demonstrable as the rebirth of the German people [*Volk*][2] from out of its own German spirit, in total contrast to that other 'Renaissance' of the newer cultural peoples of Europe, which at least in the case of the

---

[1] Emperor of France 1852–70.
[2] Unless otherwise stated, the term *Volk* will be translated in compounds and singly by the much more anaemic and neutral word 'people'.

French has visibly led, not to a rebirth, but to an unprecedentedly and incomparably arbitrary transformation imposed from above in a purely mechanical way.[. . .]

Even Prussia must and will recognize that it was the German spirit which, by rising up against French domination, originally gave it the power which it now exercises purely in accordance with the laws of expediency: and it is at this point that—to the profound benefit of all—an enlightened administration of the State of Bavaria can enter a fruitful partnership with Prussia. But only when this point is reached: there is no other basis for a positive outcome. And the German spirit is something easy to talk about rapturously in empty phrases, but which our intuition and feelings only recognize from the breakthroughs in the realm of ideas achieved by the creators of the German rebirth in the last century.[3] To provide this spirit with the basis of a German State which fully corresponds to it, so that it can reveal itself confidently to the whole world, means in effect that it must take it on itself to found the best and only durable State constitution.

['Deutsche Kunst und deutsche Politik' [German art and German politics], *Gesammelte Schriften und Dichtungen*, x (E. W. Fritsch: Leipzig, 1887; facsimile edn. George Olms: Hildersheim, 1976), viii. 32–3, 124.]

PAUL DE LAGARDE

47   The Need to Transcend Liberalism

Paul de Lagarde (né Bötticher: 1877–91) followed in the footsteps of the Grimm brothers by exploring the questions of German nationalism through an academic concern with philological and cultural issues. The main focus of his quest for a distinctive national identity was the corrosive effects of materialism and secularization and the corresponding need to create a German religious identity through a 'German Christianity'. His German Writings, published between 1876 and 1881, made him one of the most famous critics of Bismarckian Germany, especially its liberalism and the allegedly harmful influence of foreigners, particularly Jews (though his anti-Semitism remained 'ethical' rather than biological). He exerted considerable influence on the völkisch movement[4] and his writings became part of the Nazi literary canon (see Stern 1961).

The whole world is talking about the black, red, and golden International:[5] the grey International still runs around under the name liberalism. It seems to be high time to make a proper assessment of it. It is stateless like all its sisters and thus extremely pernicious for any nation. It exercises power just as readily as the other three members of the family, but it is not power that it actually aspires to. It feeds off comfort and the wish to maintain appearances: even if it has no intention to, it murders consciences and the ability to conceive life as a whole, thereby killing the personality.[. . .]

[3] e.g. Schiller and Goethe.
[4] A diffuse movement calling for Germany's cultural and political life to be rooted in the mythic qualities of the primordial German *Volk* (see Text 53).
[5] The international forces of anarchism, communism, and capitalism.

The views of liberalism have now become so much the dominant ideas of all so-called intellectuals that even current Christian orthodoxy is unwittingly corroded by it, and by having an enemy in its camp is prevented from fighting it in the open with any success.[. . .]

Even men who are not orthodox, but zealous advocates of religion who really believe that nations can only thrive through religion, have fallen under the spell of the prevailing norms of liberalism and relapse into its basic principles, which deny nature and history.

How often people have set about creating a religious reawakening. But religion cannot be reawakened, it awakes. I have called for its still glowing embers to be gathered and piled together—no one can call for more, or wish for more, than this—no human mouth may blow into these coals. The wind must come from the heights or the depths, as God pleases, once we have laid the dying fire before Him to be rekindled by Him.[. . .]

No one can resist the pressure of a [cultural] life which crowds in on him on all sides. If the Jews are at present still an alien body in Germany, this situation proves that the life of Germany is not energetic and not serious enough: but at this point the nation has the duty to remedy this serious deficiency. Every Jew that we find irksome is a serious reproach to the authenticity and genuineness of our Germanness [Deutschtum].[. . .] Our Jews will not cease to be Jews [. . .] if our governments do not put an end not only to liberalism, but also to the appalling accumulation of debts, the interest which in such an effortless and despicable manner provides the material basis for Jews to exist.[. . .] The response to the German Jewish question will be provided only by the German people in whom the same incandescent life, one capable of melting alien ice, must pulse in peacetime which in the last war,[6] to our great satisfaction, even transported those Palestinians[7] eligible for call-up into a German way of feeling and acting.[. . .]

We cannot achieve authenticity ourselves: governments must do their part for us by conscientiously ridding us of everything that has been created artificially, and by promoting with the steady gaze of expert love the growth of what will sprout up out of the old soil once it has been cleansed of rubbish: the roots of our being are still alive.

['Die graue Internationale' [The Grey International], in *Deutsche Schriften* [German writings] (Eugen Diederichs: Jena, 1944: 1st edn. 1886), 319–37.]

....

48   **The Rebirth of German Genius**

Julius Langbehn (1851–1907), autodidact in a number of disciplines and self-appointed cultural critic, wrote Rembrandt as Educator *as a call for Germans to resist the encroach-*

---

[6] The Franco-Prussian War of 1870–1.   [7] Jews.

ing materialism and artificiality of modern urban existence and return to their native rural and spiritual roots. The book struck such a deep chord that it went through forty editions in two years. It was widely read in the Third Reich (by 1935 it was in its eighty-fifth edition), especially for its celebration of the 'soil' and of Nazi cultural heroes such as Dürer, not to mention its obsession with Aryan 'blood' and national reawakening. Langbehn also advocated the creation of a United States of Europe under German leadership. He eventually renounced the heroic, Aryan image of German genius when he converted to Catholicism in 1900 (see Stern 1961).

Where there is genius there will always be triviality; where there are mountains there will always be valleys; human life is only a reflection of the life of the earth and history only an echo of geography. Of German art, of German culture, of German spiritual life what Schiller once said is true: 'the peaks of humanity will gleam with light even when damp night still shrouds the valleys'; and Germans of the present generation are called upon to turn these prophetic words into reality. Fortunate the people which listens to its prophets! [. . .] The Upper German nobleman, Schiller, was here teaching what the Low German Rembrandt taught practically: aristocracy of the spirit [*Aristokratismus*]. Aryanness, Germanness, aristocracy of the spirit are overlapping terms. The cradle of Aryanness is the whole Germanic North-West, namely Lower Germany; from this follows the necessity that a renewal of Germany must first take root in Lower Germany; where a people has been born it is also reborn. What is born or reborn is a child; and childhood is, as we said earlier, Christianity; this, as we also said before, is humanity in its noblest form. Here too it can be seen that the deepest qualities of the individual and the national soul [*Volksseele*] all gravitate towards a single point: it is from this point that the rebirth has to come forth and to this point that it has to strive. For the Germans this point is called Aryan blood; it is an aristocratic blood; it is of all human 'blood' that which has the most moral 'gold' in it.

Rembrandt is a genuine Aryan; if the still and powerful breath of the Rembrandtian spirit infuses the quality which is uniquely Germanic, then its life can be renewed once more; and it can consolidate itself; individuality, once formed, produces style. That not only German art, but German life, can once more develop style is the end-result of such an education.[. . .]

Every great shift in the axis of a people's existence means an act of rebirth; its whole existence is as it were illuminated from a new angle; it is the same, yet no longer the same. It has become new.[. . .]

Modesty, loneliness, tranquility, aristocracy, art—these are the remedies which the German must apply to himself if he wishes to escape the spiritual misery of the present. These qualities cannot be achieved without a struggle; for the immediate future of German spiritual life there is thus only one battle-cry. Swords to the ready![8]

---

[8] Literally 'bind blades': an allusion to the convention of wrapping the sword-blades just before duelling in German student circles (where the nationalist and militarist ethos was traditionally intense).

In particular, art and science must settle their differences to decide which of them is to exert dominion over German spiritual life; the contest must be fought out with honour; and the German people will judge its outcome. Its word decides!

[*Rembrandt als Erzieher* [Rembrandt as Educator] (C. L. Hirschfeld: Leipzig, 1890), 327–9.]

STEFAN GEORGE

49 | **Planting the New Reich**

Stefan George (1868–1933) was the centre of a circle of poets and aesthetes convinced that 'spiritual Germany' had to be rescued from the abyss of vulgarity and materialism into which it had fallen by a leader of exceptional visionary and creative powers, thus ushering in a 'new Reich'. The writings of the Georgekreis fed the currents of cultural anti-liberalism symptomatic of the Los-von-Weimar movement (see p. 94 above), and once the Nazis came to power they instituted a Stefan George Prize. However, their regime was too vulgarly demagogic for George's aristocratic taste and he went into exile in Switzerland. The cryptic allusion to the flag bearing the 'true symbol' of the people is particularly intriguing since it was one of George's circle, Alfred Schuler, who helped establish the swastika as a symbol of völkisch rebirth a decade before the Nazi movement was formed. Predictably, this poem was later included in Langenbucher's anthology of approved Nazi poetry (see Text 80).

> The poet is one who when the course of history runs smoothly,
> acts as an inspired child who gives voice to charming dreams
> and brings beauty into the hustle and bustle of daily life.
> But when a storm brews up from evil forces,
> and destiny knocks on the door with loud hammer blows
> He sounds like raw metal and is not heard.[. . .]
> When all were struck by blindness, he, as the only seer,
> discloses in vain the imminent crisis.[. . .]
>
> In the midst of flowing streams of mourning, the bard
> sees to it that the marrow does not rot, nor the seed wither.
> He stokes the holy fire which transcends
> and expresses itself in corporeal form. He retrieves from books
> the ancestral promise, which does not deceive,
> that those who are chosen for the highest goal
> first must traverse the deepest wastes so that one day
> the heart of this part of the globe[9] shall save the world.
> And when in the midst of the deepest distress the last hope
> seems about to be snuffed out, so his eye can already make out
> the brighter future. For him there was already growing up,

---

[9] An allusion to the myth of Germany as the 'Volk der Mitte' [People of the Middle], the heart and bastion of European civilization (see Texts 81, 82, 89).

untouched by the meretricious market,
by insubstantial wishful thinking and poisonous baubles,
steeled while the cursed years held sway,
a young race which once more measures men and things
with true yardsticks, which is beautiful and serious,
gratified by its isolation, proud before foreigners,
which keeps aloof both from the crags of intrepid arrogance
and the shallow swamp of feigned comradeship,
which spat out whatever was soft and craven and lukewarm,
which from hallowed dreams, deeds, and patience
gives birth to the only one who can help, the man [. . .]
who bursts asunder the chains, and sweeps together order
from the ruins, whips those who have lost their way home
into the land of eternal justice where greatness is once more greatness,
master once more master, discipline once more discipline.
He places the true symbol onto the people's [*völkisch*] banner,
he leads the band of loyal followers through the storm
and fearsome harbingers of dawn, to the work
of broad daylight, and plants the New Reich.

['Der Dichter in Zeiten der Wirren' [The poet in times of confusion] in *Das neue Reich* [The New Reich] (Georg Bondi: Berlin, 1928; 1st edn. 1921), 36–9.]

THEODOR FRITSCH

50　**The Need for the Nation to be Healed**

Theodor Fritsch (1852–1933) was one of the most influential and prolific anti-Semitic public-ists of the Second Reich and Weimar Republic, writing or publishing in his Hammer Press a stream of articles, magazines, and books dedicated to saving the Germans from the forces allegedly destroying them. At first these were associated with the corrosive effect of big business and finance capitalism on the traditional middle classes, but after 1900 he drew on anti-Christian, anti-Freemason arguments and biological racism, notably in the periodical the Hammer. *He became a cult-figure for the völkisch movement and the National Socialists (see Text 77; Pulzer 1988).*

On 20 January 1921 the *Hammer* began its twentieth year of publication, and it is appropriate to cast an eye over the path it has travelled.

When our periodical appeared it had set itself an ambitious, an exceedingly ambitious task: to awaken from its illusions a people which was stumbling along in blindness and the pursuit of pleasure and warn it of the terrible dangers which, like black storm clouds, were gathering over it, and which have now unleashed their fury with shattering force in the world war and revolution.[10] We saw the collapse

---

[10] i.e. the promulgation of the end of the Second Reich by Social Democrats in Nov. 1918, which led to the establishment of the Weimar Republic.

coming—even then! It had to come in accordance with unmistakable psychological laws—just as surely as a house must collapse if no one stops those who are undermining its foundations.

What motivated the publishers of the *Hammer* deep down were out-and-out positive, contructive goals. They wanted—and still want—to help create a strong, healthy German national entity [*Volkstum*], a truly German culture—by removing all the clinkers of its own weaknesses and the cinders of alien perversion [*Unarten*] which today confuse, soil, degrade our lives. We wanted to salvage from the hurly-burly of modern civilization a purely German entity, clear-sighted and resolved—prompted by the realization that every people can only fulfil its highest task by keeping pure its distinctive nature [*Art*] and by exercising its peculiar strengths and qualities.

But how far we had yet to go! To achieve such goals requires a strong, healthy national soul [*Volksseele*], a purified spirit, which, far-sighted and resolute, pursues its path and knows how to tell friend from foe. But where were these to be found? And where were the leaders [*Führer*] who recognized these tasks clearly and had the will to lead the befuddled masses on the path of salvation?[. . .]

If you yourselves want to have a positive effect, dear reader, go to your friends and neighbours and tell them what you have learnt from the *Hammer*.[. . .] Go to the poor duped workers who are completely led up the garden path by their biased press [. . .] go to them with love and confidence; pay no attention to their sullen expressions and spiteful words; remember that is the foreign poison, the Talmudic[11] misanthropy which has been injected into their soul without them realizing it. You will win them over through love.

Then go to the well-off and get them to understand that they must help to restore our ravaged national soul.[. . .]

There are 'positive tasks' to be carried out here, the most positive there can be for the time being. They are the premiss to all the others which will emerge. Only when the classes and social estates of our people work together in harmony to restore a common culture will there be a German revival. For this, though, all the poison must be removed which at present makes all members sick and stirs them all up in wild hatred of one another. A sick body, shaken by feverish spasms, can never carry out cultural tasks. The political and economic reconstruction must be preceded by an intellectual and spiritual resurrection. Go forth and help in the recovery!

['Hammer-Ziele' [The goals of the *Hammer*], *Neue Wege* [New Paths], ed. Paul Lehmann (Hammerverlag: Leipzig, 1922), 365–73; 1st pub. in the *Hammer*, Jan. 1921.]

---

[11] i.e. Jewish. It has been commonplace in the 20th cent. to blame Jews for both communism and capitalism in anti-Semitic propaganda.

ii. Non-Nazi German Fascisms

OTTO DICKEL

51   The Resurgence of the West

In the early 1920s Dr Otto Dickel was the leader of the Völkische Werkgemeinschaft [Völkisch Work-community], one of the many associations representing völkisch nation-alism which thrived in the Weimar Republic. The Augsburg Ortsgruppe of the NSDAP negotiated with him in the summer of 1921 over possible collaboration with the German Social Party, even though Hitler had expressly rejected such alliances. Hitler took advantage of this challenge to his authority by resigning from the Party, his letter of resignation specifically accusing Dickel of being an opponent of National Socialism. As he doubtless intended, this dramatic gesture prompted the Party Committee to invite Hitler back imme-diately, thereby consolidating his grip on the leadership and scotching any plans for bridge-building with other groups. That Dickel, though not a Nazi, was a national socialist in his own right emerges clearly from his riposte to Spengler's Decline of the West *from which this excerpt is taken. He stayed aloof from the Nazi Party, his 1931 pamphlet* Steuerfreiheit bringt Arbeit und Brot *[Tax-freedom brings work and bread] suggesting that his ultra-nationalism had taken on* laissez-faire *rather than corporative dimension.*

Many a time acquaintances have told me that I see the world differently from them. That is true. Who sees it correctly? Men of science with their mechanistic thinking will certainly attack me, will carp and criticize, will discover some errors and ridicule me. Let them. But if in the immediate future, perhaps even before this book is published, events take place in Russia as I have foretold, if social ferment begins in France, which is heading for the most uncompromising imperialism, and, as I fear, in England too, if the German people, overwhelmed by despair, is gripped by the irresistible force of the national resurgence, then I can only wish it men who see as I do. Men who comprehend the meaning of the world war and of contemporary events and through their bold action create a free German people on its own soil. Then in a few months a German Reich will be formed which is greater than the old one, a Reich full of inner consistency, a Reich in which our fellow Germans in Austria and neighbouring countries reach out their hands in solidarity to form a Reich which looks on the Germans abroad with pride in their eyes. Then the foundation will be laid on which the German nation can flourish, and its children, pious, patriotic, and creative, can think gratefully of their fathers who, purged by the horrors of the world war, have raised politics to the status of an art. It is not yet too late. Only cowards and egoists can say it is. The new generation, however, sets courageously about its enormous task because it sees the goal. It will act by following the precept: insight is much, but the deed to which it gives birth is everything.[. . .]

There is a stark alternative. Either those who are called upon by their culture, their possessions, and their influence to take over the leadership will point out the right paths by moving boldly ahead of the course of events, or the wheels of destiny will roll over their corpses and those of their children.

The perfection of Western culture is imminent. The great creative spirit which smooths its path will come because its hour approaches. It will prevail. For the German people will understand it, follow it loyally to the bitter end,[12] because it is a healthy and vital people. Come what may, there is one thing no one must let himself be robbed of without sacrificing himself: the faith in the German people, its world-historical task, and its fortune!

[*Die Auferstehung des Abendlandes* [The Resurgence of the West] (Gebrüder Reichel Verlag: Augsburg, 1921), 319–20.]

52   The Eternal German Reich

Moeller van den Bruck (1876–1925) was a major cultural and art historian, well known for his eight-volume history of the Germans published before the First World War. Thereafter he became increasingly associated with a current of ultra-right radicalism associated with jungkonservativ (neo-conservative) radicalism under the influence of the Nietzschean critique of democracy, H. S. Chamberlain's Ayranism, and the growing talk of a 'Prussian socialism'. The war convinced him that world history was entering a momentous new phase pioneered by the 'young peoples of the East', the 'technologically advanced' Americans, and 'the culturally gifted' Germans. The title of his most influential book, The Third Reich, provided an important Nazi slogan, but it preached cultural rather than racial awareness and purity as the key to a national rebirth and hence to Europe's salvation, which places him in a non-Nazi category of German fascism. His stress on salvaging from the past what can be used for the creation of a new order makes him one of the principal embodiments of the 'Conservative Revolution' (see Texts 193–5).

The second Reich was a transitional Reich. It collapsed because it did not have the time to create a successor.[. . .]

The second Reich was an incomplete Reich. It did not include Austria, which continued to live as a survivor of the first Reich alongside the second. It was a Small-German Reich,[13] which we can only see as a deviation on the road to creating a Great-German Reich.[. . .]

The third Reich [. . .] is a spiritual goal and simultaneously embraces a political task. If we go under, then, in the light of the experiences we have had of other peoples, Germany itself goes under, and with it everything that has ever made Germans what they are. There is no people that could raise us up again.[. . .]

[12] Literally (and prophetically) 'into death'.
[13] The terms 'kleindeutsch' (small German) and 'grossdeutsch' (great German) refer to the two solutions to the creation of Germany considered by the Frankfurt Parliament in 1848, the first excluding Austria, the second including it.

German nationalism is the protagonist of the final Reich. This Reich is always promised. And it is a promise which is never fulfilled. It is the perfection which is only achieved in imperfection.[. . .]

German nationalism fights for the possible Reich. The German nationalist of this age is, as a German being, still a mystic, but as a political being he has become a sceptic. He knows that the realization of an idea is always being postponed; that, translated into reality, spirituality normally appears very human, and that means very political; and that nations can realize the idea with which they are charged only in so far as they assert themselves historically and prevail.

It is in this sinking world, which for the time being is victorious, that the German is attempting to save what is German. He seeks the essence of what this means in values which could not be destroyed because they are essentially indestructible. He strives to perpetuate them in the world, and by fighting for them re-establishes their rightful place—and we can add, at a time when no concept is being called more into question than the concept of what is European, that he is fighting for everything which Germany has that is of consequence for Europe.

We are not thinking of today's Europe, which is too despicable to be evaluated at all. We think of the Europe of yesterday and of what can be salvaged from it to become a component of tomorrow. And we think of the Germany of all ages, of the Germany which has a two thousand-year past, and of the Germany of an eternal present which lives in the spiritual realm, but which has to be anchored in reality, and in this reality can only be anchored politically.

The animal in Man is crawling towards us. Africa is looming from the depths in Europe. We are called upon to be guardians on the threshold of values.

[*Das Dritte Reich* [The Third Reich] (Hanseatische Verlagsanstalt: Hamburg, 1931; 1st edn. 1923), 242–5.]

EDGAR JUNG
53   The Organic German Nation

Edgar Jung (1894–1934) was a First World War veteran who became actively engaged in the struggle to drive the French occupation troops out of the Palatinate in January 1924. But his nationalism expressed itself in a brand of fascism partially influenced by a Christian-monarchist conservatism and at variance with the biological racism and demagogy of Nazism, an opposition he made public in his Sinndeutung der deutschen Revolution [Interpretation of the German Revolution] *of 1933. His publicistic work for the Konservative Volkspartei as the party closest to his vision of the new order led him to be the speech-writer of von Papen, whose 'Marburg speech' of June 1934 attacking Nazism eventually sealed Jung's fate. He was killed in the Röhm Purge a week later. This extract, with its typically fascist (and anti-Semitic) palingenetic and organic conception of the nation, comes from his major work, an exhaustive diagnosis of the decadence of contemporary Germany and account of the new Reich which should replace it. The following is a classic statement of the organic conception of the nation and of Conservative Revolutionary principles.*

The Nation in the Western sense is a mass of people formed into a State, and not the organism of a people bound by destiny and blood: the individual is seen as being born not into such an organism but into the State. This Western conception of the nation, which is the basis of Western theories of the State, derives from the Roman world.[. . .]

The Romance concept of nation, which is inwardly poorer than the concept of it evolved by peoples with an uninterrupted tradition, originated in France, and is thus by its very nature alien to German thinking, just as alien as the French concept of the nation-state. The fact that the Germans cannot get to grips with it is shown by the way every German scholar and writer tailors a concept of the nation to suit himself.[. . .]

The conscious turning away from the Western theory of State is simply a necessary consequence of our history, for it was this cast of mind which caused the rise of the West and the demise of the Germans. A German resurgence demands ideas which are deeper and more in harmony with the German people, calls for a bold act of spiritual renewal so as to overcome the poverty of German thinking and German impotence. The fight against individualism cannot be simply broken off the moment we think in terms of states and peoples.[. . .]

An obsessive stress on what concerns the nation-state (chauvinism) betrays a lack of deep *völkisch* rootedness. It is not the outer belonging to a State which endows a sense of existential security, but participation in the innermost essence of an ethnic people [*Volkstum*]. Only this opens up real possibilities of self-realization and of taking part in the striving for the perfection of ethical humanity.[. . .] *Völkisch* means the bid to internalize to the full the essential quality of one's own people and collaborate in its realization, thereby serving the people's historical mission.[. . .]

Modern history is determined by great peoples. However, there are no great peoples of pure race. They are all more or less racially mixed.[. . .] Here we are dealing with relationships which are still closed to human understanding. They cannot be understood simply in terms of biological laws. But while research into race, still a comparatively young discipline, has led to few definitive results, it still cannot be denied that the racial composition of peoples has not been without influence on their historical development and cultural achievements. The fall of ancient cultures was certainly due in part to racial dissolution.[. . .]

The place of the Jews among the Germans is only to be understood if we take into account not only their traits which have been determined by blood and by spiritual factors, but also their social position.[. . .]

The Jewish people has won the battle. It has achieved a victory which no one seems capable of disputing. No one, that is, as long as the Germans themselves cling to an individualistic concept of society and State, thus corroborating the only preconditions which make Jewish power tenable. Thus when the twentieth century brings about the great showdown between individualism and the organic world-view, and once we have crossed the threshold of a new age, the Jewish question will become an issue once again.[. . .]

We are *evolutionaries* in the purest sense of the word: spiritually and intellectually we are transcending a world grown rotten and we are transvaluing values, because for us the highest value is irrefutable. If this transvaluation of all values also leads to material changes, then we may be called revolutionary as well. Our revolutionary cast of mind only applies, however, to the external aspects of the crumbling edifice of society. In truth we wish to put an end to the 400-year individualistic revolution of the West and usher in a creative age of conservation. The path to this goal is called a battle. Our justification is that the deepest will to conserve leads one to destroy. True value demands the destruction of what is the void of value.

Thus it is that from the ashes of a war which has buried an entire epoch the German arises rejuvenated, and with him a new life, a new order, but still promulgating the eternal god.

[*Die Herrschaft der Minderwertigen. Ihr Zerfall und ihre Ablösung durch ein neues Reich* [The Rule of the Inferior: Its Decay and Replacement by a New Reich] (Deutsche Rundschau: Berlin, 1930: 1st edn. 1927), 114–28.]

ERNST JÜNGER

54   The Great War: Father of a New Age

Ernst Jünger (1895–   ) rose to fame as the outstanding German writer of the war generation. In his war diary, significantly called 'The war as inner experience', and in this book In Stahlgewittern *[In Tempests of Steel] he captured in visionary prose, not only the mystic sense of communion created for some by the 'front experience', but also the conviction that the 'community of the trenches' was the basis of a new order under a new heroic élite, a strand of German fascism known as 'national revolutionary' or 'soldierly nationalism' (see also Texts 5, 12). Deeply impressed by the 'total mobilization' of human and industrial resources in the war effort of all nations, his ideas evolved to embrace (partly under the influence of a current of fascism known as National Bolshevism—see Text 172) a celebration of the dynamism and productive power of modernity in a spirit not unrelated to Futurism. This culminated in his vision of the new type of human being, the worker (see Text 56). He retained his distance from Nazism despite being wooed by the regime and allowed to publish: its fascism was too vulgar for his tastes.*

There are moments when from above the horizon of the mind a new constellation dazzles the eyes of all those who cannot find inner peace, an annunciation and storm-siren betokening a turning-point in world history, just as it once did for the kings from the East. From this point on the surrounding stars are engulfed in a fiery blaze, idols shatter into shards of clay, and everything that has taken shape hitherto is melted down in a thousand furnaces to be cast into new values.

The waves of such an age are surging around us from all sides. Brain, society, state, god, art, eros, morality: decay, ferment—resurrection? Still the images flit restlessly past our eyes, still the atoms seethe in the cauldrons of the city. And yet this tempest too will ebb, and even this lava stream will freeze into order. Every madness has always disintegrated against a grey wall, unless someone is found who harnesses it to his wagon with a fist of steel.

Why is it that our age in particular is so overflowing with destructive and productive energies? Why is this age in particular so pregnant with such enormous promise? For while much may perish in the feverish heat, the same flame is simultaneously brewing future wonders in a thousand retorts. A walk in the street, a glance in the newspaper is enough to confirm this, confounding all the prophets.

It is War which has made human beings and their age what they are. Never before has a race of men like ours stridden into the arena of the earth to decide who is to wield power over the epoch. For never before has a generation entered the daylight of life from a gateway so dark and awesome as when they emerged from this War. And this we cannot deny, no matter how much some would like to: War, father of all things, is also ours; he has hammered us, chiselled and tempered us into what we are.[. . .]

As sons of an age intoxicated by matter, progress seemed to us perfection, the machine the key to godliness, telescopes and microscopes organs of enlightenment. Yet underneath the ever more polished exterior, beneath all the clothes in which we bedecked ourselves, we remained naked and raw like men of the forest and the steppes.

That showed itself when the War ripped asunder the community of Europe, when we confronted each other in a primordial contest behind flags and symbols which many sceptics had long mocked. Then it was that, in an orgy of frenzy, the true human being made up for everything he had missed. At this point his drives, too long pent up by society and its laws, became once more the ultimate form of reality, holiness, and reason.[. . .]

What actually went on? The carriers of War and its creatures, human beings, whose lives had to lead towards War and through Him, were flung into new paths, new goals. This is what we were to Him, but what was He to us? That is a question which many now seek to ask. This is what these pages are concerned with.

[*Der Kampf als inneres Erlebnis* [Battle as an Inner Experience] (E. G. Mittler & Son: Berlin, 1929), pp. xi–xv, 1–5.]

ERNST VON SALOMON

55 The Germany of the *Freikorps*

Ernst von Salomon (1902–72) took part in Freikorps fights with Communists in the Eastern provinces as well as in the abortive Kapp Putsch of 1920. He was also the main articulator of the form of paramilitary ultra-nationalism which helped undermine the Weimar Republic with its propaganda campaign against liberalism, communism, and the Jews. His fascism (like that of Oswald Spengler and Ernst Jünger) was modelled on an idealized 'Prussiandom' rather than on the variant proposed by National Socialism, but the celebration of the Freikorps myth of the German Revolution in the best-selling novel from which this excerpt is taken was more than welcome to the Nazi regime, under which he pursued a career as a script-writer. This passage throws light on the myth of Germany which mobil- ized the Freikorps *volunteers.*

Slowly the peace terms were becoming known.[. . .] Lieutenant Kay took some of us to one side.[. . .] One by one twenty men came forward. They recognized each other in a look, a word, a smile, they knew that they belonged together.

But they were not faithful to the government,[14] heavens, they were anything but faithful to the government. They could no longer respect the man and the com- mand which they had obeyed till then, and the political order they were supposed to help create seemed meaningless to them.

They were the troublemakers in their companies. War had not yet demobbed them. The war had formed them, causing their most secret obsessions to break through to the surface and sparkle in the dark. It had given their life a meaning and sanctified their sense of duty. They were unruly, untamed. Cast out of the world of bourgeois norms, they had not returned to their regiments, but formed small groups to look for their own front to defend. There were many colours to rally round: which was flying most proudly in the wind?[. . .] They had seen through the fraud of the peace settlement, and wanted no part of it. They wanted no part of the political order which people were trying to make them digest with slippery promises. They had stayed under arms out of an unwavering instinct.[. . .]

And yet each of them was looking for something else and gave different reasons for his quest: the word for it had not yet been given them. They sensed the word, indeed they pronounced it, and were ashamed of how woolly it sounded. With fear in their hearts they tried it out and played with it, or in many a conversation avoided using it altogether, and yet it still hovered over them. The word was still shrouded in a deep haze, wizened, alluring, mysterious, emanating magic powers, sensed but not recognized, loved and yet not available. The word was 'Germany'.

Where was Germany? In Weimar? In Berlin? Once it was at the front, but the front collapsed. Then it was meant to be in the homeland, but the homeland let us down. It was heard in songs and speeches, but it sounded wrong. People spoke of the Fatherland and Motherland, but Negroes had that too. Where was Germany? Was it in people? But they cried for bread and elected those with big bellies. Was it in the State? But the State was looking for its final form amidst a torrent of words and found it only through renunciation.

Germany smouldered in daring brains. Germany existed where it was being fought for, it revealed itself where armed hands struggled to give it substance, it shone out brightly where those possessed by its spirit were prepared to make the ultimate sacrifice for its sake. Germany was where its borders were. The articles of the Versailles settlement told us where Germany lay.[. . .]

---

[14] The Republican government instituted in Nov. 1918 when the Social Democrat leader Friedrich Ebert assumed the Chancellorship, a crucial moment in the ultra-right legend of the *Dolchstoß* or 'stab in the back' by inner enemies which had allegedly delivered Germany into the hands of its foes.

On 1 April 1919, Bismarck's birthday—the right-wing parties were holding patriotic celebrations, we left Weimar and the regiment, twenty-eight men with Lieutenant Kay at the head, without any permission or an order to do so, and travelled to the Baltic.

[*Die Geächteten* [The Outcasts] (Ernst Rowohlt Verlag: Berlin, 1930), 63–4.]

ERNST JÜNGER
....
56   The Emergence of a New Type of Human Being

In these excerpts from one of his most important essays of cultural speculation—one which went on to exert a considerable fascination on some post-war fascists such as the Italian Julius Evola (see Text 171) after the war—Jünger outlines his vision of the direct lineage between the new generation formed in the trenches (see Text 54) and a new race of Spartans, the perfectly disciplined 'Workers'. These he saw as the raw material and shapers of a new civilization which he initially hoped the National Socialist German Workers' Party might be pioneering through the fusion of modern productive capacity in a hierarchical political order, a total state, led by a visionary élite. The obsession with the imminent transition to a new age is a recurrent feature of Jünger's imagination (see Text 193).

It is particularly noticeable that these carriers of a new fighting energy only manifest themselves in the last phases of war, and that their peculiar nature stands out just as the bulk of the armies trained according to the principles of the nineteenth century fall apart. They are to be found above all where the peculiarity of the age is expressed particularly clearly in the means of fighting used: in land battalions and air squadrons; in the shock troops in whom the regular infantry, broken up and worn down under the impact of machine warfare, acquires a new soul; in those parts of the navy which have been hardened by familiarity with engagements.[. . .]

Within the world of work, the type of human being who is called upon to achieve the highest form of development is one whose activity directly expresses the total character of work.[. . .]

Many signs point to the fact that we stand before the portals of an age in which we will be able to talk once more of order and subordination, of command and obedience. None of these signs is more eloquent than the voluntary discipline to which youth is beginning to submit itself, its contempt for pleasure, its warrior-like mentality, its awakening feeling for virile and unconditional judgements.[. . .]

It is in the transition from liberal democracy to the democracy of labour that the breakthrough of work from a way of life to a style of life is carried out. However manifold the permutations which this transition will adopt, its underlying significance is always the same, namely the beginning of the worker's dominion.

In fact it makes no difference whether the new type suddenly reveals itself in a party leader, a minister, or a general, or whether a party, a band of war veterans, a national or social revolutionary community, an army or a group of Civil Servants: in each case it begins to form according to the distinctive principles of organic construction. Nor does it make any difference whether the 'seizure of power' [*Ergreifung der Macht*] happens on the barricades or takes the form of a punctilious revision of the standing orders which regulate how the State's business is conducted. Finally, it is irrelevant whether the acclamation of this process by the masses is seen as the victory of collective world-views, or an individual's acclamation of it sees it as the triumph of an outstanding personality, a 'strong man'. Rather it is a symptom of the necessity of the process itself that it takes place with the approval even of those who will lose by it.[. . .]

Beyond the democracy of labour, in which the contents of the familiar world will be remoulded and reworked, the outlines can be made out of forms of State which are not comparable to anything that has so far existed. However, what can be predicted is that neither work nor labour will exist in any sense that we have known. The discovery of work as a constituent of abundance and freedom still lies before us. In the same way the meaning of the word democracy changes when the mother-soil of the people is seen as the bearer of a new race.

We can observe that peoples have set to work, and we celebrate this work wherever it is carried out. The true contest is for the discovery of a new and unknown world—a discovery more destructive and pregnant with consequences than the discovery of America. It is only with awe that we can look on as man strives to harden weapons and hearts in the midst of chaotic upheavals, and see how prepared he is to renounce any simple way out which leads to mere happiness.

To participate in this process and serve its cause: this is the task with which we are charged.

> [*Der Arbeiter* [The Worker], in Essays 2, *Sämtliche Werke* [Collected Works] (Klett-Cotta: Stuttgart, 1981: 1st pub. 1932), xviii. 116–17, 249–50, 274, 310–11.]

OSWALD SPENGLER

57   The Prussian Spirit: Salvation of the White Race

Oswald Spengler (1880–1938) became a household name in the Europe of post-war chaos and trauma with his Decline of the West *(1918–22), depicting modern 'Faustian' civilization (see Text 61) as tearing itself apart as a result of erosion by the forces of materialism and unbridled technology. Though synonymous with cultural pessimism and despair, Spengler's diagnosis of the world crisis allowed for a temporary period of resurgence following the eventual re-establishment of a heroic and authoritarian 'Caesarism', which would put an end to the reign of money. As early as 1919 his essay 'Prussiandom and Socialism' showed him applying this scheme to Germany by speculating on the emergence of an alliance between patriotic workers and a military élite able to lift Germany out of the 'swamp' of the Weimar Republic and thereby save the world. He thus became a major figure of the*

Los-von-Weimar movement (see p. 94 above), but remained an outsider within the Third Reich, refusing to see in a National Socialism obsessed with racial purity the vehicle for the national socialist revolution he longed for. That he had developed his own brand of fascist racism is clear from this passage of the book, in which he put his own gloss on the significance of the Nazi seizure of power.

The Celtic-German 'race' has the strongest will-power that the world has ever seen. But this 'I will', 'I will!'—which fills the Faustian soul to the brim, makes up the ultimate meaning of its existence and prevails in every expression of Faustian culture in thought and deed, in creative act and demeanour—awakens consciousness of the total isolation of the Self in infinite space. Will and loneliness are at bottom the same.[. . .]

If anything in the world is individualism, it is this defiance of the individual towards the whole world, his knowledge of his own indestructible will, the pleasure he takes in irreversible decisions, and the love of fate even in the moment when he goes under because of them. To submit out of free will is Prussian. The value of the sacrifice lies in its difficulty. He who has no Self to sacrifice should not talk of loyalty.[. . .] Genuine—genuinely Prussian—loyalty is what the world needs most in this age of catastrophes. One can only rely on something which stands firm. This insight is the mark of the true leader. He who comes from the masses understands all too well that no loyal following is to be expected from the masses, majorities, parties.[. . .] He who is born to lead can use them, but he despises them. He conducts the bitterest battle not against the enemy, but against the swarm of his all too devoted friends.[. . .]

It is high time that the 'white' world, and first and foremost Germany, became mindful of such facts. For behind the world wars and the as yet incomplete proletarian world revolution there looms the greatest of all dangers, the black danger, and everything the white peoples still have to offer worthy of the name 'race' will be necessary to combat it. Above all it must be remembered that Germany is not the island which political ideologues think it is, treating it as no more than an object with which to realize their programmes. It is just a tiny spot in a vast world in ferment, albeit in a crucial position within this world. It alone has the Prussian spirit [*Preußentum*] working within it as a living reality. Endowed with this treasure which enables it to be a role model of existence [*Sein*], Germany can be the educator of the 'white world', perhaps even its saviour.[. . .]

The coming phase of history will henceforth be lived out far above economic crises and the ideals of domestic politics. Elemental forces of life itself are now entering the fray where the stakes are all or nothing. The prototypes of Caesarism will soon become more clearly defined, more conscious, more brazen. The masks surviving from the parliamentary age of transition will fall away entirely. All attempts to determine the shape of the future within political parties will be quickly forgotten. The fascist formations of these decades will turn into new ones as yet unpredictable, and even nationalism as we know it will disappear. Everywhere, not just in Germany, the only formative power left is the warlike 'Prussian' spirit. Destiny, once confined within imposing institutions and weighty traditions, will make history through amorphous and unique expressions of force. The legions of Caesar are reawakening.

Here, perhaps even in this century, the final decisions are waiting for the man to take them. In front of him the petty goals and concepts of today's politics count as nothing. Whoever holds the sword which wrests victory now will be lord of the world. There lies the dice of this monstrous game. Who dares to cast them?

> [*Jahre der Entscheidung* [Years of Decision] (Beck'sche Verlagsbuchhandlung: Berlin, 1933), 142–5, 164–5.]

OTTO STRASSER

58 The German Knight as the Key to Europe's Recovery

Otto Strasser (1897–1974), brother of the major Nazi activist Gregor Strasser, was a member of the SPD and worked for the Ministry of Food before contributing articles to the Völkischer Beobachter. *After joining the NSDAP in 1925 he ran the Kampf-Verlag publishing house set up by his brother, and worked to promote his 'socialist' vision of the post-Weimar order. His espousal of anti-capitalist ideas close to those of the National Bolshevists finally led to a split with the party in 1930 after Hitler had tried in vain to bring him to heel in a 'heart to heart' (a verbatim account of which is appended to the book from which this passage is taken). He then went on to found the 'Black Front' based on a blend of* völkisch *nationalism, anti-Semitism, national socialism, and Europeanism. From the safety of exile he campaigned vigorously for his ideas, losing no opportunity to attack its Nazi 'travesty' of them. That these ideas were a form of leftist 'universal' fascism can be gleaned from this extract.*

The resolute repudiation of any form of imperialism is a core feature of the *völkisch* idea. Without reservation it affirms the right of every nation to national independence, to its autonomous control of the forms taken by its political, economic, and cultural life.

In particular this consideration leads to the rejection of the modern imperialism based on racial delusions which infers from the supposed superiority of a particular race its right to rule over and exploit other peoples and races. By the same token it rejects every form of economic, cultural, and religious imperialism, even the imperialism of particular ideas which in an identical fashion Bolshevism and Fascism are seeking to foist upon their neighbours. 'Every people should pursue happiness in its own way', that is the basic principle of this conservative world-view, which is the only one which makes the collaboration of peoples within their cultural sphere at all possible, something which in the form of a 'European Federation' constitutes the main objective of the foreign policy of the socialist German Reich.

It is increasingly evident that this Federation of the Peoples of Europe is the vital precondition for the spiritual recovery of the European nations and for the preservation of the civilization and culture of the West.[. . .]

If Europe wants to retain its high level of culture and civilization as well as its leading position in world politics it must embark on a planned programme in the structuring of its macro-political sphere.

If England (as the heart of the British world-empire) and Russia (as the centre of the Bolshevist world-empire) are not included in this scheme, it is only to establish a fact, not to proclaim an objective. For both the political and the economic (and partially even cultural) structures of these two huge empires rule out their inclusion in the European Federation.[. . .]

These fragmentary observations on the cultural programme of German Socialism [. . .] need to be rounded off with a reference to the purpose which they are designed to achieve.

This purpose is the formation of an élite of the German people in accordance with an ideal type of the essential German which is yet to take shape.

This ideal type must be anchored deeply in the *völkisch* nature of the German, and hence exhibit qualities which are familiar to us from the German past and from German prehistory—while on the other hand, to act really as a role model, he must be modern enough to fit in with the socialist order of the twentieth century.

Both requirements are satisfied by the primordial type of German, the 'knight', the chivalrous male, whom we encounter in all the great figures of German culture and who had already come into being in the earlier (conservative) epochs of German history.

Education is to be geared to producing this type of knightly German, just as the English one is geared to producing the 'gentleman' type, whose normative function has proved its strength in the selection of generations.[. . .]

This formation of a ruling cast, of an élite, is the vital issue posed by the new order, and its resolution is critical for the duration and viability of German Socialism.[. . .]

What crowns this account of the new order of national freedom, social justice, and European co-operation proclaimed here is the fact that the guiding principle of its realization, the new type of human being which it must strive to create, is the 'knight', that powerful creation of the infancy of the West. The knight was a symbol of the whole Western community which transcended all frontiers. Now with its renaissance it celebrates the resurrection of this community.

For this and nothing else is the meaning and content of the German Revolution:

The resurrection of the West!

[*Aufbau des Sozialismus* [The Establishment of Socialism] (Heinrich Grunov: Prague, 1936), 83–7, 103–4.]

iii. Nazism before 1933

ADOLF HITLER

59 **The Mission of the Nazi Movement**

Having taken over leadership in July 1921 of the Nationalsozialistische Deutsche Arbeiter-partei [originally the German Workers' Party (DAP)—'National Socialist' was added in February 1920], Adolf Hitler drastically overestimated the strength of the ultra-nationalist cause it represented to the point of attempting a putsch in Munich on 8–9 November 1923. The result was a fiasco. However, the sympathy of the judiciary for his ultra-nationalist sentiments turned the three-month trial into an extended opportunity for uncensored publicity for him, for the NSDAP, and for the cause of a fascist revolution in Germany. He emerged from the trial with the minimum sentence for high treason and as a national figure. Moreover, his short prison sentence offered an ideal opportunity to rethink his tactics and dictate the first volume of his political autobiography Mein Kampf *without losing his hold on the Nazi faithful. This passage is taken from a rambling speech which Hitler made to the court on the first day's proceedings at the People's Court in Munich, the first of many. It points to how firmly established in his thinking was the myth of national decadence and imminent rebirth which would dominate his later speeches and writings.*

No movement has operated with such a thorough knowledge of the characteristics of the masses as the Marxist movement. It knows that the mass has respect for force and decisiveness, and has replaced the weakness of the bourgeoisie and its indecisiveness with brute force and brute will-power. It has ruthlessly subjugated the individual, and has placed the worker before the alternative: 'Either you will be my brother or I will smash your skull in.' In my youth I got to know this movement in both these aspects. The bourgeois parties do not know them or do not wish to know them. Armed with this insight I had to join this young movement,[15] one which refuses to start out from the position: 'We want to see to it that we will have some share in the future, more or less.' Instead our movement has recognized that the future of Germany means 'the destruction of Marxism'. Either this racial poison, the mass tuberculosis, grows in our people, and Germany dies of an infected lung, or it is eliminated, and Germany can then thrive. Not before. Only a young movement can be inoculated with this principle, which is not perverted by any compromises or coalitions, but declares as a basic premiss: 'We can never make a pact with this world-view; for us Germany will be saved on the day on which the last Marxist has either been converted or has been broken.' There is no middle way.

Germany has not understood this, especially the bourgeois movement. That is what brought about the terrible catastrophe which has become known to us as the

---

[15] i.e. the DAP.

German Revolution.[16] The 'German Revolution' is held to be a revolution, and as such to represent a successful act of high treason. It is well known that high treason is only punished if it fails. Thereby it forms an exception among all human crimes. It is the only crime which is not punished if it is successful, that is if a new constitution gives the people the possibility of prospering. What happened on 9 November was not high treason. This act did not give the people a new constitution, but death.[. . .] If the two million who lie buried in Flanders and Belgium were to rise from the dead and be asked whether they would be prepared to recognize the state of affairs brought about by that act of high treason, but which was really just an act of base treason, they would all shout: Never! We did not fall in battle so that in five years more could be ripped away from Germany thanks to this new and so-called legalized constitutional state than had been gained in the previous 150 years with the blood of hundreds of thousands, indeed of millions. [. . .] For our new movement there could never be a reconciliation with the act of 9 November. The principle had to be established: for us this was not high treason, but a crime against the German people, a stab in the back against the heroically fighting army, against the German people, German freedom, and the German nation. Such a thing can never be legalized and recognized.

The National Socialist movement of what was then the Worker's Party adopted as its first principle the realization that the Marxist movement was to be fought to the end; second, the realization that the revolution, as the consequence of Marxism and of an unprecedented criminal act, was not a matter of the German bourgeoisie becoming national once more: the problem is that the German working people, the broad masses, must be made national again. That means not just a pure, I mean passive, relationship to nationalism, but an active fight against those who have ruined it till now. Besides it is ridiculous to want to nationalize a people at a time when hundreds of thousands are working on all sides to de-nationalize the people, and these hundreds of thousands, who also brought about the revolution, do not even belong to the race.[17] Thus the Marxist problem has become a racial problem, the most serious and deepest problem of the day. The question is: will the German people be able or not to rid itself of the essence of Marxism which has entered the whole state, its organizations, and the legislative machinery?.[. . .]

Now I would ask you, your Honours, to enter into our psyche. To what end was our movement formed? Not so that we could win seats in parliament and obtain mandates. If we had wanted that, we would have been able to achieve it more easily and cheaply. You will admit that, having once created a great movement, we would have at least managed to occupy some nook or cranny in an existing movement. We never set out to. If we founded the new movement, we did so in the hope that we would one day change the destiny of Germany, even if it was in the twelfth hour.

> [26 Feb. 1924, People's Court, Munich, first day of proceedings, in *Hitler. Sämtliche Aufzeichnungen 1905–1924*, ed. Eberhard Jäckel (Deutsche Verlags-Anstalt: Stuttgart, 1980), 1061–8.]

---

[16] The proclamation of the German (Weimar) Republic by Social Democrats in Nov. 1918.
[17] i.e. are Jews. Note the equation of Jews with Marxists, as in Texts 61, 78, 85.

Franz Pfeffer von Salomon (who also called himself simply Franz von Pfeffer, since he considered the name 'Salomon' sounded too Jewish) shared with his brother Ernst von Salomon (Text 55) a background of aristocratic militarism which predisposed him to fascism under Weimar. As leader of the Westphalian Freikorps, Pfeffer helped suppress left-wing unrest in the Ruhr and took part in the abortive military rebellion, the Kapp Putsch of 1920. Joining the NSDAP in March 1925, he soon rose to the rank of Gauleiter of Westphalia and went on to become part of the triumvirate with Kaufmann and Goebbels which headed the Ruhr Gau, formed a year later. From May 1926 to August 1930 he was Supreme Commander of the SA, but resigned after disagreements with Hitler over its role, tensions which form part of the prehistory of the Röhm Purge of 1934. After his resignation he was marginalized by the regime: he was not only excluded from the NSDAP by Hitler in November 1941, but was arrested by the Gestapo during the wave of panic arrests following the assassination attempt on Hitler in July 1944, though he survived the war. Von Pfeffer's memorandum is a response to Strasser's attempt to redefine the Party's 25-point programme. It represents an élitist and biologically racist version of Nazi ideology in contrast to Strasser's more 'socialist' vision (see Texts 62, 63). It also anticipates both the Nazis' euthanasia programme (Text 85) and the Final Solution (Text 88). Note that 'Zucht' in German means both 'breeding' and 'discipline'.

First of all I share with Strasser and all revolutionaries the view that property in Germany is wrongly distributed: property, power, culture are in the wrong hands, misery and ruin are suffered by the wrong people, and this situation is growing and consolidating itself to such an extent that only the most drastic, ruthless intervention can force German life and culture [*Volkstum*] back into the right paths. Immediately after this common assumption, however, the thinking diverges.

There are those who take as their starting-point the equality of human beings, or rather the equality of *Germans*. This premiss leads naturally to the logical conclusion that there can be no reason why among equals a different distribution of property, state power, culture should prevail. If someone who is equal is forced to live in circumstances significantly lower than the mean, then this is naturally 'unjust', or a 'scandal' with respect to other equals. If someone who is equal is treated markedly better than the average then this is likewise 'unjust', for it can only happen 'at the expense' of the share the other equals enjoy of property, power, and culture.[. . .]

In the last analysis I accuse Strasser's programme of being rooted in this basic mentality (and I fear I must accuse him of coming out with far too many arguments which in our camp are called 'socialist'). It is the Jewish-liberal-democratic-Marxist-humanitarian mentality. As long as there is even a single minute tendril which connects our programme with this root then it is doomed to be poisoned and hence to wither away to a miserable death.[. . .]

All Germans are unequal. That is the starting-point.[. . .] The first logical conclusion to be drawn from inequality is the inequality of value. Some Germans are more valuable than others ('value' is a relative concept, which I use here naturally to refer to value measured in terms of the German, Nordic world-view, and within this measured in terms of what serves the interests of collective German well-being).

A logical consequence of this inequality must be the principle of *unequal* treatment, that is, unequal share of state power, property, culture. All these must be distributed to people on the basis of how valuable they are.[. . .]

A further logical consequence of inequality in what people are worth, and the continuous changes brought about by the development of the nation [*Volk*], is the duty of the state to take charge of this development, which means influencing it in every way possible. Excellence must be increased and enhanced further. Inferiority must be reduced. In plain terms this is a question of breeding. Improving the stock of the race. Breeding human beings.[. . .] From the above considerations I can draw up the following programmatic demands of our future state, the 'Third Reich':

a. To determine the degree of higher or lower value of all inhabitants of Germany. The value will be assessed as the function of four criteria:
    (1) actual performance in their professions
    (2) physical attributes, according to health and racial characteristics
    (3) spiritual, moral and cultural traits
    (4) hereditary traits evaluated by considering parents and grandparents.[. . .]

f. No pity is to be shown to those who occupy the lower categories of the inferior groups: cripples, epileptics, the blind, the insane, deaf and dumb, children born in sanatoria for alcoholics or in care, orphans (= children born out of wedlock), criminals, whores, the sexually disturbed, etc. Everything done for them not only means taking resources away from more deserving causes, but counteracts the breeding selection process. Nor should we mourn the dumb, the weak, the spineless, the apathetic, those with hereditary diseases, the pathological, because they go under 'innocently'.[. . .]

This bottom category means destruction and death. Weighed and found wanting. Trees which do not bear fruit should be cut down and thrown into the fire.

['Zucht. Eine Forderung zum Programm' [Breeding: A demand in relation to the Party programme], internal Party memorandum, Christmas 1925, NSDAP Hauptarchiv (Hoover Institution Microfilm Collection), reel 44, folder 896, 1–11.]

<hr>

JOSEPH GOEBBELS

61   **'Christ-Socialism'**

A birth defect caused Joseph Goebbels (1897–1945) to 'miss' the First World War, and his early creative ambitions, fed by his success in obtaining a doctorate in Philosophy and Literature in 1921, came to naught. Joining the NSDAP in 1924 eventually enabled him to placate his frustrations on both counts. Having been active in helping Gregor Strasser build

up the Party organization in the North, the meeting of Party leaders at Bamberg in 1926
proved a turning point. Though his diary records deep dismay at the Führer's rhetorical
style and aspects of his policies, his personal devotion to him grew to be boundless. Hitler
reciprocated by eventually granting him extensive power over the cultural and intellectual
life of the Third Reich (see Text 69). In his semi-autobiographical diary-novel Michael
published in 1931, Goebbels' alter ego is a student obsessed with the need for the decadence
of Germany's cultural and political life to be transcended in a new order. His life is
transformed when he hears the speech of a nationalist leader, a thinly veiled portrait of
Hitler's demagogic powers. Notable in this passage is the celebration of modernism and the
dynamism of the Russian Revolution, both ideas which become taboo as Hitler imposed his
vision as the basis for Nazi orthodoxy.

15 November.
I visit [. . .] an exhibition of modern painting.[. . .] We see much new nonsense.
One star: Vincent van Gogh.

In these surroundings he already seems tame, but yet he is the most modern of
the moderns.

For modernity has nothing to do with heroic gestures. All that is just learned
through practice.

The modern man is necessarily a god-seeker, perhaps a Christ-like person.

Van Gogh's life tells us even more than his work. He combines in his personality the most important elements: he is teacher, preacher, fanatic, prophet—
mad.

In the last analysis we are all mad if we have an idea.

Fanatics of love: the capacity for self-sacrifice.

Life is an act of sacrifice for the sake of our neighbour.

And my neighbour is he who has the same blood.

Blood is still the best and most durable cement.

How unspeakably difficult is the torment of vision. What constitutes the modern
German is not so much cleverness and intellect, as the new principle, the ability to
give oneself to a cause unreservedly, to sacrifice oneself, to devote oneself to one's
people.[. . .]

Now I have found the word: we modern Germans are something like Christ-
socialists [*Christussozialisten*].

Christ is the genius of love, and as such the diametrical opposite of Judaism, which
is the incarnation of hate. The Jew represents an anti-race among the races of the
earth. He has the same function as a poisonous bacillus has in the human organism:
to mobilize the resistance of healthy forces or ensure that a living being whose days
are numbered dies more quickly and more peacefully.[. . .]

In Christ the idea of sacrifice first took visible form. Sacrifice is intrinsic to the very
nature of socialism. Devote oneself to the cause of others. Naturally the Jew cannot
begin to understand this. His socialism means: sacrifice others for one's own sake.

This is what Marxism produces in practice.[. . .]

The battle which we are fighting today till victory is secured, or to the bitter end,
is in the deepest sense a battle between Christ and Marx.

Christ: the principle of love.

Marx: the principle of hate.

10 June

Before me a new Germany rises up.

This Germany is one which I will learn to love once more. And the more shameful its shame, the more ardent my ardour for her.

If I am looking for the appearance of the new man, it is first the new German that I am looking for.

I want to root myself in the soil of my Fatherland. It is the mother of my thoughts and longings.[. . .]

The new nationalism wants Germany's future, not the restoration of a past whose continuity is now shattered.

What does nationalism mean: we stand for Germany because we are Germans, because Germany is our Fatherland, the German soul is our soul, because we all are a particle of the soul of Germany.[. . .]

The German soul is Faustian! In it lies the drive to work and the possibilities work brings, as well as the eternal longing for redemption from the intellect.

There is a German idea just as there is a Russian one. Together these two will one day contest the future.

[*Michael. Ein deutsches Schicksal in Tagebuchblättern* [Michael: Diary of a German Destiny] (Franz Eher: Munich, 1931), 124–6, 172–3.]

---

62 GOTTFRIED FEDER
. . . .
Let there be Light

Gottfried Feder (1883–1941) was one of the earliest members of the DAP. He was also among the most articulate representatives of its pre-Hitlerian national socialism in his campaign to 'break the thraldom of interest', a call aimed only at the unproductive, 'parasitic' aspects of capitalism allegedly embodied in the Jews. Early on in the regime he worked in the Ministry for Economics, but his 'leftist' stand against big business and his political career had been effectively terminated with the murder of its main spokesman, Gregor Strasser, in June 1934. Nevertheless, his various expositions of the Nazi 25-point programme were important in establishing the party's image of social radicalism in the 1920s, and 'biblical' passages such as these suggesting draconian remedies to the alleged pathological degeneracy of Weimar were to have a particular resonance when the Depression hit Germany in 1929.

From out of chaos the world came forth, from the subordinate came order, from raw eddying energy the organic.

Today chaos reigns on earth, confusion, struggle, hate, envy, conflict, oppression, exploitation, brutality, egotism. Brother no longer understands brother. Fellow-countrymen fight each other, beating men to death just because they wear a swastika.[. . .] The victims of the chaos were simple, unassuming, good-natured workers. People have lost their bearings. Marxists rally around the greatest exploiters of their own class and turn like frenzied animals on their saviours from their own ranks.

The Nationalists, the patriotic circles, the right-wing parties are simply bent on getting into government or sit there alongside the denigrators and destroyers of their ideal of the state, thus losing their honour and their character. The para-military groups[18] want to 'enter the state'.[. . .] They believe they can rule together with pacifists, internationalists, and Jews.

People have lost their bearings! The so-called legal circles do not realize that there never can and never will be a friendship between the eagle and the snake, between cattle and the lion, between human beings and a cholera bacillus—thus they put all their weight and constitutional efforts into shoring up the disorder which has become an 'order', namely political chaos, political impotence. But they opposed the National Socialists, these 'fanatics', they rejected for their alleged *Realpolitik* those who could put an end to the political chaos.[. . .]

People have lost their bearings! The whole economy has become debased, depersonalized, has been turned into joint-stock companies. The producers have delivered themselves into the hands of their greatest enemy, finance capital. Deep in debt, the creators of value in the workshop, the factory, and the office have little to show for it in wages, for every profit made by their work flows into the pockets of the anonymous financial powers in the form of interest and dividends.

Leagues, lobbies, associations for professionals, Civil Servants, employees, for savers, small property owners, creditors of the Reichsbank, paramilitary leagues, guilds, clubs, federations, trade unions, peasant and farmers organizations, clubs, or whatever other name such strange bodies may adopt—all pointless in the chaos of public life today, however reasonable in their basic idea—try to create order. They do so in vain, because they are not incorporated organically into society, into the higher totality of the people.[. . .]

The same terrible picture of chaos is presented by all the other manifestations of public life, whether we think of art, literature, theatre, cinema, radio, church, school: everywhere the 'ferment of decomposition' is at work, the great disintegra-tor and destroyer, the Jew and Freemason, is visibly at work in the key posts or behind the scenes pulling the puppet strings, as the Stresemanns and Scheidemanns dance on the public stage or quite openly with names like Jakob Goldschmidt, Warburg, Wassermann, or Levy use the press, or charge punitive interest to exploit the German people and turn them into zombies.

The will to give shape to the amorphous, the will to put a stop to chaos, to put in order a world out of joint, and to keep order as guardians (in the highest Platonic sense)—that is the enormous task which National Socialism has set itself.[. . .]

Our aim is: Germany's rebirth carried out in a German spirit to create German freedom.[. . .]

We National Socialists march behind our battle colours. Forever young, shining, and radiant, the sun-wheel, the swastika, rises before us, symbol of a life which is once more awakening.

[*Das Programm der NSDAP* (Franz Eher: Munich, 1933: 1st edn. 1928), 25–6, 35, 64.]

[18] e.g. the Stahlhelm.

63 Motherhood and Warriorhood as the Key to a National Socialism

Gregor Strasser (1892–1934), an officer in World War One, fought in the anti-Bolshevik Sturmbataillon Niederbayern before joining the NSDAP and taking part in the 'Hitler Putsch' of November 1923. As deputy to the Bavarian regional parliament he avoided imprisonment, and built up the party organization under the cover name of 'National Socialist Freedom Movement' ('Freedom' is still used today in the names of some neo-fascist parties). On Hitler's release he became responsible for the Party organization in Northern Germany, in which role he continued to pursue his 'leftist', profoundly anti-capitalist, social-revolutionary vision (see Text 60). In 1926 he was appointed Reich Propaganda chief by Hitler and then to the key post of Reich Organization chief. By 1930 he was replaced as Reich Propaganda chief by Goebbels, and, although he dissociated himself from his brother's even more 'aberrant' views on the German Revolution (Text 58), policy differences with Hitler led to his resignation from all Party duties in 1932. Hitler nonetheless had him liquidated as a potential threat in the Röhm Purge two years later. Note his critique in this passage of biological racism in marked contrast to Text 64.

We are socialists. We are enemies, deadly enemies, of today's capitalist economic system with its exploitation of the economically weak, its unfair wage system, its immoral way of judging the worth of human beings in terms of their wealth and their money, instead of their responsibility and performance, and we are determined to destroy this system whatever happens![. . .] And yet it is not enough just to change the system, to replace one economic system by another; what is needed above all is to change the spirit! The spirit to be overcome is the spirit of materialism![. . .] We must learn that work means more than possessions! Performance is more than dividends! It is the most wretched legacy of this capitalist system that the criterion for everything's value is money, wealth, possessions! The decline of a people is the inevitable consequence of the use of this yardstick, because selection on the basis of property is the arch-enemy of race, blood, life! We have never left any doubts about the fact that our national socialism [*nationaler Sozialismus*] puts an end to the privileges of wealth, and that the emancipation of the worker involves participation in profits, property, and management.[. . .]

There has been much talk in the *völkisch* movement about the emergence of a new political leadership, and the call for such a leadership is compatible with what I have been saying. But the ways which it recommends for solving the problem, examining people's blood, re-nordification, etc., etc., seem to my practical nature somewhat dubious as far as their feasibility, their value, and even their effectiveness is concerned! There is another one, however, which is an archetypally German, Prussian way, which is more appropriate than any other: selection through the army![. . .]

For a man, military service is the most profound and valuable form of participation in the State—for the woman it is motherhood! There are many African tribes where mothers who die in labour are buried with the same honours as warriors who have fallen in battle![. . .] You can call it utopian but for me it is a certainty! Given twenty to thirty years of this type of selection, Germany will have a leadership and executive class which will change the whole face of society and the State, and provide the backbone of the State and its economy![. . .]

> ['Gedanken über Aufgaben der Zukunft' [Thoughts on the tasks of the future], in Michael Geismaier [pseud.], *Männer und Mächte: Gregor Strasser* (R. Kittler: Leipzig, 1933; 1st pub. in *Nationalsozialistische Briefe* in 1926), 81–90.]

HANS F. K. GÜNTHER

64   Nordic Thinking and the German Rebirth

Hans Friedrich Günther (1891–1968), nicknamed Rassen-Günther or 'race-Günther', was a young proselyte of the Aryan theories of Gobineau, H. S. Chamberlain, and others, and as early as 1922 produced his Rassenkunde des deutschen Volkes *[An Ethnography of the German People] which had sold 270,000 copies by 1943. It claimed that, as an essentially genetic quality, Aryanism, the sole basis of a healthy civilization, could be bred back into the Germans (who were now its least contaminated carriers) if eugenics were placed at the centre of policy-making in all spheres of social and political life. In 1930 the Nazi minister of the interior for Thuringia, Wilhelm Frick, appointed him Professor of Racial Hygiene at Jena University, and under the regime he went on to hold other prestigious academic posts as well as receiving numerous honours. His voluminous writings linking racial with cultural 'health' (some still in print) helped rationalize the regime's systematic destruction of millions of human beings, principally, but by no means exclusively, Jews, by reducing them to 'specimens' of allegedly inferior human types.*

The study of the historical fates of peoples as the working out of law-bound (biological) life processes, as the working out of changing conditions of natural selection, only became possible in a fruitful way once Darwin recognized the crucial importance of natural selection for all life-forms in general.[. . .] With the rediscovery of Mendel's research into heredity in the 1900s, the theories of Galton and Lapouge concerning the laws governing life acquired a more solid basis and a deeper significance.[. . .] The work of the Germans Otto Ammon (1842–1915), Woltmann (1871–1907) and Wilser (1850–1923) lent weight to theories concerning the special importance of the Nordic race. After the turn of the century a particular way of thinking came into being and started to gain currency, that of a possible renewal of the West by maintaining the integrity of the race [*Rassenpflege*] or, to be more precise, by maintaining the integrity of the Nordic race within the racial mixture of Western people. *Nordic Thinking* was born.[. . .]

The sapping of national energies by the world war, the outcome of this war, the post-war years, and the eradication throughout all these years of valuable genetic groups—which has finally left the German people physically and spiritually with a quite different composition—all these processes, their consequences, and the concerns they have raised have been the essential reason for the spread among Germans of a certain awareness, in many even a deep consciousness, of heredity and selection, race, racial mixing, and the composition of races. Thus it is that since the war, especially now that a generation of youth has grown up which on the one hand does not feel responsible for the pre-war period, the war, and its consequences, and on the other is searching for possible ways of bringing about a total renewal of the German people, a Nordic Movement has arisen which, by increasing the Nordic racial component of all German lineages [*Stämme*], by re-nordifying [*Aufnordung*] of the German people, could lay the basis for an improvement in the genetic stock of this people.[. . .]

It is clear that since the Nordic Movement sees human beings not so much as individuals but as carriers of heredity, the key idea which informs it is that of maintaining the health of the stock (eugenics, racial hygiene).[. . .] Not just de-nordification [*Entnordung*] alone, but a degeneration (increase in inferior hereditary properties) which has spread through all the races of the historically significant peoples of the Indo-Germanic language family has led to the decline of these peoples. Those who profess Nordic Thinking will always be the most zealous advocates of a doctrine of hereditary health [*Erbgesundheitslehre*], one which takes into account all races.[. . .]

Only improvement of the stock and re-nordification will save Germanness [*Deutschheit*] from destruction.[. . .] The tall, blond, blue-eyed German is still felt to be 'genuinely German'; artists of healthy sensibility still portray in symbolic forms and heads the nobility and beauty embodied in the Nordic race.[. . .] The appeal of the Nordic still determines the sentiments of the best Germans.[. . .] Nordic Thinking demands a will which must endure down through millennia: 'We are nothing; what we seek is everything' (Hölderlin). But this act of overcoming ourselves is rewarded by the knowledge of participating in a spirit which alone can give real and durable shape to the life of peoples, a spirit which determines the course of natural selection.

> [*Kleine Rassenkunde des deutschen Volkes* [A Primer in the Ethnography of the German People] (J. K. Lehmanns Verlag: Munich, 1933; 1st edn. 1929), 138–41, 144, 146–8.]

R. WALTHER DARRÉ
....

65 **Breeding a New Nobility**

Richard Walther Darré (1895–1953) used his specialist knowledge of animal breeding techniques to evolve his own scheme for national renewal. The key to this was a genetically healthy peasantry placed at the centre of national life, secured in its ownership of land, and protected from the corrosive effects of urbanization and industrial capitalism (both closely identified with the Jews). He had already set out the eugenic, political, and legal measures necessary to realize this vision in two major books (one of which is cited here), before joining the NSDAP in 1930. He was soon promoted to the highest positions within the movement as part of Hitler's drive to recruit the peasant vote. Though given ministerial positions under the regime to realize his policies (which involved colonizing new 'living space' in the East) he was gradually marginalized from power. His schemes were not only utopian, but conflicted with the massive industrialization demanded by the Nazi war-machine. Nevertheless, his slogan 'Blood and Soil' had made a significant contribution to the rationale for the systematic inhumanity and destructiveness carried out by the Third Reich.

A reliable indication of genuine nobility is given when an individual does not allow everything he does to be determined by self-centred goals, but by goals which have a higher claim on his ego. In saying this we must consider that the first thing to which the individual self is subordinated is the people [*Volk*] as constituted by the community of Germans. Once we understand by 'people' not the purely quantitative total of all individuals whom chance has brought together within the present borders of the Reich, but only those within this mass who profess loyalty to their German blood and to a duty to their Germanness [*Deutschtum*], we thereby create a concept of people which by its nature relates to what is meant by Germanic.[. . .] To contemporary Germans who still find it difficult to understand this new stress on the value which blood shall have within the future German national community [*Volksgemeinschaft*], and to those still trapped in the anaemic concept of 'humanity', we can offer a well-known phrase from Immanuel Kant: 'This much can be judged as probable: that the mixture of ethnic groups, which gradually extinguishes their characters, leaving aside all supposed philanthropy, does not benefit the human race.'

In a word: a German national [*Volksgenosse*] in the above sense of a specific type of character determined by blood will doubtless have grown into a type of wood from which a new German nobility can be fashioned if, in everything he does, he acts according to the principle: 'As a German, always behave in such a way that your fellow countrymen [*Volksgenossen*] would want to model themselves on you.'

Today such Germans do not just occur in one class, but in every sphere of society in roughly the same proportions. The proof that this is really the case was given to us by experiences at the front of the world war in 1914, and this was probably the most decisive experience of the true front soldier: Ernst Jünger explored this insight brilliantly in his war books.[. . .]

What are the general rules governing the breeding of animals when it comes specifically to improving the stock?[. . .]

1. An ideal specimen is selected first of all to establish what the selection process is aiming at, and also to give individual breeders a sort of inner compass to point their efforts in the right direction.[. . .]
2. The best animals are paired with the best.[. . .]
3. Animals are selected according to their pedigree.
4. The qualities and yield of every animal considered for breeding are evaluated.[. . .]
5. The attributes of the offspring are carefully tested, because to some extent this provides a way of establishing whether the first four steps have been taken correctly.[. . .]

Now let us get back to human beings! At the outset we said that breeding is a technique which tries in a considered way to produce offspring whose quality is at least not inferior to that of its parents, and where possible offers the prospect of an improvement in its hereditary characteristics over time. The crucial point here is the phrase 'in a considered way'. It means that the breeder should be clear what the breeding is designed to achieve. Thus a 'breeding objective' must be set. For breeding without a goal would be a contradiction in terms, quite simply because in every case breeding involves attaching value to given hereditary traits in the light of a future objective.[. . .]

For us Germans [. . .] there can really only be one objective to pursue, which is: *Every available means should be used to achieve the goal that the creative blood in the body of our people* [Volkskörper], *the blood of human beings of the Nordic Race, should be preserved and increased, because on this depends the preservation and development of our Germanness* [Deutschtum].

[*Neuadel aus Blut und Boden* [A New Nobility from Blood and Soil] (J. F. Lehmanns Verlag: Munich, 1930), 59–60, 178–80, 190, 226.]

E. GÜNTHER GRÜNDEL
....

66   The New Human Synthesis

Written on the eve of the seizure of power, Gründel's book is an exhaustive analysis of why the Weimar Republic and the alien values it allegedly embodied was destined to collapse and give way to a new order based on a regenerated national community. Gründel himself remained an obscure figure under the regime, and is cited here mainly to illustrate one of the most recurrent themes, not just of Nazism, but of fascism in general, namely the New Man (see Texts 16, 56, 70, 107, 197). This is an archetypal myth, central to religious cultures, but also propagated by communist regimes in suitably secularized form. By envisaging the New Man as the incarnation of national palingenesis, it becomes readily fascistized.

As long as the blood that courses through the veins of the people [*Volkskörper*] is still fundamentally healthy, it spontaneously produces human beings in critical historical moments capable of rising to the challenges they pose. That is precisely the source of comfort in the apparently so hopelessly confused age of upheaval and turmoil we are living through, namely that we are today witnessing the emergence of a new man[19] and a new youth who will act as a new force: in short a new generation who will bring about the reordering of society.[. . .]

Till now the new force was in a state of seething fermentation. It reached out to affect all areas of communal existence, but only in a tentative way. It strove to find a new way of being in a new lifestyle, to achieve new forms of self-expression in a

---

[19] Literally 'new human being' (*neuer Mensch*): 'Mensch' applies to male and female in German.

new art, in new sport, in new technology. At first it imposed itself on the political arena hesitantly and ambiguously, but then ever more irresistibly, and launched attack after attack against the crumbling front of the old world which so stubbornly continued to defend itself, in waves that initially remained uncoordinated, like a mass army which was not yet fully united, but in which could be sensed the powerful new forces at work.[. . .]

Our age is once more acquiring creative momentum, it is gaining depth, direction, and future. The creative dynamic, the basic quality of the Germanic-Western cultural soul, is awakening in the dawn of its fourth day of creation in a new type of human being.[. . .]

As bearer of the new epoch, the new type of human being means the end of the age of the property-owning bourgeois,[20] and will once again forge links with the healthy roots of Western humanity by bringing about the great synthesis: from the knight he takes blood, from the pious medieval Christian the soul which rests in God, from the middle classes a free spirit. The aristocrat inherited blood—and decayed once he inherited only a name. The middle classes inherited the education of the spirit—and decayed when they inherited only money. The new man will be the comprehensive heir of his national culture [*Volkstum*].

The warrior lived according to the principle that might was right.[21] The modern property-owning bourgeois lived on the basis of individualism in rights and collectivism in duties. The new human being lives in conscious service of the community, but with a deeply personal sense of responsibility. He is not a person 'in his own right', and not the embodiment of a class, but of his people. He does not live for himself, but as an integral part of a living whole. On this basis he restores the harmonious totality of Western humanity, the living harmony of body, mind, and soul.[. . .]

The new man is still evolving. Indeed, he is not yet visible to everyone, for he does not come from the noisy centre which constantly attracts the attention of the crowd, but from the quiet periphery. Every new force that is destined to topple an age which has run its course comes from the periphery of that age with all its dominant values and pseudo-values. It is in the moments of great crisis in the emergence of the new that the 'outsiders' take on their special function of forming the nucleus of a new centre around which the coming world will henceforth order itself.

[*Die Sendung der jungen Generation* [The Mission of the Young Generation] (C. H. Beck'sche Verlagsbuchhandlung: Munich, 1933), 327–37.]

---

[20] *Bürger* in German denotes bourgeois, citizen, and (member of) the liberal or capitalist middle classes.

[21] Literally 'according to the law of the fist', i.e. jungle law.

Section B

German Fascism in Power 1933–1945

INTRODUCTION

The seven extracts in Section Bi capture some of the sense of relief and of expectancy that convinced Nazis experienced on Hitler's seizure of power. This heady palingenetic fervour was also shared by those former cultural pessimists or German fascists who now persuaded themselves that Nazism would stop the rot as it promised, or was an effective and unique vehicle for the realization of *their* vision of a reborn Germany.

The nine texts which follow (Section Bii) may not be noticeably different in basic mood, but their background is one of apparently unstoppable Nazi gains in the sphere of foreign policy which effectively rescinded the hated Versailles Treaty. This led to a growth in national self-confidence which made some nationalists look forward to the restoration and enlargement of Germany's colonial empire (Text 76). Meanwhile, a dynamic transformation of the German economy, one involving state intervention on a practically corporativist scale (though this was not how Germans were encouraged to perceive it), had practically abolished unemployment and brought all manner of material and psychological benefits to 'true' Germans. So radical was the transformation by 1938 that to the believer every sphere of life could seem to have been revolutionized by the Nazi ethos: economics (Text 74), work (Text 75), poetry (Texts 79, 80), philosophy (Text 81), and European civilization itself (Text 82). The fact that such dazzling achievements cast deep shadows over entire sections of the community deemed anti-or un-German, shadows in which many would eventually be simply disappeared, could be overlooked by 'average' Germans to whom no decadence could be ascribed, that is as long as their capacity for 'cognitive dissonance', denial, or wilful ignorance remained unimpaired. However, the regime made absolutely no secret of its campaign to eliminate physically the 'non-German' or 'non-human', as Text 77 makes clear.

The texts of Biii are written against the background of escalating war and mass murder. The unassailable belief in Nazi victory which informs Texts 83–6 gradually gives way to a mood which is often referred to as 'apocalyptic'. But this is no twilight of the gods on a par with the Book of Revelation or Norse myths. It was the dusk of idols which were all-too human: the collapse of an empire and the destruction of a military machine, both of which had committed obscene crimes against humankind. The last two passages, written as the civilian death-toll soared and German houses and factories were reduced to rubble, suggest less the persistence of propaganda than that the mythopoeic faculty of those who remained Nazis—their true secret weapon throughout the history of the movement—continued to function intact till the end. It effectively screened their minds from the devastating realities of defeat and emptiness, pain and despair they all would otherwise have felt ('guilt' would imply the penetration of their mind-set by another, quite alien value system asserting the value of *all* human beings irrespective of their physical or spiritual attributes). The rapturous evocation of the 'home' which the Germans were supposed to be fighting to defend to the last (Text 89) underlines the mysterious ability of ultra-nationalism to create a sense of a destiny transcending individual life and death, creating a fanaticism which still plagues many societies in the contemporary world. In this context Hitler's political testament (Text 90) is cited, less for the light it sheds on the 'psychopathology' of Hitler himself, than as a symptom of the resilience of fascist palingenetic myth in the face of destruction: its perverse power to wrest meaning out of the jaws of nihilism.

ALFRED ROSENBERG

67 **German Rebirth**

Alfred Rosenberg (1893–1946) had been a member of the occultist racist organization, the Thule-Gesellschaft, before joining the closely associated DAP. He then became editor of the Völkischer Beobachter *in 1921, and in 1934 was appointed 'Official responsible for the supervision of the whole spiritual and ideological indoctrination and education of the NSDAP'. In practice, however, Hitler remained unassailable as the Party's chief ideologue, and in private mocked aspects of Rosenberg's idiosyncratic 'philosophy of history', the most famous exposition of which was* The Myth of the Twentieth Century *(1930). Under the Third Reich he exerted some influence on Nazi cultural policy, and was given nominal responsibility for the conquered eastern territories, though his uncompromising paganism, and later his reservations about the regime's policy in Russia led to his further marginalization from real power. He had nevertheless succeeded in helping legitmate policies of cultural and ethnic cleansing which once put into action made systematized barbarism and mass-atrocities inevitable. This extract is taken from a speech given at the opening of the German Cultural Festival held in Cologne in October 1933.*

The political struggle within Germany is over. What we are seeing now is the death-agony of an entire epoch, and if I use these words then I do so in full knowledge of the fact that what we are living through in Germany today are no mere chance events due to a certain shift in the balance of power. For if the only aim of the whole German Revolution had been to bring down the old political class so as to help new governments come to power, even if these are laudable political aims, our great movement would have betrayed its true purpose. Instead we were fully conscious throughout these last fourteen years that much more than political goals were at stake, that the struggle for power was only the external manifestation of a spiritual and intellectual conflict. For this reason we not only attacked our opponents for their politics, but above all for their world-views [*Weltanschauungen*]. We realized from the start that a Marxist world-view can never be defeated through police or state measures.[. . .]

There have been ruthless attacks on today's doctrine of race and heredity. People said it was unchristian, that it had to be opposed, and yet in reality they are reacting in precisely the same way as four hundred years ago when people's eyes were opened to the existence of certain natural laws. Later, under the influence of the alien doctrine of humanism, countless idiots and inferior human beings were accommodated in what can be seen as palaces for the sick, while millions of physically and mentally sound Germans lay outside on the streets and hungered. But such principles were wrong. They contradict natural laws, and in the worst cases nature avenges itself by wiping out entire peoples from the face of the earth. A living example of this is the history of two heroic peoples: the Romans and the Greeks.

Today we believe that in the true sense there is no world history, but only the history of different races and peoples.[. . .]

The Second Reich did not understand its great mission [to create a German national culture]. It pursued world commerce, it prospered in an unhealthy type of economy, it had excellent armaments, but its soul had been damaged.[. . .] In this period Europe was swamped with literature promoting sickness. And just as the patient always touches his wounds, so Europe lapped up this literature so as to be constantly able to touch its spiritual wounds.

The incarnation of sickness, Dostoevsky, became the symbol for the whole of humanity.

For us the sick human being is of no interest. He no longer stands at the centre of artistic creativity, but the strong, healthy human being in the midst of his struggle, whether in victory or in heroic defeat.[. . .]

Once again the German nation is struggling to create new values, and it finds them by turning back to the oldest ones. It sees the essence of the whole National Socialist revolution encapsulated in one word: national honour! This single thought is all that is needed to build a new political state system, and foster [22] a new type of economic thinking, a new economic ethic.[. . .]

We finally want to become one with ourselves. That is the longing which is daily felt by a million German hearts. And at the end of this great longing there stands the Third Reich.[. . .]

> ['Deutsche Wiedergeburt' [German rebirth], in *Blut und Ehre. Ein Kampf für deutsche Wiedergeburt. Reden und Aufsätze (1919–1933)* [Blood and Honour: A Struggle for German Rebirth. Speeches and Essays 1919–1933] (Zentralverlag der NSDAP/Franz Eher: Munich, 1938), 257–263.]

HERMANN GOERING

68   The Third Reich as Saviour of the West

The celebrated war pilot Hermann Goering (1893–1946), took over the SA for Hitler in 1922 and was involved in the abortive putsch the following year. When an amnesty allowed his return from political exile in 1928 his social skills and chivalrous demeanour played an important role in making Hitler electable. He went on to accumulate power and responsibilities under the Third Reich, fully colluding with the most inhuman aspects of official policy, and by the time war broke out with Britain was named as Hitler's successor. As Reich Marshal he then made some major strategic mistakes in forward planning and command which led to his progressive eclipse from real power. This passage is typical of the way till the late 1930s the Nazis consistently presented the New Germany as Europe's bastion against communism and the guarantor of peace, as long as it was peace on their terms. Consistent with this logic (far from exclusive to fascism) all acts of military aggression are rationalized as defensive wars or pre-emptive strikes.

---

[22] German, *heranzüchten*: literally 'to breed'.

The last election campaign in Germany coincided with Germany's withdrawal from the League of Nations.[23] This time there were not countless domestic forces confronting each other, but a truly united nation had closed ranks to defend itself, committed to assert its rights in a concerted fight for Germany's honour against foreign countries which had hostile intentions towards her. The German people showed the world that it had every intention to work honestly and with all its might for every policy which served the true cause of peace. On the other hand it also showed the world that if other countries want to deal with Germany they must first accord her the same respect, the same rights, and the same honour as they claim for themselves. The German people, almost to a man and to a woman, stood united behind its Führer and his policy of honour and peace. Germany will continue in the future to avoid harming the interests of any other country. Germany renounces foreign conquests. Germany wishes to take nothing away from other countries, but the same Germany refuses to allow anything to be taken away from her, or harm her interests.

The other peoples should realize that Germany's Führer will be the foremost safeguard of European peace. For the task which Hitler has taken on, the fight which he has waged in the domestic sphere, is not merely a German one. Hitler's mission has a world-historical significance. By taking up the fight to the death against communism in Germany, he also created a bulwark for other European countries.[. . .]

If the Red Star had been victorious, Germany would have gone under in the bloody terror of Communism, and the West would have followed her into destruction. Through the victory of the swastika, however, this terrible danger has been averted, and we should thank God, for the possibility has been created once more for the resurgence of the German people and the creation of a healthy Germany. But Germany is and remains the heart of Europe, and Europe can only live in health and freedom if the heart is healthy and intact. The German people has arisen and Germany will be healthy, for we have the guarantee for this in Adolf Hitler, the Chancellor of the German people, the shield-bearer of its honour and freedom.

[*Aufbau einer Nation* [The Building of a Nation] (E. S. Mittler & Son: Berlin, 1934), 110–12.]

JOSEPH GOEBBELS

69 **The Total Revolution of National Socialism**

In this speech made at the inauguration of the Reich Cultural Chamber on 15 November 1933, Goebbels, now Reich Minister for Public Enlightenment and Propaganda, with almost unlimited power over the intellectual and cultural life of the state, expresses the euphoric sense of achievement that accompanied the Nazi seizure of power for many ultra-nationalists, who now felt that the real unification of the Germans had finally taken place

[23] Germany had finally withdrawn from the League of Nations on 14 Oct. 1933. The 'electoral campaign' refers to the propaganda drive leading up to the first of the regime's plebiscites, held on 12 Nov.

(cf. Mussolini's sentiments in Text 22). Goebbels also outlines the special role of the artist in the 'new age', the totalitarian implications of which would soon become only too obvious.

The revolution we have carried out is a total one. It has embraced all areas of public life and transformed them from below. It has completely changed and recast the relationship of people to each other, to the State, and to life itself. It was in fact the breakthrough of a fresh world-view, which had fought for power in opposition for fourteen years to provide the basis for the German people to develop a new relationship with the State. What has been happening since 30 January[24] is only the visible expression of this revolutionary process. The revolution did not begin here. It was only carried through to its final conclusion. At bottom it is the struggle for existence of a people which, left to its old forms of cultural life and played out values, was otherwise destined to collapse.[. . .]

There are revolutions from above and revolutions from below. Those from above generally have a limited life-span, for it is difficult, if not impossible, to force a new system of rules onto a people from above. But the readiness to adapt to a new system is an intrinsic part of revolutions from below.[. . .]

The purpose of the revolution which we have carried out is the forging of the German nation into a single people. This has been the longing of all good Germans for two thousand years. Attempts had been made through legal processes countless times; each of these attempts failed. Only the fervent explosion of the national passions of our people made it possible. The process was going to be completed all the more irresistibly, spontaneously, and wildly the longer people tried to hold it up with artificial dams. What was not possible, and often not even wanted, from above, we have achieved from below. The German people, once the most fragmented in the world, atomized into its component parts and hence condemned to impotence as a world power, since 1918 lacking the arms, and, what is worse, the will to assert its rights among other peoples, rose up in a unique demonstration of its sense of national strength.[. . .]

What fate denies us now in material blessings is made up to us two- or threefold with the blessing of new ideas.[. . .] No one orders the new world-view to march across the stage or screen. Where it does march across them, however, we must zealously ensure that in its artistic form as well it reflects the greatness of the historical process which we have completed in the German Revolution.

Over and above this, we intend to be the patron saints of German art and culture. The hunger which has gripped the German people does not only extend as far as their stomachs. It is just as much a hunger of their souls: this too needs to be sated. Like every genuine revolution, ours too aims for a radical transformation of our cultural life and spiritual creativity.[. . .]

German art needs fresh blood. We live in a young age, its protagonists are young, the ideas they are realizing are young. They have nothing in common with the past which now lies behind us. The artist who wants to find an expression for this age must feel young and create new forms.[. . .]

[24] i.e. 30 Jan. 1933, when Hitler became Reich Chancellor.

The new national art of Germany will only enjoy respect in the world and bear witness beyond the frontiers of our country to the intense cultural dynamism of the new Germany if it is firmly and ineradicably rooted in the mother earth of the national culture [*Volkstum*] which produced it. The world must discover anew what is German and genuine.[. . .]

May German art and culture be blessed and fostered by the newly formed Reich Culture Chamber.[. . .] In it the creative individual in Germany has found the way to be part of the new State. May he thereby experience the blessed feeling we all have of being pioneers, creators, and shapers of a new century.

['Die deutsche Kultur vor neuen Aufgaben' [The new tasks of German culture], in *Signale der neuen Zeit* [Signals of the New Age] (Zentralverlag der NSDAP/Franz Eher: Munich, 1939), 323–36.]

GOTTFRIED BENN

70   The New Breed of German

An early expressionist poet and a medical orderly in the First World War, Gottfried Benn (1886–1956) became increasingly obsessed after the war with the need to break out of an over-cerebral civilization and the 'nihilism' it bred. This predisposed him to see in Nazism an explosion of pent-up primordial energies which would restore meaning to the world. He thus turned to celebrating the Nazi revolution in ecstatic prose, till the violence of the Röhm Purge broke the spell. He ended up vilified by the regime and retreating into 'inner emigration', but during his brief affair with the Third Reich his readiness to glorify its leader and its grotesque eugenic fantasies knew no bounds, as this passage shows.

He who wishes his reign to last, must breed for the future.

No one can doubt any more [. . .] that behind the political events in Germany there lies a historical transformation of unfathomable consequences. The cultural sheen of an epoch is flaky and breaks up. Along sutures in the organic the forces of heredity stir; from defects in the centres of regeneration the human gene pushes towards the light. There values which were once stable and authentic melt into the shadows. There accomplishments are transformed and become unrecognizable: the centuries of propagation are at an end.

The unfathomable historical transformation initially manifests itself politically in the central concept: The Total State. The Total State, in contrast to the pluralistic State of the last epoch, the State of thwarted plans and ambitions, announces itself by asserting the complete identity of power and spirit, individuality and the collective, freedom and necessity: it is monist, anti-dialectic, enduring, and authoritarian. It is the executive principle at the most refined level of cultivation ever encountered in the history of the West: of past cultural spheres only Egypt and Yucatan bear comparison. The new, disruptive element, but simultaneously the element of synthesis involved in the transformation, reveals itself specifically in the concept of leader [*Führerbegriff*]. The leader is not the embodiment of power, and certainly not conceived as a principle of terror, but as the highest spiritual principle.[. . .]

It seems to me beyond doubt that out of this transformation a new man will once again emerge in Europe, half from mutation and half from breeding: the German man. He will stand up against no one, but he will stand out from both the Western and the Eastern type. All the preconditions for his emergence are there: behind him a quarter-century of radical crisis, shattering upheavals, of being churned up as no other people in the world has experienced, and in the last decade a growing awareness of biological dangers, one which bears out the precept that a people which becomes conscious of the dangers facing it produces genius.[. . .]

I know that this people will become free and its great spirits will come with words which once more have meaning, will be valid for other peoples, and will bear fruit. In their syllables there will be everything which we have suffered, the celestial and the transient, the legacy of our philosophical suffering. I know they will come, not gods, and not fully human either, but fruit of the purity of a new people. Then they will make their judgement and rip up the beds of idleness, and knock down the walls which have been thinly whitewashed over and where sacrilege has been committed for a handful of barley and a morsel of bread—they alone will do this. I know they will come, and I am sure that I can hear the reverberation of their footsteps. I am sure that the victims they claim deserve their fate: I see them coming.

['Züchtung I' [Breeding I], in *Der neue Staat und die Intellektuellen* [The New State and the Intellectuals] (Deutsche Verlags-Anstalt: Stuttgart/Berlin, 1933); repr. in *Essays, Reden, Vorträge* (Limes Verlag: Wiesbaden, 1959), 214–22.]

PAULA SIBER

71   The New German Woman

Fascism clearly represents an extreme form of 'male chauvinism', and one scholar (Theweleit: see Text 158) has located its basic obsession with decadence in a pathological fear (and hence hatred) of women. The official policy on women as outlined in this programmatic text could equally well have been written under the Third Reich or the Third Rome. It was written by the acting head of the Deutsche Frauenwerk (Association of German Woman), from 1933 run by the NS Frauenschaft, which had been set up in 1931 as an organization for all female NSDAP members. It should be remembered when reading such reactionary texts that fascist leaders claimed to be revolutionizing traditional womanhood and motherhood by making them vital to the creation of the rejuvenated national community. Under Nazism this was to involve in practice not just encouragement to have large families and provide a source of menial labour whenever the State required it, but collusion in the eugenics, euthanasia, war, and genocide organized by the menfolk.

To be a woman means to be a mother, means affirming with the whole conscious force of one's soul the value of being a mother and making it a law of life. The role of motherhood assigned to woman by nature and fully endorsed by National Socialism in no way means, however, that the task of the National Socialist woman within the framework of the National Community should be simply that of knowing herself to be the carrier of race and blood, and hence of the biological conservation of the people.

Over and above the duty intrinsic to her gender of conserving her race and people there is also the holy task entrusted to man and woman of enhancing and developing the inner, spiritual, and human qualities. This in the case of woman culminates in the motherhood of the soul as the highest ennoblement of any woman, whether she is married or not.

Therefore a woman belongs at the side of man not just as a person who brings children into the world, not just as an adornment to delight the eye, not just as a cook and cleaner. Instead woman has the holy duty to be a life companion, which means being a comrade who pursues her vocation as woman with clarity of vision and spiritual warmth.[. . .]

To be a woman in the deepest and most beautiful sense of the word is the best preparation for being a mother. For the highest calling of the National Socialist woman is not just to bear children, but consciously and out of total devotion to her role and duty as mother to raise children for her people.[. . .]

The mother is also the intermediary for the people and national culture [Volkstum] to which she and her child belong. For she is the custodian of its culture, which she provides her child with through fairy-tales, legends, games, and customs in a way which is decisive for the whole relationship which he will later have to his people.[. . .] In a National Socialist Germany the sphere of social services [Volksfürsorge] is predominantly the sphere of the woman. For woman belongs wherever social services or human care is required.

Apart from these tasks of conserving the people, educating the people, and helping the people, the final area of responsibility for the woman, one not to be undervalued, is her contribution to the national economy. Women manage 75 per cent of the total income of the people, which passes through her hands simply in running the home.[. . .]

The national economy includes agriculture. It is today less possible than ever to imagine the struggle for existence and the toil involved in the economics of improving crops, refining breeds, and farming new land, activities which demand constant attention and maintenance, without the contribution of woman to agriculture in overseeing and running the farm.

[Die Frauenfrage und ihre Lösung durch den Nationalsozialismus [The Women's Issue and its National Socialist Solution] (G. Kallmeyer: Wolfenbüttel/Berlin, 1933); repr. in Walter Gehl (ed.), Der nationalsozialistischer Staat [The National Socialist State] (Ferdinand Hirt: Breslau, 1933), 127–30.]

Carl Schmitt (1888–1985) was one of Germany's leading professors of international and public law between 1921 and 1945, a position which he used to become the most authoritative legal theorist of the Conservative Revolution and hence a continuing influence on an important current within neo-fascism (Texts 193–5). He became Chancellor Schleicher's adviser, but was able to make an even greater contribution to the theoretical rationale for the destruction of democracy and human life after he joined the NSDAP in early 1933. As State Counsellor for Prussia he produced articulate rationalizations of the Röhm Purge, the 'cleansing' of the judiciary and the Civil Service from 'the Jewish spirit', and Nazi imperialism. Here we see him justifying the Führer principle as the legal basis of the Nazis' 'total State'.

National Socialism does not think in abstractions and clichés. It is the enemy of all normative and functionalist ways of proceeding. It supports and cultivates every authentic substance of the people wherever it encounters it, in the countryside, in ethnic groups [*Stämme*] or classes. It has created the hereditary farm law;[25] saved the peasantry; purged the Civil Service of alien [*fremdgeartet*] elements and thus restored it as a class. It has the courage to treat unequally what is unequal and enforce necessary differentiations.[. . .] In a different way, but out of the same awareness of the specific properties of what has its own organic development, National Socialism is able to do justice to the concrete differences between the village, rural town, industrial community, city, and metropolis in the sphere of communal autonomy without being impeded by the erroneous concepts of equality imposed by a liberal democratic scheme of things.

The recognition of the plurality of autonomous life would, however, immediately lead back to a disastrous pluralism tearing the German people apart into discrete classes and religious, ethnic, social, and interest groups if it were not for a strong state which guarantees a totality of political unity transcending all diversity. Every political unity needs a coherent inner logic underlying its institutions and norms. It needs a unified concept which gives shape to every sphere of public life. In this sense too there is no normal State which is not a total State. The more varied the points of view which dictate regulations and institutions of the different spheres of life on the one hand, the more clearly a uniform, cogent, overriding principle must be recognized and adhered to on the other. Every uncertainty and dichotomy becomes the source of forces which start out as neutral towards the State and then become antagonistic to it, and hence the focus for pluralistic fragmentation and disintegration. A strong State is the precondition for the strong and autonomous vitality of its diverse constituent parts. The strength of the National Socialist State lies in the fact that it is from top to bottom and in every atom of its existence ruled

---

[25] Pioneered by Darré to preserve the peasantry from erosion by securing family smallholdings in perpetuity.

and permeated with the concept of leadership [*Führertum*]. This principle, which made the movement strong, must be carried through systematically both in the administration of the State and in the various spheres of self-government, naturally taking into account the modifications required by the particular area in question. But it would not be permissible for any important area of public life to operate independently from the Führer concept.

> ['Führertum und Artgleichheit als Grundbegriffe des nationalsozialistischen Rechts' [Leadership and uniformity as basic concepts of National Socialist law], in *Bewegung, Staat, Volk* [Movement, State, People] (Hanseatische Verlag: Hamburg, 1935), 33–46.]

ADOLF HITLER

73   The Place of Art in Germany's Political Reawakening

This sample of the special brand of palingenetic rhetoric which Hitler reserved for public speeches is taken from a pamphlet issued in English by the Nazi regime for foreign consumption. It consists of three of Hitler's addresses to the seventh Party Congress (or 'Nuremberg Rally') held in September 1935, published under the seemingly innocuous title Liberty, Art, Nationhood. *Indeed, the front cover cites the claim which the Führer made in one of the speeches that 'the German people and the German government have no other object in view than to live in peace and harmony with their neighbours'. Now that the destruction of the Weimar Republic and every trace of its liberalism was complete, Hitler was keen to allay growing fears abroad that Nazi Germany was embarked on a vast programme of militarization and imperialist expansion, a prospect which generally alarmed contemporaries much more than the regime's open commitment to a radical policy of what would now be called 'ethnic cleansing'. However, the way a reawakened Germany is identified with a cultural purge makes the pamphlet replete with implicit threats of persecution and war which utterly thwart the propagandistic intentions of its publishers.*

On February 27th 1933, when the blaze from the dome of the Reichstag was reflected in a red glow from the sky, it seemed as if Fate had chosen the torch of the Communist incendiaries to illuminate the grandeur of that historical turning-point before the eyes of the nation. The final menace of the Bolshevik revolution hovered like a dark shadow over the Reich. A terrible social and economic catastrophe had brought Germany to the verge of annihilation. The foundations of social life had crumbled.[. . .] During the months that followed it was still very difficult to discover and employ such measures as might still avert the final disaster, and doubly difficult to withstand and overthrow the last assault launched by those who wanted to wreck the Nation and the Reich. It was veritably a savage struggle against all those causes and symptoms of German internal disintegration and against our enemies abroad who were hopefully expecting the final débâcle.

At some future date, when it will be possible to view these events in clear perspective, people will be astonished to find that just at the time the National

Socialists and their leaders were fighting a life-or-death battle for the preservation of the nation the first impulse was given for the reawakening and restoration of artistic vitality in Germany. It was at this same juncture that the congeries of political parties were wiped out, the opposition of the federal states overcome and the sovereignty of the Reich established as sole and exclusive. While the defeated Centre Party and the Marxists were being driven from their final entrenchments, the trade unions abolished, and while National Socialist thought and ideas were being brought from the world of dream and vision into the world of fact, and our plans were being put into effect one after the other—in the midst of all this we found time to lay the foundations of a new Temple of Art. And so it was that the same revolution that had swept over the State prepared the soil for the growth of a new culture.[. . .]

Art is not one of those human activities that may be laid aside to order and resumed to order. Nor can it be retired on pension, as it were. For either a people is endowed with cultural gifts that are inherent in its very nature or it is not so endowed at all. Therefore such gifts are part of the general racial qualities of a people. But the creative function through which these spiritual gifts or faculties are expressed follows the same law of development and decay that governs all human activity.[. . .]

But we are convinced that in the political sphere we have discovered a fitting mode of expression for the nature and will of our people. Therefore we feel that we are capable also of recognising and discovering in the cultural sphere the complementary expression which will be adequate to that nature and that will. We shall discover and encourage artists who will imprint on the new German State the cultural stamp of the German race, which will be valid for all time.

['Art and Politics', in *Liberty. Art. Nationhood* (M. Müller & Son: Berlin, 1935), 33–42.]

WERNER DAITZ

74 **Soldierly Economics**

This article from the NSDAP monthly magazine shows how deeply the key components of Nazi palingenetic myth (anti-liberalism, anti-democracy, the organic national community, military ethos, racism, anti-Semitism, the Führer cult) had penetrated all areas of thought, in this case economics. Though inter-war Marxists saw fascism as a permutation of capitalism's onslaught against socialism, fascists conceived themselves as superseding its basic principles of laissez-faire individualism and the profit motive through the introduction of a nationally and socially healthy system: indeed a form of socialism purged of materialism and internationalism. In the case of Nazism this led first to a high degree of economic 'co-ordination', and, by 1939, to an all-out bid for autarky, which involved the creation of a vast empire of vassal states geared to supplying raw materials and finished goods to the Reich, as well as the use of slave labour on a massive scale.

National community means: a community defended from threats externally combined with social harmony at home. One without the other is impossible. Both are to be achieved only through the soldierly bearing of the German people in every field of activity, through soldierly socialism [*Soldatensozialismus*].

We therefore demand in the economy a soldierly conduct within and without. For, if the leader of a business runs it without regard to the economic independence of the nation, but only with a view to the highest possible profits, it will inevitably destroy the social peace within his company. His employees will be bound to adopt the same attitude [. . .] and for their part strive for the highest possible wage without regard for social peace and the state of the company. For Marxism always follows capitalism like its shadow. Both grow from the same root—Jewish mercenariness [*Gelddenken*, lit. 'money thinking'] which always finds a way of infiltrating Nordic economic thought once intellect has corrupted it. In the interests of a supposedly higher financial return, both destroy Blood and Soil, the biological foundations of their national culture [*Volkstum*] and hence of their own existence.[. . .]

We have before us three groups of professional activities which have grown up organically out of the farm economy, each of which has special tasks to perform in serving the totality of the people and in the defence of the economy [. . .]:

1. The agricultural economy (the Reich Nutrition Estate). This sector has the role of securing through its regulation of the market the renewal of the blood of the people and its freedom to have food.
2. The manufacturing economy (crafts, industry, trade, transport, domestic banking). This sector has the role of securing through its regulation of the market the needs of the people's civilization and technical progress and its freedom to consume raw materials.

3. The external economy (foreign trade, shipping, the financial and credit activities associated with foreign trade). This sector has the role of supplying and securing the exchange of materials abroad and the vital space [*Lebensraum*] of the national community.[. . .]

This clear division into sectors makes possible a clear and uniform formation of the bodies necessary for their self-administration and self-regulation.[. . .] They are vertical organizations which grow from the ground up like plants and once more foster the forces for the life and growth of the people.[. . .]

This concept of economics, one of primordial simplicity and naturalness, shatters the purely intellectually constructed economic theories of the last 150 years, which divorced the economy from the nation's defences and imbued it with an unsoldierly and defeatist cast of mind that subordinated the people to the economy, and freedom to mercenary principles.

The intuitive cleverness of the people senses in the promulgation of these principles the renewal of its innermost, eternal life and growth, the rebirth of all essential forces. Thus the Führer of the eternal Germany, Adolf Hitler, demonstrates every day afresh to those who dismissed him before as the most hopelessly unrealistic dreamer, that he is the greatest exponent of *Realpolitik* in every sphere of life, because he tackles everything from the point of view of a coherent vision of the world, thereby renewing it and restoring to it its eternal meaning.

['Weltanschauung und Wirtschaft [World-view and economy], *Nationalsozialistiche Monatsschriften*, 7/70 (Jan. 1936), 54–60.]

ROBERT LEY

75   The Joy of the National Socialist Economy

Robert Ley (1890–1945) replaced Gregor Strasser as Reich Organization Leader after his resignation in 1932. Under the regime he took on the task of destroying the once powerful German labour movement and subordinating workers to state control. This he did through the creation of the Deutsche Arbeitsfront (DAF), which embraced both workers and employers and by 1942 had about 25 million members. The German Labour Front in turn set up the Nazi equivalent of Dopolavoro, Kraft durch Freude (Strength through Joy). Here we see him expressing a typically Nazi puritan hedonism in his celebration of the Nazi work ethic. It was prompted by the introduction of the Four Year Plan in 1936 under the control of Goering.

Fortune has shone on us. It is as if fate wanted to compensate us a little for all the pain and the shame which we had to bear for years: first there was the enormous blood sacrifice which we had to make like no other people![26] And yet we still were denied victory; we still were defeated! And after suffering the heaviest losses of all time we had to endure the shame of defeat, subjugation, occupation. And now fate wants to make up everything to this so sorely tested people.[. . .]

[26] i.e. in the First World War.

There is one thing we must understand if we are to comprehend the greatness of this time: we are not dealing with a new state system, or a new economic system. We are not dealing with anything external like the building up of the army, or the economy—it comes down to the renewal of man, the individual man. Human beings are being transformed.

Do you believe that an idea has ever achieved this ever before? The renewal of human beings manifests itself in the fact that this idea is actually able to transform the most intimate aspects of human lives. National Socialism has the power to free the German people, the individual German, from the injuries inflicted on him which have been preventing him from performing his task. That is its ultimate, its greatest achievement.[. . .]

What the Führer demands is for us to say yes to life. He said only recently: We must demand that all institutions in Germany, whatever they are called, celebrate life. Without this positive attitude they have no value at all. Without it the logical conclusion is for me to become a Marxist, a Bolshevik.

Of course we do not have a comfortable life. Life on this earth is hard and must be earned through struggle, and earned every day afresh. All we can do is to give you the strength for this struggle, to make you inwardly strong. We can give the worker physical and spiritual health, healthy housing, and a proper livelihood with which to maintain himself and his children. Above all, thanks to Kraft durch Freude, we can offer him a great deal to nourish his spirit.

The Four Year Plan brings us a step further. It will make us economically independent of many things. The next plan will make us even more independent, the one after that even more, and we will build homes, cities, Volkswagens,[27] hotels, rest-homes, etc. Yes, there will always be work to do. I am convinced of that.

Everything that Germany is today, and that it will be tomorrow and thereafter, it owes to Adolf Hitler alone, and to no other human being or institution. Thus we must constantly offer the Führer our gratitude from the bottom of our hearts.

['Wiedergeburt aus der Freude' [Rebirth from joy], *Soldaten der Arbeit* [Soldiers of Work] (Zentralverlag der NSDAP / Franz Eher: Munich, 1942; 1st edn. 1938), 89–96.]

PAUL RITTER

76   The Expansionary Spirit of a Rejuvenated People

Hitler's own vision of how imperial expansion would proceed once Germany's irredentist claims had been met centred on Eastern Europe and Russia. However, the pressure for the return to Germany of the colonies she had lost under the terms of the Versailles Treaty (German East Africa, German South-West Africa, Cameroon, Togo, German New Guinea) was kept up by many of their former settlers. Their cause had gained invaluable propaganda when Hans Grimm's colonial novel became a bestseller in the late 1920s, its title, Volk ohne Raum *[A People without Space], bequeathing one of the more durable catch-phrases of the*

[27] Originally called the Kraft-durch-Freude car.

Nazi movement. By the summer of 1940, when final victory in the West seemed imminent, Hitler was apparently envisaging a belt of colonies stretching from the Cameroons to the East African coast, and some forward planning for a new African empire started in earnest. In this excerpt from a book of articles arguing the case for imperial expansion in Africa, Paul Ritter, of the Colonial Office of the NSDAP, makes the typical Nazi (and Fascist—see Texts 9, 11, 43) claim that German colonies were the necessity of an expropriated 'young' nation, and not the luxury of a plutocratic 'old' power like Britain or France.

For the old world of Europe only Africa, an entire area of the globe yet to be opened up, remains as a space able to accommodate the expansionary pressures exerted by the White population, which is constantly growing and looking for new opportunities. But the old world is anything but united! A two thousand year-old history, which has been written down and thus remains alive, has produced contrasts as nowhere else on earth. Irresistibly, the spirit of Indogermanic-Nordic man urges him on to undertake ever greater deeds ever further afield, and the furrows that his restlessness is ploughing in the old field of Europe are deep and terrible, while the contrasts, once determined by racial or religious factors, are now giving rise to divisions and conflicts with renewed violence only in a different guise. Just as religious sectarianism led to horrendous military struggles and the extermination of entire ethnic communities [*Volksstämme*], so today it is political belief, and the boundless lust for political power now leads to even greater crimes and more terrible atrocities.

Just as threatening for the destiny of the West as the political claim to universality, which the Comintern is pursuing through the realization of world Bolshevism, is the attempt on the part of peoples whose time has passed to rejuvenate themselves with the aid of coloured blood. In their fateful self-delusion 'gloire' and 'prestige' mean more to them than the future of the White race. Bent only on satisfying their vanity, they believe they can wantonly violate the eternal laws of blood [. . .] dutifully blind themselves to what must come, and kill culture through the impact of their mindlessly materialistic civilization. This danger was great for the German people too, as long as it was under the unbearable domination of the Marxist cast of mind, one which contradicts, negates, and undermines all the laws of national culture. What increased the danger was that many Germans were themselves hardly aware of this fact, and that even today many among us still do not understand the full implications of the warning-cry of the brownshirted[28] throngs 'Germany awake!' This awakening means not only shaking off the tutelage of the Asiatic-Jewish spirit which enslaved us, but also drawing once again on our own resources which reside in blood and race, and constitute an inexhaustible well-spring within the German people.

Under Adolf Hitler the German people has once more become a young people, a young people with the precious dynamism and resourcefulness of youth. Thanks to its youth the future belongs to this people, and its right to life has no need to be underpinned by long-outdated legal clauses.[. . .]

---

[28] The NSDAP uniform included a brown shirt (the SS wore black).

To deny Germany its colonies any longer and challenge its right to additional vital space [*Lebensraum*] and a source of raw materials would mean to compound the sin of passively tolerating Soviet domination—this the greatest crime in human history—with a new sin.[. . .]

For the German people colonies are no expression of imperialist thinking, no outer sign of the need for power and prestige, but simply a vital necessity. But since there is no political justice in the world and since throughout history the 'world-conscience' has always remained silent, there is no point in placing hopes in the goodwill of others. The only way to help the German people achieve its goal is the Führer's way: to turn the German nation into a political factor of such power and internal cohesion that the conscience of an international community, deaf to rational argument, cannot help but be suddenly awakened.

> ['Junges Volk braucht Kolonien!' [Young people needs colonies!], in Dr Heinrich Schnee *et al.* (eds.), *Das Buch der deutschen Kolonien* [The Book of German Colonies] (Wilhelm Goldmann: Leipzig, 1937), 15–19.]

HAMMER PRESS

77   Nazism's World Crusade against the Jews

After Fritsch died (see Text 50) his Handbook on the Jewish Question, which had started life as Antisemitischer Catechismus in 1887, was taken over by an editorial team and turned into a sort of anti-Semitic yearbook. This is the introduction to the 41st edition, cited as an unexceptional example of the anti-Semitic propaganda which bombarded subjects of the Third Reich from all sides and normalized the progressive removal of the Jews from society. The idea of an international Jewish 'attack' against the Third Reich was to become a major rationalization of Germany's 'defensive war' from 1939 onwards (cf. Text 41).

The history of Jewry [*Judentum*] is the history of the decline, not of the Jews, but of the people who offered Jews hospitality and rights of residence.[. . .]

It was extremely difficult for Theodor Fritsch to combat the destruction of every German sentiment through his newspaper.[29] Right from the start Jewry used the most ruthless ploys to attack him. Or it operated so cleverly disguised within the German state apparatus that the man in the street could scarcely detect when and how the Jew was at work. Thus Theodor Fritsch made unstinting efforts to win a larger group of friends; he tried to achieve his impact in the intellectual and ethical sphere by publishing essays on the racial question so as to prepare the ground for a renewal of the people and the state.[. . .]

The war, whose deeper causes unmistakably betrayed the work of Jewish instigators, brought with it the sense of community experienced by front-line soldiers [*Frontgemeinschaft*]. From this ordeal by fire suffered by the German man and the German soul the renewal of Germany was born. While the state and people

---

[29] i.e. *Hammer*.

outwardly collapsed, while parliamentarism apparently enjoyed its heyday and through its toleration of Jewry frittered away its reserves, numerous *völkisch* leagues were formed. They were an inner reaction to the collapse, the revolt of healthy spiritual forces against a decade of contamination of the body of the German people by Jewry. Out of the numerous movements of renewal which had understandably arisen it was the National Socialist German Workers' Party which soon stood out, whose leader Adolf Hitler took up the fight against Jewry in all areas of German life. This struggle, which mainly aimed to win over the German worker inveigled by Jewish Marxism and Communism, was unprecedented in its bitterness and claimed many lives [*Blutopfer*]. The NSDAP proved by overcoming purely biological and political set-backs that it was a living movement of the people [*Volksbewegung*]. By taking over power and forming the German Reich it showed that *völkisch* thinking is the irresistible creative force of the German people.[. . .]

The first years of the German renewal were characterized by a concerted Jewish attack on Germany. Hardly ever before in the history of Jewry had it showed its supranational solidarity as forcibly as now. Not only the emigrants, but also the Jewry resident in America, England, and France, tried to shut Germany out economically. The world economic consequences of this boycott[30] especially hit industries outside Germany, so that its effects, at first severe, soon wore off, particularly since Germany was intent on becoming self-sufficient in a number of areas. While in the Reich Jewry can be considered totally excluded and has no decisive influence on any area of national life, its unremitting fight against Germany has opened the eyes of foreign peoples against it. Anti-Jewish initiatives have sprung up everywhere. Their success depends on a variety of factors prevailing in individual countries. However, racial awareness, whose cultivation is the best remedy against Jewry, has grown to a greater or lesser extent in all countries, so that it is inconceivable that this world movement will lose its momentum.

[Editorial introduction (anon.) to *Theodor Fritsch, Handbuch der Judenfrage* (Hammerverlag: Leipzig, 1937; 41st edn.), 15–17.]

HEINRICH HIMMLER

78   The Divine Mission of the SS

Heinrich Himmler (1900–45) studied agriculture and was an early convert to what would be called Nordic Thinking (see Text 64) and its obsession with the need to safeguard the peasantry, breed a new German super-race, and destroy the 'subhuman' forces which stood in its way. Appointed Reichsführer of the SS (originally Hitler's bodyguard, but independent since 1925), he deliberately built it up into a 'para-state' and paramilitary force which would embody the ideal qualities of the race. As head of the SS and of the German Police from 1936, Himmler created the enormous terror apparatus which would eventually run the Gestapo, the concentration camps, and the extermination system. His Catholic

---

[30] i.e. the world Depression.

upbringing may help partly account for his zealous sense of mission, which is reflected in
this extract, one of countless examples of how readily fascism perverted religious language.

The Law of Honour of the SS-Man

In a slim volume called *50 Questions and Answers for the SS-Man* the first question is:
'What is your oath?' The answer is: 'We swear to you, Adolf Hitler, loyalty and
bravery as leader and chancellor of the German Reich. We vow to you and to the
principles laid down by you obedience to the point of death. So help us God!'
The second question is: 'Thus you believe in a God?' The answer is: 'Yes, I believe
in a Lord God.'
The third question is: 'What do you think of a person who does not believe in a
God?' The answer is: 'I consider him arrogant, stupid, and a megalomaniac; he is
not suited for us.'

I have reminded you of these three questions and answers in order to make our
attitude to religion completely clear. Be in no doubt that we would not be able to
be this body of men bound by a solemn oath if we did not have the firm belief in a
Lord God who rules over us, who has created us and our Fatherland, our people
and this earth, and who sent us our leader.

We have the holy conviction that according to the eternal laws of this world we
are accountable for every deed, for every word, and every thought, that nothing
our mind thinks up, our tongue speaks, and our hand does is completed with the
act itself, but is a cause which will have its effect, which in an inevitable, inexorable
cycle redounds on ourselves and our people in the form of a blessing or curse.
Believe me, men with this conviction are anything but atheists.

Blood and Soil

There is a second declaration I would like to make to you, German peasants, as SS
Reichsführer, being myself in ancestry, blood, and nature a peasant: the blood
principle which has always been embodied in the Schutzstaffel from the very
beginning would be condemned to death if it were not inextinguishably bound up
with the belief in the value and holiness of the soil.[. . .] I can assure you it is no
coincidence if the National Peasant Leader [*Reichsbauernführer*][31] of the German
Reich has for years been an SS leader and, as Chief Section Leader [*Obergruppen-
führer*], is head of the SS Race- and Settlement Office, just as it is no coincidence that
I am a peasant and belong to the Reichs Peasant Council [*Reichsbauernrat*].[. . .]

Bolshevism is No Transitory Phenomenon

I return to my starting-point and would like to stress once more that we do not see
Bolshevism as a transitory phenomenon which can be simply debated out of
existence or eliminated with wishful thinking. We know the Jew all too well, this

---

[31] i.e. Darré.

race which has been compounded from the dregs of all the peoples and nations of this planet and on which he has stamped his Jewish racial character [*Blutsart*], who takes pleasure in destruction, whose will is to annihilate, whose religion is godlessness, whose idea is Bolshevism. We do not underestimate him because we have known him for centuries; we do not underestimate him because we believe in the divine mission of our people and in our strength which has been renewed through the leadership and work of Adolf Hitler.

The Schutzstaffel

We, the Schutzstaffel, have been formed and grown within our newly resurrected people on the command of the Führer.[. . .] We have formed ranks, and now, obeying unalterable laws, march as a National Socialist order of soldiers infused with a Nordic sensibility [. . .] into a distant future. We believe we will be not just the grandchildren who fought the fight more resolutely, but also the ancestors of later generations necessary for the eternal life of the German and Germanic people.

[*Die Schutzstaffel als antibolschewistische Kampforganisation* [The SS as an Anti-Bolshevist Fighting Organization], Hier spricht Deutschland, 30 (Zentralverlag der NSDAP/Franz Eher: Munich, 1937), 27–31.]

WILLI F. KÖNITZER

79 The Role of Youth in Perpetuating the Third Reich

In 1938 the National Book Prize was awarded to a collection of poems written anonymously by members of Austrian sections of the Hitler Youth and published under the title Das Lied der Treuen *[The Song of the Faithful]. The symbolic value of these poems in the year of Austria's annexation (which had been promptly renamed Ostmark, a term still in vogue among some neo-Nazis today) is stressed in this propagandist piece in the Party press which brings together several key aspects of Nazism's 'civic religion': the Führer, militarism, German culture, the national community, and youth. Youth organizations had made an important contribution to the pre-Nazi völkisch movement, and now played a major role in ensuring a steady flow of ideologically sound recruits to positions within the Third Reich.*

The figure of Adolf Hitler, himself a wonderful embodiment of the union of politician with artist, impresses itself on German youth as a binding model for how to give shape to the totality of their lives. And thus a symbolic power of the volume of poetry awarded the National Book Prize lies in the fact that it was written for the German people by the youth which bears the Führer's name and who live in the newest German province.

Whatever strengthened faith and hope during the political struggle, and whatever attracted the gaze of active longing from the Ostmark towards the Reich of Adolf Hitler, found immortal expression in these poems. Can there be a more valid proof of the unity of the people, of the emergence of the new German man than the fact that the political commitment of the youth does not make them estranged from or indifferent to artistic experience, but rather causes them to express in poetic language everything which fulfils them and spurs them on to make that commitment? [. . .]

The education for Germany, which is organized by the Hitler Youth itself in accordance with the Führer's will that 'Youth must be led by youth', necessarily embraces the whole of a youth's existence. Certainly it is an education in developing a martial bearing. But here as everywhere else the example of the Führer makes any objections that might be raised invalid: a martial bearing, worlds removed from the military drill of a bygone age, does not exclude the love of art, but is what gives it its deeper meaning.

And just as the Hitler Youth is neither a league for pre-military training, nor a sports club, so it has no room, either, for the cultivation of a separate youth culture in musical groups and Hitler Youth Choirs, in literary clubs and theatrical societies. Whatever is happening within the new German youth happens exclusively in compliance with that great and unalterable law: the commitment to the Führer is the commitment to Germany.

This commitment is fulfilled in the forming of the young German in his totality, just as much in a physical and intellectual direction as in the cultivation of a spiritual sensibility and his education in the correct appreciation and evaluation of artistic achievement. The German people has become great in the eyes of the whole world through its impressive cultural achievements. Germans of the future, as they grow up as Pfimpf and Hitler Youth or as Jungmädel and members of the Bund Deutscher Mädel,[32] must be educated to recognize German cultural values and the duty to uphold them, and to feel awe for the creative powers of the German people's soul [deutsche Volkseele] which will ensure that its culture will be preserved.[. . .]

Thus the goals of the cultural work carried out by the Hitler Youth remain conditioned by political needs: the political education of the German in the National Socialist sense is to be conceived as a unity of thinking, feeling, willing, and action, one which will determine the face of the Third Reich, the lines which compose the picture of the future Germany.

['Die Hitlerjugend als Träger kulturpolitischer Aufgaben,' [The Hitler Youth as the carrier of new values], *Nationalsozialistiche Monatsschriften*, 4/39 (June 1938), 500–14.]

HELMUTH LANGENBUCHER

80 **The Successful Cleansing of German Culture**

This editorial introduction to an anthology of 'healthy' poems (which includes the one by Stefan George cited as Text 49) registers the success of the regime in creating the impression among ultra-nationalist intellectuals that society had now been purged of 'decadent' art. It

---

[32] References to the all-embracing Nazi youth organizations for young Germans of both sexes.

also underlines how indissociable beauty had become from racial principles for Nazis. Here the term 'cleansing' (Säuberung) is used in a way which predates by more than half a century the connotations of ethnic persecution and calculated atrocities it was to acquire in the Yugoslav Civil War. Indeed the whole passage can be seen as an exercise in the euphemism with which the regime systematically mystified its barbarism.

For the second time since the appearance of my *Volkhafte Dichtung der Zeit* in 1933 a new edition has become necessary. Reflecting on the way and extent to which the new edition should be modified persuaded me that the book needed a completely new form. The tasks which this volume has to fulfil today have changed since 1933. Then it was appropriate to establish the broad outlines of a new way of evaluating and presenting literary life. It was appropriate to indicate clearly the un-German manifestations of a past age which had laid claim to an intolerable degree of influence over the spiritual life of the German people. Its primary concern was to prepare the way for a general appreciation of those poets in whose works the life of the German people in all its radiant aspects has been turned into images and symbols.

Now, more than four years after the decisive change which German life experienced on 30 January 1933, the criteria and principles which had to be fought for then have penetrated the general spiritual awareness of the nation. It has long since become self-evident to the overriding majority of the German people that the norms which determine and shape our political life since 1933 must also, through a deep inner necessity, affect the whole spiritual and artistic life of the present and future of our people.

This development, for which we must thank the cleansing of German cultural life from all distortions alien to its nature [*artfremd*], a process which gathered irresistible momentum after 1933 and is now complete, has also created in the sphere of literary life those lucid, healthy relationships which alone make it possible for the work of everyone active in the creation or mediation of art to be meaningful.[. . .] I have thus been able to limit myself to drawing attention to the new principles of aesthetic presentation and judgement in the way I have described the contemporary artistic life of our people, principles which in the first version of my book I had to demand future literary criticism to adopt, since at the time they were familiar to a relatively small proportion of editors.

> [Foreword to *Volkhafte Dichtung der Zeit* [Contemporary Poetry Reflecting the Nature of our People] (Junker und Dünnhaupt: Berlin, 1937; 1st edn. 1933), ii.]

MARTIN HEIDEGGER

81 National Socialism as the Custodian of European Being

There has been much scholarly debate about how far the zealous endorsement which Martin Heidegger (1889–1976) gave to the new regime as rector of Freiburg University from May 1933 to April 1934 should affect assessments of his significance as a philosopher. His Introduction to Metaphysics, *written at a time of growing disillusionment with Nazism, was republished without modification in 1953. Such texts suggest that Heidegger's existentialism was inseparable from a philosophy of history which saw the contemporary age in terms of the erosion of authentic Being [Dasein], which he treated as dependent on suprapersonal cultural forces. This predisposed him to look for signs of a cultural revolution which was the precondition for the rebirth of Being. Heidegger then projected this typically fascist longing for a metapolitical renewal onto the Third Reich till he realized that it was not the vehicle for the type of revolution he wanted. His critiques of the mass media society and dreams of an 'existentially' sound Fortress Europe continue to exert an influence on European neo-fascists today, especially within the so-called New Right (see Text 195).*

Is 'Being' a mere word and its meaning utterly nebulous, or is it the spiritual destiny of the Occident?

This Europe, which is always in the process of tearing itself apart out of utter blindness, lies today in the great pincer-grip formed by Russia on the one hand and America on the other. Seen metaphysically, Russia and America are both the same: the same desolate frenzy of unbounded technology and of the unlimited organization of the average human being. Once the furthermost corner of the globe has been technologically conquered and opened up to economic exploitation, when every possible event in every possible place at every possible time has become as accessible as quickly as possible, when people can 'experience' an attempt on the life of a king in France and a symphony concert in Tokyo simultaneously, when time has become only speed, instantaneousness, and simultaneity, and time as History has disappeared from the existence of all peoples, when the boxer is seen as the great man of a people, when mass gatherings running into millions are regarded as a triumph—then, yes, then, the questions which hover over this whole grotesque charade like ghosts are: for what?—where to?—and what then?

The spiritual decay of the earth is so advanced that peoples risk exhausting that reserve of spiritual force which enables them just to see and take stock of this decay (in respect of the destiny of 'Being'). This simple observation has nothing to do with cultural pessimism: for in every corner of the world the darkening of the world, the flight of the gods, the destruction of the earth, the massification of man, the contemptuous suspicion of everything which is creative and free, have reached such proportions that such childlike expressions as pessimism and optimism have long become laughable.

We lie in a pincer-grip. As the people placed at the centre we experience the hardest pressure, as the people with the most neighbours we are most at risk, and on top of this we are the most metaphysical people. But this people will only be able to forge a destiny out of its fate if it first creates in *itself* a resonance, some possibility of a resonance, of this fate and achieves a creative understanding of its tradition. What all this involves is that this people as a historical people projects itself and thereby the history of the West from the core of its future development into the original realm of the forces of Being. If the great verdict on Europe is not to be reached on its road to annihilation, then it can only be reached because of the unfolding of new historically *spiritual* forces from the centre.[. . .]

In order to underpin values which have been raised to the level of a moral imperative, the values themselves are attributed Being. But in this context Being *basically* means no more than the presence of what exists. Only that what is meant is not as crude and palpable as tables and chairs. Once values are endowed with Being the high-point of confusion and rootlessness has been arrived at. However, since the expression 'value' is gradually coming to sound hackneyed, especially since it still plays a role in economic theory, values are now called 'totalities'. In 1928 there appeared the first volume of a complete bibliography of the concept value; 661 works concerning the concept of value are cited. They have presumably grown to a thousand by now. This is all called philosophy. What today is systematically touted as the philosophy of National Socialism, but which has nothing in the least to do with the inner truth and greatness of this movement (namely the encounter of a globally determined technology with the man of the new age), darts about with fish-like movements in the murky waters of these 'values' and 'totalities'.

[*Einführung in die Metaphysik* (Max Niemeyer Verlag: Tübingen, 1987; 1st edn. 1935), 28–9, 151–2.]

CHRISTOPH STEDING
....

82   The Third Reich as the Cure for the European Sickness

In the 1920s Christoph Steding (1903–38) studied widely in the humanities and social sciences in a number of 'Nordic' countries, supported in doing so by a grant from the Rockefeller Foundation. The fruit of this sustained bout of eclecticism was a vast opus on the state of European society and culture from which this extract was taken. The book so impressed Reinhard Heydrich, head of SS Security (Sicherheitsdienst) that he brought it to the attention of Himmler. Both found in it a detailed rationalization of the vision of a healthy 'Germanic' empire which could be created by the Nazis once the destruction of liberal democracy was complete, and which would act as the heartland of a vast European empire. Steding died in early 1938 of kidney disease, and thus was spared seeing his dream of a Greater Germanic Reich begin to be realized, only for it to be destroyed at the hands of the liberal and communist forces he so despised.

It goes without saying that in the aftermath of this decomposition [*Zersetzung*] of the Germanic-Nordic substance within Europe, the forcing up to the surface of wild, demonic, ruthless, bestially savage primordial forces should be seized on as an ideal opportunity to Jews, who had taken no stake in the history of our continent. They seized their chance as part of the active vanguard of Bolshevism, particularly in Russia, but in the German Reich as well, whether as advocates of tepid democracy or of the purely mercenary capitalism of the stock exchange. The result in both cases is the same. The precondition for the possibility of Jewry to infiltrate has been yet again the inner Semitization [*Verjudung*] of Europe itself which was an inevitable consequence of the decay of the German Reich: for at that point Europe becomes stripped of its history, and racial components which predominate in Jews as well, such as upper-Baltic ones, gain ascendancy.

Thus the enemy today stands right in the heart of Europe, as he threatens to arise in every European.[. . .]

It is of deep symbolic significance that the foundation of the Second Reich took place in Versailles.[. . .] Not only was the 'arch-enemy' conquered, but with it the disorder spreading out since 1789 from France as the well-spring of European anarchy. Hence even in terms of domestic politics the victory of 1870–1[33] was a victory over the destructive tendencies of the forces of social democracy and liberalism which were then gaining influence.

The Third Reich too originated in 'Versailles'. The attempt made there at the total destruction of the Reich and Europe spurred Germany to gather all its healthy forces and dig clear from the rubble in which it was buried the true substance of our part of the world.[. . .]

The process of the renewal of Europe which is spreading from the centre, from Germany, is in the first instance an affair of domestic politics.[. . .] But the higher historical right of Germans lies in the fact that restoring the health of the political organizations of Central Europe [*Mitteleuropa*] necessarily involves a simultaneous recovery of Europe as a whole.[. . .] And even if the renewal of Europe emanating from German in no way means violating or redrawing the state borders of Switzerland, Denmark, or France (as happened under Bismarck), the kingdom of Hanover, etc., the process of filling the vacuum of Central Europe and definitively rescinding the Westphalian Peace as well as the Versailles Treaty means a total shift in the status quo.[. . .]

Our topic involves investigating the relationship of the old, still pre-Bismarckian, and decidedly pre-Hitlerian Europe to the new Europe forged by Bismarck and Hitler. It thus essentially means the portrayal of a decaying world. It is a diagnosis, a diagnosis of the symptoms of what is to be seen as a disease. Where the old Europe, though afflicted by a 'mortal illness' and declining rapidly, is still regarded as the basis of existence, the analysis we have put forth will necessarily be read as a 'critique'. The diagnosis of an illness is a critique, since something can only be diagnosed as an illness where there is knowledge about what combats illness and eradicates it, namely health, and where this is seen as something close to hand and readily restorable: the quintessence of the health of Europe is the Reich.[. . .]

Only from the perspective of a world which is healing and is renewing itself is it possible for this investigation to diagnose the old world of Europe as terminally ill, and thus indirectly to point to the road to a full recovery.

[*Das Reich und die Krankheit Europas* [The Reich and the Sickness of Europe]
(Hanseatische Verlagsanstalt: Hamburg, 1938), 13–28.]

---

[33] In the Franco-Prussian War.

iii. The Third Reich at War 1939–1945

PAUL HERRE

83 **The New European Order**

This article from the NSDAP monthly, Nationalsozialistische Monatsschriften, illustrates the orthodox version of the war presented to the German public before the invasion of Russia in June 1941, namely that it was a war originally forced on Hitler by international Jewish capitalism, but had been transformed into a heroic mission to rescue Europe from chaos and create a new order. There is a close parallel between the portrayal of France and England, allies in both world wars, as the egoistic defenders of a balance of power designed to preserve their imperialist interests, and Fascist Italy's attack on them as 'plutocratic nations'. As we have seen (Text 41), the myth of the war as a crusade against an alleged Jewish world conspiracy to undermine national 'blood communities' was now being peddled by the Fascists as well. What still gives such passages a specifically Nazi tone is the reference to the peculiar historical role of the Holy Roman Empire (Reich) as a role model for a European stability based once more on a Mediterranean and Central European hegemonic nation, a myth which is closely bound up with that of Germany as the geographical and cultural heart of Europe (cf. 49, 81, 82).

History therefore demanded that the subjugated German people, whose suppression flew in the face of reason and was the main cause of the growing disorder in Europe, should take over its leadership through the imposition of a true order.[. . .] Adolf Hitler and his National Socialist movement became the vehicle through which the work of bringing into existence a new Germany and a new Europe could begin.[. . .]

Its basis was the creation of the German national community [*Volksgemeinschaft*] which was no longer the sum of Germans living within the state borders, but the German people rooted in race, soil, and history, and freed from all divisions and scission. In view of the fragmentation [*Zerreißung*] of the German people and the loss of large and valuable parts of it to states alien or hostile to Germany, the concept of national culture [*Volkstum*] prevailed over that of nation-state. Thus from out of the depths of the German soul and the German blood community the idea of a Greater Germany [*die großdeutsche Idee*] rose up to live again, and inextinguishably linked to it the old concept of the Reich as the ordering principle of the Central European area.[. . .]

The European unity which had enjoyed democratic favour, and which was nothing other than the domination of British and French imperialism, camouflaged behind hollow and misleading slogans, broke down, and the principle of nationalism, which had been crushed underfoot but which had become the central axiom of Europe and the foundation of any European order, gained ground again. In its wake the principle of vital space [*Lebensraum*] reasserted itself. This had been the foundation of the German–Italian alliance of 22 May 1939,[34] and laid the basis for

---

[34] The Pact of Steel.

the creation of an Italian empire in the Mediterranean and the Great German Reich in the heart of the continent. European history had returned to its starting-point.

But this meant a situation which was incompatible both with France's nationalist ambitions in Europe and England's claims to act as its arbiter, and once again these two made a pact to turn a critical phase in historical development to their advantage. They would fight an 'ultimate war', one intended to bring about the eternal destruction of Germany, so as to force those fighting for a true European community of existence to submit to their egoistic goals of domination.[. . .] Trusting their superiority, England and France, in league with world capitalism and world Jewry, rejected the repeated proposals for reconciliation put forward by Adolf Hitler and imposed war on Germany.

But events have taken a different turn. In the very midst of the struggle with the British arch-enemy a new Europe is arising, and the remarkable thing is that its formation is taking place without England. After long detours the principle of European order is finally being realized.

['Wesen und Wandel der europäischen Ordnung' [The nature and transformation of the European order], *Nationalsozialistiche Monatsschriften*, 12/131 (Feb. 1941), 140–3.]

HANS S. V. HEISTER

84 A National Socialist Common Market

The quick succession of military victories by the Wehrmacht from 1939 to 1941 fomented intense speculation at a high level of Nazi forward planning about the New European Order which would result from the seemingly inevitable Axis victory (see Herzstein 1982). Some of this speculation centred on the prospect of some sort of fascist Economic Community, as in this passage, which is interesting on two counts: (i) the contradiction in terms of Europe's national economies being geared to autarky (self-reliance) and yet collaborating with the Reich; (ii) the wishful thinking or euphemism of reading into Hitler's words the idea that the New European Order was aimed at securing the prosperity of any nation other than Germany itself. Apart from neutrals (like Spain) and allies (like Italy), some countries (like France) would be mercilessly exploited for their economic value while enjoying a certain measure of autonomy in their administration. On the other hand, those deemed to be inhabited by racially inferior grades of humanity (like Poland), would have even less autonomy and be run essentially as colonies suitable only for pillage, expropriation, and enslavement. Meanwhile, the Third Reich would see to it that the whole of its new empire would be systematically purged of those unfit to live according to the principles of 'racial politics' outlined in Text 85.

Recently the Nordic Society has brought out a bulletin entitled 'Economics in the New Europe'. It includes an excellent anthology of articles and lectures mostly by leading figures in the Ministry of Economics.[. . .]

Gauleiter and *Oberpräsident* Heinrich Lohse quoted the striking words of the Führer at the Party Rally held in Nuremberg in September 1939. He said:

In principle the German national economy [*Volkswirtschaft*] is organized in such a way that it can stand on its own feet at any time, completely independent of other countries. This has been achieved. Any thought of a blockade of Germany can now be safely set aside as a completely ineffective weapon. Using its own resources the National Socialist state has drawn the necessary consequences from the experiences of the world war. And we will continue to adhere to the principle that we prefer to accept restrictions in a particular area if necessary rather than become dependent on foreign countries. Above all the resolve which will dictate our economic practice will always be: the security of the nation outweighs all other considerations. Its economic existence is thus to be fully guaranteed materially on the basis of our way of life and of our need for vital space. For only in this way will the German army always be in a position to protect the freedom and interests of the Reich.

What these words of the Führer mean is thus that the autarkic economic system is the foundation of every genuine *völkisch* and national economy, and that it is only in conjunction with this system that the European macro-regional economy [*Grossraumwirtschaft*] can be built up as the complement and consolidation of the living-standards achieved through the individual national European economies once geared to the autarky principle. It is in this way that, within the common vital space of the European family of peoples, a collaboration of the national economies in Europe based on comradeship and partnership will be fostered for the common good of all concerned, as far as it is compatible with the preservation of their individuality and independence.

['Wirtschaft im neuen Europa' [Economy in the new Europe], *Nationalsozialistische Monatsschriften*, 12/136 (July 1941), 629–31.]

WALTER GROSS
....

85 Improving the Stock

From 1933 Walter Gross (1904–45) directed the Office for Education in Demographic Politics and Maintenance of the Race before it was absorbed by the NSDAP Office for Racial Policy a year later. His 1943 book Die rassenpolitischen Voraussetzungen zur Lösung des Rassenproblems *[The Racial-Political Premises for the Solution of the Racial Question] was a major exercise in rationalizing the Holocaust. However, in this article written two years earlier he is legitimating the 'Euthanasia Action' which had started in the autumn of 1939 and which led to well over 100,000 ethnic Germans classified as having 'lives unworthy of being lived' [lebensunwertes Leben] being murdered before it was slowed down in August 1941, partly as a result of protests by the Catholic Church. The article is significant because of the explicit link it makes between the euthanasia programme and the genocidal war to be carried out against the Jews within the context of racial politics. The reference to 'the definitive elimination' (the 'Ausscheidung' of a parasite can only mean physical destruction) of European Jews after the war is less euphemistic than the phrase 'total solution to the Jewish question' used by Goering in an order to Heydrich in July 1941, or the term 'Final Solution' which covered the plan for systematic genocide agreed at the Wannsee Conference held in January 1942 (while the war was still on). However, it is still less explicit than Hitler's prophecy of 'the extermination of the Jewish race in Europe' made in the Reichstag speech of 30 January 1939, several months before the war broke out.*

It is understandable that the so-called negative measures of racial hygiene, namely ones to eradicate defective elements, have always been at the centre of public interest. They are the easier ones to carry out in practical terms, but they attracted all the more attention because they seemed to conflict with the humanitarian and Christian belief in the need to make everything uniform irrespective of differences, and thus provoked particularly violent conflicts of political principles and world-views. There is the deepest imaginable gulf in outlook on life dividing us from the mentality which accorded every living creature as one of their supposed 'human rights' the right to procreation, even where the unfortunate results of this attitude could only live at the cost of their own distress and as a burden to, or even to the detriment of, society as a whole. For now our greater sense of responsibility means that we recognize it as a duty to the community to take decisions in this area too, and make procreation impossible in cases where it would only mean suffering, misery, and damage. The years which have passed since our movement took power have witnessed, and not only in Germany, the triumph of the new way of thinking. The once so vociferous dissent has fallen silent, and we are approaching with giant strides the moment where no one in the whole world will understand how only a short time before anyone could have basically thought any differently about this issue than the way prescribed by racial hygiene.

As far as the reasons for the prevention of procreation are traceable to serious hereditary diseases which can be medically established, German legislation on the prevention of progeny suffering from hereditary disease is exemplary. It stands out from the efforts made by other countries in this area for the lucidity and pragmatism which makes sterilization dependent on a legally specified medical diagnosis, one that takes no account of biologically speaking totally irrelevant factors such as economic situation, etc.[. . .]

Apart from the question of mental deficiency, the problem which still remains unresolved in the sphere of eradicatory [*ausmerzende*] racial hygiene is that of the so-called anti-social elements [*Asoziale*] or social misfits [*Gemeinschaftsunfähige*]. By this is meant that group of human beings who, without being actually criminal, never secure useful employment, even though they are completely equipped physically and mentally to do so. There is, for example, the type of professional vagabond who lives on hand-outs and petty thieving, avoiding every form of regular work and basically scrounging for a living. The records of town halls and social service offices contain shattering statistics about the sums of money squandered on this category, and at the same time about the high fertility rate that usually characterizes it.[. . .]

In principle the promotion of the purity of one's own race and its protection against the infiltration of alien races is a vital requirement of *völkisch* politics for *all* peoples and races, and extends beyond the Jewish problem.[. . .]

But in this context the problem posed by Jewry acquires a twofold significance. For a long time it constituted the only serious threat to European peoples and thus was for practical purposes largely identical with the racial problem itself. Beyond this it has become the immediate cause for a concern with questions of race and racial politics, and opened the way to fundamental insights which, even after the Jewish danger has been overcome, will be part of the tools and arsenal of truly German politics for ever more.

On the other hand the Jewish problem exhibits peculiarities which distinguish it profoundly from all present or future conflicts in the sphere of racial politics. Jewry has not confronted the European peoples as a distinctive ethnic group, but behind the deceitful mask of supposed assimilation; it has not begun to have contact with other peoples from a base in its own State, but infiltrated them and extensively conquered them as a homeless parasite people. Finally, true to its character and its historical development, it espoused the corrupting doctrine of the Communist International and of universal equality, and, as a global élite working in secret, practically secured domination over finance, over the dominant ideology [*Zeitgeist*], and finally over the politics of numerous states, which eventually had to pay for this development with two wars, with pointless economic destruction, and the grotesque mask of Bolshevism.

This explains the very special form which the defence against Jewry has taken, one which corresponds to the uniqueness of its historical manifestation and its guilt. The zeal with which Germany broke Jewish domination, the ruthless thoroughness with which the definitive elimination [*endgültige Ausscheidung*] of this parasitic foreign body from Europe will be pursued after the war, is not to be explained by the principles of National Socialist racial politics in themselves, but by the enormous suffering which the Jewish people has brought on mankind, and by the necessity to make any repetition of this baleful course of events impossible for all time.

['Grundfragen nationalsozialistischer Rassen und Bevölkerungspolitik' [Basic issues in National Socialist racial and demographic policy], *Nationalsozialistische Monatsschriften*, 12/137 (Aug. 1941), 661–6.]

JOSEPH GOEBBELS
....

86   **The True Meaning of the War**

Goebbels wrote this euphemistic justification of the Second World War and the mass atrocities it involved in the summer of 1942, when the illusion of the Third Reich's invincibility had still not been shattered. Germany invaded Russia in June 1941, and Bolshevism is once again portrayed as the offshoot of (Jewish) plutocracy, just as it was before the Ribbentropp Pact allied the two countries in August 1939. The appeal to Social Darwinian principles of 'might is right' is conflated with two other typical fascist themes, the inexorability of destiny, and the sense of historical watershed. The passage is also significant because it registers a shadow falling across the war, the sense that victory, while inevitable, is no longer imminent. In December 1941 the USA had joined the war, and the allied bombing of German cities was intensifying as Goebbels wrote. Before long the Wehrmacht would experience its first reversals in North Africa and Russia, and the shadows would grow ever longer and darker.

We are rapidly approaching the end of the third year of this war which was forced upon us. It has reached a degree of extension in space and protraction in time which very few could foresee when it broke out. The relatively insignificant issue surrounding the German city of Danzig and the need for a corridor through the corridor[35] has grown into a struggle between continents, a world war in the true sense of the word, which will decide the fate of entire peoples.

Whereas at first people only saw the immediate catalyst, now they can see the underlying cause: rich peoples, led by a refined and insatiable plutocracy and its most radical offshoot, Bolshevism, overloaded with territorial possessions and raw resources, have forced the German people along with the Axis powers to take up arms to decide the vital issue of whether in future we will have an adequate basis for our national life, or even lose the completely insufficient basis for this which we already possessed.[. . .]

The division of the earth is not ordained by God, but is decided by human beings. It can be changed at any time. It is simply a question of power, not morality. Our enemies can afford to be pious, because they have in abundance what they need for life. Once they took this too, not out of piety, but by force. Now they possess everything and we possess nothing.[. . .]

On occasion the peaceful evolution of a continent is interrupted by the stormy epochs when something new is constructed. At this point the earth is convulsed by seismic tremors which usher in a new birth amidst the most terrible labour pains.[. . .]

Every birth brings pain. But amid the pain there is already the joy of a new life. It is a sign of sterility to shy away from new life on account of the pain.[. . .] Our age too is an act of historical birth, whose pangs carry with them the joy of richer life to come. The significance of the war has grown as its scale has increased. It is relentlessly at work, shattering old forms and ideas, and directing the eyes of human beings to new, greater objectives. Think where we stood at the outbreak of war, and where we stand now! We are following the path assigned to us and cannot turn back or deviate from it. We must carry on marching towards the goal whose outlines can be made out ever more clearly in the distant haze.[. . .]

In an age which like never before offers us the choice between the highest fortune and deepest catastrophe of our Reich, we stand firm as a people, determined and ready to work and fight so as to fulfil the ultimate meaning of the war.

['Vom Sinn des Krieges' [On the meaning of the war], in *Das eherne Herz. Reden und Aufsätze aus den Jahren 1941/2* [The Brazen Heart: Speeches and Essays from the Years 1941/2] (Zentralverlag der NSDAP/Franz Eher: Munich, 1943), 436–42.]

[35] The Nazi violation of the 'Polish corridor' created by the Peace Settlement after the First World War to guarantee Poland access to the sea at Danzig (Gdansk) was a major step towards the outbreak of the Second World War.

87 The Ultimate Turning-Point: Total War

Ley wrote the pamphlet from which this extract is taken in early 1943, when his preeminence as leader of the Labour Front (see Text 75) had been eclipsed by the ruthless efforts of Todt, Sauckel, and Speer to place the country's economy and industry on a war-footing. Undaunted, he attempted to retain his influence through propaganda speeches such as this. Since the traumatic defeat of the Sixth Army at Stalingrad in January, the themes of the Wehrmacht's omnipotence under Hitler's leadership, and of the imminence of final victory, have given way in propaganda to evocations of the titanic fight to the death in which the German Schicksalsgemeinschaft (Community of Destiny) was now engaged. Hence the stoic tone of Ley's call for total war (a reference to the key phrase of Goebbels' famous do or die 'Sports Palace speech' of February 1943). The passage still testifies to the alchemical power of palingenetic myth to metamorphose catastrophe into triumph and despair into hope, at least at the level of rhetoric.

The moral front of the war experienced a decisive turning-point at the end of 1942 and the beginning of 1943. We National Socialists knew that the people we had become by 1939 was different from that of 1914. The work of the Party had borne fruit. From out of the chaos of the earlier bourgeois and Marxist parties, of trade unions and associations, there had grown up a unified and concerted national community.[. . .] National Socialist Germany no longer had political parties, it only had one party, which was called Germany and was borne along by a single will and faith, united behind one flag, and led by one leader.

Thus it was that in 1939 we had every moral and political reason to enter the global struggle which had broken out convinced that victory was ours. How right we National Socialists were in our assumption was shown by the course of the first years of the war. With irresistible *élan* and inspired by National Socialist enthusiasm, our brave soldiers routed all opposition. Poland, Norway, Holland, Belgium, France, Yugoslavia, and Greece, as well as the English divisions which had established themselves on the Continent, were swept aside by the unprecedented assault of German battalions.[. . .]

Fate made the fight ever more arduous for us. It seemed almost as if it had duped us at first so that in the ecstasy of victory we might forget that whoever wants to achieve the ultimate goal and greatest achievements must commit his ultimate and greatest efforts. The winter of 1942/3 was relentless. The great onslaught against the Volga and Caucasus last year was equally perilous. No one could have reckoned with the inconceivably barbaric methods which Bolsheviks use to conduct war. Together this created severe blows at the end of 1942 and in early 1943 which only an Adolf Hitler could cope with: they took the majority of Germans by surprise. Certainly we National Socialists knew that the battle against the Jews would be uncompromising, and that only extreme tenaciousness and toughness could bring victory over Jewry. We had often experienced in the fierce brawls which broke out at meetings before we came to power just how mean, devious, and stubborn the

Jew can be. But even we had almost forgotten that the little man is always inclined to take the easy option. Thus even we National Socialists took the set-back at Stalingrad and the subsequent withdrawal to Rostov and Kharkov very badly. Our enemies were triumphant, small-minded bourgeois in Germany hung their heads, but the broad mass of the people looked to us, its leaders, and a powerful awakening galvanized the whole nation.[. . .]

Germany stood at the turning-point in its history and understood: Stalingrad is not the beginning of the German collapse, but the beginning of the unfolding of all the moral and spiritual forces of the German nation. Germany has awakened from its ecstasy at the triumphs of 1939, 1940, 1941, and 1942, the youth has become a man, victory celebrations and premature hopes have become resolve and hardness, nebulous notions have become an unconditional certainty. That was the greatest turning-point in German history: total war.

> ['Die moralische Front des deutschen Volkes und der totale Krieg' [The moral front of the German people and total war], in *Der Weg zum deutschen Sieg* [The Path to German Victory] (Zentralverlag der NSDAP: Munich, 1943), 18–21, 26–7.]

HEINRICH HIMMLER

88 **Moral Dilemmas**

By November 1943 the Nazi system for the mass production of atrocities and murders was in place in occupied Europe and undergoing continuous expansion and refinement. This passage from a speech given by the main architect of that system, Heinrich Himmler, offers some insight into the perverse logic of the Holocaust for its perpetrators: the need to defend the German race from the vengeance of a future generation of Jews meant that it was 'unjustifiable' not to kill women and children as well as men (he enlists the sympathy of his audience for this 'difficult' decision). It also shows how thoroughly the myth of the Jews' subhuman status has been internalized in Himmler and his listeners: he invites admiration for the way his extermination system has enabled those operating it to commit genocide without losing their humanity or being traumatized. Note the way the murderers are offered the vision of themselves as stoically suffering in silence for their people, and reassured that they were not responsible for the 'idea', but 'only' for the acts.

In this context and within this intimate circle I can refer to an issue which you, my fellow Party comrades, have all accepted as self-evident, but which has become for me the most difficult issue of my life, the Jewish issue. You all take it for granted as a self-evident and gratifying fact that there are no more Jews in your *Gau*. All Germans—with a few exceptions—are clear in their minds that we would not have held out against aerial bombardments and the pressures imposed by a fourth year of war, and maybe the fifth and sixth that lie in store, if we still had this plague destroying our people. The few words of the sentence 'the Jews must be exterminated' are easy to say. Yet for those who must carry out what it demands it is the hardest and most difficult thing there is. You see, of course they are Jews, it is obvious, they are only Jews, but think yourselves how many—even Party members—have made their famous request to me or some other authority stating that of course all Jews are swines, only that so-and-so is a decent Jew and should not be harmed.[. . .] In Germany we have so many millions of people each of whom knows decent Jews that this figure is already bigger than the actual number of Jews.[. . .]

I ask you really only to listen to what I have to say in this circle, and never to talk about it. The question has arisen: What about the women and children? I resolved to find an utterly clear solution for this as well. For I did not consider myself justified to eradicate the men—that means kill or have killed—and allow the avengers of their deaths to grow up in the form of the children and grandchildren. Thus the difficult decision had to be taken to make this people disappear from the face of the earth. For the organization which had to carry out this task it was the most difficult one we had ever had. It has been carried out—I believe I can say this—without inflicting damage on the minds and souls of our men and their leaders. The danger that it might was a real one. The path between the two possibilities of either being too cruel and heartless and losing respect for human life, or too soft and so suffering distress to the point of a nervous breakdown—the strait between this Scilla and Charybdis is narrow indeed.[. . .]

With these words I would like to close the issue of the Jews. You know the score and will keep what you know to yourselves. At a future point we will perhaps be able to consider whether to tell the German people more about this matter. I believe that it is better for us all to have endured this for our people, and accepted our responsibility (the responsibility for deeds not the idea behind them), and then take the secret with us to our graves.

> [Speech to *Gauleiter* in Posen (Poznań), Poland, 6 Nov. 1943, in Gerhard Grimm (ed.),
> *Der Nazionalsozialismus* (Günter Olzog: Munich/Vienna, 1981), 277–80; orig. repr. in
> *Heinrich Himmler. Geheimreden 1933–1945*, ed. Bradley F. Smith and Agnes Peterson
> (Propyläen: Berlin, 1974), 168–71.]

SCHWARZES KORPS

89 **Heimat**

The growing inevitability of defeat brought about a significant shift in the official myths offered to the German people. It was now, like the legendary Nibelungen, a heroic 'community of destiny and blood' fighting to the last against an enemy who was sadistically enjoying the opportunity to wipe out the superior German race, and prepared to sink to any depths of inhumanity (such as terror-bombing, mass executions) to do so. The propaganda film Kolberg, produced at vast material and military cost on Goebbels' orders, allegorically reinforces this stoic vision, so far removed from the triumphant mood of the first years of the regime. Nevertheless, as this text from the SS newspaper Das Schwarze Korps *[The Black*

Corps] shows, the underlying fascist vision of reality had not been in the least dented by the imminent collapse of the regime: Germans are assured that their heroism and self-sacrifice draw on the deepest well-springs of an organic German nation, and that the basic struggle is between health and decadence: misunderstood and victimized, Germany will go under nobly fighting for the sake of European civilization.

Where does the indestructible courage come from to look every new danger calmly in the eye so as to fight against it? What is the unquenchable source of the cold-bloodedness which tenses again and again nerves already taut to the point of breaking? [. . .] Let us say it. They carry in themselves, we all carry in ourselves the spring whose inexhaustible streams nourish our lives, which make us who we are, which form our individual, our unique existence. It is the same source on which our great masters drew when they created the immortal works which now form eternal monuments of our culture. From this ancient source of our blood streams the force which from the very beginning shaped the nature of German humanity. Whatever we perceive as German ways and customs, as German culture, as the German character and outlook on life, has its original home [*Heimat*] here. The Gothic cathedrals are just as much an expression of this character as the Trutz mountains in the German East, the hymns of Hölderlin, the Friedrician[36] military spirit, the fugues of Bach, and the unbreakable resilience of German infantrymen in the two world wars of this century.

The secret lies in unity. In the totality of life, in our way of seeing, conceiving, and experiencing life as an indivisible whole. Combat and the contemplative spirit are never opposites, but two poles of an identical and unique life. Wherever the dissecting intellect of the doubter creates division, the motherly power of the heart restores unity. The soldier hurling himself against the charging hordes of the enemy knows that there lies behind him a home which embraces everything which gives his life meaning: first and foremost father and mother, wife and child, bride and lover, but also the city, the village, the farm, the field, the meadow, the forest, the realm of childhood shrouded in the distant glow of memory, the old fairy-tales, perhaps a small poem which he once heard and whose words he forgot, but whose image stays with him, joy and pain, worries and pleasures as his heart encountered them: everything which has grown and has taken shape, the fruit of centuries and the seed of the future.[. . .]

This is the secret of German power. It is from the heart of Europe that all the streams have flowed which nourished the inner life of the continent. From the German feeling for life grew the works which endowed the culture of the West with its eternal features.[. . .]

How did an English newspaper put it recently? We should exterminate this generation of young fanatics, since every measure to convert them is useless.

What do they want to convert us to? To the speculative spirit of the shopkeeper and tradesman which made the world appear to Britain's sons as a business opportunity to be turned into money? To the Hollywood ideal of slick dancing teachers? To the robotic existence of the Soviet collective?

---

[36] Lit. pertaining to Frederick the Great, king of Prussia.

No, they know nothing of us. They know nothing of the compelling magic of German inwardness which promises us a richer, deeper life. No German can resist this magic, whatever his background or education. It is a magic which expresses itself in so many varied ways. To some in the quiet family circle, in a small allotment, in the fragrance of a flower. To others in silent meditation, in a book, a verse, a song. To others in great works of art, a Wagnerian opera, a classical play, a Bach concert.

All this makes up our rich, unique, and unrepeatable world. We have answered the call to defend it with our last drop of strength, with our nails and teeth if we have to. They really will have to exterminate us, for they can convert us to nothing else. But we believe that the power of German inwardness will enable us to pass even this test.

['Die Kraft von innen' [The power from within], *Das Schwarze Korps*, 11/4 (25 Jan. 1945); repr. in H. Heiber and H. von Kotze (eds.), *Querschnitte durch alte Zeiten und Zeitungen*, xii. *Das Schwarze Korps* (Scherz: Munich, 1968), 202.]

ADOLF HITLER

90 The Rebirth of National Socialism

In this extract from the last official words of the Führer (the full text can be found in another translation in Noakes and Pridham 1974: 677–9) the dividing-line between belief and propaganda, conviction and rhetoric, is as difficult to draw as ever: Hitler may well not have intended a war against England and America, but did he really think it had been caused by an international Jewish conspiracy? Did he feel anything at all for the millions of Germans whose lives had been shattered by the war (a question not even worth asking about the countless millions of 'enemy' lives his regime had systematically destroyed)? Is it conceivable that he felt any sense of solidarity with his armed forces, hundreds of thousands of whom died unnecessarily because of his refusal to surrender? What do seem to be irreducible constants in his world-view even in the hour of his death is an anti-Semitism so pathological that he can project his hatred beyond the grave, and a palingenetic temperament so deeply rooted that he looks forward to the rebirth of National Socialism from the ashes of the Third Reich, a rebirth which would be at bottom nothing other than his own reincarnation.

Over thirty years have passed since I made my modest contribution by volunteering to fight in the First World War which had been forced onto the Reich.

In these three decades I have been inspired in thought, deed, and life only by my love of and loyalty towards my people. These gave me the strength to take the most difficult decisions, decisions which no mortal has ever had to face before. In these three decades I have consumed my time, my strength, my health.

It is untrue that I or anyone else in Germany wanted war in 1939. It was wanted and provoked exclusively by those international statesmen who are either of Jewish descent or worked for Jewish interests.[. . .] Further, I never wanted that after the first wretched world war a second would come about against England, let alone

America. Centuries will pass, but out of the ruins of our cities and artistic monuments will arise renewed hate against the people who in the last analysis are responsible for everything, the one to which we owe everything: international Jewry and its helpers!

Three days before the outbreak of the German-Polish war I proposed a solution to the German-Polish problems—one on the lines adopted in the Saar region which was placed under international control. The fact that this proposal was made cannot be denied either. It was only rejected because those in high places wanted war, partly because of the business opportunities they hoped it would open up, and partly because they were spurred on by the propaganda campaign being waged by international Jewry.

I have never let there be any doubt about the fact that if the peoples of Europe are ever treated like so many blocks of shares in the hands of these international conspirators of finance and the money markets, then the people which is the true culprit for this fight to the death will be called to account: the Jews! Nor have I ever made any secret of the fact that this time we will not allow millions of European children of Aryan stock to starve to death, millions of grown up men to be killed, and hundreds of thousands of women and children to be bombed and burnt to death in the streets, without the true culprit having to atone for his guilt, albeit through more humane means.

After a six-year battle which one day will be recorded in history, despite all the set-backs, as the most glorious and courageous testimony of a people's will to live, I cannot separate myself from the city which is the capital of this Reich.[. . .] I have thus decided to remain in Berlin and there of my own free will to choose death in the moment that I believe the seat of the Führer and Chancellor itself can no longer be defended. I die with a joyful heart in view of the staggering deeds and achievements of our soldiers at the front, of our women at home, the achievements of our peasants and workers, and the historically unprecedented effort of the Youth which bears my name.[37]

That I express to them all my thanks from the bottom of my heart goes without saying, just as much as my wish that they should under no circumstances give up the fight on account of this, but carry on fighting against the enemies of the Fatherland wherever they may be, loyal to the creed of the great Clausewitz.[38] Out of the sacrifice of our soldiers and out of my own bond with them, which extends into death, the seed will be sown one way or another to produce the magnificent rebirth of the National Socialist movement and hence the creation of a true national community.

['Politisches Testament von Adolf Hitler', dictated 29 Apr. 1945, in *Joseph Goebbels. Tagebücher 1945. Die letzten Aufzeichnungen* [Joseph Goebbels, Diaries for 1945: Last Entries] (Hoffmann und Campe: Hamburg, 1977), 550–5.]

[37] The Hitler Youth, who, despite the tender years of many recruits, were extensively deployed as front-line troops in the defensive fighting in the last stages of the war.

[38] The Prussian officer Karl von Clausewitz (1780–1831) wrote *On War*, one of the seminal works on the tactics of modern warfare.

PART III

Abortive Fascisms 1922–1945

INTRODUCTION

The General Introduction to this volume has already set out the criteria which have been used to distinguish fascist from non-fascist movements. Accordingly Part III omits the many authoritarian and 'para-fascist' regimes so often referred to as fascist, especially by the left, such as Franco's Spain and Perón's Argentina. It also ignores the 'foreign' Fascist and Nazi groups which could be found wherever there were significant concentrations of expatriate Italians and Germans (which could be as far afield as the USA, Canada, and Australia). Similarly it takes no account of the essentially mimetic (and in the main negligible) fascist movements modelled on Fascism or Nazism which surfaced in the inter-war period in countries not referred to here, such as Iceland, the Netherlands, Sweden, Denmark, Poland, Czechoslovakia, and Switzerland, even if the Sudeten-German and Austrian Nazi groups came to have a major role on political events. As for other movements closely associated with fascism: the Austrian *Heimwehren* (home defence leagues) have been omitted because in the main they stopped short of full-blown fascism, allowing themselves to be absorbed by the para-fascist regime of Dollfuss and Schuschnigg. On the other hand, the Croatian Ustasha, though exhibiting profound analogies with fascism in its mythic dynamics and cult of violence, was an ultra-nationalist secessionist movement bent on (re-)creating Croatia and not regenerating it, so that it technically does not fall within our remit. For similar reasons the various forms of Flemish ultra-nationalism pursuing secession from Belgium and fusion with the Netherlands, though closely akin to fascism, are not covered here, nor are some army movements which occurred in inter-war Lebanon, India, China, and Japan, exhibiting the external features and ethos of fascist cadre movements, but without the goal of creating a radically new national order through a populist revolution.

What is left is a relatively small cluster of inter-war movements, clearly influenced by Fascism and Nazism, but exhibiting sufficiently original specimens of home-grown ideology to throw into stark relief fascism's central paradox. On the one hand it possesses a fundamental strength of any successful political ideology, that of mutability and adaptability: the core myth of national regeneration can produce any number of surface permutations appropriate to the unique political and historical conditions prevailing in particular national cultures from Finland to South Africa, from Chile to Japan. On the other hand, when the texts sampled here are evaluated for their bearing on the concrete historical events in which the movements which generated them were involved, what stands out is fascism's recurrent impotence to carry out the revolutionary transformation of the nation promised in its extravagant ideological pronouncements. All the movements sampled here were successfully marginalized, absorbed, or crushed by established state power, whether liberal or authoritarian. In the context of contemporary concerns about the 'resurgence of fascism' it is important to bear in mind that the 'normal state' of fascism is better illustrated by the movements sampled here, namely in the state of 'air' (utopian ideology) and 'liquid' (impotent or abortive movement), than in the 'solid' form it took as the official world-view of the Fascist and Nazi regimes.

Section A

European Fascisms

i. Britain

There was no truly British fascism in the inter-war period. Northern Ireland was living through the aftermath of the creation of the Irish Free State in December 1921, while Welsh and Scottish anti-English feeling was too weak to breed significant ultra-nationalist forms of secessionist politics. In England, however, the country's nineteenth-century hegemony as a superpower was already visibly declining, and there was no shortage of admirers for what Fascism or Nazism were doing for their country: Major John Barnes (Text 131) was one of many. Nor were individual initiatives lacking to launch a movement which would emulate them, such as the British Fascisti, the Imperial Fascist League, the National Workers' Party, and the National Socialist League. It was only Oswald Mosley's British Union of Fascists, formed in October 1932, which ever showed signs of developing into a mass movement, however. In the diffuse climate of historical crisis created throughout Europe by the ongoing consequences of the Depression and by the establishment of the Third Reich, BUF membership rose as high as 50,000 in 1934. The new movement also benefited for a time from the support or financial backing of some Establishment figures in England and later of Mussolini himself. Nevertheless, despite its high media profile and the fears of many thousands of militant anti-fascists, BUF membership declined rapidly after 1934 and the party remained successfully marginalized from mainstream political life in Britain.

The BUF's initial recruitment success enabled its founder and leader, Oswald Mosley (1896–1980), to create the rudiments of a nationwide organizational structure on Fascist lines. He was also a tireless formulator of the movement's political mission and vision (Texts 91, 92). Even in the face of declining support he made sure that the party's propaganda machine continued to pour out newspapers, pamphlets, and speeches heralding Britain's transformation into a single-party authoritarian regime based on corporative economics (Text 93) and a strongly technocratic ethos. It also came to uphold a narrowly racist and anti-Semitic concept of British citizenship, as well as being committed to connivance at Nazi and Fascist aggression in Europe and beyond as long as British imperial interests were safeguarded. Nor was the charismatic dimension of fascist politics neglected. The BUF deliberately cultivated an overtly militaristic and ritual style of campaigning, its uniforms, rallies (both banned in 1936), mass meetings, leader cult, and readiness to resort to violence typical of all genuinely fascist activism. Symptomatic of this aspect of the BUF were its marching songs, two of which are reproduced here (Text 94).

Mosley's efforts to regenerate Britain were aided by countless other ideologues and activists prepared to help the BUF or use it as the vehicle for their own revolutionary schemes. Two of the better known were A. K. Chesterton (Text 95) and William Joyce (Text 96), both of whose obsession with decadence from the outset embraced different versions of a virulent anti-Semitism, something which appears to have become a central theme of Mosley's thinking and hence of official BUF policy only once it had proved to attract a degree of populist support in the East End of London. By the time war broke out and top BUF members, including

Mosley, were interned, it had long since lost any credibility as a threat to parliamentary democracy (see Thurlow 1987).

91   Christ, Nietzsche, and Caesar

Mosley took fascist ideology very seriously, and was constantly elaborating and refining his version of it. Here he presents fascism as a triumphant synthesis of ideas (see Text 170) generally considered to be incompatible, yet endowed with a unique power to heal the divisions of modern society: Christianity, Nietzscheanism, and Spengler's doctrine of Caesarism (see Text 57).

Our opponents allege that Fascism has no historic background or philosophy, and it is my task this afternoon to suggest that Fascism has roots deep in history and has been sustained by some of the finest flights of the speculative mind. I am, of course, aware that not much philosophy attaches to our activities in the columns of the daily press, and when you read that I was to lecture on 'The Philosophy of Fascism', probably many of you said: 'What has this gangster to do with philosophy?' However, I trust you will believe that those great mirrors of the public mind do not always give a very accurate reflection, and while you only read of the more stirring moments of our progress, yet there are other moments, which have some depth in thought and constructive conception.[. . .]

I believe that Fascist philosophy can be expressed in intelligible terms, and while it makes an entirely novel contribution to the thought of this age, it can yet be shown to derive both its origin and its historic support from the established thought of the past.

In the first instance, I suggest that most philosophies of action are derived from a synthesis of cultural conflicts in a previous period. Where, in an age of culture, of thought, of abstract speculation, you find two great cultures in sharp antithesis, you usually find, in the following age of action, some synthesis in practice between those two sharp antitheses which leads to a practical creed of action.[. . .]

I would suggest to you that in the last century, the major intellectual struggle arose from the tremendous impact of Nietszchian [*sic*] thought on the Christian civilisation of two thousand years. That impact was only very slowly realised. Its full implications are only today working themselves out. But turn where you will in modern thought, you find the results of that struggle for mastery of the mind and the spirit of man.[. . .] I am not myself stating the case against Christianity, because I am going to show you how I believe the Nietszchian and the Christian doctrines are capable of synthesis.[. . .]

On the one hand you find in Fascism, taken from Christianity, taken directly from the Christian conception, the immense vision of service, of self-abnegation, of self-sacrifice in the cause of others, in the cause of the world, in the cause of your country; not the elimination of the individual, so much as the fusion of the individual in something far greater than himself; and you have that basic doctrine of Fascism, service, self-surrender to what the Fascist must conceive to be the greatest cause and the greatest impulse in the world. On the other hand you find taken from Nietszchian thought the virility, the challenge to all existing things which impede the march of mankind, the absolute abnegation of the doctrine of surrender; the firm ability to grapple with and to overcome all obstructions. You have, in fact, the creation of a doctrine of men of vigour and of self-help which is the other outstanding characteristic of Fascism.[. . .]

At the moment of a great world crisis, a crisis which in the end will inevitably deepen, a movement emerges from a historic background which makes its emergence inevitable, carrying certain traditional attributes derived from a very glorious past, but facing the facts of today, armed with the instruments which only this age has ever conferred upon mankind. By this new and wonderful coincidence of instrument and of event the problems of the age can be overcome, and the future can be assured in a progressive stability. Possibly this is the last great wave of the immortal, the eternally recurring Caesarian movement; but with the aid of science, and with the inspiration of the modern mind, this wave shall carry humanity to the further shore.

['The Philosophy of Fascism', *Fascist Quarterly*, 1/1 (1935), 35–46].

OSWALD MOSLEY
....
92   **Towards a Fascist Europe**

In this article Mosley expounds his vision of a Europe united and made peaceful by the forces not of liberalism, capitalism, or socialism, but fascism—a theme which has become part of mainstream fascist thinking since the war.

Views may vary as to the causes of the division of Europe and the restoration of the Balance of Power, but dispute can scarcely arise concerning the reemergence of a situation and a system which has invariably brought war. It is to the solution of this problem thus recreated that this article is addressed, and in searching for that solution we must return to the fundamental conception of European union which animated the war generation in 1918 and has been frustrated by the perversion of the League of Nations to exactly the opposite purpose that it was intended to serve.

This examination, therefore, begins with an inquiry into the factors which divide the individual nations, and in particular into the factors which inhibit peaceful and friendly relations between Great Britain and other great nations. Having established the particular of possible friendship between Great Britain and other nations we will proceed to the general idea of European union built on the firm foundation of justice and economic reality. The sequence of thought will naturally follow the story of prior disaster and will strive to show at each stage how the previous fatality can be eliminated in the system of the future. Therefore, in proceeding to build first a system of European union we shall naturally begin with Germany.

In fact, the only policy which can logically produce another explosion on the Western frontiers of Germany is the denial of expansion; not only on her Eastern frontiers but in her limited though necessary and natural colonial ambitions. Yet Financial-Democratic policy could not be more perfectly designed to promote that explosion than by the dual policy of denying Germany colonial outlet and of circumscribing her in the East by a menacing Democratic–Soviet alliance.[. . .]

But the solution here suggested is not the partition of Russia, not merely because it is the first interest of Europe and should be the first objective of British policy to keep the peace, but also because the solution of the European problems in terms both economic and political is possible on the lines already indicated without any offensive action against Russia. Rather it is here my purpose to suggest Russia should be told to mind her own business and to leave Europe and Western civilization alone to manage their own affairs. We seek war and strife with no nation, but to Russia we say: 'Hands off Europe and back to the East where you belong!'[. . .]

While, therefore, Fascist Europe desires only peace, it can give reality to collective security by a new collective spirit in face of the common menace to Europe and the British Empire, which is the ceaseless intrigue of Soviet power that seeks to gain time, by negotiation and fair speech, for the destruction of Western civilization by the simple process of first dividing the advanced nations of Europe and then setting them at each other's throats in quarrels which have neither material nor spiritual relevance to reality.[. . .]

The system of Financial Democracy crumbles in decay to collapse throughout the world and the stricken and bewildered peoples search for an alternative which presents hope of peace and security. The alternative of the modern Movement rises with the stark realism of granite above the confusion of present politics not only as a rock on which humanity may build anew but as a conception illuminated by the highest ideal of national and world citizenship which has yet animated the soul of man. The realism of the new creed builds upon the basic fact of economic settlement and justice for individual nations, without which all else is vain. It recognizes that European leadership must rest with the great powers and that in material terms a Four Power Bloc of Fascist nations can guarantee not only the peace of Europe but the peace of the world once their policies are united in objectives which are susceptible of synthesis. But materialism alone is not enough, and upon the basic fact of an established community of interest the universalism of Fascism and National Socialism erects the majestic edifice of a new world idea which commands the mind and spirit of man with the fiery force of a new religion. The old world will not mingle: so the peace of mankind attends in all lands the passing of the Old World, and Britain by force of material power and potential of moral leadership becomes the ultimate arena of struggle between the Old and the New, within which the destiny of White civilization will be decided. Great is the responsibility that high fate imposes upon us. We fight not only for the salvation of the land we love; we fight also for the Peace of Mankind.

['The World Alternative', *Fascist Quarterly*, 2/3 (1936), 382–3, 387, 392, 395.]

93 | A Corporate Britain

Fascism is not 'anti-modern', but proposes an alternative modernity based on the principles of a 'conservative revolution'. A symptom of this in the case of the BUF was its commitment to the corporative state based on the Italian model. In the wake of the Wall Street Crash a fusion of private enterprise with state planning was looked to even by many non-fascists as a solution to economic chaos and to the social misery and political instability it generated, creating a climate which fostered Roosevelt's New Deal in the USA and Keynes's interventionist economic theory in Britain. The stress which Raven Thomson places on the organic qualities of the Corporate State and its affinities with Tudor England as the basis of Britain's 'great future' underline the fascist thrust of this text, taken from a BUF pamphlet.

No greater mistake could be made than to regard the Corporate State as a mere mechanism of administration.

On the contrary, it is the organic form through which the nation can find expression. Fascism is no materialist creed like Communism, which sets up, as its only purpose, the material benefit of the masses. Fascism is essentially idealistic, and refuses any such limitation. Fascism recognises the nation as an organism with a purpose, a life and means of action transcending those of the individuals of which it is composed. To limit such an organism to a purpose within itself, to the mere service of its constituent parts, would be a denial of the whole philosophic concept of the Corporate State.

No progressive organism can adopt a self-limiting purpose. There is always striving towards an external goal or progress would cease. Man himself, as an organism composed of many million cells, does not consider his whole purpose one of self-indulgence, or at least such men are rightly condemned by all moral authority.

The man of worth will sacrifice his immediate welfare to the needs of his career. Similarly, the Corporate State must not be considered solely as a means of good government. It is also the means of self-expression of the nation as a corporate whole in the attainment of its national destiny.

The Corporate State is then in no sense absolute, but must conform to the universal moral law as a human institution. On the other hand, it is only through co-operation with others in the organic purpose of the State that the individual can attain his highest potentiality. There is no need for any conflict between individual and the State as neither can exist without the other. An individual exiled from the civilised communion must inevitably relapse into savagery: a State deprived of loyal co-operation from its citizens must inevitably collapse into barbarism. It is only by a true balance between the needs of individual and State that progress can be achieved for both. The Corporate State, with its functional organisation of human effort in a communal purpose, best achieves this essential balance.[. . .]

What then is the purpose of the Corporate organisation of the national life?

May I, as a humble member of the nation, profess my ignorance of the divine purpose upon earth which is our destiny? All that we can do is to prepare a fitting vehicle for the attainment of that destiny, to give the nation that organic form instinct with life which will enable it to play its part in the great events of future world history.

This, however, at least we may say, that the medieval peoples who lived in hovels and built cathedrals were nearer to a realisation of the divine purpose than we are to-day; that the Tudor Period, the high point of our own national life, found its expression not only in the seafaring and Empire building of Walter Raleigh and Francis Drake, but in the philosophy and science of Francis Bacon and the poetry and drama of William Shakespeare. It will be in recovering the 'age of faith' of Christendom and the vital energy of Tudor England that we may realise in part the great future of our nation.

[*The Coming Corporate State* (Action Publications: London, 1936/7), 47–8.]

E. D. RANDELL

94   Britain Awake!

E. D. Randell, a young poet who belonged to the BUF, wrote both 'A Marching Song' (sung to the 'Horst Wessel-Lied'), which became the Blackshirts' battle-hymn, and 'Britain Awake!'. They were among the songs reproduced in the 'Official History of the BUF' (1939, unpublished) by Richard Bellamy, District Inspector for the North of England. Bellamy stresses that all 'inspired movements' need such songs 'to uplift their votaries and infuse them with that sense of sacred purpose without which nothing can be done'. The central role played in them by palingenetic myth is no coincidence.

A Marching Song

Comrades: the voices of the dead battalions
Of those who fell that Britain might be great,
Join in our song, for they still march in spirit with us
And urge us on to gain the Fascist State!
We're of their blood, and spirit of their spirit,
Sprung from that soil for whose dear sake they bled;
'Gainst vested powers, Red Front, and massed ranks of Reaction
We lead the fight for freedom and for bread!
The streets are still; the final struggle's ended;
Flushed with the fight we proudly hail the dawn!
See, over all the streets the Fascist banners waving—
Triumphant standard of a race reborn.

Britain Awake!

Britain awake! Arise from slumber!
Soon comes the daybreak of Rebirth.
We lift again thy trampled banners,
Our marching legions shake the earth.
We gather from thy lanes and cities,

With men of action at our head.
In us division and delusion,
And all hypocrisies are dead.
We follow Fascism and Mosley,
We fight for freedom and for bread!

We bring a saving Revolution,
We are aweary of deceit.
We will avenge the long betrayal,
We will acknowledge no defeat.
We breathe the spirit of our fathers,
As dauntless and as proud as they.
O'erthrow the tyranny of falsehood—
The powers of darkness and decay!
We will be victors of tomorrow,
Who are the victims of today!

Britain, assert thine ancient honour,
Who never knew a foreign yoke.
Oh, turn thy face toward the future;
Thy life and strength are in thy folk.
If Britain to herself be faithful,
And each man to his fellow true,
Through all the world come forth against us,
We even yet shall make them rue.
We'll build a Britain fit for heroes,
With courage fresh and splendour new.

[Richard Reynell Bellamy, 'Official History of the BUF' (unpublished), 1939, 95–6. The manuscript is in the care of the Friends of Oswald Mosley.]

ARTHUR KENNETH CHESTERTON

95 A Spiritual Typhus

A. K. Chesterton (1899–1973) joined the BUF in 1933, and by the time he resigned in 1938 he had been editor of the BUF newspaper Blackshirt, *Director of Publicity and Propaganda, and Mosley's biographer. He was also a prolific publicist. After the war he formed his own party, the League of Empire Loyalists, in 1954, and went on to become the first chairman of the National Front from 1967–71. As this article indicates, Chesterton nurtured a lifelong obsession with the forces of decadence allegedly threatening to overwhelm Britain, and remained till his death the exponent of a conspiracy theory focused on 'Jewish' finance.*

One of the tragedies of the democratic drift is that profound truths may become truisms without being incorporated in legislative action, especially those truths that require to be imaginatively perceived. Should forty million people find their white blood corpuscles called forth to fight against the deadly germs of typhus, their need would be sufficiently obvious for the politician to bring the resources of the State to their assistance—the more hurriedly in that to the perverted typhus germ a politician makes as appetizing a meal as anybody else. But should those forty million people be fighting a battle no less desperate against all the nameless armies of decadence and ruin that threaten the spirit, the politician can be trusted to observe nothing and therefore not to be diverted from his major business in life, which is service to his own career.[. . .] Lack of appreciation of this fact, or else a subconscious acquiescence in its implications on the part of the parasitical over-lords, has led many a civilization to disaster and many a nation to its grave.

Evidence of national neurosis today is only too abundant. The almost unbeliev-able shifts and stratagems and blundering follies of modern democratic govern-ments represent one of its facets. The brazen and suicidal rampages of vested interests represent another. The astounding depravity of the Press represents a third. Evidence even more direct is supplied by the facile and poisonous Utopian-ism of the post-War period: the meaningless catchwords and slogans, the advocacy of the brave new world by human leeches sticking frantically to the bad old order, the failure of the Conservative to conserve, the inability of the Progressive to progress, the murder of the intellect by the intellectuals, and above all the hanging, drawing and quartering of Peace by pacifists who in the frenzy of their hysteria howl and dance and shriek for war. All these things indicate something more than a mental or spiritual stammer; they indicate a strongly entrenched neurosis which is the spirit's cancer and the trumpeter of death.

The realities ferment none the less surely because on every hand they are driven underground, the result being intensified conflict between the dream-doped mind and the sharp actualities of life, a conflict that has led to wide-spread neurosis quivering on the verge of lunacy.[. . .] And in the midst of their confusion there came forth the Jew openly to claim his financial masterdom and the Bloomsbury intellectual to assume the spiritual leadership of mankind. The Lords of Decadence enter into their heritage and every vitiating influence is encouraged in order to break down what remains of a healthy, virile nationalism that alone could check and defeat the international rampage of usury and the international crowning of decay. Societies are formed for 'experimental sex week-ends' and others to press for the revision of the homosexuality laws. No anti-British traitor in Ireland, no anti-British rioter in Egypt, no anti-British agitator in India but is sure of his wounds being licked in Britain. India itself is flung away, while His Majesty's Dominions are neglected and snubbed. At home food is buried or thrown into the sea because the hungry are not given the pieces of paper wherewith to buy them. Fascism, recog-nizing the human necessity to serve a social purpose and the fact that in a very real sense man lives only in so far as he is related to others, provides every citizen with the opportunity to take control of the social life to which he belongs in so far as that social life impinges upon his own interests and is amenable to the treatment and discipline that his own specialized knowledge can give.

In the theoretical limitation of the individual's power Fascism in practice extends it illimitably by rescuing it from an impossibly large milieu and concentrating it upon the smaller field where he is able to walk with the sure tread of an expert—the field of his own special study. He is allowed at long last the corporate activity which his soul's health demands, by the simple expedient of being able to work upon the task of bringing order and decency into his own occupation, thereby functioning normally and realistically as a social being in a world where idealism and realism no longer spell antithesis.

Herein is both the meaning and the mechanism of the Corporate State of Fascism—normal functioning which is the solvent of neurosis and the conqueror of decay.

[*Fascist Quarterly*, 2/1 (1936).]

WILLIAM JOYCE

96   Hitler Shows the Way

William Joyce (1906–46) was Director of Propaganda for the BUF, but his unqualified admiration for Hitler and his virulent anti-Semitism led to his expulsion in 1937, whereupon he formed the National Socialist League (suppressed in 1939). When Britain declared war on Germany in September 1939 Joyce stayed true to his vow to fight for Hitler in order to wage 'war against Jewry', and left the country so as to work for Goebbels' propaganda machine. His countless broadcasts to the British which opened with the phrase 'Germany calling' earned him the nickname Lord Haw-Haw, and eventually led to his execution for treason after the war. The book from which this is an extract was originally published in German in 1940, though this passage is taken from a translation published by American neo-Nazis thirty-five years later. It is prefaced by an ecstatically approving editorial introduction which assures the reader that the book 'incontestably proves that a "Democracy" is the very worst form of government and has no chance of survival.[. . .] The Jews reduced England to a 5th rate power and now have identical plans for the USA.'

We have come after these laborious centuries of groping, to the greatest turning-point in world history. In general, man is free to mould his destiny, but there are exceptions. To study the career of that simple man, Adolf Hitler, to weigh his words, to observe his actions is to know that he alone, of all the German people, is the least free: for he is the servant of a Higher Destiny. A survey of the facts given in this book should show that even if he had never been born, the old system of International Finance must have rushed to its doom; even as the merchant princes realized that science had abolished time and distance, they would have sought out the cheapest labour in the world and left the white populations starving, whilst the coloured slaves did the work. The full selfishness of the whole system was about to produce its own fatal consequences, when war was declared on Germany in the vain hope of giving it a new lease of life.

Yet, it is a merciful dispensation of Providence that, in Nature's progress, the principle of destruction has never finished its dire work before the principle of construction appears. In metabolism, the breakdown of cells without their replacement means atrophy and death: and if the Good God had meant the world to die in these years, He would have entrusted its extermination to some force more in keeping with His nobility than the Jewish race.

Just as the old world, then, was crumbling, the new force of construction arose in the person of Hitler and the body of the Third Reich. There are millions of men and women today, young in mind and spirit, who cannot accept the gloomy fatalism of Spengler. There is, despite all corruption, enough eternal youth left in the world to fight to the last against the doctrine of despair. To those who preach decline and decay, there is the answer of indomitable National Socialist challenge. The men who rule England are old: the class that holds supremacy is tarnished and decayed, there is much demoralization among the British people; but the pulse of historic youth still beats, however faintly. Devoted as I am, with undivided allegiance, to my new home for the rest of my life, I hope and pray that this pulse, so feeble now, will quicken into vitality, and one day throb with life. When the smoke of battle has rolled away, when those of us who are left gaze on the cold ashes of the conflagration started on that bright September morning by the bankrupt politicians of Britain, when we count the toll of life that war has taken, when we think of the misery that it has inflicted on the millions, when we smile grimly on the charred fragments of what was once the Power of Judah, when the glory of the ancient gods has crumbled to the dust from which it came, the birth pangs of the new order will be over. Throughout the whole of his life as a Leader, Adolf Hitler has shown his love for the working people; he has offered England the hand of friendship till it could be spurned no more. In the days of his inevitable victory, when Britain is freed from the forces of darkness that have caused this war, the defeat of England will be her victory. To achieve their regeneration, her people will have to suffer much: and the longer the war lasts, the more they will have to suffer; but they will have the chance, so long denied to them, of using their genius and their character in the building of the new world to which Adolf Hitler has shown the way. In these days, it may be presumptuous to express either hopes or beliefs, yet I will venture so much: I hope and believe, that when the flames of war have been traversed, the ordinary people of England will know their soul again and will seek, in National-Socialism, to advance along the way of human progress in friendship with their brothers of German blood. That this hope and this belief shall not prove vain there are two guarantees, for me sufficient: the greatness of Adolf Hitler and the Greater Glory of Almighty God.

[*Twilight over England* (Sons of Liberty: Metairie, Louisiana, *c.*1975), 140–2.]

ii. Ireland

Irish fascism is an elusive phenomenon. In the Irish Free State the nationalist energies which had brought Home Rule about tended to flow in liberal nationalist or socialist nationalist channels. The exception were the Blueshirts, officially called the Army Comrades Association when it was taken over by former Chief of Police Eoin O'Duffy in July 1933. The ACA had been set up a year earlier as a 'non-political mass movement' for those hostile to the 'revolutionary' tendencies of De Valera's Fianna Fáil government and to the 'communist' elements within the IRA. The NG was banned a month later, but in September 1933 it changed its name to The League of Youth, modified its policies, and was incorporated into a new party, Fine Gael, formed from a merger of Cumann na nGaedheal and the Centre Party. The marches, parades, and rallies of the new movement-party had some initial success in mobilizing popular hostility to the government and concern for the plight of farmers, however it failed to dent the Fianna Fáil majority in the local elections held in the summer of 1934, after which the Blueshirts faded from the scene. Mainstream Blueshirt ideology did not envisage the creation of a radically new order, and its corporativism was more Catholic than Mussolinian in inspiration. However, some of the executive were increasingly drawn to Fascism and Nazism as models for national renewal, notably O'Duffy himself, whose leadership style was irrepressibly 'charismatic'. On being eased out of the leadership of Fine Gael in September 1934 he was able to drop the mask of constitutionalism completely, and in June 1935 he founded the openly fascist National Corporate Party (the 'Greenshirts'). After this he attended two conferences (one Nazi, the other Fascist), held to promote a fascist International. He even hosted the visit of a group of Norwegian fascists. Predictably, these initiatives too came to naught and in late 1937, after returning from Spain where he had led the pro-Franco Irish Brigade, he retired from politics.

EOIN O'DUFFY

97 The New Corporate Ireland

The extract is taken a speech which O'Duffy made to his section of the League of Youth after resigning from Fine Gael and before founding the Greenshirts. It points clearly to a fascist agenda, and to the way he saw 'his' Blueshirts as the kernel of a new order (see Cronin 1995).

In my last lecture I stressed the point that the best leadership was service. Let us dwell on this for a few moments. Service is the essence of leadership; leadership is service. Let this sink in, and dwell upon it well, for in the new Irish State which we envisage you will each and every one be called upon to play the part of leaders. That is the first function of the Blueshirts—to lead the Nation out of its present difficulties, and to set up the only Christian system of Government which will work successfully in the modern world.[. . .]

I believe that our Country's chief hope of national salvation lies in the increasing strength, manly resolve and maturing discipline of our movement. The young Blueshirt is the expression of the new Ireland. He must temper his enthusiasm with discipline: he must strengthen his body and his spirit; he must spurn danger and love daring; he must serve the Blueshirt cause with loyalty and carry out his duties cheerfully and with pleasure. In all ranks we must have affectionate comradeship. This will not weaken discipline—on the contrary it will create a spirit of obedience which will lack rigidity. Voluntary discipline is better, and harder to break, than the discipline of the schoolmaster in the classroom or of the Sergeant-Major on the Barrack Square. Our discipline is self-respect, combined with orderly unselfish behaviour and a sense of responsibility to ourselves and others. Believe and obey. Officers should inculcate sentiments of honour and duty in the rank and file, and train them to carry out their duties honourably, and with their hearts overflowing with loyalty.[. . .]

Now the last part of our motto pledges us to 'public service to the whole nation'. We have justified ourselves well on this head. Fine Gael, or Cumann na nGaedheal, made the mistake so often made by selfish politicians; they confused the Nation with themselves, the greater with the less. 'Service to the whole Nation' from their point of view meant simply that we should first perform the supreme service of giving Ireland a Cumann na nGaedheal oligarchy once more, and then perform an almost equally great service by clearing out of the picture until they would want us again. Their idea was service to the party, which was more important than the Nation in their eyes.[. . .]

For the Blueshirts themselves the setting up of an Irish Corporative State will not mark the final achievement; it will indeed be no more than the beginning of our work. No public service which we can render now will be so great or so abiding as the service which we must then undertake.

We must lead the people always; nationally, socially and economically. We must clear up the economic mess and right the glaring social injustices of to-day by the corporative organisation of Irish life; but before everything we must give a national lead to our people. At present Irish Nationality is a wilderness in which a dozen different prophets are howling so loudly and abusing each other so raucously that the listener is bewildered and wonders what sort of performance is going on.

Now what Ireland needs, and what I think only we can give it, is a sane and sincere national lead away from that wilderness. The first essential is national unity. We can only have that when the Corporative system is accepted. We shall put our National programme to the people, and it is a programme in which even the most advanced Nationalist can find nothing to disturb him. We hold the Irish people to be both wise and good, not fools to be led by the nose by any stray demagogue, and not knaves who will always sell themselves to the highest bidder. We will consult them always before taking any vital step, and if they say 'Go out of the Common-Wealth' we will go gladly, convinced that it is the right thing to do because it is their will, and we will be proud to serve in the front ranks of the Nation.[. . .]

But our main work will always be to inspire our people with a consciousness of the great destiny of Ireland as a Christian State, and to promote in the coming generations the spirit which sent and is still sending Irish Missionaries to the very ends of the earth.

When the chaos of the dark ages broke over Europe, Irishmen saved Christianity even in Italy itself; and we should never forget that our proudest traditions are cultural and Christian. Chaos seems again to be about to spread all over the world; let us resolve that once again Ireland, the last outpost of Europe, will be ready to relive her historic past and stem the tide of Communism and materialism. By discipline and service we must perfect ourselves, and our Nation, so that should the call to battle come, Ireland will be ready to play a noble part.[. . .]

The most promising feature of our movement is the manner in which it has captured the imagination of the youth. It is on the youth we rely, and we must solicit and welcome their support. We must wean them from all political parties. We must show them the futility of party strife, the waste of time and energy involved, resulting only in putting brother against brother. We must educate them towards the acceptance of the Corporative Idea.

[Speech to League of Youth Organization, O'Duffy section of Blueshirts, held at Mansion House, 16 Nov. 1934, Department of Justice, 1993 Release, B9/35: National Archives of Ireland (also printed in the *Irish Independent*, 17 Nov. 1934).]

iii. Spain

Spanish fascism is a vigorous species of the genus, though not as prolific as is generally assumed. While Franco's stand in the Spanish Civil War and the subsequent regime which he headed till 1975 is generally associated with fascism, both *Franquismo* and the anti-Republican right was in fact overwhelmingly conservative. Indeed, ultra-nationalists bent on creating a new type of order through a Spanish equivalent of Fascism and Nazism remained a highly marginalized factor in politics till the outbreak of the Civil War in July 1936. It was then that the Falange Española y de las Juntas de Ofensiva Nacional-Sindicalista, formed, as its cumbersome name implies, from the 1935 merger of two even more insignificant parties (one of them itself the result of another merger), started to become a significant mass movement as thousands flocked to join its militia. Franco, a traditionalist conservative at heart, perceived Falangists as a threat to his autonomy, yet astutely chose to emasculate them rather than liquidate them. This he did in April 1937 when he merged them with the *Requetés*, the militia of an ultra-right monarchist faction, an act signified by the addition of the adjective *tradicionalista* after *española* in the full name of the Falange. Henceforth the Falange (now FET) was reduced to an organization designed to maintain the illusion that *Franquismo* was juridically, culturally, and socially a revolutionary force, while effectively acting as a harmless safety-valve for genuine fascist energies. As the war turned against the Axis, Franco recognized the need to find an accommodation with the Allies. As a result para-fascism and true Falangism became increasingly peripheral to what remained at heart an authoritarian conservative regime.

Even if Spanish fascism failed to make headway politically, it constituted a significant phenomenon at the level of political culture, as many hundreds of individual ideologues tirelessly formulated the principles of the new Spain in monographs, newspaper articles, and speeches (e.g. Text 98). Particularly influential in spreading the word were the speeches and articles of the Falange's leader, José Antonio Primo de Rivera, son of the former dictator, Miguel (Texts 99, 100). By the time he was killed in November 1936 (like Ledesma a victim of the Republicans) José Antonio had begun to establish himself as a genuinely charismatic leader. His two years of ceaseless activity on behalf of the Falange included meetings with Hitler, Mosley, Degrelle, and Codreanu, attending the two conferences of the Fascist International in Montreux, and also producing a stream of articles and addressing numerous rallies. His admiration for Mussolini as his fascist role model was reciprocated by significant financial backing from Italy in this period. José Antonio's attempt to turn the Civil War into the birth-pangs of a new Falangist Spain which transcended the old polarity of left and right was continued by other fascists for some years after his death.

In general Falangist ideology, like *Franquismo*, was free from anti-Semitic and eugenic strains. Nevertheless, José Antonio himself made a few specifically anti-Semitic remarks, periodicals such as *FE*, *Arriba España*, and *Amanecer* (Dawn) regularly referred to the Jews as a parasitic force sapping the health of Spain or the whole of Western civilization, and at least one writer tried to inject elements of biological determinism into Spain's ultra-right. This was Antonio Vallejo-Nágera, who eventually became the first professor of Psychiatry of the University of Madrid. A passage from his writings is included here (Text 101), less for its representativeness of Spanish fascism than for its curiosity value as a sample of the outlandish racist myths which the exceptional cultural climate of inter-war Europe could nurture even in Spain (see Payne 1961).

RAMIRO LEDESMA RAMOS

98   The Voice of Spain

Ramiro Ledesma Ramos (1905–1936), was a great admirer of the elitist cultural critic Ortega y Gasset, but had increasingly succumbed to the lure of German philosophy and Nazism before he teamed up with Onésima Redondo to found the Juntas de Ofensiva Nacional-Sindicalista (JONS) in 1934. However, conflict with Falangists after the merger with Falange Española led to his being expelled. His Speech to the Youth of Spain (1935) sets out to clarify his vision of the new Spain and what separated him from the Falangists, but what this passage brings out is his typically fascist sense of standing on the threshold of a new era to which his nation is called upon to give shape.

There is nothing more opposed to the mentality, the necessities, and the tenor of our epoch than the political and economic forms elaborated by the liberal-bourgeois order. These forms have outlived their usefulness, and peoples are abandoning them like tools which are cumbersome to handle and only cause damage.[. . .]

The liberal State is simply an instrument for the individual. It must do nothing to limit the individual's freedom, nor sacrifice it for any other value. Even its coercive apparatus justifies itself as a function of freedom, guaranteeing the liberty and 'rights' of individuals.[. . .]

Everything which today acts as a germ of fragmentation, of impotence, of exhaustion, and of egoism is directly due to the social predominance of the bourgeoisie and the political predominance of its agents, advocates, and front men.

Some time ago demo-bourgeois civilization entered a final stage, characterized by hypocrisy, since, having itself lost faith in its own principles, it is endeavouring to maintain its power by cynically degrading and falsifying them. It is helped in this bid by the fact that the characteristic attitude of the demo-bourgeois spirit—a sceptical tendency, blindness to the collective, a lukewarm patriotism, a sham humanitarian sentimentality, etc., etc.—is widely spread, being not simply confined to strata and sectors of economic privilege, but extending to popular, proletarian elements, contaminated by it and its most base and degraded characteristics.

But the most active representatives of this historical attitude are now fully conscious of its sterility and bankruptcy, and realize that hardly have their political ideals leapt from their mouths than, far from constructing and building something, they turn immediately into sources of destruction and discord. They know that their system and economic order lead to gigantic crises, to their own ruin, and to masses being forced out of work and into hunger. In the same way, they see that the political and social institutions it has created turn nations into a permanent arena of bloody conflicts and undermine national solidarity more each day to the point where the very viability of peoples is jeopardized. It acknowledges that it does not know how to react to the great waves of youthful energy which keep emerging, and finally faces the prospect of their imminent collapse and final disappearance.[. . .]

A world transformation is taking place. Symptoms of it are Bolshevism, Italian Fascism, German socialist racism, and the styles and forms of life we have described above. They are eruptions, starting-points, already pregnant with what is yet to come, yet are things which are in no way definitive, permanent, or conclusive. And, of course, Bolshevism, just like Fascism and racism, are all national phenomena without world-wide scope or depth.

Perhaps the voice of Spain, the presence of Spain, if it could ever fulfil and assert itself fully, may impart to the transforming realities of our time their most perfect and fertile sense of direction, producing forms which inscribe its genius into the pages of universal history.

[*Discurso a las Juventudes de España* [Speech to the Youth of Spain] (Ediciones Tecnos: Madrid, 1954; 1st edn. 1935), 245–7, 254–6, 291–2.]

JOSÉ ANTONIO PRIMO DE RIVERA
....

99   Total Feeling

It was in association with the Montreux conference of the Fascist International held in 1934 that José Antonio made his declaration that the Falange was not a fascist movement, one often quoted by scholars reluctant to recognize the existence of generic fascism. It is clear, however, from this speech, made three months later, that he was prepared to portray Falangism as a Spanish variant of fascism, recognizing that as a generic phenomenon every national permutation of fascism would be unique.

They say that we are imitators. Onésimo Redondo[1] has already repudiated this allegation. They say we are imitators because our movement, this movement which is bringing a sea-change back towards the genuine core of Spain, is one which has come about in other places. Italy, Germany have turned towards themselves in a reaction of despair at the myths which were bent on sterilizing them; but since Italy and Germany have turned back on themselves and have totally redis-covered themselves, why should we say that Spain is imitating them in its quest to

---

[1] Co-founder of JONS with Ramiro Ledesma.

find a way back to herself? These countries turned back towards their own authenticity, and if we do so ourselves, the authenticity which we find will also be our own: it will not be that of Germany or Italy, and therefore, by reproducing the achievement of the Italians or Germans we will become more Spanish than we have ever been.

To my comrade Onésimo Redondo I would say: do not worry too much about why they say that we only imitate. If we ever succeeded in putting an end to this sort of reproach they would soon invent others. The well-spring of treachery is inexhaustible. Let them tell us that we are imitating the fascists. After all, in fascism as in all movements of all ages, underneath the local characteristics there are to be found certain constants which are the heritage of the whole human spirit and which are everywhere the same. For example, this is true of the Renaissance; it is also true of the hendecasyllable; we took the hendecasyllable from Italy, but shortly after we took it from Italy Garcilaso and Brother Martin were celebrating the fields of Spain with the Castilian hendecasyllable, and Fernando de Herrera was praising the Lord for the calmness of the sea which gave Spain victory in the battle of Lepanto.

Others call us reactionary. Some do this in bad faith so that the workers will give us a wide berth and not listen to us. Despite this the workers will listen to us, and when they listen to us they will not believe those who make this accusation, because it is precisely when the aim is to restore, as we do, the idea of the indestructible integrity of fate that it is not possible to be reactionary.[. . .]

Finally there are those who claim we have no programme. Do you know anything serious and profound which has ever been achieved with a programme? When have you ever seen decisive things, eternal things which involve love, life, death being carried out by following a programme? What is needed is a total feeling of what is required: a total feeling for the Fatherland, for life, for History, and it is that total feeling, clear not on paper but in the soul, which will tell us in every concrete situation what we must do and what we must prefer. In the best epochs there were never so many study circles, statistics, censuses, programmes as now.

[Speech proclaiming the formation of the FE de las JONS, 4 Mar. 1934, repr. in *José Antonio Primo de Rivera. Escritos y Discursos, Obras Completas 1922–1936* [Writings and Speeches. Complete Works 1922–1936] (Instituto de Estudios Politicos: Madrid, 1976), i. 327–33.]

JOSÉ ANTONIO PRIMO DE RIVERA
....

100   Bread and Justice

Far from being a natural ally of the bourgeoisie, José Antonio saw in National Syndicalism, a version of corporatism, a way of reconciling class conflict and creating a national socialism which would benefit workers. This passage is a classic statement of the widespread belief among fascists that by blending existing ideas they were forging a new synthesis unclassifiable as either right or left, and thus uniquely able to solve the problems of the modern age.

Well then: if communism puts an end to many good things, such as family attachments and national sentiment; if it provides neither bread nor freedom and makes us subservient to a foreign country, what is to be done? We are not going to resign ourselves to the continuation of the capitalist regime. One thing today is painfully obvious: the crisis of the capitalist system and its devastating consequences which communism is doing nothing to attenuate. What is to be done, then? Are we in a cul-de-sac? Is there no way of placating the hunger of the masses for bread and justice? Do we have to choose between the desperation of the bourgeois regime and the slavery of Russia?

No. The National Syndicalist Movement is convinced that it has found the right way out: neither capitalist nor communist. Faced by the individualist economy of the bourgeoisie, the socialist one arose, which handed over the fruits of production to the State, enslaving the individual. Neither of them have resolved the tragedy of the producer. To address this issue let us erect the syndicalist economy, which neither absorbs the individual personality into the State, nor turns the worker into a dehumanized cog in the machinery of bourgeois production. The national syndicalist solution is the one which promises to bear the most fruit. It will do away once and for all with political go-betweens and parasites. It will free production from the financial burdens with which finance capital overwhelms it. It will overcome the anarchy it causes by putting order into it. It will prevent speculation with commodities, guaranteeing a profitable price. And, above all, it will pass on the surplus value not to the capitalist, not to the State, but to the producer as a member of his trade union. And this economic system will make a thing of the past the depressing spectacle of unemployment, slum housing, and misery.[. . .]

Workers! Comrades! Decisive moments are approaching. No one can stand back with his arms folded. The fate of everyone is in the balance. Either the workers, forcefully, implacably, will put an end to finance capital and join the National Syndicalist Movement to impose a regime of national solidarity, or internationalism will turn us into the stooges of some foreign great power.

The National Syndicalist Movement, conscious that it has strength and reason on its side, will keep up the assault on all its enemies: the right, the left, communism, capitalism. For the Fatherland, Bread and Justice. We are sure to win. It is essential in the interest of both the producers and the nation. We will impose a new order of things, without people starving, without professional politicians, without bosses, without usurers, without speculators.

Neither right, nor left! Neither communism nor capitalism! A national regime. The National Syndicalist regime!

Long live Spain!

['An appeal to Spanish workers', *Arriba*, 20 (21 Nov. 1935); repr. in *José Antonio Primo de Rivera. Escritos y Discursos, Obras Completas 1922–1996* (Instituto de Estudios Politicos: Madrid, 1976), ii. 823–5.]

101 A new Breed of Spaniards

Antonio Vallejo-Nágera's Eugenesia of Spanishness (1937), Regeneration of the Race (1937), and Racial Politics of the New State (1938) show the unmistakable influence, not just of Nazi racial theory, but of the international eugenics movement (which was well represented in liberal nations as well by the 1930s). He also drew on the concept of limpieza de sangre (purity of blood) cultivated by the Spanish aristocracy in the sixteenth century, and looked to a resuscitated Inquisition to police Spain's racial laws. According to Vallejo-Nágera Spanish Marxism was a product of Jewish and Moorish blood, while foreign Marxism derived from pure Semitic stock. However, his vision of a regenerated Spain also allowed for a degree of racial mixing, as this passage makes clear.

It is the patriotic spirit which has raised up the peoples fallen into shame and ruin after the catastrophe of the Great War. Races which have rediscovered themselves, which have contemplated their history, the peoples which have struggled to recuperate their spiritual values and revive ancient traditions, are those which, like a phoenix, have been reborn from the ashes and have been able to stand up to the whole world in order to maintain their racial personality.[. . .]

A patriot is someone who wants for his country prosperity, the respect of his rights, and his rightful place in the world order. Territorial patriotism is dangerous because it ignores the fact that the life of peoples must adjust to general principles of justice and morality. If a nation robs other nations and kills to grow at their expense, and subordinates universal morality to its own caprice, it will be ignoble in its conduct, and its thought will not acquire universality.[. . .]

The regeneration of a race calls for a policy which neutralizes the damage which can be caused to its germ plasma by pathogenic agents, both physical and psychological, material and moral. *We share the view of the National Syndicalists that every race has a particular cultural significance,*[2] and is endowed with bio-psychological features which must be raised to become its external characteristics. The Spanish do not fear and have never feared bastardization. We have casually cross-bred with the most diverse races not only without losing our individuality, but asserting it as forcefully as ever, while at the same time conserving the essence of Spanishness which nourished our psychological personality.

It is far from our minds to promote a racial policy rooted in the endogamic sense of primitive societies.[3] We will never attack the mixing of superior and inferior castes of our race. What we call for is a *Hispanic supercaste*, ethnically improved, morally robust, spiritually vigorous. For this we need to stimulate the fertility of select groups, for in biology quantity is not opposed to quality.[. . .] But we do not confine ourselves to stimulating the fertility of élites. Our programme strives to spread among individuals of all classes a desire to rise to the level of select hierar-

---

[2] 'National Syndicalists' was another expression for Falangists.
[3] i.e. of marrying only within the tribe.

chies, aristocrats of body and spirit, an ambitious programme which demands the collaboration of sociologists, economists, and politicians. We refer here to the politics of doctrine, not of parties, for these exert a disastrously harmful influence on the race.

The regeneration of the race has to be backed up by the *regeneration of the family institution*, because the family constituted in accordance with traditional principles of Christian morality represents a storehouse of social virtues, a bastion against the corruption of the social environment, a sacred depository of traditions.[. . .] The family acts as a type of cell in the social body which forms the race. If many cells are vigorous and healthy, besides ensuring the vitality of the body, they defend it from becoming infected and poisoned. If many families are healthy and prestigious they eventually can revitalize a decadent race.

Culture and religion are consubstantial with the Christian family, which suffuses the atmosphere with a morally purifying influence that consolidates and preserves racial values. The Greek and Roman civilizations lasted twenty centuries because of the purification effected by Christianity. The Arab people, equally heirs to Greek civilization, after a few centuries suffered a degenerative collapse from which it has not been able to recover. If we reflect a few moments on the bases of the family institution as Catholicism understands them, we will soon be convinced of the solid basis which it provides for the regeneration of the race.

[*Eugenesia de la Hispanidad y Regeneración de la Raza* [Eugenesis of Spanishness and Regeneration of the Race (Editorial Española: Burgos, 1937), 113–19.]

iv. Portugal

Portuguese fascism never gained the necessary momentum to be incorporated into Salazar's para-fascist regime, even in an emasculated form. In 1930 the minister of economics turned dictator had created a single party, the União Nacional, which was to become the official outlet for mass political 'participation' in the Estado Novo [New State] inaugurated in 1934. Yet by 1932 there was still enough political and civic space left for Rolão Preto to form a genuinely fascist movement, the blueshirted National Syndicalists. Despite the absence of a profound social crisis, or the threat of a Bolshevik revolution, National Syndicalism had by the end of 1933 managed to attain a membership of some 25,000, many among the disaffected youth of Lisbon, Braga, and Oporto. It also recruited elements within government and the armed forces who longed for a more dynamically modern and heroic Portugal than Salazar seemed to promise. A few months later National Syndicalism felt strong enough to flex its muscle in conflicts with the União Nacional in the rural north. Not surprisingly this put an end to Salazar's tolerance: a political safety-valve had become a potentially dangerous rival force. In July 1934 he dissolved the movement and sent Preto into exile in Spain. His resolve to take pre-emptive action was no doubt strengthened by the assassination in the same month of Dollfuss, in some respects his kindred spirit, at the hand of Austrian Nazis. An attempted coup by a few die-hards a year later was put down effortlessly.

Preto's influences were typically eclectic: Lusitanian Integralism (a Portuguese equivalent of Maurras's Action Française), the nationalist forms of syndicalism elaborated in France, Italy, and Spain, and the image of Nazism as a dynamo of populist anti-bourgeois and anti-communist energies. Preto spurned Aryan mythology and anti-Semitism, though: like its Spanish counterpart, Portuguese National Syndicalism still nominally upheld Christian principles, or at least the mythic power of Catholicism to form the basis of social cohesion, spiritual values, and national reawakening (see Gallagher 1990).

ROLÃO PRETO

The Wind of Change

The weekly newspaper of Preto's Nacional-Sindicalismo was União Nacional (the same name as Salazar's official party). He saw his movement as part of a world-wide wave of spiritual and social renewal which would go beyond liberalism, democracy, and right-wing or left-wing authoritarianism to create a new type of order. As these articles, published shortly before his exile, make clear, a major component of it was anti-materialism, a recurrent fascist theme.

A terrible wave of utilitarianism and baseness is sweeping through the world, and is threatening to subvert and vulgarize everything, plunging it into a quagmire of tragic moral degradation.[. . .] Where are we going? Day by day more is being chopped away. The clear and holy light of ideas is covered up and lost sight of under a cheap blanket of unfettered commercialism which darkens the soul. Justice, independence, nobility of feeling or thought: empty words. Contemporary man feels increasingly a pawn in a game of material interest, more a slave of gold than ever.[. . .]

Every so often these acts of extraordinary moral decadence sweep over the world. Man abandons his supreme position in the scale of what is valuable on this earth to surrender to the lure of material objects and the state of supreme wretchedness which goes with them. Only his vanity, his comforts, his material possessions seem to him a worthwhile goal, a path to follow. To achieve this goal, to follow this path, any contradiction of his spirit, any abdication of responsibility, any amount of baseness or shame are justified. Now more than ever all means serve to fulfil this end.

This is the way of the world.

But there are independent spirits, free spirits, those who are prepared to embark on a hard road of sacrifice to preserve their pride and the glory which their independence and freedom give them. They should not despair. Already the signs of reaction are becoming manifest in the noisy protest on every side from those able to resist the temptation to trade their own dignity for material comforts, to swap strength of character for the possibility of making money.

This reaction against the materialist and corrupting utilitarianism of a whole age is the beginning of the great Revolution whose spirit is going to burn and purify the earth. It is a singular aspect of the human condition that the onset of man's decadence and death always create the conditions of his salvation and deliverance.[. . .]

The Revolution is under way. It will redeem man, raising him to the height of all the divine greatness that is his. Friends, the glitter of gold, however intense and brilliant, will never obscure the light of the ideal which we carry inside our breast and which is like the pure, redeeming brightness of the dawn in the tragic night of human distress.

['Oiro' [Gold], *União Nacional*, 25 Feb. 1934.]

Across changing epochs and institutions the path of Revolution stretches into the distance, moving out beyond Liberalism and Democracy, beyond materialist or communist Caesarism,[4] inalterable, sovereign, inexorable. It is the destiny of human personality. In vain the spirit of the times will try to hold it back; in vain political or economic tyrannies will strive to crush it. Causing upheavals, toppling governments, ever marching onwards, the spirit cannot pause in its urge for renewal, which stems from the distress of the humble and the revolt of the

---

[4] Here used as a general term for authoritarianism.

downtrodden, and strides on relentlessly in search of new forms which correspond to its freedom, its dignity, its supreme exaltation. It is easy to know where the world is going, because it is this spirit which moves it.

The National Syndicalist movement in Portugal is part of this wind of creativity which is moving the world. It can be nothing else.

> ['Para onde vai o mundo? O verdadeiro sentido do Nacional-Sindicalismo' [Where is the world going? The true path of National Syndicalism], *União Nacional*, 3 June 1934.]

ROLÃO PRETO

103   Ersatz Fascism

In this passage, written from exile, Preto writes a thinly disguised attack on Salazar by portraying authoritarian Austria (run under Dollfus and Schuschnigg, like the Estado Novo, *on Catholic corporatist lines) as an ersatz fascist (para-fascist) state led by a politician out of touch with the true fascist spirit (which Preto clearly believes both he and Mussolini embodied). Since Austria had now been incorporated into the Third Reich as a result of the* Anschluss, *this is a bitter indictment of Portugal's inner weakness and vulnerability.*

The error of Dolfuss–Schuschnigg lay above all in a basic contradiction: that of creating a fascist organization from which the Leader felt apart and divorced through an exclusively Catholic temperament, education, and spirit.

What would really be the point of the 'single party', the armed militias, the youth organizations, the corporative formations, etc., if they all lacked the fervent soul of the Leader, sincerely believing in the system and supplying an exhaustible source of enthusiasm and faith. The Revolution can only be made with revolutionaries, and fascism has only been realized by fascists. Schuschnigg, cold, calculating, a melancholy ghost wandering around among the other gloomy ghosts of the Hofburg,[5] someone by temperament and through experience mistrustful of others, whom he sees only motivated in their turn when induced by base interests; sceptical about the very ideas he is advocating, but which basically he does not even live out himself—poor Schuschnigg was the perfect negation, the total negation of a fascist leader.

The way the Duce sees it, the fascist leader must not only serve as the fulcrum around which all national activity turns and is orientated, but, more important, he has constantly to reveal himself to be the dynamo at the heart of the whole system, generating, augmenting, and radiating the energy which permeates it.

The fascist leader must always take up a vanguard position, pointing out new courses of action, channelling people's desires, arousing enthusiasm, constantly creating reasons for hope.[. . .]

---

[5] The palace in Vienna used by the head of State.

Therein lies the central difficulty. He can never afford to be *behind, marching* because others are pulling him along, *seeing* because others are showing him, *having faith* because others are inspiring him to believe.

All the acts and words of a fascist leader must be forcefully inspired by two watchwords: imagination and courage.

Everything else is a waste of time and, consciously or not, a betrayal of the methods which can bring about a fascist reality. The Austrian example clearly teaches us these lessons. Dollfuss and Schuschnigg did not succeed in founding a fascist system in Austria, they barely managed to create a substitute, an *Ersatz*, as it is called in their language. A substitute the militias, the corporations, the youth organizations, a substitute the ideas and their implementation. Finding it impossible to mobilize people to act in the present or future, they then tried to rouse their spirits through evoking examples of glory from a petrified past. A procession of ghosts going round a tomb while the miserable people looked on confused and indifferent, that was the Austria of Schuschnigg.[. . .] It is true that the new generations believe in History, but only on condition that they themselves continue to write its triumphal pages.[. . .]

Those who try to create a fascist type of situation when they themselves are not fascists inevitably place themselves in the following dilemma: either the system remains soulless and everything ends up by collapsing, dragging the country into ruin with it and depriving it of any possibility of a vital reaction; or else, by way of a miraculous paradox, the country manages to preserve itself by drawing on its deepest reserves of strength, generating a mystic climate of exaltation despite its spineless leaders, and, in this case, the tidal wave which sooner or later must arise, will flood the coasts and violently sweep across the country in an inexorable surge of destiny.

[O Fascismo (Guimarães, Lisbon, 1939), 10–11.]

v. France

French fascism was no closer to seizing power in the inter-war period than the Spanish or Portuguese. Nevertheless, ideologically speaking, it produced an even richer variety of permutations of fascist thought, drawing on a long indigenous tradition of ultra-nationalist critiques of liberal democracy and the threats to civilization posed by the left, materialism, cosmopolitanism, and Jews. Georges Valois (1894–1945) was a member of Maurras's ultra-conservative and royalist Action Française, but the influence of Sorelian revolutionary syndicalism via the Cercle Proudhon on the eve of the First World War predisposed him to be favourably impressed by Mussolini's fascism after it to the point of trying to emulate it in Le Faisceau. It was formed in 1925 as the embryo of a new corporatist social order, complete with sections for youth, civilians, producers, and a paramilitary wing (Text 104). Valois's ultimate goal was for the New France made possible by his fascism to join forces with a New Spain and a New Italy to form a Latin block in the Mediterranean. He broke with any anti-Semitism he might have imbibed as a Maurrassian to the point of inviting Jews to contribute to the 'New Age' (also the title of the movement's newspaper). By 1927 he had dissolved Le Faisceau, recognizing that the 60,000 members it had initially attracted were an insufficient basis for revolutionary change, but continued his publicist activity on behalf of a new European order. He was to die in Bergen-Belsen concentration camp.

Another attempt to found a mimetic Fascist party was Bucard's Francisme (1933–44), which hardly made a ripple. Much more significant was the attempt by Jacques Doriot (1898–1945), a former communist mayor in Paris, to create a mass movement based on a synthesis of socialism and patriotism to counteract the forces of Bolshevism, liberalism, capitalism, and class conflict which he saw tearing France apart. His crusade led to the formation of the Parti Populaire Français in 1936 as the basis for a counter-attack against the Popular Front, and for a time this showed signs of becoming a mass movement, with some 60,000 members by 1938 and a widely read newspaper, *L'Émancipation Nationale*, which became a forum for French fascist thinking. Despite the heady optimism of the party's manifesto (Text 105), the PPF too came to nothing, and was in any case eclipsed in size and impact by De La Roque's extreme right Parti Social Français, which rallied forces convinced that the State could crush the Popular Front and reform itself without mutating into a new order on fascist lines. However, it continued in new guise as a collaborationist party under Nazi occupation after 1940, Doriot convincing himself that his movement could provide the driving force for a new France, partner on equal terms with Germany within the Nazis' new European order.

The final bid to create a fascist party as the basis of the new France was made during the war by Marcel Déat (1894–1955), who, in a way reminiscent of Mussolini and Mosley, shifted by stages from revolutionary left to revolutionary right without ever feeling he was contradicting his basic principles. After the defeat of France in 1940 he persuaded himself that Nazism really was a dynamic, anti-capitalist, and classless form of national socialism, and hence was realizing the highly statist and authoritarian vision of the planned economy which he had been promoting in his 'neo-socialism' during the 1930s. In 1941 Déat formed his own party, the Rassemblement National Populaire, which he insisted was the fulfilment of the French revolutionary tradition and the vanguard of a mass movement of all productive Frenchmen (Text 106). The RNP's anti-Semitism was not biological, but more than implicit in the relentless attacks on capitalism. No matter how authentically French, this fascism too remained a dead letter for the mass of the French and was tolerated by the Nazis simply for its propaganda value.

Ever since the second half of the nineteenth century French culture has provided an ideal habitat for countless aesthetes and intellectuals to indulge in speculation about the decadence of the nation or of the West and possible remedies (see Sternhell 1986). This forms a major factor in explanations of why liberal Republican France could so quickly give way after its defeat in 1940 to the France of Vichy and of widespread collaboration with the Nazis in the occupied zone. An extensive collaborationist publicism and literature of rare sophistication grew, Drieu La Rochelle, Céline, Rebatet, and Brasillach being only the more famous of hundreds of literati who preached fascism as the way out of the malaise. Drieu La Rochelle (1893–1945), for example, had been obsessed with cultural and national decadence since the First World War, commuting between pessimism and the manic optimism which fascist fantasies of rebirth could engender. He was thus predisposed to reading into the creation of a Nazi empire in Europe the birth-pangs of a new phase of Western civilization in which heroic spiritual values would replace the degenerate ones of contemporary modernity (Text 107).

GEORGES VALOIS
....

104   Empty Portfolios

On creating Le Faisceau, *Valois took the trouble to announce the good news to his fellow Fascists in Italy in a book called* French Fascism *which was published in Italian in 1926. In this passage he expresses his belief in the fascist (corporativist) state as the cure to the problems created by the failure of liberalism to harness properly the forces of capitalism and modernization.*

It is important to realize that all the convulsions of France and Europe (communist and fascist convulsions) are caused by the incapacity of the liberal and parliamentary State to govern in a world which has undergone enormous economic transformations, transformations demanding state organs which those who drew up the constitutions of the nineteenth century had never foreseen. The State as it is constructed today, compared to the State which is needed, what a horse-drawn carriage is compared to a 40-horsepower motor vehicle, or a candle compared to an electric lamp.

This is more or less understood by all. Awareness of this fact has caused people to say, especially after the war, that the State has stopped being political to become economic. This is a silly thing to say, because the State is always political: it is the organ via which citizens are obliged to live in peace. What is perfectly true, however, is that the State nowadays has an enormous economic function to fulfil: as long as the institutions needed to carry out the new functions of the State do not exist everything will go to pieces, and we will go from convulsion to convulsion until we finally collapse, or achieve a new greatness.[. . .]

Doubtless many citizens enjoy the benefits of this civilization on a scale which, fifty years ago no one could have imagined possible. But many citizens suffer cruelly: peasants are wrenched from the earth and fall prey to the city. Thousands upon thousands of workers lack the bare essentials in an extraordinarily rich era of civilization. Producers and savers are ruined overnight by the financial forces unleashed by these economic forces, and never even understand what has happened to them.

Economic and financial forces hold sway over everything, fight among themselves, and struggle to control the State, or the ministers and deputies who run the State.

These powers are men who represent scores and hundreds of millions of men, and sometimes thousands of millions of men. Faced by these powers, the State is armed with ministers who have long nails and empty portfolios, by deputies and ministers who think they are still living under Louis-Philippe, or by Civil Servants who do not take a taxi because they cannot afford one with their salary. There are men who, faced by this spectacle, long for the time of St Louis, others who would like to burn down banks and factories.

The only solution is to put an end to all this chaos. It is not a question of destroying these forces which are irresistible, because they are not harnessed. It is a question of imposing a discipline on them which is national, social, and human. They are not to be destroyed or reduced, but rather exalted. But it is vital that the State is stronger than them, and that it is structured in such a way as to exercise control over this new world.[. . .]

Thus the solution to the European problem seems to have been found. It is the creation of the unitary or fascist State existing above parties and classes and capable, by basing itself on veterans, workers, and peasants, of harnessing these prodigious economic forces which have been unleashed onto the modern world, forces which unchannelled would put the whole of Europe at risk, but which channelled properly will provide it with a prosperity which is unimaginable today.

A unitary national State which presides over the rational organization of production based on a systematic collaboration of science and industry in turn provides the basis for social justice: this is what social Catholics, socialists, and communists themselves have been seeking for fifty years. In present conditions, the men of these parties, raising themselves above their old class habits, will find in the national State what they have not found elsewhere.

[*Il fascismo francese* [French Fascism] (Giuseppe Marino: Rome, 1926), 21–3, 25.]

105 Saving France

In this extract Doriot expresses the naïve faith, typical of so many fascist leaders, that his new movement will transcend political polarization and class barriers to forge a new national community.

If we had a State able to carry out this recovery it would be one strong enough to reorganize France and the Empire. It would restructure the economy of France by creating professional organizations which regulate problems of production and the relationships between the various elements involved in production. It would reorganize France into large economico-administrative regions. Once its authority had been restored it would be strong enough to decentralize the outmoded and antiquated system of administration which is now stifling the country instead of stimulating activity.

By encouraging regionalism it would foster the blossoming of the culture in our beautiful French provinces, which live on in the memory and in the great traditions of our country. Under the uncontested authority of France, it could thus carry out reforms which would be dear to our friends in Alsace and Lorraine.[6]

Once restored to being the animator and guide of the Empire, and mindful of its economic tasks, it could enlist the collaboration of the peoples of our colonies in our great undertakings, though they would still take into account their own political, religious, and national aspirations. Under its protection the peoples who live under our flag would feel happy to be alive, because it would be a reign of authority, justice, and prosperity.

Such a State would make France respected abroad. There would be no foreign powers which would dare attack our country if it spoke our language clearly and pursued our political aspirations resolutely. Led and reorganized in this way, France could contemplate the future serenely and would once more be a nation admired throughout the world. It can become one: its fate is in our hands.

To achieve this it is enough to rouse it from its torpor, to appeal to its heart and reason: it is the mission with which all members of the Parti Populaire Français are charged.[. . .]

Our party is already a microcosm of a reconciled France. It is the model of what the whole of France will be tomorrow. Yet we formed it at the most difficult moment, a moment when class hatreds were at their peak, when the orchestras of right and left were making more din than ever to fight in opposing camps. It was almost a miracle to bring it about, and yet this miracle has been achieved before our very eyes.[. . .]

What we have started within the party must be continued: hundreds of thousands of men are destined to join it. You will go back to them and you will tell them what the Parti Populaire Français is. You will tell all of them, you the workers, you the

---

[6] Reintegrated into France only in 1918 after half a century of German occupation.

bosses, you the intellectuals, you the peasants, you will all tell everyone that their place is with us and that they must take it up.

And then, when they have joined this brotherly party, you will be conciliatory towards them to allow them to complete the rest of their evolution. Yes, we are destined to receive the former communist, or the man who was active in the extreme right. Who could dispute the fact that there will be some issues on which they disagree or have different shades of opinion? But the strength of our party lies precisely in the way it allows for such disagreements, such different shades of opinion, but subordinates them all to our great national ideal!

A few months after joining us there will no longer be former right-wingers, ex-communists, ex-socialists, former *camelots du roi*.[7] I only want to know soldiers of the PPF, bent on saving their country!

[*La France avec nous!* [France Is With Us!] (Ernest Flammarion: Paris, 1937), 117–21.]

MARCEL DÉAT

106 **The European Revolution and the New State**

This passage is taken from an article which Déat wrote for the RNP organ, L'Œuvre [Work] in late 1943, when the war had already started going against the Germans. It shows that he still retained an unshakable belief that the Nazis were creating a genuinely 'national socialist' order in Europe, based on the principle of the 'strong State', which he attempts here to present as entirely compatible with French political theory. The antagonism to capitalism and the bourgeoisie he expresses links his fascism structurally with the 'neo-socialism' which before the war he had prescribed as a cure to the ills of the modern world.

Liberal capitalism was only interested in the State in as far as it served its own purposes. It needed a docile agent to translate the needs of bankers and the captains of industry into laws and regulations. This gave rise to the theory of the 'night-watchman State', whose function was to make sure the people, especially the proletariat, remained law-abiding, but which was ordered not to stick its nose in the affairs of these gentlemen. Translate that into the euphemistic language of academics and you get the doctrine of *laissez-faire* and *laissez-aller*, which very conveniently proves that any interference by public agencies in the economy is a malevolent heresy.

However, the interventions of the State multiplied. Increasingly it had to assume functions in the sphere of economic control, and it had to draw up and put into effect a whole programme of social legislation. The reason for this is that capitalism had the effect of bringing about the spectacular growth of the industrial masses condemned to live at the mercy of crisis and permanent misery. It is understandable

---

[7] Militants of the royalist and anti-Semitic Action Française.

that in its early days socialism turned to the State, even the theoretically democratic but actually bourgeois State, to obtain from it a minimum of aid and protection. But socialism was impregnated by the same spirit as the capitalism against which it was rising up. It too bathed in the democratic atmosphere of the nineteenth century and never grasped clearly the idea of what the true State had to be, namely a strong State, capable of instigating the revolution.

This new function of the State has only been realized and understood, and the new State has only been constructed, by the first European revolutions, and first and foremost by Germany.[. . .] The great novelty of the German State, the Third Reich, is that it succeeded in being both authoritarian and popular, so that it no longer expressed class interests, and offered something much better than a compromise between the interests of rival classes, or a precarious and constantly challenged balance between antagonistic forces. That was precisely the dangerous stage which our democracy had reached, leading to a visible paralysis of public institutions, a lack of authority, the breakdown of the State.

This time the mass of the people was integrated into a national community in which social rank found its place without the hope of imposing its pre-eminence or dictatorship. Neither bourgeois capitalism nor the proletariat took over, so that the regime which emerged was tainted neither by Anglo-Saxon hypocrisies nor by Bolshevik brutalities. And the mass of workers ceased to be so much dust and instead took on organic form: it was plucked from its isolation and desolation, and integrated instead in the collective, at last a collective provided with armour and spirit, a head and vigorous arms.

It is this aspect of the German Revolution which we are most blind to, but which is probably the most important. Certainly it has some specifically German traits, and it is easy to find the sources of this doctrine in the great tradition of German philosophers and economists which was inaugurated at the end of the eighteenth century. But if we are taken aback at this new concept of the State, it is because we have forgotten the teachings of Saint-Simon, it is because we have not reread Auguste Comte, it is because Fourier's ideas which adumbrate such a State have been dismissed as too puerile, it is because the very quantity of Proudhon's works has made us lose sight of their cogency. By the way, these old masters will doubtless become fashionable again, which is vital if France intends to make an original contribution to the great reconstruction of Europe.[. . .]

A State only prevails if it is upheld by men who are decisive, you may even say fanatical, men who in any case have a keen sense and a concrete vision of what is demanded for the sake of the public well-being [salut publique], dedicated with all their soul to a future which must be realized at all costs. These men do not comprise a class or a clan, they come from every walk of life. In other words, this necessary élite, which will carry the nation with it and guarantee the creation of the State, will be the élite of the revolutionary party.

Such a party was formed in Germany by the war, by defeat, by misery, by the horrendous spectacle of an unprecedented decadence, then by fourteen years of epic struggle. We do not have to wait this long, for we have before us the example of those who have succeeded, and in our turn we have experienced defeat and witnessed major episodes of failure and of almighty disintegration. This should suffice for us to undertake the task and see it through to success. Besides, we have no choice: succeed or perish.

[L'État et la Révolution [The State and the Revolution], *L'Œuvre*, 1/3. Nov. 1943, 1–2.]

PIERRE DRIEU LA ROCHELLE

107 **The Rebirth of European Man**

Under the Nazi occupation Drieu La Rochelle like Doriot and Déat, became an ardent collaborator. As this passage shows, he convinced himself that he was living through a turning-point in European history, the foundation of a new European order, and the emergence of the 'new man', all recurrent hallmarks of the fascist mentality when the Nazi war-machine seemed unstoppable.

A certain way of thinking characteristic of the late nineteenth and early twentieth century had provided European humanity with the basis of a renaissance such as it had not seen for centuries, for a revolution as total as that of an hour-hand returning to the same point on a clock-face.

In this moment the new ways of being have fused with the ways of thinking which called them forth. A new man has been born, reacting against the city, half-way between the countryside and the town, restoring to the soul and the body the values of force, of courage, of affirmation, eager to experience and to be tested and to base his life on an immediate and constant relationship between what is thought and what is accomplished. This fusion of practice with reason, transcending the diverging excesses of rationalism and romanticism, could not help but enter the political sphere and seek its crowning expression within it.[. . .]

This man retrod the path of Nietzsche. Taking as his starting-point the ultimate excess of intellectualism, he plunged headlong into books which might have been fatal. In the event they were not, and so he became imbued instead with their ideas, and found he had become a nihilist before a *tabula rasa* where all categories and outdated restrictions had been abolished, along with a reason which had turned to rationalism, and a mortality which had turned into hypocrisy. In an age where the vitality of old norms is completely spent, the most immoral men are the most moral.[. . .]

The new man has appeared in uncompromised fullness in Italy and Germany. He first appeared multilated and compromised in Russia, because the 'barbarians' who are 'primitives', thrown into disarray by the decadence of their neighbours, like dogs without masters, rummage for scraps in dustbins; they are forced to digest rotting filth.

The first task of the new man is to restore the values of the body. He starts out from the demands and attributes of the body.

This is the great revolution of the twentieth century which a section of French intellectuals has dimly sensed, but which they have not been able to grasp clearly and communicate to the nation: the revolution of the body, the restoration of the body.[. . .]

The new man starts with the body, he knows that the body is the articulation of the soul, and that the soul can only express itself, reveal itself, acquire substance in the body. There is nothing more spiritual than this recognition of the body. It is the soul which calls, which wants salvation, which saves itself by rediscovering the body.

Nothing is less materialist than this movement. The pathetic mistake of the last generation of rationalists, one which summed up all the dissolution, all the bastardization of their pseudo-humanism, was to accuse of materialism a revolution which salvages and restores the sources and mainstays of the spirit.[. . .]

The Hitlerian has been formed from the convergence of all these elements: the fighter of the Great War moulded in the Sturmtruppen or airforce, and who turned into the fanatic of the Freikorps, the terrorist-assassin who killed Rathenau; the boy scout, the Wandervogel trekking from youth hostel to youth hostel from one end of Europe to the other in search of an ill-defined salvation; the communist hit-man; the neurasthenic inspired by the example of the Italian Fascists as well as by the American gangsters, the mercenaries of the Chinese wars, the soldiers of the Foreign Legion.

It is a type of man who rejects culture, whose resolve is stiffened in the midst of his sexual and alcoholic depravity and dreams of giving the world a physical discipline with radical effects. It is a man who does not believe in ideas, and hence rejects doctrines. It is a man who only believes in acts and carries out these acts in line with a nebulous myth.[. . .]

Totalitarian Fascism and Hitlerism go beyond socialism and nationalism just as they annihilate capitalism and liberalism. Action breaks up these separate systems, these particular morphologies: this does not mean it does not analyse them or reinstate elements of them which are viable again. Action shatters the old links which existed between ideas, and so liberates many a valid one, all the more able to do so because it breaks up and disperses the old groupings of men who uphold the rigidity of ideologies.

Totalitarianism offers the chances for a double restoration, corporeal and spiritual, to 20th century man, to the man who demands wholeness and imposes it on the inadequate conditions which he has found.[. . .]

The Revolution which is taking place in Europe is total because it is the revolution of the body, the restoration of the values which have come forth from the body and are linked to the body, and because, by virtue of this very fact, it is the revolution of the soul which discovers and redefines its values through the values of the body.

['Renaissance de l'homme européen' [The rebirth of European man], in *Notes pour comprendre le siècle* [Notes to Understand the Century] (Gallimard: Paris, 1941), 149–62.]

vi. Belgium

Once militant Flemish separatism is excluded from the category of fascism, Belgian permutations of it are thin on the ground before the war. Originally Rex started out as a movement of Catholic moral rearmament which drew heavily on Maurras and his Action Française, and which used the monthly *Rex* (from *Christus Rex*, Christ the King) to fight a journalistic campaign for cleaning up the country's social and political life. Against the background of mounting political tension in Europe, its editor Léon Degrelle (1906–94) rapidly gained a reputation for the rhetorical powers displayed in vociferous attacks against Communists, finance capitalism, and governmental corruption. In 1936 Rex became the name of Degrelle's own party, set up to take the campaign into the political arena (Rex supporters carried brooms as a symbol of the urge to sweep clean). Despite his growing admiration first for Mussolini and then for Hitler, the party adopted a platform of radical social reform through state intervention which stopped well short of fascism, since it did not call for the overthrow of the liberal democratic system as such. It was only when he challenged the prime minister directly to an electoral duel in April 1937 and was soundly beaten that Degrelle and a number of Rexist radicals abandoned any lingering commitment to parliamentary democracy and 'genuine' Christianity. After the Nazi invasion of Belgium in May 1940, Degrelle threw his efforts into transforming Rex into an openly pro-Nazi party, and his organization collaborated with the Gestapo to the point of raising volunteers for the Walloon Legion which fought on the Eastern front (Degrelle among them). The subtle transition from a proto-fascism to fully-fledged Belgian fascism is illustrated by two passages, the first from Degrelle when he still technically pursued an electoral route to power (Text 108), the second from one of the party's principal ideologues, José Streel, after Rex had thrown its lot in with Nazism (see Conway 1993).

LÉON DEGRELLE

108 **The Revolution of Souls**

The preface to Degrelle's The Revolution of Souls *(1938) registers his extreme disappointment at not being swept into power in the by-election the year before. Though the remedies which he proposes for the creation of a 'new world' are too nebulous to count as full-blown fascism, they bear witness to Degrelle's heightened palingenetic political temperament at the time. This predisposed him to the enthusiastic collaboration with the Nazi's 'New European Order' during the war, when his insistence on wearing a fascist uniform in church led to his excommunication (a weapon which the Vatican under Pius XII refrained from using to discourage the collusion of Catholics with Nazi atrocities). Degrelle went on to become one of the most important figureheads of the continuity between inter-war and post-war fascism (Texts 174, 180).*

What is surprising is that in its revolt the whole of the new generation—and so many older men who think like it, who share its nausea and anger—have not turned to anarchy. And that, rather than indulging in the perverse joy of smashing everything to pieces in a blind rage, they have preferred to undertake the ungrateful task of uplifting souls and rebuilding a country from top to bottom. If they had put so much zeal into whipping up the masses and leading them into the arms of communism, where would the country be now?

The intransigence of the new generation will turn them into arsonists or crusaders. They will no longer tolerate half-baked solutions. They will create a new world, a complete social order, a seamless system of justice, a real fraternity among people, a society no longer based on physical degradation, hatred, the stifling of thought, but on human dignity, on profound virtues, and on the peace which stems from spiritual growth. Our century will either be a century of the soul, or it is doomed to burn like a funeral pyre.[. . .]

Europe is going mad. Mad with scandals. Mad with egoism. Mad with revolt against Heaven. Mad with blood.[. . .] Corrupt in its morality, debased in its faith, puffed up with individualism, fanaticism, and pride, having lost touch with charity, with the love of God and man, anaemic, modern Europe is waiting for the final blow, the last convulsions, the last corpses. The hour is approaching when all accounts will be settled. The hour is also coming when to save the world it will need a handful of heros and saints who will carry out the Reconquest.[8][. . .]

A country soon gets back on its feet after financial set-backs. It is not too hard for it to find a new political structure. It just calls for able technicians and a collective will to join forces.[. . .] The real revolution is much more complicated, the one which puts right not the mechanism of the State, but the secret life of each soul.[. . .]

It is only the quality and vibrancy of the soul which matters, the capacity for giving oneself unstintingly, its will to place an ideal above all other considerations in a spirit of total disinterest. Only faith counts, burning confidence, the complete absence of egoism and individualism, the striving of the whole being towards service, however lowly it is, wherever it may be, however it may be fulfilled, for a cause which transcends man, asks everything of man, and promises him nothing.

In a century where people only live for themselves, hundreds, thousands of men must no longer live for themselves, but for a collective ideal, and be prepared in advance to endure for its sake every sacrifice, every humiliation, every heroic act.[. . .] I can hear in the night's darkest hour crowds of people rising to their feet to protest their will and their faith. I see these thousands of men and women renewing their vow. How can one doubt that this heroism will bear fruit? It is these souls which will change the world.

[*Révolution des âmes* [The Revolution of Souls] (Éditions de la France: Paris, 1938), 145–54, 161–2.]

---

[8] Reference to the 16th-cent. *Riconquista* in which the Moors were finally driven out of Spain as an 'alien' population.

José Streel was one of Rex's leading ideologues. In The Revolution of the Twentieth Century, *written when an Axis victory still seemed inevitable, he offers a sustained analysis of the cultural and political sea-change which he believed world history was passing through, namely the transition from the age of liberalism to the age of fascism, confirming the prediction Mussolini had made in the* Enciclopedia Italiana *article on* Fascism *a decade before (see Text 32), and producing in each national culture an appropriate manifestation of the new genus of political energy (cf. Text 99). Note the attempt to turn the Nazi* Volksgemeinschaft *into a universal principle, the 'community of the people'.*

Thus whatever area of society is considered, it only confirms the impotence of traditional forces. None provided an adequate response, based on realities, to the needs which surfaced in a society profoundly modified after the 1914–18 war. Most of these forces spent their strength in pursuing pointless goals on the margins of real events.[. . .]

Well, peoples could not wait indefinitely or be satisfied with partial or provisional remedies to the ills that assailed them. They needed a radical reassessment of the conditions in which they lived. They were waiting for a force which, completely new and hence totally flexible, could manage to synthesize the needs of the age and come up with a way of meeting them all in a satisfactory way. Or rather, they did not wait for this force: in so far as they still constituted relatively healthy organisms, the peoples themselves were about to make this new force well up from out of their own substance: this force is called fascism, national socialism, the new order. It is this force which is everywhere at work giving birth to the revolution of the twentieth century, namely the adaptation of the peoples of Europe to the new historical climate which recent processes have brought about. It is not the arbitrary creation of a few fanatical minorities resorting to violence to impose their will: it is the life-asserting reaction of a social body on the verge of exhaustion, and responding through those parts of it which are still healthy, to the effects of a slow intoxication.

This revolution is an organic phenomenon, almost a physiological one. Any other way of seeing it cannot take account of its scope and originality or its defining features. It has emerged naturally from the decomposition of the liberal regime whose creative well-springs have run completely dry within the forms it has created. Just as at the beginning of the nineteenth century liberalism brought a solution to the new problems which the *ancien régime* was incapable of envisaging, so fascism, in the second third of the twentieth century, is presenting itself as the life-form most rigorously adapted to contemporary conditions.[. . .]

The revolution of the twentieth century has not succeeded everywhere all in one go—even if movements have arisen everywhere to lay the basis for it; it has succeeded in certain countries which did not seem particularly well suited for it, while it has not broken through in others where the ground seemed more favourable. It has got to power by very different means, it has taken specific forms, and followed its own course in each country. Each national revolution forms a particular, self-contained whole which has taken a gamble with its own resources and found its own way in the light of its own genius. Its course has not been dictated by fate but by realities.[. . .]

We are witnessing the crystallization of what historians will call the century of fascism or national socialism, on a par with the great periods of the Middle Ages, the Renaissance, the *ancien régime*, and the liberal epoch, [. . .]

The community of the people [communauté populaire]—which in the present stage of historical development is fundamentally confused with the nation—is the nation considered as a complete social environment in which man can blossom. It pre-exists the individual and is not dependent on an unstable set of conditions. It is above all conflicts of interests which can manifest themselves within it; it imposes on its members links powerful enough, and a solidarity effective enough, to transcend all ideological and economic differences.[. . .] It is perpetuated through the heritage which is passed down to each generation from its forebears, and through the duties which unite it to future generations. The solidarity in which it binds the same people to each other with countless ties is not a sentimental or voluntary act of generosity, but an organic condition of its existence from which no one is free to opt out; the community is the real source of this solidarity and all the consequences which flow from it. Hence its unity and cohesion are the fundamental values outside of which human societies cannot achieve a viable form of life. Through its party and class struggles and its individualism the liberal regime has broken down the community. By doing this it has sinned against what is real, for the community of the people is the primordial reality whose empirical existence cannot be denied and which must serve as the basis of all historical development.

It is the need to reestablish such a community, its unity and cohesion, which we find lies at the basis of all the achievements of the revolution of the twentieth century, for it is towards community that the whole movement of adaptation to the real which inspires this revolution is geared.

[*La Révolution du vingtième siècle* (Nouvelle Société d'Éditions: Brussels, 1942), 63–5, 72–3, 80–1.]

Norwegian fascism and treacherous collaboration have become synonymous with Vidkun Quisling (1887–1945) who founded Nasjonal Samling[9] in 1933 to create a movement of national regeneration based on a blend of anti-Communism, Christian corporativism, autarky, and traditional Norwegian values. His urge to do so was prompted by no narrow nationalism, but a keen sense of the need to counter the threat of communism through a revival of the Nordic Principle at the root of Western civilization. He took up this theme in an article published in the *British Union Quarterly* in 1937 (vol. 1, no. 1) calling for a Nordic World Federation, which opens with the declaration 'an old world falls, a new is being born', and concludes with the call for 'all people of Nordic race and outlook in every country' (including Britain) to fight the 'diabolical' force of Jewish liberalism and Marxism'. Clearly this brand of fascism placed Quisling on a collision course with Nazism, especially after he was granted an audience with Hitler in 1942. He lost no time in setting up an NS government when the *Wehrmacht* overran Norway in April 1940, and two years later he found himself titular head of state, and leader of the only legal party. By now his ideology required minimal adaptation to accommodate the official aspirations of the Third Reich. However, the NS comprehensively failed in its task of Nazifying the Norwegians *en masse*, and his dream of achieving Norwegian sovereignty within Hitler's new European order remained what he accuses Marxist ideals of being, a godless chimera. He was shot as a traitor in 1945 (see Hoidal 1989).

VIDKUN QUISLING

110   **The Nordic Revival**

This extract from Russia and Ourselves, *published in English in 1931, shows that even before Hitler came to power Quisling was contemplating a regenerated Norway as part of a Nordic alliance.*

We have seen how the Bolshevists are working against the world. How is the world to defend itself against Bolshevism, and Bolshevist-ridden Russia, which, with her resources, her means, and her aims, is not only a danger, but the greatest of all dangers to the civilization of the world, and the welfare of mankind?[. . .]

The Nordic nations must strive towards a fuller knowledge of themselves, their own character, and their place and task in the world. We must realize that we do not stand alone, but that we are members of a common Northern stock, which

---

[9] Lit. 'The Rallying of the Nation'. The word *samling* (German *Sammlung*) has the connotations of the French *rassemblement* in the name of Déat's party Rassemblement National Populaire (see Text 106), suggesting a vast movement of populist energies.

represents the most valuable contribution to the human race, and has always been the chief exponent of world-civilization. Not only Greece and Rome, but Europe and America owe their greatness to the Nordic element, and the fate of the modern world is bound up with its preservation or decay, as was the case with the ancient civilizations. Efforts towards the national revival of our countries are futile unless the Nordic spirit is reanimated. The progress of our nations is inextricably bound up with the preservation of their Nordic blood; and in order to ensure this survival of our typical stock we must observe a set of rather primitive laws, already discovered by science. Unless we guard our Nordic character, it will be lost to us.[. . .]

Our civilization, created and borne forward by the Nordic race and by Nordic elements in other races, is now threatened by the devastating activities of inferior races. If this crisis is to be safely passed, it is an essential condition that the various Nordic peoples, and people with Nordic sympathies, should join hands and initiate honest and intelligent co-operation for world organization and peaceful progress.[. . .]

Our policy, apart from being abreast of the times, must conform to the needs and aims of our Nordic stock. Our political creed and our political activities must be grounded upon and permeated by a sane nationalism, and by a profoundly moral outlook on the world. Like Bolshevism itself it must be a politico-religious movement, in a sense a Puritan movement. And the only useful basis for this will be found in a Nordic revival. In our countries where the Nordic stock predominates, the notion of 'race' ought to supply as workable an ideology as that of 'class'. By combining the 'Nordic idea' with a religious and moral perception of the world, and attention to the requirements of modern progress, a scientific political doctrine may be evolved (religious in aim, national, social, and Nordic, or, if you will, social-individualistic) which will possess the necessary strength and conviction to overcome the ogre which oppresses our communities. A national renaissance in Nordic spirit; a peaceable and just solution of the social problem; and a world-embracing co-operation between the various Nordic peoples and people of Nordic sympathies to promote the world's organization and peaceful development—this is not merely an anti-Bolshevist, but primarily a positive policy founded upon realities, and with a strong and noble aim in view, something really worth living and dying for. Far more so than the Godless chimeras of Karl Marx and Lenin.

[*Russia and Ourselves* (Hodder & Stoughton: London, 1931), 274, 280–4.]

VIDKUN QUISLING
111 A Greater Norway

Just how totally Quisling's fascism had accommodated Nazism once Norway was occupied can be seen from his collection of speeches and articles published in translation by the Third Reich in 1942, from which this extract is taken. The explanation of the war is the standard

*Nazi one of an Anglo-Jewish conspiracy (see Texts 41, 83, 86), and is full of the triumphalism
still possible before Stalingrad.*

Throughout the nineteenth century all the works of our great poets resonate with
the same theme: first the evocation of a great Nordic past, then the tragic recognition of a national decay, 'our shame, our night and our distress' (Aukrust), and then
the confident promise of a rallying of our nation and its imminent resurrection. As
Henrik Ibsen wrote in 1872:

> One day generations may come after us
> Who form the mainstay of popular unity [*Sammlung*].
> At this point the old greatness will arise once more
> And wise words will become gloriously true.

This great poetic theme of our past greatness, our present decay, and the new force
we will be in the future is in fact intimately bound up with the overwhelming
feeling and the living faith of the whole Norwegian people, and prophetically points
forward to the battle which we are fighting today.

> A seer's spirit infuses the poet's word
> When he sings from the midst of woes, affliction, and hard battle.
> He senses the meaning at the core of bitter human distress,
> And how from it the new age is arising.

This whole line of thought is all the more penetrating because it is in harmony with
our forefathers' vision of the struggle which is taking place throughout all lives
lived in this world: a vision which is apparently deeply rooted in the national soul
[*Volksseele*], and is based on the belief that our own world only perishes in the battle
with the evil, destructive forces of darkness in order to arise again more gloriously
than ever.

*Only the greatest and strongest peoples can boast myth, poetry, and national history as
intimately bound up with each other as the Norwegian people can.*[. . .]

The national decay and collapse of Norway are the result of a set of debilitating
and corrosive forces which over generations have been able to gather momentum.

These currents of corruption are all closely linked with each other and finally
merge in the mighty stream which we call Anglo-Jewish world capitalism. That is
the Midgard snake which wraps itself round the world and gnaws at the roots of the
Nordic tree of life. To remove Anglo-Jewish, capitalist influence from every area,
dynastic, political, social, economic, and cultural, is the premiss for the resurrection
of Norway, and hence the principal goal of our movement for national unification
[*Sammlung*].[. . .] And England will go under with the death of the doomed capitalist
system, whose creators and leaders are the members of international Jewry resident
there, and on whom English world dominion depends. It is now obvious that the
English policy of 'divide and rule' in continental Europe is played out. It is precisely
in the Balkans that the English attempt to balkanize Europe is rapidly approaching
its moment of truth, in which the whole of Europe with a population of over 300
million people economically and militarily united confront the English island,
while its dominion in the East is being simultaneously threatened by Japan.[. . .]

The followers and the members of the Nasjonal Samling movement are the social group which forms the backbone and leadership of the State, one which identifies with the national interests and, through its power over the State, will bring about the national resurrection.[. . .]

A complete transformation of the outlook of our fellow countrymen is necessary if the Norwegian people is to rise again as a national and free people within the New Europe. And the expression of this spirit to which the Norwegian people must be converted is national socialism, a national community organized on national soil, brotherly love at its most practical, the incorporation of the individual in the people and of the people in the global community, sustained by national self-discipline, national solidarity, and national organization. *The new Norway must build on Germanic principles, on a Norwegian and a Nordic foundation.*[. . .]

The war has shocked the Norwegian people out of its deep slumber and the thought of national reconstruction is born once more.[. . .] With the foundation of the Nasjonal Samling we have safeguarded the new national autonomy of the Norwegian people and created the basis of a national rebirth in the spirit of the historical tradition of our people. And as good Norwegians we are now building the new Norway on this basis without regard to personal sacrifice.[. . .]

I am no prophet. But what I said in the past has come to pass. And today I tell you that what Norway was it will be again, despite the difficulties that lie in its path.

Norway will grow into a great political alliance and thus contribute to laying the spiritual and economic foundation of a new civilization.

Norway shall not only be free. Norway shall be great.

['Nationaler Verfall und nationale Wiedererhebung' [National decay and national resurgence], in *Quisling ruft Norwegen!* [Quisling Calls Norway], trans. Günther Thaer (Franz Eher Verlag: Munich, 1942), 118–19, 132, 134–6, 140–1.]

viii. Finland

The political roots of Finnish fascism lay in the Civil War between communists (Reds) and nationalists (Whites) which broke out shortly after the country had won independence from Russia in 1917. Ideologically it drew on a powerful movement of cultural nationalism which had grown up in the nineteenth century and culminated in the Academic Karelia Society (AKS) founded in 1922, which asserted the need to eradicate Swedish influence and create a Greater Finland (Suur-Suomi) stretching to the Urals. Elements of Lutheran fundamentalism and Social Darwinian ideas commingled incongruously in the myths underpinning of the cult of Finnishness, which found particular favour amongst *Jäger* [hunters], volunteers who had fought with the Germans during the war.

The political expression of Finnish ultra-nationalism surfaced in 1929 when farmers in the Ostrobothnian commune of Lapua violently broke up a communist meeting. The nationwide Lapua movement was born, backed by elements of the peasantry, the farming community, middle classes, intellectuals, Civil Servants, the Church, and the armed forces, united in a crusade to purge Finland of communism (Text 112). The activist wing of Lapua took the law into its own hands, smashing Communist printing presses and even abducting the former president and his wife in 1930. The promulgation of anti-communist laws shortly afterwards, largely as a result of the threat Lapua posed to the government, did not placate the Lapuan hard-liners, least of all its leader Vihtori Kosola, who had started modelling himself on Mussolini and campaigning for the overthrow of liberal democracy itself. However, the banning of communism signalled the end of Lapua as a genuine mass movement and when Lapua militia attempted a *coup d'état* in February 1932 the revolt was easily crushed. Lapua's banning followed soon after.

Finnish fascism resurfaced immediately in the founding of Isänmaallinen Kansanliike (IKL), or People's Patriotic Movement, in April 1932, subsuming both Lapua and the AKS. It set out to act as the nucleus of a broad White front to eradicate communism, establish an authoritarian corporate state, and create a Greater Finland (Text 113). It talked of a regenerated Finnish national community (*kansankokonaisuus*), created a hierarchical structure complete with a Fascist-style youth movement, the Blue Blacks (Lapuan activists wore a black shirt and blue tie), and developed a distinctive style of ritual politics. Despite gaining 100,000 members, its electoral popularity peaked at 8 per cent in 1936, and growing political stability sapped the IKL of its strength. After some of its leaders had contributed to government during the period of co-operation with Germany (1941–3), the IKL was dissolved in 1944 (see Karvonen 1988).

Lapuan ideology drew deeply on bourgeois anti-Marxism and Lutheran Christianity, both of which come to the fore in this editorial taken from the movement's newspaper, Lapuan Päiväkäsky, The Lapua Daily Order. *Note the typically fascist equation of Marxism with anarchy, Judaism, and materialism.*

Between God and Satan, white and red, no middle road exists. The hour of our destiny has arrived, we must align ourselves with the one or the other.

Two spirits are today fighting for world supremacy, one of them destructive, the other constructive. The former spirit wants to tear asunder all conceptions of justice, and all divine and moral laws, along with the social order built upon them. It endeavours to overturn thrones and established churches, to eradicate loyalty and humbleness from human hearts, and to foment such general dissatisfaction that it will lead to a war in which everyone is pitted against everyone else. The aim is to enable someone—a Dictator-Jew, or some small faction?—standing on the ruins of burnt-down homes and bloodstained churches, to exert tyrannical power at will in the name of the 'proletariat' while in fact solely pursuing his own interests. The second spirit, by contrast, endeavours to preserve those values already created, and to build a new Finland based on godliness and the rule of law.[. . .]

Communism is the spirit of terrible persecution, hatred, and destruction, a spirit which has sworn to wipe out the time-honoured foundations of our society. Nothing is sacred or worthy of respect to communists. Everything from family life to the highest echelons of government should be ridiculed and destroyed. We hate this spirit, and wish to spread this hatred as far and wide as we possibly can.

There are only two kinds of people: the righteous and the godless. The divine world order and the teachings of the Christian Church know of no third possibility. In reality there are no 'centrists' or 'humanists of the golden middle road'.

Between good and evil, life and death, peace and war, light and darkness, Christ and Satan, white and red, the gospel of the Churches and atheism, there is no intermediate form, no third possibility. What it is all about is a struggle between an ethical bourgeois world-view and materialist Marxism. 'The golden middle road' is simply an impossibility, a paradox. He who woos pagan anti-Christianity woos the Devil himself.

[Editorial from *Lapuan Päiväkäsky*, 1931, quoted in Juha Siltala, *Lapuan liike ja kyyditykset 1930* [The Lapua Movement and the Abductions of 1930] (Otava: Helsinki, 1985), 444–5.]

113 **The Revolution of the Finnish Heart**

The continuity between the AKS and the IKL is illustrated in these extracts from two speeches by the Reverend Elias Simojoki, who made the first one as a founding member of the AKS, and the second thirteen years later as IKL deputy and head of the Blue Blacks.

A revolution in the hearts of our people—that is what we are preparing and that is what we believe in. It is a tremendous goal, next to which even goals such as a Greater Finland, a free Karelia, and a liberated Ingria may be secondary. We firmly believe that only a national reawakening can furnish the basis for victory in that great marathon which we are approaching minute by minute; in the hour of that reawakening our dreams of Greater Finland and a free family of Finnish peoples will come true as if by themselves, as the result of natural necessity. We shall charge onward towards this goal and will not have the time to look out for those who may be trampled by our feet. In the struggle which lies ahead we shall demand nothing for ourselves. We accept being small as long as our Fatherland and our people become great. We accept being poor, if by that the Fatherland can become rich. We joyfully accept being humiliated, if the road to the Fatherland's and our nation's glory must pass through our personal shame. We will throw ourselves in the dust to be the stepping-stones of our nation, if the upward road for our nation must go this way. The treasure which recompenses us for our heavy sacrifices and enriches our hearts may be invisible to others, but it is sufficient for us. That treasure has been given to us by the Fatherland, and therefore we offer ourselves in return.

[Speech delivered in 1923 by Elias Simojoki, in *Palava pensas* [Burning Bush] (Werner Söderström: Porvoo, 1942), 52–3.]

Today, there is great fear of the fascistization of our young. If by fascism one means the national revival which has begun to fight for the National State, there is every cause to fear the fascistization of youth. Whatever measures our opponents may take, in this sense our youth will be fascistized: it will take up the struggle for a new State and a new society, one from which class hatred has been eradicated. The most important mission of this youth, indeed of our entire national movement, it is to win the soul of the Finnish working people back to the Fatherland. For achieving this cause, no sacrifice may be too great, no programme can be too radical. It is on this issue that the Finnish nation will stand or fall.

[Speech by Elias Simojoki, at an IKL rally in Helsinki on 15 Sept. 1935, in *Palava pensas*, 154.]

ix. Estonia

The only candidate for an Estonian fascism is Eesti Vabadussõjalaste Liit, or the Estonian War of Independence Veterans' League (EVL) formed by the ex-soldiers who had fought to preserve the country's newly declared independence from Russia in the fighting of 1918–20. It was formed in 1929 with a view to creating a more socially cohesive, politically stronger national state (*rahvusriik*), and imitated the ritual, militaristic style of fascism to whip up patriotic spirit and appeal to energies of youth as the core of an integrated national community (*rahvuslik tervik*). However, the EVL (sometimes erroneously called 'vaps', which referred to an individual EVL member) sought to reform the state system through the electoral process rather than overthrow it, operated within the bounds of legality, and never developed a consistently revolutionary vision of a post-liberal new order.

The outstanding achievement of the movement was to mobilize support for constitutional change in the referendum of October of 1933, when it won 73 per cent of the vote. It was only after the head of state, Konstantin Päts, had banned the EVL in March 1934 as part of measures to eliminate opposition and create his own, partially fascistized dictatorship, that some EVL members planned a coup on fascist lines, but it was pre-empted by the police. The EVL thus falls short of being fascist, its ideologues themselves seeing only the crusade against Marxism and corruption as the common denominator of their goals with those of Fascism and Nazism. Nevertheless, given the rarity of English translations of Estonian material relating to the radical right, it seems opportune to print these two extracts from editorials published in the EVL newspaper *Võitlus* (Struggle) shortly after the 1933 referendum. Significantly, they present the success of the movement's campaign to renovate the nation in terms, not of a new order and a new man, but of a revitalized republic based on Estonian reasonableness (see Kasekamp 1993).

EVL

114 A New Estonia

The secret of the Veterans' League's success is simple. The Veterans worked hand in hand with the people for the people's rights and freedom. The political parties worked against the will of the people for their own personal and factional interests. The Veterans carried in this battle the desire to establish the right foundation for our State's life so that the Estonian nation can become internally strong.[. . .] Now the question arises: how to put the new constitution properly into practice in actual life so that its basic idea will be achieved.[. . .] We must set to work to scare away the old dissolute spirit. We must set to work to ensure that the new constitution will be put into practice in the sense and spirit that it was conceived.[. . .] The political parties have not yet correctly evaluated the significance of the 14, 15, and

16 October.[10] The parties wish to play down the significance of those days as if no more than the changing of a few paragraphs was involved. Actually those days mark the beginning of the rebirth of the Estonian nation in the moral and political, as well as the economic sphere. On those days the people finally put an end to the profiteering and vested interests of the existing party-political system. On those days the people initiated a bloodless national revolution corresponding to the Estonian people's characteristically reasonable and considered way of acting. The Veterans do not intend to stop half-way, but will work and struggle for our high ideals from our newly won positions.[. . .] The Veterans' movement will win, or we will die fighting for our beliefs. For us a third way—surrender or compromise—does not exist.

[*Võitlus*, 19 Oct. 1933.]

The second republic must not only be different numerically, but must be ordered differently, justly. Where class interest ruled, there the whole Estonian people's common interest must arise and grow. Where greedy sharks lived the high life, from now on there must be men who are honest like our people, true to them to the bone. Where greasy internationalizing socialism flourished, there must develop and blossom the nationalist Estonian future, which is sustained above all by the honest and conscientious Estonian working man. When over 416,000 enfranchized and conscious citizens led by the Veterans carried out the constitutional revolution against the political parties' baseness so long desired by our people, then all unbiased historians must later recognize that the Veterans for the second time in history became the backbone which finally straightened the Estonian people, which enabled the birth of the Estonian nation, nationalist Estonia. At the moment of the crumbling of the political parties' fortress of avarice, the Veterans' popular movement was blessed and consecrated by 416,000 citizens as the only true and rightful leader of the Estonian people.

The nucleus of this popular movement are the Veterans, who together with the Estonian people not only created the independent Estonian state in the War of Independence, but afterwards have fought with all their might on the internal front for the sake of a better and more just future for our State, finally mobilizing the people to take part in the referendum and securing the victory of the sovereign people over its party-political servants.[. . .] With unshakeable spirit, courage, and bravery, the Veterans' movement wants to work tirelessly so that the Estonian people, not only in form, but also in content, can achieve the second republic so fervently desired by all classes, the republic which is truly based on justice and fairness. That republic can only be led by the EVL spirit. The first republic belonged to the political parties. The second republic, however, belongs to the EVL spirit. And therefore the second republic will be a genuine people's republic—an Estonian national state.

[*Võitlus*, 21 Nov. 1933.]

[10] The dates of the referendum on which the EVL won 73% of the vote for a new constitution.

x. Latvia

Like Estonia, Latvia was a Baltic state which gained independence in the wake of the Russian Revolution. Its liberal democracy was soon exposed to the socio-economic pressures ensuing from the Depression, as well as from the political pressures emanating from the Europe-wide shift towards authoritarianism. Eventually democracy was snuffed out by the leader of the Peasant Union, Karlis Ulmanis, whose palace revolution in 1934 led to a para-fascist regime partially modelled on Mussolini's. It had to contend with a genuinely fascist threat, however, in the form of the Ugunkrust (Fire Cross), subsequently renamed Pērkonkrust (Thunder Cross), whose greyshirted paramilitary troops pursued a revolutionary solution to the crisis which would turn Latvia into an authoritarian state based on a new élite and a new corporatist economy. It also stood for an integral nationalism which extolled the values of Latvianness, the peasantry, and the land, which turned the country's many non-Baltic ethnic minorities, particularly the Jews, into a 'problem'. Ulmanis tried to crush the Thunder Cross in 1935 and 1937, but it survived his regime, which was terminated by the Nazi–Soviet Pact of 1939, to emerge as a collaborationist force when the Third Reich's troops occupied the Baltic States in 1941. Its members took an active part in the Nazi death squads' 'actions' against the Jews and provided men for the Latvian division of the German Sixth Army.

GUSTAVS CELMIŅŠ

115 **A Latvian Latvia**

This extract is taken from a speech by Pērkonkrust's leader Gustavs Celmiņš reported in the movement's newspaper six months after the liberal government had tried unsuccessfully to ban it.

Today the Latvian people ask us: are you the ones who will make the Latvian master in his own land, who will save our nation from misery and collapse?[. . .] We are the ones![. . .] Our programme with its explanations is sufficient to form the foundation on which a Latvian State for Latvians can be built. These four principles make up the Pērkonkrust's political platform:

1. Supreme power in Latvia belongs to the Latvian people.
2. The good of the nation is of higher value than individual freedom.
3. The premiss of the state economy is the inner colonization of the nation's resources.
4. A state president elected by the people for five years, a parliament for the representation of commerce, a government subordinate to the president.

In a Latvian Latvia the question of minorities will not exist. Only Latvians will rule themselves and the other nations which live here. This means that once and for all we renounce unreservedly bourgeois-liberal prejudice on the national question, we renounce historical, humanistic, or other constraints in pursuit of our one aim—the good of the Latvian nation. Our God, our belief, our life's meaning, our goal is the Latvian nation: whoever is against its welfare is our enemy.

Our relations with other peoples who have come to our land is not determined by their degree of worth or belonging. We divide them into two groups: (1) Estonians and Lithuanians, who for us are not foreign peoples; (2) Jews, Germans, Poles, Russians. All of them are 'non-Latvians' and in a Latvian Latvia there is no place for them.[. . .]

Since our programme is not artificially conceived for the sake of agitation, our position is wholly vindicated. (1) We assume that the only place in the world where Latvians can settle is Latvia. Other peoples have their own countries. (2) The only way to keep national independence in these specific geographical boundaries is through unity.

In one word—in a Latvian Latvia there will be only Latvians.[. . .]

We renounce the right to individual freedoms for the good of the nation and the state. In a Latvian Latvia the individual will be valued only in so far as he is useful for the nation.[. . .] The Pērkonkrust acknowledges only the united nation and therefore there will be no classes in a Latvian Latvia.[. . .] The Pērkonkrust considers that the individual, nation, and State constitute an indivisible whole. One without the other cannot exist alone, but they must complement and support each other in an unbroken rhythm of labour.[. . .] The State has not only the right but the duty to make demands of those who do not participate in common work.[. . .] We acknowledge only a united Latvia, and equally harmful in our opinion are both the Marxists who undermine that unity, and the bourgeois with their narrow-mindedness or their unwillingness to understand the justified needs of their fellow national workers.[. . .] We acknowledge private enterprise and private property, but we do not acknowledge individual anarchy which leads to economic chaos and to excesses in the cultural and social sphere.[. . .] Our time is coming. A Latvian Latvia is coming. There honesty, work, and justice will rule.

[Speech of 17 Sept. 1933, published in *Pērkonkrust*, 24 Sept. 1933.]

xi. Romania

Romanian fascism is principally associated with Corneliu Codreanu, who in the course of the 1920s evolved a highly original and virulently anti-Semitic form of rebirth nationalism. To implement it he formed in 1927 a paramilitary terrorist organization, the Legion of the Archangel Michael (better known by the name of the movement created in 1930 to form its mass base, the Iron Guard). Despite attempts by liberal administrations to crush it, the movement grew to become the third largest party by 1937. A year later King Carol staged a *coup d'état* and set about eliminating the Legion, which he rightly saw as a threat to his authority. But his unpopularity when Romania lost large tracts of territory in 1940, at the hands of the temporarily allied Third Reich and Russia, forced him to woo the Legion to give himself a popular base. This desperate move failed in its objective and the king was forced into exile. His successor, General Antonescu, then created the National Legionary State with Iron Guardists appointed to important government posts, notably their leader Horia Sima, who became deputy prime minister. But by their nature para-fascism and fascism are mortal enemies. The Legion continued to operate as if they were the true masters of Romania, and in January 1941 Antonescu took Hitler's advice to crush it. After two days of bloody fighting in which the Nazi-backed government forces suppressed a Legionary revolt, Romania officially became a National and Social State, in other words a puppet State of the Third Reich.

An early embodiment of the Legionary ethic of heroic self-sacrifice was Ion Moţa (Text 116), who gained a reputation in his student days as a fanatical anti-Semite and the translator of *The Protocols of the Elders of Zion*. In 1923 Codreanu appointed him leader of the Brotherhood of the Cross (a forerunner of the Legionaries of the Archangel Michael) and he remained his right-hand man. He represented the Legionaries at the meeting of the Fascist International in Montreux in 1934, made major speeches at party rallies, and edited the movement's journal *Libertate* [Liberty], dedicated to the 'education of peasant and worker'. In late 1936 he formed a Legionary unit and left along with another prominent Legionary, Vasile Marin, to fight the Republican forces in Spain. Both were killed on the battlefield on 13 January 1937. By far the most important ideologue of the Iron Guard, however, was Corneliu Codreanu (Text 118). His murder in prison in 1938 by the henchmen of Carol's 'State of National Renaissance' assured him the status of martyr, not just for the Legionaries, but for fascists the world over ever since (see Ioanid 1990).

ION MOŢA

116 | **The Romanian Legionary's Mission in Spain**

On 3 December 1936, the day of his departure from Lisbon to Spain, Moţa foretold his death in this letter, published posthumously in the Legionary magazine, Libertate, *with the epigraph 'Those who have died under the enemy bullets march side by side with those left behind.' It is imbued with the pseudo-Christian obsession with sacrifice and death so central to the ethos of Romanian fascism.*

Beloved comrades and readers of *Libertate*, God has chosen to include me—perhaps along with others of my comrades in the Romanian Legionaries of the Captain[11]— among those blessed soldiers who have fallen in Spain for the defence of the Cross. There, I have said that they are 'blessed', these soldiers—even if many of us leave behind children, wives, dear creatures with no one else to support them but us—because the only way a man can be really happy is to live this earthly life in such a way as to be able to hope for the salvation of his soul. And we whom God has accepted to defend him at the cost of our blood and our lives may have a strong hope in the salvation of our soul, despite all the sins we have committed up till now. No force, no love exists which is higher than that of the race (and can only be realized in the race), except for the force of Christ and love of Him. Christ is the same in Spain as in Romania.[. . .] We are defending Christianity in a foreign land, we are defending a force which wells up from the force of our people, and, spurred on by our love for the Cross, we are obeying here in Spain our love for the Romanian people.

Thus we fight, we die here for the defence of our ancestral law, for the happiness of our Romanian people, for its rebirth through the struggle of the Legion, through the reconstruction of the country which the Captain is carrying out. Our action is the corner-stone of this new Legionary Romania which is being built, an edifice which—following the will of fate which is unchanged since the time of Mastro Manole[12]—has demanded that we should be buried in its foundations and which, henceforth, the centuries will never be able to demolish again.

This is why I too have now taken leave of my nearest and dearest, why I will no longer be with you physically, beloved comrades and readers of *Libertate*. But as the song puts it so eloquently:

> Those who have been cut down by the enemy's bullets,
> March in the ranks of those who remain.

As the Legionaries know full well, when they are mustered at the front they carry out the 'roll-call of the dead', and the names of those killed in battle are called out, all the Legionaries reply, loudly and with conviction, in place of whoever no longer has a voice:

PRESENT!

[*Testamento di Ion Motza* (All'Insegna del Veltro: Genoa, 1984), 40–1, 1st edn. 1937.]

---

[11] i.e. Corneliu Codreanu.
[12] Reference to a Romanian legend concerning the building of a famous Romanian church which could not be completed by Mastro Manole until he had walled his wife inside it.

117 The Resurrection of the Race

This passage is taken from a German translation of an anthology of Codreanu's pre-war writings published in 1940, which implies that the Nazis themselves recognized the ideological affinity between the SS and the Legionaries, even if for pragmatic reasons Hitler generally preferred provinces of his European empire to be in the hands of a compliant para-fascist like Antonescu rather than independently minded fascists. It gives a flavour of the pathological conspiracy theory Codreanu held concerning the Jews, and his quasi-Christian myth of the organic Romanian nation. (He claimed to have been told to found the Legion by the Archangel Michael himself, who appeared to him while in prison.)

I will underline this once again: we are not up against a few pathetic individuals who have landed up here by chance and who now seek protection and shelter. We are up against a fully-fledged Jewish state, an entire army which has come here with its sights set on conquest. The movement of the Jewish population and its penetration into Romania are being carried out in accordance with precise plans. In all probability the 'Great Jewish Council' is planning the creation of a new Palestine on a strip of land which, starting out on the Baltic Sea, embraces a part of Poland and Czechoslovakia and half of Romania right across to the Black Sea.[. . .]

To carry out the plan the Jews take over the press. They welcome every opportunity to whip up discord in the Romanian people and where possible to divide it into several opposing camps which bitterly fight each other. They attempt to take possession of more and more sources of Romanian life. They drive the people systematically into the arms of vice, and intoxicate the people with all kinds of drinks and poisons.

Whoever wants to destroy a people will do it in the following way: destroy the link between heaven and the soil, foment fraternal conflicts and discord, sap all the vital energies of a people to the verge of extinction, resort to physical poisoning, etc. All these measures destroy a people more surely than guns and bombers![. . .]

The worst thing that Jews and politicians have done to us, the greatest danger that they have exposed our people to, is not the way they are seizing the riches and possessions of our country, destroying the Romanian middle class, the way they swamp our schools and liberal professions, or the pernicious influence they are having on our whole political life, although these already constitute mortal dangers for a people. The greatest danger they pose to the people is rather that they are undermining us racially, that they are destroying the racial, Romano-Dacian[13] structure of our people and call into being a type of human being that is nothing but a racial wreck. They present us with the type of politician who has nothing left of the nobility of our race within him, but only dishonours our race, degrades it, and condemns it to oblivion!

[13] The Dacians were the alleged root race of the modern Romanians.

If this breed of men continues to govern our country much longer, the Romanian people will soon close its eyes for ever. Romania will collapse, despite all the great programmes with which these tricksters want to glue down our eyelids.[. . .]

When we speak of the 'Romanian people' we mean by this not just all the Romanians who are now alive, who have the same past and the same future, the same way of dressing, the same language, the same daily pursuits.

We mean by Romanian people all the Romanians, living or dead, who have lived on this soil since the beginning of our history, and all who will live on it in the remotest future. The people includes therefore:

1. all the Romanians alive today;
2. all the souls and remains of our ancestors;
3. all those who will come into the world as Romanians.

A people only achieves true consciousness of itself if deep in its soul it is alive not only to its personal interests, but to its great unity and inner bonds.

The people has:

1. a physical and biological heritage: flesh and blood;
2. a material heritage: the soil of the fatherland and its treasures;
3. a spiritual heritage.[. . .] The ultimate purpose of a people is spiritual resurrection! The resurrection of the people in the name of the Redeemer Jesus Christ.

Creativity, culture are only means to this, and never ends in themselves. They are means to achieve this spiritual resurrection. Culture is the fruit of the talents and abilities with which God has endowed our people.

There will come a time when all the peoples of the earth will fight their way through to this final resurrection, all the peoples with their dead leaders. Then each people will be given a special place before the throne of God. This final act, this overwhelming moment, this resurrection of the dead, is the highest and most sublime goal which a people can aspire to.

A people is thus an entity whose life continues beyond the earth!

['Das Program der eisernen Garde' [The Programme of the Iron Guard], in *Die eiserne Garde* (Brunnen-Verlag: Berlin, 1940; translation of C. Z. Codreanu, *Pentru Legionari* [For the Legionaries], Bucharest, 1936), 111–13, 274, 394, 396.]

xii. Hungary

Hungarian fascism came into its own only in the last year of the war. Inter-war Hungary provides another example where a strong conservative right denied genuine fascism the space to break through. After the collapse of Béla Kun's Soviet Republic in August 1919 the country was ruled by a nominally parliamentary but effectively authoritarian right-wing government headed by Admiral Horthy. Though supported in its irredentist territorial claims by Mussolini, the regime resisted fascistization even when the prime minister was the pro-fascist Gömbös (1932–6) and mass patriotic rallies became the order of the day. The ultra-nationalism and anti-Semitism endemic to the country bred numerous attempts to launch fascist movements modelled on Nazism. The two notable ones were Böszörmény's Scythe Cross, which in 1936 attempted to mobilize peasant discontent through a mass march on Budapest, which in the event was a fiasco.

The other was launched by Ferenc Szálasi, who in 1935 founded the Party of National Will, renamed the Arrow Cross Party (Nyilaskeresztes Pártot) in 1937. Its programme was based on an original form of rebirth national socialism called 'Hungarism', but its rapid growth in popularity was due largely to the radical irredentist stand it took on the need to reverse the Treaty of Trianon of 1919, which had excluded 3 million Magyar-speaking people from the new Hungary. In the elections of May 1939 the party obtained 37 per cent of the vote, despite the fact that Szálasi had been imprisoned in 1938 for subversion. He was set free in 1940, but the Arrow Cross had by now passed its peak, and would have faded from the scene had not the Nazis installed him as head of state in October 1944 after Horthy had tried to protect his country by declaring neutrality. As the murderous end-game of the Second World War approached his country, Szálasi, with the extraordinary ability to confuse dreams with reality so typical of fascist leaders both in and out of power, now thought his time had come to implement his nebulous vision of a 'social-national' Greater Hungary with hegemony over the Carpathian–Danube Basin. Curiously, though his Hungarism was anti-Semitic it rejected the policy of mass extermination in favour of mass deportation, and he tried in vain to help the many thousands of Jews destined to die as Eichmann enforced the Final Solution on Hungary's Jews (see Deák 1965).

FERENC SZÁLASI
118 **Hungarism**

This sample of Hungarist thinking is taken from an anthology of pronouncements made by Szálasi over the years. It was published in the middle of the war while Horthy was still in power and Szálasi was an increasingly marginalized figure. (The only two significant references to the Jews are contradictory: one refers to them as 'an oozing wound, moral, mental and material, in the life of the state and people', while the other declares that they should have a 'proportional participation in the life and work of the State'.)

Has a national-socialist state an ideology?
Our ideology is new, still unknown. Until now the national-socialist states have not been able to formulate a new ideology. Their only concept is the negation of the practices of communism and Marxism.

What is the ideology of national socialism?
It has no ideological system yet. One can only see its political and social aspects. And because it has no ideology yet, for the moment it only denies and rejects Marxism. The ideology has to provide a content for it and in a positive sense it is about life, the life of workers, the morality and ethical spirit of material life.[. . .] The new ideology is actually a 'social nationalism'.[. . .]

What is social nationalism?
Social nationalism is the only true form and biology of life. The only viable basis for a nation is the social-national.[. . .]

How can we become national socialists?
The ideological basis of the national economy and programme of Hungarism is: social nationalism and its conscious practice. The individual can become a conscious national socialist only through the ideology and function of social nationalism. National socialism is a nationalist order in socialism, and social nationalism is a social order within nationalism. Spiritual order in the body and corporeal order in the spirit.[. . .]

What is the use of Hungarism?
In the perfection of Hungarism social nationalism is the ideological instrument, which provides the ideological basis for all national-socialist states and communities to realize and practise their nationalism and socialism.

What is the future of Hungarism?
We are sure it will be accepted not only by the Hungarian workers, but in all the states where one can already find national-socialist systems without the workers of such nations being provided with an ideological basis or practice. The Marxist workers' International started off in England, but it is the Hungarian workers in the Danube Basin who are going to initiate the spread of the social-national dimension of real national socialism so that it is taken up by the workers of all working nations.

How should Germans in Hungary greet us?
We expect our brothers to greet us with conviction and with all their heart in the salute 'Heil Hungary!' [Heil Ungarn], because we give our lives and blood to Hungarism and its implementation. Let's stop saying 'Heil Hitler!' because that would pave the way for a strong German influence and, through that, for German power-seeking. We are ashamed that 'Heil Hungary!' does not come naturally to the lips of Hungarians. We are about to change this situation quickly and fundamentally [15 March 1937].[. . .]

How will the reorganization of Europe take place?

The system and power can only be conquered through an individual belief in truth, not through opportunism. I am convinced that to reorganize Europe we have to start from the Hungarist principle, even though Hungary has been looked down on by the Germans. The New Hungary has to be based on my personal prestige. Luckily I am here, because there cannot be a New Hungary without me, and only with the expansion of the Hungarist principle will the reorganization of Europe be possible. Without my Hungarist principle there cannot be a new Europe either (summer 1942).

Who is going to realize Hungarism?

I will never give up Hungarism and everyone who cannot identify himself with Hungarism, or does not want to recognize me as the only leader, or does not want to accept that I have been chosen by higher divine dispensation to redeem the Hungarian nation, or does not understand me, or loses my confidence, can go. With the help of the secret strength inside me I am going to create the Hungarist State, even if I have to do it on my own [July 1942].

What is the instrument of Hungarism?

Every party member has to accept Hungarism as an ideology, and the Arrow Cross Party as the practical instrument for the realization of Hungarism [18 April 1942]. [. . .]

What is the objective of the state?

To create and organize, with centralized administration and leadership, and with distributed executive powers, the Hungarian United Territories [Hungària Egyesült Földek] stretching from the Carpathians to the Adriatic coast, formed out of Hungary, Slovakia, Ruthenia, Transylvania, Croat-Slovenia, and West-Gyepü. The Hungarian United Territories will have to be recognized as independent, free, and indivisible by England, Germany, Italy, Poland, and Russia through international treaties.

About the use of the mother tongue?

In state administration and government we want and demand the constitutional legitimization of the Hungarian language. In the enforcement of the law and in local administration we want the constitutional legitimization of the mother tongue.

What do we mean by freedom of religion?

We do not accept atheism. Every citizen must belong to one of the established and accepted Churches. We are going to be the strongest support of the Church.[. . .]

What should the Hungarian culture be careful about?

The culture of the Hungarians should always defend its unity, its racial independence, and its equality against any other culture.[. . .]

What will bring catastrophe to South-East Europe?

The greatest tragedy and catastrophe of the states of South-East Europe will be if they do not unite with the Hungarian Socialist State to fight for their rights.[. . .]

What will happen if the foundations are rotten?
They cannot be rotten, because for twenty years we have been struggling mentally and physically [. . .] and thus have built the base and the foundation.

[*Szálasi Ferenc Ideológiája: Idézetek Szálasitól* [The Ideology of Ferenc Szálasi:
Quotations from Szálasi] (Zaltán Kostyán: Budapest, n.d. [*c.*1943]), 3–6, 8, 11–15.]

Section B

Non-European Fascisms

i. South Africa

Curiously, most works on generic fascism have concentrated on inter-war Europe. This is not only to ignore the unabated profusion of post-war fascism, but also several highly original permutations of it which emerged outside Europe in the 1930s. A perfect habitat for the generation of home-grown myths before the Second World War was Afrikaner South Africa, where white supremacist and anti-British sentiment were channelled into a distinct form of ultra-nationalism through the efforts of the Broederbond (Brothers' Association). This was a semi-clandestine patriotic organization which created a potent ideological force out of a blend of Dutch Reformed Christianity with a historical myth of the Boers' national characteristics exhibited in the Great Trek of 1838. The anti-British sentiment of Afrikaner radicals, the affinity Dutch settlers felt with Germanic culture, and the presence in South Africa of many German émigrés also meant that by the mid-1930s Nazi overseas organizations were flourishing and the anti-Semitic Greyshirts had been formed to emulate the Sturmabteilung, the paramilitary wing of the NSDAP (see Bloomberg 1981).

The centenary of the Great Trek in 1938, when a symbolic re-enactment of the original journey inland from the Cape was staged, led to the creation of an authentic fascist movement in the shape of the Ossewabrandwag (OB; Ox-Wagon Sentinel). Its vision of South Africa's transformation into a 'Christian Nationalist' state soon attracted enough members for its leader, van Rensburg, to be able to offer Nazi agents a deal once Germany was at war with Britain. If supplied with enough arms by the Third Reich the 170,000 OB members, or rather its paramilitary formation, the Stormjaers, would stage a coup to overthrow the government, split between pro-British interventionists and neutralists. South Africa would then annex Southern Rhodesia and three British protectorates in exchange for naval and air bases. This led to Operation Weissdorn to topple Smuts's Government in 1941, plans for which were well under way before they were foiled by astute police action. Henceforth the OB ceased to be a credible revolutionary force, but remained a significant source of pro-Nazi Afrikaner ultra-nationalism till the war turned against the Third Reich. It also exerted considerable influence on the Afrikaner Werstandsbeweging formed after the war (see Text 206).

119   **The Reawakening of the Boerevolk**

This extract is taken from an OB pamphlet published during the war outlining the fundamental principles of the organization, and articulating the myth of the Boerevolk as an organic people forged by faith, culture, history, and race.

The first trek, the Great Trek, was the great pioneering period in the Afrikaner's pursuit of his own Fatherland. It united the Boer people and culminated in the Republic. The second trek, the Ox-Wagon Trek, drew together an expanded Afrikanerdom in the Ossewabrandwag and must result in a larger Republic. Through the Ox-Wagon Trek the Afrikaner was returned again to his past in a remarkable way, and thereby was put in touch with the ideals fostered by his ancestors, their world-view, and the strength that made them victorious. The festival gave rise to *a national renaissance, and this awakening had its roots in the Ossewabrandwag;* what was intended simply as a delightful folk festival developed into a mighty national movement.[. . .]

[In a national movement] the entire nation is drawn together in an invincible unity and all differences of class are wiped out. A national movement is concerned both with assimilating the most valuable elements of the past, and with realizing the full potential of the future. In the mirror of the past, the wishes of the people for the future lie revealed. The invisible thread binding the past to the future is the world-view of the nation. A nation is guided by its world-view, inspired and spurred on by it to its greatest deeds.

The *world-view* has its origins in the past, and is made up of the organic union of all the aspirations and ideals emerging out of the highest and best experiences of the nation while it is being shaped. In this way the Ossewabrandwag, which is the fruit of the people's deep and dedicated contact with its past, became the vehicle for the nation's world-view and, for this very reason, the expression of the nation's direction and future.[. . .]

The Development of a Specific World-View

One of the most powerful factors in the unification of the developing Afrikaner nation, and the determination of its national life, was the Christian Faith. The degree to which the people felt this faith, the manner in which it was practically manifested, and the perspectives it opened up gave rise, as a result of the specific experiences and reactions of the people—far removed from the circle of civilization and in contact with barbarism—to a specific world-view, in accordance with which the nation developed. We prefer to style it Christian-Nationalism.

It entailed a belief in God and the acceptance of his guidance. Free Will and Liberalism were ruled out and had to give way to conscious and responsible leadership with a specific purpose.

It also recognized the diversity of life, in nature and among human beings and peoples: the root of the deep-seated desire for national self-determination. This desire, in conjunction with the principle that every human being and every nation has equal rights, and is equal, gave rise to our nation's heartfelt and vital desire for freedom. This is why our people cannot bear to be shackled and will never be slaves. From the very first the principle of a spiritual brotherhood, and the clash with the ruling power, strengthened a conviction of unity in spite of individual differences.

The original religious instinct of the Afrikaner is responsible, too, for the spiritual dimension of his world-view. The spiritual and not the material predominates, and in the social order relations must be determined according to moral criteria and not materialistic ones.[. . .]

As we demand freedom from the outside world, so we also insist on inner *self-determination*. The people do not only have a right to ensure their survival as a nation, but must also safeguard themselves against cultural decay and degeneration. The people may not commit suicide through a liberalistic indifference.

The OB intends, therefore, in accordance with our Christian world-view and our history, to safeguard the biological and spiritual composition of our people. The miscegenation of races will not be allowed, and all elements which do not agree with our world-view will be eliminated. Only those who are able to assimilate themselves to us and assist in the realization of our ideal will be included in our people. Only those who can be at one with the people in every aspect will become citizens of our State.

Let it thereby be stated clearly that only citizens who love the nation will be permitted to participate in the various educational institutions responsible for building it up. The radio, the theatre, the press, and the school will be national in the fullest sense of the word. Only in this way will the people be given the pure formation that will enable it to achieve its full national expression, and fulfil its calling.

[*Die Grondslag van die Ossewabrandwag* [Founding Principles of the Ossewabrandwag] (Britz: Bloemfontein, n.d. [*c.*1942]), Department of Historical Papers, University of the Witwatersrand Library, A726/Ba2.]

ii. Chile

Though Latin America is widely perceived, especially by Marxists, as a breeding-ground of fascism, the hegemony of propertied, religious, and military (and hence conservative) élites has been generally so powerful that genuinely populist forms of rebirth ultra-nationalism have been systematically denied the space to establish themselves as regimes. The Perónist regime in Argentina at first seems to constitute an exception to this rule, but it lacks the radical palingenetic and ultra-nationalist thrust to constitute an example of fascism. As for movements, there has been no shortage of radical right-wing groups, whether paramilitary or populist, some of which have gone beyond crude anti-communism to share common ground with fascism (for example, the inter-war Mexican Sinarquistas, the Paraguayan Febreristas, or the post-war Frente Nacional Patria y Libertad in Chile), but almost all have lacked the radicalism necessary to carry through a social and ideological revolution. The two exceptions to this have been the National Socialists in Chile and the Brazilian Integralist Action (see Alexander 1973).

Chile's Movimiento Nacional Socialista (MNS) was formed by the Hispano-German Jorge González von Marées in 1932 with the backing of numerous *émigré* Germans. It soon ceased to be a crudely mimetic Nazi party and, though profoundly influenced by European models (its newspaper extensively published articles by German, Italian, and British fascists), it developed an ideology peculiarly tuned to the unique historical, cultural, ethnic, and economic situation of Chile. It suffered the fate of so many of its European counterparts of being crushed by a right-wing regime when its attempted coup was suppressed by government troops in 1938. An attempt to relaunch itself as Vanguardia Popular Socialista came to naught: it unceremoniously disbanded in 1941 after González had been interned on suspicion of insanity (see Sznajder 1993).

CARLOS KELLER

120   *Chilean Action* and National Regeneration

This sample of MNS ideology is taken from an article in the first issue of the movement's newspaper Chilean Action, *written by its leading ideologue, Hispano-German Carlos Keller in the heady days of its initial expansion.*

Since the Pacific War[14] and the revolution of 1891,[15] the Chilean people has entered a period of decadence, characterized by the prevalence of negative factors.

There is no doubt that the material progress which we have witnessed since the Pacific War is a consequence of the wealth it brought us. But this material progress

[14] The 'Nitrate War' of 1879–83 in which it gained naval supremacy over Peru.
[15] The congressional revolution which overthrew the military government.

has been a simple reflex reaction to the material boom of other nations which have come to make us part of their economic system.[. . .]

The chimera of gold started to infiltrate every aspect of national life. The zeal to grab a share of the booty destroyed the honesty, integrity, and modesty of the period when we were known as the 'Prussia of South America'. The people were sacrificed wretchedly. No one was concerned to develop their talents and improve the conditions in which they were living. Despite the enormous increase in educational bureaucracy, its effective impact on generating a sense of progress at the level of popular culture has been next to nothing.

Yet we must ask ourselves, was it really necessary for everything to turn out as it has? Are there not vital forces in our people which are prepared to react vigorously against these conditions and perpetuate the honourable traditions of the period before the revolution of '91?

It is beyond question that such forces exist. They are embodied in the rancher who intelligently works his land, transforming the soil into a productive tool; in the industrialist who with much integrity and tenacity has been able to create a business; in the craftsman who wants to create and develop his skill; in the worker who has created a home and wants to move up in society; in the student who diligently spends his nights making himself useful to his country; in the teacher in a remote village who loves the young entrusted to him and seeks to instil in them a sense of duty, of discipline, and the longing to improve the situation.[. . .]

Forty years of the trappings of democracy have been enough to bring Chile to the edge of the abyss. The nation finds itself in a create state of complete anarchy and division. Parliament has broken down into an infinity of groups and factions which defend particular interests.[. . .] But on the margins of this world, separated from it by an abyss, the true Chilean people carry on living out their quiet, hard-working lives, having withdrawn from the political chaos. They represent an immense family of resilient, enterprising, and patriotic individuals who do not recognize class differences, who are willing to obey, but not to obey leaders who have put them in their current situation. It is to this Chilean people that the *Acción Chilena* is addressed.[. . .]

To destroy the parliamentary-democratic regime now in power all we have to do is absolutely nothing: the only thing to do is to let it carry on a little longer. Its collapse will be the logical and inevitable consequence of its own actions.[. . .] Our present duty is not to destroy but to build.

We must ask ourselves: what will come after formalist democracy? And with this we return to my earlier question: will it be Marxism or fascism?

There is indeed a third possibility. There is also the possibility of a personal dictatorship, of *caudillismo*,[16] which has brought such misery to our continent. However, probably this will not come about here, and in any case it would not last long.

The real choice is between Marxism and fascism. We must, in an unequivocal and absolute way, opt for one or the other of these two solutions.

---

[16] An authoritarian system in which power is invested in a (would-be) charismatic leader (*caudillo*).

It is this basic issue which *Acción Chilena* is tackling.[. . .] [T]he stance it adopts means struggle, but a struggle with clear weapons, driven by unshakeably held convictions, to make Chile a greater, more beautiful country.

[*Acción Chilena*, 1/1 (Jan. 1934, 1–8.]

JORGE GONZÁLEZ

121 The Soul of the Race

In this article, written a few months before the MNS's abortive coup of 5 September 1938, Jorge González, 'el Jefe', demonstrates not only the manic overestimation of the strength of his movement typical of true fascist 'believers', but how convinced he was that Chile's rebirth was part of a global historical process.

Yet it was this very frenzy of moral anarchy and destruction which in the last few years has provoked a vigorous reaction from the spiritual reserves which have been stored deep down in the soul of the people. In the short space of a decade we have seen in every part of the civilized world powerful movements of rebellion rise up one by one against the materialist tyranny. From the depths of the nation, from the very heart of the masses brought low by the Marxist contagion, and even from within the strongholds of democratic furore, fervent phalanges of youth have sprung up ready to put up a fight to reconquer the primacy of the spirit for its peoples.[. . .]

Chile cannot be left outside this process of spiritual reconstruction. Its heroic and austere past, the centuries-old national virtues could not be engulfed by the flood of materialism. Despite the general disintegration of society, the spirit of the race was kept intact and the deeply felt appeal of some men was enough for this spirit to be awakened, virile and forceful once more, from its prolonged lethargy.

This is the historical mission of *Nacismo*. It was *Nacismo* which, in times of disorientation and uncertainty, when political and social chaos seemed to be dragging us once and for all into disaster, was able to make its clear and energetic voice heard: to save our country it is not programmes which are necessary, but vigorous action against the prevailing materialism; we will only be able to over-come the material and moral evils which afflict the Chilean people if this people shows itself capable of rallying around a national ideal which, rooted in the noble traditions of the country's past, arouses in the masses the spiritual energies necess-ary to combat the germs of destruction.

This is how the founders of *Nacismo* spoke. Doubtless an alien language in the circles of materialist frenzy, but nevertheless one which did not fall on deaf ears. Many young men could understand it and joined *Nacismo* eager to turn words into reality. Thus it was that, as days and months went by, the old spineless, negative, morbid spirit faded away and it began to turn back towards life. At first in small circles, then in close-knit groups, this spirit, rejuvenated and dynamic, is now galvanizing every stratum in every corner of the nation.

[*Acción Chilena*, 4/2 (Feb. 1938), 73–5.]

iii. Brazil

Brazilian Integralist Action (AIB) was altogether a more impressive phenomenon, and perhaps the only non-European fascism to bear direct comparison with Fascism or Nazism in their movement phase before seizing power. It was launched in 1932 by Plínio Salgado, who had been deeply impressed by a visit to Fascist Italy two years earlier. What turned the AIB into a highly original permutation of non-European fascism, however, was the importance which Salgado attached to Catholicism (reflected in the choice of a Maurrassian name for his movement), together with his urge to achieve an original synthesis of ideas and an organizational style appropriate to Brazil's unique size, history, and multi-ethnic society (*Brasilidade* or Brazilianness embraced in principle the whole of the country's multi-ethnic population, though anti-Semitism became an active ingredient through the agency of some high-ranking Integralists).

For a time the AIB was highly successful. By the end of 1934 it had achieved an active membership of anything up to 200,000, and was not only holding impressive mass rallies, but building up a vast cellular structure, and a network of party organizations on a scale reminiscent of the NSDAP in the late 1920s when it sought to become a 'shadow state'. In mass meetings it developed a distinctive ritual style, its followers sporting green shirts bearing black and blue armbands inscribed with the letter Σ (sigma), the mathematical sign for summation, and reciting the movement's anthems and slogans. However, the designation of 1932 as Year I of the new era (on Fascist lines) was premature. The movement was suppressed by the parafascist Vargas regime in 1937, and two Integralist revolts were easily quelled the following year. When Salgado went into exile in Portugal in 1939 Integralism was effectively dead. The parallels with the fate of Preto's National Syndicalism under Salazar are obvious (see Levine 1970).

PLÍNIO SALGADO

122 A Fourth Era of Humanity Dawns

Salgado was one of the most prolific theorizers of all fascist leaders. In this extract from one of his many books he associates the growth of the AIB with the dawn of a fourth era of humanity (a variation on the triadic scheme of historical evolution generally beloved of fascist ideologues, e.g. Third Reich, Third Rome). Note the emphasis on synthesis (see Texts 91, 170).

From out of this heartless civilization, whose last throes are accompanied by the death-rattle of economic crises, a new civilization will rise up. Atheist Humanity will give way to Integralist Humanity. It is the 'fourth humanity'. Just like a rising sun it is already casting its first rays of light. A new light shines out in the world. It is Atlantis which is resurfacing. The new civilization will realize the great synthesis. Philosophical synthesis. Political synthesis. But most of all, the synthesis of the Eras of Man.

In the ancient cradle of Latin culture the 'fascio' arose as the accumulation of 'national energies'; in the Baltic,[17] where there were Aryan residues, the 'Swastika Cross' appeared, the expression of a sense of race and symbol of human movements; in the 'steppe' the red flag unfurled in the old Semitic spirit of human totality in its materialistic sense; here in Brazil, sophisticated man, filled with the percussive instincts which he inherited from his savage ancestors, Keyserling's 'telluric man'[18] moulded within pure spiritual and Christian sentiment, is unfurling the Sigma flag. The hoisting of this flag declares the supreme synthesis in the widest human and universal spirit.

Here will be born the new Law, the new politics of the Revolutionary State with a pre-established moral purpose. It will not only be a Totalitarian State with an all-embracing absolutism, but the Integral State, which serves as the arbiter of the relationships between social movements. Within it revolution ceases to be disorder provoked by individuals, classes or parties, and becomes instead the spiritual right to intervene in the unfolding of the material forces of society, re-establishing equilibrium in the light of social justice. Law will cease to be a rigid taboo, the crystallization of despotic power, and instead acquire the flexibility which so long ago was preached in the Gospel when Jesus declared: 'The Sabbath was created for Man and not Man for the Sabbath' (St Mark 2).

Though it starts out from a spiritual conception of the Universe, the New State will nevertheless be realistic and practical. The experimental and scientific contribution of the nineteenth century, the input of the knowledge of nature which derives from Atheist Humanity, will give the Integral State elements on which it can draw in a continuous effort to impose moral harmony on the material world. Science is not rejected, but becomes the servant of the State instead of the tyrant which enslaves it.

This is why our movement, which has come into being on the eve of the appearance of the new type of Humanity, has to start with a revision of the Past, using all human resources to realize the great synthesis. In the midst of a dying world of disorientated masses, we can already clearly make out the approaching steps of the Fourth Humanity.[. . .]

The Brazilian Integralist movement is a cultural movement which embraces:

1. a general revision of the philosophies which dominated up to the beginning of this century and, hence, of the social, economic, and political sciences;
2. the creation of a new way of thinking, based on the synthesis of the fragmented knowledge which the last century has bequeathed us.

Brazilian integralism, then, is very different from the French integralism of Charles Maurras, because it does not derive from an 'integral nationalism' con-

[17] This appears to be a somewhat geographically aberrant reference to Nazism.
[18] i.e. 'earth-bound' man, a reference to the esoteric cultural philosophy of the Austrian Hermann Keyserling (1880–1946) who seems to have influenced Salgado.

cerned with the restoration of traditions. It is equally distinct from Lusitanian integralism,[19] which imported the Gallic traditionalist mentality along with its tendency to reconnect the modern social process to the medieval spirit; on the other hand, it is different, not only from German 'racism', whose thesis of ethnic supremacy expresses a cultural prejudice, but also from Italian 'Fascism', with which we only have in common the new attitude to the State in the face of class struggle.

What we are dealing with, therefore, is an original movement, genuinely Brazilian, with its own philosophy, a clear set of values which stands out from the confusion of the contemporary world.

[*A Quarta Humanidade* [The Fourth Humanity] (Livraria José Olympio: Rio de Janeiro, 1934), 82–8.]

PLÍNIO SALGADO
....

123 **The Soul of the Nation Awakens**

This passage from Salgado's Let's Wake up the Nation *expresses sentiments about nationalism and the precondition of national renewal which would ring true to all fascists.*

The soul of a nation does not awaken with laws; it does not spring into creative activity simply through the actions of administrations, even when they are honest and well-intentioned; it does not rise up through simple governmental measures, however well conceived they may be.

The best governments in the world cannot succeed in pulling a country out of the quagmire, out of apathy, if they do not express themselves as national energies. At most they will be able to construct good roads, sound bridges, excellent dams, beautiful buildings, magnificent scientific laboratories. All this will, however, have the ephemerality of passing initiatives, and mean nothing as expressions of a Fatherland. The most perfect laws will be unable to adapt themselves to the realities of a country whose soul is asleep. The people will not understand them, respect them, value them, because they will not speak to the instinct of the race, to the national spirit, to the feelings of the masses.[. . .]

Strong governments cannot result either from conspiracies or from military coups, just as they cannot come out of the machinations of parties or the Machiavellian game of political lobbying. They can only be born from the actual roots of the Nation. They can only see the light in the wide open spaces of the countryside or the eddying energies of the popular masses. Because in that case, at least for the time being, they will have awakened the soul of the Fatherland. Historically speaking, a people does not exist without a soul. Without spiritual energy all the material forces which can be unleashed serve only to make evils worse than

[19] The Portuguese derivative of Maurras's Action Française which influenced Salazar.

ever, increase anxieties, destabilize even more situations already catastrophic in themselves.

This is why Brazilian Integralism will do no deals, will have no truck with the trivial game of party-politics, is not interested in the situations the government creates for itself, neither offers nor denies support to administrations, leaves alone those who are running a Dead Nation, is not concerned with details of laws and regulations, does not go to the trouble of criticizing the constitutional charter voted by a Constituent Assembly which was no more than a gathering of tailors cutting out the burial clothes for a corpse.

The Brazil for which they were working out a constitution already died long ago when the first gunshots rang out at Copacabana in 1922.[20] The one still alive is a New Nation, whose soul we are starting to rouse to new life.

Unless this soul comes to life, the laws will count for nothing, neither will the wisdom of the legislators, for they are already on their way out and are looking to new generations to put them out of their misery.

The soul of a people, however, can only awaken through sacrifice and pain. The sacrifice of all vanity and of any impulse to conquer power immediately. A moral sacrifice in the face of the horde of the unaware, the sleepwalkers, the incompetent who smile the bitter smile that goes with intellectual obtuseness. A perpetual sacrifice to put up with the stench of putrefying corpses which liberalism, material-ism, scepticism, oligarchism, and factional politics leaves wafting over the fields where voices still ring out from demagogues, disguised as separatists or socialists, the last costume they can don before being overwhelmed by the irresistible waves of the 'Green Shirts'.

The soul of a people awakens through courage, through faith, through continu-ous regimentation, through permanent indoctrination, through perfect discipline, through ever-renewed hope, through spiritually uplifting moments, through high morale, through ceaseless struggle against soporific liberals and literary prejudices, against depersonalizing cosmopolitanism, against crude opportunism, against the general aimlessness which peoples without historical destiny are forced into by degrading pragmatism, against the premature decrepitude of generations corroded by scepticism, and, most of all, against the pestilential stagnation, the moral swamps in which decadent races go under and nationalities are enslaved.

The soul of a people awakens through the spread of sound, generous ideas, ideas of courage, force, national ambition, in complete contrast to emasculating passiv-ity, to the gangrene of negativity, to the cancer of materialism.

The soul of a people is awakened in battle, the tremendous battle of ideas which forces the opposing energies into retreat and changes the state of mind of the Fatherland, compelling it to lift up its head and march into History.

[*Despertemos a Naçāõ* [Let's Wake up the Nation] (Livraria José Olympio: Rio de Janeiro, 1935), 193, 196–9.]

---

[20]   A reference to the abortive rebellion of *tenentes* (lieutenants) against the State.

iv. Japan

Japanese fascism is as elusive as Latin American fascism, and for a similar reason: it had to contend for space with a formidably entrenched radical right. In the aftermath of the World Depression Japan embarked on an aggressive scheme of conquest and colonization to create a new Asian Order under its hegemony, culminating in the bombing of Pearl Harbor in December 1941. However, though Imperial Japan joined the Axis Powers in November 1936, its own authoritarian regime was headed by a conservative ruling élite for whom ultimate authority resided in the divinity of the Emperor, something which sets it quite apart from fascism. Even the highly active and diffuse radical right which grew up in the 1930s did not abandon the emperor principle. The only conspicuous exception is Nakano Seigō (1886–1943), who even before the First World War was formulating a scheme for the renewal of Japan which he gradually refined ideologically by blending the Samurai ethic, Ōyōmei intuitionism (a form of Neo-Confucianism), and the concept of popular nationalism associated with the French Revolution. Spurning the putschist road to revolution favoured by militarists, he worked for change to be brought about through the spread of a new spirit of populist Japanese nationalism. From early on his palingenetic vision came to crystallize round Takamori Saigō, a Samurai outlaw or *hayato* (literally 'falcon') who led the unsuccessful 1877 Satsuma Rebellion. Nakano saw in Saigō a fusion of revolutionary individualism with service to the nation which for him epitomized the 'true spirit' of the Meiji *ishin* (generally translated 'Restoration' but which has connotations of renovation as well), which lasted from 1868 to 1912, during which time the modernization of Japan started in earnest. For Nakano this true spirit had soon been betrayed by the Meiji government, and the task of modern Japan was to recapture it.

Nakano's growing despair of liberal or conservative parties as vehicles for Japan's renewal led him to joining forces with Adachi Kenzō in December 1932 to form Kokumin Dōmei (National Alliance). In May 1936 he left this group with a splinter group which became Tōhōkai (Far East Society). Its debt to the two fascist regimes' ritual style of politics was evident in the series of rallies the movement held where supporters wore black shirts and an armband fusing a cross with a circle in a way which curiously prefigures the Celtic Cross favoured by a number of fascist movements after the war, including Britain's National Front. A personal audience with Mussolini in Italy in late December 1937 convinced him more than ever that the Duce was not merely Italy's *soō-oyabun* or paternal leader, but its Saigō. In other words, he embodied his role model's heroic rebellion which he led on behalf of his people in accordance with the Ōyōmei principle of 'union of thought and action' (*iwayuru chigyō gōitsu*), and was thus uniquely able to create a new political order based on an integrated (and hence 'social') national community. Meetings with Ribbentrop and Hitler a month later only confirmed his sense that European fascism showed Japan and other Asian countries the way forward.

Though Nakano gathered thousands of followers, Tōhōkai never remotely resembled the mass revolutionary movement needed to overthrow traditional élites.

In 1940 his frustration led him to resort to verbal attacks on the Tōjō regime, becoming especially scathing of the Imperial Rule Assistance Association (formed in October 1940 as a single organization welding together all political parties), criticizing it for being a bureaucratic institution aloof from the minds and lives of the people. After Japan had so dramatically declared war on the USA, such criticism became intolerable to the Tōjō regime. Nakano was forbidden to make public speeches or publish articles. Finally he was placed under house arrest in October 1943, whereupon he committed *seppuku* (ritual disembowelling) near a five-volume biography of Saigō (see Najita 1971).

NAKANO SEIGŌ

124 The Need for a Totalitarian Japan

This passage from a speech made to Tōhōkai's first National Congress in January 1939 reflects how thoroughly Nakano had taken on board fascism's critique of liberalism and the positive connotations it gave to totalitarianism.

Some people say that neither Fascism nor Nazism are appropriate for our nation. However, I believe that there are no differences in the ultimate spirit of people who try to overcome difficulties, whether it is Germany, Italy, or Japan [*applause*]. Both Fascism and Nazism are clearly different from the despotism of the old period. They do not represent the conservatism which lags behind democracy, but are a form of more democratic government going beyond democracy. Democracy has lost its spirit and decayed into a mechanism which insists only on numerical superiority without considering the essence of human beings. It says that the majority is all good. I do not agree, because it is the majority which is the precise cause of contemporary decadence. Totalitarianism must be based on essentials, superseding the rule of numbers [*applause*]. We should not be satisfied with the consensus of the majority nor just participation in elections. Individuals have to be organically united for solidarity and for combat, sharing common ideals and a common way of feeling, otherwise they will not form a perfect national organization. We should not tolerate an individualism which shows no concern for others. We must be concerned with the problems of others as if they were our problems: our problems as other people's problems, the people's problems as our problems, and the State's problems as our problems. At this point a nation's people will be able to understand each other perfectly, keep in step, and proceed with a distinctive unity. In other words, this will be a government ruled by a majority which is more positive and essential than a democratic majority. Moreover, totalitarianism is, I believe, the means by which such a political system can best be advanced and closely monitored.

[Nakano Yasuo, *Seijika—Nakano Seigō* [Nakano Seigō the Politician] (Shinkoukaku: Tokyo, 1971), ii. 365–6.]

Nakano's last major public appearance was at Waseda University on 10 November 1942, when he made the three-hour speech from which this extract is taken. In it he explored once more the paradox that Japan could only become an integrated people and occupy its rightful place in the world if Japanese could, like Hitler, individually recover the spirit of freedom and moral courage of the true Meiji Restoration embodied in Saigō. The allusion to the Jews is striking, since they were not a factor in Japanese society. It shows just how Westernized Seigō's fascism had become.

'Give me freedom or give me death': what a heroic phrase that is! Neither liberals nor Jews have such mettle. I believe that the spirit of freedom should be respected exactly in terms of this expression. In the medieval period Protestants rose against the privileged ruling classes ridden with religious superstition. Luther showed great courage with his answers at the Diet of Worms. The first cry of freedom was born, at the risk of death, of the need to recognize the value of human beings felt by people who desired to live in truth and overthrow the oppression of despotic injustice. There were good reasons for the birth of Protestantism or liberalism. A totalitarian Hitler, who possesses a great Protestant spirit, is demanding freedom and autonomy from the United States and Great Britain, who dominate it through the power of money and productive capacity. What is wrong with wanting this freedom? Nothing is wrong. It is the decadence of liberalism which is responsible.[. . .]

Hitler understands the absolute evil of social democracy, based as it is on a parliamentary system where everything is decided by the majority. The parliamentary mechanism is manipulated by a boss who does not need talented parliamentarians because it is more convenient for him to gather around him those who are weak, dependent, or untalented, and manipulate them through pressure, bribery, or by involving them in dishonourable machinations. As a result he succeeds in gaining the support of a considerable number of people in a way which tramples underfoot those with true quality and denies the existence of a holy people. This is the way social democracy has worked according to Hitler.

In today's Japan we consider enemies all those who insult the pure spirit of humanity and act dishonourably in collusion with authority and groups to take advantage of the current situation. In contrast, we count as comrades all those who decide on independent courses of action in the light of their autonomous conscience, asserting their identity with pride even in this unstable and critical period. Hitler lived in the midst of the politics of vested interests cultivated by social democracy, yet he resisted them implacably by asserting the values of Germanic humanity.[. . .] Although social democracy developed out of liberalism, it is a form of government which suppresses individual freedom, enslaving the masses.[. . .] Hitler bravely stood his ground against the Weimar mentality. He declares that the truly strong man is strongest when he is alone. This is the true cry of a spiritual individual who has been awakening the forces of democratic totalitarianism. If I translate this cry into an Eastern context it means 'I do it despite ten million enemies' [*senannin to iedomo ware yukan*].[. . .]

The Japanese passion for a political idea seems to fade away very quickly.[. . .] An individual like Saigō started regretting the decline of the spirit of the Meiji Restoration [*ishin*] when it was only in its fourth year [1872]. It is Saigō himself who represents the great passion for renewal among the leading figures of the Meiji period. Is it not Saigō who can bear comparison with the world reformers such as Hitler, Mussolini, and Garibaldi, not only in the lucidity and sophistication of his thought, but also in the sense of elegance and profundity which he inspires? The other Meiji personalities are doubtless outstanding, yet it is Saigō who stands out as an innovator. His innovative ideas are the source of his passion, or, to put it another way, his passionate character is rooted in his ideas.[. . .] When I had just graduated from Waseda University I wrote *Meiji minkenshi ron*,[21] with a sense of urgency despite my youthful years. In the book I discussed the great Saigō who, I concluded, was the core figure of the Meiji spirit of restoration. I also insisted that his ten years' war was not fought in the spirit of reaction, but of the revolutionary action which truly embodied the Meiji Restoration.[. . .]

I know that many quote Hitler, but only a few have read *Mein Kampf* carefully. Read it in German, if possible.[. . .] It provides very good material to discipline your Japanese spirit.

Japan is facing a most difficult period, one which I believe has affected your families. I said before that our Japanese spirit has been weak. The reason is that neither national nor individual life has suffered enough. At the moment you are being thrown into an unprecedented crisis. This means that you are being given a serious opportunity. You should write your own *Mein Kampf* on your own reality, as a testimony to your personal physical struggle on this earth.[. . .]

You are students of the historic Waseda University. Do not swim with the current. Do not choose to become Civil Servants or enter similar occupations. Challenge the movement of history with the power to rise up alone in the world [*tenka hitori o motte okoru*]. Strive to embody this phrase in your own life.[. . .] The war has entered an extremely critical phase summed up in the military slogan 'conquer or be conquered'. To overcome this great crisis Japan needs to undertake drastic reform.

[Nakano Yasuo, *Seijika—Nakano Seigō* [Nakano Seigō the Politician] (Shinkoukaku: Tokyo, 1971), ii. 668–9, 672, 682–3.]

---

[21] *On the Popular Rights Movement in the Meiji Era*, published in 1913.

PART IV

Theories of Fascism

INTRODUCTION

Now that some impression has been given of the sheer variety of fascisms which had sprung up before 1945, it is appropriate to review some of the approaches adopted by commentators and scholars intent on making sense of this new 'ism' which had burst so dramatically onto the scene. If they were not so varied, and in many cases contradictory, this would be unnecessary. However, as was indicated in the General Introduction, the phenomena denoted by the term 'fascism' shrink, expand, and change in their historical and geopolitical extension according to which ideal type is applied. As a result, the definitional map being used for orientation within this field of studies can never be taken for granted: it has become an intrinsic part of the understanding of fascism itself. Indeed, as one commentator observed, 'The history of fascism is at the same time the history of the theoretical analysis of fascism'.[1]

One aim of this section, then, is to document some of the different ways a phenomenon called 'fascism' has been refracted by the lenses through which it has been scrutinized, and, by allowing numerous conflicting positions to be scanned in a series of brief extracts, convey a cumulative sense of how indissociable the ideas and events subsumed under the term are from the way it is conceived. This indirectly underlines the strictly tentative and heuristic nature of the definition which informs this anthology, which was stressed in the General Introduction. It should also encourage students at all levels of expertise to formulate their own position and so participate directly in the highly open debate which has always existed over basic definitional issues in fascist studies.

Part IV is divided into two sections. Section A covers the period 1920–45. It shows how even before Mussolini started establishing an authoritarian (and would-be totalitarian) regime in Italy in 1925, some commentators already saw in Fascism the manifestation of a new genus of political ideology distinct from the traditional, conservative, or military extreme right. In addition it provides a sample of the varied reactions, ranging from sympathetic or intrigued to deeply hostile, which this recognition provoked, mainly drawn from publications in Britain or the United States. These should be treated very much as sample countries: in the inter-war period the academic, publicistic, and journalistic establishments of every nation in the 'developed' world produced assessments of the political upheavals in Italy and the prospects of them spreading to other countries.

What is common to many of the reactions in Section A is the underlying assumption that world history was at a crossroads, whether the crisis was conceived as the replacement of liberal democracy by something potentially better, the final stage of capitalism and the dawn of socialism, or the end of civilization and the beginning of totalitarian barbarism. In other words, the brooding sense of historical turning-point which is so central to fascism's vision of a new order also informed

[1] Ernest Mandel in his introduction to Trotsky 1971: 9.

much of the thinking of anti-fascists before 1945. Indeed, a generalized feeling of crisis and malaise underlies some prognostications about how history was to develop (for example in the extracts from H. G. Wells and Peter Drucker) which may now seem wide of the mark, but only serve to emphasize how threatened the survival of liberal democracy/capitalism could seem, not just to Marxists and fascists, but to democratic socialists and liberals alike by the end of the 1930s. The diffuse sense of the failure of democracy and liberalism in the year of Hitler's accession to power is captured in Bernard Shaw's play *On the Rocks* of 1933, and has been surveyed in the chapter 'Weariness of Democracy and Admiration for Dictators' in R. Griffiths' *Fellow Travellers of the Right* (1983). Section B reviews some of the main approaches to fascism developed in the very different climate of the post-war era.

It should be borne in mind while reading Part IV that the task of defining and understanding fascism is not simply an academic issue. Fascism has become a marginalized, but endemic, ingredient of political culture in many areas of the Westernized world where a multi-ethnic society has not enjoyed the economic or social preconditions which foster liberalism, while the immigration pressures on the 'First World' combined with structural unemployment are only aggravating the situation. Meanwhile, in the former Soviet empire the Cold War has created an ideal habitat in which racism and fascism can thrive. Equally disturbingly, fascists are present at the heart of the democratic process in Italy and Russia, and applying pressure from the wings in many other nation-states on such issues as immigration, cultural identity, and family values. In such circumstances a clear-sightedness about fascism's dynamics, goals, and prospects of achieving them is as important as ever. In the 1970s Ernest Mandel claimed that 'fascism was able to develop successfully over two decades only because its real nature was not understood (Trotsky 1971: 10), and Kitchen stressed the need to be aware of fascism's capacity for assuming new forms if it is to be successfully combated (Text 152). In the 1990s their words have taken on a special resonance, though there are still few signs of progress towards a consensual approach to the 'real nature' of fascism among those concerned with fighting it, whether in the street or on the page.

Section A

....

Reactions to Fascism 1920–1945

....

INTRODUCTION

As a latecomer to the political scene, fascism, both the Italian original and the new movements or regimes associated with it elsewhere, took political commentators and academics by surprise. By 1914 most liberals and Marxists were ensconced in philosophies of history which convinced them that they were in the vanguard of history, and moving ineluctably towards the realization of their own myth of progress. As a result ultra-conservatives could be easily dismissed by them as an irrelevant constituency of reaction and cultural pessimism. At the time there was no room in either liberal or Marxist schemes of history for a new form of political energy which sought to use nationalist myths to mobilize the masses in a spirit which was both reactionary and revolutionary, traditionalist and modernizing, élitist and populist. Nor was there any scenario which foresaw such a movement creating an authoritarian military state in a major European nation-state.

The nine extracts of Section Ai give just a hint of the difficulties experienced by contemporaries of the rise of European fascism, especially those with no strong prior commitment to an ideological or party-political position, to make sense of the international implications of what Mussolini was achieving in Italy. It should also be borne in mind that the context in which the pieces were written varies enormously from country to country, and even more so over time. In the immediate post-war period the spectre which frightened most European leaders was political instability and social unrest, especially the threat of Bolshevism. As a result Mussolini's coup of 1922 was widely welcomed by many foreign observers in liberal democracies as a positive way of solving Italy's domestic crisis and eliminating that threat. Indeed, Mussolini was given the Order of Grand Commander of the Bath by King George V in 1923, and in a press statement to *The Times* on 21 January 1927 made during his visit to Fascist Italy, Winston Churchill made the famous remark: 'If I had been an Italian, I am sure I should have been entirely with you from the beginning to the end of your victorious struggle against the bestial appetites and passions of Leninism.'

After 1927 the scene rapidly changed. The Great Depression which set in after 1928, the Nazi seizure of power in 1933, and the series of international crises leading up to the Second World War meant that the context which conditioned how commentators reacted to fascism changed rapidly, raising spectres of a showdown between civilization and barbarism. In particular it became increasingly tempting to see in fascism the harbinger of a general drift towards the destruction of liberalism by ultra-right authoritarian regimes in Central, South-Western and Eastern

Europe. Such a view of contemporary history could not help but modify the evaluation of fascism's significance as a new determinant in shaping history. When Mussolini announced the existence of the Rome–Berlin Axis in November 1936, only his most ardent 'fellow-travellers' could still delude themselves into thinking that he had been showing the Western world a benign way out of the 'crisis of civilization'. The impotence of the League of Nations to stop the Fascist conquest of Ethiopia, the course of the Spanish Civil War, Hitler's *Anschluss* with Austria, and the occupation of the Sudetenland were to confirm the worst fears for the fragility of the post-Versailles world-order.

In the main Marxists (Section A ii) proved more flexible than liberals in adapting their theoretical frameworks so as to make sense of the degenerating international situation. Right from the start the violence meted out by *squadristi* (see Text 12) against 'Bolsheviks' and priests defending workers' interests convinced them that Mussolini represented desperate counter-revolutionary reaction on behalf of the property-owning classes. As ultra-right movements and regimes came to dominate parts of Europe, and Japan emerged as a major imperialist power, they had few problems in revising their teleological vision of History's movement towards communism to take account of fascism—quickly recognized as a generic force not confined to Italy—as the quintessential manifestation of the anti-proletarian violence which socialists had always believed was latent within the liberal system: with its back to the wall, capitalism was showing its true colours. Democratic socialists, too, found much in this analysis, even if their gradualism meant that they could afford to be less simplistic about the nature of this new enemy to their cause. However, the debate over the nature of fascism within Marxism was pursued more energetically than in the liberal camp. There are several reasons for this: (i) in the inter-war period fascism was a rival revolutionary (or as Marxists would have it, counter-revolutionary) creed; (ii) fascism displayed a degree of activist violence towards revolutionary Marxism which far surpassed the animosity of liberalism; (iii) Marxist orthodoxy suggested that a precondition for fighting fascism was the scientific analysis of its dynamics; (iv) the debate reflected deep cleavages both between factions of revolutionary Marxists and between these and reformist social-ists, especially social democrats. This aspect of fascist studies has been covered by scholars in some detail elsewhere (notably in the excellent anthology of texts provided by Beetham 1983).

Sections Aiii and Aiv sample the writings of a number of commentators who did not operate within the relatively narrow confines of Marxist orthodoxy, though seven of them (Texts 139, 140, 142, 144–7) are informed by Marxist assumptions. Taken together they underline how idiosyncratic analyses of fascism became at the height of its threat to liberal democracy, each commentator being thrown back onto his own political or religious convictions in the attempt to make sense of its dynamics and chances of ultimate success.

i. Ambivalent or Positive Reactions to the Spread of Fascism

VILFREDO PARETO

126   **Black Sheep**

One of the most significant early reactions to Mussolini's success in forming a coalition government in the aftermath of the March on Rome (October 1922) was from Vilfredo Pareto (1848–1923), Italy's most distinguished sociological theoretician. His analysis of the structural weaknesses of liberal democracy and the need for new élites directly influenced Italian Fascist thought. In this interview he already anticipates the notion of fascism as a generic phenomenon (that is, not confined to Italy) by seeing the values embodied in Mussolini's movement as a potential remedy for a perceived European malaise. Consistent with this positive evaluation is Pareto's assumption that Fascism is the product of political idealism and desire for national renewal, not of sectional class interest or nihilism.

Let's consider Fascism. Admittedly, every flock has its black sheep, and even among the Fascists there were individuals who were in it for their own immediate gain, but these were exceptions. The vast majority followed a line of conduct in the pursuit of an almost mystical ideal: the celebration of national sentiment and the power of the State, the reaction against pseudo-liberal, pacifist, and humanitarian forms of democratic ideology. This feeling was often nebulous: but the majority I speak of was guided steadfastly and ably towards the conquest of centralized power. It won. It applied a law, one which in my *Sociologia*[2] I had deduced from countless facts, according to which a movement whose leaders have a highly developed instinct for exploiting unforeseen conjunctures of events and whose rank-and-file is motivated by powerful idealism will win out over all other forces.

Another difference between Fascism and its opponents: economic or financial conditions. All the problems which depend on these conditions have two solutions: either the maximum utilitarian benefit for all concerned, or the greatest possible satisfaction of demands issuing from sectional interests. Weak governments tend to adopt the second solution, while only powerful governments who depend on armed force and on idealistic aspirations are able to adopt the first systematically.

As long as a society is wealthy and prosperous the utilitarian solution can be ignored in favour of the sectional one, but when prosperity disappears and crises start occurring, to persist in jeopardizing the economy through vested interest or prejudice can lead to the worst catastrophes.

The whole of Europe is wrestling with similar difficulties at present and its ruling classes are unable to find any quick or appropriate solution: in Italy Fascism has

---

[2] *Trattato di sociologia generale* (G. Barbèra: Florence, 1916), translated into English as *The Mind and Society* (Jonathan Cape: London, 1935).

effectively embarked on a solution by substituting a new ruling class for one which had shown itself to be completely inept at exercising power. State power was at a low ebb, and Fascism tried to restore it. The future will tell us if this has inaugurated a new era, or if there will be a relapse into the ancient errors of policy which created the impression that we are being led into an anarchy of medieval proportions.[. . .]

In Italy Fascism has succeeded in [. . .] giving to the nationalist religion the goal of defending the State and bringing about social renewal: this is where the essence of the Fascist Revolution basically lies.

> [Interview published in *La Tribune*, 24 Apr. 1923; repr. in *Scritti politici*, ed. G. Busino (UTET: Turin, 1974), ii. 1896–1923, 739–41.]

KENNETH ROBERTS

127   **A Plague of Amateur Mussolinis**

The observations on contemporary Italy and Germany offered by the American writer Kenneth Roberts are of interest on several counts: (i) his book is a detailed account of 'pre-totalitarian' Fascism; (ii) it invites the reader to see in Fascism a role model of a benign form of military dictatorship through which a nation-state can protect itself from the menace of communism to which weak democratic governments expose it; (iii) it portrays Nazism (even before the abortive putsch of November 1923) as a perverted form of Fascism based on fanaticism and anti-Semitism, thus anticipating the debate about Nazism's relationship to fascism in general and Italian fascism in particular which is still alive today.

The Salvage of a Nation

Mussolini's dictatorship is a good dictatorship; and a dictatorship in Italy is a national necessity. Those kindly souls in other countries who have never known the joys of successful communism and rampant socialism may speak deprecatingly, pessimistically and indignantly of Mussolini's strong-arm methods, but they are what Italy deserved and must continue to have before she can climb from the hole in which she deliberately sunk herself.

There must of course be an end to individual government of this sort; but nobody can predict the future of Mussolini and the Fascisti Party. Mussolini may last long enough to put Italy on a sound basis, and he may be overthrown by politicians and their dupes before his work can be completed. The party may get rid of its discordant elements and maintain a strong position because of the soundness of its common-sense beliefs, or it may fall to pieces through the selfish aspirations of its subordinate leaders. Nobody can say what will come of it except the ouija-board experts and the astronomers [*sic*], neither of whom is regarded as a reliable source of information.

This much, however, is certain: The rise of Mussolini and the Italian Fascisti should be a lesson to all governments and to all politicians.[. . .] The Fascisti showed the world that a nation doesn't have to endure the progressiveness that is based on lies and demagoguery and stupidity and perversity, and that progresses inevitably to communism and its necessary accompaniments of unbearable taxes, poverty, misery, degradation and chaos.[. . .]

Beer-Fascisti of Bavaria

It is entirely within the bounds of reason that a movement calling itself the Fascisti movement might overturn the existing government and seize the reins of power in any country; but it may be regarded as certain that if the movement were not of truth, directness and common sense, it would be no better than the government it replaced, and it would probably be worse.

Hitler, in Bavaria, chose to put the blame for Bavaria's troubles—which he proposed to rectify—on the Jews. By doing so he showed that he was using common sense in the same proportion that a good cook uses powdered glass in making fudge.

Hitler—in common with sundry other near-Fascisti leaders in central Europe—argued that the war[3] was conceived and started by Jewish bankers, and that its long duration was due to the same cause. This theory is borne out by facts in the same manner that facts bear out the theory that the earth is flat and doesn't revolve on its axis.

In order to obtain as large a following as possible, Hitler advocated all sorts of changes and reforms which appealed to all sorts of people, but which could not further the general welfare in any way. These are the tactics of the demagogue and blatherskite; and such tactics are the ones which any genuine Fascisti movement must attack and destroy.[. . .]

All the countries of the world, including America, are troubled by amateur Mussolinis who are only like Mussolini in that they would like to run everything in sight. They are not honest; they are not direct; and their brand of common sense is the same that one might expect to find in the inmates of an asylum for the violently insane.

[*Black Magic* (Bobbs-Merrill: Indianapolis, 1923), 135–7, 162–3.]

ROBERT MICHELS

128   **A Sunny Disposition**

Robert Michels (1876–1936), a sociologist by training and a proponent of élite theory, is another German academic who responded favourably to Mussolini's 'conquest of the state' in October 1922, settled in Italy, and went on to become one of Fascism's principal apologists. This article was published in German and is one of the earliest examples of an attempt

---

[3] i.e. the First World War.

to make sense of the new regime to an academic audience outside Italy (note the reference to the 'trains running on time' which became a cliché about the new Italy), while assessing the chances that Fascism might catch on elsewhere in Europe (which here he portrays interestingly as a 'danger', but with no reference to Hitler's abortive putsch in Munich the year before).

The essential thing is that Fascism has found in Benito Mussolini someone with a natural gift for leadership in the grand manner, someone who combines a sunny disposition with a keen intuition for the possible and the achievable, an unshakeable belief in himself and his mission as well as an extraordinary influence over the masses with a really unusual readiness to take bold decisions.

Politically Italy was longing for a firm hand. Now that the Fascists are at the helm, the general reaction for the time being is 'A government at last!' That the machinery of the Italian State works better today is undeniable. The post and railway do their duty. The trains no longer dawdle on anything like the scale they used to. Even the risks of being robbed on boats and trains have stopped. Foreigners are unanimous: officials now go about their duties with an unusual discipline and a surprising zeal. Order now reigns in the country. Even in the economic sphere. The stabilization of the Italian lira can be considered as good as complete.[. . .]

The prospect of returned stability can be looked forward to in the sphere of foreign policy as well. The Italians are a circumspect, down-to-earth, hard-working, peace-loving people. Apart from the fact that there are financial limitations to Italian foreign policy and that an ambitious scheme of expansion would be hardly compatible with the commitment of the new regime to frugality, the Italian people, whose history taken as a whole is one of struggle for its own freedom and that of others, would put a stop to any extravagant departure from the constraints of political reason. Clearly this by no means precludes the new government undertaking a more energetic defence of Italian interests abroad. Here too it is a matter of *tempo secondo*.[4]

The greatest danger lies in the possibility that some parties outside Italy will succumb to the understandable temptation to imitate the method and success of the Fascist putsch, and that a regenerated Communist Party might one day also try its luck (though such a day is a long way off). Even if, against all the odds, Fascism has so far given a good account of itself in a number of spheres, it still has to prove itself politically (for it is history itself which always has the last word). As far as today's Italy is concerned, however, if all the indicators are to be believed, Fascism will not constitute an element of international instability, and perhaps has ceased to be a factor of national instability as well.

['Der Aufstieg des Fascismus' [The rise of Fascism], *Archiv für Sozialwissenschaft und Sozialpolitik*, 52/1 (1924), 91–2.]

---

[4] An interesting anticipation of subsequent Fascist expansion into Ethiopia, the Adriatic, and the Balkans.

129 The Italian *Volksstaat*

Johann Mannhardt was one of the first social scientists in Germany to write a detailed account of early Fascism. Under the influence of the idealist and organic concepts of nationhood which have been a feature of German political thought since Herder, he saw in Fascism a spiritual and ethical force for the renewal of Italy which had enabled the country finally to achieve a form of statehood appropriate to its inner nature. Such ideas point to an underlying affinity both with the State theory of Giovanni Gentile (Texts 20), and the German organic theories of State (Texts 95, 98). What is implied by Volksstaat is not the liberal democratic nation-state (Staatsnation), but a form of State which corresponds to a particular Volk ('people', 'nation' conceived as a 'natural' organic entity). Mannhardt is particularly lucid about the possibility of fascism becoming a generic force which adapts itself to the habitat of each national culture, and the threat this posed to Germany.

What sense can Fascism have for the development of Italians, who, as we have already said, first started to become a people with Dante? Here too Mussolini's words point the way. So far the Italian State has never become one with the Italian people. As an incomplete people it had not yet found an appropriate form of state. The Fascist state simply sets out to be the State of the Italian people. Perhaps it will succeed. It would then achieve its greatest significance. Italy would become a *Volksstaat* just as England and France are, because to be a *Volksstaat* does not mean putting into practice vague notions about the nation and the State plucked out of the air, but that a particular nation has found the form of State which corresponds to its essence. Thus Fascism would be for Italy what puritanism was for England and liberalism was for France.[. . .]

Puritanism and liberalism have not only been determining influences on the formation of the *Volksstaat* in England and France, but have been the dominant intellectual forces throughout the whole of the West. Fascism draws its best energies from what is for the time being a completely nebulous value system in which the rejection of liberalism is much more evident than any positive content. Even the longing to overcome the Enlightenment and thereby both liberalism and democracy is something encountered throughout the whole of the West, if not the whole 'civilized world'. It must be considered a surprising contrast to earlier intellectual climates that the *political* expression of this longing for a new set of values should manifest itself so early. It was this factor which from the outset gave the Fascist movement the expressly political character that it did not necessarily have in its own terms. Above all, Italy is in a position to win a great lead and a dominant position over other countries in crystallizing this new value system and in implementing so decisively the inferences to be drawn from it. We have seen that in its nature and external features Fascism is totally Italian, but that it has an impact abroad independent of the will of the Italians themselves. The significance of Fascism may well be that in a specifically Italian form it transmits to the rest of the world the new intellectual climate which is emerging, just as liberalism made an impact on the world in its French or English form. At this point Fascism would acquire, apart from its Italian connotations, supranational meaning. The word Fascism would thereby express a general set of values, like the word liberalism before it.[. . .]

European liberalism senses the danger that this represents for it, and it is only right in being on the defensive.[. . .] In terms of domestic politics England and France would have nothing to fear for the stability of their *Volksstaat*, even if the fascist wave one day were to break on their shores. In Germany the situation is quite different.[. . .] Fascism could jeopardize the domestic politics of the German people if Italian Fascism were seen and used as the recipe for the German situation. Whether the stream of new intellectual currents which are welling up out of the soil of Europe could ever allow the Germans to become a proper *Volksstaat* as well, we cannot say. At present the preconditions for this are nearly all missing. Even if the German nation-state were able to grow out of the same roots as the Fascist State, one thing is certain: if it were to happen it could only come about on the basis of our own people drawing on its own nature and its own strength.

[*Der Faschismus* (Beck: Munich, 1925), 392–4.]

ERWIN VON BECKERATH

130 **The Italian Experiment**

With his book Essence and Development of the Fascist State, *Erwin von Beckerath established himself in non-Marxist academic circles as the foremost German expert on fascism, and was invited to write the chapter on fascism in the* American Encyclopedia of the Social Sciences *published in 1931 (one year before Mussolini's famous article on Fascism for the Italian Encyclopedia). Approaching Fascism in terms of what might now be called a 'structural-functionalist' concern with how the new regime functioned, he saw in it a 'thrilling experiment' in the creation of a new type of State: a modern variant of absolutism which was 'reshaping the capitalist order'. Note the way fascism is now being treated very much as a generic phenomenon.*

The Italian experiment which is playing itself out before the eyes of Europe is of extreme interest for these reasons. First, what is being undertaken is the creation of an authoritarian State in true eighteenth-century fashion, which simultaneously is infused with the energies of modern life. Secondly, it is the attempt to consolidate the supremacy of the state over a new type of economic system,[5] one in which political-economic considerations take priority over private activity. Finally, it is the bid to solve the problem of distribution, which is liable to generate conflicts of interest which can be politically dangerous, through higher political authorities. The primacy of the political over the economic is nevertheless an eminently European concept.

[5] i.e. the corporatist system (see Texts 10, 17, 31, 93).

In all this Europe is no disinterested onlooker. Since the end of the war Bolshevism and fascism have been fighting for its soul. The chaos which followed the world conflict promoted communist experiments in parts of Central and Southern Europe which were of brief duration because they were in contradiction with the social structure in those areas. Since 1922 a wave of nationalism has rippled across the continent taking over Spain, Hungary, Poland, and Lithuania, not to mention the fascist parties which sprang up everywhere.

The peculiar revolutionary force of Bolshevism lay in the destruction of the bourgeois and feudal means of production, and it was in the nature of things that within Europe this was only possible in Russia. As long as Fascism represented a purely political system without intervening in the social system, it could be adopted despite its specifically Italian traits, especially since its neo-absolutism inevitably found a deep resonance in powerful parties accustomed to hold the reins of power. How will things develop now? Apart from the fact that the increasing concentration of economic and political power in the hands of the few means the disintegration of an ideology based on majority rule, the constitution of the state is, as history shows, dependent on the economic and political situation. It is significant in this respect that in a tense situation Italy was the first to return to an absolutist form of State. If, as is to be assumed, the economic and political tensions which Europe is subject to in the twentieth century continue to deepen, it is probable that the authoritarian state will regain lost ground in the Western world in conjunction with a restructuring of political ideology.

[*Wesen und Werden des faschistischen Staates* [The Essence and Development of the Fascist State] (Wissenschaftliche Buchgesellschaft: Darmstadt, 1979; 1st pub. Springer: Berlin, 1927), 154–5.]

JAMES STRACHEY BARNES

131   To Each Country its Own Fascism

Major James Strachey Barnes was a member of the Royal Institute of International Affairs and one of Britain's most important apologists of Fascism. He was so impressed by events in Italy that he became Secretary-General of the Centre International des Études Fascistes in Lausanne and wrote a eulogy of the New Italy in the volume Fascism *published in 1931 in the Everyman Home Library series (co-edited by Julian Huxley). He convinced himself that Fascism was showing the world how a modern state under inspired leadership could put an end to a long period of decadence and become the latest in a series of the major revolutions to have changed the course of European history: the 'Pagan Renaissance', the Reformation, the French Revolution, the Industrial Revolution, and Capitalism. Barnes sums up what he calls the* Weltanschauung *of Fascism in the word 'Youth' and sees its essential spirit in Rudyard Kipling's poem 'If'. These passages bring out his vision of a variegated 'Eurofascism'.*

The post-war crisis, in fact, brought matters to a head; liberal statecraft was found bankrupt; and to save Italy from economic ruin there was nothing for it but for a minority of souls, acting in advance of, but not against, public opinion, to seize the State and to achieve Fascism by Revolution. By great fortune, the movement also produced the man, gifted with all the true marks of a leader, a man of the people, who could read deep into the soul of the people and thereby be able to drive the movement closer and closer to the Italian Nation's true traditions, ridding it, as it developed, of its impurities and moderating its excesses.

For this reason alone Fascism has come to stay in Italy. For Europe it stands at the cross-roads looking back to the two Romes, Imperial and Catholic, that made her civilisation, and pointing to its straight continuation as the only safe road by which to advance. Thus its historical function and mission is simply this: to prepare the ground for a new European political and social synthesis, founded on the sure traditions of the past, when Europe was yet one.[. . .]

Those who come to approve of the doctrine must take their own steps to realize it in accordance with the conditions of the country of which they are members; and in an old country like Great Britain, with a long national history and tradition, the constitutional path is undoubtedly the right one for the people to take. The coming of Fascism in England, we hope, need not be accompanied, as in Italy, by violent Revolution, so that English men and women must above all begin by learning to dissociate in their minds Fascism and the various violent and dictatorial accompaniments that happen to be associated with it in Italy.[. . .]

Fascists in each country must make Fascism their own national movement, adopting symbols and tactics which conform to the traditions, psychology and tastes of their own land. Do not seize on the accidentals of the movement or you will be in danger of missing the essentials. Remember that, though truth is universal, its acceptance need never make the world the same colour, for in its application to the individual case is born variety. It is only falsehood that is drab. The infinite variety of the Universe is in reality a perpetual testimony to its essential unity, a chorus of harmony in praise of its Maker, One God in three persons.

[*The Universal Aspects of Fascism* (Williams & Norgate: London, 1928), 63, 240–1.]

GIUSEPPE BORGESE

132 The Makers of Europe

G. A. Borgese (1882–1952) was associated before the First World War with the Florentine avant-garde around Papini and was the author of an influential book on D'Annunzio. He wrote extensively on Italian and German cultural history, which made him well placed to discuss the nature of fascism after he had gone to the USA in 1931, where he taught at the University of Chicago. In the 1934 article from which the following excerpts are taken he is prepared to concede fascism a modernizing, renovating function in national and even European life. He went on to develop a far more critical attitude, however, and wrote

Goliath: The March of Fascism (*Victor Gollancz: London, 1938*), *to expose the dangers it posed to civilization.*

Not a single prophet, during more than a century of prophecies, analyzing the degradation of the romantic culture, or planning the split of the romantic atom, ever imagined anything like fascism. There was, in the lap of the future, communism and syndicalism and what not; there was anarchism, and legitimism, and even all-papacy; war, peace, pan-Germanism, pan-Slavism, Yellow Peril, signals to the planet Mars; there was no fascism. It came as a surprise to all, and to themselves too.[. . .]

Hitler is only the shadow of Mussolini; but such a broad one that it seems doubtful if many sun rays for autonomous development are still left to Italian fascism. For the time being Mussolini, the creator, already looks like the precursor of Hitler, the imitator: a destiny allotted to many such geniuses.[. . .]

There are, beyond doubt, positive and creative elements in fascism. First the appeal to energy (although energy must know its aim, and the aim must be a good one). Second, the appeal to social order, and discipline (though the basis of this order must be shifted, and the aim must be collaboration among freely ordered nations, not war, which is the worst of disorders). Third, the criticism of democracy and parliamentarianism in their decay (although a better democracy, not despotism, must be the inference).

Fourth, and best of all, Italy and Germany came last, not yet two thirds of a century ago, into the row of modern national states. They were immature. Fascism is giving them the inner experience of struggle and character that France and Germany had in the late Middle Ages, and America in the Civil War. Much of Germany is still a storage place for the pious safekeeping of medieval memories; Italy is still a peninsula jutting out from the ancient world into the new. Involuntarily, but at highest speed, fascism is burning in both countries all the material of the past: personal and dogmatic authority, monarchy and church, classic and romantic pedantry, day-dreaming and involuted introversion. From fascism both nations will emerge, soon or late, renovated, quite European and modern, and makers of Europe.

['The Intellectual Origins of Fascism', *Social Research*, 1/4 (Nov. 1934), 475–6, 84–5.]

SIR CHARLES PETRIE
....
133 **A Sense of Humour**

Sir Charles Petrie, Irish baronet and foreign editor of English Review, *the major journal of High Toryism in Britain, was a Catholic, and a monarchist with a great nostalgia for the era when the Habsburg Empire held sway. He was also a great admirer of Mussolini as an inspired leader who had reconciled the Vatican to the Italian state and was orchestrating the nation's ascendancy to the status of a great European Power. He was less impressed by*

Nazism, as the following passage makes clear. Its interest lies in the intuitive recognition that there is an underlying kinship between Fascist Italy and Nazi Germany at the level of ideology ('faith'), but that differences in national culture ensure that at the level of socio-political reality they are like chalk and cheese (as an example he points out that, whereas Italian Fascism is inseparable from the corporate state, 'in Germany corporative ideals have made no appeal').

The two movements are alike in their authoritarianism and in their opposition to Communism and to Liberation, but there the resemblance ends. Fascism is based upon the principles of Christianity, and it has come to an understanding with the Church of Rome: National Socialism is continually looking over its shoulder at paganism, and it is in conflict with all organized religion. The Italian, too, has a keen sense of humour, whereas the German has none at all; so that the regime in the latter case is able to interfere with the liberty of the subject in social matters to an extent that would never be tolerated south of the Alps. A few years ago the authorities in Rome altered the numbers of the bus routes without due warning, and there was nearly a revolution: in Berlin this inconvenience would have been accepted without grumbling. Even when movements have much in common, they soon begin to develop differences due to local traditions, heredity, or environment. To-day, Italy and Germany are both armed to the teeth, but the outlook of their citizens is in marked contrast: at heart the Italian will never be a militarist, while the German will never be anything else. Even when the faith is the same, as it is not in the case under consideration, national differences make themselves felt. The Roman Catholic Church is one all over the world, but the atmosphere of a Catholic service in England is more like that of an Anglican service than of Catholic service in France or Italy. In these circumstances not only have Fascism and National Socialism very little in common, but what they have is bound to diminish with the passage of time.

[*Lords of the Inland Sea* (Lovat Dickinson: London, 1937), 62–3.]

H. G. WELLS

134   **A Bad Good Thing**

H. G. Wells (1866–1946) became famous for his prolific output as a writer of science fiction and futuristic novels. He was also a keen essayist on political and social issues and a writer of popularized non-fiction, such as A Short History of the World. *Before 1914 he shared the prevailing optimism of the time concerning the benefits which science might bring to humankind, though even then* A Modern Utopia *looked forward to a world state ruled by an enlightened 'Samurai Order'. The First World War shattered his optimism and* The Shape of Things to Come, *a futuristic novel which was the basis for the 1936 film* Things to Come, *foresaw the decade ending in the collapse of liberal democracy in horrendous wars. The orgy of destruction would reduce the world to pre-industrial levels of technology till eventually the one technocratic caste left, the airmen, would set up a global Air Dictatorship leading to a benign form of world government which, as this passage makes clear, he sees dimly adumbrated in Mussolini's regime.*

Before the end of the thirties it was plain to all the world that a world-wide social catastrophe was now inevitably in progress, that the sanest thing left for intelligent men to do was to set about upon some sort of Noah's Ark to salvage whatever was salvageable of civilization, so that there should be a new beginning after the rising deluge of misfortune had spent itself. A few prescient spirits had been saying as much for some years, but now this idea of salvage spread like an epidemic. It prepared the way for the Modern State Movement on which our present order rests. At the time, however, the general pessimism was little mitigated by any real hope of recovery. One writer, quoted by Habwright, compared man to a domesticated ape, 'which has had the intelligence and ability to drag its straw mattress up to the fire when it is cold, but has had neither the wit nor the foresight to escape the consequent blaze'. Habwright's brief summary of the financial operations that went on as the sense of catastrophe grew justifies that grim image very completely.

The conviction that Parliamentary Democracy had come to an end spread everywhere in that decade. Already in the period between the vacillation in international affairs after Versailles and the warfare of the forties, men had been going about discussing and scheming and plotting for some form of government that should be at least decisive. And now their efforts took on a new urgency. There was a world-wide hysteria to change governments and officials.

At its first onset this craving for decisiveness had produced some extremely crude results. An epidemic of tawdry 'dictatorships' had run over Europe from Poland to Spain immediately after the war. For the most part these adventures followed the pattern of the pronunciamentos of the small South American republics, and were too incidental and inconsequent for the student of general history to be troubled about them now. But there followed a world-wide development of directive or would-be directive political associations which foreshadowed very plainly the organization of the Modern State Fellowship upon which our present world order rests.

The Fascist dictatorship of Mussolini in Italy had something in it of a more enduring type than most of the other supersessions of parliamentary methods. It arose not as a personal usurpation but as the expression of an organization with a purpose and a sort of doctrine of its own. The intellectual content of Fascism was limited, nationalist and romantic; its methods, especially in its opening phase, were violent and dreadful; but at least it insisted upon discipline and public service for its members. It appeared as a countermovement to a chaotic labour communism, but its support of the still-surviving monarchy and the Church was qualified by a considerable boldness in handling education and private property for the public benefit. Fascism indeed was not an altogether bad thing; it was a bad good thing; and Mussolini has left his mark on history.

[*The Shape of Things to Come* (Hutchinson: London, 1933), 136–8.]

ii. Interpretations of Fascism by Marxists

135

(a) Opening the Door to Fascism

This passage is taken from the Resolution of the Third Enlarged Executive of the Communist International (ECCI) Plenum on Fascism, which had been influenced by a powerful speech by the veteran German communist Klara Zetkin, who had stressed that fascism 'had attracted thousands of disappointed proletarians who hoped that the will to build a new and better world would rise above class contradictions and find its embodiment in the nation'. The resolution acknowledges four points about fascism which contrast with the orthodox position which later emerged under the sway of Stalinism: (i) it has a genuine revolutionary dimension; (ii) its revolutionary rhetoric appeals to some workers; (iii) it has an autonomous anti-capitalist and anti-liberal dynamic, but is liable to become a tool of the bourgeoisie; (iv) as a manifestation of capitalism it has an intrinsic international dimension (a point already recognized by the Fourth Comintern Congress held in November 1922, shortly after the March on Rome).

Fascism is a characteristic phenomenon of decay, a reflection of the progressive dissolution of capitalist economy and of the disintegration of the bourgeois State.[. . .]

In the period of revolutionary ferment and proletarian risings, fascism to some extent sympathized or at least flirted with proletarian revolutionary demands. The masses which followed fascism vacillated between the two camps in the great and universal class contradictions and class struggles. But with the consolidation of capitalist rule and the general bourgeois offensive they threw themselves definitely on to the side of the bourgeoisie, where their leaders had stood from the beginning. The bourgeoisie immediately took fascism into paid service in their fight to defeat and enslave the proletariat.[. . .] The old, allegedly non-political apparatus of the bourgeois State no longer guarantees the bourgeoisie adequate security. They have set about creating special class-struggle troops against the proletariat. Fascism provides these troops. Although fascism by its origin and its exponents also includes revolutionary tendencies which might turn against capitalism and its State, it is nevertheless becoming a dangerous counter-revolutionary force. That is shown where it triumphed in Italy.[. . .] In Italy the door to fascism was opened by the passivity of the socialist party and the reformist trade union leaders; its revolutionary phraseology won over many proletarian elements, which made its victory possible.[. . .] The triumph of fascism in Italy spurs the bourgeoisie of other countries to take the same course in defeating the proletariat. The working classes of the entire world are threatened with the fate of their Italian brothers.[. . .]

The fascist forces are being organized on an international scale, and it is consequently necessary to organize the workers' struggle against fascism internationally.

['Extracts from a Resolution of the Third Enlarged Executive of the Communist International Plenum on Fascism' (23 June 1923), in J. Degras (ed.), *The Communist International 1919–1943* (Oxford: Oxford University Press, 1965), i. 41–3.]

(b) White Terror

By the time the Communist International adopted this pronouncement on fascism at its sixth annual congress the European situation had changed significantly. In Italy much of the institutional apparatus of Mussolini's dictatorship was now in place, though the Lateran Pacts, finally reconciling the Vatican to the State, would be signed only the following year. Meanwhile in Germany Nazism was rapidly building up its nationwide organization to become a 'shadow state'. References to fascism's anti-Semitism show the way Nazism has modified the image of generic fascism (official Fascism would only adopt Nazi-style anti-Semitism a decade later). This account of fascism prepares the ground for the highly influential definition adopted by the Comintern shortly after the Nazi seizure of power which forms the next extract. It is also notable for the way it stressed the Comintern's bitter enmity with Social Democracy, which Stalin had first described as fascism's 'twin' in an article written in late 1924 (the Resolution of the Fifth Comintern Congress of July 1924 had already declared that 'fascism and social-democracy are the two sides of a single instrument of capitalist dictatorship'). This would lead to the fatal tactical flaw of treating the German Social Democrats as 'social fascists'.

Alongside social-democracy, which helps the bourgeoisie to oppress the working class and blunt its proletarian vigilance, stands fascism.

In the imperialist epoch the intensification of the class struggle, the expansion of the elements of class war—particularly after the imperialist world war—led to the bankruptcy of parliamentarism. Hence the 'new' methods and forms of governing (e.g. the system of 'inner Cabinets', the operations of oligarchic groups behind the scenes, the deterioration of 'representative assemblies' and distortion of their function, the restriction and elimination of 'democratic freedoms', etc.). In certain historical conditions this process in which bourgeois-imperialist reaction conducts its offensive assumes the form of fascism. The relevant conditions are: instability of capitalist relationships; the presence in large numbers of socially declassed elements; the impoverishment of broad strata of the urban petty bourgeoisie and the intelligentsia; discontent among the rural petty bourgeoisie; finally the constant threat of proletarian mass action. To secure greater durability, solidity, and stability for their power, the bourgeoisie are to an increasing degree compelled to abandon the parliamentary system in favour of fascist methods of rule, which are independent of party relationships and combinations. Fascism is a method of directly exercising the bourgeois dictatorship, ideologically disguised under ideas of 'the national community' and representation according to occupation (i.e. in fact representation of the various groups of the ruling classes). It is a method which uses its own peculiar brand of social demagogy (anti-Semitism, occasional attacks on usury-capital, impatience with the parliamentary 'talking-shop') to exploit the discontent of the petty-bourgeois masses, the intellectuals, etc.; and which corrupts by creating a compact and paid hierarchy of fascist fighting squads, a fascist party machine, and a fascist bureaucracy. Fascism also seeks to penetrate the ranks of the working class by winning over its most backward strata by exploiting their discontent, the passivity of social-democracy, etc. Fascism's chief function is to annihilate the revolutionary vanguard of the working class, i.e. the communist strata of the proletariat and their leading cadres. The combination of social demagogy, corruption, and active white terror, and the most extreme imperialist aggressiveness in foreign policy are characteristic features of fascism. When the position is particularly critical for the bourgeoisie fascism resorts to anti-capitalist phraseology, but once it is certain of its power it is revealed more and more openly as the terroristic dictatorship of large capital, and discards its anti-capitalist lumber.

['Extracts from the Programme of the Communist International Adopted at its Sixth Annual Congress' (1 Sept. 1928), ibid., i. 484–5.]

(c) Fruit of the Womb

This passage is taken from the theses of the thirteenth ECCI Plenum on 'fascism, the war danger, and the tasks of communist parties'. In the first meeting of the ECCI to be held since the Nazi seizure of power in March 1933, a major discussion took place to reassess the threat which fascism posed to the prospects of world revolution. Speaker after speaker insisted on the impossibility of a pact with the social-democracy, now called social-fascism. The debate produced several optimistic evaluations of the situation, portraying the forces of international socialism as still having the upper hand over fascism and capable of overthrowing the various regimes it had erected (by now Marxists considered all right-wing dictatorships, such as those of Poland, Spain, and Portugal, as fascist). In its final Resolution the Congress produced the classic and highly crude characterization of fascism as the dictatorship of finance capital, repeated verbatim by Dimitrov at the Seventh Comintern Congress of 1935. It went on to become the orthodox definition for every generation of political scientist working within the Soviet empire up till its collapse (see Texts 136, 150).

Fascism is the open, terrorist dictatorship of the most reactionary, most chauvinist and most imperialist elements of finance capital. Fascism tries to secure a mass basis for monopolist capital among the petty bourgeoisie, appealing to the peasantry, artisans, office employees and civil servants who have been thrown out of their normal course of life, and particularly to the declassed elements in the big cities, also trying to penetrate into the working class.

The growth of fascism and its coming into power in Germany and in a number of other capitalist countries means:

(a) that the revolutionary crisis and the indignation of the broad masses against the rule of capital is growing;

(b) that the capitalists are no longer able to maintain their dictatorship by the old methods of parliamentarism and of bourgeois democracy in general;

(c) that, moreover, the methods of parliamentarism and bourgeois democracy in general are becoming a hindrance to the capitalists both in their internal politics (the struggle against the proletariat) and in their foreign politics (war for the imperialist redistribution of the world);

(d) that in view of this, capital is compelled to pass to open terrorist dictatorship within the country and to unrestrained chauvinism in foreign politics, which represents direct preparation for imperialist wars.

Born in the womb of bourgeois democracy, fascism in the eyes of the capitalists is a means of saving capitalism from collapse. It is only for the purpose of deceiving and disarming the workers that social-democracy denies the fascization of bourgeois democracy and draws a contrast in principle between the democratic countries and the countries of the fascist dictatorship. On the other hand, the fascist dictatorship is not an inevitable stage of the dictatorship of the bourgeoisie in all countries. The possibility of averting it depends upon the forces of the fighting proletariat, which are paralysed by the corrupting [disintegrating] influence of social-democracy more than by anything else.

['Extracts from the Theses of the Thirteenth ECCI Plenum on Fascism, the War Danger, and the Tasks of Communist Parties' (Dec. 1933), ibid., iii. 296–9.]

PALMIRO TOGLIATTI
....

136 Erroneous Definitions

In the spring of 1935 the most influential Italian member of the Comintern, Palmiro Togliatti, gave a series of lectures to the Party School in Moscow on the nature of fascism. They are interesting on several points: (i) they reveal how the definition evolved by the Thirteenth Plenum of the ECCI in December 1933 had now become gospel to Comintern members; (ii) they register the major U-turn in orthodox policy taken by Comintern at the Seventh Congress of 1935, Social Democrats now being belatedly regarded as allies rather than traitors in the fight against fascism; (iii) they reflect the tension between intellectual freedom and urge to toe the line experienced by all communists in the Stalinist era. Togliatti had originally recognized the mass base of fascism, then denied it when it was officially identified only with capitalism, and now conveniently passes over his own dogmatic promulgation of the 'erroneous definitions' which turned social democrats into enemies.

The most complete definition was given by the 13th meeting of the Enlarged Executive of the Communist International and is as follows: 'Fascism is the open terrorist dictatorship of the most reactionary, most chauvinistic, most imperialist elements of finance capital.'

Fascism has not always been defined this way. Diverse, often erroneous definitions have been given of fascism at different stages and different times. It would be interesting (and it's a job I advise you to undertake) to study the diverse definitions we have given of fascism at various stages.[. . .]

Why has fascism, the open dictatorship of the bourgeoisie, arisen today, precisely in this period? You can find the answer in Lenin himself; you should look for it in his works on imperialism. *You can't know what fascism is if you don't know imperialism.* You know the economic features of imperialism. You know the definition Lenin gives. Imperialism is characterized by: 1) the concentration of production and capital, the formation of monopolies which play a decisive part role in economic life; 2) the merging of bank capital with industrial capital, and the creation, on the basis of finance capital, of financial oligarchy; 3) the great importance acquired by the export of capital; 4) the rise of international capitalist monopolies; and, lastly, the repartitioning of the world among the great capitalist powers, which can now be viewed as complete.

These are the features of imperialism. Based on them, there is a tendency of all the bourgeoisie's political institutions to undergo a reactionary transformation. This, too, you will find in Lenin. There is a tendency to make these institutions reactionary, and this tendency appears in its most coherent forms with fascism.[. . .]

At this point I must caution you against another error: schematism. You must be careful not to consider the transition from bourgeois democracy to fascism fatal and inevitable. Why? Because imperialism does not *necessarily* have to give birth to the fascist dictatorship.[. . .] England, for instance, is a great imperialist state in which there is a democratic parliamentary government (although here, too, it cannot be said that reactionary features are not present).[. . .] This tendency toward the fascist form of government is present everywhere, but this still does not mean fascism must perforce be arrived at everywhere.[. . .] This is the first element to spell out in defining fascism.

The second element consists in the nature of fascism's mass base. The term fascism is often used imprecisely as a synonym for reaction, terror, etc. This is incorrect.[. . .] We must use it only when the fight against the working class develops on a new mass base with a petty-bourgeois character, as we can see in Germany, Italy, France, England—anywhere a typical fascism exists.

Hence, the fascist dictatorship endeavours to possess a mass movement by organizing the bourgeoisie and petty bourgeoisie.

[*Lectures on Fascism* (Lawrence & Wishart: London, 1976), 1, 3–4, 5.]

R. PALME DUTT

137 The Purging Fires of Fascism

Another symptom of how Comintern pronouncements became canonic for communists the world over is to be found in R. Palme Dutt's monograph on fascism, written as editor of the British Communist Party's Daily Worker. *He attacks social democracy, warning that 'Where the majority of the working class has followed the line of Reformism (Germany, Italy, etc.), there at a certain stage Fascism inevitably grows and conquers' (p. 88). He is also alarmed by the internationalization of fascism, which he sees fully-fledged in Italy,*

Germany, and Austria, threatening the infant Republic in Spain, embryonic in Ramsey Macdonald's National Government and the British Union of Fascism in Britain, Roosevelt's 'New Deal' (and the Ku Klux Klan) in the USA, and the 'Government of National Concentration' and the Croix de Feu in France. He ends his book with this assessment of the future of fascism, infused with his unshakeable faith in the ultimate triumph of communism.

Marx and Engels long ago pointed out the inevitable working out of capitalism in barbarism and decay, if the working-class revolution should fail to conquer in time. Stage by stage, through imperialism and its world orgies of brutality and destruction, through the slaughter of the world war, and to-day through Fascism, we are tasting the first beginnings of this alternative.

It is time to end this chapter of human history, before we have to tread this path still further, and to open the new one throughout the world which has already begun over one-sixth of the world. Only the working-class revolution can save humanity, can carry humanity forward, can organise the enormous powers of production that lie ready to hand.

The working-class movement in the first period after the war was not yet ready outside Russia for its world historic task. The organised working-class movement was still soaked with reformist and pacifist illusions, with opportunism and corruption in its upper strata. Fascism is not only the punishment of history for this weakness; *Fascism is the weapon of history for purging and burning out this weakness.* In the fires of Fascism the revolutionary working class is drawing close its ranks, steeled and hardened and clear-seeing, for the final struggle; and the revolutionary working class, thus steeled and strengthened, will rise to the height of its task and save the world.

Whatever the black hells of suffering and destruction that have still to be passed through, we face the future with the certainty and confidence of approaching power, with contempt for the barbarous antics of the doomed and decaying parasite class-enemy and its final misshapen progeny of Fascism, with singing hearts and glowing confidence in the future. *'The last fight let us face. The Internationale unites the human race.'*

[*Fascism and Social Revolution* (Martin Lawrence: London, 1934), 288–9.]

E. J. STRACHEY

138   The Return of the Dark Ages

John Strachey, a British Marxist theorist, was one of the Labour MPs who signed the Mosley Manifesto and became a founding member of the New Party (April 1931), an attempt to break the mould of British politics by taking radical measures to save Britain from industrial stagnation. After the failure of this party in the General Election later that year, Oswald Mosley went on to found the British Union of Fascists in October 1932 after a visit to Mussolini's Italy had confirmed his shift to the right. Strachey, meanwhile, returned chastened to his ideological fold and wrote The Menace of Fascism *to warn his readers of the threat it posed to modern civilization. At one point he takes issue with the opinion of a certain Professor Scott Nearing that the practical result of fascism's animus against big business and industry combined with its pursuit of autarky would be to return the West to the primitiveness of medieval village life.*

No, Fascism will actually foster the highest forms of modern technique in the short period of preparation for a new war, but it will do so only to smash them, and, with them, if Fascism is allowed to run its course, all modern civilization, in a series of vast new Imperialist wars for the partition, then the re-partition of the world.

But it is inconceivable that Fascism will be allowed to run its full course. Each of its wars will involve the arming of important sections of the working class. Each will put unbearable pressure, unimaginable suffering, frightful privations on the workers. Each will certainly be accompanied by working-class revolutions. Nor can we doubt for a moment that these revolutions will be successful, and that there will arise working-class powers which will be able to abandon Imperialist policy and yet to solve the economic problem, because they will be willing to end the private ownership of the means of production.

Thus, the alternative which faces the world is not between a working-class civilization based upon planned Socialist production, and a Fascist civilization of Corporate States, 'Third Empires', or whatnot. Our alternative is a working-class Socialist civilization, or the destruction of all civilization and a return to the dark ages.[. . .]

We face either the destruction of civilization in a series of Fascist wars 'for space and employment', or the overthrow of Fascist Imperialism by the workers. For the workers alone can end the private ownership of the means of production, and so set humanity once more on the path of progress. The self-destructive nature of Fascism, doomed as it is to ruthless internecine conflict, gives us the assurance that the workers will triumph, albeit perhaps, after terrible and unnecessary sacrifice, and that humanity will go forward to a new epoch in the history of civilization.

[*The Menace of Fascism* (Victor Gollancz: London, 1933), 148–50.]

G. D. H. AND M. I. COLE

139 **Tribal Loyalties**

G. D. H. Cole (1889–1959), was Chichele Professor of Social and Political Theory at Oxford University from 1944 to 1957 and president of the Fabian Society from 1952 till his death. Between 1913 and 1920 he had been the major theorist of guild socialism. The widely read Guide *quoted from here is one of several introductions to modern politics written with his wife Margaret. In the section devoted to 'currents of political opinion' the authors argue that the emergency programme of state intervention undertaken by the United States under Roosevelt's New Deal is not to be confused with 'European Fascism': the fascist Corporative State is to be seen as an attempt to create an alternative to laissez-faire Capitalism to bring about 'permanent change both in the political structure of the State and in the State's relation to economic affairs'. This recognition that nationalist sentiments were likely to prevail over socialist internationalism sets this passage apart from orthodox Marxist analysis.*

Fascism is State-controlled Capitalism operated in the interests of the broad mass of property-owners, its conception being of course wide enough to include the possession of a superior type of education reserved for a few as in effect a form of property.

But it is also highly relevant that Fascism is nationalist. For there is an economic as well as a political reason for its nationalism. It must be nationalist because the national State is the only available instrument for guarding the rights of property against Socialist attack. This necessity explains the eagerness with which Fascist leaders play upon nationalist sentiment. But it does not, of course, explain the existence of the strength of the sentiment to which they are able to appeal. For the nationalist sentiment itself, though it is reinforced by economic considerations, does not depend mainly upon them, but arises rather in its present heightened state from the power of fear and the threat of insecurity to drive men back to primitive loyalties. Nationalism in its more exaggerated forms is the outcome of a fear complex expressing itself no longer in a group or tribal loyalty on a small scale but in a sense of the nation as the embodiment of collective power. International Socialism or anything else that requires world-wide collaboration is apt to seem terrifying to the minds of men who can think or feel only in terms of things nearer to home. This is the fatal weakness that besets the present propaganda of internationalism.[. . .] [S]trong as Socialism has become in many countries it is still in its internationalist appeal only skin-deep among the greater part of those who have become accustomed to give it political support in national affairs.

[*A Guide to Modern Politics* (Victor Gollancz: London, 1934), 55–6.]

R. A. Brady wrote his Marxist analysis of the Third Reich when he was Associate Professor of Economics at the University of California, applying an orthodox Marxist diagnosis of it as the tool of monopoly capitalism. In his chapter 'The Looming Shadow of Fascism over the World', he portrays 'the people of every nation' being 'slowly separated into warring camps. Left and right, Popular Front and Fascist, red and reactionary, capital and labour—the terms vary with time and circumstance, but the cleavage remains the same.' Another feature typical of Marxist analysis is the way he sees Italy and Germany as 'the major exponents of Fascism', but 'only less so are Portugal, Hungary, Austria, Greece, Romania, Brazil, Bolivia and Japan'. In Spain too, where civil war is in the air, the struggle is between the Popular Front and fascists. For Brady fascism is the 'wedding of a condition and a myth': the condition is the application to the whole of society of the hierarchical organizational structure and authoritarian ethos of big business and the military; the myth, the Social Darwinian concept of the survival of the most predatory, already firmly entrenched within the capitalist business ethic.

Here we have the modern parallel to the ancient story of the hero, Cadmus, who, in the quest for the Golden Fleece, slew the fiery dragon. Following the voice of an unseen oracle, he sowed the dragon's teeth in the soil where the battle took place, and from thence sprang a race of warriors who rose and fought each other to death. When the business forces of the world openly sow the dragon's teeth of discord amongst otherwise peaceful peoples, they prepare, if not themselves, coming generations for the wasteland shambles; for ten to fifty or a hundred years of sanguinary war and terror-ridden struggle in what may be the growing darkness of a fading and broken civilisation.[. . .]

There is no hope against all this, except that of sweeping away the very foundations on which fascism constructs its brittle edifice. If the world-wide fascist trend of things is to be reversed, what is left of democracy must be reinforced, and the sweep of the tide turned. But this means an erosion of fascist foundations, not by humanising business enterprise, but by arraying together all those forces whose face is turned the other way.

Against an opponent who believes singly and solely in force and guile, force must be massed. The hope of the people of the United States is to be found, not in giving free rein to monopoly-oriented and fascist-inclined capitalism, but in turning back its fields, factories, and workshops to those who fought its war of freedom against a tyrannical power, and who built, with their muscles and brains, all the real wealth and all that there is in America which deserves the name of culture. But it will not come to them as a 'gift'; they must learn that the only solution to recovery of their heritage lies within themselves.

And the solution is no different for any people or nation in the world.

[*The Spirit and Structure of German Fascism* (Victor Gollancz: London, 1937), 353–4.]

141 The Hopeless Task

Karl Polanyi was an Austrian sociologist who emigrated to Britain after Hitler came to power. In his chapter on 'The Essence of Fascism' he concentrates on the aspects of fascism which deny the primacy of the individual over society, a premiss which found concrete expression in its destruction of democratic institutions, its suppression of cultural, intellectual, and religious freedoms, and its bid to impose its own supra-individualist vision of the world. Thereby fascism comes into direct conflict with the Christian tradition.

For the idea of Man and the idea of Society cannot be dealt with separately. What Fascism is contending with is the Christian idea of man and Society as a whole. Its central concept is that of the person. It is the individual in his religious aspect. The consistent refusal of Fascism to regard the individual in this aspect is the sign of its recognition that Christianity and Fascism are completely incompatible.

The Christian idea of society is that it is a relationship of persons. Everything else follows logically from this. The central proposition of Fascism is that society is *not* a relationship of persons. This is the real significance of its anti-individualism. The implied negation is the formative principle of Fascism as a philosophy. It is its essence. It sets to Fascist thought its definite task in history, science, morals, politics, economics, and religion. Thus Fascist philosophy is an effort to produce a vision of the world in which society is *not* a relationship of persons. A society, in fact, in which there are either no conscious human beings or their consciousness has no reference to the existence and functioning of society. Anything less leads back to the Christian truth about society. But that is indivisible. It is the achievement of Fascism to have discovered its whole scope. It rightly asserts the correlatedness of the ideas of Individualism, Democracy and Socialism. It knows that either Christianity or Fascism must perish in the struggle.

At first sight it seems almost inconceivable that Fascism should have undertaken a task which to our conventional minds seems so utterly hopeless. And yet it has. That its assertions and propositions are more startling than anything which Radicals of the Left have ever produced ought, however, not to surprise us. Revolutionary Socialism is but a different formulation and a stricter interpretation of truths generally accepted in Western Europe for almost two thousand years. Fascism is their denial. This explains the devious paths which it has been driven to explore.

['The Essence of Fascism', in J. Lewis, K. Polanyi, D. K. Kitchin, *et al.*, *Christianity and the Social Revolution* (Victor Gollancz: London, 1935), 370–1.]

142 Rabbits Ruled by Stoats

George Orwell is more famous for his anti-totalitarianism than for the idiosyncratic brand of democratic socialism articulated in The Road to Wigan Pier, *a bitter indictment of the atrocious living conditions still endured by millions of Britons in the late 1930s. Towards the end of the book he alerts the reader to 'the urgent danger of Fascist domination in Europe' (p. 100), and argues that if this comes about it will be largely the fault of Socialists themselves, who have underestimated fascism's positive appeal to the millions drawn to its defence of spiritual, patriotic, and military values. Only when socialism becomes once more associated with justice and liberty will it be able to counter the global threat which fascism now poses.*

It was easy to laugh at Fascism when we imagined that it was based on hysterical nationalism, because it seemed obvious that the Fascist states, each regarding itself as the chosen people and patriotic *contra mundum*, would clash with one another. But nothing of the kind is happening. Fascism is now an international movement, which means not only that the Fascist nations can combine for purposes of loot, but that they are groping, perhaps only half consciously as yet, towards a world-system. For the vision of the totalitarian state there is being substituted the vision of the totalitarian world. As I pointed out earlier, the advance of machine-technique must lead ultimately to some form of collectivism, but that form need not necessarily be equalitarian; that is, it need not be Socialism. *Pace* the economists, it is quite easy to imagine a world-society, economically collectivist—that is, with the profit principle eliminated—but with all political, military, and educational power in the hands of a small caste of rulers and their bravos. That or something like it is the objective of Fascism. And that, of course, is the slave-state, or rather the slave-world; it would probably be a stable form of society, and the chances are, considering the enormous wealth of the world if scientifically exploited, that the slaves would be well-fed and contented. It is usual to talk of the Fascist objective as the 'beehive state', which does a grave injustice to the bees. A world full of rabbits ruled by stoats would be nearer to the mark. It is against this beastly possibility that we have got to combine.

The only thing *for* which we can combine is the underlying ideal of Socialism: justice and liberty. But it is hardly strong enough to call this ideal 'underlying'. It is almost completely forgotten. It has been buried beneath layer after layer of doctrinaire priggishness, party squabbles and half-baked 'progressivism' until it is like a diamond hidden under a mountain of dung. The job of the Socialist is to get it out again. Justice and liberty! *Those* are the words that have got to ring like a bugle across the world.

[*The Road to Wigan Pier* (Penguin: Harmondsworth, 1962; 1st pub. 1937), 200–1.]

PETER DRUCKER

143 **Black Magic**

Peter Drucker fled Nazi Austria in 1939, and went on to a highly successful career as a political scientist. His analysis of fascism is based on the premiss that the economic (materialist, mechanistic) conception of human life central to liberalism and socialism has broken down and that fascism simply negates it without putting anything positive in its

*place (cf. Text 148). He is confident that the Nazis need the Jews 'as personified demons' to
maintain the momentum of their nihilism and will never attempt 'a real solution'. In a
curiously abstract way he also believes fascism will evaporate once a positive conception of
a new order emerges based on the original European values of spirituality, freedom, and
equality. Despite such grave misreadings of fascism, particularly of Nazism, the book is
significant testimony to the widespread liberal feeling by 1939 that the rise of fascism
threatened the very survival of Western civilization, and also to the fact that some anti-
fascists too were awaiting the appearance of a 'New Man'.*

The totalitarian revolution is clearly not the beginning of a new order but the result
of the total collapse of the old. It is not a miracle, but a mirage which will dissolve
as soon as a new order, a new concept of man, appear. Fascism can only deny the
concept of Economic Man which has broken down. It cannot create the new
concept which should take its place. But unless a new order and new concept based
upon the European values of freedom and equality can be found, Europe and the
Occident are doomed.

The form which the totalitarian revolution has been taking indicates in itself that
such an order will eventually arrive. That the masses substitute organization for
order when they cannot have a real order, that they worship a demon when they
have no God to worship and no concept of man to respect, shows by its very
intensity that they must have an order, a creed, and a rational concept of man. The
more fervently they turn fascist, the more feverishly do they search for something
else. And the more eagerly will they embrace the new order when it appears.
Armaments, the totalitarian organization of society, the suppression of freedom
and liberties, the persecution of the Jews, and the war against religion are all signs
of weakness, not of strength. They have their roots in blackest, unfathomable
despair. The more desperate the masses become, the more strongly entrenched
will totalitarianism appear to be. The further they push on the totalitarian road, the
greater will be their despair. As soon as they are offered an alternative—but no
sooner—the whole totalitarian magic will vanish like a nightmare.[. . .]

But the dynamic character of our history, which is all our strength, is also our
weakness; for it makes periods of transition like the present one inevitable. Yet that
today the European masses flee into the black magic of totalitarianism rather than
tolerate a world without order and a society without meaning, only shows that the
force that is Europe is still alive.[. . .]

The Western democracies have to realize that totalitarian fascism cannot be
overcome by socialism, by capitalist democracy, or by a combination of both. It can
only be overcome by a new noneconomic concept of a free and equal society. The
fascist countries might be destroyed; they might be reduced to anarchy. But neither
capitalism nor socialism can be restored thereby. On the contrary, the Western
European democracies themselves will be forced into totalitarianism unless they
produce a noneconomic society striving for the freedom and the equality of the
individual.

[*The End of Economic Man* (Harper & Row: New York, London, 1969; 1st pub. 1939), 236,
241, 242.]

Max Horkheimer (1895–1973) was one of the most important theorists of neo-Marxist Critical Theory and director of the Frankfurt Institute of Social Research, which in 1933 had transferred to the USA to avoid being closed down by the Third Reich. He was also a Jew. It is in this article, finished in September 1939, only days before the outbreak of the Second World War, that Horkheimer coins the dictum, later beloved of Marxist theorists, 'whoever is not prepared to talk about capitalism should also remain silent about fascism' and gives his own gloss on the argument that fascism was a direct product of the crisis of capitalism. This passage captures something of the anguish of those clear-sighted enough to sense the enormity of the catastrophe which was about to break over the world, not least over his own people, while yet fully aware of their impotence to stop it.

Today to appeal to nineteenth-century liberal thought in the struggle against fascism is to invoke the very force which has enabled it to triumph. As victor it can appropriate the slogan 'let the most able rise to the top'. Fascism has triumphed so conclusively in the competitive struggle between nations that it can actually eliminate competition altogether. '*Laissez-faire, laissez-aller,*' it might well ask, 'why can't I do what I want? Am I not the employer and provider for just as many of the masses as any freewheeling economic giant? I am even at the cutting edge of chemistry. Labouring masses, colonialists, dissatisfied elements complain. My god, haven't they always?'

Jews have little to hope from the Second World War. However it ends, a seamless process of militarization is leading the world ever deeper into authoritarian-collective forms of life. The German war economy in the First World War was a forerunner of modern 'five-year plans'; the compulsory conscription used in modern warfare between nations is a major constituent of totalitarian social engineering. Mass mobilization brings the columns of workers who have been assigned to the armaments industry and the construction of ever more motorways, underground railways, and blocks of flats little that is new, except, that is, for a mass grave.[. . .]

In the totalitarian order anti-Semitism will come to a natural end, when there will be no humanity left, but perhaps still a few Jews. Hatred of Jews is associated with the rise of fascism. In Germany anti-Semitism serves as a safety-valve at most for younger ranks of the SA.[6] It is used as a means of intimidating the population at large. It is a way of showing that the system is ruthless and will stop at nothing. Politically speaking pogroms are aimed at the onlookers. To see if anyone raises a finger. There is nothing to be gained from them any more. The slogans of anti-Semitic propaganda are for foreign consumption. It is all very well if Aryan captains of industry or other prominent people still make indignant protestations, especially

---

[6] *Sturmabteilung*, the paramilitary wing of the Nazi Party, by 1939 superseded by Himmler's SS or *Schutzstaffel*.

if their countries are at a safe distance, their potentially fascist populations do not take them very seriously. In secret people approve of the cruelty which they sound so outraged about. In continents whose profits could feed the whole of mankind, every beggar fears being robbed of his food by Jewish immigrants. Armies of the unemployed and of petty bourgeois love Hitler the world over precisely for his anti-Semitism, and the hardcore of the ruling class share this love with them. By intensifying the cruelty *in absurdum* horror at it is appeased. The impunity which the divine Power concedes to the perpetrators, no matter how sorely it is tested, is permanent proof that it does not exist. By reproducing inhumanity people simply prove to themselves that humanity, religion, and the whole liberal ideology count for nothing. All totalitarian society has to do now is do away with guilty consciences. Compassion is really the last sin.[. . .]

There is nothing to be hoped of the alliance between the major powers. The totalitarian economy cannot be relied on to collapse. Fascism fixes the social results of the collapse of capitalism. It is utterly naïve when people outside the country encourage the German workers to revolt.[. . .] Intellectuals simply cannot take in the idea that progressive forces have been defeated and that fascism can last indefinitely. They think that any system which works must also be good, and therefore set about proving that fascism cannot work. But there are periods in which in terms of force and efficiency it is bad which has come to prevail. Jews were once proud of their abstract monotheism, the rejection of idolatry, the refusal to treat anything finite as if it were infinite. Their distress makes them turn to this faith once more. The refusal to have respect for an ephemeral phenomenon which wants to be treated like God is the religion of those who in a Europe subjected to an Iron Heel persist in dedicating their lives to prepare for better days.

['Die Juden und Europa' [The Jews and Europe], *Zeitschrift für Sozialforschung*, 8 (1939), 132–3, 135–6.]

iv. Four Wartime Analyses of Fascism

WILHELM REICH

 145 **Forcing Elephants into Foxholes**

Like Drucker, Wilhelm Reich (1897–1957) fled Austria for the USA in 1939, but his attempt to blend Freudian psychoanalysis with communism led him to devise a theory of sexual repression, and of techniques for removing it, which ran foul first of American law and then of McCarthyism. Though highly unorthodox, his theory of fascism complements later psychological approaches in its insistence of the central role played by repression and life-denial in generating the fanaticism and destructiveness it inspires.

The case of fascism, in contrast to liberalism and genuine revolution, is quite different. Its essence embodies neither the surface nor the depth, but by and large the second, intermediate character layer of secondary drives.

When this book was first written, fascism was generally regarded as a 'political party', which, as other 'social groups', advocated an organized 'political idea'. According to this appraisal the fascist party was instituting fascism by means of force or through 'political manœuvre'.

Contrary to this, my medical experiences with men and women of various classes, races, nations, religious beliefs, etc., taught me that 'fascism' is only the organized political expression of the structure of the average man's character, a structure that is confined neither to certain races or nations nor to certain parties, but is general and international. Viewed with respect to man's character, *'fascism' is the basic emotional attitude of the suppressed man of our authoritarian machine civilization and its mechanistic–mystical conception of life.*

It is the mechanistic–mystical character of modern man that produces fascist parties, and not vice versa.

The result of erroneous political thinking is that even fascism is conceived as a specific national characteristic of the Germans or the Japanese. All further erroneous interpretations follow from this initial erroneous conception.

To the detriment of genuine efforts to achieve freedom, fascism was and is still conceived as the dictatorship of a small reactionary clique. The tenacity with which this error persists is to be ascribed to our fear of recognizing the true state of affairs: fascism is an *international* phenomenon, which pervades all bodies of human society of *all* nations. This conclusion is in agreement with the international events of the past fifteen years.

My character-analytic experiences have convinced me that there is not a single individual who does not bear the elements of fascist feeling and thinking in his structure. As a political movement fascism differs from other reactionary parties inasmuch as it is borne and championed by masses of people.[. . .]

It follows from all this that the social measures of the past three hundred years can no more cope with the mass pestilence of fascism than an elephant (six thousand years) can be forced into a foxhole (three hundred years).

Hence, the discovery of natural biological work-democracy in international human intercourse is to be considered the answer to fascism. This would be true, even if not a single contemporary sex-economist, orgone[7] biophysicist, or work-democrat should live to see its complete realization and victory over irrationality in social life.

[Preface to 3rd (1942) edition, *The Mass Psychology of Fascism*, trans. Vincent Carfagno (Simon & Schuster: New York, 1970; 1st pub. in German 1933), pp. xiii–iv, xxvii.]

ERICH FROMM

146   The Fear of Freedom

Reich was not the first to attempt to blend Marx with Freud. The 'Critical Theory' of the pre-war Frankfurt Institute for Social Research worked on a similar synthesis in order to develop a new methodology with which to expose the totalitarianism explicit in both Fascism and Stalinism, and latent in liberal democracy. The Institute was re-established in the USA after Nazism had closed it down, but, like Marcuse, Erich Fromm (1900–80) did not accompany Horkheimer and Adorno when they transferred the Institute back to Frankfurt in 1950. Fromm's analysis locates the 'human basis of Fascism' in the sado-masochistic predisposition of 'normal' (as opposed to 'neurotic') people which lies at the root of 'the authoritarian character'. His account thus relates closely to the approach adopted in the Frankfurt School's later contribution to understanding the psychology of fascism (see Text 156).

Since the term 'sado-masochistic' is associated with ideas of perversion and neurosis, I prefer to speak of the sado-masochistic character, especially when not the neurotic but the normal person is meant, as the *'authoritarian character'*. This terminology is justifiable because the sado-masochistic person is always characterized by his attitude towards authority. He admires authority and tends to submit to it, but at the same time wants to be an authority himself and have others submit to him. There is another reason for choosing this term. The Fascist system calls itself authoritarian because of the dominant role of authority in its social and political structure. By the term 'authoritarian character', we imply that it represents the personality structure which is the human basis of Fascism.[. . .]

We thus come to define a genuine ideal as any aim which furthers the growth, freedom, and happiness of the self, and to define as fictitious ideals those compulsive and irrational aims which subjectively are attractive experiences (like the drive for submission), but which actually are harmful to life. Once we accept this definition, it follows that a genuine ideal is not some veiled force superior to the

---

[7] The occult energy which Reich postulated to be the source of all biological and psychic health and whose existence he claimed to have demonstrated empirically.

individual, but that it is the articulate expression of utmost affirmation of the self. Any ideal which is in contrast to such affirmation proves by this very fact that it is not an ideal but a pathological aim.

From here we come to another question, that of sacrifice. Does our definition of freedom as non-submission to any *higher* power exclude sacrifices, including the sacrifice of one's life?

This is a particularly important question to-day, when Fascism proclaims self-sacrifice as the highest virtue and impresses many people with its idealistic character. The answer to this question follows logically from what has been said so far. There are two entirely different types of sacrifice. It is one of the tragic facts of life that the demands of our physical self and the aims of our mental self can conflict: that actually we may have to sacrifice our physical self in order to assert the integrity of our spiritual self. This sacrifice will never lose its tragic quality. Death is never sweet, not even if it is suffered for the highest ideal. It remains unspeakably bitter, and still it can be the utmost assertion of our individuality. Such sacrifice is fundamentally different from the 'sacrifice' which Fascism preaches. There, sacrifice is not the highest price man may have to pay to assert his self, but it is an aim in itself. This masochistic sacrifice sees the fulfilment of life in its very negation, in the annihilation of the self. It is only the supreme expression of what Fascism aims at in all its ramifications—the annihilation of the individual self and its utter submission to a higher power. It is the perversion of true sacrifice as much as suicide is the utmost perversion of life. True sacrifice presupposes an uncompromising wish for spiritual integrity. The sacrifice of those who have lost it only covers up their moral bankruptcy.

[*The Fear of Freedom* (Routledge & Kegan Paul: London, 1942), 141, 230–1.]

HAROLD LASKI

147   Market Forces

Harold Laski (1893–1950) was professor of political science at the London School of Economics from 1926 to 1950 and a prominent member of the Labour Party executive. The position he arrives at in his wartime analysis of fascism follows orthodox Marxist thought in seeing its essence as 'the outcome of capitalism in decay' (p. 95), but departs from it in two key respects: (i) by stressing the fact that the social base of fascism was heterogeneous (for example, it attracted among others demobbed soldiers, intellectuals, the young, and women), and not to be reduced to the middle classes; (ii) fascism was bent on the destruction of laissez-faire capitalism. Nevertheless, in this passage Laski agrees with the bulk of fascist studies till the 1960s, whether Marxist or 'liberal', in denying fascism any genuine ideological content.

Much effort has been expended to discover a philosophy of Fascism. It is a waste of effort. Fascism is power built upon terror and organized and maintained by the fear of terror and the hopes to which conquest gives rise. It is the disciplining of society for a state of war in which martial law is permanent because the nation is forced to spend any brief period of peace in the preparation for war. It survives in peace by the intensity of the terror it imposes; it survives in war just to the degree that it is successful in war. Its authority depends, in the period of peace, partly upon its power to prevent the organization of its opponents, and partly upon the expectations of benefit near at hand it is able to arouse. In time of war, its authority depends upon the continuous achievement of victories, and the recognition, by the nation, that the price of defeat is bound to be heavy.

There is no philosophy, in short, in Fascism in any of the forms in which we have known it. All the fustian of doctrine its exponents have presented us with reveal themselves, on examination, as propaganda expedients which have no meaning except their power to bolster up the particular regime. The doctrine of Nordic superiority works in Germany; the doctrine of the Latin genius works in Italy. Anti-Semitism is the historic weapon of every ruler who needs an enemy to exploit and property to distribute; and it is always popular with the illiterate masses in a period of economic strain. The insistence on the 'manifest destiny' of the nation, whether Germany or Italy, is, at bottom, simply the search for new sources of wealth to be exploited as a means of maintaining acquiescence in the regime. Conquest means posts, investments, a market to be politically controlled. The attack on the democratic principle necessarily follows from the need of the leader to justify his own exercise of absolute power. If a constitutive principle in Fascism exists at all, it is simply and solely the principle that power is the sole good and that values attach only to those expedients which sustain and enlarge it.

[*Reflections on the Revolution of Our Time* (Allen & Unwin: London, 1943), 96–7.]

TALCOTT PARSONS

148 Rationalism Debunked

With Talcott Parsons (1902–79) American sociology arguably broke free from the tyranny exerted by the myth of objectivity and became a genuine social science. His approach synthesizes into a sophisticated conceptual framework elements drawn from three of the discipline's founding fathers: Weber's theory of rationalization, which sees it as eroding the 'magic' from the world; Durkheim's theory of 'anomie' (the spiritual vacuum created by the erosion of traditional sources of a sense of belonging, especially religion); Pareto's emphasis on the socio-political power of non-rational forces, associated with nationalism and religion. The result was a pioneering essay published in 1942 in which the dynamics of fascism are analysed in terms of structural dysfunctions within society which create diffuse psychological and symbolic needs. Such needs cannot be as successfully catered for (or understood) by the liberal, socialist, or Enlightenment traditions as by overtly irrational political movements such as fascism. Fascism offers a substitute religion to the disaffected while advocating policies which locate the alleged causes of the problems in human scapegoats while proposing violent measures to solve them, thus creating the illusion of providing a way out of the impasse.

With the wisdom of hindsight, it can now be clearly seen that this rationalistic scheme of thought has not been adequate to provide a stably institutionalized diagnosis of even a 'modern' social system as a whole, nor has it been adequate to formulate all of the important values of our society, nor its cognitive orientation to the world. It has been guilty of the fallacy of misplaced concreteness in neglecting or underestimating the role of what Pareto has called the 'non-logical' aspects of human behavior in society, of the sentiments and traditions of family and informal social relationships, of the refinements of social stratification, of the peculiarities of regional, ethnic or national culture—perhaps above all of religion. On this level it has indeed helped to provoke a most important 'anti-intellectualist' reaction.

On another level it has 'debunked' many of the older values of our cultural tradition, and above all the cognitive patterns of religion, to a point well beyond that to which common values and symbols in the society had moved. Even apart from questions of its metaphysical validity it cannot be said adequately to have expressed the common orientations of the members of society.

But on top of these inherent strains a crucial role has been played by the emergence within the rationalized cultural tradition itself of a definition of the situation which has thoroughly 'debunked' many of the institutionalized products of the process of rationalization itself. Surely the stage was set for a combination of this definition of the situation with a reassertion of all the patterns which the utilitarian scheme had omitted or slighted—an acceptance of its own indictment but a generalization of the diagnosis to make 'capitalism' appear a logical outcome of the whole process of rationalization itself, not merely of its perversion, and the fact that in certain directions it had not been carried far enough. By the same token it is possible to treat both capitalism and its leftist antagonists, especially communism, not as genuine antagonists but as brothers under the skin, the common enemy. The Jew serves as a convenient symbolic link between them.

This reaction against the 'ideology' of the rationalization of society is one principal aspect at least of the ideology of fascism.

It characteristically accepts in essentials the socialist indictment of the existing order described as capitalism, but extends it to include leftist radicalism and the whole penumbra of scientific and philosophical rationalism.

The ideological definition of the situation in terms of which the orientation of a social movement becomes structured is of great importance but it never stands alone. It is necessarily in the closest interdependence with the psychological states and the social situations of the people to whom it appeals.[. . .] The fundamental fact is that the incidence of the process within the social structure is highly uneven— different elements of a population become 'rationalized' in different degrees, at different rates, and in different aspects of their personalities and orientations.

['Some Sociological Aspects of the Fascist Movements', *Social Forces*, 21 (1942), 138–47; repr. in *Essays in Sociological Theory* (Free Press Glencoe / Collier Macmillan: London, 1964), 134–5.]

Section B

Post-War Judgements on Fascism

INTRODUCTION

The post-war period has seen the development of fascist studies into a major branch of the historical and social sciences. Academics within the Soviet empire had little option but to apply to pre-war Comintern orthodoxy to demonstrate empirically the nexus formed by capitalism and state power in Mussolini's Italy, the Third Reich, and what were assumed to be 'weaker' fascist regimes such as Franco's Spain or Perón's Argentina. Their limited perspective produced a steady flow of data-cum-propaganda about how such regimes functioned as socio-economic systems of production and destruction at the expense of the 'people'. Western Marxists, on the other hand, were free to elaborate their own conceptual framework, drawing on the significant modifications to historical materialism pioneered by Gramsci, the Frankfurt School, or structuralists, which have allowed the power of ideology and the irrational to be recognized as well as the complexity of class relations under fascism. All were spurred on by the conviction that fascism cannot be safely consigned to 'history', but is a latent tendency in all modern states.

Meanwhile in the liberal camp the disarray over the nature of fascism registered by Borgese before the war (Text 132) continued after 1945 against the background of several historical events that influenced the climate which informed their approach. These included (i) the uncovering of the full scale of inhumanity wrought by Nazi racial policies; (ii) the surprisingly rapid recovery of liberal democracy in the West; (iii) the division of Europe by the Iron Curtain and realization of the full horrors of Stalinist totalitarianism. The combined effect was to make them tend to see fascism as an exclusively European phenomenon devoid of ideological coherence, whose time had passed, but which was structurally linked to the Communist dictatorships through the concept of 'totalitarianism'. This foreshortened perspective has been remarkably durable, especially among 'empirical' historians, despite the enrichment of the debate about fascism through several developments within academia itself: the increasing impact of social sciences on historiography; the growth of empirical knowledge on specific movements and regimes which challenged simplistic theoretical positions; the publication of several highly individual theories which set out to give as comprehensive an account of fascism as any Marxist could wish (though on markedly un-Marxist premises).

In the last few years the collapse of the Soviet empire and proliferation of nationalism, racism, and fascism in its wake are bound to generate renewed interest in the dynamics of generic fascism and may well help enlarge the focus of enquiry so that post-war and non-European fascism, as well as newer forms of ultra-nationalism such as Hindu fundamentalism in India or Ba'athism in Iraq, are recognized as casting important light on the genus. In the meantime this section can only hope to illustrate the lack of consensus which caused one academic taking stock of the situation to observe:

Although the last 25 years have seen the appearance of a vast amount of work in many languages on the phenomenon of fascism, and although enormous amounts of research time and mental energy have been put into the study of it, historians and other social scientists have been unable to reach a consensus of what fascism is or was. Explanations for it and interpretations diverge possibly more widely than any other historical topic. 'Fascism' has stubbornly remained the great conundrum for students of the twentieth century (Robinson 1981: 1).

The first part (Section Bi) takes its cue from the essay 'Contemporary Approaches to Fascism: A Survey of Paradigms' in the monumental (both for its length and influence) *Who Were the Fascists* published in 1980. The passage exemplifies the way positions within the debate have proliferated since the war. It also provides a context for the selection of extracts which follow. Not all the positions categorized in the passage are represented. Approaches 1 (fascism as Hitlerism or Mussolinianism), 3, and 10 (fascism as product of an aberrant process of national or cultural development confined to Italy and Germany) have no bearing on this book in so far as they implicitly deny the relevance of the concept of fascism as a generic phenomenon. As for the attribution of fascism to a moral disease (2) or an aesthetic aberration (9), both of these are categories which few academics would now regard as scientifically sustainable. By definition the accommodation of fascism within theories of totalitarianism (5) deals only with fascist *regimes*, and most scholars applying it have tended to treat Fascism and Nazism simply as separate manifestations of an autocratic system, ignoring the whole issue of a generic fascism (e.g. Arendt 1967, Radel 1975). In any case the Cold War vogue for totalitarianism as an explanatory category had distinctly waned by the 1980s. On the other hand, the idea of fascism as part of the European counter-revolutionary tradition (11) is too idiosyncratic to have had any impact and can safely be ignored.

Approaches which remain influential enough to merit inclusion are: Marxist theories (4), attempts to relate fascism to a particular class within the social structure (7a), psycho-social theories (7b), and investigations of fascism's relationship to modernization (8). Nolte's theory (6), though it is highly idiosyncratic and has not been applied by other experts, has become so often referred to that it warrants inclusion in Section Bii, which surveys some major individual theories of fascism.

i. Some Approaches to Fascism

BERNT HAGTVET AND STEIN LARSEN

149 **Paradigms of Fascism**

Who Were the Fascists (1980) is the most comprehensive and ambitious multi-author work to appear on fascism to date, and does full justice to the complexity of phenomena and range of issues involved in its manifestations, at least in the context of inter-war Europe.

Writing the history of fascism today inevitably means writing the history of scholarship on fascism. From its very inception fascism provoked analysis. A typology of the existing body of literature could also be organized along *chronological* lines. Leaving principles of organization aside, we would like to survey the main strands of theorizing in the field. Here we shall confine ourselves to a mapping of the intellectual landscape.[. . .] In subsequent sections we shall single out a few of these traditions for analytic discussion.

We would suggest that the body of literature on fascism can be divided into the following sub-fields:

1. Fascism as the product of a 'daemonic' *Führer* personality. This mode of analysis gained widespread popularity after World War II and is prominent in the interpretations of scholars like Golo Mann, Meinecke, Tellenbach and Fabry. It is also part of the implicit message of quite a few of the most recent biographies of Hitler, most notably in Fest.

2. Fascism as the result of Europe's *moral disease*, an interpretation propounded among others by Croce, Ritter, Hans Kohn and the Catholic tradition.

3. Fascism as a product of a particular *developmental sequence* confined to Germany and Italy, both peripheralized within the European economy, both suffering the impact of an accumulation of 'development crises'. This tradition has assumed many forms, from the earlier theories of a German road to Nazism (Vermeil, McGovern, Viereck) to later attempts to view fascism within the context of national history (Lukacs, Bracher).

4. Marxist theories: Fascism as a *product of capitalist society* and as an expression of anti-proletarian hysteria. Fascism can be seen as 'the power of finance capital itself' (Dimitrov), or as the result of *class equilibrium* and the formation of a relatively independent state executive which determines the way in which the economic domination of society by the bourgeoisie should be organized (Bonapartism). There is also a growing literature on fascism as a *partner* in alliance with the traditional Right. This interpretation avoids the sterile economism of the agent theory and can be found in a variety of forms.

5. Fascism as a manifestation of *totalitarianism*, which holds that there is an essential similarity between communist and fascist dictatorship.

6. Fascism as a 'revolt against transcendence': Ernst Nolte's phenomenological approach which exercised an important influence on scholarship on fascism in the 1960s and generated the renewed interest in the phenomenon.

7. Fascism as the outgrowth of the *social structure*. This theory can be subdivided into two groups: a. Sociological theories which portray fascism as an independent movement of the frustrated *middle class*, and b. *psychosocial theories* which focus on the impact of the economic infrastructure on the authoritarian character structure of individual members of fascist parties.

8. Fascism as a particular stage in broader processes of *modernization* (Moore, Dahrendorf, Schoenbaum, Turner, Organski).

9. Fascism as an *aesthetic* aberration.

10. Fascism as the product of a pathological *cultural tradition*.

11. Fascism as the expression of a specifically European syndrome of *counter-revolution*.

['Contemporary Approaches to Fascism: A Survey of Paradigms', in S. Larsen, B. Hagtvet and J. Myklebust (eds.), *Who Were the Fascists* (Universitetsforlaget: Bergen, 1980), 28–9.]

a. Marxist Approaches

A SOVIET POLITICAL DICTIONARY

150 **The View from Moscow**

This is a sample of the orthodox position on the nature of fascism maintained within the Soviet empire till its collapse at the end of the 1980s. It is clearly a perpetuation of the (highly simplistic) position adopted by the Comintern before the war (see Text 135c), pointing to the inhibiting effect of Stalinist orthodoxy on research in the social sciences. Note the characterization of Franco's Spain as fascist, and the insistence that fascist regimes have continued to form in the post-war period.

FASCISM, a political trend which emerged in capitalist countries in the period of the *general crisis of capitalism* and which expresses the interests of the most reactionary and aggressive forces of the imperialist *bourgeoisie*. *F. in power is an openly terroristic* dictatorship of these forces. F. is characterized by extreme *chauvinism, racism* and *anticommunism*, by the destruction of democratic freedoms, the wide practice of social demagogy and the strictest control over the public and private life of citizens. The foreign policy of F. is one of imperialist conquests and of wars of aggression. The first fascist regime was established in Italy in 1922. Fascism came to power in Germany in 1933 and in Spain in 1939. The military defeat of the fascist bloc in the Second World War (1939–45) was accompanied by the collapse of the fascist regimes in Italy and Germany and of fascist-type regimes in several other countries.

The overthrow of F. in Portugal and Greece in 1974 and the downfall of the fascist regime in Spain after Franco's death (November 1975) testify to the weakness of fascist regimes in present-day conditions. However, the military fascist coup in Chile (September 1973), the influence wielded by reactionary military circles in several countries, the racist rule in the Republic of South Africa, as well as some other facts indicate the gravity of the fascist danger in several regions of the world. Creation of a united front of antifascist forces would be a most effective barrier to F.

['Fascism', in *ABC of Political Terms: A Short Guide* (Novosti Press Agency Publishing House: Moscow, 1982), 29–30.]

JOACHIM PETZOLD

151   The View from East Germany

Joachim Petzold's work The Demagogy of Hitler-Fascism *was published in West Germany as one of the major contributions to fascist studies by East German scholars. In the introduction he reasserts some axioms of Soviet orthodoxy in the debate as a riposte to the inadequacy of those being generated in the capitalist West. Note that the Frankfurt School Marxist Max Horkheimer (see Text 144) is referred to as a 'bourgeois sociologist'.*

The reasons why Nazi ideology grew out of the *Zeitgeist* which so many refer to and took on a quite specific political form, are sought by bourgeois historians in every possible sphere, but very rarely in the monopoly capital stage of capitalist society's development. It was on this point even before the Second World War that the bourgeois sociologist Max Horkheimer made the extremely perceptive observation, 'Whoever is not prepared to talk about capitalism should remain silent about fascism.' The question of what relationship the Nazi movement and fascist activism have at all to monopoly capital has become the main focus of the controversy between Marxist and non-Marxist historians in the field of fascist studies. It will also lie at the heart of the present investigation.

The very intensity of the controversy over this key issue points to the fact that an analysis of fascist phenomena touches on basic class interests.[. . .] Bourgeois historiography has made repeated attempts to refute the thesis of the Thirteenth Plenary of the Executive Committee of the Communist International, namely that 'Fascism in power' is 'the open terrorist dictatorship of the most reactionary, most chauvinist, and most imperialist elements of finance capital'.[8] It has even been denied that there ever was a fascism in a global sense at all. According to this point of view there were such profound differences between German National Socialism, Italian Fascism, the Spanish Falange, and similar political phenomena that a generic concept was inappropriate. Whenever the social roots were looked into, forms of fascist activism were at most characterized as middle-class movements directed against both the proletariat and monopoly capitalism. But even this sociological line of

[8] See Text 135c.

enquiry is going too far for some bourgeois historians. They dismiss fascism as the work of outstanding personalities such as Mussolini, Hitler, and Franco, or as the result of national peculiarities.

[*Die Demagogie des Hitler-Faschismus* (Röderberg-Verlag: Frankfurt-am-Main, 1983), pp. vii–ix.]

MARTIN KITCHEN
....

152 **The View of a Western Marxist**

Martin Kitchen's Fascism *is an example of the theoretical sophistication which has been evolved to address fascism by some Western Marxists in the post-war period, one which allows considerable room for original synthesis and individuality of approach. In the chapter from which this passage is taken he specifically criticizes the failure of orthodox Marxist analysis to come to terms with the complexity of the phenomenon. He shows a perceptiveness unusual in Marxist circles concerning the radical distinction to be drawn between military dictatorships and fascist regimes. His remarks on the importance of immigration to neo-fascism are particularly pertinent today.*

Although the regimes of Nazi Germany and fascist Italy provide the best examples of fascism in action it would be a serious mistake to limit a definition of fascism to these two forms, or even to the period between the two World Wars. Such a definition would make it impossible to analyse fascist dangers in the present day. The fact that changing circumstances are liable to produce differences in fascist movements, at least at the phenomenological level, has led many writers to talk of 'neo-fascism'.[. . .]

A new fascism is bound to adapt itself to a new situation. This is already apparent in the fascistic movements such as the N.P.D.[9] in Germany, the M.S.I.[10] in Italy or the National Front[11] in Britain. Their style is not as rowdy and violent as that of their predecessors. They are more concerned to appear respectable. Anti-Semitism, although often present, is less pronounced. Immigrant workers are frequently blamed for economic problems such as unemployment. Anti-communism takes the place of anti-capitalism. Fascist mass-movements, if they reappear, will probably be more restrained and civilised, but they will be no less menacing. When the manipulation of mass opinion is no longer sufficient to maintain the consensus then the state repression of the opposition groups may well be deemed necessary. Again this need not imply the physical brutality of previous fascist regimes, but may well be of a more subtle and insidious nature. For all the talk of 'structurally immanent state fascism' a mass party, a charismatic leader and a distinct ideology will still be necessary. The nature of all three components is likely to be quite distinct from their historical forms. Such differences combined with a changed economic, political, social and psychological situation may, perhaps, make it more meaningful to

---

[9] See Text 209.
[10] See Text 211.
[11] See Texts 182, 202 for passages which have a bearing on the NF.

speak of 'neo-fascism'. A theory of neo-fascism would take the essential features of the fascism of the past, examine how these factors are likely to have changed, and see under what socio-economic crisis situations in contemporary advanced capitalism such drastic measures are likely to be employed. But such a task lies outside the scope of this present work.

Thus the danger of fascism is still with us. Contrary to the commonly held belief, the dictatorships of the undeveloped world, although they have clearly learnt much from fascist practice, are not themselves fascist. The regimes of Generals Pinochet[12] and Amin[13], for example, differ in many essential points from our model of fascism. This does not make them in any sense less revolting and inhuman, but to analyse such regimes in terms of fascism does nothing to provide a true understanding of the nature and dynamics of such systems of domination. It is rather in the highly developed capitalist states that the fascist potential continues to exist. The socio-economic system which produced fascism to overcome its difficulties still exists, the problems which it faces still remain acute. A society which restricts its democratic practice to the functioning of the parliamentary system, and which denies the extension of such democratic forms to vital sections of society including the economic sector is ever prone, under certain specific conditions, to resort to fascism. The struggle against fascism can thus only be effective if it is also a struggle for the extension and the deepening of democratic forces. Such an inhuman, repressive and tyrannical system can only be combated by the determination to strengthen and extend the humane, emancipatory and democratic forces within society. Anti-fascism is thus part of the struggle for the emancipatory society, and an analysis of fascism an essential precondition for effective action.

[*Fascism* (Macmillan: London, 1976), 88–91.]

b. Fascism as the Product of Structural Forces

SEYMOUR M. LIPSET

153   **Extremism of the Centre**

The American sociologist Seymour Lipset developed his theory of fascism as 'extremism of the centre' as part of his highly influential investigations into the social basis of political movements. The major premise of his position, the essentially middle-class nature of fascist support, has since been refuted by empirical research, such as that of D. Mühlberger (1991) into Nazism.

Before 1917 extremist political movements were usually thought of as a rightist phenomenon. Those who would eliminate democracy generally sought to restore monarchy or the rule of the aristocrats. After 1917 politicians and scholars alike began to refer to both left and right extremism, i.e., Communism and fascism. In this view,

[12] Dictator of Chile in the 1970s.   [13] Dictator of Uganda in the 1970s.

extremists at either end of the political continuum develop into advocates of dictatorship, while the moderates of the center remain the defenders of democracy. This chapter will attempt to show that this is an error—that extremist ideologies and groups can be classified and analyzed in the same terms as democratic groups, i.e. right, left, and *center*. The three positions resemble their democratic parallels in both the compositions of their social bases and the contents of their appeals. While comparisons of all three positions on the democratic and extremist continuum are of intrinsic interest, this chapter concentrates on the politics of the center, the most neglected type of political extremism, and that form of 'left' extremism sometimes called 'fascism'—Perónism—as manifested in Argentina and Brazil.

The center position among the democratic tendencies is usually called liberalism. In Europe where it is represented by various parties like the French Radicals, the Dutch and Belgian Liberals, and others, the liberal position means: in economics—a commitment to *laissez-faire* ideology, a belief in the vitality of small business, and opposition to strong trade-unions; in politics—a demand for minimal government intervention and regulation; in social ideology—support of equal opportunity for achievement, opposition to aristocracy, and opposition to enforced equality of income; in culture—anticlericalism and antitraditionalism.

If we look at the supporters of the three major positions in most democratic countries, we find a fairly logical relationship between ideology and social base. The Socialist left derives its strength from manual workers and the poorer rural strata; the conservative right is backed by the rather well-to-do elements—owners of large industry and farms, the managerial and free professional strata and those segments of the less privileged groups who have remained involved in traditionalist institutions, particularly the Church. The democratic center is backed by the middle classes, especially small businessmen, white-collar workers, and the anticlerical sections of the professional classes.

The different extremist groups have ideologies which correspond to those of their democratic counterparts. The classic fascist movements have represented the extremism of the center. Fascist ideology, though antiliberal in its glorification of the state, has been similar to liberalism in its opposition to big business, trade-unions, and the socialist state. It has also resembled liberalism in its distaste for religion and other forms of traditionalism. And, as we shall see later, the social characteristics of Nazi voters in pre-Hitler Germany and Austria resembled those of the liberals much more than they did those of the conservatives.

[*Political Man: The Social Bases of Political Movements* (William Heinemann: New York, 1960), 132–3.]

BERNT HAGTVET AND STEIN ROKKAN
....
154 **Defective Nation-Building**

This passage is taken from the attempt by two Norwegian professors to develop a sophisticated model of the structural factors which enabled 'fascist-type' forces to seize power in

Germany, Italy, Austria, Spain, and Portugal, though, as the authors imply, the question of how far any of the regimes which established themselves in these countries apart from Italy were truly fascist is still unresolved.

Scholars have diverged in their definitions and their interpretations of fascism ever since the March on Rome. The divergences increased dramatically after Hitler's *Machtergreifung* [seizure of power] in 1933 and the Dollfuss coup in 1934: what did these ideologies, these movements, these strategies have in common? Was there a core concept of fascism and how could this essence be identified in the welter of complex interactions in each concrete development?

However difficult this search for conceptual communalities, there was, by the time of the final confrontation during World War II, not much doubt about the actual alignment of cases:

Five of the countries of Western Europe had succumbed to movements of this general type and had been turned into plebiscitary one-party dictatorships.

However divergent their national trajectories, these five countries, Italy, Germany, Austria, Spain and Portugal had succumbed to similar fates.

1. They had all experienced a number of *competitive elections* under broadening suffrage criteria and had passed through a shorter or longer period of *rapid mobilization* of new strata of the territorial population under mass parties and parallel movements and agencies:

2. They had all run into a series of *constitutional crises* in the management of these waves of competitive mobilization, and had finally succumbed to a movement determined to put an end to such pluralistic tolerance and to introduce *monolithic control* of mass politics:

3. Finally, these monolithic movements had all reached their positions of dominance through extensive use of *extra-legal violence* against political opponents and had maintained their power through ruthless mobilization against internal no less than external enemies.[. . .]

To avoid misunderstanding: we do not claim that the *régimes* established in each of these five cases were 'fascist'. There were indeed important differences in the structure and contents of the victorious ideologies and these were clearly reflected in the institutions built up and the practices followed by the victors. Our analysis concentrates on the one feature these five cases have in common: the sequence leading from a series of competitive elections under multi-party systems to the victory of a monolithic alliance and the abolition of pluralist opposition. This is the sequence we find in our five cases and not in the other twelve.[14] How can we account for these differences in the outcomes of the mobilization processes between these five and the others? How can we identify the prerequisites for success and the conditions leading to failure in the struggle to maintain competitive pluralism under full-suffrage mobilization?[. . .]

We might conclude, at least for the period up to 1939, that the chances for the *survival* of competitive multi-party politics was greatest within the capitalist *core* of

[14] i.e. the non-fascist European nation-states taken into account in the article.

the world economy, that the likelihood of *fascist-type* victories was greatest in the *semi-peripheralized* territories of earlier city-studded empires—and that the probability of *communist-type* victories was greatest in the much more markedly *peripheral* areas of earlier empires of the 'agrarian bureaucracy' type, empires with poorly developed commercial-industrial bourgeoisies.

['The Conditions of Fascist Victory', in *Who Were the Fascists* (see Text 149), 131–2, 149.]

GEOFFREY ELEY

155   Redemptive Potential

In the article from which this is taken Geoffrey Eley, a British historian whose work specializes in the transition from the Second German Reich to the Third, focuses on the relationship between industrialization, capitalism, and political crisis. It points to a fertile blend of Marxist with liberal insights into the structural causes of revolutionary movements of the right in modern society. Note the insistence that fascism lacks a revolutionary dynamic of its own.

Fascism thus prospered under conditions of general political crisis, in societies that were already dynamically capitalist (or at least, that had a dynamic capitalist sector) but where the state was incapable of organizing for the maintenance of social cohesion. The political unity of the dominant classes and of their major economic fractions could no longer be organized successfully within the existing forms of parliamentary representation and party government. Simultaneously the popular legitimacy of these forms also went into crisis.[. . .]

The problem of defining fascism is therefore not exhausted by describing its ideology, even in its expanded sense. Fascism was not just a style of politics, it was also inscribed in a specific combination of political conditions (themselves the structured, mediate effect of complex socio-economic determinations), namely, the kind of dual crisis of the state just referred to. Although such a crisis is normally associated with the Great Depression after 1929, the postwar political crisis of 1917–23 was equally important. The global ideological context of the Bolshevik Revolution and its international political legacy gave enormous impetus to the radicalization of the right, and the more vigorous fascist movements generally arose in societies that experienced serious left-wing insurgencies after 1917–18. Hungary, Austria, Finland, and Spain, as well as Italy and Germany, are all good examples.[. . .]

Fascism may be best understood, therefore, as primarily a counter-revolutionary ideological project, constituting a new kind of popular coalition in the specific circumstances of an interwar crisis. As such it provided motivation for specific categories of radicalized political actors in the immediate aftermath of the Great War, who were embittered by national humiliation and enraged by the advance of the left. As working-class insurgency defied the capacities of the existing liberal politics to achieve the necessary stabilization, this radical-nationalist cadre became an important pole of attraction for larger circles of the dominant classes and for others who felt threatened by the reigning social turbulence. In Italy, where the socialist movement was further to the left than in Germany and where no equivalent of the SPD[15] functioned as a vital factor of order, this process of right-wing concentration around the redemptive potential of a radical-nationalist, anti-socialist terror was far more advanced. But later, in the renewed but differently structured crisis of 1929–34, a recognizable pattern recurred. Elsewhere, Spain and possibly Austria were the closest examples of a similarly enacted fascist solution. Other countries certainly generated their own fascist cadre—in some cases very large (France, Finland, Hungary, Rumania) and in some, quite small (Britain, Scandinavia). But the severity of the political crisis, and the degree of resilience of established political forms, determined the broader attractions of the fascist ideology.

['What Produces Fascism: Preindustrial Traditions or the Crisis of the Capitalist State', *Politics and Society*, 12/1 (1983), 78–82.]

....

c. Psycho-Historical Approaches

....

THE FRANKFURT SCHOOL
....

156   **Fear and Destructiveness**

This passage is taken from the conclusion of the Frankfurt School's major publication explaining the socio-psychological structures underlying fascism, and in assessing the task of eradicating fascism combines insights drawn from Marxism, Freudian psychoanalysis, sociology, and political theory in a way characteristic of 'Critical Theory' (see Texts 144, 146). Note the key role in combating fascism attributed to social scientists.

It seems obvious therefore that the modification of the potentially fascist structure cannot be achieved by psychological means alone. The task is comparable to that of eliminating neurosis, or delinquency, or nationalism from the world. These are products of the total organization of society and are to be changed only as that society is changed. It is not for the psychologist to say how such changes are to be brought about. The problem is one which requires the efforts of all social scientists. All that we would insist upon is that in the councils or round tables where the problem is considered and action planned the psychologist should have a voice. We believe that the scientific understanding of society must include an understanding of what it does to people, and that it is possible to have social reforms, even broad and sweeping ones, which though desirable in their own right would not necessarily change the structure of the prejudiced personality. For the fascist potential to change, or even to be held in check, there must be an increase in people's capacity

---

[15] Social Democratic Party.

to see themselves and to be themselves. This cannot be achieved by the manipulation of people, however well grounded in modern psychology the devices of manipulation might be; and it is a judgement which finds support in the present study that the man who is first to seize power will be the last to give it up. It is safe to assume, however, that fascism is imposed on the people, that it actually goes against their basic interests, and that when they can be made fully aware of themselves and their situation they are capable of behaving realistically.[. . .]

It is the fact that the potentially fascist pattern is to so large an extent imposed upon people that carries with it some hope for the future. People are continuously moulded from above because they must be moulded if the overall economic pattern is to be maintained and the amount of energy that goes into this process bears a direct relation to the amount of potential, residing within the people, for moving in a different direction. It would be foolish to underestimate the fascist potential with which this volume has been mainly concerned, but it would be equally unwise to overlook the fact that the majority of our subjects do not exhibit the extreme ethnocentric pattern and the fact that there are various ways in which it may be avoided altogether. Although there is reason to believe that the prejudiced are the better rewarded in our society as far as external values are concerned (it is when they take short cuts to these rewards that they land in prison), we need not suppose that the tolerant have to wait and receive their rewards in heaven, as it were. Actually there is good reason to believe that the tolerant receive more gratification of basic needs. They are likely to pay for this satisfaction in conscious guilt feelings, since they frequently have to go against prevailing social standards, but the evidence is that they are, basically, happier than the prejudiced. Thus, we need not suppose that appeal to emotion belongs to those who strive in the direction of fascism, while democratic propaganda must limit itself to reason and restraint. If fear and destructiveness are the major emotional sources of fascism, *eros* belongs mainly to democracy.

[T. W. Adorno *et al.*, *The Authoritarian Personality* (Harper & Row: New York, 1950, 975–6.]

GERALD M. PLATT

157   Making Sense

The essay from which this passage is taken underlines the fallacy of treating fascist movements such as Nazism as if they drew their support from a cohesive social grouping such as 'the lower middle class'. It quotes empirical evidence for the essential heterogeneity of the social basis of Nazism, and proceeds to construct a sophisticated model of the genesis of new ideological forces like Nazism, which not only give their followers a new way of making sense of the world, but the illusion of belonging to the 'same' movement. This arguably represents a considerable advance on earlier attempts to model the socio-psychological dynamics of fascism.

The loss of familiar social orders and one's place in them is potentially chaotic. People who cannot sustain a biographically achieved sense of personal identity, continuity, feelings of worthiness, self-esteem, membership in a community, and so on, are easily overwhelmed by affective experiences. When these conditions are widespread the society is undergoing a sense-making crisis.

In the face of a sense-making crisis, of course, different people perceive the situation differently; there will not be a single response to the crisis throughout the population. For private reasons people may be capable of denying the disorder or of perceiving the disorder and not responding to it. Other people in the society may continue to use the routine sources for sense making despite their ineffectiveness and the personal and social discomfort experienced with producing variant and even deviant forms of familiar world-views. These individuals attempt to normalize the experience of chaos by retrospectively reviewing their accomplishments as only temporary variants on traditional and familiar experience. Another class of people may use its categorical identities for making sense of the chaotic situational conditions. These people interpret the world, even disruptive economic and political events, in terms of class, religion, age, psychological disposition, and so on, to make the events meaningful and thus cognitively and emotively organized according to subjective interpretive principles embedded in the categorical identities.[. . .]

A substantial portion of the population whose relation to material conditions, to their place in the world and their relations to others is undermined by these circumstances; that portion of the population who experience these circumstances as enduring unendingly, unresolvable in traditional terms, experiences a sense-making crisis. Those individuals cannot continue to employ routine sources of sense making to organize their meaningful actions and they experience bewilderment and loss. They cannot make sense of the emotional arousal they experience. They cannot harness and give direction to the emotional arousal. Once the familiar sources are inapplicable, unavailable, or disrupted individuals experiencing this cannot resolve and make meaningful the sources of arousal in constructive directions.

It is at this point that situationally produced chaos leads to the search for new situated rules for interpreting the world; that is, the search for new methods for cognizing and experiencing the world and making sense of the emotional arousal. These situated rules of interpretation provide meaning to the experienced chaos by providing for alternate world-views. They harness emotional arousal and they guide persons to a renewed sense of meaning in the world. The emerging interpretive rules accomplish this by informing their adherents of the meaning of chaotic experiences, pointing to the modes for resolving such experiences.

However, the system of rules which arises is characterized by an intermingling of the traditional with the new interpretive sources. A population thus is being offered simultaneously both an explanation of the failure and a reason for hope. A temporal relationship exists between the routine sources of meaning and the new interpretive rules. The latter slowly emerge from and are dialectically related to the former. The new system incorporates parts of the old systems as the new rules are being institutionalized in a significant portion of the population. This evolution permits a transition to the new sources of meaning, a new mode of constructing meaning without a total abdication of the past. As the dialectical interplay between the failing and rising modes of construction of the new system is sharpened, the population becomes attuned to the failures of the traditional sources and the effectiveness of the new interpretive procedures. Finally, a leadership for the new sources arises in society either expressing or simply codifying the new rules of interpretation. And if this leadership gains access to sources of power it makes attempts at superimposing the new interpretive system upon broad ranges of the society's population.[. . .]

The new interpretive system is codified in the language of ideology, determining the meaning of emotional arousal, suggesting the re-establishment of a coherent world and one's place in it. The language of ideology points to new modes of cognizing and making sense of the material circumstances, past failures, present circumstances, future hopes, and the meaning of the whole society.

['Thoughts on a Theory of Collective Action: Language Affect, and Ideology in Revolution', in M. Albin (ed.), *New Directions in Psychohistory* (Lexington Books: Lexington, Mass., 1980), 82–3.]

KLAUS THEWELEIT

158   Raising the Dead

The German academic Klaus Theweleit has attempted to model the psychology of fascism by bringing to bear insights culled from various currents of Marxism, psychoanalysis, and radical feminism on the writings of members of the Freikorps, *a paramilitary movement closely bound up with the genesis of Nazism (see Text 55). The result is a demanding book which offers some revealing insights into the inner world of (at least some) fascists in their struggle against forces which they feel are threatening to engulf them.*

We may at last arrive at an understanding of fascism's triumph in Germany. What the texts cited have most clearly demonstrated is a refusal by fascism to relinquish desire—desire in the form of a demand that 'blood must flow', desire in its most profound distortion. In the German Communist Party (KPD) desire was never seen as the producer of a better reality: that party never so much as intimated that there might be pleasure in liberation, pleasure in new connections, pleasure in the unleashing of new streams. Instead, desire was channelled into plotting and scheming tactics and strategies—literary ones included—while fascism screamed, 'Germany awaken!' What was 'sleeping' had ears to hear its call as a bell-peal of immediate resurrection: 'the dead' could now return from the entrails.

Fascism's most significant achievement was to organize the resurrection and rebirth of dead life in the masses—'strange as it may sound to men who have never struggled for existence'. In the contemporary context, dead life can hardly be called a rarity; and its resurrection remains an important political process—perhaps the most important political process of all. The task of the nonfascist, however, is not to organize dead life, but to release it from its bonds, to intensify, accelerate, and transform it into a multiplicity whose best quality is that it cannot be organized as fascism, nor in any way assembled into blocks of human totality-machines, knitted into interlocking networks of order: a multiplicity that will not fit into the slot of power-hungry bodies of party formations, that refuses to function as the liver or the little finger of institutions and rulers, but instead holds the promise of a lived life that must not scream endlessly for rebirth.[. . .]

The texts of the soldier males perpetually revolve around the same central axes: the community of the male society, nonfemale creation, rebirth, the rise upward to hardness and tension; the phallus climbing to a higher level. The man is released from a world that is rotten and sinking (from the morass of femaleness); he finally dissolves in battle. The biting clarity of all these images allows them to be traced to a source in these men's most intense compulsions; and indeed the writers themselves explicitly indicate that it is these compulsions, and not what are traditionally termed 'political' convictions, that determine their actions.

[*Male Fantasies*, 2 vols. (Polity Press: Cambridge, 1987, 1989), ii. 189, 360–1.]

d. Modernization Theories

BARRINGTON MOORE

159   Blood and Death

Barrington Moore's work, written when theories of development were in vogue, attempts to establish a relationship between the paths taken by various societies towards industrialization and the degree of democracy which their ensuing political systems accommodate. Note that he assumes Imperial Japan to have been fascist (a highly contentious assumption), and makes cryptic allusions to fascism in Russia, China, and India.

Though it might be equally profitable to undertake a parallel consideration of democratic failures that preceded fascism in Germany, Japan, and Italy, it is enough for present purposes to notice that fascism is inconceivable without democracy or what is sometimes more turgidly called the entrance of the masses onto the historical stage. Fascism was an attempt to make reaction and conservatism popular and plebeian, through which conservatism, of course, lost the substantial connection it did have with freedom, some aspects of which were discussed in the preceding chapter.

The conception of objective law vanished under fascism. Among its most significant features was a violent rejection of humanitarian ideals, including any notion of potential human equality. The fascist outlook stressed not only the inevitability of hierarchy, discipline, and obedience, but also posited that they were values in their own right. Romantic conceptions of comradeship qualify this outlook but slightly; it is comradeship in submission. Another feature was the stress on violence. This stress goes far beyond any cold, rational appreciation of the factual importance of violence in politics to a mystical worship of 'hardness' for its own sake. Blood and death often acquire overtones of erotic attraction, though in its less exalted moments fascism was thoroughly 'healthy' and 'normal', promising return to a cosy bourgeois, and even prebourgeois peasant, womb.[. . .]

Plebeian anticapitalism thus appears as the feature that most clearly distinguishes twentieth-century fascism from its predecessors, the nineteenth-century conservative and semiparliamentary regimes. It is a product of both the intrusion of capitalism into the rural economy and of strains arising in the postcompetitive phase of capitalist industry. Hence fascism developed most fully in Germany where capitalist industrial growth had gone the furthest within the framework of a conservative revolution from above. It came to light as only a weak secondary trend in such backward areas as Russia, China, and India. Prior to World War II, it failed to take much root in England and the United States where capitalism worked reasonably well or where efforts to correct its shortcomings could be attempted within the democratic framework and succeed with the help of a prolonged war boom.

[*The Social Origins of Dictatorship and Democracy* (Penguin: Harmondsworth, 1977; 1st pub. Beacon Press: Boston, 1966), 447–8.]

HENRY A. TURNER JUN.

160 Utopian Anti-Modernism

Henry Turner, an American academic, wrote the chapter from which this is taken under the influence of Nolte's theory of fascism as 'resistance to transcendence' (see Text 162) and of the rise of a youth counter-culture in the 'Hippie 1960s' (which seemed to many to be the denial of Western progress). In it he articulates the common argument that Nazism sought to establish an anti-modern utopia, and hopes that it is in this (highly questionable) aspect of Nazism that the elusive 'fascist minimum' may be found, while recognizing that such an approach may call into question how far Fascism was actually fascist at all.

A good many widely-held beliefs about who was a fascist and who was not might thus be overturned if utopian anti-modernism should prove to be a central and common characteristic of the Italian and German movements. The implications for traditional thinking about fascism as a generic phenomenon would, however, be far more dire if, as also seems possible, such a definition were inapplicable to Italy. For if Italian Fascism should, upon closer examination, turn out to have been predominantly pro-modernist then the two paradigmatic manifestations of fascism would stand opposed to one another on what many now hold to be the fundamental issues of modern times. One, that is, would have been committed to furthering the process of modernization by repressive, authoritarian methods, the other to employing similar methods but as a means of reversing that same process through a fanatical and ultimately suicidal pursuit of an unattainable, archaic utopia. If this should indeed be the case, there would be grounds for arguing that, in terms of underlying socio-economic issues, Italian Fascism and Nazism do not belong in the same category at all. And if the paradigms of fascism are revealed as fundamentally different, what basis is there any longer for a generic concept? It should not be forgotten that the generic category in political analysis is at bottom metaphoric, a borrowing from biology. Nor should it be forgotten that biologists have abandoned or revised their application of the term genus wherever they have recognized that what had previously been regarded as constituent species were in actuality set apart by basic differences.

['Fascism and Modernization', in H. A. Turner (ed.), *Reappraisals of Fascism* (Franklin Watts: New York, 1975), 131–2.]

EMILIO GENTILE

161   Fascist Modernity

The Italian scholar E. Gentile has produced a number of highly sophisticated analyses of Fascism, placing particular emphasis on the debt of the early movement to various currents of thought which focused on the creation of a new type of State, and on the crucial role played by attempts to create a 'civic religion' in the Fascist bid to realize this palingenetic vision once in power. Reviewing recent advances in the study of fascism, he stresses how important it is to recognize its compatibility with modernity.

The first really important and fundamental change has been to place back on the agenda the image of an international fascism, so as not to relapse into a view of Fascism as something wholly Italian, domestic, home-grown. The tendency of new historiography is to probe more deeply into the specific reality of phenomena considered fascist so as to establish alongside the similarities the differences as well, some of which were substantial.

The other aspect of this change has been for scholars to start considering fascism as a phenomenon which had its own ideology and its own culture, if only—as it is prudent to emphasise—in an anthropological sense, not in an academic sense, a culture whose motivations, matrices, values have to be uncovered or highlighted even if they are negative values, alien and opposed to our world of values.

The next step has been to acknowledge that it is in the nature of fascism as a mass movement to be not just the product of demagogy or manipulation.[. . .] Demagogy and manipulation are not terms which can readily account for the mass conversion to fascism. I am not talking of consensus. I am talking of the mass following which fascism achieved on the basis of explicit declarations of its objectives. One merit should be granted fascism: it never hid its goals, it never claimed to consider the masses the depositories of all virtues; that it intended to liberate man;

that it wished to spread freedom and rationality through the world. It always declared that the masses are a raw material to be moulded, that it cannot rule by itself; that material well-being was important, but that sacrifice, austerity, privation, and discipline were also important; that reason counted for little in the world and that the masses are moved by myth, by faith; that it is necessary to believe, to obey, and fight.[. . .]

Another aspect of the new historiography is thus the way it reflects on the variety of fascist regimes and movements, taking account of the various historical and social situations, at least in Europe, if we wish to limit fascism geographically to Europe. This raises the question, a fundamental one as I see it, within the fascist debate, and one which probably requires much further study, reflection and discussion, namely the connections between fascism and modern society. Because fascism cannot, I believe, be seen as an expression of anti-modernity, just as totalitarianism cannot be seen as an expression of anti-modernity.

Certainly if we identify modernity and liberalism, understood in its widest sense, it seems to me that fascism is automatically excluded from modern phenomena. But is it true that modernity and liberalism coincide? Is it true that traditional and modern societies are two totally opposite realities, so that where tradition is involved there can be no modernity? Does the presence of political myths, of political religion, exclude modernity?[. . .]

In reality there have been intense processes of modernization—Eisenstadt[16] observes—under the aegis of traditionalist myths and symbols. The crisis of the rationalist, progressive, Enlightenment model, if we want to call it that, has led us to recognize that authoritarianism and modernity, irrationalism and modernity, fascism and modernity are not at all incompatible.[. . .] As one of the greatest sociologists of modernity, Gino Germani, points out, there are forms of authoritarianism, under which he included fascism, which are not a reaction to modernity or a resistance to modernity, but which are born from the very heart of modernity, from the contradictions intrinsic to modern societies, and which should be studied in these terms.

['Fascism', in Lucia Morra (ed.), *L'Europa del XX secolo fra totalitarismo e democrazia* [Twentieth-Century Europe between Totalitarianism and Democracy] (Tools: Faenza, 1991), 106–10.]

[16] e.g. in S. N. Eisenstadt (ed.), *Patterns of Modernity*, 2 vols. (New York University Press: New York, 1987).

ii. Some Individual Theories of the Fascist Minimum

162 **Resisting Transcendence**

It is common to attribute to Three Faces of Fascism *(1965) by the West German scholar Ernst Nolte the merit of reviving scholarly interest in generic fascism and establishing the need to take fascist ideology seriously. The work concentrates on underlying parallels between the Action Française (which most historians do not consider to have been a fascist movement), Fascism, and Nazism. In the concluding section he erects a highly abstract theory of generic fascism which centres on its anti-Marxism (though stressing its underlying kinship with Marxism), and its bid to 'resist transcendence'. By this he seems to mean that fascism aimed to reverse or find a refuge from the forces of secularization, democratization, and globalization—sometimes equated with 'modernization'—which both in theory (that is, ideologically) and in practice (the type of society created) have led to the breakdown of the closed material and spiritual social system of tradition. In other words Nolte's theory is a highly abstruse and convoluted version of the common theory of fascism as a bourgeois revolt against Enlightenment rationalism (Text 148) and modernization (Text 160), a position which obscures the fact that fascism offers to believers both its own form of transcendence from the anomie of modern society (Text 157), and an alternative form of modernity (Text 161). Nor was its social basis only middle-class.*

It has now become evident what fascism actually is. It is not that resistance to practical transcendence which is more or less common to all conservative movements. It was only when theoretical transcendence, from which that resistance originally emanated, was likewise denied that fascism made its appearance. Thus fascism is at the same time resistance to practical transcendence and struggle against theoretical transcendence. But this struggle must needs be concealed since the original motivations can never be entirely dispensed with. And insofar as practical transcendence from its most superficial aspect is nothing but the possibility of concentration of power, fascism pursues its resistance to transcendence from within that transcendence and at times in the clear consciousness of a struggle for world hegemony. That is the transcendental expression of the sociological fact that fascism has at its command forces which are born of the emancipation process and then turn against their own origin. If it may be called the despair of the feudal section of bourgeois society for its traditions, and the bourgeois element's betrayal of its revolution, now it is clear what this tradition and this revolution actually are. Fascism represents the second and gravest crisis of liberal society, since it achieves power on its own soil, and in its radical form is the most complete and effective denial of that society.

It is precisely in this broadest of all perspectives that the observer cannot withhold from fascism that 'sympathy' of which we have spoken. This sympathy is directed not toward persons or deeds, but toward the perplexity underlying the colossal attempt to overcome that perplexity, which is the most universal characteristic of an era whose end cannot be foreseen. For transcendence, when properly understood, is infinitely remote from the harmlessness of safe 'cultural progress'; it is not the couch of the finite human being, but in some mysterious unity his throne and his cross.

Nevertheless, fascism as a metapolitical phenomenon still serves as a means of understanding the world today: only when liberal society, after steadfast and serious reflection, accepts practical transcendence as its own although no longer exclusive product; when theoretical transcendence escapes from its ancient political entanglements into genuine freedom; when Communist society looks at itself and its past with realistic but not cynical eyes and ceases to evade either one; when the love of individuality and barriers no longer assumes political form, and thought has become a friend of man—only then can man be said to have finally crossed the border into a postfascist era.

[*Three Faces of Fascism* (Weidenfeld & Nicolson: London, 1965), 453–4.]

A. JAMES GREGOR

163   The Total Charismatic Community

Like Nolte, the American scholar A. J. Gregor also takes both ideology and structural factors seriously in his analysis of fascism. On the basis of a thorough study of Fascist social and political thought he comes to see the core of generic fascism in an attempt made by modern States, based on a relatively coherent social theory, to integrate the masses within societies which have been subject to rapid economic development. He sees Fascism in Italy as paradigmatic of totalitarian mass-regimenting regimes in many developing nations, such as the one that formed in Russian and Communist China, Latin America, and the Third World.

What have been traditionally identified in the literature as a 'fascist' regime can best be characterized as totalitarian, revolutionary mass movements that have come to power in relatively or partially advanced industrial environments; environments in which there already exist entrenched and vital propertied classes as well as peripheral elements threatened with status deprivation. Fascist movements thus come to power in circumstances in which some accommodation with established interest groups must, at least initially, be effected if the revolution is not to drown in blood and/or the productionist aspirations of the movement are not to be faulted. Thus, those revolutionary mass-movement regimes that have been identified as 'fascist' in the literature of political analysis are radically disposed mass movements supported by elements of the traditional and conservative propertied elites.[. . .]

National Socialism came to power with the connivance of the propertied and strategic elites of the old order. Some commentators misconstrued[17] this to mean that National Socialism was a movement dedicated to the protection of vested

---

[17] Notably Marxists.

interest. The conservative forces which had allied themselves with National Socialism, however, rapidly capitulated before its evident power. National Socialism, like paradigmatic Fascism, was intrinsically neither procapitalist nor antilabor. It aspired to a society in which class, category, and confession would merge in one total charismatic community.

Fascisms of this kind develop in industrial communities in which classes are reasonably well articulated and vital and in which a traditional aristocracy exists that is threatened by displacement or downward mobility. These forces lend support to fascist movements and either contain it, as is the case in Spain, render it quiescent, as was the case for a considerable length of time in Fascist Italy, or submit to it, as was the case in National Socialist Germany.[. . .]

In a significant sense it can be said that contemporary radical revolutionary mass movements possessed of nationalist and developmental intentions, and animated by totalitarian aspirations, are variants of paradigmatic Fascism.

Such fascist and quasi-fascist movements occupy one end of the continuum occupied by contemporary revolutionary mass movements. They constitute an extreme type: their purpose is the rapid attainment of status for status-deprived national communities. To this end all energies are mobilized and directed, under single-party auspices, in a communalist regime of totalitarian character.

[*The Ideology of Fascism* (Free Press: New York, 1969), 378–82.]

JUAN B. LINZ

164 The Latecomer

Juan Linz, Professor of Sociology and Political Science at Yale, has established himself as one of the major experts on authoritarianism, fascism, and the breakdown of democratic regimes. His main contribution is in stressing the way, as a latecomer movement, fascism is highly eclectic in its ideology, its fortunes determined largely by the political space available to it. His definition is a sophisticated example of the 'check-list approach' adopted by many non-Marxist scholars since the war.

How can we define fascism? Any definition of this latecomer movement has to emphasize the things against which it stood; we noted earlier its anti-dimension but we should also consider its new appeal and its conception of man and society. In addition to those ideological elements, no definition can ignore the importance of its distinctive style, its rhetoric and its symbolism, its chants, ceremonies, and shirts that attracted so many young people in the years between the two wars. But neither ideology nor style, given its electoral weakness, except in Germany, would have made it a decisive factor in the political life of many societies without the new forms of organization and political action.

We shall use a multi-dimensional typological definition of fascism in our analysis, a definition which in our view covers all the movements discussed here even when some dimensions might be more central to one or another of them. We define fascism as a hypernationalist, often pan-nationalist, anti-parliamentary, anti-liberal, anti-communist, populist and therefore anti-proletarian, partly anti-capitalist and anti-bourgeois, anti-clerical, or at least, non-clerical movement, with the aim of national social integration through a single party and corporative representation not always equally emphasized; with a distinctive style and rhetoric, it relied on activist cadres ready for violent action combined with electoral participation to gain power with totalitarian goals by a combination of legal and violent tactics. The ideology and above all the rhetoric appeals for the incorporation of a national cultural tradition selectively in the new synthesis in response to new social classes, new social and economic problems, and with new organizational conceptions of mobilization and participation, differentiate them from conservative parties. The appeal based on emotion, myth, idealism, and action on the basis of a vitalistic philosophy is initially directed at those least integrated into the class structure—youth, students, demobilized officers—to constitute a self-appointed elite and later to all those disadvantageously affected by social change and political and economic crisis against the political system. In a plebiscitarian mobilization of the masses, the fascist appeal is based on an inflation of national solidarity and the rejection of the institutionalization of conflict and cleavages in modern societies and therefore a destruction and/or demobilization of the parties that organize those cleavages, particularly working-class but also clerical parties. Hypernationalism is reflected in a deep-seated hostility to all organizations and movements that can be conceived as international in character—that is communism, even socialism, international finance capitalism, the Catholic church or at least the Vatican, Freemasonry, the League of Nations, pacifism, and the Jews, even in those movements that are not initially anti-Semitic and even less racist.

['Some Notes toward a Comparative Study of Fascism in Sociological Historical Perspective', in W. Laqueur (ed.), *Fascism: A Reader's Guide* (Penguin: Harmondsworth, 1979), 24–6.]

RENZO DE FELICE
165 Verbal Revolutionarism

Renzo de Felice is an Italian scholar renowned for his multi-volume biography of Mussolini. In his pronouncements on generic fascism he stresses the gulf between Fascism's progressiveness and Nazism's bid to return to an idealized past. He too adopts the 'check-list' approach to define it, blending structural, ideological, and organizational features.

As a preliminary working hypothesis, I propose this twofold typology:

Typology of countries. Fascism established itself wherever:

social mobility, particularly of a vertical nature, was the most rapid and intense;

a predominantly agrarian and latifundium-type economy existed, or massive residues of this sort of economy were not substantially integrated into the national economic complex;

there was an economic crisis (inflation, unemployment, high cost of living, and so on), or such a crisis had not been completely surmounted;

there was a confused process of crisis and alteration of traditional moral values;

there was a crisis of either growth or senility within the parliamentary system that caused either the Socialists and Communists or certain sectors of the bourgeoisie to question the very legitimacy of the system and occasioned the feeling that there was no valid alternative government;

war had aggravated or left unresolved certain national and colonial problems such as Irredentism and the presence of powerful alien minorities, thereby encouraging nationalistic tensions and the rise of revisionist tendencies with regard to the configuration of Europe as determined by the treaties of Versailles, Trianon, Saint-Germain, and others.

Typology of forms of power. Fascism established itself through:

mystical concepts of life and politics based on the primacy of irrational activism and faith in direct and revolutionary action; denigration of the ordinary individual and exaltation of the national collectivity and extraordinary personalities (elites and supermen), thus providing the basis for the myth (so essential in Fascism) of the 'leader';

a political regime of the masses (in the sense of a continual mobilization of the masses and a direct relation between the leader and the masses), based on a single-party system and a party militia and enforced by a police regime and control of all information and propaganda media;

verbal revolutionarism, coupled with substantial conservatism and alleviated by social concessions of a welfare nature;

an attempt to create a new managerial class, existing as the expression of the party and, indirectly, of the petty and middle bourgeoisie;

the creation and improvement of a strong military apparatus;

an economic system based on private enterprise but characterized by expansion of the public sector, by transfer of economic leadership from the capitalists and entrepreneurs to high state officials, and by state control of the major aspects of economic policy including mediation labor controversies (corporativism) and promotion of autarky.

[*Interpretations of Fascism* (Harvard University Press: Cambridge, Mass., London, 1977), 11–12.]

GILBERT ALLARDYCE

166 **A Mulish Concept**

This article by the American scholar Gilbert Allardyce is worth citing as the expression of an understandable exasperation with the endless and increasingly complex debate over the fascist minimum. His response is one of radical scepticism about the value to the social sciences of using 'fascism' as a generic term at all.

'Perhaps the world fascism should be banned, at least temporarily, from our political vocabulary', S. J. Woolf wrote in 1968. Historians who have confronted the problem of defining this mulish concept may sympathize with this modest proposal. Unfortunately, the word 'fascism' is here to stay; only its meaning seems to have been banned. Nevertheless, the German philosopher-historian Ernst Nolte is probably correct in stressing that historians do not have the responsibility to invent new terms simply because the existing ones seem inadequate. But they do have the responsibility to confess how truly inadequate the term fascism has become: put simply, we have agreed to use the word without agreeing on how to define it. This article is concerned with the reasons for this unfortunate state of affairs.

Although some scholars attempted from the start to restrict the use of the term fascism to Mussolini's movement in Italy, most have joined in a process of proliferation that began as early as the 1920s. After Mussolini's success, observers thought they recognized men and organizations of the same type arising in other nations. From this beginning emerged a popular image of fascism as an international movement, a phenomenon that found purest expression in Italy and Germany, but also appeared in a wide number of other countries. When stripped of national trappings, it is commonly believed, all of these movements had a common characteristic that was the essence of fascism itself. Although that essence is difficult to define, the prevailing hope is that continuing research will eventually reveal the nature of fascism more clearly. Thus, while the thinking itself continues to elude us, the name goes on as before.

First of all, fascism is not a generic concept. The word *fascismo* has no meaning beyond Italy. Yet it was applied from the beginning to movements that arose in other nations, movements whose fate it was to be interpreted in terms of Mussolini's organization. Such parties presumably corresponded to foreign 'models,' first the Blackshirts, and later the Nazis. 'They claim that we are fascists, but they know that this is a lie,' protested Jacques Doriot, the leader of the *Parti populaire français*, in 1937. 'We do not think that the regime of Hitler or Mussolini can be fitted to our country.' Such men, however, could no more get rid of the word in their time than historians can be rid of it today. Even those outside Germany and Italy who adopted the term for their own political purposes came to recognize the curse of its association with things foreign. Oswald Mosley, leader of the British Union of Fascists, contended that his own movement was a form of English patriotism that became so confused in the public mind with alien powers that it was denounced as unpatriotic. Students of politics, of course, must always distinguish between movements already in control of the state and those still competing for power. Few were more aware of the difference than the so-called fascists themselves. Mosley complained in later life that, whenever some success appeared possible in the 1930s, his organization received a 'knock-down blow' from the actions of Hitler and Mussolini themselves, blustering into some new European crisis for purely national interests and spreading alarm and opposition in England.

['What Fascism is Not: Thoughts on the Deflation of a Concept', *American Historical Review*, 84/2 (1979), 367, 370.]

G. L. Mosse, Professor of History at the University of Wisconsin, is one of the world's most prolific and distinguished experts on Nazism and fascism. He has paid particular attention to the forms, socio-cultural sources, and dynamics of fascism's anti-rationalism and ultra-nationalism.

The building blocks for a general theory of fascism now seem to lie before us. Fascism was everywhere an 'attitude towards life', based upon a national mystique which might vary from nation to nation. It was also a revolution attempting to find a 'Third Way' between Marxism and capitalism, but still seeking to escape concrete economic and social change by a retreat into ideology: the 'revolution of the spirit' of which Mussolini spoke; or Hitler's 'German revolution'. However, it encouraged activism, the fight against the existing order of things. Both in Germany and Italy fascism's chance at power came during conditions of near civil war. But this activism had to be tamed, fascism had to become respectable: for activism was in conflict with the bourgeois desire for law and order, with those middle-class virtues which fascism promised to protect against the dissolving spirit of modernity. It also clashed with the desires of a head of state who represented the old order and who could not be ignored. While Hitler was freed from this constraint by President von Hindenburg's death in 1934, Mussolini always had to report to King Victor Emmanuel. The result was that activism had to exist side by side with the effort to tame it. This was one of the chief problems faced by Hitler and Mussolini before their rise to power and in the early years of their rule.

Fascism could create a consensus because it annexed and focused those hopes and longing which informed diverse political and intellectual movements of the previous century. Like a scavenger, fascism scooped up scraps of romanticism, liberalism, the new technology and even socialism, to say nothing of a wide variety of other movements lingering from the 19th into the 20th century. But it threw over all these the mantle of a community conceived as sharing a national past, present and future—a community which was not enforced but 'natural', 'genuine', and with its own organic strength and life, analogues to nature. The tree became the favourite symbol, but the native landscape or the ruins of the past were also singled out as exemplifying on one level the national community, a human collectively represented by the fascist party.

Support of fascism was not built merely upon appeal to vested interests. Social and economic factors proved crucial in the collapse after the First World War, and in the Great Depression the social and economic successes of fascism gave body to fascist theories. But, and this seems equally crucial, political choices are determined by people's actual perception of their situation, their hopes and longings, the utopia towards which they strive. The fascist 'attitude towards life' was suffused by cultural factors through which, as we have attempted to show, the movement presented itself: it was the only mass movement between the wars which could claim to have a largely cross-class following.

In the end, the fascist dream turned out to be a nightmare. It is not likely that Europe will repeat the fascist or the National-Socialist experience. The fragments of our Western cultural and ideological past which fascism used for its own purposes still lie ready to be formed into a new synthesis, even if in a different way. Most ominously, nationalism, the basic force which made fascism possible in the first place, not only remains, but is growing in strength—still the principal integrative force among peoples and nations. Those ideals of mass politics upon which fascism built its political style are very much alive, ready to absorb and exploit the appropriate myths. The danger of some kind of authoritarianism is always present, however changed from earlier forms or from its present world-wide manifestations.

['Toward a General Theory of Fascism', in G. L. Mosse (ed.), *Masses and Man* (Howard Fertig: New York, 1980), 194–6.]

STANLEY PAYNE

168 **A New Nationalist Authoritarian State**

Stanley Payne, also Professor of History at the University of Wisconsin, has made major contributions to the history of Spanish fascism. He has also published the most influential theories of generic fascism of the last two decades, at the heart of which stands a 'typological description', in other words a sophisticated form of 'check-list'.

The descriptive typology in table 1 is suggested merely as an analytic device of limited scope for purposes of comparative definition. It does not propose to establish a rigidly reified category, but a loose wide-spectrum description that can identify a variety of differing allegedly fascist movements while still setting them apart from other kinds of revolutionary or nationalist movements. Individual movements might then be understood to have possessed further beliefs, characteristics, and goals of major importance to them that did not contradict the common features but were simply added to them or went far beyond them.

The term fascist is used not for the sake of convention alone but because the Italian movement was the first significant force to exhibit those characteristics (or at least most of them) as a new type and was for long the most influential ideologically. It constituted the type whose ideas and goals were the most easily generalized, particularly when compared with racial National Socialism.

Table 1. Typological Description of Fascism

A. The Fascist Negations:

    Antiliberalism
    Anticommunism

Anticonservatism (though with the understanding that fascist groups were willing to undertake temporary alliances with groups from any other sector, most commonly with the right)

B. Ideology and Goals:

Creation of a new nationalist authoritarian state based not merely on traditional principles or models
Organization of some new kind of regulated, multiclass, integrated national economic structure, whether called national corporatist, national socialist, or national syndicalist
The goal of empire or a radical change in the nation's relationship with other powers
Specific espousal of an idealist, voluntarist creed, normally involving the attempt to realize a new form of modern, self-determined, secular culture

C. Style and Organization:

Emphasis on esthetic structure of meetings, symbols and political choreography, stressing romantic and mystical aspects
Attempted mass mobilization with militarization of political relationships and style and with the goal of a mass party militia
Positive evaluation and use of, or willingness to use, violence
Extreme stress on the masculine principle and male dominance, while espousing the organic view of society
Exaltation of youth above other phases of life, emphasizing the conflict of generations, at least in effecting the initial political transformation
Specific tendency toward an authoritarian, charismatic, personal style of command, whether or not the command is to some degree initially elective.

[*Fascism: Comparison and Definition* (University of Wisconsin Press, Madison, 1980), 6–8.]

ZEEV STERNHELL

169 A New Civilization

Zeev Sternhell is an Israeli scholar who has written extensively on French and Italian fascism. He is particularly keen to demonstrate how fascism represented a synthesis of ultra-right and ultra-left aspirations towards a post-liberal society rooted in the late nineteenth-century revolt against positivism and liberalism, and going 'beyond right and left'. One peculiarity of his approach is that he regards the biological racism of Nazism as too exceptional and extreme to qualify it as a form of fascism.

FASCISM   Of all the major ideologies of the twentieth century, fascism was the only one to come into being together with the century itself. It was a synthesis of organic nationalism and anti-Marxist socialism, a revolutionary movement based on a rejection of liberalism, democracy and Marxism. In its essential character, fascist ideology was a rejection of materialism—liberalism, democracy and Marxism being regarded simply as different aspects of the same materialist evil. It was this revolt against materialism which, from the beginning of the century, allowed a convergence of anti-liberal and anti-bourgeois nationalism and a variety of socialism which, while rejecting Marxism, remained revolutionary. This form of socialism was also, by definition, anti-liberal and anti-bourgeois, and its opposition to historical materialism made it the natural ally of radical nationalism. The fascist synthesis symbolized the rejection of a political culture inherited from the eighteenth century and the French Revolution, and it aimed at laying the foundations of a new civilization. Only a new communal and anti-individualistic civilization was deemed capable of assuring the permanence of a human collectivity in which all strata and all classes of society would be perfectly integrated, and the natural framework for such a harmonious, organic collectively was held to be the nation—a nation enjoying a moral unity which liberalism and Marxism, both agents of warfare and disunity, could never provide.

From this perspective, it is clear that fascism was a pan-European phenomenon, and it existed on three levels—as an ideology, as a political movement, and as a form of government.

From the point of view of the history of ideas, the first world war was not the watershed it appears to have been in so many other areas. Fascism did not belong only to the inter-war era but to that whole period of history which began with the modernization of the European continent at the end of the nineteenth century. The intellectual revolution of the turn of the century, the entry of the masses into politics, produced fascism as a system of thought, as a sensibility, as an attitude to the essential problems of civilization. The First World War and the economic crisis of the 1930s produced the sociological and psychological conditions necessary to the construction of the fascist movement, but they did not produce fascist ideology.

['Fascism', in David Miller (ed.), *The Blackwell Encyclopedia of Political Thought* (Blackwell: Oxford, 1987), 148.]

ROGER EATWELL

170 **The New Synthesis**

Roger Eatwell teaches at the University of Bath and has specialized in the study of the right, with particular attention to Poujadism, the Holocaust denial, and British fascism. He has also contributed a sophisticated model with which to grasp the underlying coherence of fascist ideology in terms of the way, in evolving positions on a cluster of basic themes, it synthesizes elements of right and left, conservative and revolutionary currents of thought. This approach has the merit of highlighting the structural affinity both between apparently conflicting forms of inter-war fascism, and between inter-war and post-war fascism or 'neo-fascism', which in some cases has moved a long way from its antecedents.

Most attempts to produce a generic definition of fascist ideology have been linked to a particular conception of where fascism stands on the left–right spectrum. It is normally seen as 'extreme right', thought right-wing terminology is often used erratically, and fascism is sometimes also conceived as 'radical right', 'far right' and 'ultra right'. Moreover, left–right terminology fails to bring out that ideologies are better seen as multidimensional, and that at some levels there can be significant overlaps between ideologies.

One recent definition from a major commentator[18] holds that: 'fascism was primarily a new variety of authoritarian conservatism and right-wing nationalism which sought to defeat the Marxist threat and the political liberalism which allowed it to exist in the first place'. Such a definition completely fails to see fascism's radical side. In an attempt to solve this problem, others have seen fascism as 'neither left or right', as a doctrine of the 'revolutionary centre' (notably Sternhell's major works[19]). The problem here is the opposite one; such approaches fail to see fascism's right-wing aspect.

The approach delineated above tries to resolve this problem by seeing fascism as a spectral-syncretic ideology. In other words, there was a series of core themes in European fascist ideology, notably synthesis, but these did not produce a unique set of conclusions. Some commentators, notably Sternhell, have already stressed Valois's formulation of: nationalism + socialism = fascism. However, there are misleading aspects to this formula. Moreover, fascism sought a much broader set of syntheses. Among the most important were: between a conservative view of man constrained by nature and the more left-wing view of the possibilities of creating a 'new man'; between a commitment to science, especially in terms of understanding human nature, and a more anti-rationalist, vitalist interest in the possibilities of the will (one of the factors which attracted the philosopher Heidegger to Nazism was his belief that the fall into inauthentic mode of existence in modern society was reversible); between the faith and service of Christianity and the heroism of Classical thought; between private property relations more typical of the right and a form of welfarism more typical of the left. The Mussolini–Gentile entry in the 1932 *Enciclopedia Italiana* underlines this point when it notes that fascism was '[a]nti-positivistic, but positive', that the fascist state was 'the synthesis and unity of all values'.

[‛Towards a New Model of Generic Fascism', *Journal of Theoretical Politics*, 4/2 (1992), 161–94.]

[18]   Robert Soucy, 'French Fascism and the Croix de Feu: A Dissenting Interpretation', *Journal of Contemporary History*, 26 (1991), 159–88.

[19]   Z. Sternhell, *La Droite révolutionnaire, 1885–1914. Les Origines françaises du fascisme* (Seuil: Paris, 1978); *Ni droite ni gauche* (Seuil: Paris, 1983).

PART V

Post-War Fascisms

Those who approach fascism with the preconception that it is ideologically barren are likely to assume that it has undergone no significant modifications in the post-war period. This section will hopefully demonstrate how erroneous such an assumption would be. While there is no shortage of slavish imitation and mindless regurgitation of canonic Fascist and especially Nazi ideas by new generations of fascists, the more theoretically demanding among them have embarked on a thoroughgoing programme of modernization to adapt the dream of the regenerated nation to new historical realities. In doing so they have lost no time in identifying any new 'enemies' that they can claim stand in the path of its realization, as well as raising a number of new issues with which they hope to mobilize support.

Unfortunately, little authoritative secondary literature exists to help compile or classify texts representative of this important development. Indeed, there has been a conspicuous lack of scholars prepared to trace the continuity between the inter-war and post-war fascism, either at an organizational or ideological level. This may be attributed partly to the persistent lack of consensus among non-Marxists over the definition of fascism itself, as well as to a prevalent assumption that 'real' fascism was interred with Mussolini or Hitler. It may also be connected with the curious hiatus which has grown up in the coverage of fascism as a historical phenomenon. Almost without exception monographs or edited volumes on the subject have focused on events up to 1945 (usually in Europe), and have been content to confine their reflections on developments thereafter to a few perfunctory remarks or a superficial chapter at most. For the period after 1945 the subject has fallen into the domain of political scientists and journalists, whose tendency to concentrate on contemporary events in particular countries has led to an unassimilable mass of specialist studies but a distinct paucity of overviews. Ó Maoláin's *The Radical Right: A World Directory* (1987) is a rare exception to this generalization, but sensibly confines itself to being an inventory of specimens of a broadly conceived illiberal right without offering extensive analysis of this huge topic.

Ó Maoláin's work underlined just how intractable the subject of post-war fascism had become by the mid-1980s. It recorded the vital statistics of thousands of groupings with an apparent kinship with Fascism or Nazism, ranging from publications and publishing houses to pressure groups, from paramilitary terrorist groups to electoral parties, from minute *groupuscules* to fully-fledged tentacular organizations, from the highly ephemeral to the extremely durable. Given the complex formal and informal connections, both national and international, which exist between them, not to mention the links between current and past movements or the activities of individuals who are liable to move from organization to organization or even be associated with several simultaneously, the subject of post-war fascism has clearly become, as far as the resources of a single academic are concerned, infinite. This is hardly surprising when it is considered that half a century has passed since 1945, three decades longer than the inter-war period when 'classic' fascism flourished, and in that time it has spread to more countries, assumed new forms, and, as ever with marginalized opposition ideologies, has been extraordinarily fragmented and 'fissiparous'.

Clearly each competing ideal type of fascism would have placed a different taxonomic grid over this area and produced a different pattern of phenomena to be included and excluded, different categories and subcategories. One effect of applying mine, which makes a mythic core of palingenetic ultra-nationalism its key definitional component rather than its features as a particular type of mass or cadre movement or regime, is that the 'purely' cultural campaign against liberal democracy fought by the French New Right and its associated currents of thought figure prominently in the following selection. At the same time, many obvious candidates for inclusion, such as Perónism, various paramilitary right-wing movements and authoritarian regimes that have continued to spring up all over the world, whether Le Pen's Front National, the warring factions in the former Yugoslavia, or the 'colonel' regimes in Greece and Argentina, have all been excluded as lacking a sufficiently radical palingenetic (that is, revolutionary) thrust.

Another criterion which has determined the contents of Part V is the decision to abandon the idea of chronological sequence in favour of a thematic approach. Passages have been chosen to illustrate a number of categories which have been devised specifically in order to reduce the topic to some semblance of manageability, and should not be taken as any sort of authoritative or definitive breakdown of the subject. The first of these is devoted to 'verdicts on the "fascist era" from veteran fascists', and is intended as a bridge from Part III (inter-war fascism) to this part. The immediate problem for those convinced that some form of fascism offered the solution to the crisis of their nation or the entire 'West' in the 1920s and 1930s was to come to terms with the fact that the Fascist and Nazi permutations of it had been defeated by the combined efforts of 'actually existing' liberalism and communism. Given the crucial role played by 'cognitive dissonance' in human affairs, it would be naïve to assume that convinced fascists would see in the Allied victory the refutation of their convictions. Rather they tended to diagnose what had gone wrong in such a way that it only confirmed their own brand of palingenetic myth. Thus for Julius Evola (Text 171) Fascism had failed to pursue the opportunity to reinstate the Traditionalist concept of empire, while for the National Bolshevik Ernst Niekisch (Text 172), Nazism had been a demagogic travesty of the German Revolution that he had envisaged. For both thinkers fascism's historical moment had passed, whereas for Maurice Bardèche (Text 173) it is the post-war period which has disclosed its true mission, one which only became apparent in the course of the war: the creation of a Europe sufficiently powerful to withstand the twin threat posed by Russia and the USA. In similar key Léon Degrelle (Text 174), once the Rexist leader and writing from the security of exile in Franco's Spain, having been condemned to death by the Belgian government, rhapsodizes about the original palingenetic ideals of international fascism, clearly not contaminated for him by the realities of the Third Reich.

Two veteran British fascists provide equally idiosyncratic angles on the way the fascist dream could be perpetuated. A. K. Chesterton (Text 175) fully accepts that fascism not only failed, but that Nazi atrocities have discredited the whole fascist enterprise. However, he reserves his rancour in this passage for Mosley, whom he had served so prominently in the mid-1930s, and before long will have launched his own ultra-right party. Mosley had spent his internment in refining his fascist vision, and on his release threw his energies into becoming the driving force of a thoroughly modernized Eurofascism at home and abroad. This meant a new party, the Union Movement, and a flood of new writings in which he sought to retrieve the fascist ideal intact from the disaster of what happened. Part of this exercise involved qualifying his pre-war admiration of Hitler and turning Mussolini into a hero of modernization, corporatism, and anti-communism drawn by miscalculation into a ruinous war (Text 176).

These appetizers are followed by the main course. In practice perpetuators of the fascist dream of any sophistication recognized that they now had to operate in a radically different climate than the one provided by the inter-war period. First, not only had Fascism and Nazism been defeated militarily, but their bid to create a new order under charismatic leadership was now fatefully associated for the vast majority of the world's population with state terror, imperial expansion, war, and attempted genocide: in short, a period of mass death, systematic destruction, and barbarism on a scale unknown in human history. Secondly, the chaos which ensued at the end of the Second World War, in contrast to the First, did not give rise to a chronic crisis of both democratic and feudal societies and a proliferation of authoritarianism throughout Europe. Instead, liberalism recovered rapidly in the West, which marginalized fascism, while the formation of the Soviet empire in the East effectively prevented the emergence of any form of ultra-right. Any rerun of the fascist seizure of power through a paramilitary coup or electoral machinations was thus ruled out. The response to this situation has been the appearance of a number of new 'discourses' which post-war fascists can draw on when articulating their ideals or producing propaganda.

For the more pathologically driven fascists and racists the world over it is the Third Reich rather than Fascist Italy which has become a role model for the perpetuation of their 'struggle' against 'degeneracy': its unprecedented success in transforming German society within a few years into a vehicle for the realization of a programme of stated domestic and foreign policies of unprecedented radicalness, and its ruthless implementation of its fantasies of establishing a racially pure national community have made it a bottomless reservoir of mythic archetypes. As a result Nazism, though originally a specifically German permutation of fascism, has undergone a significant modification: it has been internationalized to become a sort of 'Universal Nazism', the equivalent of the 'Universal Fascism' which won a significant following among fascists before the war (see Text 29). As the foundation of the monthly magazine *Nation Europa* by an ex-SS officer in the late 1940s indicates, many German fascists proclaim a pan-Aryan or pan-European mode of international Nazism, while white supremacists and anti-Semites outside Germany also portray Hitler's movement as a struggle on behalf of all Aryans. Examples of this are an article by the British fascist Colin Jordan printed in a global Nazi publication produced in the USA (Text 177), the declaration of the West European chapter of the World Union of National Socialists (Text 178), and a piece by the founder of the New European Order based in Switzerland (Text 179).

The more intelligent Nazi-sympathizers, who are concerned with preaching to the non-converted, have recognized the need to launder away as far as possible the annoying historical stains which have soiled the original fascist vision. The detergent they use is history itself, rewritten as if the mass destruction, the state terror, and the eugenic and genocidal atrocities of the Third Reich could somehow be spirited away. The most blatant tack is 'Holocaust Denial', which involves such techniques as claiming that the systematic destruction of European Jewry in the Final Solution was scientifically and logistically impossible (Text 180), using the status of 'eye witness' to dismiss it as a lie (Text 181), or accusing those who offer documentary proof that it took place of being 'establishment historians' bent on fabricating a legend (Text 182). Another, perhaps more pernicious, ploy is to contribute to 'Historical Revisionism' by doctoring or decontextualizing facts in a way which puts a different gloss on the events associated with fascism. The result is apparently 'factual' historical scholarship whose subtext is an apologia for fascism's onslaught against humanity. A past master in this technique is David Irving (Text 183), who has produced a series of dense monographs on aspects of the Third Reich and Second World War which in one way or another deflect the charge of inhumanity away from Hitler and onto his subordinates or the Allies who fought him—though an article from Irving's own paper (Text 184) shows him prepared to publish documentary sources suggesting that Hitler was as early as 1922 proposing the physical extermination of the Jews. In 1989 Irving changed his public position to one of unashamed Holocaust denial when he wrote the introduction to the English edition of the infamous *Leuchter Report* (published under his own imprint, Focal Point Publications), which claimed to adduce forensic evidence that the mass gassings of Jews in the camps were a scientific impossibility.

Revisionism is not only the province of Nazi sympathizers, however, but can be reinforced by more orthodox academics. An outstanding example is Ernst Nolte (Text 185), not a fascist but one of the leading figures in fascist studies (see Text 162). He caused some consternation at the height of the debate over recent German history known as the *Historikerstreit* in the late 1980s when he published a book presenting the atrocities of the Third Reich as the result of a European 'civil war' in which Germany pitted itself against the twin enemy of Bolshevism and Western decadence, rather than as the natural and deliberate fruit of a Nazi ideology which had roots deep in the pre-1914 period. How readily revisionism lends itself to purely journalistic expression is shown by an article by Gerhard Frey (a true fascist apologist) written at the time of the trial of a former Gestapo head for war crimes, which draws attention to the criminality of Germany's enemies (Text 186).

Another crucial development since 1945 has been the shift of 'Eurofascism' from its marginalized position under inter-war Fascism and Nazism to become a central plank of European fascist ideology and policy. Eurofascism is much more variegated than neo-Nazism (which as we have seen can also assume a pan-European form), and is here illustrated in the declaration of the Malmö conference (Text 187) at which the European Social Movement was formed, Julius Evola's 'Traditionalist' version (Text 188) which was already embryonic in his key 1934 text *The Revolt against the Modern World*, and Mosley's permutation (Text 189), which had been first formulated in 1936 (see Text 92).

Europe is also a key theme of the most original recasting of the fascist vision, the *Nouvelle Droite* or 'New Right', generally associated with Alain de Benoist, who is but the figurehead of a specialized branch of cultural industry with contributors from all over Europe (and now Russia). The New Right has not only abandoned paramilitary violence and electioneering as the high road to power in favour of a cultural war, but translated the 'classic' fascist obsession with national decadence and rebirth into a critique of egalitarianism, liberalism, multi-ethnicity, and pluralism as the cause for a wholesale loss of (Indo-)European roots, 'difference', and identity. New Rightists often accuse liberals of racism, alleging that their encouragement of racial mixing and the globalization of consumerist materialism is what is destroying the integrity and distinctiveness of ethnic groups (*ethnies*), while they are attempting to preserve them (and hence are the true anti-racists—cf. Text 178). This insidious ideological dialect, which feeds eclectically on the works of a wide range of mostly unsuspecting social scientists, genuinely deserves the term 'neo-fascism'. It is sampled here in articles by French (Text 190), Franco-German (Text 191), and English (Text 192) contributors.

New Right spokesmen would doubtless reject the term fascist, but they make no secret of their debt to a form of political myth-making which our ideal type has revealed unmistakably to be a mode of palingenetic ultra-nationalism, the 'Conservative Revolution'. This term was first used to cover all non-Nazi forms of German fascism by Armin Mohler (Text 193), who produced a *catalogue raisonné* of this vast and complex area of German cultural history. Articles on aspects of the Conservative Revolution (exemplified here in Texts 194 and 195) are commonplace in New Right literature, because it enables the fascist dream of ultra-nationalist regeneration to be pursued specifically shorn of its awkward associations with historical Fascism and Nazism, just as anti-Stalinist Marxists are not embarrassed by the Gulags: indeed for Mohler the authors he studied so devotedly were the 'Trotskyites' of the German Revolution.

'Third Position' is a blanket term for those who, in order to distinguish themselves from 'classic fascism' or neo-Nazism, have recourse not just to this label but to others such as Third Way, Strasserite, National Democratic, National Revolutionary, or Political Soldier. In doing so they have much in common with the New Right, and indeed draw extensively on its ideas, as well as on the Conservative Revolution, Eurofascism, and what they see as 'kindred' manifestations of a Third Way tactic. The important distinction is that they are not simply concerned with cultural revolution, but work on two fronts simultaneously, ideological and paramilitary, in order to create a new type of élite which would blend physical heroism with spirituality. An example of the sort of New Right spirituality which influences them is an article on the 'sacred' (Text 196), while Derek Holland's piece on the 'political soldier' (Text 197) is a classic of its kind. In the manifesto of Groupe Union

Défense (Text 198) can be seen elements of both New Right and Third Position Eurofascism.

The final section sets out to illustrate some of the inventive ways in which fascism has adapted to the historical realities of contemporary society. It can turn itself into the words of lyrical ballads, or of the heavy metal numbers (Text 199) consumed at skinhead concerts (skinhead fascism is now a truly international phenomenon which gives the lie to fascism's allegedly middle-class nature). It can dress up in the language of rights and the call for 'identity' (Text 200), the buzz-word of the politics of the 1990s. It can go Green and claim the primacy in ecological matters (Text 201). It can cite the breakdown of law and order and the structural economic crisis of modern capitalist societies as the proof of liberalism's bankruptcy and imminent collapse (Text 202). Meanwhile its militants can pick on the threat posed by immigrants and 'anti-racists' to European values and traditions and hence to the 'true nation' (Text 203), or fantasize about the final showdown between Aryans and the rest of humanity, which they would of course deny is fully human (Text 204). Alternatively they can call for a heroic rebellion against all those who are desecrating the Motherland (Text 205), or for the preservation of the primordial nation through its unification within a racially and culturally pure sovereign state (Texts 206, 207).

Nor has the 'democratic' path to the fascist state been abandoned. The Reader ends with four examples (Texts 208–11) of how deeply illiberal concepts of nationhood and national mission have been translated into electoral programmes whose hidden agenda could well remain opaque to those not versed in fascism's more euphemistic utterances, but not to the 'nazi-skin' who took to the streets to celebrate the success of Italy's National Alliance in the 1994 elections. We finish, however, with a piece of party literature which does not even pretend to abide by the democratic 'rules of the game', and offers instead a blatant exercise in ultra-nationalism (Text 212). It would perhaps be tempting to dismiss such palingenetic fantasizing in the organ of Zhirinovsky's Liberal Democratic Party as symptomatic of the teething troubles of an infant democracy, were it not for the fact that the LDP had won 23 per cent of the votes in one part of the general elections of December 1993, and at the time of writing (July 1994) even serious 'Russia-watchers' were suggesting that Zhirinovsky or some equally extreme ultra-nationalist might just conceivably become the next president of Russia. The text must stand for all those dreamers, famous or obscure, who continue to prepare for the day when they can inflict their utopian vision of a new order on the world and in practice create another hell on earth for entire sections of humanity.

i. Verdicts on the 'Fascist Era' from Veteran Fascists

JULIUS EVOLA

171 **Fascism: Myth and Reality**

Julius Evola (1898–1974) spent much of his life elaborating into a highly sophisticated 'total' vision of the world his lifelong obsession with the notion that the Westernized 'modern world' represented the rotten fruit of two thousand years of decadence. As a result the primordial 'Tradition' which he alleged preceded it had all but vanished. In his voluminous and massively erudite pseudo-scientific writings he argued that this Tradition had expressed itself historically in several organic, hierarchically structured, and metaphysically based States which, under the leadership of an élite caste of warrior-priests, formed the core of vast empires through which superior races and their superior values prevailed. During the 1930s he convinced himself that if Fascism could ally itself with the more 'aristocratic', un-demagogic forces within the Third Reich it would create the basis for the re-establishment of such a Traditional empire in Europe (he wrote the Synthesis of Racial Doctrine for Mussolini's regime in 1941). However the defeat of the Axis caused him to adapt his philosophy to the age of 'ruins' in which cultural rebirth was indefinitely postponed.

Fascism has undergone a process which can be defined as *mythologization*, and the attitude which many adopt towards it is of a passionate and irrational kind rather than a critical, intellectual one. This is especially true of those who retain an idealistic loyalty towards the Italy that was.[. . .] Mythologization has naturally gone hand in hand with *idealization*, so that only the positive aspects of the Fascist regime are highlighted, deliberately or unconsciously playing down the negative ones. The same procedure is practised the other way round by those who represent anti-nationalist forces, their mythologization leading to systematic denigration, the construction of a myth of Fascism which only focuses on its most problematic aspects with a view to discrediting it and making everyone hate it.[. . .]

Over and above any polemical one-sidedness, those who, unlike the 'nostalgics' of the younger generation, have lived through Fascism and have thus had a direct experience of the system and its men, know and acknowledge that not everything about it was in order. As long as Fascism existed and could be considered a movement of reconstruction in the making, one of yet unrealized and uncrystallized possibilities, it was still permissible not to criticize it beyond a certain limit. And those who, like ourselves, while defending a set of ideas which only partially coincided with Fascism (and with German National Socialism), did not condemn these movements, even though fully aware of their questionable or aberrant aspects, did so precisely because we counted on future possible developments—to be encouraged with every means and strength we could muster—which might have corrected or eliminated these aspects.

Today, when that Fascism lies behind us as a historical reality, our attitude cannot be the same. Instead of idealizing it in a way consistent with the 'myth' of Fascism, what is necessary now is to separate the positive from the negative, not just for theoretical reasons, but for practical guidance with an eventual political struggle in mind. Thus we should not accept the adjective 'fascist' or 'neo-fascist' *tout court*; we should call ourselves fascist (if we feel we must) in respect of what was positive about Fascism, not fascist in respect of what Fascism was not.[. . .]

Even in the search for the positive, there is in practice an essential difference between on the one hand those whose only reference point is Fascism (or possible analogous movements of other nations—German National Socialism, Belgian Rexism, the early Falange in Spain, Salazar's regime, the Romanian Iron Guard: at one point it was possible to talk of a 'world revolution', a general movement of opposition to the proletarian revolution), seeing in it the be-all and end-all of their political, historical, and doctrinal horizons, and on the other those who consider what emerged from such movements as particular manifestations, some more perfect than others, of ideas and principles based in that earlier Tradition of which we have spoken, but adapted to particular circumstances. These principles are to be associated with 'normality' and permanence, relegating what is original and in the strict sense 'revolutionary' about those movements to secondary, contingent traits. In other words, it is a question of making linkages as far as it is possible between the great European political Tradition and discarding what at bottom can be seen as compromises, divergent or even deviant possibilities, or phenomena which were products of the very evils which people set out to take a stand against and fight.

[*Il fascismo* (Giovanni Volpe: Rome, 1979; 1st edn. 1964), 13–17.]

ERNST NIEKISCH

172 **The Third Reich: The Triumph of the Demagogues**

Ernst Niekisch (1889–1967) was a leading exponent of 'National Bolshevik' fascism in the inter-war period, who looked to a close relationship between the national renaissance he read into Communist Russia and that of Germany to save the West from terminal decline. Hitler's anti-Bolshevism thrust him into 'inner emigration', but he did not alter his analysis of Europe's predicament. Niekisch's non-Nazi version of radical anti-capitalism is still regarded as significant by some neo-fascists who associate themselves with the 'Conservative Revolution' (see Texts 193–5).

The way things will go from now on is quite clear. It will be difficult to help Europe to its feet: its decline and descent would appear to be inexorable. The Russo–Asiatic bloc is such a reserve of energies that the future belongs to it.

At this point a major problem arises: is there any possibility of salvaging the best cultural values of Europe and perpetuating them in the new age which is dawning? Ancient Rome faced a similar problem.[. . .] The Christian religion and Christian

Church were 'cultivated': they were spiritualized through the heritage of classical culture. This heritage did not perish, but was preserved.[1]

Were there still ways to transfer the best of the Western–European heritage to the new Russo-Asiatic world which was arising? This was the question which had been asked [after the First World War] and which was the basic question posed by the *Widerstand* movement. Prussia of old, which had never been completely incorporated into the West, appeared a potential instrument for transmitting Western values to the East. If the whole German people could understand this, its existence could still acquire a deeper significance. *The destiny of Hitler was to destroy this possibility.*[. . .]

Since 1917 I have been convinced that the bourgeois world, the West, is caught up in a process of decomposition, that Asia is reclaiming the peninsula of Europe which juts out from it, which ever since the time of the Persian wars has retained its independence from it. This process, I believed even then, was manifesting itself in the most varied spheres of life, and I saw in the Russians the arbiters of this great Asiatic claim on Europe.[. . .]

Now it was my fundamental conviction that there is only one type of élite which can legitimately exercise power. The élite I am talking about is the élite of the spirit.[. . .] The spiritual élite derives its authority from the power of the masses and has the prospect of an exalted political position only in so far as it is able to win the trust and devotion of the masses. With the help of the masses it can unsaddle the landowning and plutocratic élite. The seductive appeal which the communist idea exerted on much of the intelligentsia is to be attributed to the opportunity which it seemed to offer to the power of the spirit, especially in the context of tasks which presuppose the development and mastery of technical production machinery.

But this élite has a dangerous rival in the form of individuals obsessed with power and glory who descend to the level of the primitive masses and are able to win a mass following not through the way they selflessly pursue their real interests, but through irresponsible predictions and promises of good times ahead. These are the demagogues who, armed with pseudo-dogmas and pseudo-ideologies, turn the heads of the masses and thwart the attempt of the spiritual élite to establish the rule of reason and morality. The Hitler-Reich was an example of the triumph of demagogy over a spiritual élite. The demagogue is the travesty of the spiritual leader: he eclipses him and makes everything play into the hands of the landed or money élite.

[*Gewagtes Leben* [Living Dangerously] (Kepenheuer & Witsch: Cologne, 1958), 145–55.]

MAURICE BARDÈCHE
....

173   **Lenin was Right**

The literary critic Maurice Bardèche (1907–   ) was brother-in-law of the French fascist Robert Brasillach, executed for treason in 1945, and frequented ultra-right circles during the

[1] The German *aufheben* refers to the Hegelian concept of realities being simultaneously destroyed and preserved in a higher synthesis.

Second World War. Soon after the Liberation he wrote books defending collaboration and Vichy's collusion with the Third Reich, and produced one of the earliest exercises in Holocaust denial with Nuremberg ou la terre promise *(1948). This was followed by a work arguing for a strong (fascist) Europe to withstand the American and Russian super-powers, a vision he tried to implement as leader of the French delegation at the congress of Malmö of 1951, when plans were finalized to create a pan-European fascist movement.* What is fascism? *was written against the background of the Algerian War which did so much to mobilize ultra-nationalists in France and elsewhere, and confirmed his reputation as one of the most important fascist ideologues of the post-war years. Note the identification of the 'new man' as the fascist minimum.*

Fascism starts out as an empirical medicine which is born of crisis or the threat of crisis. That is why it has arisen in every country of the world and why it wears such different guises. This defensive reaction takes its form and inspiration from the image which the most aware and robust men of each country have of their past and of the genius of their race. Every fascism is a reaction to the present and every fascist reaction is a resurrection. Fascism is thus in its essence nationalist, and its deepest aspirations are often untranslatable to a foreign context: it is sometimes not for export. And this explains the idea that even objective opponents of fascism have made of it, namely that it can only be an upsurge of national conscience of no use to other peoples, and that it can only lead to a foreign policy designed to enhance prestige through egoistic expansion and conquest.[. . .]

The way fascism developed during the war passed unnoticed by almost all observers, intent as they were only on condemning it and unconcerned with getting their history right. At the outset of the war fascism is nationalistic, arrogant, impassive. It declares the triumph of a particular human quality over human mediocrity, it pursues this triumph in the face of all opposition, it promises nothing, and it does not even care about being admired or imitated. Then the gigantic scale of the war, the appearance of the two awesome poles of modern times looming out of the mist in which they were shrouded before, caused fascists to become aware of its significance. At this point Hitler's government starts talking about Europe: it points to it as a future, a reward, something to be rehabilitated. It matters little if it was sincere or was trying to deceive people. For those who are fighting the war and those who are living through it, the fascist idea now has a dramatically new content it has lacked so far. They had been told that fascism was the best bulwark against communism and was also a struggle against the destructiveness of liberalism. But now they know that fascism is a life-and-death struggle, a desperate last-ditch stand. They know that fascist victory is the only chance to establish a *third order*, a *third world*, and that the defeat of fascism will condemn men henceforth to know nothing except the sterile confrontation of liberal democracies with communism. They also know that the idea and unity of Europe is not only a propaganda theme: this unity is necessary, it is the only path of salvation between the two monsters which have appeared: and if fascism loses this war, they know that this unity will never be realized, for Europe will be a conquered territory, it will belong either to the United States or to Soviet Russia, it will lose its independence and become a new type of colony. It will never be possible to realize the original political concept, the new idea of man which is the only thing which can come to its support.[. . .]

It is this new image of man which is essential.[. . .] The single party, the secret police, the public displays of Caesarism, even the presence of a *Führer* are not necessarily attributes of fascism, let alone the reactionary thrust of political alliances.[. . .] The famous fascist *methods* are constantly revised and will continue to be revised. More important than the mechanisms is the idea which fascism has created for itself of man and freedom.[. . .]

It was Lenin who prophesied that fascism would be the last form which societies would adopt in order to survive so as not to capitulate to communist dictatorship. If the West has no more strength left, if it disappears like an old man who is drowning, then we can do nothing for it. But if it can rise up to defend itself, Lenin's prophecy will be fulfilled. With another name, another face, and with nothing which betrays the projection from the past, with the form of a child we do not recognize and the head of a young Medusa, the Order of Sparta will be reborn: and paradoxically it will, without doubt, be the last bastion of Freedom and the sweetness of living.

[*Qu'est-ce que le fascisme?* [What is Fascism?] (Les Sept Couleurs: Paris, 1961), 175–6.]

LÉON DEGRELLE
....
174 **The Ideals of the Fascist Era**

By the time the Nazis occupied Belgium Léon Degrelle (1906–94), the leader of the Rexists, had already moved from the Christian extreme right to fascism. He went on to become the country's most high-profile collaborator, becoming part of the Waffen SS in 1943 and commander of the volunteer Wallonie SS Brigade in 1944. Having helped defend Hitler's bunker, he secured asylum in Franco's Spain. From here he became one of the most important figures in the perpetuation and internationalization of Nazism, both through his books and through organizations such as the New European Order and CEDADE which he helped set up.

You can see that the Spain of 1939 was not Germany of 1939.[. . .] Yet the same dynamism was at work everywhere stirring the crowds, the same faith moved them, and a similar ideological bedrock could even be discerned underlying it. They shared the same reactions towards the old parties, all so sclerotic and corrupted by sordid compromises and devoid of imagination that they had nowhere brought social solutions on a sufficiently large scale or which were genuinely revolutionary. Meanwhile the people, worn down by long hours of work, miserably paid, inadequately protected against accidents at work, illnesses, or old age, waited full of impatience and anguish to be treated at last with humanity, not just materially but morally.[. . .]

In the 'fascist' ideal the respect for ordinary people and desire for social justice went hand in hand with the will to restore order in the State and continuity of service to the nation.

There was also the need to be spiritually uplifted. Throughout the whole continent youth rejected the mediocrity of professional politicians, pettifogging irrelevances, lacking education, culture.[. . .] This youth wanted to live for something great, something pure.

'Fascism' had sprung up everywhere in Europe, spontaneously, in very different forms, out of a vital, total, and general need for renewal: *renewal of the State*, a strong, authoritarian State with time for itself, and the possibility to surround itself with competent people so as to break out of the uncertainties born of political anarchy; *renewal of society*, liberated from the asphyxiating conservatism of the bourgeois with his gloves and starched collars, with no vision, red in the face through eating too much rich food and drinking too much claret, intellectually, emotionally, and above all financially resistant to any idea of reform; *social renewal*, or more precisely, social revolution, eliminating the paternalism so dear to the well-off, who made out they had big hearts with a calculated quavering of the voice, and preferred the condescending distribution of wealth through small-scale and highly subsidized charities to recognizing social justice; a *social revolution* which would put capital back in the position of being merely a material instrument, while restoring the people to their rightful place as the essential base, the primordial element of the life of the Fatherland; and finally *moral renewal*, by teaching a nation, and especially its youth, to rise up and give of itself.

There was not a country in Europe between 1930 and 1940 which did not hear this call.

[*Hitler pour mille ans* [Hitler for a Thousand Years] (Éditions de la Table Ronde: Paris, 1969), 31–2.]

ARTHUR KENNETH CHESTERTON
....
175   **The Lunacy of Fascism and Nazism**

After the war A. K. Chesterton (1899–1973) maintained his distance from Mosley's attempts to revive fascism. His own analysis of the crisis of history was based on a conspiracy theory of the pernicious influence of Jewish finance (expounded in The New Unhappy Lords *published in 1965), and focused not on a regenerated Europe but a revitalized imperial Britain. This led to the formation in 1954 of the ultra-conservative League of Empire Loyalists with its own organ,* Candour. *In 1967 he became the first chairman of the National Front, formed from the merger of the LEL with some smaller fascist groups. He resigned in 1971, alienated by the shift towards neo-Nazism promoted by John Tyndall and Martin Webster, but also in response to his growing unpopularity within the party.*

Now it is curious that while the Press pretends to take Mosley seriously, in truth it takes his policies so little seriously that nobody to date has thought worthy of comment the fact that he makes his new bid for public attention, not by preaching Fascism, but by advocating its direct opposite—internationalism. Nationalism or internationalism, it is clearly all one to the Press, which has some undisclosed reason for being interested in the man, but which cannot conjure up the slightest interest in his programme. His own followers seem to be in the same peculiar position. They cried 'Hail Mosley' when he came before them as a nationalist leader and see no reason to vary this greeting now that he presents himself to them as an internationalist leader. Indeed, Mosley goes out of his way to affirm the shift of emphasis. Fascism, he asserts, was too narrowly nationalistic. He will not repeat that mistake. He will, instead, unite Europe and exploit Africa that he may succeed where Fascism failed. 'Hail Mosley!' shout his followers in ecstatic agreement.

Fascism certainly failed. It failed so disastrously that it is impossible even to mention the word without invoking, not what its adherents meant when they used it, but what its deadliest enemies intend people to believe it to have meant. And that is defeat indeed! In the inter-war period, when mankind was menaced by militant Communism and made desperate by the rampages of international finance, which swung the world helplessly between glut and scarcity, there was nothing in my view sheerly unreasonable in the original Fascist case. It has only been made to appear unreasonable because National Socialist Germany and Fascist Italy both turned lunatic, preferring military glory to ordered tranquillity and thereby furthered the cause of their own destruction. Because of their excesses—the German excesses against the Jews, in particular—these regimes invested Fascism with so rank an odour that even such sanity as it contained is now held suspect. Not the least sane of its concepts was that which insisted that internationalism must always be a racket run by the world's only international people. How thoroughly in keeping with the hapless Mosley temperament it is that he should seek to return to political life without the least hope of ever being able to escape the odium, whether deserved or undeserved, of his Fascist past, and yet having divested his political stock-in-trade of the one part of the Fascist argument which was demonstrably true!

Spare Them!

['The Importance of Being Oswald', *London Tidings*, 85, 29 Nov. 1947.]

OSWALD MOSLEY

176 Hubris and Miscalculation

Oswald Mosley studiously used his internment during the war to elaborate and modify his fascist vision. He emerged convinced of the need for the narrow nationalism of Fascism and Nazism to give way to a pan-European new order and attended the congresses in Rome (1950) and Malmö (1951) which launched the European Social Movement. In 1948 he had created the Union Movement, a Europeanized version of the BUF which distanced itself from Fascism and Nazism, which was defunct by 1978, though not before some of its former members had set up an important ultra-right umbrella group, The League of St George, in 1974. This passage is taken from one of a number of Mosley's books articulating his new faith.

Question 175. What do you think of Hitler?
[. . .] His outstanding quality was will. He banished the hopeless mood of Germany after the First World War, he broke the chains of his people, restored their

self-respect, confidence and hope in the future, and, in the material sphere, solved the unemployment problem and restored their economy. All this was done in an unnaturally confined space under conditions of extraordinary difficulty. It is not surprising at this point of great achievement that the Germans were grateful to him for his outstanding will and energy.

The basic reason for his downfall and the disaster to all his work was that he understood no kind of practical or moral limitations to his will.[. . .] He suffered in extreme degree from what the Greeks called *hubris*: the belief that man can usurp the place of the gods in complete determination of his own fate.[. . .] Hitler in the final period [. . .] tried to inflict on a whole people a cataclysm of nature; he usurped a higher function than that of man.[. . .]

Hitler's duty was to lose himself but to save his idea. The only thing that then should have mattered to him was to preserve and transmit whatever truth he possessed to posterity. He should in his moral terms have committed suicide long before, directly it was clear the war was irretrievably lost.[. . .] As it was he prolonged his own life for a few weeks as a last exhibition of ineffective will, but tarnished his idea and jeopardized the future by the wanton deed of the concentration camps and the useless sacrifice of German youth. If he had gone a little sooner, leaving his idea and his fame inviolate, he might have been among those who in the German proverb must succumb in life in order to achieve an immortality in the minds and hearts of men.[. . .]

Question 176. What did you think of Mussolini?
He was ruined by a world war he did not desire, because he was not a man who would risk much for small gain. His actual entry into the war, I believe, was a miscalculation inspired by the narrow concept of national interests prevalent in those days. He left behind something of his work for Italy, which ranged from such practical tasks as the reclaiming of the Pontine Marshes into prosperous farm lands to a certain resistance to decadence which still endures in the elite of that nation. In the larger sphere his concept of corporate action has influenced, and will influence, the thinking of the world. Some of these ideas are in no way incompatible with a democratic system.

The roughness of the young fascists to their red opponents (the castor oil,[2] etc.) can only be excused at all by the incredible savagery and brutality of the reds, which were proved among other things by an exhibition held in Rome in 1932.[3] When they found the dead bodies of comrades who had been killed by having their heads held in furnaces, etc., some of them lost their tempers when they next met the party of assassins. We now live in a world where everything is permitted to communists of any race, and nothing—not even one per cent of such deeds—to their opponents. History will one day correct some of these remarkable errors; unless their consequences prevent any truthful history ever being written, owing to the victory of communism.

[*Mosley—Right or Wrong?* (Lion Books: London, 1961), 167–72.]

[2] Used by Blackshirts to 'punish' socialist and Catholic trade unionists during the years of *squadrismo* (1919–22).
[3] See Text 34.

ii. Discourses of Post-War Fascism

a. Universal Nazism

COLIN JORDAN

177 The Revival of National Socialism

Colin Jordan has been one of Britain's most active neo-Nazi agitators. He founded the White Defence League in 1958 with the help of the widow of Arnold Leese, founder of the inter-war Imperial Fascist League, and after a brief time with the British National Party formed by John Bean in 1960 (the present party of that name was formed by John Tyndall in 1982), he left to form the National Socialist Movement in 1962. In the same year he set up the World Union of National Socialists (WUNS), and remained the commander of its European section throughout the 1960s, abetted in this by his wife Françoise Dior, daughter of the world-famous couturier Christian Dior. In the 1980s he put his energy into reviving Gothic Ripples, originally the organ of Leese's movement, as his personal mouthpiece. This article was published by the National Socialist White People's Party, affiliated to WUNS, and led by George Lincoln Rockwell, till his assassination in 1967 the doyen of American neo-Nazism.

Twenty-one years after the physical defeat of National Socialist Germany in the outcome of her heroic struggle against the overwhelming array of men and materials marshalled against her by the Bolshevist–democratic alliance, the appearance of this journal in 1966 reflects that revival of National Socialism which is a feature of the day.

That the creed should live on and manifest itself as it does now, after being subjected to two decades of the greatest campaign of defamation which the world has ever known, is a proof of its continuing validity and appeal and its worthiness for the future. It has survived the flames of war and the tempest of vilification because, when war has done its worst and vilification run its entire gamut, National Socialism remains, in the final analysis, synonymous with higher man's will to survive, his instinct for health and strength, and his desire for beauty in life; and, as long as that will, that instinct, and that desire remain on this earth, the creed of National Socialism will remain, indestructible.[. . .]

It revives the blood feelings and sense of community of the Nordic tribes of early Europe: the feeling that man is essentially a member of the folk, and that all members of the folk are bound together closely with reciprocal duties and obligations.

National Socialism, in this way, reaches back to the old, healthy, organic values of life in revolt against the whole structure of thought of liberalism and democracy, with its cash nexus; its excessive individualism; its view of man as a folkless, interchangeable unit of world population; its spiritual justification in a debased

Christianity embracing a sickly 'humanitarianism', which will always tolerate a greater harm for the sake of avoiding a lesser one; and its fraudulent contention that the artificially induced and numerically determined wishes of the mass are the all-important criteria.

History is a saga of social decay and renewal. National Socialism is the twentieth century's remedy of renewal for the great degeneration of modern times under the disintegrating, debasing, and emasculating thought and practice which emerged with the disruption of the old medieval order of stability by the developing forces of capitalism and the industrial revolution; flourished under the *laissez-faire* liberalism of the eighteenth and nineteenth centuries; came to a climax under the democracy of the nineteenth and twentieth centuries; and will result in the world triumph of communism by the end of this twentieth century unless National Socialism comes to power in time, over a sufficient area of the globe.

National Socialism, therefore, is immensely more than a transitory political scheme. It is a historic tendency of rebirth: our age's movement of renaissance, a movement revolutionary in scope and spirit, seeking no compromise with the present order, its pernicious practices, and its false values, but their complete replacement.[. . .]

As such it is worldwide, and it is life-wide. It is worldwide in that, in its essentials, it is valid and vital universally, qualified only by the fact that it is Aryan in emanation and tradition, and upholds and depends on qualities to be found par excellence in the Aryan people.

It is life-wide in that it is not an aspect of life, but the whole of life seen from one aspect. It is an attitude of mind expressible in respect of virtually anything and everything. National Socialism stands relentlessly opposed to every manifestation of ill health, ugliness, and degeneracy in the cultural and spiritual, no less than in the political and economic spheres. In fact, it constitutes a way of life. A man does not call himself a National Socialist as a mere label of intellectual-endorsement. He is born with a propensity to National Socialism, his mind aesthetically craving the discernment and fulfilment of a healthy pattern of life, and he not only thinks and feels, but acts as a National Socialist, if he is really and entirely one.[. . .]

National Socialism's belief in the folk as the basic value, and its totality of outlook, result, figuratively speaking, in *thinking with the blood* on all questions.

This immediately and inevitably gives rise to the definition of citizenship as a matter of race: only those who are members of the folk are members of the nation, and only those who are members of the nation can be citizens of the state—to paraphrase the fourth of the Twenty-five Points of Adolf Hitler's NSDAP.

It also generates the belief that it is necessary not merely to preserve the racial character of the folk, but also, by eugenic measures, to improve the quality of the folk. It is National Socialism's revolutionary contention that the way of real progress lies in breeding better human beings.

Since all citizens are of the same race, they have a transcendent bond of kinship uniting them as blood-brothers above all sectional and class differences and personal distinctions. National unity, i.e., cohesion and corporate life in place of the class warfare of Left and Right, is one of the great secondary principles of National Socialism.

['National Socialism: A Philosophical Appraisal', *National Socialist World*, 1 (1966), 5–7.]

178 A Racist Catechism

The *Fédération ouest-européenne (FOE or West European Federation) was set up in 1963 at a meeting of Colin Jordan, Françoise Dior, and the French neo-Nazi Yves Jeanne as a chapter of WUNS responsible for keeping the Nazi dream alive in francophone Europe, its fiefdom being divided into six areas on allegedly ethnic lines. Its constitutive charter accused the Jews of causing the outbreak of war in 1939 which prevented Hitler from establishing his ethnically based new order, and celebrated the creation of non-German SS divisions. Till it was banned in 1964, its organ,* Le National-Socialiste, *stood for Holocaust denial, the vindication of Hitler, the vision of a Europe of* ethnies *(i.e. distinct ethnic groups), and crude anti-Semitism. It made no bones about its acceptance of Nazi racist doctrine, as can be seen from this manifesto.*

- Life is of plural origins, the unit of type is the race;
- the racial structure of man displays a profound interdependence between psychological and physiological traits;
- the behaviour of man is determined by two factors: heredity and milieu;
- the racial group is determined by the predominance of the heredity component; milieu cannot modify the racial and heredity component, it allows it to show its true worth;
- races are immutable except through interbreeding which cause a weakening of racial characteristics;
- each race can hope to achieve racial perfection through the progressive improvement of the elements which constitute it;
- racial hierarchy is an irrefutable and natural fact; the Aryan race is hierarchically superior to other races;
- the Aryan race naturally possesses the most complete racial genius;
- the Aryan race is made up of different racial groups: Nordics, Dalic Nordics,[4] Oriental Nordics, Celts.
- positive racism is a sound philosophical concept;
- negative racism is anti-racism, which tends to encourage the physiological destruction of races;
- the area into which the Aryan race has expanded is Europe, North America, the Union of South Africa, Australia, New Zealand, certain South American countries;
- WUNS is the only custodian and steward of the greater Aryan racial destiny.

[*Le National-socialiste,* Mar.–Apr. 1964, quoted in J. Algazy, *La Tentation néo-fasciste en France 1944–65* (Fayard: Paris, 1984), 317.]

---

[4] In the fantasies of 'racial experts' such as H. F. K. Günther (see Text 64), 'Dalic' referred to a particular genetic type associated with Scandinavian valleys (in Swedish *Dal*).

Some idea of the Byzantine interconnections of post-war fascism can be gleaned from the fact that the author of this piece is a Swiss closely associated in the late 1940s with La Sentinelle, published by the indefatigable French Eurofascist organizer, René Binet. Both had been active in setting up the Zurich conference for the hard-line racists who had split with non-Nazi fascists at the Malmö international congress of 1951. It was this which led to the creation of Le Nouvel Ordre Européen based in Switzerland, which produced L'Europe réelle, published in Brussels, and Europae, 'official organ of NOE'. It was produced by the Barcelona branch of CEDADE, a Universal Nazi organization formed in 1965 by Spanish fascists and fugitives from the Axis Powers. The first issue contained, apart from the piece reproduced here, articles by Bardèche on 'the real Europe', Evola on 'the problem of decadence', a piece on eugenics, one on 'genetic pollution', and another on the dangers of democracy, all translated into German, Spanish, English, French, and Italian.

Our friends and comrades Jacques de Mahieu and Jacques Bauge-Prevost have exposed why it is necessary to return the Afro-Asians, set on aryan land by unlucky politicians to their countries of origin and why a biological politic, scientifically based, must include the whole of our racial community.

Nevertheless, this double postulate is unworkable in the present world situation.

In fact, the USA leaders, in the name of Judeo-masonic bleating humanitarism [*sic*], do not only want to keep foreign populations within their country, do not only want to force them to mix with the Whites, but they also force the governments of Western Europe, their servants, to open their countries to colour immigration. They are, besides, in opposition to every biological politic, as this would rapidly ruin their power, based upon decadence and strengthened by decadence. Sick populations, hindered by hospitals and asylums for lunatics and weak persons, will revolt less against the plutocratic parasites. And as the evil utopians of New York have atomic arms and a potential of more than 200 million people, our double racist proposition requires to constitute a power at least equal.

An aryan government who wished to repatriate the Afro-Asians would need to be strong enough to face the United States on the field of battle.

Unless an astonishing aryan revolution should take place in the United States,[5] in which we hope but in which we do not dare to believe, it is only Europe, politically united, who will provide our race with the sword she needs. It is then a question of weaning half of our continent away from the communist yoke, from an ideology which goes against nature, even more harmful, if that's possible, than the American humanitarism. Because communism kills whilst plutocracy is satisfied with poisoning. Nevertheless, we have not to choose between cholera and plague. That our populations prefer to die in the XXIst century rather than in the XXth is a derisory aim. We must assure their survival for millions of years.

[5] Cf. Text 205.

A politically united Europe, endowed with a regime of social justice and placed in the service of the aryan racial community, is an aim quite distant from the present chaos and which many people might be tempted to find impossible.

But have we a right to allow that the White race is assassinated?

We must begin by the beginning: to spread the idea. And the New European Order seeks to devote itself to spread the idea. It groups personalities who agree to dedicate themselves to make the postulates of defense of the race acceptable.

The New European Order is not therefore a political movement of the party kind. It will not present rolls for elections. It will not compete against any party of the national European opposition, but it would not know how to be unselfish in their activities.

In fact, we, that are destined to work within the American colony called Western Europe, recognize the non-marxist forces of the opposition to plutodemocracy, a first gathering of healthy elements, frequently instinctive and without a coherent doctrine, but sometimes fitted with a vanguard programme in certain dominions. These elements represent a biological élite looking for their destiny.[. . .]

But this élite has grown in the ignorance of social-racism. Every means of mass diffusion: books, press, radio, television, subject to an inexorable and hidden censorship, keep silent about every racial thought. Vacher de Lapouge, Gobineau, Rosenberg, René Binet, Friedrich Ritter, José Antonio, Redondo, Gentile, Evola and many other people do not exist for the 'democrats'. Even more, racism is shown as a will of genocide, as a synonym of murdering. Cross-breeding deserves every praise.

Alright, we want to help this élite. We want to bring them the thought of the great aryan thinkers. We want to enlighten their own nature and their own will. We want to help them in the struggle they have begun.

Indeed, we cannot offer them neither money nor power [*sic*]. But we offer them more: the spiritual weapons, the only ones which can [*sic*] save not only the aryan world but the whole life in our planet.

['How to Save Europe', *Europae*, 1 (1979), 86–7.]

b. *Holocaust Denial*

The Miracle of the Telephone Box

Here we find Degrelle still invoking his Catholic roots while seizing on the Pope's visit to Auschwitz to deliver a piece of vulgar Holocaust denial which deploys two classic techniques: first he uses mathematical calculations to pour ridicule on the logistical feasibility of mass extermination; secondly he seeks to relativize the Nazi atrocities which he has minimized by referring to the Allied 'terror bombing' of Germany, the crimes against humanity committed in the history of the United States, and the horrors of Stalinism.

TO HIS HOLINESS POPE JOHN-PAUL II
The Vatican City

Most Holy Father,

I am Léon Degrelle and I was the Leader of Belgian Rexism (The 'Rexist' Movement) before the Second World War. During the War I was the Commander of the Belgian Volunteers on the Eastern Front, and fought in the 28th Walloon Division of the Waffen SS. This will certainly not be regarded as a recommendation by everyone. I am, however, a Catholic like you, and I believe that I am thus entitled to write to you as a brother in the faith.

I am concerned by the announcement in the press that during your coming visit to Poland, from 2nd to 12th June 1979, you are going to concelebrate Mass with all the Polish Bishops at the former concentration camp of Auschwitz. Let me say straight away that I find it very edifying to pray for the dead, whoever they may be and at any place, even in front of the brand-new crematory ovens with their immaculate firebricks.[. . .]

I fear above all that your prayers, and even simply your presence in such places, may be immediately diverted from their profound significance and used as a smokescreen by unscrupulous propagandists, who will employ them to launch hate campaigns under your cover. These campaigns are based on lies and have poisoned the whole subject of Auschwitz for more than a quarter of a century.

Yes, I mean lies. The legend of the massive exterminations at Auschwitz exploited the collective psychosis which, owing to uncontrolled gossip, had unhinged numerous World War Two internees. Since 1945 the whole world has been assailed by this legend. Hundreds of lies have been repeated in thousands of books in an increasingly virulent rage. They are reproduced in full colour in apocalyptic films, which are outrageous in the way they flay not only truth and probability, but commonsense, the most elementary arithmetic, and the facts themselves.[. . .]

It is ridiculous to imagine, and above all to pretend, that 24,000 people could have been gassed at Auschwitz each day—in batches of 3,000 at a time—in a room of 400 cubic metres. Still less could this have happened, in batches of 700 or 800, in buildings with a floor space of 25 square metres and a height of 1.9 metres, as has been claimed with regard to Belzec. Twenty-five square metres is equivalent to the floor space of a bedroom! Would you succeed, Most Holy Father, in putting 700 or 800 people in your bedroom?

Seven hundred to 800 people on 25 square metres works out at 30 people to the square metre. A square metre 1.9 metres high is the size of a telephone box! Can you picture, Your Holiness, thirty people piling into a telephone box in St Peter's Square or at the Great Seminary of Warsaw? Or on a simple shower stand?

If the miracle of thirty human bodies planted like asparagus in the goldfish bowl of a telephone box, or the one of the 800 people crowded around your camp-bed, had ever been realised, a second miracle would have immediately been indispensable. Otherwise the 3,000 people—the equivalent of two regiments—crammed together so fantastically in the Auschwitz chamber, or the 700 to 800 people piled up at Belzec (on account of having 30 occupants to the square metre), would have perished almost immediately as they would have been asphyxiated by the lack of oxygen!

There would not even have been any need for gas.[. . .]

And what about Britain, with its bombardments of unfortified cities like Copenhagen, its execution of Sepoys tied to the mouths of cannons, its crushing of the Boers, and its Transvaal concentration camps, where thousands of women and children perished in indescribable misery? And what of Churchill unleashing his abominable terror bombings on the civilian population of the Reich, which burnt them in their cellars with phosphorous, and annihilated about two hundred thousand women and children in one night in the gigantic crematory of Dresden? I use the word 'about' because only an approximate estimate could be made by calculating the weight of the ashes!

And what about the United States? Did it not rise in power thanks to the frightful slavery of millions of Blacks, who were branded like animals, and thanks to the almost complete extermination of the Red Indians, who had been the original owners of the coveted territory? Was it not the dispenser of the atomic bomb in 1945? Even yesterday, did it not number undoubted torturers amongst its troops in Vietnam?

And we have not even dwelt on the tens of millions of victims of the tyranny of the USSR, or on its *present day* gulags. I strongly fear that no one will breathe a word about them at the time of your next visit to the 'restored' Auschwitz camp, which has itself been void of occupants for decades!

[*Letter to the Pope on his Visit to Auschwitz* (Historical Review Press: Chapel Ascote, Warks., England, 1979), 3–10.]

THIES CHRISTOPHERSEN
....

181   A Monumental Lie

Thies Christophersen is one of the leading 'eyewitnesses' of the Holocaust denial industry. A member of the SS, he claims to have been deployed at Auschwitz as army agricultural researcher from January to December 1944, precisely the period when the high-tech crematoria of the Birkenau camp reached their maximum output. He rejects any idea that the camp was ever used for systematic extermination of Jews or anyone else. The pamphlet was originally published in 1973 as Die Auschwitz Lüge *by the Deutsche Bürgerinitiative, a fascist group which specializes in disseminating revisionist, pan-German and Eurofascist ideas, and run by Manfred Roeder, who in 1981 was sentenced to thirteen years' imprisonment as intellectual leader of the Deutsche Aktionsgruppen which had bombed asylum hostels the year before, killing two refugees. (I have used the Italian edition to emphasize the internationalism of post-war fascism, which knows no frontiers.)*

In a book published in Brazil one can read: '. . . this documentation (UNO) has been used by the Canadian Anti-Defamation Committee of Christian Lawmen and establishes that in the twelve years that Hitler's regime lasted (1933–45) 200 thousand Jews died in a wide variety of ways: political assassination, capital punishment, execution of terrorists and saboteurs, the (allied) bombing of concentration camps, and other causes associated with war; others died of natural causes such as illness and old age.'[. . .]

As for me, I have never made a secret of having served at Auschwitz. Every so often I have been asked about the alleged annihilation of Jews, but I have always replied that I knew nothing about it. What amazed me was the speed with which the fairy tale of 'gassing' was accepted and believed, spinelessly, without any attempt to refute it or examine it closely.[. . .]

My lodgings were at Raisko, about three kilometres from the main camp. Here there was a women's camp with greenhouses and the laboratory complex for our cultivation programme.[6][. . .] Every day parcels arrived with luxury items for the internees from CARE (a North American aid organization: if the Germans were criminal sadists who daily exterminated hundreds of thousands of Jews, what was the point of continuing to send this aid which only would have benefited the camp executioners?).[. . .] No, the immates of Raisko were not hungry. And when a new internee joined the camp undernourished and gaunt, after a few days his skin became silky smooth.

'The extermination camp was not at Auschwitz, but at Birkenau.' This is what I read and heard after the war. Well, I was at Birkenau too. I did not like this camp at all. It was overcrowded and the inmates did not make a good impression. Everything was dirty and in a run-down state. I saw entire families with children, and it pained me to see this. They explained that the children had not wanted to be separated from the parents when they were interned. However, I also saw boys happily playing football. Nonetheless, I remain of the opinion that children should not be placed in internment camps, and that, even if the English did this in the Boer War, it is not a valid justification. I raised this matter with my superiors. The reply was: 'We share your opinion, but there is nothing we can do about it. In any case it was the parents themselves who opposed being separated from their children.'

I was at Birkenau with the task of selecting a hundred or so workers for our plantations of *kok-sagis*. The procedure was as follows. In the course of an assembly the inmates were asked if they were prepared for such work and if they had any experience of it. In general more volunteered than were needed. Therefore a 'selection' took place.[7] Subsequently people wanted to construct diabolic interpretations on the basis of this term. Obviously the aim was to put to work internees who were idle, and they themselves were keen to be employed. To select meant to use them in accordance with their aptitudes and capacities while taking their condition of physical fitness into account.[. . .]

In my whole stay at Auschwitz I never noticed a shred of evidence that could suggest to me the possibility of mass extermination through 'gas chambers'. Even

---

[6] Christophersen claims that the main function of the Raisko camp was to grow a plant, *kok sagis*, used for the production of artificial rubber at the notorious Buna works attached to Auschwitz (see Text 213).

[7] 'Selection' was the Nazi euphemism for the process by which inmates of extermination camps were sorted into those condemned to be murdered immediately and those who were to be worked to death slowly.

the smell of burning flesh, which, according to what was related later, often spread round the camp, is a monumental lie [*una fandonia piramidale*]. Near the camp there was a large blacksmith's forge. The smell, cause by horseshoes being fitted onto the hoofs of horses, was certainly not particularly pleasant.[. . .]

I have related my experiences exactly as I lived them and remember them. I have told the truth as God commands. If this testimony can help restoring to our youth the respect which its fathers merit, as fighters for Germany and not as criminals, I will be more than satisfied.

[*La Fandonia di Auschwitz* [The Auschwitz Lie] (Edizioni la Sfinge: Parma, 1984), 29–30.]

JOHN DAY
....

182 An Ever-Flowing River

The monthly Spearhead *is edited by John Tyndall to 'reflect a cross-section of contemporary British Nationalist opinion', especially that of the NF in the 1970s and the BNP in the 80s and 90s in which he has played a leading role (see Text 202). John Day, the author of this review article of an English translation (provided with a disturbingly 'neutral' preface by a Cambridge don) of Frédéric Reider's* L'Ordre SS, *takes the opportunity it offers to serve up some of the major themes of Holocaust denial, and alludes at the end to another component of post-war fascism, the vision of the SS as the basis of a new supra-national aristocracy on which Europe's regeneration could have been based. Reider's history reproduces some of Himmler's chilling 'secret' speeches to SS henchmen (see Text 88) without a note of condemnation, and bemoans the dilution of the élite qualities of the original order once its ranks were swelled by substandard recruits. The title 'professor' seems to have been con-ferred on Reider by Day himself. On the equally spurious academic credentials attributed to revisionist luminaries Butz and Faurisson, see Eatwell (1991). In granting permission to quote from this article,* Spearhead *stressed that it was printed 'only to maintain free debate on issues on which that kind of debate is not normally these days permitted'.*

The Taking of Power

In 1933 Hitler was made German Chancellor. In 1934 he learned that Ernst Röhm's SA—millions of 'super-rowdies' as Reider calls them—were virtually in open revolt. Then followed the so-called Knight [*sic*] of the Long Knives, in which Himmler's SS executed many of the chiefs of the SA.

By the mid-thirties, the size and power of the SS had mushroomed, Himmler and Heydrich now controlled all German police forces, including Goering's creation, the Gestapo, whose very name even today turns many to 'zero at the bone'—par-ticularly, cynics might add, when the bones in question belong either to reds, pornographers or Hollywood film-producers.

And it is Hollywood we must thank for depicting National Socialist Germany as one vast concentration camp. Professor Reider might have corrected this impression by pointing out a rather dull but recalcitrant fact, albeit one that is a well-kept secret: Germany in the Hitler years employed fewer police per thousand of the population than does 'free', 'democratic' West Germany today—and without the computers and data-banks of the 1980s.

What no-one would dispute is that the SS was merciless in rooting out and crushing communism.[. . .]

As for Jews, these 'were indeed the leaders of the leftist movement', as Reider tells us; but it was never a crime just to be Jewish. Hitler had commissioned the SS to solve the country's Jewish problem equitably and humanely, and the first proposal offered was to encourage Jewish emigration to the then British Mandate of Palestine. Reider casually mentions that, tales of persecution to the contrary, Jews in Germany 'were not at all to go to the Promised Land'.

After war erupted in 1939 the SS tried another approach: Jews were relocated to occupied Poland. Not at all pleased, Poland's Governor-General had the influx halted. Then arose the plan, approved of by both Himmler and Heydrich, to create a Jewish homeland in Madagascar, though this too came to naught.

'Extermination' Legend

Establishment historians insist that the next solution put forward was the alleged 'Final Solution', i.e. the organised liquidation of European Jewry. Reider does not venture as deeply into the barely questioned realm of the 'Holocaust' as, say, Professors Butz and Faurisson have done, but at times he gets close:–

When Goering was tried (at Nuremberg), he writes, 'a directive he had sent to Heydrich was produced. In this he wrote: "I give you all powers to make preparations for . . . a final solution to the Jewish Question in those of the European territories which are under German influence"'. Goering was able to show quite easily that 'final solution' did not necessarily signify destruction or extermination.[. . .]

Allies Had Camps Too

Whatever the precise figure of Jews who died during World War II, none was as a result of Zyklon-B poisoning or any other kind of gassing. German policy in the war was simply to intern Jews in concentration camps on the grounds that their ethnic background made it likely that they would be sympathetic to the enemy. In this respect such a policy was no different to that of the British Government of the time, which interned all nationals of the Axis countries (even including Jews!) and that of the Roosevelt administration in the United States, which set up internment centres not basically different from Germany's concentration camps for the purpose of placing in custody many thousands of US citizens of Japanese descent following the attack on Pearl Harbour and the entry of the US into the war. The German assessment of which people might be a potential 'fifth column' in the country's midst would seem at least a little more logical than the British one, which included Jewish refugees from Hitler merely because Germany was the country of their origins.[. . .]

Raising of German Stock

Separating Jews from Germans made up merely the negative half of Hitler's racial programme; there was a positive side too, which was the improvement of the German péople through the use of the science of eugenics. Within the SS, a racial department called *Rusha* (which also looked after ideological education) ensured the racial worth of all SS members and of their wives and fiancées, encouraging SS members to have large families and promoting German settlements in Eastern Europe.

Founded in 1931 by Walter Darré,[8] *Rusha* operated a stringent selection procedure for this 'association of German men defined according to their Nordic Blood', as the SS described itself. Himmler allowed into the organisation only 15 out of every 100 applicants, and between the years 1933 and 1935 he lopped the branches of an overgrown tree by cashiering some 60,000 less than ideal men. Himmler always sought quality, for he envisaged his Black Order as an aristocracy—an aristocracy based, not on riches or inherited titles, but on blood, on race.[. . .]

Like his Führer, Himmler refuses to be forced into a stereotype—he was both 'peaceful bookworm, discoursing on things of the spirit and . . . implacable political policeman'. He respected hugely the heroes of Germandom; revered, especially, the Order of the Teutonic Knights, those medieval German nobles who warred against the Slavs—took them for his model even: yet his mind remained focused on the problems of this 20th Century.

For The Race

For the past, present and future were all as one to Himmler. He viewed his Northern European race—*our* race—as like an ever flowing river. And whatever actions he took he did for the welfare, as he saw it, of the race.

['The SS Re-Examined', *Spearhead*, 216 (Feb. 1987), 12–14.]

....

c. Historical Revisionism

....

DAVID IRVING

183 **The Bicycle Thief**

....

David Irving is perhaps the world's most prolific and high-profile producer of sophisticated revisionist literature, though his jokes mocking the Holocaust made to German ultra-nationalists gathered under the slogan 'The Truth Set You Free' in 1990 reveal a considerably more 'vulgar' side to his character. His nomination of Rudolf Hess (at one time Hitler's second-in-command) for the Nobel Peace Prize during a lecture tour in 1984 was found distinctly unfunny by the Austrian authorities. As this extract shows, Hitler's War

---

[8] See Text 65.

explicitly denies that the Führer gave the order for the Final Solution, and manipulates evidence to suggest that over-zealous henchmen such as Himmler organized the exterminations behind his back: Hitler's repeated public and private threats to eradicate the Jews from Europe referred simply to a scheme of mass transportation to Madagascar. Irving was awarded a prize by Dr Gerhard Frey (see Text 186) for consistently denying that the Nazis had any systematic policy to commit genocide of the Jews, that the camps were ever used as extermination centres, or that Hitler gave direct orders for the 'Final Solution' (which allegedly only meant mass deportation). He explains the mass killing of Jews carried out by Einsatzkommandos in the East as a symptom of the polycentric nature of the Third Reich, which left local commanders free to commit atrocities on their own initiative.

No documentary evidence exists that Hitler was aware that the Jews were being massacred upon their arrival.[. . .] In most circumstances Hitler was a pragmatist. It would have been unlike him to sanction the use of scarce transport space to move millions of Jews east for no other purpose than liquidating them there; nor would he willingly destroy man-power, for which his industry was crying out. Heinrich Heim recalls one exasperated comment by Hitler when Allied radio broadcast an announcement that the Jews were being exterminated: 'Really, the Jews should be *grateful* to me for wanting nothing more than a bit of hard work from them.' It was Heydrich and the fanatical Gauleiters in the east who were interpreting with brutal thoroughness Hitler's decree that the Jews must 'finally disappear' from Europe; Himmler's personal role is ambivalent. On November 30, 1941, he was summoned to the Wolf's Lair for a secret conference with Hitler, at which the fate of Berlin's Jews was clearly raised. At 1.30 PM Himmler was obliged to telephone from Hitler's bunker to Heydrich the explicit order that Jews were *not to be liquidated*, and the next day Himmler telephoned SS General Oswald Pohl, overall chief of the concentration camp system, with the order: 'Jews are to stay where they are'.

Yet the blood purge continued. The extermination program had gained a momentum of its own.[. . .] The precise mode of 'elimination' met with varying interpretations. Hitler's was unquestionably the authority behind the *expulsion* operations; on whose initiative the grim procedures at the terminal stations of this miserable exodus were adopted, is arguable.[. . .]

Starting in March and April the European Jews were rounded up in occupied France, Holland and Belgium, and in eager Nazi satellite Slovakia; for political reasons Hungary—which had nearly a million Jews—and Romania were not approached yet but were told that their Jewish 'problems' would be left unresolved until the war was over. From Hans Frank's Generalgouvernement of Poland too—beginning with the ghettos of Lublin—the Jews set out eastward under the direction of one of the cruellest SS leaders, Brigadier Odilo Globocnik, the Trieste-born former Gauleiter of Vienna. Upon arrival at Auschwitz and Treblinka, four in every ten were pronounced fit for work; the rest were terminated with a maximum of concealment. Two documents shed some oblique rays of light on the level of responsibility for this. At a cabinet meeting in Cracow on April 9, Hans Frank disclaimed responsibility for the disruption in the work process caused by the order to turn over all Jews for liquidation. 'The directive for the liquidation of the Jews comes from higher up.' In a letter of June 26 it became clear that Himmler was anxious to conceal the massacre, for Globocnik was quoted as being eager to get it over with as quickly as possible in case one day *force majeure* should prevent them completing it: 'You yourself, Reichsführer, once mentioned that you felt the job should be done as quickly as possible if only for reasons of concealment.' The concealment was almost perfect, and Himmler's own papers reveal how he pulled the wool over Hitler's eyes. On September 17, while the murder machinery was operating at peak capacity, the Reichsführer still calmly jotted down in his notes for that day's Führer conference: 'Jewish emigration—how should we proceed?' And March 1943 he was to order a too-explicit statistical report rewritten to remove a stray reference to the massacre of Europe's Jews before it was submitted to the Führer!

The ghastly secrets of Auschwitz and Treblinka were well kept. Goebbels wrote a frank summary of them in his diary on March 27, 1942, but evidently held his tongue when he met Hitler two days later, for he quotes only Hitler's remark: 'The Jew must get out of Europe. If need be, we must resort to the most brutal methods.'[. . .]

As late as July 24, Hitler was still referring at table to his plan to transport the Jews to Madagascar—by now already in British hands—or some other Jewish national home after the war was over.[9]

Hitler still referred to the 'Madagascar plan' in Table Talk, July 24, 1942. SS General Karl Wolff estimated—in a confidential post-war manuscript—that altogether probably only some seventy men, from Himmler down to Höss, were involved in the liquidation program. The only evidence of a 'Führer Order' behind the program came from post-war testimony of SS Major Dieter Wisliceny, Eichmann's thirty-one-year-old adviser on Jewish problems attached to the Slovak government (e.g. in pretrial interrogations at Nuremberg on November 11 and 24, 1945, and a written narrative dated Bratislava, November 18, 1946). He claimed the Slovaks had sent him to Berlin in July or August 1942 to check up on the fate of 33,000 next of kin of the 17,000 able-bodied Jews supplied for the German arms industry. Eichmann admitted to him that the 33,000 had been liquidated, and—said Wisliceny—pulled from his safe a red-bordered Immediate Letter, stamped 'Top State Secret', with Himmler's signature and addressed to Heydrich and Pohl. It read (from memory): 'The Führer has decided that the Final Solution of the Jewish Question is to begin at once. I herewith designate [Heydrich and Pohl] responsible for the execution of this order.' However, there is a marked difference between Wisliceny's 1945 and 1946 recollections of this text; and when years later Eichmann was cross-examined about this in his trial on April 10, 1961, he testified that he had neither received any such written order nor shown one to Wisliceny (who had long since been executed himself). He had only told Wisliceny verbally, 'Heydrich sent for me and informed me that the Führer has ordered the physical annihilation of the Jews'.

This kind of evidence, of course, would not suffice in an English magistrate's court to convict a vagabond of bicycle stealing, let alone assign the responsibility for the mass murder of six million Jews, given the powerful written evidence that Hitler again and again ordered the 'Jewish Problem' set aside until the war was won.

[*Hitler's War* (Hodder & Stoughton: London, 1977), 331–2, 291–392, 858.]

[9] The rest of this extract forms the notes to the reference to Hitler's 'Madagascar plan'.

The true position of Irving on the Final Solution can be gleaned from this item in Focal Point, *the organ of the Focus Policy Group, which he formed as an abortive attempt to create a broad-based international network of ultra-nationalists in the early 1980s. The cover of this issue featured a bronze head of Hitler and bore the headline 'The Voice from beyond Valhalla'. This passage is taken from the transcript, 'never before published', of a stenographer's record of the clarification of his long-term policy which Hitler made in private to 'one of his financial backers' on 21 December 1922 at the Hotel Regina Palace in Munich. The piece is entitled 'Hitler Lays it on the Line' with the heading 'In talk with German financier Hitler revealed his Secret Plans twenty years before he implemented them: Dictatorship, War, Conquest, the Jews'. Here we reproduce only the section concerning the Jews.*

Answers to Some Problems

The Jewish Question: the Jewish question could be dealt with the way that Frederick the Great solved it. He eliminated [*ausgeschaltet*] the Jews from everywhere where they were bound to have a noxious effect, but on the other hand he made demands on them where they could be of use. In our political life the Jews are unquestionably noxious. They are methodically poisoning our people. I always used to regard antisemitism as inhuman but now my own experiences have converted me into the most fanatical enemy of Jewry, in which connection: I combat Jewry not as a religion, but as a race.[. . .]

The Jews have no right to rule, because they are bereft of the slightest spark of organisational talent.

The Jews seek to restructure the nation along caste lines. While an Aryan nation keeps pumping fresh blood from its innermost depths into the highest reaches and thus keeps eternally rejuvenating its substance, the Jews try to divide mankind into castes and this will slowly but surely strangle it to extinction. If you want proof of the harmful effect of caste, look at ancient Egypt and India.

The Catholic church offers the opposite example: without gainsaying its many shortcomings, it forms and reforms its leadership by drawing upon the fresh and unused forces that grow upwards from its depths . . .

Two Possibilities

IT IS CLEAR that there is nothing Jews can do about their character and shortcomings. But in our own case what matters is not whether they are to blame, but whether or not we are obliged to put up with the Jewish yoke any longer.

The lion is a beast of prey.

There's nothing he can do about that—it lies in his nature. But no way is Man obliged to stand for being mauled by a lion; he must save his skin as best he can, even if the lion comes to harm.

A solution of the Jewish Problem must come. If the problem can be solved by common sense, then so much the better for both parties. If not then there are two possibilities: either a bloody conflict or an Armenianisation.

[*The Turks are claimed to have secretly liquidated 1,500,000 Armenians at the beginning of this century.*][10]

['Hitler Lays it on the Line', *Focal Point*, 31 May 1983, 3, 5–6.]

185 ERNST NOLTE
....
From Class War to Race War

Ernst Nolte has the curious distinction of having not only written one of the most famous definitions of fascism in his Three Faces of Fascism *(1965), but of having indirectly contributed to historical revisionism, one of its post-war discourses. As early as 1974 comments in his* Deutschland und der Kalte Krieg *[Germany and the Cold War] presented the atrocities committed under Hitler as typical of all modern states undergoing a period of vigorous expansion and internal reconstruction: mass murder thus becomes a symptom of national vitality. At the height of the intense debate over how best to interpret the place of Nazism in Germany's history (known as the Historikerstreit), he then produced a scholarly work portraying the Third Reich as a symbiotic product of Stalin's terror state, its eugenic and genocidal policies not the result of its own ideological dynamics, but a mere counterpart to the Gulags.*

In the ideology of National Socialism everything was repudiated which had existed as a long-term trend in the West before being taken over by communism. Yet the world dominion of the Germanic or Aryan Man for which it strove was nothing other than the perpetuation of European domination in the world which was in the process of decaying from within, because it was exporting throughout the world ideas and processes which within Europe had led to the spread of the Industrial Revolution from England, and had resulted in the formation of nation-states from areas which had previously been neither independent nor unified. What the struggle against the Jews meant was precisely this: that it was imperative to fight simultaneously against the messianic claims of Bolshevism and Western *decadence* so as to free the world from a twin evil whose common origin people believed they had identified in this people. In as far as National Socialism was an ideology and a messianic creed, it therefore attacked whatever was genuinely common to Bolshevism and *the West*, such as the commitment to pacifism, which was countered by the celebration of war for its own sake.[. . .]

[Himmler] must have been thinking of the Soviet Union when he made one of the most revealing of his pronouncements with which he wanted to justify the killing of the Jews, for this was something which could not have derived simply from the experience of the collapse of the Second Reich or even from the setting up

---

[10] Irving's own note.

of the Soviet Republic in Munich: 'We had the moral right, we had the duty to our people to murder this people which wanted to murder us.'[11]

The empirical truth underlying this pronouncement is that the party of Bolsheviks had in fact undertaken to bring down the *world's bourgeoisie*. It was also true that the fall of the Russian bourgeoisie through total extermination was not far off. There are also good grounds for maintaining that, like countless other petty bourgeois and skilled workers, Himmler confounded the expectations of the Bolsheviks by choosing to side with the *bourgeoisie* rather than the *working masses*. As a result the period became *a period of fascism* and of European civil war.[. . .] The most serious historical and at the same time moral injustice lay in the fact that this great clash of classes and cultures was understood as a fight to the death between two peoples, the Germans and the Jews. The only element of truth this contained was that special circumstances and conditions had meant that a conspicuous number of Jews took part in the Russian Revolution, most of whom no longer saw themselves as Jews anyway. But many other Jews had in fact fallen victims to this revolution, or else been deprived of their rights and driven into emigration. Hardly any other group was affected as much as Jewish communists by Stalin's Great Purge. But the Jews in the West were as differentiated in the party affiliations as the society in which they lived. By making *the Jews* responsible for a process which had caused them to panic, Hitler and Himmler gave a new dimension to the concept of destruction pioneered by the Bolsheviks and eclipsed those genuine ideologues through the awfulness of their deeds by replacing social premises with biological ones.

[*Der europäische Bürgerkrieg* [The European Civil War] (Propyläen Verlag: Berlin, 1987), 535, 544–5.]

GERHARD FREY

186 Truth and Fiction[12]

Over the last twenty years Munich publisher Dr. Gerhard Frey has built his Deutsche Volksunion into the most important umbrella organization for the dissemination of extreme right and revisionist propaganda in Germany. It comprises six 'action communities' for lobbying on various issues (e.g. abortion, the environment), a publishing house, and two newspapers. Since 1987 it has also operated as a 'Germany First' electoral party under the name DVU—Liste D. This article from its weekly paper Deutsche Wochen-Zeitung *was written at the time of the trial of Klaus Barbie, head of the SS in Lyons during the war, when the need to relativize Nazi atrocities and minimize any sense of national guilt was particularly strong.*

On Monday the trial by jury began in Lyons before a French court of Klaus Barbie, who was the German head of the police in Lyons during the Second World War

---

[11] See Text 88.
[12] Frey has chosen as the heading for his article the title of Goethe's autobiographical novel *Dichtung und Wahrheit*, which translates into English both as *Poetry and Truth* and *Truth and Fiction*.

and is accused of the deportation and death of a large number of people. Barbie was extradited to France four years ago in circumstances reminiscent of a kidnapping.[. . .] A French press which is not renowned for its goodwill to Germany is anticipating the proceedings of Barbie's trial with conspicuous unease.[. . .] *Liberation* comes to the realization that 'The Federal Republic has seen itself for the last ten years obliged to recognize its collective guilt only to discover that the France which is making the accusation still has some dirty linen of its own.' Yet no one dares tell the whole truth:

1. Even after the Thirty Years War when the German people was reduced from a population of about 30 million to 7 million, the belligerents drew a line under the orgy of mass murder in the Peace of Munich: *tabula rasa*.[. . .] After the Second World War the victors only gave an amnesty to their own criminals, including the murderers who caused the deaths of more than 6 million Germans, either in the Allied prisoner of war camps or through the crime against humanity of mass expulsions and terror-bombing.

2. The victors of the last war are clearly intent on destroying the national identity of the German people, as can be seen from the way accusations of collective guilt and collective responsibility made exclusively against the Germans have been increasing in regularity over the last few years.[. . .]

3. On the other hand it does not bother France in the least that at the time of the so-called Liberation between 250,000 and a million human beings were killed, often in appalling agony, or that as a result of its brutal colonial policy Paris has a terrible blood guilt on its conscience (in the Algerian War alone half a million of the native population were tortured to death or executed).

4. It is also true that the fraternal alliance of the French with the German conquerors posed no problems from 1940 till at least 1942.[. . .]

5. The relentless perpetuation of extreme anti-German versions of the past, in which war-crime trials and the exercises in contrition of influential German politicians play a major role, is of crucial importance for those who commit crimes in our age or have done so in the past. For example Washington does not turn a hair at the extermination and exploitation of so many Indian nations, but instead builds a Holocaust museum dedicated to the German persecution of the Jews at the expense of DM 200 million. Moscow does not remember a single one of the more than a hundred million corpses which litter the path of Soviet imperialism from the glorious October Revolution onwards. Instead, like Chancellor Kohl, it identifies evil with the years 1933–45. And thus both the conquerors and their helpers all become honourable people.

6. Finally there is that fact that Bonn's policy of an unconditional acknowledgement of sole and total guilt, which means that even unborn generations will bear the burden of German Collective Guilt, is leading to ever more comprehensive and outrageous demands (for example Warsaw would now like, 'compensation' on top of the East Germany that has been stolen from us and the millions in reparations already received). It is easy to see that the policies pursued by West Germany, and this goes for the CDU and FDP as well, are depriving the population of the Federal

Republic of equal rights with the rest of the international community for years to come, perhaps for ever.

['Der Fall Barbie—Dichtung und Wahrheit' [The Barbie Case—Truth and Fiction], *Deutsche Wochen-Zeitung*, 29/21 (15 May 1987), 1.]

d. Eurofascism

THE MALMÖ MANIFESTO

 187   The European Revolution

The Malmö conference of May 1951, which brought together the internationalist fascists from fourteen European countries, succeeded in founding the 'Malmö International', or European Social Movement, to which sixteen national movements were affiliated. Despite divisions over the degree of anti-Semitism and active racism to adopt, delegates had little difficulty agreeing that the role of a regenerated Europe was to act as a citadel of healthy values to ward off the threat posed by the two superpowers, a position expressed in this manifesto of ESM goals, one of the first major post-war statements of Eurofascism.

1. Defence of Western culture against communism;
2. Creation of the European Empire;
3. Prices and salaries controlled throughout the European Empire;
4. The armed forces of all countries under the control of the central government of the Empire;
5. The right for colonial peoples to enter the Empire once they have attained a certain educational and economic level;
6. The election of heads of government through plebiscite;
7. Regulation of social and economic life through the organs of a corporate State;
8. The aim of education will be to produce men and women who are *strong*;
9. The co-operation of idealists who found themselves on either sides of the lines during the last war will be sought;
10. The aim of this European Revolution will be the spiritual regeneration of man, society, and the State.

[*Droit et Liberté*, 2 June 1951.]

JULIUS EVOLA

188   The True Europe's Revolt against the Modern World

Even before the war Evola was an outspoken critic of narrow nationalism, and was urging the Fascist regime to follow the example of the Nazis in their uncompromising commitment to expansionism, hierarchy, and militarism. In 1940 and 1941 he published essays on 'the European idea', the need for a 'European law', and the vision that a new version of the State and empire could result from the symbiosis of the Roman and the Germanic. After the war, though the end of the kali yuga *(the black age of decadence) was now no longer in sight, he continued to campaign for a Europe united not on Western (that is, American) premisses, but on those of the 'eternal' spiritual values of 'the Tradition'. His essays on the subject have become classics not just for Evolians, but for Italian neo-fascists, Third Positionists (seeking a third, allegedly un-Nazi way between capitalism and communism), and the New Right. This essay, for example, is taken from the foremost organ of New Right political analysis in Britain (see Text 192).*

The first political step in forging a united Europe would be the withdrawal of all European governments from the United Nations, a hypocritical organisation if there ever was.[. . .]

The ground for a European initiative must be carefully prepared; but the problems of concrete political tactics fall outside the scope of this essay. Here we can only point to what we believe must be the form and the spiritual and doctrinal basis of united Europe.

'Federalist' and 'associative' solutions, economic and military co-operation—these are all the manifestation of presuppositions about the *organic* character of Europe (or the lack of it). The condition of a truly *European* entity must be the binding force of an idea and tradition with which Europe is irrevocably linked. Some argue that the nation state, being not divinely ordained but the creation of determined groups successfully rising to a historical challenge, is a model for the merging European nation. According to this view the spiritual precondition for a united Europe exists in the myth of a common destiny defended by the 'national revolutionary' groups of Europe. This view is inadequate. The birth of the European nations was largely the work of dynasties representing a tradition of loyalty to a particular crown. In any case, the factors which created the European nations have been the very ones which have maintained European *disunity* from the Hundred Years War to the present day.

Among those who possess a spiritual and traditional understanding of Europe we can distinguish between those who believe in an *Imperium* of the kind referred to above, and those who talk of Europe as a *nation*. The concept of nationhood is in my opinion inappropriate. The notion of European unity is spiritual and supranational. Homeland nation, ethnic group subsist at an essentially naturalistic 'physical' level. Europe (*Europa una*) should be something more than this. The old nationalisms and resentments are only grafted onto Europe when a particular national domination is imposed by one nation upon the rest of Europe. The European *Imperium* will belong to a higher order than the parts which compose it, and to be European should be conceived as being something qualitatively different from being Italian. Prussian, Basque, Finnish, Scottish or Hungarian, something which appeals to a different aspect of our character. A European *nation* implies the levelling and cancelling of all 'rival' nations in or beyond Europe.[. . .]

So far as 'European culture' is concerned it is these days the stamping-ground of the pragmatic European, the liberal, humanist intellectual. His 'European culture' is an appendage of 'democracy' and the 'Free World'. In this sense 'culture' is the stock-in-trade of the so-called 'aristocrat of thought', in reality the clothing of the parvenu, his badge of success. A genuine aristocracy of the intellect would not in any case be adequate for the task in hand; the re-animation of the European will and the sustaining of a revolutionary elite who could make this a political possibility. What is more, every time that we try to give the notion of 'European culture' concrete significance, we seem to run up against innumerable 'interpretations' which leave us with nothing conclusive at all. Everyone has their own idea about what European culture is and many Europeans feel reticent or even guilty about championing it and so the parvenus can speculate to their hearts' content in the reviews and colour supplements about all the latest developments in this or that field of art in such a way that 'culture' becomes entirely divorced from the 'serious world', from what matters. Ironically, much of what the defenders of culture admire plays a major role in helping to bring about a spiritual crisis and lack of confidence in European culture. The 'Westernisation' of the world has meant that this decomposition extends across the world—thus Europe, from illuminism to communism has become the breeding ground of the very forces which work to destroy everything which is specifically European.[. . .]

We must create a 'unity of fighters'. That is a pre-requisite. To set a vision of the world and of Europe aside as 'irrelevant' would be to sink into the morass of political partisan politics, a cynical affair without identity, without spiritual meaning. A united Europe, without a communal spiritual identity and sense of direction would become just one more power bloc. In what way would such a United States of Europe be spiritually distinct from the United States of America or China or be anything nobler than the organisation of African Unity? Europe must not be a stage towards the Westernisation of the world but a move against it, in fact a revolt against the modern world in favour of what is nobler, higher, more truly *human*.

['United Europe: The Spiritual Prerequisite', *Scorpion*, 9 (1986), 18–20; adapted from *Gli uomini e le rovine* [Men and the Ruins] (Giovanni Volpe: Rome, 1972; 1st edn. 1953), 239–46.]

OSWALD MOSLEY
. . . .
189 **Europe a Nation**

Until the 1970s Britain's major contributor to Eurofascism was Oswald Mosley. His geopolitical vision of a revitalized Europe using Africa as a resource base was nothing new. It had been entertained by Nazi ideologues such as Alfred Rosenberg and Werner Daitz when the war in the East started going against the Wehrmacht, was adopted as official policy by the Republican Fascist Party in November 1943, and had been explored at length by the former French fascist Georges Valois in his 1931 work War or Revolution. *However, to propose it just when a 'wind of change' was ushering in an irresistible movement of decolonization was a remarkable exercise in wishful thinking even by fascist standards.*

EUROPE a Nation is an idea which anyone can understand. It is simple, but should not on that account be rejected; most decisive, root ideas are simple. Ask any child: what is a nation? He will probably reply, a nation has a government. And, in fact, this is the right answer, for the first thing to note about a nation is that it is a country consisting of a people with their own government. Many deeper reflections naturally follow; questions of geography, race, history, which contributed to the evolution of this fact, a people with a government which is a nation. But the simple, decisive point which defines as nation, is that it has a government. That is why the dividing question of modern Europe is whether or not we desire a European government. It is the purpose of this book to answer, yes. And in the end all will find it necessary to make up their minds on which side of this question they stand.[. . .]

In the end the only way to get great things done is to do things in a great way. If we meet a vital necessity with a clear decisive idea which everyone can understand and which evokes a high ideal, the people will respond directly they see the necessity, understand the plan, and feel the appeal of a moving cause. That is why in life it is often easier to get great things done than to get small things managed. In a supreme moment, like the wars of the past, the peoples of Europe were capable of every exertion and of every sacrifice. There is now a real need to evoke the same fervent spirit for a decisive act, not of destruction but of construction, for a work not of division and death, but of union and life. This can only be done by an idea which is clear, and an idea which is great. Europe a Nation alone can awaken the vital response of the peoples.[. . .]

If the countries of the West are certain to be confronted on world markets with a competition they cannot face, what is the remedy? The only possible answer is to withdraw from world markets into a viable economy, which is large enough to contain its own essential supplies and to provide its own markets. The only one available is Europe–Africa. South America is a conceivable economic alternative to Africa, but no one in the West can afford to leave a vacuum in Africa to be filled by communism, and a too close economic tie-up between Europe and South America can create political difficulties with North America which it is in the interests of the whole West to avoid. South America would appear to be rather a meeting ground for both the economics and the cultures of Europe and America.

So the creation of a Europe–African economy with considerable speed is now vital to the life of Europe.[. . .] The civilisation we intend to create must be durable and humane. This means that the Blacks cannot be subjected to the Whites in Africa, and exploited as a pool of cheap, inferior labour. There is plenty of room for both White and Black in Africa, which is still relatively an empty continent. There is ample room for two nations, each with access to the necessary wealth for a full life and a high standard. But they must be separate nations if we are not to revert to the sweating and exploitation of the old colonialism. Whatever illusory guarantees of political liberty are given to backward peoples—even if the resistance of the White population to being in a numerical minority could be overcome, and it cannot be surmounted without the force which none are prepared to use—the less advanced peoples will in practical experience again become the bondsmen of the more advanced, if they live among them. An endless heritage of racial hatred will be the result, culminating in an explosion which will be repressed with bloodshed. So it is necessary to create two nations in Africa, and no one can claim that the necessary space or wealth of potential foodstuffs and raw material are not there. Again, this is a task which is out of the question for the weak individual nations of Europe, but by no means beyond the strength and power of a united Europe.[. . .]

From every sphere of enquiry we return to our original questions: how can something so big as Europe–Africa be made at all without European Government; how can it be done without European Government in the short time available which is certainly much less than the fifteen years now believed to be necessary to make even the common European market; and what hope is there of anything short of a united Europe with a Europe–African economy providing a solution for the economic problems now facing the nations of Western Europe? Something so big cannot be done with such speed without real unity. And real unity now means the European Government of Europe a Nation. We must now think, feel, act as Europeans.

['Europe a Nation', in *Europe: Faith and Plan* (Euphorion Books: London, 1958), 18–19, 29, 35, 38.]

e. The New Right

ALAIN DE BENOIST

190   Regenerating History

The (palingenetic as opposed to monetarist) New Right is made up of scores of intellectuals, autodidacts, and publicists from every corner of the Europeanized world. By far its most prestigious ideologue is Alain de Benoist, awarded a prize by the Académie Française in 1978 for Vu de droite, *a dense anthology of short essays on themes and thinkers which, to the initiated, cumulatively delegitimize many assumptions of liberal democracy. This passage brings out the typically fascist sense of living through the watershed between a played-out system based on egalitarianism and a new phase of history which will inaugurate cultural rebirth and forge once more into a powerful civilization the Europe divided by Roosevelt, Churchill, and Stalin at the Yalta Conference in 1945 (the political and economic dynamics of this transformation are, of course, left vague). It was translated by a major representative of the Italian New Right (Nuova Destra), Marco Tarchi, whose edition has been used here rather than the French, to emphasize the internationalization of new currents of neo-fascist thought.*

What is the greatest threat today? It is the progressive disappearance of diversity from the world. The levelling-down of people, the reduction of all *cultures* to a *world civilization* made up of what is most *common*. It can be seen already how from one side of the planet to the other the same types of construction are being put up and the same mental habits are being engrained. Holiday Inn and Howard Johnson are the templates for the transformation of the world into a grey uniformity. I have travelled widely, on several continents. The *joy* which is experienced during a journey derives from seeing differentiated ways of living which are still well rooted, in seeing different people living according to their own rhythm, with a different skin colour, another culture, another mentality—and that they are proud of their *difference*. I believe that this diversity is the wealth of the world, and that egalitarianism is killing it. For this it is important not just to respect others but to keep alive everywhere the most legitimate desire there can be: the desire to affirm a personality which is unlike any other, to defend a heritage, to govern oneself in accordance with what one is. And this implies a head-on clash both with a pseudo-antiracism which denies differences and with a dangerous racism which is nothing less than the rejection of the Other, the rejection of diversity.

We live today in a *blocked* society. Globally speaking we are only now beginning to become aware of ways to break out of the order established at Yalta. Nationally speaking there has never been such marked divisions between various political factions in peacetime. Philosophically and ideologically, we oscillate constantly between different extremes without managing to find a balance. The cause and remedy for this situation is to be located within man. To say that our society is in crisis is just a platitude. Man *is a crisis*. He is a tragedy. In him nothing is ever definitively *said*. Man must constantly find within himself the theme of a new discourse corresponding to a new way of being in the world, a new *form* of his humanity. Man is in crisis through the very fact that he exists. The originality of our age does not lie in this fact. The originality—the sad originality—of our age lies in the fact that for the first time man is retreating in the face of the implications which flow from his instinctive desire and will to resolve the crisis. For the first time man believes that he is overwhelmed by the problems. And indeed they do overwhelm him *in as far as he believes they do*, when in fact they originate within him, and fall within the range and scope of the solutions which he carries within himself.[. . .]

The old right in France has always been reactionary.[. . .] It is a type of attitude which has always proved sterile. History repeats itself but never serves up the same dish twice. It offers a wealth of lessons not because it allows us to know what will happen, but because it helps us rediscover the *spirit* which has produced a certain type of event. This is what Nietzsche meant when, in the very moment he was preaching the eternal return, he declared, 'it is impossible to bring back the Greeks'. To spell this out: the Greek miracle cannot be repeated,[13] but if we allow ourselves to be imbued with the spirit which produced it we will perhaps be able to create something analogous. It is what we could define the *regeneration* of history.[. . .]

If egalitarianism is reaching its '*final* stage of affirmation', what will succeed it will necessarily be something different. Moreover, if the present world is the materialization of the end of a cycle, it is equally clear that the only source of inspiration possible for what must be born is something which has preceded what has just occurred. The projective force for the future resides in the *spirit* of the

[13] i.e. the achievements of Greek civilization and culture.

remotest past. The 'positive nihilism'[14] of Nietzsche has only one sense: one can only build on a site which has been completely cleared and levelled. There are those who do not want to construct (a certain kind of left) and do not want to raze to the ground (a certain right). In my view both these two attitudes are to be condemned. If a new right is to be brought into being we have to start from scratch. And given the time which has to be made up it will need about a century to succeed. Which means there is not a minute to lose.

[*Le idee a posto* (Akropolis: Naples, 1983), 76–81; translation of *Les Idées à l'endroit* [Ideas Put Right] (Albin Michel: Paris, 1980).]

PIERRE KREBS

191 The Metapolitical Rebirth of Europe

The most prolific ideologue of Germany's New Right (Neue Rechte) is Pierre Krebs. Armed with a clutch of French and German qualifications ranging from law and Scandinavian philology to journalism, he has edited a review of 'metapolitics', written numerous books on the issues in which literature, philosophy, and politics meet, and devoted his publicistic and editorial energies to establishing the premises for a 'cultural revolution'. This involves the rejection of egalitarianism for 'differentiation', Judaeo-Christianity for Indo-Europeanism, Enlightenment humanism for 'organic humanism', and pluralism and racial mixing ('Pan-mixie') for the right of peoples to have a separate identity. In 1980 he founded the Thule Seminar (its name peculiarly reminiscent of the Thule Society which had deep links with the early Nazi Party) to help bring about an 'all-encompassing European rebirth'. In this passage he articulates the theme of 'right-wing Gramscianism'—the idea that 'metapolitical' cultural transformation is the precondition for political transformation—beloved of the European New Right.

An Italian Marxist, Antonio Gramsci, was the first to understand that the State is not confined to a political apparatus. In fact he established that the political apparatus runs parallel to the so-called civil apparatus. In other words, each political apparatus is reinforced by a civil consensus, the psychological support of the masses. This psychological support expresses itself through a consensus on the level of culture, world-view and ethos. In order to exist at all, political power is thus dependent on a cultural power diffused within the masses. On the basis of this analysis Gramsci understood why Marxists could not take over power in bourgeois democracies: they did not have cultural power. To be precise, it is impossible to overthrow a political apparatus without previously having gained control of cultural power. The assent of the people must be won first: their ideas, ethos, ways of thinking, the value-system, art, education have to be worked on and modified. Only when people feel the need for change as a self-evident necessity will the existing political

[14] Cf. the concept of 'German nihilism' in Text 193.

power, now detached from the general consensus, start crumbling and be overthrown. Metapolitics can be seen as the revolutionary war fought out on the level of world-views, ways of thinking, and culture.[. . .]

It is precisely the metapolitical level which is our starting-point. We want to take over the laboratories of thinking. Hence our task is to oppose the egalitarian ethos and egalitarian socio-economic thinking with a world-view based on differentiation: this means an ethic and a socio-economic theory which respects the right to be different. We want to create the system of values and attitudes necessary for gaining control of cultural power.

Our strategy is dictated neither by the immediate contingencies of reality nor the superficial upheavals of political life. We are not interested in political factions but in attitudes to life. Commentators will carry on writing irrelevant articles categorizing us under 'New Right' but also under 'left-wing'. Such terms are pathetic and leave us cold, for neither the right nor the left are our concern. It is only basic attitudes to life which people have that interest us. And all those who are aware of the American as well as of the Soviet danger, who realize the absolute necessity of the cultural rebirth of Europe as the harbinger of its political wakening, who feel rooted in a people and a destiny, are our friends and allies, irrespective of their political and ideological views. What motivates us and what we are striving for cannot be accommodated within the activities of a political party, but—and we insist on this point—solely within the framework of a metapolitical, exclusively cultural project. A programme which sets out once again to make us conscious of our identity through awakening the memory of our future, as it were. In this way we aim to prepare the ground for what is to come.

We have defined our programme as the total rebirth of Europe. We have also established the strategy for realizing this project: metapolitics and cultural war. We still have to consider the basis and material framework within which this programme can be carried out: the Thule Seminar, a New School of European culture.

The tragedy of the contemporary world is the tragedy of disloyalty: the uprooting of every culture, estrangement from our true natures, the atomization of man, the levelling of values, the uniformity of life. A critical and exhaustive engagement with modern knowledge—from philosophy to ethology, from anthropology to sociology, from the natural sciences to history and educational theory—if carried out with the appropriate intellectual rigour and sound empirical methodology, can only contribute to throwing light on the general confusion of the world. It is with such fundamental considerations that the Thule Seminar is concerned. Open to the intellectual and spiritual life of our age, yet critical of all ideological dogmas, its research is based on a sense of commitment to Western culture. The Thule Seminar is concerned with clarifying the basic questions at the heart of the movement of ideas, with redefining the key cultural concepts, and the discovery of new alternatives to the core problems of the age.[. . .] The Thule Seminar proclaims a European Europe which must become aware of its identity and its destiny.

[*Die europäische Wiedergeburt* [The European Rebirth] (Grabert: Tübingen, 1982), 82–6, 89.]

A Breath of Fresh Air

Scorpion was founded in 1981 (originally under the name National Democrat*) and is the most important (if not only) British organ of the New Right, even if it has tended to blend indiscriminately the (logically incompatible) Evolian Traditionalism with the pseudo-Nietzschean 'nominalism' of GRECE. As long as the Soviet system lasted this magazine was a regular mouthpiece for the New Right's vision of a European Empire, a bulwark of spiritual values warding off the materialism of the USA and the USSR. Its other major theme is the preservation of Europe's distinctive 'ethnies'. Its founder, Michael Walker, had been a National Front organizer for central London, but in 1984 started weaving an apparently independent New Right strand of fascism as part of the diversification which occurred within the movement once its leadership was no longer dominated by neo-Nazis. This is Walker's own account of GRECE.*

The original and still most important group belonging to what is termed the European New Right is GRECE, a cultural organisation based in Paris. The letters stand for *Le Groupement de Recherche et d'Études pour la Civilisation Européenne* (The centre for the study and search [*sic*] for European civilisation). The word is an acronym for the French word for Greece, which underlines the group's strong sense of attachment to the Greek heritage in particular, with its cult of heroism, elitism and beauty, and perhaps most importantly, its pagan values and outlook. The group was created on 5th May 1968 by the sons and daughters of mainly very conservative parents.[. . .]

The starting-point of GRECE was to undertake an analysis of the *meaning* of ideas. They wished to preserve an identity, a collective identity as Europeans: on that they were agreed from the beginning; but that was all. Nothing else would be 'assumed', not the sanctity of the White race, not the need to defend Christendom, not the Western world, nor NATO, nor any of the other bastions of the old right. All would be examined critically in order to grasp their completing meaning. Taking its example from Nietzsche's creation of a genealogy of morality, GRECE examined the history of ideas in order to better understand the relevance of each idea in the modern world.[. . .]

Pierre Vial, the general secretary of GRECE, Michel Marmin, film critic and leading GRECE member, and Guillaume Faye, a new and passionate advocate of GRECE, confirmed the total break of the New Right with one of the most sacred cows of all in the old right corral; the West. The leading article in that issue of *Éléments* was written by Guillaume Faye: 'This is the hideous face of a civilisation, which, with an implacable logic, has forced itself onto every culture, gradually levelling them, bringing all peoples into the gamut of the one-world system. What use is the cry "Yanks out!" when those who shout the slogans are Levi customers? More successfully than Soviet Marxism this civilisation is realising the project of abolishing human history in order to ensure the perpetual well-being of bourgeois man . . . This system, this civilisation, which is eradicating the identity of the peoples of Asia, Africa, Europe and the Americas has a name: it is called Western civilisation.'[. . .]

Alain de Benoist has adopted a famous aphorism of Oscar Wilde for his own use: the *societé marchande*[15] is one which knows the price of everything and the value of nothing. This is echoed in Faye's assessment of liberalism as the creed which 'tolerates everything and respects nothing'. To quote Robert de Herte again: 'The inherent materialism of liberalism and Marxism is nothing other than the dissolution of the soul, the abandonment of all human motivation, which cannot be rationalised in terms of personal interest or immediate existence. The only world which is permitted to impinge on our minds is the here-and-now of *my* world. There exists no place in 'my' world for what has a value *beyond me*, which constrains me, which gives me a *form*. The 'rule of quantity', to use René Guénon's expression, is formless, *hic et nunc*, nothing more. The paradigm of decadence: a falling off from spiritual to material, from soul to spirit, to body alone: the era of *homo economicus*, linked closely to the coming of the bourgeois, the bourgeois not so much as the representative of a *class* as a type who imposes a certain *system of values*. The aristocrat seeks to preserve what he *is*, the bourgeois what he *has*.'[. . .]

The New Right can be described as *a revolt against the formless*: formless politics formless culture, formless values. That modern society pays scant attention to measure, order, style, is self-evident, nowhere more so than in the United States. According to the New Right, utility and ugliness are the deadly twins of the Western world. When a society reduces all facets of life to the dictatorship of economics, then beauty, honour, loyalty—in a word everything we call intangible—is made tangible, rentable, and thus destroyed. If it is true that style maketh the man, then the man created by the modern world is inhuman, deprived of what is specifically human, cultural, and reduced to his materiality.[. . .]

Above all GRECE loves life and with irrational resilience will champion the cause of excellence against the mediocrity of the egalitarians and the hypocrisy of the sectarians. For those of us who felt disillusioned and depressed by the level of political and philosophical debate in a Europe which is rapidly losing all identity, the French New Right has initiated a kind of *revolution*. We need to think through all our nations again from the beginning. Someone has opened the windows and brought a fresh breeze into a muggy, malodorous study.

['Spotlight on the New Right', *Scorpion*, 10 (Autumn 1986), 8–14.]

....

f. The Conservative Revolution

....

ARMIN MOHLER
193 **German Nihilism**

A recurrent source of inspiration for the New Right is the rich seam of non-Nazi German fascism of the inter-war period exhaustively explored and classified by Armin Mohler in a

---

[15] 'Market society'.

doctoral thesis written under Jaspers in the late 1940s. It was Mohler who popularized the term 'Conservative Revolution' for this species of fascism (see Texts 52, 53, 57), and who identified it with a 'healthy' ultra-right revolution in contrast to the Hitlerian 'travesty' (he called its writers 'the Trotskyites of the German Revolution'). In this passage from the book, based on the original thesis, what emerges is the typically fascist sense of living at a watershed between an age of liberal decadence and a rebirth which could come at any moment.

We posited as the premiss of this investigation that we find ourselves in an inter-regnum in which an old order has broken down and a new order is not yet visible.[. . .] We have described this breakdown as a crumbling of the central position that Christianity occupied as the force which determined everything, including what grew up in opposition to it and which for about one thousand years has conditioned the structuring of the West in a changing interaction with the classical heritage and the dynamism of peoples who entered history for the first time.[. . .]

The present work is being written in a second post-war period in which the ideas of the Enlightenment and the French Revolution have flared up again but have been called into question even faster than after the first war, and in which all intellectual activity henceforth is destined to take place under the sign of Nietzsche.[. . .]

In the context of our investigation of the 'Conservative Revolution' we are basically concerned with the type of nihilist who consciously takes action filled with a sense of moral responsibility and with positive faith in the possibility of breaking through. It is this type of nihilist which, for lack of a better term, we want to call 'German'.[. . .] The most impressive document of this 'German nihilism' in its fully developed form is the first edition of *Das abenteuerliche Herz* [The Adventurous Heart] by Ernst Jünger[16].[. . .] In it we find the expression which most succinctly sums up the ambivalence of negation and affirmation we have referred to: 'In times of sickness, of defeat, poisons become medicines . . .'.[. . .] It is the lonely, adventurous heart alone which, now that traditional connections have broken down and become meaningless, must seek out the new way of connecting up with the world on the other side of isolation.[. . .] 'For a long time now we have been marching towards a *magic zero*, which can only be passed beyond by someone who has access to other, invisible sources of energy.'[17] At this point, at the magic zero, we get to the heart of 'German nihilism'. It is the belief in unconditional destruction which suddenly metamorphoses into its opposite [*umschlagen*]: unconditional creation. For 'the essential core does not decay [. . .] Our hope is placed [. . .] in what is left over.'

Destruction metamorphoses into creation—the word 'metamorphosis' [*Umschlag*] here is a characteristically German word, above all particularly characteristic of the type of thinking we are exploring. It originates in a mind-set for which spheres that in other contexts are carefully kept separate, are no longer differentiated clearly if at all, for which things normally considered in opposition to each other are seen as two sides of a single entity.

The 'metamorphosis into the opposite' which the nihilist sees at the end of his path is probably the most difficult aspect of the process we are attempting to

[16] See Text 54.
[17] The quotation is from Ernst Jünger, *Das abenteuerliche Herz* (1929).

describe here, and is something which even more than the others can only be evoked allusively.

According to the nihilist, the modern age cannot stop plunging ever faster into the abyss by changing course or by slowing down, but only by transcending it altogether on another plane—a transcendence which leads to a metamorphosis into the opposite.[. . .]

As far as the authors under consideration are concerned there is no passage in which the metamorphosis is presented as having already occurred or is prophesied as taking place in a prescribed year in the future. Rather the metamorphosis from negative to positive seems for those who think cyclically to be a process which individuals are continually experiencing down through the age of the 'linear' view of time and will continue to carry out. The assumption that there could be a single, all-embracing metamorphosis would of course imply an acknowledgement of the reality of the 'linear' world to be 'transcended'. However those who think in terms of cyclic time consider the 'linear' world an optical illusion, whereas *their* world is always present and is only lost sight of when eyes are fixed exclusively in that single direction.[. . .]

This is the basis for understanding the curious phenomenon of 'rebirths' which are one of the essential spiritual characteristics of our time. There have been 'renaissances' for centuries: a complete list of all those postulated from the 'Carolingian renaissance' onwards would be amazingly long. But these are 'induced' rebirths which have a limited impact, and mostly affect the external forms of art and science.[. . .] Once the parenthesis of the 'linear' historical period starts losing its universal validity, however, sunken worlds seem to burst through the smooth surface created by the 'linear' world-view on all sides. These rebirths have something irresistible about them and a force which stirs from the depths, both qualities which earlier renaissances did not have in anything like the same degree.

We have gone into the image of the return [*Wiederkehr*] in so much detail because it provides us with a key image for the entire 'Conservative Revolution'. It is the only starting-point which makes most of its pronouncements fully comprehensible, even if all its representatives were not fully aware of its relevance. And where such individuals still cling to outmoded conceptions—which is not surprising in this time of transitions and intermediary stages—they might try to compare their pronouncements with this image.[. . .] It is the conception of return which is the starting-point to any attempt to understand what meaning the word 'conservative' assumes for the 'Conservative Revolution'.[. . .] The term has established itself as a blanket term for all attitudes which deny progress, and has become a central term for the 'Conservative Revolution' as well. Thus we will ignore all meanings it has acquired outside this context and will only be concerned with what 'conservative' means within the movements under consideration.[. . .]

It would be false to see in this 'Conservative Revolution' something approximating to 'reform'. Apart from the fact that 'reform' is always something unbloody, while it does not surprise these conservatives that birth has to be paid for with destruction, 'reform' involves something being added on to what is already there. For the conservative it is already there and 'revolution' can only result from a restructuring of what is already there.[. . .]

In the 'Conservative Revolution' there exists a will to a violent change of certain conditions which justifies the use of the word 'revolution' and which is again and again referred to by its opponents as 'revolutionary'.[. . .]

> [*Die Konservative Revolution in Deutschland 1918–1932* (Friedrich Vorwerk Verlag: Stuttgart, 1950), 117, 121, 127–30, 137, 142, 147, 149–51.]

LOUIS DUPEUX

194 The Will to Modernity of the Conservative Revolution

Liberals and socialists naïve enough to consider their own scheme of human progress to be the only one which is 'rational' or viable often tend to see fascism as a form of 'cultural pessimism', as intrinsically reactionary, backward-looking, or 'anti-modern'. Such assumptions are profoundly called into question in the impressively scholarly paper from which this passage is drawn. It was given by Louis Dupeux to a conference on Cultural Pessimism, Conservative Revolution and Modernity held by the Groupe Français d'Étude de la 'Révolution Conservatrice' Allemande in March 1981. The proceedings were published first in the Strasburg-based Revue d'Allemagne, *then in* Diorama letterario, *one of Italy's more important New Right publications closely associated with the ideological van-guard of the neo-fascist MSI (see Text 212). The introduction to this issue was written by Marco Tarchi (see Text 190).*

The 'vitalism' of the German New Right, which expresses itself particularly in Blood and Soil vocabulary, gives rise to a notion of the greatest importance: the notion, or rather the image, of 'development' [*Entwicklung*], which is the perfect response to the rationalistic concept of 'progress'. The image of 'organic' development is a supremely energizing and fertile one [. . .] because it leads to the key concept of the 'replacement' or 'exchange' of one thing for another [*Ablösung*] being natural and hence inevitable: the changing of generations, the substitution of human or social 'types' seen as 'worn out' by new ones, for example the 'bourgeois' by the 'Soldier' or the 'Worker', the replacement of peoples held to be 'old' by peoples who claim to be 'young' (which the German people is of course considered to be). Finally, the image of organic development, with its connotations of Life and Death and above all of Rebirth [*Wiedergeburt*], Resurrection [*Auferstehung*] is central to the call for the reintroduction of the 'heroic sense of life' and of history into a world considered anaesthetized by rationalism and hedonism.

The conjunction of a cyclic vision of history and belief in the permanence of the 'core' of true values is the basis of the faith in a 'conservative dynamic' and gives the neo-conservative confidence that his 'values' will eventually re-emerge within all regimes to triumph over the disorder they engender. 'The Tradition', says Moeller,[18] 'is perpetually being interrupted by catastrophes which assail it and by revolutions we cannot avoid. But the Tradition constantly renews itself.'[. . .] In

---

[18] See Text 152.

contrast to 'cultural pessimists', 'revolutionary conservatives' no longer feel prisoners of a hated century. They see themselves 'at a historical turning-point' [*Zeitwende*]. They feel they have 'a grip on reality' which enables them to live in their own age, not only by coming to terms with the alleged 'decline' through a heroic stance, like the legendary Spengler,[19] but by remodelling it in accordance with their precepts. Beyond the 'heroic realism' of Nietzsche, Spengler, or even Jünger,[20] their attitude culminates in affirmation [*Bejahung*], the 'joyful' acceptance of the challenge of the age. The 'Faustian' spirit of the New Right here corresponds to the Promethean spirit of the Left. Indeed, it claims to be the only way of overcoming the problems of the modern world precisely because it proceeds from another essence. The fervent nationalism of the period adds an extra ingredient to this supreme self-confidence, because it allows them to see in the German the incarnation of 'Faustian man', the born soldier, the organizer, the engineer.[. . .]

It will be the task of a radically 'new' State to integrate [*eingliedern*] the classes and to structure [*gliedern*] the masses, at the same time promoting the emergence of a new aristocracy, in the context of which it is appropriate to stress that without exception all the 'Conservative Revolutionaries' claim to be resolutely 'modern' in their sincere commitment to social mobility.[. . .] To deny this, as vulgar Marxists do, and to present 'Conservative Revolutionaries' as pure and simple defenders of the old social order means adopting a nonsensical position which denies the very existence of the 'Revolutionary Conservative' idea. It also means condemning oneself to understanding nothing of the essence of certain practical achievements of 'fascism' once it became a reality.[. . .]

The movement of ideas which has come to be called the 'Conservative Revolution' seems to us to combine (sometimes even in the same author and often in the same magazine) two currents born of different phases in Germany's modernization process. First the current of 'cultural pessimism'[. . .] characterized by the belief in irreversible decline, in open or thinly disguised hostility to the industrial revolution and technology, to the metropolis, to mass society, to the breakdown of social order and traditional values.[. . .] Superimposed on this current and tending to conflict with it more and more to the point of open contempt, invective, and polemic, we find a new 'voluntarist' and even 'optimistic' current, whose importance has generally been underestimated to date in historical studies and which represents a new element and the true nature of the 'Conservative Revolution'.

Far from accepting the theme of decadence, this young (at times even juvenile) current accepts the 'challenge of modernity', is in favour of heavy industry, technology, and a certain form of rational organization of society. Accepts mass society and the possibility that a partial remodelling of it might bring about the emergence of new élites.[. . .]

If our theory is correct it means that the study of the problem of modernity is the key to understanding the 'Conservative Revolution' and, by cautious extension, what is, rightly or wrongly, generally defined as 'fascism'.

['Rivoluzione conservatrice e modernità', *Diorama letterario*, 79 (Feb. 1985), 5, 6, 7, 10, 11, 15.]

[19] See Text 57.   [20] See Texts 54, 56.

195 **Heroic Realism**

Among the heroes of the Conservative Revolution to whom the New Right regularly pay homage in their quest for cultural regeneration are Oswald Spengler, Gottfried Benn, Carl Schmitt, Friedrich Nietzsche, Ernst Jünger, and Moeller van den Bruck. Martin Heidegger (see Text 81) is particularly treasured as a role model by the New Right, however, for his sustained campaign for Europe's 'metaphysical' awakening. Robert Steukers, editor of Vouloir, is Belgium's most prominent spokesman of the New Right and a close associate of Alain de Benoist. In the early 1990s he was helping disseminate in the new Russia a version of New Right ideology called 'Eurasianism', which presents Russia as part of an Indo-European geopolitical and ethno-cultural bloc vital to keep the inroads of alien cultures at bay. The wanton eclecticism of this passage is typical of New Right thinkers, who feel emancipated from the 'pedantry' of a 'decadent' liberal academia.

In Heidegger's works two modes of writing exist side by side. The one is palpable, exalting the earth, the soil, the forest and the work of the woodcutter: the other consists of a seemingly impenetrable philosophical jargon. It is Heidegger's remarkable achievement that he was both a bucolic poet and an extremely rigorous philosopher, who allowed no concept to escape him. How is it possible that two such qualities could coexist in one man?

Martin Heidegger was born on September 26th 1889, in Messkirch in Swabia and for Heidegger himself there was nothing incidental about this fact, for he was always deeply attached to his Germanic origins. A sense of belonging, according to Heidegger constitutes one of the essential pre-conditions of being 'fully human'. To be 'fully human' man must fashion and inhabit a world in his image. All Heidegger's work is impregnated with a sense of belonging to Swabia, that part of southern Germany which includes the Black Forest and gave us Schiller, Schelling, Hegel and Hölderlin. The rhythm of the Swabian forests, mute but omnipresent in Heidegger's world, distinguishes him from Sartre. Sartre, who was in many ways a disciple of Heidegger, was also profoundly influenced by his milieu—in this case the frenzy and hubbub of the great city, where it is impossible to grasp the originality of nature.[. . .]

Heidegger's philosophy sought to be an ontology which posed the central question of the problem of what 'being' actually means. Ever since Plato this problem had been forgotten, thanks to the dominance of metaphysics. Our ignorance of Being is the root of the nihilism of the post-Christian society. Heidegger, who always emphasised the importance of time and place in our lives, drew on the example of German society after the defeat of 1918. Here we can see how Heidegger's philosophy is involved in the Conservative Revolution, for it too was marked by a search for wholeness. Peter Gay, in *The Outsider as Insider* (Penguin), a study of Weimar Germany, speaks of a 'hunger for wholeness' in the Conservative Revolution. The social and spiritual chaos of the Weimar years provoked a febrile quest for whatever would prove itself substantial, intense, to discover the quiddity of life and how modes of being become tangible reality.[. . .]

The nub of the problem lies in our notion of being as a static essence, but being according to Heidegger, 'is' not but 'is becoming'. (*Das Sein an sich 'ist' nicht, es 'west.'*) Being is not pure presence but pure potentiality. In German the word *Wesen* is at the origin of the verb. We must labour in order that a new manifestation of being is called forth and the name we give to our vocation is *destiny*. The categorical imperative of Kant will be no longer an affirmation of phenomena as 'non-absent' and define being in this negative way, but will be the labour which brings forward new phenomena. The stance of man tomorrow will be *heroic realism*.[. . .]

In the arguments of the Conservative Revolution there is a mixture of aspiration to rediscover a stable world philosophically marked by a certain substantialism and on the other hand a wish to extirpate the remnants of substantialism. In Germany the chief representatives of what is called 'heroic realism' were Josef Weinheber, Ernst Jünger and Gottfried Benn. They called themselves *radikal unbürgerlich* [radically unbourgeois] and gave themselves the task of tearing people out of a complacent attitude in which they are not truly themselves. The man of action must acquire structure, form and attitude: the world justifies itself not by morality but by aesthetics. Even if the heroic gesture is ethical, it is by its beauty that it has value. The heroic gesture does not serve necessarily a supreme rational cause. This aestheticism is of a kind which penetrates the world and does not flee it.[. . .]

The poets of the thirties were fascists, communists, nationalists—committed at any rate, and some were even active on the streets. Benn[21] chose to remain just a poet: for Germany he hoped that the destructive force could be harnessed to a metaphysics of form and a severe code of ethics. Clearly this was not Heidegger's view, although in many ways Heidegger and Benn do indeed belong to the same tradition. The Conservative Revolution was not a movement as such in that it did not move in one direction. It was rather a grouping of thinkers who were convinced of the inadequacies of liberal, bourgeois society. Their antidotes varied according to their personal and ideological provenance. National Socialism, which brought an abrupt end to the intellectual vitality of the Conservative Revolution, was described in some instances as 'plebian', in others 'reactionary' and 'Catholic'.[. . .]

This latter opinion was forcibly expressed by the 'national bolshevik', Ernst Niekisch.[22] He was unequivocally in favour of a German–Russian alliance against the West. The German–Slavic union would destroy the detested heritage of Rome. In *Widerstand*, the magazine which he edited, he wrote (No. 3, 1930): 'We are the generation at the crossroads. If we come to realise that fact, we shall be capable of the exceptional, the extraordinary, the unheard of . . . The world cannot change without a shattering and a shimmering.'

['Heidegger in Time and Place', *Scorpion*, 11 (1987), 26–31.]

[21] See Text 70.   [22] See Text 172.

g. Third Position

ADOLFO MORGANTI

196 The European Genius and the Rediscovery of the Sacred

Morganti's article appeared in Elementi, *the self-styled organ of the Italian New Right dedicated to 'cultural rebirth', and clearly modelled on* GRECE's Éléments. *However, insistence on the human need for the 'sacred' is one that constantly occurs in the writings of the more 'metapolitically' orientated ideologues of the Third Position. In fact Morganti took part in a conference held in 1981 by the Italian neo-fascists, whose proceedings were later published under the title* Beyond Right and Left. *Another symptom of the overlap is the way in the 1980s Evola was invoked in the British New Right publication* Scorpion, *which stresses cultural revolution as a prerequisite to political change, as well as in the Third Positionist* Rising, *calling for a guerrilla war against the 'system'.*

Alongside the thousands of pseudo-Hindu charlatans, there are also oriental organizations operating in the West which offer a complete sacred path and whose followers have begun to address the problem of how it is possible realistically to live out, for example, a Buddhist spirituality in contemporary Europe. This line of enquiry opens up thorny issues which are particularly relevant to the debate on *how* to rediscover the mythic and sacred roots of European civilization and *what* form this work of revitalization should take.[. . .]

What is involved here is avoiding the confusion often made between the rational and the meta-rational, the source of the Sacred. This ambiguity is a typical product of cultural colonialism by Enlightenment ideologies [. . .] and it is only through intensive research work, and hence through 'cultural' activity, that authors like Eliade, Dumézil, Benveniste, Kerényi, etc. have brought to light once again the meta-rational foundations of *ideational* and organic civilizations of ancient Europe. It is once again down to 'culture' to play the key role in elaborating contemporary forms within which the same world of values can become actualized. This contradiction is only apparent and is resolved immediately it is understood that every rationalistic activity subsumes a preconscious mechanism of interpretive 'selection', or reference to particular values and archetypes which constitute the psychological reality of the philosophical concept of a 'world-view'.

If the story of the common European cultural heritage [*ecumene*] is surveyed in the light of this approach, with the help of a wealth of scholarship which is already well established, what is immediately thrown into relief are the *mythic figures* which throughout the centuries in which society and culture formed an organic whole operated subliminally as the *atemporal archetypes* of European civilization.[. . .] These archetypes, being not mere associative forms but concrete projections of a meta-historical universe, may in the long run, despite centuries of existing in the ghettos of political archaeology, prove more vital than the opposing values. Maybe the *Genius Europae* which has continued to form centuries of civilization despite the mutations of history, the decline of religious belief, and upheavals in the economy, may still rise up with the force of ancient trees, drawing strength from the crisis of a bourgeois world which is less and less contingent and increasingly structural. At this point the *symbols* of this atemporal construction could make available a whole range of operational and creative fronts: for example uniting work and professional expertise in 'skill-communities'; engendering a new mentality of *militia*, one which avoids anachronisms and even gives a metaphysical meaning to its daily presence geared to the cultural reconquest of civil society; finally surging clear from the shallows of a deceptive intellectualism, opening up access to the sources of the Sacred in its expressions which are most appropriate to binding together *practically* a supranational community through the rediscovery of the sacredness of the world and the liturgy of existence.

It is useless to point out the risks involved in a reductionism which denies that man has a mythic atemporal dimension to circles which have spontaneously organized under the inspiration of the *idée-force* of community, the organic nature of culture, the centrality of the Sacred, and the struggle against a cultural imperialism which is constantly eating away at Europe with the jaws of the power blocs and the gastric juices of the American way of life. Certainly it is more useful and productive to stress the mobilizing power of an undertaking whose starting-point is an experiential and cultural fact, the crisis of the West, and to point out the splendour of a world in which human reality stretches from a down-to-earth concreteness to the peaks of a sacredness restored to its constitutive role, and where man can take up his rightful place in the centre of the cosmos.

['Il sacro è un albero dalle lunghe radici' [The Sacred is a tree with long roots],
Elementi, 2/1 (Jan.–Feb. 1983), 42–5.]

DEREK HOLLAND

197   The Political Soldier and National Revolution

In the wake of the National Front's rapid electoral decline after Margaret Thatcher's 1979 victory, the crudely neo-Nazi, narrowly patriotic line that had been followed under the leadership of John Tyndall and Martin Webster gave way to a more intellectually pretentious and internationalist 'Third Position' line imposed by a younger generation of Strasserites who took over in 1983. The urgent need to create an élite of heroic 'Warrior-Philosophers' required to implement a Third Positionist strategy prompted Derek Holland, one of the NF leaders behind the 1983 bid to 'modernize' British fascism, to write a trilogy of booklets as the credo of the 'political soldier'. This passage is taken from the second, Thoughts on Sacrifice and Struggle, *which appeared in 1990, by which time the National Front weekly* Nationalism Today *had also adopted a Third Positionist approach. The pamphlet's cover showed a priest and a knight standing either side of a Celtic cross.*

In the past five years or so, enormous changes have taken place within the National Revolutionary Movement, both in Britain and in the various countries of Europe. Such changes have undoubtedly been for the better—despite their many and obvious imperfections—and are solid evidence of a certain maturity of mind. But it must be made clear to all who would build the New Age, inspired by a living ideal, that such changes are *not* the end, but the beginning of a process of revalorization which has as its overriding objective the material and spiritual salvation of our countrymen. Now, the fact remains that the adaptations that have taken place in terms of strategy, tactics and organizational infrastructure, as well as ideology—and I do not underestimate their importance—have only touched the surface, have only dealt with *external things*. If we are to have a redeeming National Revolution, that will act as a cleansing fire of purification, we must go below the surface, we must go to the heart of the matter: the New Man that will build the New Social Order must of necessity appear *before* the National Revolution because the Builder must precede, in time and place, the Building which he has undertaken to construct.[. . .]

There are those, claiming to be Nationalists, who have glorified Thought almost to the exclusion of Action; they have formed numerous debating societies and clubs; they have given lectures of the highest calibre on a range of subjects; they have produced innumerable highly sophisticated and intellectual works. But what has been the sum total of this effort? Virtually nothing, for it has taken place in a vacuum; it has *not* made the necessary connection with the real world of families and communities, of languages and cultures—the very real victims of the bloody tyranny swamping the globe. A people oppressed by the Stalinist jackboot or the slick mind distortion techniques of the capitalist salesmen do *not* want words, rhetoric, over-learned volumes: they want a programme for survival which links their ideals and desires to concrete effective action. A good example of this defective type of thinking is the 'New Right' which has rallied writers and intellectuals; which has bought newspapers and magazines with all the persuasive powers that such things entail. Why has the decline of France not been stemmed? Simply, it has forgotten the French people, it has refused to dirty its hands on street politics—the lives of ordinary people if you like—because it is 'below' the *salons* of the intellectuals. *Such an attitude is not merely useless, it is utterly contemptible.*[. . .]

The European Motherland was once the Jewel of Jewels in a world where Life had meaning; she is tired and torn, cast down under the weight of the Death System which operates out of Washington, Moscow and Tel Aviv. Her beauty and nobility have faded, her partisans have surrendered and gone over to the enemy in droves. We, unworthy though we are, are the last of her Loyal Sons. *We dare to hold high the banner of Tradition and Order.*[. . .]

The rekindling of that Spirit which made Europe breath-taking can only come through the rekindling of sacrifice and struggle. It will *not* come from votes and elections, nor will it come from debates about the standard of living. *It will only come when the New Man, who will build the New Ethos, is forged and tempered in the fire of love generated by our fanatical devotion to our Holy Cause.* That Cause, that sacred duty, is in your hands; it is for you to commit yourself heart, mind and soul to the strengthening of the Revolutionary Fighting Front that proclaims its loyalty to the European Motherland.

> [*Political Soldier: Thoughts on Sacrifice and Struggle* (Burning Books: Croydon, Surrey [*c*.1989]), 4–5, 26.]

GROUPE UNION DÉFENSE
....
198   **A Community of Destiny**

A less metaphysical, more 'nominalist' version of Third Positionism is exemplified in Groupe Union Défense (GUD), a university-based fascist movement which invokes the names of Sorel, Nietzsche, and Alain de Benoist as some of its mentors. It was founded against the background of the abortive left-wing revolution of May 1968, and in the 1980s was still striving to persuade students to become part of a 'third force' to create a nationalist 'new order' purged of American capitalism and Russian communism. When this pamphlet was written it had links with another ultra-right group, Troisième Voie (Third Way), an inter-university nationalist movement, as well as with skinhead fascists. Anti-fascists claimed that GUD militants did not shrink from violence themselves. Typical of the 'modernization' of fascism is GUD's stress on the unity of Europe, the emphasis on identity, the corresponding rejection of the multi-racial society, and the importance given to ecology.

The Basic Principles of the Militant

1. *Struggle against Marxism and Capitalism.* The central objective of this struggle is the formation of a third political force, a genuine alternative to petty-bourgeois parties and to Marxist and social democratic movements.

We reject: the Marxist idea of historical materialism which reduces political consciousness to the product of social and economic relations and thereby conjures away the concepts of the nation, spirituality, etc.; the idea of class struggle, which divides the national community in two, the Nation being according to Renan 'a Community of Destiny'; the one-world vision of communism as well as the messianic vision of history which is opposed to our Nietzschean conception of life; the superseded character of Marxism which predicted the proletarianization of the working class, whereas this is constantly diminishing owing to the automation of production.

We fight political and economic liberalism because we reject the primacy of the economic over the political.[. . .] We are not individualists, just as we do not embody social class. The community of destiny which is the nation and our nationalist political option leave no room for individualism. National solidarity and social justice are at loggerheads with this notion.

2. *Struggle against the bipolar world.*[. . .] To break with the American–Soviet empire we recommend: the creation of an axis of mutual interest between Europe and the Third World.[. . .] The establishment of a specifically European military defence

system. This involves the destruction of NATO and the definitive withdrawal of American bases in Europe. Our rallying-cry must be: 'against Moscow without Washington'.[. . .]

3. *Struggle for our national identity.* Let it be clear that we are not xenophobes. We do not hate the foreigner. What needs to be criticized is the incoherent immigration policy pursued for the last twenty years by liberals and socialists.

The struggle for our national identity is also the rejection of the Anglo-Saxon subculture which is colonizing our screens and airways.

We want: the closing of borders to cheap imported labour; a tax on employers of foreign labour; draconian measures against employers of illegal immigrants; a complete revision of the naturalization legislation: the notion of *jus sanguinis* (transmission of nationality on the basis of blood) must replace that of *jus soli* (nationality on the basis of residence).

4. *The necessity of revolution and the inanity of democracy.* Our fight is revolutionary. No nationalist state without revolution![. . .] Politics is a noble and aristocratic activity and can only be engaged in by an enlightened politicized minority. This is why we reject universal suffrage and democracy in general. The term 'revolution' should be clarified. Our revolutionary nationalism is in no way the product of the revolutionary heritage of 1789 (rights of man, Enlightenment liberalism, etc.). In this sense the opposition revolution/counter-revolution is false. We are revolutionaries, counter-revolutionaries, while remaining resolutely modernist!

5. *Defence of the environment.* Ecology was originally a nationalist topic (Barrès, for example) before being picked up by the extreme left. The nationalist state is concerned with the environment and will introduce very strict regulations in this area, unlike the liberals on all sides who have passively put up with several oil-slicks as well as the destruction of the French forest so that property developers can profit.[. . .]

6. *Critique of the consumer society.*[. . .] Under this heading we condemn hedonistic practices (more and more of everything) as well as their many indecent avatars: waste, individualism. Materialism is opposed to the idea of spirituality which underlies our militant struggle. Consumption is not an end in itself, but merely a means to live.

7. *Fight for a new university.*[. . .] European recognition of qualifications to give substance to the idea of Europe (co-operation of research teams, etc.)

[*Principes de base du militant, Union et Défense*, Institut d'Études Politiques: Paris, 1987; repr. in *Droite extrême et Extrême droite en milieu universitaire*, Supplement to PSA, Letter 52 (Pour un Syndicalisme Autogestionnaire, Paris, 1988), 42–5.]

iii. Contemporary Expressions of Fascism

a. Ideological Fascism

SKREWDRIVER
199 **Songs for Europe**

An important development within post-war fascism has been the recruitment of elements of contemporary youth culture associated with punk rock, heavy metal, and football supporter hooliganism. While Fascism and Nazism would have seen such phenomena as symptomatic of the decadence they were bent on purging, in the United States, Europe, and the new Russia some ultra-nationalists have recognized the enormous scope they offer for channelling the diffuse frustrations and resentments of the disaffected young into energies which further 'revolutionary nationalism'. The National Front's White Noise Records and Germany's Rock-O-Rama ensure a steady supply of illicit racist CDs to neo-Nazis the world over, some of the most famous of which are by Ian Stuart, till his death in September 1993 leader of the group Skrewdriver and from 1986 manager of his own music company, Blood and Honour. Stuart himself reputedly observed: 'A pamphlet is read only once, but a song is learnt by heart and repeated a thousand times.' The burgeoning skinhead counter-culture in the former Soviet empire has become a natural constituency for gut-sentiments of racism, and is ripe for indoctrination with fascist myths.

Mother Europe's Sons

We are Mother Europe's sons, and we are the chosen ones
We are Mother Europe's songs, and if a fight's worth fighting [I'm] goin' to carry on.[. . .]

Don't care too much for Tories, Labour want to flood this land,
Don't care too much for Liberals, with their wishy-wash plans.
I just care for my country, and the people who belong.
And 'cos I'm proud to say it, they'll probably ban this song,
When I say, I want my freedom in this world today.[. . .]

One Land

Once a mighty nation was split asunder
A calm blue sky possessed by thunder—Donner
Once the land so proud and free
Until the war: the shame came down on Germany—Deutschland,

And now you're one land: free once again.

They may have split the flesh, but they could not split the blood,
And they could not split the spirit of the people—das Volk.
And they tried to grind you down, tried to knock you to the ground
Tried to beat you with the hammer and the sickle—Sichel.[. . .]

And now you're one land: free once again.[. . .]

Oh No! (Here Comes a)

He looks to the East and worships the Beast
Nothing but air in his head.
Appears in your eyes, peddling lies,
Selling ideas that are dead.
He's out there every single morning
Talking about his new day that is dawning.

Oh no! Here comes a Commy
Red star on his breast.
Oh no! Here comes a Commy
Won't you give him a rest.

In your land he's got a plan, to bring it all down the ground:
Confuse you with lies, he's brought his spies
To bring destruction all around.
He just wants to see our nations dying.
His desire is for the red flag flying.

Oh no! Here comes a Commy [. . .]

All for his plans [are] from alien lands,
People that don't belong here.
They came to these shores, they always want more
With their lies and crocodile tears.
The red gets his support from these invaders,
Hopes that their sheer numbers will evade us.

Oh no! Here comes a Commy [. . .]
Won't you—off and die!

[*Freedom? What Freedom?*, Rock-A-Rama Records, n.d. [c.1990].]

Europe on my Mind

So many lives have been wasted,
Scattered as the leaves upon the ground,
In the cause of the freedom they had tasted,
For the liberty they found.
Ground beneath the heels of red jack-boots,
With half of Europe ruled by the red beast,
Whilst the other half were fooled to thinking they were free
As kosher power ruled at every feast.

Chorus
Beloved Europe's on my mind now,
It's on my mind and in my soul
Liberty and justice is our goal.
[. . .]

Our Time will Come

Now the battle's over, your country is in chains
No land was the winner, no-one ever gained,

Apart from shady money-lenders high up in ivory towers
Where they look down on the nation and plot away for hours.

Chorus
New order, our time will come.

You marched forth to battle, to misery and pain,
You believed another war would free your sacred land.
But all you did was the bankers' bidding,
Another war they'd planned.[. . .]

[Ian Stuart, *Patriotic Ballads II*, Rock-A-Rama Records, n.d. [*c.*1992].]

HARTWIG HUBER

200   The Immortal Principle

Nation Europa was set up in the German Federal Republic in 1950 by former SS officer Arthur Erhardt and has established itself as the major German-speaking forum for ecumenical fascism and the 'Europe a Nation' principle. It regularly publishes articles in support of far right and neo-fascist parties and movements in Germany (e.g. the Republikaner Party) and abroad (Le Pen's Front National in France, South African white supremacists), and foments anti-immigrant feeling with its regular column 'Nachrichten von der Überfremdungsfront' (roughly 'News from the front in the battle against being swamped by aliens'). The influence of New Right and Conservative Revolutionary fascism can be seen in this declaration of an additional human right, published in a special issue on 'identity', one of the major themes of modern racist and neo-fascist discourse.

When two hundred years ago the rights of man were solemnly declared, anthropology as a natural science was still in its infancy. Human rights are the creation of jurists and philosophers. The premiss of their thinking was an isolating and speculative one: Man was abstractly conceived as an individual; not as a man, or a woman, or a child, or as someone with ties to a family, an ethnic group [*Stamm*], a people [*Volk*]. The heterogeneous world which had grown up over centuries, and which even in the age of absolutism had started to become rationally organized, was now radically simplified.

An abstractly conceived being, Man, was recognized to have fundamental freedoms in 1789, but not to be a communal being. In those days nothing was known of genetics and the like. They were building on speculations about a noble savage, who was contrasted with the European who had been corrupted by his society.[. . .]

Charles Darwin discovered the natural history of man. The history of his development was uncovered step by step.[. . .] Modern man emerged in the Ice Age, the quaternary.[. . .] Research into human behaviour, which made leaps and bounds with the work of the Nobel prize-winner Konrad Lorenz, who died recently, has done a lot to establish a realistic and scientific picture of man. However, the resistance of older, better established sciences such as sociology is still strong. The conflict between empirical natural science and speculative human sciences has not yet been fought out to a conclusion. The picture of man founded on the natural sciences should be taken into account in a redrafting of human rights.[. . .]

Man is a territorial being. That was not yet known in 1789. Every man strives to possess space to dispose of as he alone sees fit. These are the roots of the right to a home [Heimat]. But the right to a home can be found in no constitution which incorporates human rights. If human rights are to mean anything, however, then the right to a home should be included in the list!

Man is as much an individual as a collective being. In every human group a hierarchy establishes itself very quickly and instinctively: men are unequal. Every scientist knows that to establish differences he must experimentally create the same conditions. (Before the law all men are equal.)

The development of man is a combination of natural and cultural factors. This has given rise to an abundance of ethnic groups. American ethnographers have counted at least 4,000 cultures on the earth. The wealth of the human species is in its abundance of cultures.

Let us sum up: the human rights of 1789 were incomplete. The right to a home and an identity must now be added to them. The human rights of the Enlightenment are abstract, individual rights. If they are to be complete and to be implemented, they must include collective human rights, namely the human rights to home and identity! In other words, the human rights of the individual and those of the community should complement each other harmoniously. *Every people has a right to its own identity. Whoever violates this right is playing with fire.*

['Menschenrecht auf Heimat und Identität' [The human right to home and identity],
Nation Europa, 39/7 (July 1989), 5–6.]

PADRAIG CULLEN

201   The Greening of Nazism

In 1987 Scorpion dedicated a whole issue to reporting on a conference on the theme 'Ecology: The Growing Dilemma', run jointly with Iona, an 'independent cultural society for British nationalists' created by a former NF organizer. It was chaired by Robert Steukers (see Text 195) and one of the speakers was Anna Bramwell, who talked on the link between the aims of Walther Darré (see Text 65) and those of 'post-war environmentalists' in the light of her recently published biography of him. In the same issue Padraig Cullen, a frequent Scorpion contributor on 'blood and soil' issues, wrote a review of Bramwell's book, from which this extract is taken, showing how easily a revisionist message can be read into this work by those keen to ignore the National Peasant Leader's collusion with Nazi eugenics, mass 'resettlement', and genocide in his bid to overcome the decadence of urban civilization and the Jews. (The Italian New Right Diorama letterario has also praised the book, while Spearhead has cited it as evidence that Darré is 'edging towards rehabilitation'. America's racist Noontide Press *paid it the dubious compliment of advertising it in the same flier as an English edition of Rosenberg's* The Myth of the Twentieth Century!*)*

Blood and Soil, Walther Darré and Hitler's 'Green Party' by Anna Bramwell. The Kensal Press. 1985.

Dr. Bramwell describes her book as a 'political and intellectual history of a man described in highly coloured terms by admirers still living today as the "last peasant leader" '. But *Blood and Soil* is much more than a fascinating biography, it is also a vigorous iconoclastic attack upon the academic coterie that dominates historical writing, and an informative and surprising look into a hitherto little known aspect of National Socialist Germany. In addition, the topics of organic farming, ecological awareness, and rural versus urban life, are of the greatest current interest and further heighten the importance of this work.[. . .]

She tells of the way in which the history of Nazi Germany has been abandoned by historians who feel some sympathy for aspects of the National Socialist ideal. Instead the ground has been left to 'internationalist social democrats, who can only examine the exceedingly broad church manifestations of National Socialism through their own progressive prejudices'. These latter are limited by their own attempts to systematise the experience of Germany within their own preconceived frameworks, a process that is fatally limited in its ability to throw light on the Nazi enigma. Dr. Bramwell makes an appeal for real history, a call for the establishment of 'what actually happened', instead of the juggling of facts to fit unresponsive models and popular prejudices:

It is the core of my argument that one should not let the existence of the uniforms and the swastikas interfere with the evaluation of Darré's attempt to 'watch over the inviolability of the possible'. He was a guardian of a radical, centrist, republican critique which pre-dated National Socialism, and still lives on.[. . .]

Darré himself stressed a view of European history familiar to readers of this journal. Instead of the history of the conquerors, princes, kings, merchants and the Church, Darré's history was that of the 'other' Europe; the history of the peasantry, its struggles and rebellions. The cultural qualities, and the independent anti-state nature of the peasants were also stressed by their new, and welcomed, spokesman, Darré. He was a trenchant critic of all things urban, whilst believing in the applicability of technology to the farms of the peasant. For him a revival, rescue, of the peasantry would lead to a new, Nordic, peasant international that would ensure the rebirth of that 'other' Europe; so long weakened by capitalist values, introduced, interestingly enough, in Darré's view, by the Teutonic Knights.[. . .]

Dr. Bramwell draws a lovely picture of Darré's 'Peasant Capital', the old city of Goslar. Here his dream nearly took permanent shape.

The dream was to make Goslar the centre of a new peasants' international: a green union of the northern European peoples. Here he made speeches condemning the *Führerprinzip* and attacking imperial expansion. Visitors flocked to him. Organic farming enthusiasts from England now welcomed Darré's plans, and admired the hereditary tenure legislation. Representatives from Norwegian and Danish peasant movements joined the conferences on 'Blood and Soil'.[. . .]

Yet even by 1933 Darré was falling out of step with the centralist tendencies of the State.[. . .] Darré's final disillusionment during the twilight years of the Third Reich, along with his subsequent arrest and trial in 1949 in the Wilhelm-strasse Trials of top civil servants, making painful reading. Released from prison in 1950, Darré, now a sick man, continued his writings for practical peasant solutions until his early death in 1953. In the conclusion it is stressed again that Darré's belief in the 'holistic trinity' of peasant–nature–God (God in all things), was not a mere reaction to industrialism, but a practical programme for a revolution, a green revolution.

I feel that *Blood and Soil* is in many ways an important work. It courageously challenges many academic sacred cows. In addition, it asks many questions, both of historical and contemporary importance, that point the way for future research, and policy. For Darré, it is a fitting testimony.

Darré, the stubborn individualist, went on to fight his corner till his death in 1953. In politics, as in art, ends and means, the virtue of the performer and the virtue of the end result, are strangely unrelated.

[Review of Anna Bramwell, *Blood and Soil: Walther Darré and Hitler's Green Party*,
Scorpion, 11 (1987), 36–7.]

JOHN TYNDALL
....

202   **Spiritual AIDS**

Neo-Nazism has not just 'universalized' itself, but has updated its catalogue of symptoms of alleged decadence with reference to such phenomena as AIDS, immigration, urban decay, abortion, unemployment , drugs, and crime. This is exemplified in the following passage from a full-length book by John Tyndall, who had already played a leading role in six ultra-right groups, notably the National Front, before founding the British National Party in 1982. However much BNP spokesmen show themselves willing to abide by the parliamentary 'rules of the game' officially, their leader is still prepared to indulge in a sustained outpouring of vitriol on everything liberal democracy stands for.

We live under a state that is terminally sick, in the manner of a political, economic, social and spiritual AIDS. Lacking the built-in natural immunity that is to be found in all healthy body organisms, it is vulnerable to every germ and shock that the world climate may blow its way. For this, state, every week is a crisis, as it wriggles vainly to cope with some fresh problem arising from out of its own insoluble internal tensions and contradictions. Its death is certain; the only remaining uncertainty is that of the precise moment when it expires.[. . .]

In every aspect of contemporary British politics the habit is to try to 'square the circle', to make work that which will not work. The present form of parliamentary 'democracy' as a method for the translation of the popular will into political action has become a stale joke. Yet the greater the evidence of this, the greater the intransigence with which the system is defended and the shriller the cry of 'wolf!' against those who would question it. An economic doctrine that has emaciated industry and delivered over 3 millions to idleness is persisted in as if no other were conceivable. The response to inner city deterioration is yet more promises of open cheques, bearing the signature of the taxpayer, while almost everyone with a wit to rub against the other knows that money has almost nothing to do with the problem. Pious speeches against mounting crime are a weekly ritual, while those making them know in their bones that, within the limits of what is 'acceptable' policy, nothing will be done, or can be done, to reverse the trend.

Meanwhile, the lunacy of 'race equality' has become the national religion in a manner reminiscent of pre-reformation frenzy, with every unbeliever a candidate for the stake.

And in the global field the phantoms of internationalism and 'one world' paralyse all searchings for a policy that will ensure British survival.[. . .]

The political rot, however, is only a part of a much more general rot. Our entire national life is in the grip of degenerative forces, which barely leave one small area of affairs unaffected, as they run amok like maggots invading a diseased carcass, filtering through everywhere as resistance wanes.[. . .]

But what is not yet fully grasped is the depth of the root of the sickness and the radical nature of the means needed to overcome it. Too many people still see and talk about only the *symptoms* of what is wrong. Only a few are prepared to give their minds to the *causes*—and fewer still to the *causes of the causes*. It is my conviction that if we really are to understand the ills of Britain in the 1980s we must see them as the logical and inevitable result of a process of faulty national development extending well back into the previous century. Institutions do not lend themselves to infiltration, take-over and internal corruption on the present scale unless they possess in the first place some fundamental weakness. Likewise the fashionable doctrines of national degeneracy that hold such wide sway today could not ever have infected a climate of ideas that was basically healthy.

What many people regard as the 'lunatic left', for instance, is a growth that first needed fertile soil for its germination. That soil existed in the atmosphere of *liberalism* that preceded the growth, and in the system of values which in that atmosphere had gained widespread acceptance in our society. It was liberalism which, over many decades, eroded the once sturdy national and racial spirit of our educated classes, thus paving the way for a marxist creed which requires the elimination of that spirit as an essential precondition for its advance.[. . .]

If we are seriously to grapple with the chaos of the present day and formulate a creed and movement for national rebirth, our thinking must begin with an utter rejection of liberalism and a dedication to the resurgence of authority.

As such, it must entail the embrace of a political outlook which is, in relation to the present, *revolutionary*. Nothing less will suffice.[. . .]

It is precisely a creed of heroism that is needed now to turn the tide of British history at this eleventh hour, a creed that will call forth all the finest attributes of manhood that sent our forebears across the oceans in their small boats in the drive to empire, a creed that will unite the British Nation into a true *community*, capable of undertaking the gigantic works of national reconstruction to which we must apply ourselves if we are to have a future, a creed by which we may achieve a new renaissance of the British genius in all the creative arts and sciences and hurl back the forces of decadence that now threaten to engulf us.[. . .]

In this book I have emphasised the national and British interest, and called for the building in Britain of a movement of nationalism. This is necessary because Britain is our country and it must come first in our priorities—along with those other countries sharing with us the British heritage.

But none of this should obscure the fact that, at a certain level our struggle is global—just as we are confronted by a global enemy. I have acknowledged our spiritual and intellectual debt to nationalist thinkers of the era preceding 1914, and it is a considerable one. But in our thinking today and in the future nationalism must take on something of a different dimension to the one dominant at that stage of history. Over and above the rivalries of nations, there is the transcendent interest of Western Civilisation, Western Culture and—as the creator of these things—the White European Race. Here we must see 'The West', not in the form currently fashionable: as a coalition of nations organised in mutual defence of the dubious blessings of 'liberal democracy' and 'capitalism', but as a *cultural* and above all *racial* entity. In this regard, the peoples of Eastern Europe currently under communist rule are in truth part of the same entity.[. . .]

Our creed is one of heroism, and the coming epoch calls for the return of the heroic virtues. Not for us the cosy tranquillity of the political soft option; for us only the long march through the cold night—which must precede the glorious dawn. These conditions demand a special quality of steel in those who rally to our banner, and if the forthrightness of the message put forward in this book frightens and puts off the delicate of fibre and of spirit, that is good; for their place is not with us and we would not wish to encumber ourselves with their presence.

Today, from out of the chaos and the ruins wrought by the old politics, new men are rising. These new men of the new age are now working night and day across the land to forge the sinews of the movement to which their lives and mine are dedicated. Above them as they work are the spirits of legions of mighty ancestors whose bones lie at the bottom of the oceans and beneath the soil of five continents where the men and women of our blood have borne the British flag and stamped the mark of British genius. Today we feel the voices of these past generations calling down to us in sacred union, urging us to be worthy of their example and their sacrifice. To them we owe it to fight on, and to dare all, so that a great land and a great race may live again in splendour.

[The Way Ahead, *The Eleventh Hour: A Call for British Rebirth* (Albion Press: London, 1988), 585–90, 602–3, 608–9.]

b. Militant Fascism

 203 **Blood, Soil, and Faith**

L'Œuvre Française was formed in 1968 by ex-collaborator Pierre Sidos partly as a reincarnation of Jeune Nation, which, as founder member and secretary, he had helped become one of France's most violent neo-fascist groups at the time of the Algerian War in the 1950s. It distinguishes itself from overtly Nazi groups, preferring Pétain to Hitler as a role model, and hence cultivating a blend of fundamentalist 'national' Catholicism, pan-Europeanism, and anti-Semitism. The tirade against anti-racism as a war against the integrity of races, and hence the true racism, is typical of neo-fascist Newspeak (for example, it is an argument used by Guillaume Faye of the French New Right—cf. Text 178). The leaflet from which this passage is taken also shows the influence of Third Positionist critiques of the Right–Left cleavage. This is no simple 'cultural organization', however. Several members were arrested in 1994 for plotting to kill a minister who was planning to crack down on fascism in France.

International Anti-Racism is the Negation of National Patriotism

In government, in the Church, in parliament, in political parties, in the media and art, in the judicial system, in the street, the insolence and maliciousness of those who claim to be 'anti-racist' seem no longer to have any limit.

Their aim is to ensure the victory of cosmopolitanism through the use of all intellectual and material forms of subversion.

Their plan involves the negation of the Christian essence of our national existence and the denial of the European source of our French identity.

Their tactic consists in systematically accusing French people of good stock, and who are prepared to defend themselves, of 'fascism' and 'nazism'. It is what they call 'the struggle against racism', 'anti-racism'.[. . .]

Anti-racism is the negation of French France

Self-styled anti-racism is an internationalist ideology which abusively exploits phoney humanitarian sentiments to encourage the invasion of the nation's inner world, to the detriment of the physical and moral health of France. It is the negation of natural rights—never called into question till now—of the French to live peacefully as masters in their own homes in accordance with the genius of their blood, the nature of their soil, the faith of their heaven.

The pretext invoked is the pseudo-philosophy of the 'rights of man', the ideology of the so-called liberation, the frenzy of what was supposed to be the 'resistance'.[. . .] This has culminated in the anomaly of a new state doctrine: anti-racism, which leads to the hatred of every normal society, i.e. one which is hierarchical, traditional, and national.[. . .]

The result which anti-racism banks on achieving is a France which is under occupation, disfigured, changed beyond recognition: a cosmopolitan 'Hexagon' which would no longer be historical France, the France of the French.

Anti-racism is the enemy of our freedoms, our jobs, the future of our children, the enemy of civil peace at home and a fruitful co-operation between states abroad.

L'Œuvre Française wants to safeguard national identity

A strictly nationalist movement, L'Œuvre Française, was founded and directed by Pierre Sidos. Its symbol is the Celtic cross, its slogan 'France for the French', and its action is based on a political creed which affirms the existence of a single France, historically constituted as a sovereign state, whose unity and continuity is assured by a principle of authority allied to personal responsibility. It is composed of a people of European extraction, generally of French language, of a Christian tradition, of a classical education, and of a millennial nationality, living in Western Europe within fixed boundaries. The power of integral nationalist thought on all acts of public life must form the basis of the preservation of its spiritual and intellectual identity, its physical and moral integrity, its political and cultural independence, for the common good of the French and the healthy balance of the international community.

This profession of nationalist faith rejects the division of France into 'left' and 'right' by asserting a national sentiment which transcends the various cleavages within society, and exists over and above elections and parties. It obviously rejects anti-social theories, anti-national machinations, anti-natural practices, all engendered by cosmopolitanism and its modern successor, anti-racism.

The precondition for safeguarding French national identity is first and foremost not to confuse but to differentiate, to make selections between people, to make choices between ideas, by opting for definite preferences and establishing hierarchies. In this respect, L'Œuvre Française, the most intransigent contemporary nationalist movement and the most rigorous in theoretical terms, as well as being the best organized and best led in terms of practical activity, is superbly well placed to make a valuable contribution to the re-establishment of France in every sphere.

[Leaflet circulated by L'Œuvre Française, n.d., *c*.1993.]

WILLIAM PIERCE
204   **The Cleansing Hurricane**

The Turner Diaries *could be described as the* Mein Kampf *of Universal Nazism. Its author, William Pierce, played an important role in the 1970s as editor of* National Socialist World, *the organ of the World Union of National Socialists (see Texts 177, 178)* *and leader of the National Alliance. Using the fictional diary form (as Goebbels had before him, see Text 61), Pierce describes how the neo-Nazi terrorist Organization led by the élite Order finally wins the civil war against the System in California, North America, Europe, and eventually the whole world—taking the trouble to nuke Israel on the way—enabling the White race finally to claim the whole planet as its homeland 'uncontaminated' by non-Aryans: the ultimate paranoid fantasy for a Nazi. The book inspired the Order, a terrorist group which in 1983–4 stole $4,000,000 and murdered two people, one of them Alan Berg, a Jewish radio chat-show host (a deed which formed the basis of Oliver Stone's 1984 film* Talk Radio *(see Flynn and Gerhardt 1990). (The 'Great One' is, of course, Adolf Hitler.)*

The Organization's enclaves continued to expand, nevertheless, both in size and number, all through the five Dark Years preceding the New Era. At one time there were nearly 2,000 separate Organization enclaves in North America. Outside these zones of order and security, the anarchy and savagery grew steadily worse, with the only real authority wielded by marauding bands which preyed on each other and on the unorganized and defenseless masses.

Many of these bands were composed of Blacks, Puerto Ricans, Chicanos, and half-white mongrels. In growing numbers, however, Whites also formed bands along racial lines, even without Organization guidance. As the war of extermination wore on, millions of soft, city-bred, brainwashed Whites gradually began regaining their manhood. The rest died.

From the liberation of North America until the beginning of the New Era for our whole planet, there elapsed the remarkably short time of just under 11 months. Professor Anderson has recorded and analyzed the events of this climatic period in detail in his History of the Great Revolution. Here it is sufficient to note that, with the principal centers of world Jewish power annihilated and the nuclear threat of the Soviet Union neutralized, the most important obstacles to the Organization's worldwide victory were out of the way.[. . .]

From as early as 1993 the Organization had had active cells in Western Europe, and they grew with extraordinary rapidity in the six years preceding the victory in North America. Liberalism had taken its toll in Europe, just as in America, and the old order in most places was a rotted-out shell with only a surface semblance of strength. The disastrous economic collapse in Europe in the spring of 1999, following the demise of the System in North America, greatly helped in preparing the European masses morally for the Organization's final takeover.

That takeover came in a great, Europe-wide rush in the summer and fall of 1999, as a cleansing hurricane of change swept over the continent, clearing away in a few months the refuse of a millennium or more of alien ideology and a century or more of profound moral and material decadence. The blood flowed ankle-deep in the streets of many of Europe's great cities momentarily, as the race traitors, the offspring of generations of dysgenic breeding, and hordes of Gastarbeiter met a common fate. Then the great dawn of the New Era broke over the Western world.[. . .]

The Organization still required time to reorganize and reorient the European populations newly under its control before it could hope to deal in a conventional manner with the enormous numbers of Chinese infantry pouring across the Urals into Europe; all its dependable troops at that time were hardly sufficient even for garrison duty in the newly liberated and still not entirely pacified areas of eastern and southern Europe.

Therefore, the Organization resorted to a combination of chemical, biological, and radiological means, on an enormous scale, to deal with the problem. Over a period of four years some 16 million square miles of the earth's surface, from the Ural Mountains to the Pacific and from the Arctic Ocean to the Indian Ocean, were effectively sterilized. Thus was the Great Eastern Waste created.

Only in the last decade have certain areas of the Waste been declared safe for colonization. Even so, they are 'safe' only in the sense that the poisons sowed there a century ago have abated to the point that they are no longer a hazard to life. As everyone is aware, the bands of mutants which roam the Waste remain a real threat, and it may be another century before the last of them has been eliminated and White colonization has once again established a human presence throughout this vast area.

But it was in the year 1999, according to the chronology of the Old Era—just 110 years after the birth of the Great One—that the dream of a White world finally became a certainty. And it was the sacrifice of the lives of uncounted thousands of brave men and women of the Organization during the preceding years which had kept that dream alive until its realization could no longer be denied.

Among those uncounted thousands Earl Turner played no small part. He gained immortality for himself on that dark November day 106 years ago when he faithfully fulfilled his obligation to his race, to the Organization, and to the holy Order which had accepted him into its ranks. And in so doing he helped greatly to assure that his race would survive and prosper, that the Organization would achieve its worldwide political and military goals, and that the Order would spread its wise and benevolent rule over the earth for all time to come.

[*The Turner Diaries* (National Alliance: Washington, DC, 1980; 1st edn. 1978), 207, 209–11.]

205 Patriots of the World Unite!

One of the first movements which succeeded in forming a significant political constituency out of frustrated nationalism in the Russia of perestroika was Pamyat (memory), which by the late 1980s was rapidly recruiting passive and active support in the larger cities with a blend of orthodox Christian fundamentalism, monarchism, ultra-nationalism, and anti-Semitism. By 1990 Pamyat had formed an electoral wing in St Petersburg (the Republican People's Party of Russia) and had started to infiltrate the Green movement. The British anti-fascist periodical Searchlight (224 (1994), 18–19) claims that by late 1993 Pamyat had become a successful nationwide ultra-right umbrella organization bringing together over

100,000 members of individual groups. It thus helped prepare the ground for Zhirinovsky's electoral breakthrough in December of that year, when he obtained 24 per cent of the vote. This extract comes from an eleven-page appeal to the Russian people to understand 'what is really going on' in their country, made at a time when the degree of destabilization that lay before it could hardly be imagined. By 1994 it had been joined by dozens more specimens of ultra-right, thriving in the hothouse conditions created by Russia's post-communist (and pre-liberal) era.

Pamyat represents and is the expression of *the will of public opinion* in the country—in the three years of its existence this has become *a fact*. And who would dare act against their own people? Only those who are remote from it and have not known its soul for a long time and are unable to understand it. It is they who are now trying to convince everyone that there are no dark forces in the state and no conspiracy. No?! Then let them answer the following questions publicly:

Who has been inciting political terror in the country for 70 years? Who is destroying and crushing any independent thinking? Who is flagrantly violating the Constitution and the Law?

Who has blackened our history and culture? Who has destroyed the huge number of monuments of world renown which belong to the Russian people and other people? Who has reduced our historical sacred places—our churches, temples, monasteries, graveyards, and graves of national heroes of our Motherland—to a state of extreme desolation and destruction?

Who has been ruining the economy all this time and destroying [our] agriculture?

Who has reduced the ecology of the country to a catastrophic state?

Who arranged the disaster at Chernobyl and made a vast region of land unusable?

Who is depleting our raw materials and selling off our natural wealth abroad for a mere trifle?

Who is destroying our nation with ideological and alcoholic dope?

Who at the word Russian rushes like a watchdog to accuse us of chauvinism and nationalism? Who is trying to change the meaning of the word Russian to that of enemy?

In whose hands are the mass media?[. . .][23]

We call upon all honest and courageous people to close ranks around the Pamyat Patriotic Association and support the healthy forces of the Party who do not separate themselves from the people, and to protect the ideals of the Motherland.[. . .]

We, together with the people, demand that all forces be mobilized to explain the danger Zionism represents in our country and that an end be put to the actions of those who are selling their homeland for 30 pieces of silver!

Stop the cosmopolites! Morally wasted children are following them.

We must do everything we can to bring up our children to be true heroes of the Land of Russia for future glorious victories in the name of love and goodness!

Raise up the deepest layers of the history and culture of the Motherland! Penetrate with solicitude the people's traditions, folklore, epos, and all the wisdom

---

[23] The assumed answer to these questions is, predictably, the Jews.

accumulated by our people and all the peoples on earth! The secrets of the future are locked in this wisdom!

A people that loses its national language ceases to exist! And what has the 'great and mighty' Russian language been turned into?! Soon, unless active measures are taken, the media will start talking to the people in Esperanto! Is it not clear in which school or country studied the numerous propagandists, Party and leading officials, and all those who today have a public platform? Their speech has lost its figurativeness, poetic quality and passion, and consists of clichés, foreign words and technical terms. How can one speak to a people in such gibberish? Or strike a spark and flame in its spirit? This machine-like language is causing us irreparable harm—like an asphalt tumour on the skin of the earth.

Let us protect our national language!

[*An Appeal to the Russian People*, Pamyat Patriotic Association of the Russian People, samizdat circulated 8 Dec. 1987; repr. in *Soviet Jewish Affairs*, 18/1 (1988), 61–70.]

AFRIKANER-WEERSTANDSBEWEGING

206 God's Own

The apartheid policies pursued so relentlessly by the Republic of South Africa after 1948 were not radical enough for those Afrikaners who felt that their identity as a Boer nation was still under threat. As a result the 'African Resistance Movement' came into being in 1973, its commitment to Christian Nationalism underlining its kinship with the Ossewa-brandwag (see 119). Though the AWB's ultimate goal may be the creation of a 'modern Christian Afrikaner-Boer national state' [volkstaat], in practice it has behaved like a radical fascist movement, lashing out in its propaganda against liberals, blacks, Jews and communists, and committing numerous terrorist outrages on neo-Nazi lines through the paramilitary activities of its shock-troops, the Storm Falcons, and vigilantes, the Brandwag. Its violence reached a crescendo in the run up to democratic elections in April 1994, making it for a time the most high-profile fascist movement of the post-war era.

Permission was refused to quote from the AWB's party programme, *Programme of the AWB* (Aurora, Pretoria, nd., c.1991). The letter from Oxford University Press was returned with the laconic comment written at the bottom 'The AWB is *not* a fascist movement, thus under no condition will permission be granted for publication.'

In terms of the ideal type on which this anthology is based the AWB is technically correct, for it is a separatist nationalist movement, and does not strive to regenerate an existing nation-state drawing on the myth of a past (pre-modern) golden age. In the words of its own programme the movement's main goal is 'The founding of an independent Christian, republican Afrikaner-Boer national state, *separate* from the RSA, on the basis of the inalienable claim of the people according to history and international law to the Boer Republics'. In this way it believes it can fulfil its mission to bring about 'The unification of all Afrikaner-Boers, and other assimilable

Christians who desire assimilation, into a single Afrikaner-Boer nation', and 'the perpetuation of the Afrikaner-Boer nation [Boerevolk], free in its own land, and growing in both spiritual and material prosperity.'

However, it can be safely assumed that it was not this taxonomic nicety which provoked the AWB's adamant reaction. More likely it stems from the tendency of all fascist movements to take umbrage at the suggestion that it is the blood relation of another movement, especially since any derivativeness would conflict with the claim of all fascist movements to incarnate the unique essence of the national community they seek to regenerate (cf. Text 99). It may also have a lot to do with the exclusively negative connotations which the term fascist has acquired in liberal politics, the social sciences, and the 'Western' media, which the AWB rightly perceive to be their sworn enemies and a major obstacle to the realization of their dream of an independent homeland within the New South Africa.

Nevertheless, the programme bears all the traits of the palingenetic mindset which our ideal type makes central to the definition of fascism in this Reader. For example, its commitment to the 'Detection, exposure and resistance with every available means of forces detrimental to the people such as the inimical power of Mammon, Liberalism, Humanism, Communism and Marxism' points to an acute sense of the corrosive effects exerted on an allegedly racially pure nation by the dominant forces of the modern age. It is significant in this respect that the AWB does not consider itself to be anti-modern as such, for it envisages the Afrikaner-Boer national state becoming a 'highly developed First World state', even if its major duty is to 'look after the current interests of the nation and honour the spiritual foundations and principles of the Boer Republic'. That the new State would not feel confined to parliamentary and diplomatic measures to fulfil this task is clear from the statement that 'the hegemony must use the military power which it has received to maintain law and order and protect its subjects'.

The corollary of this ultra-nationalism is a distinctively racist version of the regenerated Boerevolk, as is clear from its pledge to the following principles:

The fostering of a powerful awareness among Afrikaner-Boers of their white lineage and heritage, their blood relationship and nationalism, and of the importance of racial purity; the fostering of love for family, kith and kin, nation, and fatherland; the encouragement of a keen awareness of tradition and history among the youth, and the maintenance and development of their Afrikaner-Boer culture.

That this is intimately bound up with linguistic nationalism is seen from the fact that the programme commits the AWB to 'The maintenance, development and protection of Afrikaans as the national language.'

Perhaps the most distinctive trait of the AWB variety of fascism, and the most eloquent testimony to its continuity with the Ossewabrandwag, is the stress placed on Christianity in the definition of the nation and of the source of ultimate authority. What the AWB envisages is what Romanian ultra-nationalists now call an 'ethnocratic State' (see Text 207) which is simultaneously a theocratic State, reminiscent of the one aspired to by the Romanian Iron Guard before the Second World War (see extracts 116, 117). This is made explicit when the programme declares that the axioms of the AWB's concept of statehood are that:

1 The supreme sovereignty of the triune God, and His guidance in the fates of nations and individuals, are recognized and professed.

2 The Word of God is accepted obediently as the sole guideline for all expressions of national life.

3 The Protestant faith, and the Christian-national world-view which has arisen from it, determine the development of national life in every sphere.[. . .]

The programme goes on to declare that 'The Afrikaner-Boer nation had its origins within God's providential scheme and is called to a life of service to Him out of gratitude for His grace'. As a consequence of such premisses the AWB programme constantly blends Christian fundamentalism with ultra-nationalism. For example, the policy towards youth is 'The establishment and maintenance of a Christian-national upbringing and educational system so that the young will grow up with a fear of the Lord, will know Him, honour and love Him; and so that they will also be prepared for appropriate professional work and service to the people.'

In short, the AWB leadership has every right to reject the taxonomic label 'fascist' in its own minds, but liberal academics have every right to suggest that the movement constitutes a major example of a post-war, non-European form of fascism with a high degree of originality. In this respect one only has to ponder on the AWB's ubiquitous symbol: three sevens arranged in a radial design encircled in red. Ostensibly it conveys the struggle of Christian Nationalism against the Beast of the Apocalypse (whose Biblical number is 666). Yet it seems more than a coincidence that it also evokes for many the Nazi swastika, the emblem of the most virulently destructive form of fascism and white supremacism the world has ever seen.

NOUA DREAPTĂ

207 **The Romanian Ethnocratic State**

Given the close causal relationship of objective conditions of social, economic, and political crisis with the rise of ultra-nationalism, it was tragically predictable that the former Eastern bloc would experience a burgeoning of racism and fascism once the Soviet empire collapsed, especially in Hungary and Romania, which, as in the former Yugoslavia, had deeply rooted traditions of ethnic hatred. Within a few years literally scores of neo-fascist movements had surfaced, both parliamentary and terroristic, ranging from attempts to revive indigenous inter-war fascism (the Arrow Cross and the Iron Guard), to various new concoctions blended from Christian fundamentalist nationalism, neo-Nazism, and Third Positionism. Almost without exception they serve a dangerous cocktail of anti-Roma (gypsy) sentiment, anti-Semitism, xenophobia, anti-Islam, and anti-Americanism, often associated with a claim to represent 'a return to Europe': not the Europe of the EU, of course, but the 'Indo-European' or Christian Europe of fascist fantasy. This text must stand for any number that could be cited from the vast output of ultra-nationalist publicists. It is taken from Noua Dreaptă (New Right), the organ of the Party of the National Right, founded in 1993 by Radu Sorescu, who also edits the newspaper. It offers the fascist international a handy new concept, 'the ethnocratic State', which would replace Western-style democracy with an ethnically cleansed corporative system.

Preamble

The Romanian nation is today living through a moment of shame. The democratic political parties in their struggle for power are reducing the country's population to misery. The Hungarians want to secure official autonomy by involving international organizations. The gypsies proclaim themselves king, spurning order and national sovereignty. Arabs, Turks, Chinese, and Africans are taking over Romanian business. The nation is disintegrating, cripples and beggars are becoming the symbol of the nation. Moscow, Washington, and Paris are dictating to Bucharest. Russia has placed Bessarabia in a state of siege and is hand in glove with revisionist Hungary. Ukraine is illegally occupying Romanian territories. On top of all this our state leadership lacks firmness.

The National Right summons the Romanian people to the barricades of honour. Thousands of the youngest are leaving the country in disgust, millions of hungry unemployed people, undervalued workers, and intellectuals feel stranded and powerless. We make no bones about it: we are nationalists! We do not have rights, but only duties. We are not the nation. The nation is ancient. We can only serve it. Till death!

I. The Ethnocratic State

A. The Ethnocratic State The ethnocratic State rejects from its own organism all minorities as long as they refuse to be assimilated by the Romanian nation. Minorities transform themselves wholesale into a political problem by sowing discord and using blackmail against the State, thus bringing about situations which tend to compromise the image of Romania in the world. For this reason, the only guarantee of our survival is the ethnocratic State.

The ethnocratic State sanctifies the power of the Romanians within their Fatherland. Its foundation is nationalism. Nationalism and the national will to assert and defend itself: the land of our forebears, history, culture, religion, language, and race. The ethnocratic State is the institutional and material expression of Romanianism.

The ethnocratic State is fundamentally distinct from the democratic State. The democratic State is constituted for the entire population, irrespective of race or creed. The democratic State allows and fuels inter-ethnic tensions, it tramples on national dignity. In short, it is the generator of anarchy and misery. The basis of the ethnocratic State is the will of the Romanian people. To defend the dignity of the Romanian nation, the National Right considers that all the functions of the State should be carried out only by native Romanians. Minorities who prove to be enemies of the ethnocratic State forgo their citizenship and are to be expelled.

B. Right-Wing Nationalism Right-wing nationalism puts moral values before the material interests of the Nation. It therefore openly conflicts with the communist as well as social-democratic and liberal theories. In our concept the State is supreme. The State is the depository of ideals. Nothing can exist outside the State, nobody can be against the State, because the people is the body of the State, but the State is the spirit of the people. Outside the State man is nothing, within the State he is everything. Before there can be rights there must be duties. When man is born he has no rights.[. . .] The rights of man, invented by some utopian thinkers such as Jean Jacques Rousseau, is no more than a slogan designed for the idle and the poor. Because people of this sort cannot aspire to the dignity of the hero, because people of this sort run away from sacrifice and are frightened of inequality and natural law, because people of this sort do not accept law and order, they are always demanding rights which they have not earned. People can only have rights when they face up to their duties to the nation.[. . .]

E. *The Offensive of Romanianism* The National Right has launched the Offensive of Romanianism. Our Latin spirit prevails over Judaeo-Masonic mercantilism, and will use the law to combat the primitive and anarchic views of unintegrated gypsies, while resolutely opposing the revisionist demands of some Hungarians and Slavs. The ethnocratic State, based on the collective identity of Romanians, has three principal virtues: legislative spirit, organizational spirit, and military spirit. The Romanian nation has the historical duty to defend its vital space. In these conditions, every struggle is justified, every war has historical legitimacy. Romania must once again become the most powerful state in the Balkans by imposing conditions at the conference table. If you are not willing to stand firm, you will die as a nation. Other powers will relish transferring us to the cemetery of oblivion.[. . .]

IV. *The Foreign Policy of the National Right*

The ethnocratic State, supported by the National Right, does not recognize the legitimacy of European and international institutions created during the Cold War, because it was based on balance of force. This led us to a global policy which does not take account of the national will. The ethnocratic State promotes direct, bilateral relationships. Romania must align itself economically and militarily with Germany and Japan.[. . .]

['The National Right's Manifesto to the Nation', *Noua Dreaptă*, 1 (1993), 8–9.]

c. *Electoral Fascism*

FRENTE NACIONAL

208 Living Stones of the New Spain

Nearly four decades of authoritarian rule under Franco seem to have left most Spaniards disenchanted with ultra-right solutions to the problems of State, and both the nostalgic and neo-fascist right have remained highly marginalized. The only potential leader figure with some charisma has been Blas Piñar, who founded the Frente Nacional in 1986 after the failure of his Fuerza Nueva (New Force), which had effectively folded in 1982 after only six years of activity. This speech, made to the first Youth Congress of the Frente Nacional on 14 May 1988, attempts to modernize the discourse of the Falangism (for example, the allusion to José Antonio and syndicalism) and Franquism (for example, the stress on Catholicism and the family) by avoiding overtly revolutionary attacks on liberal democracy and confining itself to vague references to 'saving Europe'. Given the party's pathetic performances in both the 1987 and 1989 elections in which it won no seats at all, the call for 'new men' rings particularly hollow, testifying to the grotesque degree of self-delusion which has been a recurrent feature of fascist visions of an imminent transition to a new order.

I would like, with the necessary brevity and clarity, to establish precisely what we see when we look at the Spain of today, the Spain in which we live, in which we survive. It is a Spain which is in tatters, unstable, desperate, timid, frightened, oscillating between being atonic and epileptic. I invite you to accompany me in this task, which cannot be exhaustive but only partial, and which does not mean dwelling on the negative and tragic, for its basic aim is to arouse the desire to revive and rally the national energies which seem to have either gone to waste or gone to sleep. For this purpose we are not going to use the eyes of the flesh or the eyes of the intelligence, but, above all, the eyes of the heart, because the eyes which love the Fatherland in ruins with the will to serve it can stimulate the spirit of struggle which is so sadly lacking in most.

Build on rock using living stones. This is an absolute premiss of all serious politics. Let us try to look with the loving eyes of the heart for the living stones with which, on the foundations of solid rock, it is possible to build a society which will serve man and, at the same time, fashion a man who will perfect the society he belongs to. If we think of Spain as a nation and society, we mean a historical entity which has created itself in the course of centuries, which still remains today, however wounded and infirm, and which is moving into an uncertain future, I would like to suggest that the following are just such living stones: theological faith, patriotism, the family, justice, and the mission.

A. Faith   [. . .] If the theocratic State is an absurdity, so is the lay State, which secularizes politics, declares itself independent of any higher norm, and falls prey to the tyranny of positivism, which never recognizes any rights other than those granted by a framework of laws which has been instituted by a majority. José Antonio asserted that the lay State, as a neutral State, does not exist. For this reason José Antonio had no hesitation in wanting the reconstruction of Spain to be made following a Catholic path which, besides, is the only path proper to a Christian nation.[. . .]

B. Patriotism   [. . .] This love of our Fatherland must stir us to denounce lack of love and adulterous love. For it is lack of love for the country when it is regarded with indifference, or when, out of egoism, convenience, or cowardice we refuse to defend it. It is adulterous love towards the Fatherland when it is betrayed in the service of bastard or foreign interests, when in its place is substituted love for a land which claims the right to tear itself away from the whole.[. . .]

C. The Family   [. . .] Without a strong family a corner-stone of Spain's reconstruction would be missing.

D. Justice   [. . .] It is clear that Syndicalism is an integral part of a modern society and plays in it a role of supreme importance. Of course there are three types of Syndicalism: the syndicalism of attack which is used as an instrument by a party— generally a Marxist one—which aspires to seize State power; syndicalism of defence, which is formed as an independent instrument by professional groups on the margins of the state. Then there is the syndicalism of integration, independent and professional but, while remaining distinct from the State, is integrated within the state in the form of a Corporation and assumes two functions within it: a political one, via its representation within legislative bodies and the organs of public administration, and an economic one by intervening through its consultative or decision-making capacity in the elaboration of short-term policies and long-term strategy.[. . .]

E. Our Mission   [. . .] Spain, a Christian nation, has always had and still has an ecumenical mission, and has taken on the task of going forth and spreading the Gospel. This vocation has been manifested in the way it responded to two great challenges, the challenge of Europe and the challenge of the Hispanic world.[. . .] We saved Europe from Islam in the South, from the Turk in the East, and from Communism in the Crusade of 1936.[. . .] The Hispanic World was our work of genius.[. . .]

Hence Europe and the Hispanic World are for us Spaniards a call to arms which we cannot ignore. In both spheres we have a decisive mission to accomplish, and the call of Europe cannot make us forget the Hispanic World, nor can the call of the Hispanic World weaken our resolve to contribute to the task of rebuilding the continent of Europe on the basis of its true roots.[. . .]

These are the five living stones. Either we use them or we throw them away. However, there are two ways to throw them away: one is to hurl them into the abyss; the other is to use them, but only after weakening them and breaking them down so much that instead of being living stones they start flaking and crumbling. This is how the liberal right normally operates, flinging them into a System which kills them off through its own ideological basis. As Le Pen said in one of his electoral addresses: 'All those who contribute in any way to maintaining the System promote the destruction, whether fast or slow, of the values of Christian civilization.' This is not our politics, a politics of ambiguity and compromise, a politics which is neither hot nor cold, and which makes God vomit.

We need men. We are looking for men [. . .], but men of our time who are able to reap the harvest of the past and intend to build in the future without forgetting that times have changed since 1936, society is different, and the global context is distinctive.[. . .] Hence immutable Principles demand a different strategy to make an impact and give shape to the nation.

[Blas Piñar, *Fuerza Nueva*, 963 (28 May–11 June 1988), 28–34.]

Until it was eclipsed by the Republikaner and the Deutsche Volksunion in the late 1980s, the National Democratic Party of Germany was the Federal Republic's most successful crypto-fascist party. The nostalgia for the Third Reich of its hard-core membership was translated into the muted policies of heightened patriotism, reunification, end to immigration, and anti-communism compatible with a 'radical right' rather than an 'extreme right' movement (a distinction critical to its legality in Germany). Its leader shows here that he has mastered the encoded language of neo-fascism by his obligatory references to self-determination, identity, the environment, revisionism, and Europe. The assumption that the Germans constitute a homogeneous Volk *still betrays the fundamental illiberalism of his position.*

In my opinion an authentic German-national social people's party such as the NPD is to be founded on the following principles:

1. The German people is the centre and goal of all national politics. The German people has a right to its *völkisch* national autonomy. This raises the question of German being, Germanness, or, in modern terminology, of German identity. This approach and basic consideration determines how questions concerning immigration in whatever form—via the EC or political asylum, etc.—are to be tackled. For me Germany [*Deutschland*] is and remains the land of the Germans [*Land der Deutschen*], and it should not degenerate into an exotic country.

2. Principle 1 is the basis of the demand for the self-determination of the Germans, and hence the question of sovereignty, which in turn frames questions relating to NATO, the EC, and immigration. We reject NATO and the EC as instruments for the international regimentation of the Germans and of their control by foreigners. We are opposed to a policy of 'open borders'. We want to determine our own affairs in every respect and in every sphere.

3. The stress on national criteria goes hand in hand with the call for social justice for Germans in Germany, because a just social order can bring about equality and solidarity both inwardly and outwardly. We are a people, want to remain a people and not become an EC, UNO society or any sort of 'something else' society.

4. Whoever wants a people, a nation also wants a healthy environment in which national life can develop. The protection of nature, of the organic natural world, as well as the protection of life, especially within the family, and towards every new life, enjoy the same priority as Principles 1 to 3.

5. The economy must stay national in spite of international collaboration. Hence no decisions affecting us are to be made by foreign capital in whatever area and on whatever scale. There must be no sell-out of German industry or German territory to foreigners. Our goal: the socially controlled market economy on the principle 'as much freedom as possible and as much state as necessary' for the protection of the individual just as much as the whole people against exploitation, lack of control of their lives, and oppression.

6. A people that is healthy, or wants to become it, must know where it comes from. It must know what was, what it objectively has been, so as to prevent historiography or re-education bringing about alienation from its own people, or even hatred towards its own people. Therefore I support all efforts of scientific revisionism, and I am committed to make my own contribution to it especially through translations. A book entitled 'Contributions to Revisionism' is planned in which I am involved as both editor and translator. In this context it is in order to avoid misunderstandings if I explicitly state that Germany is for me more than the old Federal Republic plus the new Federal Republic. Germany for me is Germany within the *völkisch* frontiers which have historically grown up. The old JN/NPD slogan of the 1970s which I helped formulate was 'National solidarity—Social justice!' This message, taken together with the principles of sovereignty and German identity, does not only have a future in Central Germany (which is not Eastern Germany). Europe for me is not the EC. Europe is the home [*Heimat*] of the Europeans with whom we feel bound in partnership. We reject an artificial EC-state. An International of Nations, of Fatherlands bound in partnership is a practical goal and one worth striving for.

[Günter Deckert, *Deutsche Stimme*, 7/8 (Feb. 1993), 9.]

BRITISH NATIONAL PARTY
....

210 **Saving the Nation**

The British National Party caused a brief 'moral panic' in the media when in September 1993 its candidate Derek Beackon was one of the town councillors elected to represent Tower Hamlets, a particularly run-down part of the East End of London. It was formed by the veteran fascist agitator John Tyndall in 1982 as a result of schisms which occurred within the National Front in the wake of its eclipse after the 1979 general election, and has effectively replaced it as Britain's most important fascist movement. The party's 'esoteric' ideology emanating from the top is a virulent neo-Nazism adapted to the British situation (see Text 202). However, in its pronouncements for more public consumption (as in this regular insert in the party organ British Nationalist: BNP) *the vision of a white supremacist post-liberal corporate state under an authoritarian leader is translated into as 'democratic' a discourse as possible, though it is not difficult to decode its 'subtext'.*

- The establishment of a government of national unity that will put an end to nationally divisive party warfare; the return of leadership and statesmanship to British affairs.
- An end to immigration and a start to repatriation.
- British withdrawal from the Common Market.
- The disbanding of the multi-racial Commonwealth and its replacement by a new Commonwealth of self-governing white states.
- British ownership and control of British industry and resources.

- Protection of British industry by the selective exclusion of foreign manufactured goods from the British market.
- An end to the financial swindle that causes inflation and slump, and its replacement by a sane and fair financial system that will give the people the purchasing power to buy the goods they produce.
- The subordination of the power of the City to the power of government, and the harnessing of the City to the needs of British industry.
- The regeneration of British farming, with the object of achieving the maximum possible self-sufficiency in food production.
- Rejection of both the poll tax and its substitute, the new 'property tax' and a return to the old rates system, though with fairer rebates allowing for differences in income and in the numbers occupying properties.
- A healthy environment for a healthy people—the protection of our countryside and an end to the architectural disfigurement of our towns and cities.
- Tougher treatment of criminals, including the return of the death penalty.
- A return to traditional methods of education, with stronger discipline in the classroom and the sacking of 'trendy' teachers.
- An alternative defence strategy: withdrawal from NATO, closure of all foreign military and air bases in Britain, the strengthening of Britain's defences and a position of armed neutrality.
- An end to overseas aid and the allocation of the money saved to the financing of repatriation and greater help for the needy at home.
- The crushing of the IRA, the termination of the Anglo-Irish Agreement and firm support for the Loyalist majority in Northern Ireland.
- Repeal of the laws permitting homosexuality and abortion (except where the latter is the result of rape or necessary on medical grounds), the wiping out of AIDS and a return to healthy moral values aimed at strengthening the family and community.

['What We Stand for', *British Nationalist: BNP*, May 1993, 8.]

MOVIMENTO SOCIALE ITALIANO

211   **For a New Italy**

In the Italian general election of March 1994 the Movimento Sociale Italiano/Alleanza Nazionale bloc won 12.7 per cent of the vote and 109 seats in the Italian parliament as part of Berlusconi's right-wing 'Freedom Alliance'. The MSI/AN leader, Gianfranco Fini, chose to avoid controversy by refusing to accept a portfolio, but four MSI deputies became ministers. Furthermore, in the Euro-elections held in June the same year the MSI/AN vote was 12.5 per cent and resulted in the appointment to Strasburg of veteran MSI deputy Pino Rauti, whose Le idee che mossero il mondo *[The Ideas which Moved the World] of 1965 is an undisguised celebration of European Fascism in Evolian key (see Texts 171, 188). The long-term implications of this dramatic turn of events in a campaign to 'clean up' Italian political life are impossible to predict. The MSI is in direct line of descent from the Partito fascista repubblicano (see Text 43), but has gone to great lengths to translate its fundamentally illiberal vision into the language of democracy (thereby alienating the movement's hard-liners) in the extended MSI/AN manifesto, from which these excerpts are taken. However, the Fascist connotations of the calls for a new Italy, a new State, and revised borders with Dalmatia, together with the stress on moral values and youth, would not be lost on any historically literate voter, and Fini's declaration shortly after the elections that Mussolini had been Italy's greatest statesman of the century was hardly reassuring.*

The year 1993 was crucial. It marked the end of the old and the beginning of the new. Until a few years ago in the era of the democracy of parties,[24] the Italians were convinced of exercising sovereignty by always voting 'for someone' or sometimes 'against something', but never 'for something'. It was only in 1993 that the scandal of the irrelevance of their vote as a means of showing who should govern became apparent.[. . .]

The State is the image of the Nation, epitomizing its values by perpetuating hate. It exalts the qualities of the people whose rights it safeguards; it tells them their duties; it promotes development; it is the inspiring force behind national education and the artefact of justice; it is the guarantor of social equilibrium through the principle of solidarity understood as a synthesis of rights and duties. In this indissoluble identity the roots of the Nation-State extend deep into history and tradition, and it identifies the path to progress by pursuing the maximum common good— the good of the nation—on the basis of which it ensures that all individual needs of individuals and groups are met. With the disappearance of the sense of the State and the travesty of the State itself into a regime of parties, the sense of Nation has disappeared, and with it the awareness of the value of the 'national community' so that the State has come to take material form in its worst aspects: bureaucratic centralism, draconian tax regimes, partitocracy.[. . .]

The identity of the Partito democratico della sinistra[25] has been aptly described as a 'radical mass party', that is, a confederation of groupings promoting causes which range from the politicization of homosexuality to the most extreme and irrational forms of ecologism and feminism, and all lead to the complete laicization of the Italian people. In contrast, our identity is based on the integral respect for the reality of the human person and his or her sacredness.[. . .]

Now a great chance for the introduction of a new model of political representation has been created by the failure of the partitocratic system, by the wiping out of the old parties brought about by the electorate, and by new personalities entering the political stage who are more representative and more reliable than their predecessors.[. . .] The concomitant of a government made strong by direct popular investiture is a strong parliament with extensive powers of policy-making and control.[. . .]

---

[24] An allusion to the pejorative Italian term 'partitocrazia' or 'party-ocracy', which evokes the chaos and corruption of Italy's political system.

[25] The rebaptized Communist Party.

The present situation is the result of the total failure of the absurd and suicidal race for the paradise of possessions and appearances instead of pursuing the only world which gives quality and substance to a person, namely the world of 'being'. This is the difference which has always distinguished the Youth Front [Fronte del Gioventù] from other youth organizations.[. . .] It is because of its way of being, its history, its tradition, its presence in the country, that today the Youth Front must form the nucleus of a youth alliance (like the MSI–DN[26] in the national alliance), a broad based movement which enables different souls to identify with a political project in which values such as national identity, freedom, right to life, the family, and solidarity provide the base for the reconstruction of the nation.[. . .]

After German unification, Italian unification with the return, sanctioned through international agreements, of Istria, Fiume, Dalmatia. [. . .] An allied Europe [. . .] no more subordination, but European strength, independence, and autonomy in political and military decisions.[. . .] There is an Italian people living and working beyond the frontiers of the Fatherland [. . .] nearly 60 million of Italian extraction according to the estimates of the Foreign Minister: a huge potential force, totally ignored and even discriminated against by Italian governments and the forces of Italian politics.[. . .] We will obtain their electoral participation for the reconstruction of the Italian state.

['Il Programma della destra per la Nuova Italia' [The Right's programme for the New Italy], *Secolo d'Italia*, 27 Feb. 1994, 1–4, 7, 10, 12.]

RUSSIA'S LIBERAL DEMOCRATIC PARTY

212   King Kong Meets his Match

The success of Vladimir Zhirinovsky's Liberal Democratic Party in obtaining 23 per cent of the votes for the 'all federal list' in the 1993 Russian elections (giving it sixty-four deputies and making it the third largest parliamentary faction) sounded alarm bells for all those concerned about the future stability not just of Russia itself, but of the post-Cold War world order. Zhirinovsky, a prolific self-promoter, has made enough contradictory statements in his brief but spectacular career to make him difficult to categorize in conventional political terms. There can be no doubt, however, that he espouses a radical irredentist programme for reintegrating Russians within new frontiers, and intends to teach Europe a lesson in how to put an end to the multi-ethnic and pluralistic society espoused by all truly democratic liberals and socialists. His article was published by one of the LDP party newspapers, Sokol Zhirinovskogo *(Zhirinovsky's Falcon), and betrays an unmistakably fascist mind-set. Though now unlikely to replace Yeltsin as next president, Zhirinovsky's impact in legitimizing ultra-nationalist ideas as an integral part of the parliamentary rather than the extraparliamentary political arena could make comment by many a historian to the effect that fascism effectively died in 1945 ring hollow indeed.*

---

[26] In 1971 the MSI merged with the Monarchist Party and changed its name to MSI–Destra Nazionale (MSI–National Right).

The bearers of white civilization are disappearing. The world is turning yellow, and red, and black. No place is being left on the planet for the White person. As we approach the year 2000 the White race comprises just 7 or 8 per cent of the population of the globe. The old film-clip about King Kong gripping in his paw the beautiful blonde woman carries its ominous subtext: soon—very soon—that is precisely how the European will feel in the face of other races and peoples.

Yes, we can say with pride: contemporary world civilization has been built by the White person; all other peoples aspire to imitate and copy us, feeling through that a humiliating dependence on us and their own second-rateness in the established world order.[. . .]

Two civilizations cannot go on living together in North America.[. . .] White America will be violently swallowed up by non-White ethnic groups; those of Anglo-Saxon, European, and Jewish extraction not worthy of counting themselves amongst Europeans will find themselves amongst a terrified minority facing the huge mass of black, yellow, and red dwellers on this earth. There will come a demand for the setting up of ethnically pure states on the territory of the former USA. The coloured majority subject to such a fearful and destructive aggravation could then receive moral and material support from Russians (in the shape of Russian weapons).[. . .] The Whites can then of course either live as small colonies on reservations in the midst of these deeply antagonistic states, or return to their historic homeland.[. . .] There is another possibility, of course: when the Whites of America, moved by a healthy impulse for survival and by racial instinct, carry through the deportation of the dark part of the population to their historic homeland. Into the space thus freed up, and with the active help of the Russian government, could be sent representatives of those nations and peoples which, under the guise of national right to self-determination, took part in the destruction of the historic Russian state: a section of Ukrainian nationalists; the leftovers of the non-Russian population in the Baltic region; and the refugees of the virtually disappearing Armenia. These immigrants will make a fine sauce for the ethnic stew in America. At the same time, the enforced expulsion of anti-state elements will make room for the development and improvement of the quality of the population of the renewed Russia.[. . .]

In the political long term, there can be no doubt that once the system of occupation in the Greater Germany is complete there will begin a time for new and joyful changes in Europe. The Germans have truly recognized their own position and the lessons of history: the great racial qualities of Russians. Only with Russians will they be able to find genuine support in their struggle against the rottenness of North American civilization. Together with Russians they will be able to wreak revenge on America for its fierce internationalism and anti-Germanism. Russia and Germany together will be able to ensure the violent end of the United States and the establishment of a healthier racial balance on the continent of Europe.[. . .] And, as our leader Vladimir Zhirinovsky truly points out: 'The joint exit (*vykhod*) of Europe's two great powers towards the shores of the warm Indian Ocean can refresh more than one generation of German and Russian youth.'

Effeminate Europe may still not be completely ready for such a turn of events. There's no doubt, however, that with Russian help Germany should be able to return to itself the historic lands of Alsace-Lorraine (Elsass and Lothringia), for which so much German blood was shed, as well as the Sudetenland and the Baltic coasts of Prussia. Together we shall be able to create on the southern shore of France a new Arab state with the population of those derived from the countries of North Africa.[. . .]

For the first time in world history it will also be possible to create a state along sexual lines: homosexuals should permanently get their own little corner of lust where they will feel genuinely at home. Various regions of Holland or even Amsterdam could be converted into such self-nurturing states.[. . .]

Above all, as the first stage of the new politics, there will be a strong return of nations to their own languages—even by an enforced route. We Russians shall need to demand of non-Russian peoples who insist on their own states that they cease the use of our language in all areas of life, or perhaps the introduction of a charge for using our language. The instruction of non-Russians will only be possible in the local language. No more conversations, negotiations, or interviews of local tribal leaders in Russian! Temporary rulers from the margins of Russia must stop it, and never, anywhere (even in their sleep) use Russian words—and must order their relations to do the same. We must bring in severe laws forbidding the use of Russian as a language of international intercourse.[. . .] We Russians shall at long last stop experiencing the feeling of shame for our precious language corrupted by ridiculous accents.

We Europeans must put all our efforts into returning peoples artificially transplanted into our White civilization to their national roots and their natural way of life. Less contact, no technical aid, no instruction of specialists and students! To cultivate in the end a United Nations of peoples of White race.[. . .]

We shall build a world of hope, stability, and happiness, giving the opportunity for all races, nations, and peoples to develop their civilizations IN PARALLEL, without mixing and with minimal interaction. The grievous experience of the past thousand years, and especially of the twentieth century, has shown emphatically that any kind of intermingling and mutual influence is the way only to death and degradation for the White race. But in parallel civilizations lie paths to the achievement of true internationalism and friendship of peoples.

[Andrei Arkhipov, 'Novyi poriadok: parallel'nye tsivilizatsii' [The New Order: parallel civilizations], from a section called 'Belyi Mir' [White world], in *Sokol Zhirinovskogo* [Zhirinovsky's Falcon], 2 (1992), 8–9.]

213 **The Deadly Trunk of Fascism**

Primo Levi (1919–87) was born in Turin, where he graduated in chemistry shortly before the Fascist racial laws of 1938 made it impossible for Jews to take academic degrees. After the armistice of 1943 he joined a partisan group, and was finally arrested in 1944, sent to Auschwitz, and condemned to be worked to death at the Buna artificial rubber works. It was his knowledge as a chemist which enabled him to survive till the Russians arrived in the area, and a fortuitous illness which spared him the death march of prisoners from the camp. After the war he took up a successful career as an industrial chemist, but devoted his spare time to writing a series of works bearing witness to the atrocities committed at the camp, and to the extraordinary forces of human resilience in inwardly resisting the extremes of brutality and degradation to which he was exposed. This passage is taken from an appendix to the English paperback edition of his most famous work, If This Is a Man (1958), published in the year that he committed suicide. One of the factors contributing to the depression which prompted this act was Levi's sense that a new generation had arisen who either were oblivious of the realities of fascism in power, or who were swayed by the efforts of historical revisionists to cast doubt on the very existence of the Nazis' extermination camps and their policy of systematic genocide.

There is no rationality in the Nazi hatred: it is a hate that is not in us; it is outside man, it is a poison fruit sprung from the deadly trunk of fascism, but it is outside and beyond fascism itself. We cannot understand it, but we can and must understand from where it springs, and we must be on our guard. If understanding is impossible, knowing is imperative, because what happened could happen again. Conscience can be seduced and obscured again—even our consciences.

For this reason, it is everyone's duty to reflect on what happened. Everybody must know, or remember, that when Hitler and Mussolini spoke in public, they were believed, applauded, admired, adored like gods. They were 'charismatic leaders'; they possessed a secret power of seduction that did not proceed from the credibility or the soundness of the things they said, but from the suggestive way in which they said them, from their eloquence, from their histrionic art, perhaps instinctive, perhaps patiently learned and practised. The ideas they proclaimed were not always the same and were, in general, aberrant or silly or cruel. And yet they were acclaimed with hosannas and followed to the death by millions of the faithful. We must remember that these faithful followers, among them the diligent executors of inhuman orders, were not born torturers, were not (with a few exceptions) monsters: they were ordinary men. Monsters exist, but they are too few in number to be truly dangerous. More dangerous are the common men, the functionaries ready to believe and to act without asking questions, like Eichmann; like Höss, the commandant of Auschwitz; like Stangl, commandant of Treblinka; like the French military of twenty years later, slaughterers in Algeria; like the Khmer Rouge of the late seventies, slaughterers in Cambodia.

It is, therefore, necessary to be suspicious of those who seek to convince us with means other than reason, and of charismatic leaders: we must be cautious about delegating to others our judgement and our will. Since it is difficult to distinguish true prophets from false, it is as well to regard all prophets with suspicion. It is better to renounce revealed truths, even if they exalt us by their splendour or if we find them convenient because we can acquire them gratis. It is better to content oneself with other more modest and less exciting truths, those one acquires painfully, little by little and without short cuts, with study, discussion and reasoning, those that can be verified and demonstrated.

It is clear that this formula is too simplistic to suffice in every case. A new fascism, with its trail of intolerance, of abuse, and of servitude, can be born outside our country and imported into it, walking on tiptoe and calling itself by other names, or it can loose itself from without with such violence that it routs all defences. At that point, wise counsel no longer serves, and one must find the strength to resist. Even in this contingency, the memory of what happened in the heart of Europe, not very long ago, can serve as a warning and support.

[*If This Is a Man* (Sphere Books: London, 1987), 396–7.]

Select Bibliography

....

(Restricted to secondary sources on fascism published in English and not used as sources of extracts)

I. GENERIC FASCISM

The Debate on Fascism

BERGHAUS, G. (1995) (ed.), *Fascism and Theatre: Comparative Studies on the Aesthetics and Politics of Performance in Inter-war Europe* (Berghahn Books: Oxford, forthcoming).

BLINKHORN, MARTIN (1990) (ed.), *Fascists and Conservatives* (Unwin Hyman, London).

DE FELICE, RENZO (1977), *Interpretations of Fascism* (Harvard University Press: Cambridge, Mass.).

—— and LEDEEN, MICHAEL (1976), *Fascism: An Informal Introduction to its Theory and Practice* (Transition: New Brunswick, NJ).

GREGOR, A. JAMES (1974), *Interpretations of Fascism* (General Learning Press: Morristown, NJ).

GRIFFIN, ROGER D. (1993), *The Nature of Fascism* (Routledge: London).

—— (1993), *Europe for the Europeans. Fascist Myths of the New European Order, 1922–92* (Humanities Research Centre Occasional Papers, 1, School of Humanities, Oxford Brookes University: Oxford).

—— (1994), *Modernity under the New Order: The Fascist Project for Managing the Future*, no. 2 in the series Modernity and Post-Modernity: Mapping the Terrain (Thamesman Publications, School of Business, Oxford Brookes University: Oxford).

ROBINSON, R. A. H. (1981), *Fascism in Europe* (Historical Association: London).

STERNHELL, ZEEV (1979), 'Fascist Ideology', in Walter Laqueur (ed.), *Fascism: A Reader's Guide* (Penguin: Harmondsworth).

TURNER, S., and KÄSLER, D. (1992), (eds.), *Sociology Responds to Fascism* (Routledge: London).

WEBER, EUGEN (1964), *Varieties of Fascism* (Van Nostrand: New York).

Marxist Theories of Fascism

TROTSKY, LEON (1971), *The Struggle against Fascism in Germany*, ed. Ernest Mandel (Pathfinder Press: New York).

POULANTZAS, N. (1974), *Fascism and Dictatorship* (New Left Books: London).

BEETHAM, DAVID (1983), *Marxists in Face of Fascism* (Manchester University Press: Manchester).

Fascism and Totalitarianism

ARENDT, HANNAH (1967), *The Origins of Totalitarianism* (Allen & Unwin: London).

RADEL, J.-LUCIEN (1975), *Roots of Totalitarianism: The Ideological Sources of Fascism, National Socialism and Communism* (Crane, Russak & Co.: New York).

II. ITALIAN FASCISM

ADAMSON, W. L. (1989), 'Fascism and Culture: Avant-Gardes and Secular Religion in the Italian Case', *Journal of Contemporary History*, 24.

ADAMSON, W. L. (1992), 'The Language of Opposition in Early 20th Century Italy: Rhetorical Continuities between Pre-War Florentine Avant-Gardism and Mussolini's Fascism', *Journal of Modern History*, 64/1.

—— (1993), *Avant-Garde Florence: From Fascism to Modernism* (Harvard University Press: Cambridge, Mass.).

CANNISTRARO, P. V. (1982) (ed.), *A Historical Dictionary of Fascist Italy* (Greenwood Press: Westport, Conn.).

DE GRAND A. J. (1978), *The Italian Nationalist Association and the Rise of Fascism in Italy* (University of Nebraska Press: London).

GRAZIA, V. DE (1994), *How Fascism Ruled Women* (University of California Press: Berkeley).

GREGOR, A. JAMES (1979), *The Young Mussolini and the Intellectual Origins of Fascism* (University of California Press: Berkeley).

KOON, T. (1985), *Believe, Obey, Fight: Political Socialization of Youth in Fascist Italy 1922–43* (University of North Carolina Press: Chapel Hill, NC).

LEDEEN, M. A. (1972), *Universal Fascism* (Howard Fertig: New York).

—— (1977), *The First Duce: D'Annunzio at Fiume* (Johns Hopkins University Press: Baltimore).

LYTTELTON, ADRIAN (1973), *Italian Fascisms from Pareto to Gentile* (revised edn.; Jonathan Cape: London).

—— (1987), *The Seizure of Power: Fascism in Italy 1919–1929* (2nd edn.; Weidenfeld & Nicolson: London; 1st edn. 1973).

MICHAELIS, M. (1978), *Mussolini and the Jews* (Clarendon Press: Oxford).

ROBERTS, D. D. (1979), *The Syndicalist Tradition in Italian Fascism* (Manchester University Press: Manchester).

SBACCHI, A. (1989), *Ethiopia under Mussolini* (Zed Books: London).

STERNHELL, ZEEV, with SZNAJDER MARIO, and ASHERI MAIA (1994), *The Birth of Fascist Ideology* (Princeton University Press: Princeton, NJ).

STONE, M. (1993), 'Staging Fascism: The Exhibition of the Fascist Revolution', *Journal of Contemporary History*, 28.

SZNAJDER, MARIO (1989), 'The "Carta del Carnaro" and Modernization', *Tel Aviv Jahrbuch für deutsche Geschichte*, 18.

TANNENBAUM, E. R. (1972), *The Fascist Experience: Italian Society and Culture 1922–1945* (Basic Books: New York).

III. GERMAN FASCISM

ADAM, P. (1992), *The Arts of the Third Reich* (Thames & Hudson: London).

BRACHER, K. D. (1970), *The German Dictatorship* (Penguin: Harmondsworth).

GRUNBERGER, R. (1974), *A Social History of the Third Reich* (Penguin: Harmondsworth).

HERF, J. (1984), *Reactionary Modernism* (Cambridge University Press: Cambridge).

HERZSTEIN, R. E. (1982), *When Nazi Dreams Come True* (Abacus: London).

HILDEBRAND, K. (1984), *The Third Reich* (Allen & Unwin: London).

HITLER, A. (1972), *Mein Kampf*, tr. R. Mannheim (Hutchinson: London).

Hitler's Table Talk 1941–1944 (1953) (Weidenfeld & Nicolson: London).

KERSHAW, IAN (1987), *The Hitler Myth* (Oxford University Press: Oxford).

—— (1990) (ed.), *Weimar: Why Did German Democracy Fail?* (Weidenfeld & Nicolson: London).

—— (1991), *Hitler* (Longman: London).

—— (1993), *The Nazi Dictatorship*, (3rd edn.; Edward Arnold: London).

LOCHNER, L. P. (1948) (tr. and ed.), *The Goebbels Diaries* (Hamish Hamilton: London).

MOSSE, G. L. (1966), *The Crisis of German Ideology* (Weidenfeld & Nicolson).
—— (1980), *Masses and Man* (Howard Fertig: New York).
MÜHLBERGER, DETLEF (1991), *Hitler's Followers: Studies in the Sociology of the Nazi Movement* (Routledge: London).
NOAKES, J., and PRIDHAM, G. (1974), *Documents of Nazism 1919–1945* (Jonathan Cape: London).
—— —— (1984, 1988), *Nazism 1919–1945: A Documentary Reader* (Exeter University Press: Exeter; vols. i and ii 1984, vol. iii 1988).
PEUKERT, D. J. K. (1987), *Inside Nazi Germany* (Penguin: Harmondsworth).
POIS, R. A. (1970) (ed.), *Alfred Rosenberg: Selected Writings* (Jonathan Cape: London).
PULZER, PETER (1988), *The Rise of Political Anti-Semitism in Germany and Austria* (revised edn.; Peter Halban: London).
SMELSER, R. (1988), *Robert Ley* (Berg: Oxford).
STACHURA, P. D. (1983) (ed.), *The Nazi Machtergreifung* (Allen & Unwin: London).
—— (1983), *Gregor Strasser and the Rise of Nazism* (Allen & Unwin: London).
STERN, F. (1961), *The Politics of Cultural Despair* (University of California Press: Berkeley).

IV. OVERVIEWS OF INTER-WAR FASCISM

CARSTEN, F. L. (1967), *The Rise of Fascism* (Methuen: London).
KEDWARD, H. R. (1969), *Fascism in Western Europe 1900–45* (Blackie: London).
LAQUEUR, W. (1979) (ed.) *Fascism: A Reader's Guide* (Penguin: Harmondsworth).
MOSSE, G. L. (1979) (ed.), *International Fascism: New Thoughts and Approaches* (Sage: London).
ROGGER, H., and WEBER, E. (1966), *The European Right* (University of California Press: Berkeley).
WOOLF, S. J. (1981) (ed.), *European Fascism* (Weidenfeld & Nicolson: London).

V. ABORTIVE INTER-WAR MOVEMENTS

ALEXANDER, R. J. (1973), *Latin American Political Parties* (Praeger: New York).
BLOOMBERG, C. (1981), *Christian-Nationalism and the Rise of the Afrikaner Broederbond in South-Africa 1918–48* (Macmillan: New York).
CONWAY, M. (1993), *Collaboration in Belgium: Léon Degrelle and the Rexist Movement 1940–1944* (Yale: Newhaven-London).
CRONIN, M. (1995), 'The Blueshirt Movement 1932–5: Ireland's Fascists?', *Journal of Contemporary History*, 30/2.
DEÁK, I. (1965), 'Hungary' in H. Roger and E. Weber (eds.), *The European Right* (University of California Press: Berkeley).
GALLAGHER, TOM (1990), 'Conservatism, dictatorship and fascism in Portugal, 1914–45', in M. Blinkhorn (ed.) *Fascists and Conservatives* (Unwin Hyman: London).
GRIFFITHS, R. (1983), *Fellow Travellers of the Right* (Oxford University Press: Oxford).
HOIDAL, O. (1989), *Quisling. A Study in Treason* (Oxford University Press: Oxford).
IOANID, RADU (1990), *The sword of the Archangel: Fascist Ideology in Romania*, trans. Peter Heinegg (East European Monographs: Boulder Colo.).
KARVONEN, L. (1988), 'From White to Blue-and-Black. Finnish Fascism in the Inter-war Period, *Commentationes Scientarum Socialium*, No. 36.
KASEKAMP, A. (1993), 'The Estonian Veterans' League: A Fascist Movement?', *Journal of Baltic Studies*, 24/3.
LEVINE, R. (1970), *The Vargas Regime: The Critical Years, 1934–38* (Columbia University Press: New York).

NAJITA, T. (1971), 'Nakano Seigō and the Spirit of the Meiji Restoration in Twentieth-Century Japan' in J. W. Morley (ed.) *Dilemmas of Growth in Prewar Japan* (Princeton University Press: Princeton, NJ).

PAYNE, STANLEY (1961), *Falange* (Stanford University Press: Stanford, Calif.).

STERNHELL, ZEEV (1986), *Neither Right nor Left: Fascist Ideology in France*, trans. D. Meisel (University of California Press: Berkeley).

SZNAJDER, MARIO (1993) 'A Case of Non-European Fascism. Chilean National Socialism in the 1930s', *Journal of Contemporary History*, 28/2.

THURLOW, RICHARD (1987), *Fascism in Britain: A History 1918–1985* (Basil Blackwell: Oxford).

VI. POST-WAR FASCISMS

CHELES, L., FERGUSON, R., and VAUGHAN, M. (1991), *Neo-Fascism in Europe* (Longman: London).

EATWELL, R. (1991), 'The Holocaust Denial: A Study in Propaganda Technique', in Cheles *et al.*, *Neo-Fascism in Europe*.

FLYNN, K., and GERHARDT, G. (1990), *The Silent Brotherhood: Inside America's Racist Underground* (Penguin: Harmondsworth).

FORD, G. (1992), *Fascist Europe: The Rise of Racism and Xenophobia* (Pluto Press: London).

From Ballots to Bombs: The Inside Story of the National Front's Political Soldiers (1989), (Searchlight Publishing: London).

HAINSWORTH, P. (1992) (ed.), *The Extreme Right in Europe and America* (Pinter Press: London).

HARRIS, G. (1990), *The Dark Side of Europe: The Extreme Right Today* (Edinburgh University Press: Edinburgh).

HILL, R. (1988), *The Other Face of Terror* (Grafton: London).

HOCKENOS, P. (1993), *Free to Hate: The Rise of the Right in Post-Communist Eastern Europe* (Routledge: New York).

LARSEN, S. (1995) (ed.), *Modern Europe after Fascism* (Princeton University Press: Princeton, NJ).

Ó MAOLÁIN, C. (1987), *The Radical Right: A World Directory* (Longman: London).

SCHMIDT, M. (1993), *The New Reich* (Hutchinson: London).

SEIDEL, G. (1986), *The Holocaust Denial* (Beyond the Pale Collective: Leeds).

THURLOW, RICHARD (1987), *Fascism in Britain: A History 1918–1985* (Basil Blackwell: Oxford).

Valuable sources of up-to-date information on the evolution of the contemporary ultra-right, racism, and fascism published in English:

1. the British monthly *Searchlight* (37B New Cavendish Street, London W1M 8JR);
2. the Intelligence Reports of the Institute of Jewish Affairs (79 Wimpole Street, London, W1M 7DD);
3. the Bulletins of the Center for Democratic Renewal (PO Box 50469, Atlanta, Georgia 30302–0469, USA);
4. for Eastern Europe: the Research Reports of Radio Free Europe/Radio Liberty, Inc. (Oettingenstrasse 67, 8000 Munich 22, Germany; US Office, RFE/RL Research Institute, 1201 Connecticut Avenue, NW, Suite 410, Washington, DC, 20036, USA).

Acknowledgements

Adorno, T. W., excerpt from *The Authoritarian Personality*, E. Frenkel-Brunswick and D. Levinson, N. Sanford. © 1950 by the American Jewish Committee. Copyright renewed. Reprinted by permission of HarperCollins Publishers, Inc.

Allardyce, Gilbert, *What Fascism is not: Thought on the Deflation of a Concept*, American Historical Review, 84 (1979), 367, 370, reprinted by permission of the author.

Amaudrez, Guy, *How to Save Europe*, Europae, 1 (1979), reprinted by permission of Cedade.

Beckerath, Erwin von *Wesen und Werden des fascistischen Staates*, pp. 154-5, © 1927 by Springer Verlag GmbH & Co. KG.

Benn, Gottfried, *Zuchtung, Der neue Staat und die Intellektuellen*, © 1933 by Deutsche Verlags-Anstalt GmbH, Stuttgart.

Benn, Gottfried, *Sämtliche Werke. Stuttgarter Ausgabe. In Verb, mit Ilse Benn hrsg. von Gerhard Schuster. Vol. IV: Prose 2*, Klett-Cotta, © 1989 by J. G. Cotta'sche Buchhandlung Nachfolger GmbH, Stuttgart, 1989.

Benoist, Alain de, tr. of *Les Idées à l'endroit*, © 1979 by Albin Michel—Éditions libres Hallier.

Borgese, G. A., *The Intellectual Origins of Fascism*, by permission of *Social Research*, 1: 4 (1934).

Brady, Robert A., from *The Spirit and Structure of German Fascism*, © 1937 by Robert A. Brady. Used by permission of Viking Penguin, a division of Penguin Books USA, Inc.

British National Party, reprinted by permission of *British Nationalist*, May 1993, PO Box 117, Welling, Kent, DA16 3DW.

Cullen, Padraig, Review of Anna Bramwell, *Blood and Soil: Walther Darré and Hitler's Green Party*, by permission of *The Scorpion*, BCM 5766, London WC1, No. 11 (1987), 36-7.

Day, John, *The SS Re-examined*, by permission of *Spearhead*.

Drucker, Peter, *The End of Economic Man*, © by Transaction Publishers, New Brunswick, NJ (1995): first published 1939, pp. 236, 241, 242.

Eatwell, R., reprinted with permission, *Towards a new model of generic fascism*, Journal of Theoretical Politics, 4: 2 (1992), © by Sage Publications, Ltd.

Eley, Geoffrey, 'What Produces Fascism: Pre-industrial traditions or the crisis of the capitalist state,' *Politics and Society*, 12: 1 (1983), 78-82, © 1983 by Sage Publications, Inc.

'Fascism', *ABC of Political Terms: A Short Guide*, pp. 29-30, © 1982 by Novosti, Moscow.

Felice, Renzo de, *Interpretations of Fascism*, (1977), pp. 11-12, reprinted by permission of Harvard University Press.

Fromm, Erich, *The Fear of Freedom*, (1942), pp. 141, 230-1, reprinted by permission of Routledge, International Thomson Publishing Services, Ltd.

Gregor, A. James, *The Ideology of Fascism: The Rationale of Totalitarianism*, pp. 378-82, adapted with the permission of The Free Press, a Division of Simon & Schuster, © 1969 by The Free Press.

Gründel, E. Günther, *Die Sendung der jungen Generation*, © 1933 by Verlag CH Beck, Munich, pp. 327-37.

Hagtvet, B. (et al.), 'Contemporary Approaches to Fascism: A Survey of Paradigms', in S. Larsen, B. Hagtvet, and J. Mycklebust (eds.), Who Were the Fascists, pp. 28–9 © 1980 by Scandinavian University Press, Norway.

Hagtvet, B. and Rokkan, Stein, 'The Conditions of Fascist Victory', Who Were the Fascists, pp. 131–2, 149, © 1980 by Scandinavian University Press, Norway.

Heidegger, Martin, Einführung in die Metaphysik, (1953: first edition 1935), pp. 28–9, 151–2, © by Max Niemeyer Verlag GmbH & Co. KG.

Hitler, Adolf, 26 February 1924, People's Court, Munich, first day of proceedings, Hitler Sämtliche Aufzeichnungen 1905–1924, ed. Eberhard Jäckel, 1980, pp. 1061–8, reprinted by permission of Deutsche Verlags-Anstalt, GmbH, Stuttgart.

Huber, Hartwig, 'Menschenrecht auf Heimat und Identität', Nation Europa, 39: 7, July 1989. © by Nation Europa Verlag GmbH.

Junger, Ernst, Sämtliche Werke: Vol 8: Essays 2: Der Arbeiter, Klett-Cotta, © 1981 by J. G. Cotta'sche Buchhandlung Nachfolger GmbH, Stuttgart.

Kitchen, Martin, Fascism (1976), pp. 88–91, by permission of Macmillan Press Ltd.

Krebs, Pierre, Die europäische Wiedergeburt, pp. 82–6, 89, © by Grabert Verlag.

Lipset, Seymour M., from Political Man: The Social Bases of Political Movements, by permission of the author.

Mannhardt, Johann W., Der Fachismus, © 1925 by Verlag CH Beck, Munich, pp. 392–4.

Moore, Barrington, from The Social Origins of Dictatorship, pp. 447–8, © 1966 by Barrington Moore, Jr. Printed by permission of Beacon Press.

Niekisch, Ernst, Gewagtes Leben, © 1958 by Verlag Kiepenheuer & Witsch, Köln.

Nolte, Ernst, Three Faces of Fascism, (1965), pp. 453–4, © by Weidenfeld and Nicolson.

Parsons, Talcott, 'Some Sociological Aspects of the Fascist Movements', Social Forces, 21, pp. 138–47. © by The University of North Carolina Press.

Payne, Stanley, Fascism: Comparison and Definition, © 1980 by Stanley Payne, (Madison: The University of Wisconsin Press).

Piazzesi, Mario, diary entry for 24 November 1921, Diario di uno squadrista, ed. M. Toscano, © 1981 by Bonacci Editore, Rome.

Pierce, William L., 'The Turner Diaries', The National Alliance, 1980, pp. 207, 209–11. By permission of the author.

Platt, Gerald M., Thoughts on a Theory of Collective Action: Language Effect and Ideology in Revolution, from New Directions in Psychohistory, by Mel Albin. Reprinted with the permission of Lexington Books, an imprint of The Free Press, a Division of Simon & Schuster. © 1980 by Lexington Books.

Reich, Wilhelm, Excerpts from the Preface to the Third Edition of The Mass Psychology of Fascism, translated by Vincent R. Carfagno. Translation © 1969 by Mary Boyd Higgins as Trustee of the Wilhelm Reich Infant Trust Fund. Reprinted by permission of Favrar, Straus & Giroux, Inc.

Salomon, Ernst von, Die Geächteten, © 1930, 1962 by Rowohlt Verlag GmbH, Reinbek bei Hamburg.

Spengler, Oswold, Jahre der Entscheidung, © 1953 by Verlag CH Beck, Munich, pp. 142–5.

Sternhall, Zeev, 'Fascism,' Blackwell's Encyclopedia of Political Thought (1987), p. 148, © by Blackwell Publishers.

Steukers, Robert, 'Heidegger in Time and Place', by permission of *The Scorpion*, BCM 5766, London WC1, Vol. II, pp. 26–31.

Theweleit, Klaus, *Male Fantasies*, 2 vols, (1987, 1989), vol. 2, pp. 189, 360–1. Reprinted by permission of Blackwell Publishers.

Togliatti, Palmiro, *Lectures on Fascism*, (1976), pp. 1, 3–4, 5. Reprinted by permission of Lawrence and Wishart Ltd.

Turner, Henry A. Jr., 'Fascism and Modernization' in H. A. Turner (ed.) Reappraisals of Fascism, pp. 131–2. Franklin Watts, by permission of Grolier International, Inc.

Tyndall, John, *The Way Ahead, the Eleventh Hour: A Call for British Rebirth*, 1988, by permission of the Albion Press, PO Box 117, Welling, Kent, DA16 3DW.

Walker, Michael, *Spotlight on the New Right*, by permission of *The Scorpion*, BCM 5766, London WC1, No. 10, Autumn 1986, pp. 8–14.

Any errors or omissions in the above list are entirely unintentional. If notified the publisher will be pleased to rectify these at the earliest opportunity.

Index